D1432165

ÐOUGLAS
LiBRARY

QUEEN'S UNiVERSiTY
AT KiNGSTON

KiNGSTON ONTARiO CANADA

BULLION JOHANNESBURG

BULLION JOHANNESBURG

Men, Mines and the Challenge of Conflict

John Lang

Jonathan Ball Publishers
Johannesburg

HD9506. S74 C455 1986u

All rights reserved. No part of this publication
may be reproduced or transmitted, in any form or
by any means, without permission.

© John Lang

First published in 1986 by
Jonathan Ball Publishers
P O Box 548
Bergvlei 2012

ISBN 0 86850 130 1

Design and phototypesetting by Book Productions, Pretoria
Printed and bound by National Book Printers, Goodwood, Cape

This book is for Joan, with love

Historians with too much of an eye on the present can write history that lacks compassion and understanding, that fails to see the complexities of the lives of those societies and individuals who although now gone lived once in what was, to them, the very difficult and uncertain present.

Harrison M Wright: *The Burden of the Present.*
David Philip, Cape Town, with Rex Collings, London, 1977.

Contents

Illustrations

SECOND SECTION

Between pages 160 and 161

Boers leave for the Front (Africana Museum).
Ships in Lourenço Marques (Africana Museum).
Georges Rouliot (John Heydenrych: Chamber of Mines).
Drummond Chaplin (John Heydenrych: Chamber of Mines).
Lord Milner drives through Johannesburg (Africana Museum).
Lord Milner at Garden Party (Africana Museum).
Joseph Chamberlain in Johannesburg (Africana Museum).
Arrival of the Chinese at ERPM (Africana Museum).
Tube Mills (Africana Museum).
George Farrar electioneering in 1907 (Africana Museum).
Afrikaners replace British immigrants as miners (cartoon: Frank Holland: 'The Star').
Sir Percy FitzPatrick celebrates the Defeat of Louis Botha (Africana Museum).
General Strike: Mass Meeting (Africana Museum).
Police Charging (*Strike Album* published by the Central News Agency, Johannesburg, a copy of which is in the possession of the Strange Library of the Africana Museum).
Woman Strike Leader (*The Illustrated Star: Town and Country Journal*).
Unions bury their strike dead (Africana Museum).
South African Institute of Medical Research (Africana Museum).

THIRD SECTION

Between pages 256 and 257

Anglo American's First Profit (*Optima*).
Curlewis Conference (Africana Museum).
Sir Evelyn Wallers (John Heydenrych: Chamber of Mines).
P M Anderson (Africana Museum).
Strike Commando with Brass Band (Africana Museum).
Arrest of Strike Leaders (Africana Museum).
Murder Scene at Brakpan Mine Offices (Africana Museum).
Burial of Trooper H J Coetzee (Africana Museum).
Smuts and Martial Law (Boonzaier cartoon).
Smuts counter-attacks (Africana Museum).
Aftermath of Bombardment of Fordsburg (Africana Museum).
Aerial photograph of Battle of Fordsburg (South African Defence Force Military Archives, Pretoria).
John Martin (Africana Museum).
Guy Carleton Jones (Gold Fields of South Africa).

Rudolf Krahmann with Magnetometer (Gold Fields of South Africa).

FOURTH SECTION

Between pages 352 and 353

British Royal Family underground (Africana Museum).
Dr D F Malan, Prime Minister, opening First Uranium Plant (Chamber of Mines).
Stowe McLean (Africana Museum).
Harry Oppenheimer at Opening of President Steyn (*Optima*).
President Brand Gold Mine (Chamber of Mines).
Shaft-sinking (Chamber of Mines).
Gold Producers' Committee in Session: 1960 (Chamber of Mines).
Raiseborer (Chamber of Mines).
Migratory worker (Chamber of Mines).
WNLA airlift (Chamber of Mines).
Homeward Journey (Chamber of Mines).
Western Deep Levels (Chamber of Mines).
Sir Ernest Oppenheimer (*Optima*).

FIFTH SECTION

Between pages 448 and 449

Harold Macmillan at West Driefontein (Chamber of Mines).
West Driefontein Flood: First Report (Gold Fields).
West Driefontein Flood: Water pouring through the Main Plug (Gold Fields).
Robin Plumbridge (Chamber of Mines).
Gold Rush Headlines, 1967 (Chamber of Mines).
Americans turn in their Gold, 1933 (Intergold).
Krugerrand Pan-European Advertisement (Intergold).
Life-President Hastings Banda of Malawi visits Western Deep Levels (Anglo American Corporation of South Africa).
Signing of Coal Export Contract (Mr George Clark).
Giant Dragline shifts Overburden to expose Coal (Chamber of Mines).
Richards Bay Coal Port (Chamber of Mines).
Coal miners at Arnot (Anglo American Corporation).
Peter Ngobeni, champion sprinter (*Mining Sun*).
Daniel Mapanya, middleweight champion (*Mining Sun*).
Helicopter lifts Injured Miner (Chamber of Mines).
Japan Gold Jewellery Show: Official Opening (Intergold).

Foreword

by
Professor Burridge Spies,
Professor of History, University of South Africa

The true starting-point for the historian of the Chamber of Mines is the discovery of the Main Reef Series of the Witwatersrand in February 1886.

That influential event was followed at the end of 1887 by the formation of the short-lived first Chamber of Mines. Based as it was on individual rather than corporate membership and with the aim to disseminate authoritative information about the new goldfields, it was much narrower in concept, composition and function than the body that was to replace it less than two years later. Yet it paved the way for the modern Chamber of Mines.

By mid-1889 the leading mining houses had become aware of the urgent necessity to replace the Old Chamber with an organization with wider powers, fully supported by the whole industry. The establishment on 5 October 1889 of the Witwatersrand Chamber of Mines 'to promote and protect the mining interests and industries of the Witwatersrand Gold Fields' was the response to those needs.

This book, fittingly published one hundred years after the great gold discovery on the Witwatersrand, presents the history of the Chamber of Mines from its beginnings. The mineral revolution and the momentous social, economic and political consequences initiated by diamonds less than two decades earlier, were accelerated by gold. The role of mining capital in laying the foundation of a modern industrial state, and in particular, the evolution of class, race and labour relations in twentieth-century South African society have attracted the attention of historians. Much of their work touches on the role of the Chamber of Mines as the co-ordinator of mining policy and the spokesman for the industry at the interface with governments and trade unions. However, no historian has focused directly on the history of the Chamber of Mines for the full period of its existence.

In this book, the Chamber of Mines occupies for the first time a central, pivotal position. John Lang, who has had full access to the Chamber Archives, has presented a history from the perspective of the Chamber of Mines. The author is well qualified for the task. His close association with the mining industry over a period of twenty-three years gave him valuable insights into that perspective. There are other perspectives and John Lang is not unaware of them. He has deliberately not tried to avoid controversy. He has sought to balance the Chamber's role against other relevant forces, and he has told his story within the context of the political, social and economic framework of the last hundred years. This is no dull institutional history. Many remarkable, colourful personalities, who have been prominent in the mining world and who helped shape the developments of their time, are vividly portrayed.

This is a readable short history which provides a cohesive picture of the Chamber of Mines of South Africa. It has something to say to the mining specialist, the student of history and the general reader.

S B SPIES

Preface

I have called this book *Bullion Johannesburg*, the telegraphic address of the Chamber of Mines since the turn of the century, to symbolize the dynamic the Chamber and the mining industry have imparted to South Africa. In writing it I was able to draw on my service with the Chamber from 1957 to 1980, experience which enabled me to observe at first hand the making of policy in the mining industry, its negotiations with trade unions, and the conduct of relations with the Government at Cabinet level. At the same time, these years at the Chamber made me wonder whether or not I should accept the commission to write its history, for nobody can get to know the South African mining industry as well as I did without being captivated by the quality of the people who work its mines and serve its institutions. However, as Pulitzer Prize winner Barbara W Tuchman pointed out to the American Historical Association in 'The Historian's Opportunity',* the historical writing of a purely objective person, if such existed, would be as indigestible as the eating of sawdust. Tuchman proclaims also the importance of the historian's involvement in the grandeur of his theme. These are the realities of the historian's stance; but they do not absolve him from taking account of all possible points of view.

This requirement led me to Burridge Spies, Professor of History at UNISA, who kindly agreed to act as consultant. Professor Spies is a distinguished contributor to South African history. I was remarkably fortunate to have his appraisal - and friendly encouragement - at each stage of this work and, while the view of events and the conclusions are my own, his scholarly advice has been of fundamental importance.

I am particularly indebted, too, to Dennis Etheredge, an historian turned mining house executive, who became Anglo American's member on the Chamber's Executive Committee from 1977 to 1983, for encouraging the writing of this history, and for agreeing to read it in manuscript..

Many mining personalities gave of their time to recall past events. They included nine former presidents of the Chamber who, all told, held the office for eighteen years in the period from 1954-1982: C B Anderson, P H Anderson, Dr A A von Maltitz, R S Cooke, the late T Reekie, J W Shilling, R C J Goode,

---

* *Practising History:* MacMillan, London 1982.

R A Plumbridge, and A W S Schumann. Olive McLean was most helpful in recalling memories of her late husband, C S McLean, three times President between 1945 and 1953, and a dominant figure in the post-war Chamber. A Tracey Milne, successively Secretary, Manager and General Manager of the Chamber, between 1951 and 1968, gave me valuable guideposts. Particular thanks are due as well to Dr T W de Jongh, Governor of the South African Reserve Bank from 1967 to 1980, who recalled for me the little-known background to the monetary and gold crises of the sixties and seventies.

Peter H Bosman, General Manager, and Tom R N Main, Assistant General Manager, provided my liaison channel with the current Chamber. They responded promptly to requests for assistance, and granted me unrestricted access to information, while refraining from any attempt to influence content. I owe special thanks, too, to the many Chamber officials, past and present, who furnished factual and statistical detail, personal recollections, or photographic material. The personnel of the correspondence and library departments were untiring in searching the archives and in meeting my unceasing requests for books and unpublished documents.

The resources of Johannesburg's Strange, Reference and Newspaper Libraries and its Africana Museum proved invaluable. The staff of the Transvaal Archives in Pretoria was always helpful, and so was *The Star*.

Finally, I thank the Providence that led Rosemary Burke to become Secretary to the project. Her role soon expanded to include research, and by her dedication over more than three years she made an inestimable contribution to the compilation of the book.

The many others who helped, both in South Africa and abroad, have been thanked personally.

JOHN LANG

NOTE ON MONETARY TERMS AND
ON SYSTEMS OF MEASUREMENT

In the Prelude and the first four parts of the book, the monetary unit used is the £, which was in use in South Africa until 1961 when the decimalization process was started with the introduction of the rand (equivalent to ten shillings South African or sterling) as the unit of account.

Similarly, the British Imperial system of measurement, with other systems in use in South Africa in the past, have been used for much of the book, giving way at the appropriate stage in Chapter Thirty-Four of Part Five to the metric system introduced in South Africa in 1971.

Forerunners and Foreglow

When young Victoria ascended the throne of England in 1837 the interior of southern Africa was viewed, depending on the extent to which distance lent enchantment, as an empty land that beckoned with mystery and romance, or as a savage *terra incognita*. Its potential as a prime source of the world's day-by-day needs of metals and minerals was wholly unsuspected.

The regions of settlement were clustered on or near the coastline of the Cape Colony. The Mother City of Cape Town, at the south-western tip, was the only town with a population of more than ten thousand. Five hundred miles away, on the Colony's troubled eastern frontier, colonists advancing across the Gamtoos River in search of hunting and fertile watered land had mingled and clashed with Xhosa tribes moving south and westward with the same things in mind.

The colonists were a mix of people of European descent. The forebears of some had come from Holland during the rule of the Dutch East India Company which had established a supply base for shipping at the Cape in 1652. The original Dutch settlers were joined by people from all over Europe, mainly French Huguenots and Germans. Then came the British. During the Napoleonic Wars in 1795 Britain occupied the Cape as part of her ever-dominant strategy of sea power. Ceded briefly to a Batavian (Netherlands) administration after the Treaty of Amiens in 1803, the Cape was re-occupied by Britain in 1806. It was finally ceded to her in 1814 as part of the general peace settlement. Intermittently, through the long period of British rule, there would be waves of British settlement, but never enough to match the growth of other European stock which merged to constitute the Afrikaner race.

In the 1820s, intrepid and almost-forgotten explorers, hunters and missionaries like Cornwallis Harris, Hume and Archbell, forded the Orange far to the north-west of the Cape's eastern boundary and opened wagon trails across the Witwatersrand and the Magaliesberg ranges. They found there Bantu-speaking tribes with an Iron Age culture, preserved in being long after its supercession in most other parts of the world. Some of these Iron Age people were still excavating and smelting iron-bearing shale on what is today Melville Koppies (Hills) in suburban Johannesburg. Their clay smelters cast a pale foreglow of the monster blast furnaces of the future Transvaal.

Stand on the summit of Melville Koppies today and look to the north. If you ignore the modern suburban sprawl in the foreground housing some of the Witwatersrand's teeming millions, you will see a landscape of immense age that has not changed a great deal in 10 000 000 years, but was once the habitat of antelope, zebra and buffalo and the carnivores that preyed upon them. The earliest known inhabitants of this environment were of the Stone Age. They expressed command of their universe by skilfully fashioning axes, cleavers and flakers of flint and other handy materials. They were the first to satisfy the human yearning for self-expression by painting on rocks the animals, peoples and events that were the highlights of their lives, and among these Stone Age people were the forerunners of the great army of miners that have tunnelled deep into the land's crust.

Ancient workings of these first Stone Age miners have been uncovered just across the present Transvaal border with Swaziland at Emabomvini, 'the place of the red'. In the winning of 50 000 000 tons of haematite (iron ore in the form of red ochre) ordered by Japan, the modern miners of the Swazi Iron Ore Development Corporation found that primitive man had been there before. The writer Lyall Watson has recorded that crews in the Japanese bulk carriers amused themselves on the journey home by collecting samples of the ancient stone implements that abounded in the ore.[1]

Charcoal nodules were collected at Emabomvini and sent abroad for carbon dating. The results enabled the modern miners to claim discovery of the oldest known mine in the world.[2] But what were Stone Age men doing driving tunnels through an iron ore deposit? They were seeking pigments, found as a derivative of iron ore, for purposes of adornment and for ritual use in the burial of their dead.

The Iron Age tribes that superseded them from, perhaps, the fifth century AD were part of a movement southwards across the Limpopo, in the never-ceasing land search of the Bantu. It was not long before the Iron Age tribes found metal deposits and soon they were operating small furnaces to forge metal ores for weapons and tools, and for personal adornment. Their way of life appears to have been based on a large group working together for the production of food and metal. They left evidence of ancient trade routes for metals linking the far interior with the coast of Moçambique.

The Transvaal high plateau that the white settler entered in the 1830s abounded with evidence of ancient mine workings. Copper was mined from the earliest times at Messina and at Phalaborwa, each today the location of modern mining on a vast scale. The early inhabitants won gold at Pilgrim's Rest and elsewhere. Tin was worked in the central regions and iron ore over most of the northern parts.

These individual smelting furnaces of days-gone-by produced only a few pounds of metal at a time. Nor do the ores worked seem to have been rich; though they were sometimes meagre surface indications of huge low-grade deposits that awaited the magic of modern infrastructure and capitalist enterprise.

Revil J Mason, the Transvaal archaeologist, has described[3] iron working on Melville Koppies.

We may imagine the Melville women collecting haemetite lumps ... or in places actually mining it with ... the men. They then mixed the lumps with charcoal inside the furnace and fired the mixture early in the morning, perhaps using magical ritual .... Most of the furnace apertures were sealed with clay to retain heat and speed of fusion of the iron ore. All day relays of men worked the skin bellows on either side of the furnace, directing the airblast into the furnace through clay blowpipes. Slowly the temperature of the ore mass rose higher, fusing the furnace sides and melting the clay blowpipe nozzles. ... The bellowsmen sweated in the heat, cooled by the light breeze moving up over the lip of the krantz a few yards away. Towards sunset the gasping of the bellows died. The men broke the clay seals of the furnace and raked out about twenty pounds of crude iron from the furnace base. Next day they hammered the iron into hoes, knives, adzes, axes and assegai blades. Some may have been drawn into wire for making beads or bangles.

The time was not far distant when white traders would pour a flood of cheap metal goods from European factories into the Transvaal. Its people would no longer require the product of furnaces of the Melville pattern. But the Melville iron smelters were doomed to be slaughtered or driven headlong from their traditional home in the great tribal upheaval known as the *Difaqane*.

During the 1820s the interior of southern Africa became a cauldron of savagery. Catastrophe struck not only the iron smelters but all the indigenous peoples between the Drakensberg escarpment, the Kalahari Desert and the Limpopo River. The explosive source of disaster was the rise of the Zulu kingdom of the Nguni people under Shaka, the principal agents of destruction three bands fleeing from Shaka's wrath, and marauding as they went. They were Hlubi led by Mpangazitha and Ngwane led by Matiwane, both operating between the Vaal and the Maluti Mountains to the southward; and Ndebele under Mzilikazi, operating mostly north of the Vaal. Several displaced Sotho communities became auxiliary agents of disaster.[4] Highly disciplined warriors carried death far and wide, not only in the regions north of the Orange and the Vaal but in Natal, Pondoland and northwards into central Africa. A number of varying demographic and economic factors have been advanced as contributing to this mass upheaval, but the major underlying cause was the universal competition for land, grass and water that was a constant feature of southern Africa before ever white colonists pressed upon the fringes of the old Cape Colony.[5]

About one-sixth of the size of the United States, South Africa is essentially a poor country agriculturally; eighty-six per cent of its land is arid or semi-arid and only one-third receives the twenty-five inches of rain annually necessary for the cultivation of most crops. It lacks the extensive, rich and well-watered

3

farming areas of the eastern United States. As a rule of thumb, the lower the average rainfall in a region, the more erratic its incidence, the more regular the ravage of drought. Not for nothing did the names of so many Boer farms derive from the *fonteine*, the springs, that gave them life.[6]

Whatever the cause of the *Difaqane*, its consequence was chaos as Sotho tribes clashed with Nguni invaders and with one another in competition for diminishing supplies of grass and cattle. Old settlements were abandoned, ancient chiefdoms disappeared; new groups came into being and in turn dissolved; and as food became scarce, progressive demoralization led to widespread cannibalism. [7] The time of trouble, known in the Sotho language as *Difaqane*, is called *Mfecane* in the Nguni, meaning respectively the 'hammering' or 'crushing', the words carrying something of the connotation of 'forced migration' or of modern-day labels like 'total war', 'scorched earth' and 'genocide'.

The historical significance of scattering displaced tribes across half the African continent probably equalled that of the Great Trek which followed the *Difaqane* closely, and which in some respects was shaped and facilitated by it.

Over many years the Cape developed into a multiracial, stratified slave-owning society. It was increasingly exposed to the impact of the ideological revolution which erupted on both sides of the Atlantic in 1776 and 1789, preaching the liberty and equality of Man. The crusade was taken up, sometimes with unbridled zeal, by church and mission groups. Under a law of 1833 Britain set in train the emancipation of slaves throughout the Empire. The Cape slave owners, like their counterparts elsewhere, resented the chosen method of implementation and, in particular, the arrangements for compensating the owners of freed slaves. It was however the large, settled owners of the western Cape who suffered, rather than the restless trek-boers of the eastern frontier. Coincidentally, the trek-boers were becoming restless over the policies of a distant, but uncomfortably efficient, British administration for a number of reasons, including the handling of race relations and the thorny issues of disputes on the troubled frontier.[8]

In and after 1835 many Boers disposed of or abandoned their farms, bought large supplies of gunpowder, mustered their livestock, bundled the rest of their movable property onto their wagons and headed northwards across the Orange. They became known as Voortrekkers. The burden of their justification in contemporary documents was that the authorities, under the influence of persons acting dishonestly 'under the cloak of religion' had mishandled master-servant relations, and, in doing so, offended both the law of God and human susceptibilities.[9]

For whatever reason, and these surely varied from Boer to Boer, they took great risks and endured much in seeking a new country, with plenty of land for all, away from interference by the British or any other government.

They trekked to two main areas, southern Natal and the central plateau, the Highveld, on both sides of the Vaal. This leap forward in settlement turned the flank of the southern Nguni chieftains, and advanced the frontiers, after bloody massacre of trekking whites and retaliatory slaughter of blacks, to the Tugela River in Natal and across the Vaal to the Limpopo.

Among those who forded the Vaal with the women and the wagons was an eleven-year-old boy named Stephanus Johannes Paulus Kruger, later to become Commandant-General and four times President of the Transvaal Republic. As they crossed the Highveld they found a vast stretch of country that seemed almost devoid of human habitation. But the destruction of the *Difaqane* was being followed by a process of regeneration with the consolidation of Ndebele power in the central Transvaal, and the rise of the Southern Sotho Kingdom under Moshoeshoe, the founder of Lesotho.

Paul Kruger was in the Voortrekker laager at Vegkop, close to the site of the Free State town of Heilbron, on 11 October 1836, when it was attacked by the Ndebele. The laager was not penetrated but nearly all the flocks and herds were driven away at the price of many dead. There followed retaliation and conquest. Mzilikazi, beaten in a nine days' battle, fled northwards across the Limpopo. After more wanderings, he carved out the 'Matabeleland' of modern Zimbabwe at the expense of the Shona. There, close to a hundred years old, he died in 1868, and bequeathed his kingdom to his son Lobengula, destined to be defeated by the forces of Cecil John Rhodes's Charter Company.

The Voortrekkers claimed possession of the Highveld by right of their conquest of Mzilikazi and as a consequence of the protection they offered the tribes scattered by the *Difaqane*; they laid claim to an area embracing everything between the Vaal and the Limpopo and the Kalahari Desert and the Drakensberg. And they hankered for access to the sea to bolster their independence.

The impact of new competing groups seriously disturbed the already delicately poised balance of soil and settlement. The incursion of the white settler upon the hinterland served to hasten the inevitable conclusion of the pastoral cycle, enlivened by hunting, that was a favoured way of life for both white and black, but which had no prospect of long enduring. The end of the age-old nomadic movements to pastures new on the African continent, as rhythmic as the slow movement of the great game herds, was already written large in the pressure of migrant millions on the barren, drought-seared land. And while the Indians of North America succumbed to the epidemics of European origin, especially smallpox, the Bantu-speaking tribes displayed relative immunity. Moreover, Western ways of health and hygiene increasingly afforded them a way of escape from their ancient bondage to the endemic diseases of Africa. Southern Africa was to witness a population explosion among the Bantu tribes that could only be contained and fulfilled in an urban, industrial environment.

Moreover, white settlement in southern Africa was insignificant compared to the mass exodus from Europe to accessible North America, with its great rivers penetrating deeply the interior, and its vast forests. Incredible as it must seem to Americans, South Africa possesses hardly any natural harbours and does not have a single navigable river or arterial lake.

At the outset of the eighteenth century only about twelve hundred Europeans were living in the Cape Colony, compared with about two hundred thousand in the English colonies of North America. In 1800, there were four million in the United States and only twenty thousand in southern Africa; and in 1900, when the frontier era closed in both regions, about sixty-seven million in the United States and just over one million in South Africa. The North American Indian population, cruelly diminished by disease, war and land starvation, numbered only two hundred and fifty thousand or one-twenty-fifth of its pre-Columbian size. In contrast, the Bantu-speaking African population numbered about six million or eighty per cent of the whole population and easily maintained its overwhelming numerical superiority.

As settlement was extended in the nineteenth century, the white Africans and white governments, inhibited by a harsh geography, entered painfully, often reluctantly, upon the inhospitable hinterland. As they did so they progressively subjugated the tribes and absorbed them into the South African political and economic system.

Not surprisingly tribal unrest and uprising were not infrequent, and the fear of revolt became an established part of South African life. Not surprisingly again the troubles came most frequently in time of drought:

> Burned under a cruel sky, as empty of moisture as the soil was of nourishment, the cracked and cropless land was often the trigger of revolt.[10]

British Government rule was periodically extended over colonists and tribes – and periodically withdrawn. The recurring desire to be rid of the costs and responsibilities of African rule was expressed in the Sand River and Bloemfontein Conventions (1852 and 1854) which created the Transvaal Republic and its sister republic of the Orange Free State, and gave the Boers the right to manage their own internal affairs. But disentanglement was set back sharply by an event that in long-term implication would have as shattering an impact as *Difaqane* and Great Trek – the discovery of diamonds.

Modern mining in southern Africa can be dated from 1852 when the first systematic attempts were made to recover copper from deposits in the Namaqualand region of the Cape Colony. It was another fifteen years before alluvial diamonds were discovered near Hopetown. A few months later the first signs of gold were reported by Karl Mauch, the discoverer of the Zimbabwe Ruins, on an expedition in the Tati district of present-day Botswana, about 625 miles to the north of the Orange. The gold find yielded little; the diamond discovery changed the course of history. It ushered in South Africa's mineral revolution, which was to end the region's unenviable position as the least promising and most economically retarded of the settler societies of northern European origin.

The first diamond diggings were along the Vaal, Harts and Orange Rivers in the geographical centre of the country, in a desolate land of sun-scorched earth, stony koppies and scattered, flat-topped thorn trees. Bitterly cold in winter, scorching hot in summer, the land was bare and waterless away from the rivers. Diamonds apart, it was rich only in the diversity of its wild life. The postcart from Bloemfontein departed daily for the Cape in full daylight to protect the horses from attack by lions.

Prior to the discovery the Cape Colony was at a rudimentary stage of development. Industrial activity was small-scale and widely dispersed. Wool was the staple, accounting for much of the country's exports. Whites working as farm foremen and head shepherds earned an average of £3 2s 1d a month. There were little more than two miles of railways and in all that huge country the ox-wagon was the sole means of carrying merchandise. Total Government revenue in 1860 was only £742 000.[11]

The first diamond of twenty-one carats was christened the 'Eureka', but its discovery occasioned little excitement. In due course there came along the 'Star of South Africa', a beautiful pure white stone of eighty-three and a half carats. Schalk van Niekerk, who had found the 'Eureka' among the playstones of a Boer's children, bought the 'Star of Africa' from a Griqua for a Griqua's dream of riches – five hundred sheep, ten oxen and a horse. The Griqua thought Van Niekerk crazy. The next buyers were Hopetown merchants who paid £10 000 for it.[12] Before the 'Star of South Africa' started on its journey to London, Richard Southey, the Colonial Secretary at the Cape, laid it on the table of the Cape Assembly with the words: 'Gentlemen, this is the rock on which the future success of South Africa will be built.' London jewellers fashioned the stone into an oval three-sided brilliant of great lustre and of the first water, and mounted it into an ornament for the hair, for the Countess of Dudley. Its whereabouts today is a mystery.[13]

The discovery of the 'Star of South Africa' made the world sit up and take notice. The 'Star' and the 'Eureka' were the first of a flood of gems that would surpass the treasure of the shahs and maharajahs of the Orient. It triggered a rush of diggers from every corner of the land and of the globe, from all walks of life. Many walked 435 miles from the coast to the diggings.

Three years after the rush to the river diggings, which yielded the heaped-up alluvial treasures of uncountable years, came a flood of prospectors to the 'dry' diggings at Bultfontein and Du Toit's Pan. In 1871, the most significant find of all was made at De Beer's 'New Rush' at Colesberg Kopje, which was to become the tent town and then the city of Kimberley.

The diggings lay in a wilderness of vague boundaries and doubtful ownership. Suddenly, where nobody had bothered much who ruled, there was a fistful of claimants – the Transvaal Republic, the Orange Free State Republic, a number of Bantu tribes, and the Griquas, a tribe largely of mixed white and Khoikhoi origin. R W Keate, Lieutenant-Governor of Natal, was appointed to arbitrate by the British Government. The resultant Keate Award was controversial and much disputed. It gave sovereignty to Griqualand West, whereupon Nicholas Waterboer, the Griqua chief, invited the British Government to annex his country. Later, in 1877, the Cape Colony was persuaded to accept the responsibility of incorporation and the Orange Free State received compensation, some would say conscience money, of £90 000. The dispute left a legacy of bitterness between Britain and the Boer republics.

Within five years of the discovery of the dry diggings, £1 million worth of gems was exported, the first of a seemingly endless stream of such millions. With the discovery that the volcanic pipes of the dry diggings were diamondiferous at depth, diamonds ceased to be a fortune hunter's gamble and became the stable foundation of a large-scale modern industry. The demands of practical mining and the needs of human safety dictated the amalgamation of claims under control of large companies. From them would come the wealth that would back the widening search for gold, coal and other minerals, and the discovery and early development of the Witwatersrand gold-fields. On the Kimberley diggings, too, were to be tested and proved those who would construct the industry's triumphs and taste the bitterness of its defeats. The men who emerged at the top were able and ambitious, and often incredibly young. They quickly dominated in the free-for-all of the diamond diggings, and the self-confidence derived from hard-won expertise would bring them fairytale riches and the headiness of power.

The future gold magnate J B Robinson was among the first to arrive. He began digging on the Vaal River at Hebron in 1867 at the age of twenty-seven. Cecil Rhodes was only eighteen when he arrived at the dry diggings in 1871. He speedily built up a position of dominance in between intermittent terms at Oxford. His absences were eased by an enduring friendship with Charles Rudd, nine years older, which would culminate in their being Joint Managing Directors of Gold Fields of South Africa in Johannesburg. Alfred Beit was twenty-two when he arrived from Germany in 1875 as a diamond buyer. Progressively bewitched by Rhodes's charisma, he came in course of time to take uncharacteristic risks, involve himself in bizarre adventures. They were often seen together, 'Rhodes tall, moody and taking long vigorous strides, and Beit shorter, vivacious and hard put to it to keep up with his companion'.[14]

John X Merriman, the future statesman, arrived at New Rush in the early days to try his luck. He found that 'most of the Grahamstown church choir, about half the Cape Parliament, and some forty thousand white diggers, speculators, and cosmopolitan adventurers ... had arrived there before him'.[15] He did not enjoy the experience and counted his friendship with Rhodes almost the only benefit.[16]

Julius Wernher (twenty-one), after service in the Prussian Dragoons in the Franco-Prussian War, was in at the beginning as a buyer to Jules Porges of Paris. In the course of time he would establish a partnership with Beit and become the London end of Wernher, Beit and Company. J B Taylor, too, began his mining career in 1871, working at his father's sorting table at New Rush when he was ten years old. He would retire on the Witwatersrand at thirty-four with a fortune and enjoy for another fifty years a squire's life of sport and leisure.

Another early arrival, with a wagonload of merchandise, was young Sammy Marks, son of a Lithuanian tailor, accompanied by his cousin, Isaac Lewis. Together they would establish Lewis and Marks, one of the so-called 'Big Ten' of finance houses on the Rand in the mid-1890s.

George Albu set up as a diamond merchant at age twenty with his seventeen-year-old brother Leopold. In the 1890s he would form the General Mining and Finance Corporation on the Rand. Sigismund Neumann, who would head another of the Rand's 'Big Ten', was on the diggings in his teens.

Perhaps the most tragic, most colourful figure of all, was Barney Barnato who, with his elder brother Harry, established Barnato Brothers when he was twenty-two. He went on to amalgamate large diamond holdings into Kimberley Central Mining Company which Cecil Rhodes would finally force him to merge with his company, De Beers, in exchange for a life governorship and a share of the profits. He was joined at an early stage by his nephews, Solly, Woolf and Jack Joel. Woolf made a considerable fortune while still in his teens and played a leading role later on in the development of the Johannesburg Consolidated Investment Company. When Barnato committed suicide in 1897, Woolf took over control of Barnato Brothers, only to be fatally shot in his office the following year.[17]

Later arrivals included Dr Leander Starr Jameson, who would strike up an enduring friendship with Rhodes, and lead at his behest the ill-fated Jameson Raid. Another newly-qualified young doctor was Hans Sauer, an Afrikaner who in days to come would, on the issue of the denial of the franchise to new-comers to the Transvaal, join the Johannesburg rebels against Kruger. Courtly Georges Rouliot was General Manager of the Cie Generale des Mines des Diamants, Kimberley's famous 'French Company', at twenty-one.

By contrast Hermann Eckstein was a mature thirty-five when he arrived to manage the Phoenix Diamond Mining Company in 1882. On the Rand seven years later he would form 'The Corner House', in the Wernher, Beit interest. Lionel Phillips, another future magnate and head of Corner House, arrived in his twenty-first year to work for J B Robinson. Like Robinson he would be a 'loser' at Kimberley, but a big 'winner' on the Rand.

These young men of star quality among the dramatis personae of Kimberley included three future Prime Ministers of the Cape Colony (Rhodes, Merriman and Jameson); and three future Presidents of the Chamber of Mines (Eckstein, the founder President, 1889-1892, his successor, Lionel Phillips, 1892-1896, and 1908-1909,[18] and Georges Rouliot, 1898-1902). Six were to be created baronets for public service (George Albu, Jameson, Neumann, Phillips, Robinson and Wernher).

The entrepreneurs who emerged at Kimberley took with them to the Rand a gift for getting things done in the face of seemingly insurmountable difficulty. Not surprisingly, perhaps, they were sometimes short on patience, and

9

sometimes short on wisdom. But they were rich in faith in the future greatness of South Africa.

Also making their bow at the diggings were the first of the great army of mineworkers who would provide the skill and the muscle essential to the creation of what was destined to be the greatest industrial complex in the southern hemisphere.

Labour on the diamond fields was for the most part divided into two classes: a small élite group of skilled white workers earning high wages and a large group of unskilled black workers earning relatively low wages. This was not simply the result of colour prejudice. The blacks had no skills to sell. The absence of these seemed to substantiate preconceived ideas of the structure of colonial society:

> While the full significance of occupational colour differentiation first began to emerge with the expansion of mining after 1870 ... many of the underlying attitudes were already formed long before the end of the nineteenth century.[19]

However, the cash wage offered on the diamond fields gave the black man new hope. Before the discovery of diamonds, farming had provided the only important field of employment. Throughout most of the country such workers were hired by the year and paid in livestock. Small as wages paid on the diggings were, they were the highest in South Africa and larger than those paid to rural labourers in Britain. The black workers were enabled to get drunk on 'Cape Smoke', to buy clothing and other goods and to acquire 'that symbol of equality, a gun'.[20] They came for short periods and left after a few months with the goods they had acquired. The whites made permanent homes on the fields.

Nor, for the most part, were the white skilled workers South African-born. Like their black fellow-workers, white South Africans were lacking in industrial skills and apart from a few wagon builders, there was no substantial cadre of craftsmen to draw on. Thus the wages of skilled workers had to be set at levels that would attract craftsmen from abroad. The report of the Inspector of Diamond Mines for 1889 showed that fifty-five per cent of white employees at the Kimberley mine during that year were of British extraction, forty-three per cent of colonial origin, ie from the Cape or Natal, and two per cent from other countries; at De Beer's mine sixty-five per cent were British, thirty per cent colonial and five per cent from other countries. Some of the skilled workers came in the early days as diggers in their own right, and they insisted that the different spheres of employment of black and white should be maintained as amalgamation of claims proceeded and the big companies took over. This insistence was progressively strengthened as black workers demonstrated their adaptability to industrial employment. Through the growing strength of organized white trade unionism the racial separation of levels of employment was to be of continuing importance in the subsequent social and industrial development of the country. The diversity of mineral wealth awaiting discovery would in general prove to be in low-grade deposits, requiring a massive labour force and the tightest cost control.

The historian C W de Kiewiet has commented:

> South Africa's new prosperity was not built up on diamonds alone nor upon the gold whose discovery was at hand. Of the resources which permitted South Africa at long last to take its place beside the Australian colonies, New Zealand, and Canada in the economy of the world, native labour was one of the most important. What an abundance of rain and grass was to New Zealand mutton, what a plenty of cheap grazing land was to Australian wool, what the fertile prairie acres were to Canadian wheat, cheap native labour was to South African mining and industrial enterprise.[21]

But while the Orange Free State, Natal and the Cape Colony prospered after the discovery of diamonds, the Transvaal was drawn ever deeper into crisis. Finally in 1877 the finances and administration collapsed and the burden of war against the Pedi under Sekhukhune, and the demoralization of the territory, was such that the arrival of Sir Theophilus Shepstone with an escort of twenty-five was sufficient to permit the annexation of the Transvaal to the Crown. But the swing from British withdrawal to intervention was sufficient to resurrect its counterforce, Afrikaner nationalism.[22] The new British Government, under Gladstone, was faced with revolt. It thought it wise and proper to withdraw, and did so, with a loss of face on the local scene that irked the British settler. British authority was withdrawn, leaving the Transvaal still poverty-stricken, but independent, to enter upon its age of gold.

While the world was agog with the splendour of the Kimberley discoveries, prospectors drawn to South Africa in search of diamonds began to fossick around for gold and other minerals. Their activities made inevitable the discovery of gold deposits. Gold mining made a modest beginning, however, because the prospectors were seeking alluvial deposits and related veins, and were attracted to the mountain streams of the Drakensberg. The first real mining was at Eersteling in the northern Transvaal, but this was small-scale. Then as the search intensified, new gold-fields were opened up at Murchison, Lydenburg, Sabie, Pilgrim's Rest and Barberton. The Kimberley entrepreneurs, or their representatives, such as J B Taylor, soon headed that way. They were joined by others like J Percy FitzPatrick and Abe Bailey who were to play leading roles on the Rand. The Sheba mine at Barberton, which would be controlled by Lewis and Marks, showed astonishing values. There followed the shortest, wildest gold boom the world has ever known. The bursting of the bubble left behind the Sheba and a few other respectably payable mines, an army of disgruntled investors and a nasty odour around investment in gold mining.

Meanwhile, the development of the Kimberley diamond fields caused men like Sir Henry Barkly, High Commissioner and Governor of the Cape, to

11

impress upon the Cape Colony Government the urgency of prospecting for coal. He recommended the well-known George William Stow, but the Government was disinclined to appoint experts. It was instead the Orange Free State Government which commissioned Stow to prospect for coal in the Bethlehem district. Here Stow found no coal, so he went to look for it farther north, as far as Maccauvlei, and crossing the Vaal River, he prospected the farm Leeuwkuil on which a portion of the town of Vereeniging is situated. This was in 1879 and is probably the first record of coal found in payable lodes in the Transvaal. He found a seam or layer twelve feet thick. To his disgust the Orange Free State Government decided that the great distances and lack of transport prevented any development.

In Kimberley Stow met Sammy Marks and told him of his find. Marks at once created The South African and Orange Free State Coal and Minerals Mining Association – De Zuid-Afrikaansche en Oranje-Vrij Staatsche Kolen en Mineralen Mijn Vereeniging. He then authorized Stow to purchase surrounding farms which he assessed as containing coal reserves.

On 25 November 1880, G W Stow bought the farm Leeuwkuil, 5 675$^{1}/_{2}$ morgen in extent (about 12 000 acres) for £5 000. This worked out at 9s 6d an acre – one of the highest prices paid up to that time in the Transvaal. On 14 October 1881, J G Fraser, agent for Marks, travelled to the farm Maccauvlei where the owner of the farm Klipplaatdrift lived. This latter farm adjoined Leeuwkuil. The owner sold the farm to Fraser for £15 000. During and after 1881 coal from the area was taken to Kimberley, mostly by ox-wagon.[23]

The ground had been laid for the coal industry that was to power the industrialization of the Transvaal.

The scene was set, and waiting in the wings was the discovery that was to move South Africa onto the world stage. It came in 1886, with the proving of the conglomerate beds of the Witwatersrand Geological Basin, halfway between Barberton and Kimberley. As the full potential of the Witwatersrand conglomerates became known, the finance houses built on Kimberley diamonds moved to the Rand, and with the backing of the banks of Britain, France and Germany, began the development that was to amaze the world. The importance of the rapid accretion to available world stocks of gold, and of the revealed potential of southern Africa, aroused the attention of the great European nations. They tightened their hold on their possessions in Africa and scrambled for African territories still unclaimed.

Meanwhile, on the new gold-field burghers of the Republic and 'uitlanders' of many nationalities scrambled for claims, competing for a slice of the new bonanza.

[1] L Watson, *Lightning Bird: The Story of One Man's Journey into Africa's Past*, p 204.

[2] *Ibid*, p 206.

[3] R J Mason, *Prehistoric Man at Melville Koppies, Johannesburg*, Johannesburg Council for Natural History: Occasional Paper 6, March 1971, p 48.

[4] M Wilson and L Thompson, eds, *A History of South Africa to 1870*, p 391.

[5] C W de Kiewiet, *A History of South Africa Social and Economic*, p 50.

[6] Modern farming methods and water conservation have made a big difference. Today South Africa has the distinction of being the only nation in Africa that is both self-sufficient in food production and a major exporter of foodstuffs.

[7] Wilson and Thompson, eds, p 391.

[8] T R H Davenport, *South Africa: A Modern History*, p 27 *et seq*.

[9] *Ibid*, p 40, quoting the Manifesto of the Voortrekker leader, Piet Retief, and the diary of his niece, Anna Steenkamp.

[10] De Kiewiet, p 75.

[11] M Wilson and L Thompson, eds, *The Oxford History of South Africa, II: South Africa: 1870-1966*, pp 3-4.

[12] I Balfour, *Famous Diamonds*, pp 9, 25.

[13] *Ibid*, p 25.

[14] H A Chilvers, *The Story of De Beers*, p 47.

[15] P Lewsen, *John X Merriman: Paradoxical South African Statesman*, p 30.

[16] P Lewsen, 'Merriman' in *Dictionary of South African Biography*, II, p 464. (The friendship did not survive the Jameson Raid.)

[17] He was killed in a shoot-out with the international swindler Von Veltheim who was demanding money from Solly Joel.

[18] While in office in 1896, he would be sentenced to death for leading the rebellion against the State, but escape with a fine.

[19] G V Doxey, *The Industrial Colour Bar in South Africa*, p 6.

[20] Lewsen, *Merriman: Paradoxical South African Statesman*, p 38.

[21] De Kiewiet, p 96.

[22] P Lewsen, ed, *Selections from the Correspondence of J X Merriman: 1870-1890*, p v.

[23] G A Leyds, *A History of Johannesburg: The Early Years*, pp 17-18.

PART ONE

The Chamber of Mines in Kruger's Republic

CHAPTER ONE

The Trail of '86

The old coach track from Kimberley to the Transvaal capital, Pretoria, went by way of Klerksdorp and Potchefstroom, and then passed to the north of Krugersdorp. Descending to Mulder's Drift on the final thirty-five mile stage of their journey, travellers admired the cascades that fell from the hills to the southward. They understood – as their modern counterparts do not – how years before the range had come to be dubbed the Ridge of White Waters, *die Witwatersrand*.

There were falls nearby at Witpoortjie, spectacular after heavy rain. Then if you travelled from east to west along the range there were lesser falls to enjoy at the places now known as Melville, Parktown, Munro Drive in Upper Houghton, and at Orange Grove and towards Bedfordview. Engineers have long since channelled and drained the cascades; they are lively only in images of days gone by.

J B Taylor, on a visit from Barberton, came up by Orange Grove in 1884, with his brother Bill and some others, travelling by ox-wagon from Pretoria to shoot over Sammy Marks's farms at Vereeniging. Threatened by a thunderstorm, they outspanned near ground that afterwards became the fabulous Robinson gold mine. Close up, the Witwatersrand was not an attractive place. The veld was barren, rocky and treeless, and largely uninhabited. There was a Boer family every six miles or so, working farms of perhaps 5 000 acres. When they were at home, that is; for the Boer farmers, with wives, children, and servants, were accustomed when winter came to trek, in a kind of patriarchal cavalcade, to the warmer bushveld, so as to give their flocks and herds the benefit of better pasturage. Their lonely homesteads were solidly built with thick walls and with windows and doors brought by ox-wagon from Delagoa Bay, and a roof of thatch. The floors were of red earth smeared over with cow dung and water, and covered with softened hides and skins of zebra and buck or the kaross of a lion. Interior doorways commonly had home-made reed or bamboo curtains, strung in long vines from the lintels. Anthony Trollope, the novelist, wrote after his visit in 1878 that he never entered a Boer's home without being made to feel welcome. But he added: 'It should be understood ... that their courtesy is very superior to their coffee.'[1] By 1884 that famed hospitality and courtesy, so far as prospectors on the Witwatersrand were concerned, was wearing thin.

Taylor set down long after his memories of that outspan on the bleak Witwatersrand:

> When we had outspanned, my brother and I went ... to fetch water, in the hopes of also getting a snipe in the vlei. Our route lay along an outcrop of reef, which stuck out as much as two or three feet from the ground in places, traceable for miles. It was a conglomerate with large pebbles, many of which were easily detached. These pebbles were embedded in an oxidised casing and looked worth sampling for gold. We took half a dozen chunks of the reef, with a view to crushing and panning when we got back to Pretoria. I confess that my brother was keener than I, since I had never heard of gold being found in conglomerated reef matter. Anyhow, the samples were put in a bag and taken to the Vaal River. There the Kaffir boy used them to support pots and kettles at the camp fire, and forgot to return them to the bag when we proceeded on our journey. This we discovered on our return to Pretoria. My brother, who was then resident there, said he would take the first opportunity of acquiring further samples when next he visited the Rand.[2]

He failed to do so, and Taylor's story joins a host of tales of the might-have-been, for numberless people, including Voortrekkers, had followed the wagon trails that criss-crossed the outcrop of gold-bearing ground. But the treasure chest did not readily yield its key.

There were no golden clues in the watercourses to point the way to the conglomerate beds, and when the conglomerate beds were observed, their significance was not understood. In no other part of the world had auriferous conglomerate been mined on any scale.

The conglomerates look dull and grey. They consist of water-borne pebbles forming a matrix with a silica cement containing iron pyrites and, sometimes, uranium oxide. They contain gold, if indeed they contain it at all, in specks so minute as rarely to be visible to the naked eye – and conglomerates form a relatively small part of the massive rock layers that make up the Witwatersrand Geological System.

Its origins go back to the beginnings of time. When the earth was young, gold-bearing debris scoured from ancient mountains by natural forces was carried by glaciers and rivers and deposited along the shoreline of an ancient sea. There, by some geological freak, it was concentrated in successive layers. Over millions of years the basin, which may have been the size of the Caspian Sea, was silted up and became dry, and high, land. Extremes of climate and volcanic action caused the land surface to buckle and change until finally, the Witwatersrand projected above the plateau to form a watershed, a continental divide. The run-off into the tributaries of the Limpopo and the Crocodile that rise on the northern slopes flows nearly 400 miles into the Indian Ocean. The run–off feeding into the Vaal finds its way twice as far to the south and west to discharge into the Atlantic.

The gold-bearing reefs of the system have been likened to a few widely-separated pages in a vast book, each such page a few feet or a few inches thick. Time has buried the 'book' deep in the earth's crust and tilted and twisted its pages. The first clue to its existence was the outcropping rock signalling the deep-running 'Main Reef'. Australian diggers had earlier coined the term 'reef' because mineralized rock sometimes outcrops, breaking the surface of the earth, rather as coral formations of the Great Barrier Reef off the north-east coast of Australia break the surface of the sea.

In 1885 Stephanus Johannes Minnaar found payable gold on the farm Kromdraai about ten miles north of Krugersdorp. Kromdraai was proclaimed as a public diggings, the first farm in the neighbourhood of the Witwatersrand to be so proclaimed. Little gold was found there, but the discovery focused attention on geological manifestations elsewhere along the Rand and aroused great interest in the area. Two brothers, Fred and Harry Struben, were already busy on large-scale prospecting. The previous year they had discovered an area of gold-bearing quartz at Wilgespruit, south-east of Kromdraai. They had great hopes for the so-called Confidence Reef but it did not justify expectations.[3]

A P Cartwright has written that studying the history of events was like watching an exciting film being run through in slow motion.[4] The prospectors bumbled around as though blindfold, following false trails. They panned in all the wrong places, crushed samples of the wrong rock with a 'dollie' – a length of timber hung from a sort of gallows on which it could be hauled up and dropped. They observed the conglomerate, but like J B Taylor were not overly impressed. In the end it fell to an Australian gold-digger and storeman named George Harrison who had seen gold-bearing conglomerate in Australia to discover the Main Reef Series. The story is told that on a Sunday stroll on the farm Langlaagte in February 1886, he stumbled over the outcrop and realized that it might be gold-bearing. He broke off pieces and sampled them. Later he signed an affidavit:

> My name is George Harrison and I come from the newly discovered goldfields Klipriver[5] especially from a farm owned by a certain Gert Oosthuizen. I have a long experience as an Australian gold digger, and I think it a payable goldfield.[6]

A number of others, like the Strubens, Japie de Villiers, Colonel Ignatius Ferreira, Henry Nourse, Jan Bantjes, and Harrison's partner George Walker, were hot on the trail as well. In July 1886 samples were sent to Kimberley. They were crushed and panned publicly. The results created a sensation. It was as though Cartwright's slow-motion film had been switched to 'fast forward'. Alfred Beit formed the Robinson Syndicate, consisting of himself, J B Robinson and Robinson's partner Maurice Marcus. Robinson left im-

19

mediately for the Transvaal and so did a number of others including Rhodes and Hans Sauer. The Rush to the Rand was on.

Gerrit Ockerse, who is commemorated in Johannesburg's Ockerse Street, was one of those appointed to the hurriedly organized Mining Commissioner's Office. He made the journey from Pretoria on horseback, a six-hour ride. After passing the Halfway House and crossing the Jukskei River, he finally came to a lone house near Orange Grove. Here the road forked, one to the left to Heidelberg and Natal, and the other to the right – to the diggings. Ockerse dismounted to ask the way. An old woman came to the door and in response to Ockerse's enquiry, replied indignantly, '*Kan jy dan nie sien nie waar die vuilgoed fortuinsoekers die land platgetrap het om die aardse slyk te soek?*' ('Can you not see where the filthy fortune-seekers have trodden down the lands going their way to seek the earthly dross?')[7]

Those taking part were by no means only from across the borders of the Republic. A list of registered owners of the mining leases in 1887 suggests that as many as two-thirds of the leaseholders were Transvaal burghers.[8] As it happened only relatively few, of Transvaler and Uitlander alike, would make fortunes, but the pioneers would leave more than their footprints on the Highveld.

Fourteen years later, a young war correspondent for *The Morning Post* of London, Winston Spencer Churchill, marching to Pretoria with the British Army under Lord Roberts in the Boer War, rode up from the south and afterwards wrote:

> The whole crest of the Rand ridge was fringed with factory chimneys. We had marched nearly 500 miles through a country which, though full of promise, seemed to European eyes desolate and wild, and now we turned a corner suddenly, and before us sprang the evidences of wealth, manufacture, and bustling civilization.[9]

Once the Main Reef had been discovered and shown to be consistently auriferous, the prospectors and diggers quickly traced it in a line running east and west through Langlaagte for an astonishing thirty miles or more. The newcomers settled in two main areas, at Ferreira's Camp on the farm Turffontein, where Fordsburg Dip now is, and on the southern portion of the farm Doornfontein[10] a few miles to the east. The camp at Doornfontein was established by the Veldkornet, Johannes Petrus Meyer, who was the government representative with full authority in his ward Klip River under the Landdrost of District Heidelberg. So many diggers up from Natal on the Heidelberg road made Meyer's Camp their headquarters that it quickly became known as Natal Camp. By July 1886 both camps were already of considerable size and importance, but the road from Kimberley passed through the camp to which Ignatius Ferreira gave his name and more newcomers settled there.

Ferreira, one of the most colourful of the pioneers, had served in both Boer and British forces and received the CMG for service in the second war against

Sekhukhune, the Pedi paramount chief, and in other campaigns, including those against the Zulu chief, Cetshwayo.

Ferreira's Camp grew with astonishing rapidity. Wood and iron buildings in sections ready for erection arrived quickly on ox-wagon and were speedily placed in position. In a very short time the camp became the main centre of business activity.

Ferreira ran it military fashion; from the first, tents had to be in line, roadways aligned. Without any official or recognized authority, Ferreira held sway, exercising by the strength of his personality a restraining influence on the camp's cosmopolitan population.

The Government in Pretoria handled the extraordinary situation well. A commission consisting of Christiaan Johannes Joubert, Head of the Mines Department (also described as the 'Minister of Mines'), and Johann Friedrich Bernhard Rissik, the Acting Surveyor-General, was sent to the Rand to hear evidence, recommend the steps necessary to create a public diggings, and to decide on the site of a village. The Commission had an excellent reception. At a meeting held near Ferreira's wagon on 5 August, about 250 were present. Among them were Rhodes, Rudd, Robinson, H S Caldecott, Dr Hans Sauer, T W Beckett, and Henry Nourse. After the meeting, the group went to Edgson's canteen, where the health of President Kruger was proposed and 'heartily responded to', according to the official report. Liquor of all kinds was sold and soon nothing was left but *mampoer* (peach brandy).[11]

There followed, on 20 September 1886, the proclamation of Driefontein and Elandsfontein as public diggings. The newly-appointed Mining Commissioner, Carl von Brandis, commanding in appearance with military bearing and a huge, bushy white beard, read the notice at nine o'clock that morning, standing on a whisky box in front of his tent. The proclamation of the southern portions of Doornfontein and Turffontein followed a week later. The government ground, Randjeslaagte, and the farm Langlaagte were proclaimed on 4 October. Roodepoort, Paardekraal (adjoining Langlaagte) and Vogelstruisfontein, the most western parts, were proclaimed on 11 October.

At the end of September 1886, D P Ross, Manager of the Philipstown (Cape) branch of the Standard Bank, was sent to examine the prospects of opening a branch of the bank on the Rand. In his report, he estimated that the population was already two thousand five hundred. He wrote of Ferreira's Camp:

> It has about 400 inhabitants; there are twenty-four iron buildings, a considerable number of reed and one or two brick houses, fourteen stores and canteens (two of a very fair size), and two hotels one of which is of a very fair appearance and creditably conducted.[12]

Ross recommended the establishment of a branch agency of the bank and on 11 October he opened for business in a marquee at Ferreira's Camp.

But the decision had already been taken to proclaim a village a mile or two to the east on Randjeslaagte, the government-owned farm which fortuitously occupied a position almost exactly in the middle of the strike of the Main Reef, but was not itself to prove gold-bearing. The farm was '*uitvalgrond*', a triangular piece left over after survey of neighbouring farms. Nobody at the time seemed to bother about how it came to be called Johannesburg. It became accepted in later years that the town was named for all, some or one of four men who were prominent at the time. They are President Kruger whose second name was Johannes; Christiaan Johannes Joubert, Head of the Mines Department, Johann Rissik, the Acting Surveyor-General, and Johannes Petrus Meyer, Veldkornet of the ward.

Right until recent times there was controversy about the naming. As late as 1974, a book was published suggesting, incredibly, that the town was named after a Portuguese gold coin known as a *Ioannes*.[13] James Gray who with his wife Ethel did the most exhaustive researches on the beginnings of the city, is certain that it was named for Meyer. Professor L Fouché, the historian, on rather stronger grounds, plumped for the first three.[14] The issue was however resolved by Dr M S Appelgryn, the historian, with the discovery in the Transvaal Archives of a memo to the State Secretary from Rissik dated 1896 which confirms that the town was named for Rissik and Joubert.[15]

On 4 November of that year, Von Brandis was appointed Special Landdrost with jurisdiction over the whole of the proclaimed gold-fields. Jan Eloff became Mining Commissioner. Hans Sauer has recorded that the Rand had no occasion in those early days to complain of its officials. Von Brandis, from a German family of long military tradition, was a 'charming old soldier, energetic, straight, and easy to work with'.[16] His humanity and generosity were generally acknowledged. He was to play a key role in the formative, early years of the Rand, remaining Special Landdrost until the capture of Johannesburg by Lord Roberts on 31 May 1900.

In the closing months of 1886, work on the reefs came more or less to a standstill for a while, because it was realized that this was no poor man's diggings as the California fields had been. The remarkable feature of the field was not so much the richness of the ore but the vast extent of the deposits. There was bonanza ground about, but the average grade overall was not high. The unique feature was the reliance that could be placed on its continuance at payable levels. The security offered made possible the large-scale employment of machinery. Indeed the reefs could not be mined on an economic scale without it. Nor could such expenditure be justified on a single, or even small groups of claims. As a result, syndicates were quickly formed to acquire claims to permit the mining of amalgamated blocks. The syndicates ordered machinery and sat back to await the lumbering ox-wagon trains that would transport it from the coast or railhead at Kimberley. In the meantime, the buying and selling of claims and the general wheeler-dealing went on amid the mushrooming hotels and bars of the future city.

During the waiting period, some individual diggers moved back to the eastern Transvaal, George Harrison among them. He sold his discoverer's claim to F W Marsden for £10, and disappeared from the scene. George Walker, who may have been with Harrison when the Main Reef was discovered, failed to turn his digger's claim to advantage and died a poor pensioner. Bantjes was another prominent pioneer who died indigent. He had crushed reef on the farm Roodepoort in early 1886 but it did not yield much gold, and he sold for a song rights in what became a fabulous gold mine.

The Gold Law gave authority for the Mining Commissioner in every proclaimed gold-field to take the necessary steps for the election of a diggers' committee of nine members. They were elected from and by the holders of diggers' licences granted by the Mining Commissioner who was *ex officio* Chairman of the committee. Those elected held office for twelve months and could then be re-elected. The first election for a diggers' committee on the Rand took place on 8 November 1886. A sandwich-man carried calico posters through the crowd, bearing the inscription in large letters 'Vote for Ferreira, the Man'. Nobody else adopted this method of self-promotion. Ferreira, undoubtedly for better reasons, headed the poll with ninety-six votes. Others elected were J S Harrison, H J Morkel, Dr Hans Sauer, W P Fraser, J J Eloff, T Y Sherwell, and W Bissett. J J Eloff, the representative of Langlaagte (not to be confused with Jan Eloff, the Mining Commissioner), resigned in March and Harry Struben was elected to fill the vacancy.

The Diggers' Committee did work that in the circumstances could be called distinguished in obtaining basic amenities for the fast-growing population – and the Government seems at first to have responded reasonably to petitions.

There have been misconceptions about the role of the Diggers' Committee. Various historical writers, including Gray, have stated that it was, after about a year of life, transformed into a Sanitary Board or Committee at the end of 1887. It has been shown however that these two institutions functioned side by side, the Diggers' Committee continuing for another six months before it became redundant and died a natural death.[17] The Sanitary Board, with wider functions and elected representatives from five wards, was to lay the foundations of municipal government in Johannesburg.

A further popular misconception is that the Diggers' Committee was a forerunner of the Chamber of Mines.[18] In fact, it had an entirely separate existence. The Chamber was founded as a consequence of the realization of the early mine-owners that it had become necessary to create a body that could publish authoritative information on the fields which would be accepted as such both in South Africa and the financial capitals of the world.

[1] A Trollope, *South Africa*, II, p 20.

[2] J B Taylor, *Recollections of the Discovery of Gold on the Witwatersrand and the Early Development of the Gold Mines*, pp 3-4.

[3] M S Appelgryn, 'Die Ontdekking van Goud aan die Witwatersrand', *Kleio*, II, 2 October 1970.

[4] A P Cartwright, *The Gold Miners*, p 39.

[5] Langlaagte was administratively in the Klip River Ward of the Heidelberg District.

[6] J Gray, *Payable Gold*, photograph of G Harrison's affidavit facing p 96, transcription, p 253-254.

[7] Leyds, p 3.

[8] Cartwright, *The Gold Miners*, pp 79-80, map of the Witwatersrand showing the farms on which the Main Reef outcrop had been traced between Roodepoort and Driekop, published in 1887 by E P Mathers. With the map a list of the registered owners of the mining leases is given.

[9] W S Churchill, *Ian Hamilton's March*, p 238.

[10] Bought by F Bezuidenhout in 1879 for a span of oxen and a trek chain. The family sold off the farm piecemeal across the years and made a fortune. The suburb of Bez Valley recalls the Bezuidenhouts.

[11] Gray, p 99.

[12] J A Henry (H A Siepman, ed), *The First Hundred Years of the Standard Bank*, pp 336-337.

[13] N Hirschon, *The Naming of Johannesburg as an Historical Commentary*, quoted by M S Appelgryn in 'The Naming of Johannesburg – a Radical Theory', *Kleio*, VII, 1, May 1975.

[14] L Fouché, 'Johannesburg in South African History', *South African Journal of Science*, XXXIII, March 1937, pp 1128-1129.

[15] Transvaal Archives (SSa 338 Ra 831/96) quoted in Hirschon.

[16] H Sauer, *Ex Africa*, p 174.

[17] M S Appelgryn, 'Die Ontstaan van die Eerste Gesondheidskomitee van Johannesburg', *Kleio*, III, 2, October 1971.

[18] See for example, P Richardson and J J Van-Helten, 'The Gold Mining Industry in the Transvaal 1886-99', P Warwick and S B Spies, eds, *The South African War: The Anglo-Boer War 1899-1902*, p 20.

CHAPTER TWO

The Old Chamber

The first Chamber of Mines in Johannesburg held its foundation meeting at the Central Hotel on 7 December 1887 to elect a Council of twenty-five from a hundred and forty members who had paid their annual subscriptions (two guineas, payable half-yearly in advance) and were thus eligible to vote. The membership list reads like a roll of honour of South African pioneers, or a rogues' gallery, depending on your perspective of those robust times.

That Chamber made an impressive start, briefly flourished, declined and died, all in eighteen months or so. Little formal record remains of its short life, but it had proved a need and its departure left a gap which would swiftly be filled by the launching on 5 October 1889 of the Witwatersrand Chamber of Mines, organized on the much more substantial base of mining company representation, instead of on individual membership.

The first report of the Witwatersrand Chamber of Mines contains a single reference to its precursor, the Old Chamber. The Chairman of the Council, Carl Hanau, in the Council's half-yearly report dated 27 January 1890, states: 'The outstanding liabilities of the Old Chamber have been taken over ... and paid.' (They amounted to £117 2s 6d.)

This was certainly a too cursory reference to a body which, by its achievements and, more importantly, by its failures, set guidelines that were to be followed with advantage by its successor.

For long years the Old Chamber was forgotten and little was known about it except that it had existed. Memories of pioneer times were overlaid by those of more eventful days that followed upon each other, and written records of the Old Chamber remaining were scanty. One letterbook survives in the archives of its successor, with smudgy copies of correspondence, dating from 26 January to 27 November 1888, in the crisp copperplate hand of a procession of secretaries. Otherwise there are a few documents in the Transvaal Archives and some slight sketches in contemporary notes.

Fortunately, meetings were generally public and open to the Press which fully reported them. When Dennis Etheredge wrote his 'Early History of the Chamber' for his master's degree in 1949, there were no copies of newspapers available dated earlier than April 1889. In recent years the Johannesburg Newspaper Library has acquired full microfilm of copies of *The Eastern Star* from the first issue on the Rand in October 1887. Study of the microfilm has made it possible to give for the first time a fuller picture of the Old Chamber's activities and the problems it faced. Posterity is in debt to the journalists of the day who followed their industrious calling, under circumstances of remarkable difficulty. They were wordy by modern standards, but their often elegant prose is rich in detail for the historian.

The honour of producing the first newspaper in Johannesburg was secured by *The Diggers' News*, which came into being on Thursday, 24 February 1887. The following day saw the first issue of *The Transvaal Mining Argus*, printed in Pretoria. *The Standard and Transvaal Mining Chronicle* was issued in March. In October arrived two evening papers, *The Daily News*, and *The Eastern Star*. *The Eastern Star* had been moved up from Grahamstown, an operation entailing a twenty-three-day haul by three teams of oxen of the newspaper's printing plant from railhead at Kimberley.

The two Johannesburg newspapers which came to exercise the greatest influence during the Kruger Administration were *The Standard and Diggers' News* (an amalgamation of *The Diggers' News* and *The Standard and Transvaal Mining Chronicle* took place in January 1891) and *The Star* (as *The Eastern Star* became known from April 1889). *The Standard and Diggers' News*, under its owners, Emmanuel Mendelssohn and R S Scott, received a government subsidy and became such a critic of capitalist interests that Lionel Phillips and his associates tried to purchase the newspaper in 1894. When that attempt failed, the Corner House group of companies subsidized *The Standard and Diggers' News* to the tune of £87 6s 8d per month 'so long as they support the true interests of the place [Corner House]'.[1] The newspaper, however, remained a supporter of the Kruger Government which apparently paid Mendelssohn a larger subsidy of £720 per month.[2] In 1889 *The Transvaal Leader*, in which Eckstein had a controlling interest, was launched in an attempt to counteract the influence of *The Standard and Diggers' News*.

In 1889 a new company, The Argus Printing and Publishing Company Limited, was established to finance and control *The Star*. The mining magnates, Hermann Eckstein, J B Robinson and Cecil Rhodes, now had interests in the newspaper, which came to identify itself with the industry and to criticize the policies of the Kruger Administration.

The Eastern Star from the outset referred to itself as *The Star*. Unlike the others, it would flourish down to the present day. Valuable social commentary of pioneer days was provided, too, by the Pretoria newspaper, *De Volkstem*, which from an early date stationed a representative at Ferreira's Camp.[3]

The Eastern Star first appeared in Johannesburg on Monday, 17 October 1887, and thereafter on each Monday, Wednesday and Friday with a guaranteed circulation of 2 000 copies in the Transvaal and Colony. Its opening leader was headed 'Ourselves':

Today the *Eastern Star* makes its first appearance in its new sphere, and starts afresh upon its course, which had been arrested for a short space by transference to this more northern portion of our South African hemisphere.

It [Johannesburg] has arrived at its present stage of advancement years before Kimberley even approached it. An exchange, a club, a theatre, grand hotels, and all the adjuncts of civilized life ....

The Eastern Star went on to signal how it would continue. It certainly came out from its corner fighting:

... the *Star* will be loyal to the institutions of the land which gives it shelter and the protection of its laws. But loyalty to the institutions of a country does not mean subservience to those who are in power for the time being.

True loyalty to the State consists in doing for it that which is best calculated to preserve its Constitution intact, at the same time endeavouring to bring about such reforms as will give to all who submit to its laws a voice in the Government of it. Taxation and representation are all but synonymous terms in every country in which the democracy, and not the autocracy, rules. In countries under Republican forms of Government, the widest freedom and liberty for all are the chief boasts. Can that be said of a country in which a very large proportion of the people are shut out from exercise of the franchise for five years, and in which no person is eligible for a seat in the Legislature who has not been a resident in the State for fifteen years?

An important motivation for the moves that led to the founding of the Chamber was the need for authoritative information about the output of the new field on a basis that would be acceptable in the financial capitals of the world. It is forgotten today that the published yields of the diamond fields of Kimberley and of the Witwatersrand gold-fields were regarded at first with scepticism because mining experts had rejected on geological grounds the possibility of major deposits in South Africa. And the climate of opinion generally was not improved by over-speculation and bogus promotion. It was even claimed in London that Brazilian gems were used to falsify the volume of Kimberley production.[4]

Cecil Rhodes himself was discouraged by expert advice about the Witwatersrand field – to the chagrin of Sauer who obtained valuable options on the Rand in the early days which Rhodes allowed to lapse. Gardner Williams, the famous American mining engineer and distinguished General Manager of De Beers, advised him against any kind of participation. Williams insisted that there never had been – and never would be – a paying gold-field in South Africa. He knew that conglomerates had not been a substantial proposition elsewhere in the world, and he was not wrong when he described the Rand as a 'ten pennyweight proposition' – but he did not allow for the vastness of the gold deposits and the economies of scale that would make them uniquely profitable. Three of the pioneers who backed their hunches against the judgement of the experts commented in their memoirs as follows:

Hans Sauer:[5] All the wonderful mineral riches of Africa ... were in the first instance found by men who were quite ignorant of mining matters .... The discoveries were almost always condemned as valueless by the engineers, as in the case of the Rand ....

Carl Jeppe:[6] ... it is wonderful how often the gentlemen with theoretical knowledge – and sometimes those with practical experience too – proved to be utterly at fault in South Africa, both as to diamonds and gold.

J Percy FitzPatrick[7] – somewhat poetically: Perhaps there is something in Africa itself which makes it a huge exception to the rules of other lands; the something which is suggested in the 'rivers without water, flowers without scent, and birds without song'; a contrariness which puts the alluvial gold on the top of mountain ranges and leaves the valleys barren; which mocked the experience of the world, and showed the waterworn gravel deposit to be the biggest, richest, deepest, and most reliable gold reef ever known; which placed diamonds in such conditions that the greatest living authority, who had undertaken a huge journey to report on the occurrence, could only say, in the face of a successful wash-up, 'Well, there *may* be diamonds here, but all I can say is they've no right to be' ....

The early pioneers of the Reef, as their optimism was justified by results, found it of vital importance that the reputation of the field should be established as soon as possible on the basis of orderly development and reliable statistical information.

Accordingly, in the issue of *The Eastern Star* on Friday, 21 October 1887, there appeared a report under the following headings:

PUBLIC MEETING.
DISSEMINATION OF MINING NEWS.
A CHAMBER OF MINES TO BE FORMED.

The meeting, held at the Central Hotel, considered a report of a committee appointed earlier which recommended 'after very careful consideration as to the best means of obtaining authentic information as to the output of gold on the Witwatersrandt, and of making the same public in the interests of these fields, and of guarding mining interests generally, recommends ... That a body be formed, to be called the Chamber of Mines ....' After discussion the meeting adopted an amendment proposed by Ed Lippert:[8] 'That it is desirable to form a Mining Institute for the purpose of watching over, promoting and representing the mining interest.'

The meeting also agreed that membership should be 'open to all interested in mining'. It appointed a Provisional Committee, which included Carl Jeppe, the lawyer and Transvaal burgher, to draft rules and attract members.

The Provisional Committee worked with commendable speed so that on the following Wednesday, *The Eastern Star* could comment:

> We have been permitted to inspect the draft of the Constitution of the Chamber of Mines, with the Rules and Regulations which are to govern its proceedings, and it appears to us that it is so complete and comprehensive in every detail that it cannot fail to meet with the general approval of the members, when submitted to them at the adjourned meeting to be held tomorrow .... The preamble stating the objects of the Chamber ... declares them to be: 'to collect, arrange and from time to time publish, facts connected with the mining industry, particularly the Witwatersrandt Gold Fields, and to watch over and promote that industry generally.'
>
> It provides at some length for the manner in which members are to be proposed and admitted, especially with regard to the taking of a ballot. ... Subscriptions when payable, absent or defaulting members, and the expulsion of members, and for what causes, are all carefully dealt with, as well as all the details necessary to the establishment and working of an institution which should become one of the most important in the town.
>
> But all the care ... will be of little avail unless shareholders of Mining Companies also interest themselves in it. It is most important that the different Companies and their managers and administrative representatives – the men, in fact, who are responsible for the working of the Companies – should be well represented upon the Council and Executive Committee.

According to the next issue of *The Eastern Star* on Friday, 28 October, the draft constitution was read clause by clause at the adjourned meeting and adopted with some amendments. *The Eastern Star* concluded its report with a statement in parentheses that it published as an extra the draft Constitution, up to the last clause adopted. Alas! This section of the newspaper, though widely searched for, has not yet been found. However, *The Eastern Star* on 11 November reported:

> The amended draft of the Rules, as published in an extra in our last, was submitted, and after some little discussion adopted, with the exception of the clauses referring to the duties of the Secretary and Treasurer, which were ordered to be held over .... The draft was referred back to the Committee, with several suggestions for their further amendment.

The revised rules were adopted on Wednesday, 16 November 1887.[9] It is from this day that the Old Chamber can be regarded as having been formally constituted.

At the meeting of Foundation Members which followed on 7 December, the election of the Council duly took place. W J Quin and Thomas Sheffield were appointed scrutineers. The scrutiny was a 'somewhat tedious business'. When completed the result of the ballot was: E Jones, C Jeppe, C Hanau, H W Struben, J Stroyan, R W Murray, Jnr, J G Maynard, C W Deecker,

H Eckstein, W St John Carr, J Dell, J B Robinson, F Clench, E Hancock, G Tilney, A C Baillie, W P Fraser, H Wright, C Cowen, G Brown, A A Stanton, Dr T G Lawrence, T W Farrell, and Quin and Sheffield, who were candidates as well as scrutineers.

Murray then proposed Harry Struben as the first Chairman of the Chamber. He described him as 'the pioneer of the Randt Gold Fields'. As such it was only appropriate and proper that he should be elected. Struben was elected unanimously. E Jones, a consulting engineer, was then proposed as Vice-Chairman and elected unanimously as well. A tradition of unanimous election of office-bearers continues to the present day.

In accepting office, Jones announced to applause a donation of £50 for the purchase of books and papers for the proposed Chamber library. Jeppe then said that he would take the hat around and raised a list, headed by Jones's donation, that totalled £160.

Two weeks later, on Wednesday, 21 December, the Council met for the first time and elected an Executive Committee to run the affairs of the Chamber in the periods between Council meetings. They chose Carl Jeppe, Hermann Eckstein, J B Robinson, J Stroyan, Captain J G Maynard, J Dell, E Hancock, H Wright, and A C Baillie. The first three were to play key roles in the future of the industry and of the Transvaal.

The requirement that membership should be open to all individuals 'interested in mining' was a broad one. There were important mining people among those who paid their foundation guinea, apart from those elected to the Council and Executive. Among them were Alfred Beit, S Neumann, J B Taylor, Dr Sauer, Fred Struben, H S Caldecott, C D Rudd and Henry Nourse. There were people who were important, or who became important in other spheres, like James Sivewright who became a Cabinet Minister in the Cape and was influential in Transvaal railway and telegraph affairs; Richard Kelsey Loveday who became the Volksraad Member for Barberton; W St John Carr who would be the first Mayor of Johannesburg; Sir Drummond Dunbar who would be the first Secretary of the Johannesburg Stock Exchange; Colonel Ignatius Ferreira, and H B Marshall, the financier and industrialist, who gave his name to Marshallstown. There was much cross-membership with the Diggers' Committee (Colonel Ferreira, J Spranger Harrison, Dr Sauer, W P Fraser, Captain J G Maynard, T Y Sherwell) and with a Vigilance Committee formed to counter attempts at claim jumping (Hancock, Harrison, Newman Marks, Dr Lawrence, Cowen and Stroyan). There were others whose interest in mining was peripheral. Jeppe is described in the *Dictionary of South African Biography* as a jurist, businessman and politician. He did establish mining claims. His brother Julius, also a Foundation Member, is described as a mining and property magnate but seems to have been mainly interested in land at the time. Thomas Sheffield was owner and Editor of *The Eastern Star*, and in partnership with his brother George, another Foundation Member. C W Deecker was owner and Editor of *The Transvaal Mining Argus* (no connection with the Argus Group). An organization in which the vote of the owner of a claim or two, or a share broker, could carry the same weight as the head of a major mining group was likely to run into difficulty before long.

It was to come. On Saturday, 3 March 1888, at a meeting of the Executive Committee, Jeppe, in the chair, referred to the difficulty experienced by the Executive in carrying out the work of the Chamber owing to members of the Committee failing to attend its meetings, or to there being no quorum. In the same month the Chamber, the prisoner perhaps of its Rules, declared that J B Robinson and Hermann Eckstein, who represented the two most powerful mining groups on the Rand, had rendered their seats vacant through non-attendance at meetings. Carl Hanau, partner in the powerful S Neumann Group, who had apparently been added to the Executive after the initial election, was also declared to have rendered his seat vacant. St John Carr, Fraser and Quin were elected to fill their places. Harry Struben quietly moved off stage and at some time unknown Carl Jeppe became Chairman of the Chamber.

Meanwhile the Chamber continued to exercise its intended functions. Soon after the founding of the Chamber, on 23 November 1887, St John Carr had read a paper on the future of the gold-fields at St Mary's Hall under Chamber auspices, entitled 'Our Position and Our Prospects'. The attendance was thought fair considering the shortness of notice given. The first letter in the old letterbook that survives is a copy of one written to E J Roberts on 26 January 1888, informing him that members of the Chamber would be pleased to hear him read his paper on 'Scientific Milling of Gold Ores'. On Thursday, 15 March of that year, Ramsay Collins read a paper on 'Auriferous Conglomerates'.

In pursuance of its initial object to disseminate authoritative statistical information, the Chamber published monthly a return of the output of gold on the fields. As receipts from gold sales leapt month by month, the Chamber's announcement of the results by the 10th of each month became a highlight of public interest. *The Eastern Star* commented that the Chamber had fulfilled the purpose of its foundation.[10]

The Chamber opposed the bogus flotations and false prospectuses which characterized mining in the early days. It wrote to the Stock Exchange, the Colonial Institute, *The Times* and other newspapers in London in January 1888, and warned them to carefully investigate companies before writing favourably about them. The Chamber offered to provide relevant information. In the following month the Chamber was empowered by its members to deal with false statements and misrepresentations in prospectuses.[11]

This sphere of the Chamber's activities, not surprisingly, occasioned some difficulty. At the monthly meeting of members on 4 April, Carl Jeppe reported numerous applications for information about the capacity of engineers who had reported on mining ventures placed before the public, and even requests for quotations for scrip. He gathered there was some misapprehension in England as to the objects of the Chamber. The Executive had supplied what information it could, exercising, at the same time, every caution; but it had not lost sight of the fact that the Chamber 'could easily be made a tool of'.

In the same month, the Secretary wrote the following in reply to a letter from France:

> I am instructed by the Executive Committee of the Chamber of Mines to inform you that you have evidently mistaken the purpose for which the Chamber of Mines was formed. They do not act as Brokers, nor do they advise Investors, but are a public body, composed of the leading men on the Gold Fields, formed for the purpose of watching over and protecting the Mining Interests of Witwatersrand.[12]

The activities of the Old Chamber were many and varied. Early reports refer to the appointment of a committee to consider the revision of the Gold Laws in conjunction with the Diggers' Committee, and in co-operation with the Barberton Mining and Commercial Chamber. Representations were made to the Government with regard to the prevention of gold and amalgam thefts; the jumping of claims; in opposition to the granting of patents and the Dynamite Monopoly; against the granting of monopolies in general; and supporting proposals for the dispatch of gold through the Post Office.

Discussions were held with Christiaan Joubert, Head of the Department of Mines, when he visited the gold-field in April 1888, the Chamber's representatives being Bill Taylor, C F Liddle, C W H Kohler, C W Deecker, H S Caldecott and H Wright. One of the subjects discussed was the jumping of claims on the property of the National Gold Mining Company of which Kohler was Manager. Joubert also raised the point that he was neither a member of Kruger's Executive nor of the Volksraad and suggested that the Chamber might press for him to be appointed to the Executive and be present at meetings of the Volksraad. The Chamber took no action on this, apparently because it was found that he had the right to be present at both bodies, and to address them, when mining matters were under discussion.

For its part, the Chamber deputation urged that the Chamber should be recognized as a public body. Joubert was not forthcoming on the point, and in fact the Old Chamber was never officially recognized.

The Chamber entertained Joubert to a banquet on Thursday, 29 March 1888, at the Rand Club (founded earlier by Cecil Rhodes), covers being laid for fifty guests. The table was decorated 'in most elegant style, while the catering was simply superb'. The menu was:

SOUP
Jardiners
FISH
Salmon Mayonnaise

ENTREES

Lamb Cutlets with Green Peas

Supreme of Chicken and Piquante Sauce

Fillets of Beef with Champignon, etc

Ragout of Wild Duck

JOINTS

Boiled Turkey and Oyster Sauce

Roast Saddle of Mutton

Roast Beef

Ham

VEGETABLES

Potatoes, Peas, Cauliflower, Asparagus

Chicken Curry

Marrow Bones

PASTRY

Compote of Pears with Whipped Cream

Chocolate Cake Queen's Pudding

Lemon Jelly Custards

The pioneers not only enjoyed a party. They had a stamina unknown today. There were toasts to 'The President' and 'Queen Victoria', 'The Minister of Mines', 'The Civil Service' (with special mention for J Marais, the Auditor-General, Carl von Brandis and Jan Eloff), 'The Collector of Customs', 'The Ladies', 'Our Guests', 'The Press' (coupled with the names of Thomas Sheffield of *The Eastern Star* and Crosby of *The Diggers' News*), 'The Managers of Mines', 'The Pioneers of the Gold-Fields', 'The Vice-Chairman' and finally 'The Chairman'. All the toasts were replied to, sometimes by more than one speaker (Joubert in true political tradition making a long and graceful speech without saying anything in particular). That makes more than twenty speeches. The remainder of the evening was spent 'in conviviality'.[13]

The Old Chamber had no fixed abode. It met first at the Central Hotel, which collapsed in 1889 but was rebuilt in substantial fashion and stood for more than seventy years at the corner of Sauer and Commissioner Streets. The Chamber also met at the Stock Exchange, at Quin's Boardroom and in the Government Buildings.

The first Secretary was A W Macintyre. In July 1888 St John Carr, a member of the Executive, became Secretary and one of his first duties was to write to his predecessor asking him to furnish a cash statement, a list of members of the Chamber and of subscriptions received. Two months later Ramsay Collins, another member of the Executive, was Acting Secretary as St John Carr had resigned.

In November 1888 the Chamber advertised for a secretary and at the end of the month it unanimously elected Henry Wright to the post. He resigned in June 1889 and was voted a gratuity of fifty guineas. There was difficulty in finding the wherewithal to pay the Secretary's salary.

Despite the imposing array of activities, the Old Chamber was seldom an effective body. On 6 June 1888 *The Eastern Star* commented

> The Chamber of Mines is, unfortunately, not heard of so frequently as it ought to be, nor as its promoters and founders intended that it should be. We are not in a position at present to lay the blame on the right, or indeed upon any, shoulders for the laxity which has of late been displayed by that body. But we do hope that ... the failure of the Chamber in the performance of the duties for which it was established will impress upon the Committee the necessity of showing that there is still some vitality left in it. The community, however, even if the Chamber did nothing else, is much indebted to it for the action it took in the early days of its career which led to the publication of the monthly statistics showing the out-put of gold by our several Companies. For nothing is calculated so much to impress people at a distance with a correct impression as to the value of these fields as these monthly returns, showing as they are doing a constantly increasing yield.

The Chamber still had 'vitality' enough to organize a public meeting at the Stock Exchange on 4 July 1888 to hear Ed Lippert, who had recently been awarded the concession for the manufacture of gunpowder, dynamite and explosives in the Transvaal, reply to public opposition to the concession. It was the beginning of a controversy that was to play a dominating role on the mining scene until the end of the century and in which the Chamber would be endlessly engaged. After Lippert had addressed the meeting at length in justification, J B Robinson commented that if there was a gentleman present able to protect his own interests it was Lippert. He had handled his case in a very able way which showed him to be a smart man of business. He had tried to persuade them that his dynamite at £7 10s a case would be better than the imported stuff at £5. If he would give them an assurance that, while he had the right to charge £7 10s, he would never charge more than the price of the imported article, Robinson would be satisfied.

Lippert was unable to comply with Robinson's request. He could only say that the price would not be as much as £7 10s.

The Chairman (Jeppe) commented that he took that as an assurance that the price would be £7 9s 9d.[14]

Lippert left the meeting amid 'cheers, groans and hisses'. It was then proposed by Robinson and agreed:

> That as the concession granted ... to Mr Lippert for the manufacture of dynamite and explosives will have a very serious effect upon the mining industry ... a petition to Government be drafted, respectfully urging upon them the advisability of re-considering the price fixed, so as not to exceed the cost of the imported article ....[15]

Meanwhile on 11 June had taken place an extraordinary general meeting which discussed possible dissolution of the Chamber and then adjourned. A further meeting on 31 July appointed a provisional committee to reconstruct it. On 6 September the provisional committee reported that it had met five times and had arranged for a deputation and a public meeting to protest against the proposed Bank Concession, had revised the Rules of the Chamber and secured a guarantee fund for the Secretary's salary for six months.[16]

Significantly, the funds came mainly from the banks who furnished the Chamber with information on which it based its published statistics – the Standard Bank, the Natal Bank, the Bank of Africa, and the Cape of Good Hope Bank, each guaranteeing £10.

The provisional committee reported that it had found that only one member had paid his guinea for the current half-year. They urged members to do so to enable the incoming committee to pay off outstanding debt.

The changes to the Rules proposed were not radical. They did away with the Council and substituted an arrangement whereby business would be directed by a committee, meeting weekly and reporting their transactions to a general meeting of members to be held monthly.[17]

The result of the ballot for a new executive was: Birkett, Britten, Jeppe, Murray, Wright, Liddle, Quin, Deecker, Birbeck, Nourse, St John Carr and Collins.

The Old Chamber battled, largely in vain, to obtain improvements in conditions for the mining industry. It did not always confine itself to strictly mining matters, and indeed there was little that affected the general public of Johannesburg that did not impinge on the mines. The Chamber opposed an attempt by a company to get a sanitary concession; it opposed the suggested closing of the overworked Telegraph Office on Wednesday afternoons and urged an increase in staff instead. It asked the Government to establish a municipality and it scrutinized the powers of the Sanitary Board over water rights and made recommendations.

When confronted with the resolution, in September 1888, urging the Government to establish a municipality in Johannesburg, the State Secretary, Willem Eduard Bok, wrote on the letter: 'Who or what is the Chamber of Mines and what has that body to do with town administration – I thought the Sanitary Board was concerned with all that?'[18] It has become a popular legend that Bok was genuinely ignorant of the existence of the ten-month-old Chamber. But closer examination of the evidence suggests otherwise.

Bok was not a simple Boer elevated to a position of unexpected responsibility. He was an able and cultured Hollander who had emigrated to the Transvaal in response to an appeal made by President T F Burgers. He had been educated in Amsterdam, concentrating on the study of French, German and English. He spent a year thereafter at St John's Collegiate School in London to improve his English. In 1876, he was Secretary to the deputation consisting of Paul Kruger and E J P Jorissen which went to Britain to protest against the annexation of the Transvaal. As a secretary, he also accompanied the 1878 deputation to London of Kruger and General Piet Joubert. He was present at the historic meeting at Paardekraal in 1880 which sparked the re-bellion leading to the First Anglo–Boer War, and was sworn in as State Sec-retary of the Republic. Reappointed in 1884, his second term was 'noted for the establishment of Johannesburg'.[19] He visited the town in October 1887, and toured mine properties. In the same year, Boksburg, the second town of the Reef, was named after him. By 1888 Johannesburg had become the largest town in the Transvaal, outstripping the capital, Pretoria.

It is too much altogether to believe that Bok was unaware of the existence of the body which had raised a series of important issues with the Head of his Department of Mines – and wined and dined him so sumptuously; who had held discussions on the dispatch of gold through the Post Office with Dr W Leyds, then State Attorney, and with the Postmaster; whose activities were chronicled week by week in the Press and which each month published the details of the gold yield on which the State depended for solvency. However ineffective a body the Chamber may have been, it was not possible for the State Secretary to be unconscious of the build-up of grievances on the gold-fields for the relief of which the Chamber regularly called on the Govern-ment in a restrained and responsible manner. Nor were its representatives nonentities or unfamiliar. Both Struben and Jeppe were, in fact, burghers and well-known personally to Kruger and almost certainly to Bok. Struben had appeared before the Volksraad and received its thanks for his part in the dis-covery of the gold-field.

It must regretfully be concluded that Bok's stance was one of an arrogant disregard for the views and aspirations of the Uitlander population which was to become all too familiar in official circles in Pretoria. When the Chamber sent a memorial asking the Government not to grant concessions affecting the mining industry without consulting the Chamber, a clerk made the following note for the State Secretary: 'Shall I reply that the Chamber of Mines is meddling in affairs which have nothing to do with them?'. Bok's emphatic reply was 'Ja!'.[20]

Jeppe, commenting at a Chamber meeting on Tuesday, 6 November 1888, said the Government's answer to its communication on concessions was a 'snub'. The Chamber existed for the protection of mining interests, and it was its duty to make representations. The meeting thought it advisable to reply to the Government's letter, but in a manner which would give no offence. Deecker was deputed to draft a reply.[21]

In May 1889 the Chamber sent a memorial to the Volksraad stating that it had heard that the Gold Law, which provided the legislative and regulatory background for mining, was to be revised, and asking to be allowed to submit practical suggestions. The Raad unceremoniously rejected the proposals on the grounds that the Witwatersrand was represented in the Raad and an approach could have been made through its representative.

That representative was Meyer, the Veldkornet with whom the mining community was on good terms, but those who put forward the needs of the mines did not have an easy passage. Eloff, the Mining or 'Gold' Commissioner, sent in his resignation because of ill-health, lack of staff, and because his proposals for improvement on the gold-fields were consistently disregarded. Fortunately, the communication gap that was widening between Johannesburg and Pretoria did not exist on the local scene. Relations were generally good and Eloff was persuaded by public petition to withdraw his resignation.[22]

The Old Chamber, with dwindling support, and little to show for the effort of those who worked loyally for it, moved inevitably to its demise. Several efforts were made to revive it but it at last became clear that radical reconstruction was needed. This finally led to the negotiations which resulted in the establishment on 5 October 1889 of a powerful and permanent Chamber.

[1] C T Gordon, *The Growth of Boer Opposition to Kruger (1890-1895)*, p 89, quoting the Leyds Papers, 670. (Letter of Lionel Phillips to London headquarters, 8 December 1894.)

[2] *Ibid*, p 88, quoting the Leyds Papers, 679, No 45.

[3] Gray, pp 108-109.

[4] R W Murray, Snr, *South African Reminiscences*, pp 113-114.

[5] Sauer, p 146.

[6] C Jeppe, *The Kaleidoscopic Transvaal*, p 115.

[7] J Percy FitzPatrick, *The Transvaal from Within: A Private Record of Public Affairs*, pp 44-45.

[8] Edouard Amandus Lippert (1853-1925), a Pretoria financier of German origin and sympathy, who was to become notorious as a concessionaire, was a cousin of Alfred Beit. He made a fortune which he lost in the hyper-inflation of the German mark which followed the 1914-1918 War.

[9] *The Eastern Star*, 18 November 1887.

[10] *Ibid*, 7 March 1888.

[11] D A Etheredge, 'The Early History of the Chamber of Mines: Johannesburg: 1887-1897', pp 7-8.

[12] Letterbook of the Old Chamber, 1888, p 37, 6 April 1888, to M Raveneau.

[13] *The Eastern Star*, 4 April 1888.

[14] *Ibid*, 6 July 1888.

[15] *Idem*.

[16] *Ibid*, 7 September 1888.

[17] *Idem*.

[18] Etheredge, p 2, citing State Secretary, incoming correspondence, R 8641/88.

[19] J Ploeger, 'Bok' in *Dictionary of South African Biography*, I, p 87-88.

[20] Etheredge, p 9, citing State Secretary, incoming correspondence, R 9669/88.

[21] *The Eastern Star*, 7 November 1888.

[22] *Ibid*, 17 April 1889.

CHAPTER THREE

To Promote and Protect

By mid-1889 the Witwatersrand was an established phenomenon. A chain of mines was blasting out the outcrop from Roodepoort to Germiston. Ox-wagon trains had drawn huge quantities of machinery from railhead at Kimberley along dreadful tracks and through drifts imperilled by the flash floods that follow Highveld storms. Everywhere the stamp batteries, crushing the reef by night and day, had begun the unceasing roar that was to characterize the Rand for years to come. The output of gold had risen steadily month by month. In January 1888, when monthly declarations began, the output was 11 269 ounces; in May 1889 it exceeded 36 000 ounces for the first time.[1] By then that lusty infant, the Johannesburg Stock Exchange, had been through a sustained boom and experienced its first, sobering slump. The town of Johannesburg continued to burgeon, seemingly magically, in the centre of the strike of the reef, and the rudiments of municipal government and services had been established. The population of the Witwatersrand had soared, outstripping the food and water supply and the primitive transport system. The problems of supply were exacerbated by crippling drought. As winter gave way to spring, the gusty winds, bringing no relieving rain, conjured malevolent dust clouds from the unmetalled roads and the mounting dumps of tailings. The Government was struggling to meet the postal, police and other administrative requirements. And the mine-owners, scanning the mine plans and totting up the numbers, saw that, while there were quick profits to be made, the real bonanza lay in long-term operation. They had steady, expanding business on their hands. Like businessmen the world over who market a common product they were going to need an enduring institution to promote and protect their interests.

The Old Chamber had failed principally because it did not confine its membership to those directly engaged in mining operations, and did not have the full support of the mining houses.

The leading mining house was Corner House, led by Hermann Eckstein and J B Taylor, which represented Wernher, Beit, London. The other great mining houses of the time were those led by J B Robinson, Rhodes (Consolidated Gold Fields) and Barnato (Johannesburg Consolidated Investment Co). The Old Chamber did not receive the support of either Corner House or the

Robinson Group. Its dismissal of Eckstein and Robinson from the Executive Committee because they failed to attend its meetings can hardly have helped to maintain accord.[2]

There was little hiatus between the death of the Old Chamber and the birth of the new. J B Taylor recalled in 1936[3]:

> Mr W Y Campbell, who represented the interests of Sir Donald Currie, called at our office one day and told us that he and Edward Lippert had come to the conclusion that as long as the Mines had no corporate body to express their views the Government would not pay sufficient attention to the needs of the industry. They suggested that a Chamber of Mines should be formed. Mr Herman Eckstein was not on friendly terms with Lippert, so he asked me to attend a meeting convened by Mr Campbell for the purpose of discussing the matter. The only persons ... present ... were Messrs John X Merriman[4] (representing J B Robinson), W Y Campbell, Edward Lippert and myself. A skeleton charter for a Chamber of Mines was drawn up and later submitted to representatives of all the Mines. H Eckstein was elected President and I was elected one of the Vice-Presidents.

Old men forget. Taylor's memory was at fault on the latter. Although a prominent member at the start of the new Chamber, he was never a vice-president. Soon after, Eckstein sent him to watch the interests of the Corner House in Pretoria and his involvement with the Chamber declined.

R R Hollins in an article written in 1926 mentions a joint committee whose negotiations and efforts led to the formation of the Chamber.[5] He includes himself, but not Taylor, among its members. However, according to *The Star*, both were elected to a committee chosen at a public meeting held on 6 May 1889 under Hollins's chairmanship. At a further meeting on 6 June 1889, Campbell said that it was a matter of history that the Old Chamber had failed, and new blood would have to be infused into it. He laid on the table draft rules which he had prepared, as the rules of the Old Chamber had proved unworkable. It was agreed that they be referred to the 'Council' (presumably the committee chosen in May) whose decisions would be accepted.[6]

The corollary to the public meetings and announcements was considerable behind-the-scenes activity. There were a number of cross-currents, including a movement to form a so-called Mining Union. At some stage the seal was set on the negotiations when Taylor received Eckstein's agreement to the formation of the Witwatersrand Chamber of Mines. Eckstein made his agreement conditional upon his being elected the first President and Lippert's being excluded from the Executive.[7]

Accordingly, about the middle of August Campbell addressed a circular to members of the Old Chamber in which he stated:

> I have pleasure in reporting to you that an amalgamation of interest and purpose has been effected between your Chamber and the gentlemen who

proposed forming a Mining Union. I have caused the rules as now agreed upon to be transcribed for the printer .... In the event of no other member ... moving in the matter, I propose shortly to secure a practical amalgamation of forces, and also the canvass of Companies which will nominate representative members of the new Chamber.[8]

Campbell then carried out his intentions. At the beginning of October he was received by President Kruger and asked him to become Honorary President of the Chamber:

His Honour having intimated his consent to accept the Honorary Presidency of your Chamber, with the Minister of Mines as Honorary Vice-President, I presented a copy of our Articles of Association with the intimation that a copy of same in the legal language of the State would be forwarded.[9]

A later Press report indicated that Lippert may have been associated with Campbell in the negotiations.[10]

The first meeting of Representative Members of the Witwatersrand Chamber of Mines was held on Saturday afternoon, 5 October 1889, in the Board Room of Natal Chambers. On the motion of Taylor, Campbell occupied the chair. It was resolved that the Articles of Association as presented to the meeting should be the Articles of the Chamber. These Articles, in the form then approved, cannot be traced. The earliest copy available is in the Second Annual Report of the Witwatersrand Chamber and they had by then been considerably amended. However, no changes had been made to the objects initially laid down, for those published in the 1890 report were identical with those published in *The Star* on 3 September 1889. They were:

1. To promote and protect the mining interests and industries of the South African Republic, and in particular the mining interests and industries of the Witwatersrand Gold Fields.
2. To consider all questions connected with the mining industry, and to promote public discussion thereon.
3. To promote Legislative or other measures affecting such mining industry.
4. To collect and circulate statistics and other information relating to such mining industry.
5. To communicate with and exchange information upon mining matters with Chambers of Mines or Government Departments of Mines in the South African Republic and other countries.
6. To procure information as to mines, mining companies, and all matters relating thereto.
7. To establish, form, and maintain a library, and museum of models, specimens, designs, drawings, and other articles of interest in con-

nection with the mining industry, for the use of members.

8 To act as arbitrators in the settlement of any disputes arising out of mining.

9 To sell, improve, manage, lease, mortgage, dispose of, turn to account, or otherwise deal with any part of the property of the Chamber.

10 To invest the moneys of the Chamber not immediately required upon such security or securities, and on such terms or otherwise, in such manner as may from time to time be determined.

11 To borrow any money required for the purposes of the Chamber upon such securities as may be determined.

12 To obtain, whenever determined upon, an Act of the Volksraad, for the incorporation of the Chamber, and any other Act that may be deemed conducive to any of these objects.

The members present at the first meeting on 5 October 1889 signed the Articles on behalf of the mines they represented as follows:

Aurora	C W Seccombe
Balmoral	W F Lance
City and Suburban	W Hosken
Crown Reef	C Hanau
	R O G Lys
Driefontein	S T Bain
	J Gardner
Eclipse	A C Baillie
	Sir Drummond Dunbar
Geldenhuis Estate	W H Rogers
George Goch	E Hancock
	J O C Potter
Langlaagte Block B	H Eckstein
	A Lilienfeld
Langlaagte Estate	G Richards
	H L Webster
Langlaagte Western	C E Hollings
	Sydney Morris
Luipaard's Vlei	J Durham
Nigel	F A Laughton
Odessa	F C Liddle
Randfontein	J Brooks
	L Phillips
	J G Schultze
Riet Vlei	P Groen
Robinson	H A Rogers
	F Spencer
	J B Taylor

Stanhope Geldenhuis	F J Dormer
	W P Fraser
Transvaal Montana	John Morty
White Reef	T Palmer
	D C Stevens
Witwatersrand	W Y Campbell
	A Osborne

A Council of twenty-one was then chosen from Representative Members nominated for election (not necessarily those present at the meeting). R R Hollins topped the poll. There followed in descending order of votes received:

W Y Campbell, C Hanau, G Goch, E Lippert, H A Rogers, J B Taylor, W H Rogers, H Eckstein, F C Liddle, T M C Nourse, J Hay, W Hosken, W F Lance, G Richards, G Farrar, F Spencer, H L Currey, L Phillips, F J Dormer and W Ross.

Eckstein seems to have relented somewhat on his embargo on the irrepressible Lippert, perhaps in recognition of the part he played in securing Paul Kruger's acceptance of the Honorary Presidency – and thus obviating the possibility that Dr W J Leyds, who had succeeded Bok as State Secretary on 2 May that year, would disclaim knowledge of the new Chamber's existence.

A further meeting of the Chamber took place on 10 October 1889, with Campbell again in the Chair. Apparently only a handful of members was present. Eckstein was duly elected President; Hollins and Hanau were elected Vice-Presidents. Taylor, Goch, Lance, Dormer, Richards, Rogers and Liddle were elected members of the Standing Committee. A vote of thanks to Campbell was recorded for his invaluable services in the organization of the new Chamber. He was elected to the office of second Honorary Vice-President. The Acting Secretary, J Sheldrick, despatched on the same day the first letters of which record exists, to give formal advice of the appointments.

The underlying motive of the reconstituted Chamber was to contain the costs of mining, especially those which resulted from the action or inaction of the Government, or from unbridled competition for goods and labour in short supply. These normal preoccupations of business interest were intensified on the Rand by the low grade of the ore deposits overall and the fixed price of gold. Any reduction in the costs of mining moved ore from the unprofitable to the profitable category; similarly any increase rendered ore 'unpay', and in a field of the incredible dimensions of the Rand this could result in catastrophic loss of revenue to the State – and of profits to the industry. Indeed, cost escalation could be catastrophic in terms of the solvency of one and the viability of the other. Not surprisingly, a century later, despite the diversification of the modern Chamber, the containment of mining costs remains its all-important preoccupation.

At the outset in 1889 the problems facing the new institution were legion. The cost of mining stores was high as a consequence of distance from port and railhead, and of customs and excise duties, popularly regarded as excessive, which were imposed on goods entering the Republic. These impositions were made the harder to bear by government reluctance to allow the thrusting rail links to 'come on' from Natal and the Cape, ahead of construction, by the Netherlands South African Railway Company,[11] of the Transvaal's own link with the Portuguese harbour of Delagoa Bay. Not surprisingly the cost of living was high too and this inflated the wages necessary to attract men to the fields. The scarcity of black labour in particular had led not only to the bidding up of pay rates to levels which the mining companies regarded as excessive, but to wholesale desertion as workers yielded to the blandishment of touts. These parasites trafficked in labour, poaching from one employer to supply another at a useful margin of profit. High costs stemmed too from the government grant of concessions permitting the creation, for the benefit of favoured individuals, of monopolies of essential goods and services. On the technical side there was a need for the exchange of information. Mining was still primitive and many properties required re-design and re-development to permit full exploitation of the ore body, and to make conditions in the shafts tolerable for workers. Mining laws and regulations were in need of thoughtful review; there were legal obscurities and unsolved problems of tenure arising from the confusion of the early scramble for claims. Despite some notable achievements neither the infrastructure nor the State's administrative provision matched the growth of the field. There was need for scrutiny of applications for patents that might hold the industry to a king's ransom. It was vital to mining that it should possess a voice that could speak authoritatively and responsibly for it – and which could command a hearing.

The Chamber was able to act usefully in all these fields because although it enjoyed powerful mining house backing, it never infringed managerial prerogative. It did not control mines nor share in profits; it was itself controlled by member mines and provided services for them paid from subscriptions. It could by a simple decision of policy stand aside from any area seen as controversial, or competitive *vis-à-vis* its members. In essence, the Chamber provided a means whereby mining companies could act in concert where this seemed to them prudent and desirable, and facilitated co-operation and consultation among them.

The Articles of Association provided for five classes of members but only one class, that of Representative Member, had any voting powers or was of any importance in regulating the Chamber's affairs. The qualifications of Representative Members were defined as follows:

Any syndicate working a mining property or any owner or association of owners of digger's claim or claims, paying an annual subscription of not less than Twenty-five Guineas to the funds of the Chamber, shall be entitled to nominate one Representative Member to the Chamber.

43

Any registered mining company, paying an annual subscription of Fifty Guineas, shall be entitled to nominate one Representative Member to the Chamber, and in similar manner to nominate two such Representative Members for an annual subscription of One Hundred Guineas; and three such Representative Members for an annual subscription of One Hundred and Fifty Guineas; provided that no nomination shall exceed three Representative Members by any such company.[12]

(In practice, mining companies became known as First, Second or Third Class Members depending on whether they had three, two or one Representative Member.)

There was provision for the election of Associate Members at an annual subscription of three guineas. The first was elected in 1892. Honorary Members could be elected without liability to subscription. It was stipulated that they 'shall be elected from persons benefiting the Chamber by donations of useful objects, contributions of money, or by any special furtherance of, or ability to further, the aims of the Chamber'. The first Honorary Member, elected in 1889, was Johannes Petrus Meyer, who represented the Rand in the Volksraad. Carl Jeppe was elected the following year.

Two further classes provided for those outside the Republic: Foreign Members and Visiting Members, who paid subscriptions of five guineas and two guineas respectively. A visitor could be a Visiting Member for no longer than three months and, unlike the other members, could not attend meetings of the Chamber unless invited.

Initially, real power lay in the hands of the Council of twenty-one members established under the original Articles, and especially in the seven members of it elected to form its Standing Committee. However, this arrangement did not long endure. It was found that this system gave insufficient say to the general body of Representative Members who, as such, met only at the half-yearly general meetings and then transacted little other than formal business. In May 1890 the Council was abolished and it was agreed that the general body of members should meet not less than once a month. The Council was replaced by an Executive Committee consisting of the President and Vice-President and eleven elected members. The eleven included the seven members of the former Standing Committee with the exception of Taylor and Liddle, and added W Hosken, L Phillips, T M C Nourse, E Hancock, G H Farrar and F von Hessert. In October 1890 Dormer (who had founded the Argus Group of newspapers and taken over as Editor of *The Star*) resigned – and in came Ed Lippert.

The Chamber's Articles made the usual provision for the vesting of its property, and for legal proceedings; for the operation of a banking account and the maintenance of accounts. Finally, it provided that the Articles could not be altered or amended save by a Special Resolution duly carried at a general meeting of the Chamber.

The creation of the Witwatersrand Chamber did not arouse much public interest to judge by Press reports which accorded less prominence and comment to the foundation of the new than they had to the old. Optimism was tempered by past failures. And only twenty-one companies became members at a time when there were a hundred and fifty on the Stock Exchange List. It is not surprising that *The Diggers' News* did not feel that the new Chamber had been widely accepted by the industry. However, its base was to prove solid and it grew steadily.

Coincidentally, the Chamber was immediately thrust into a position of public importance by the threat of famine on the gold-field as a consequence of the long-sustained drought. Early in October information came in from all over the Transvaal, and from districts outside from which supplies of grain were principally drawn, that the quantities on the road and immediately available would not be enough to feed the population.

Measures were at once put in hand to assess the probable needs and the quantities of stores available in 'Camp' (as Johannesburg and the other mine villages were still collectively, and quaintly, called). Special committees were appointed to ascertain the stocks of meal at the various mines and the number of people to be provided for.

A report dated 17 October 1889 showed that there were 770 000 lb of flour, meal and mealies in store; and 690 000 lb on the road, two days' journey away. According to the report, 686 000 lb had been issued during the previous three days, and 700 000 lb were on the border awaiting transport. The stock position was: 'Sugar and Milk, very low; Coffee, Tea, and Sundries, fair supply. Paraffine [*sic*] almost *nil*. Candles, good stocks. Chaff and Forage coming forth pretty freely.'

On the assumption that the population of the Witwatersrand was twenty-five thousand whites and fifteen thousand blacks, it was estimated the stocks issued during the previous three days ought to last until Friday, 25 October, at least, and on the same basis the stock in store and to arrive would last till 5 November (eleven days) for whites and till 15 November for blacks.

The Chamber telegraphed the Landdrosts and Resident Magistrates at Kimberley, Bloemfontein, Harrismith, Ladysmith, Aliwal North, Kroonstad, Newcastle and other places, inquiring what were the stocks of meal and grain, and the available transport.

Public petitions, supported by the Chamber, were sent to the Government praying that the special duties on vital foodstuffs might be suspended, and the Government responded by issuing a proclamation temporarily withdrawing the special duty on meal, flour, butter and tinned meat. The Government also set aside £5 000 for the relief of distress. On 19 October the Chamber proposed to the Government that the money should be used in paying a bonus of £20 each to the first 250 wagoners who arrived in Johannesburg from beyond the border, and who had crossed the border after announcement of the bonus.

The Government after some argument agreed, subject to the condition that a committee be appointed to certify that carriers claiming the bonus had not maltreated their animals.

As a result of this timely action by Government and Chamber there appeared the following in *The Star* of 31 October:

STATE OF THE COUNTRY.
ARRIVAL OF PRODUCE.
Twelve Wagons Claim the Bonus

No little surprise was caused in town last evening when a number of transport riders showed up at the Mining Commissioner's office, and claimed the bonus of £20 offered by the Government for wagons laden with produce coming from beyond the borders of the State, and starting after the 24th last. The first to arrive was Mr W R van der Merwe, from Vredefort district, Orange Free State, with a load of thirty-five muiden[13] of mealies. The Commission, consisting of two members of the Chamber of Mines, and the Acting Secretary, were speedily called together, and set to work to investigate the validity of the carrier's claim. Meanwhile, Mr Eloff wired to the Landdrost of the district whence Van der Merwe came, and received a reply substantiating the transport rider's statement. The commission certified that the claimant's mules were in good condition and showed no sign of ill-treatment. The bonus of £20 was accordingly paid. Since then eleven other wagons all laden with grain and mealies have arrived ... from the Free State ....

In all a partial or total bonus was paid to 282 wagoners, of which seventy-six per cent came from the Free State, seven per cent from the Cape and seventeen per cent from Natal. They brought in nearly five million lb of grain and general provisions. The Chamber's Commission reported that a certain Jas Bloiff brought six teams of oxen from Natal in fifteen days, sustained only by roadside grazing. They arrived in excellent condition as did four teams of mules that made the journey from Kimberley in thirteen days.

The Chamber also acted to obtain assistance from the Natal and Cape Governments. Natal responded by publicizing the Transvaal bonus and offering one of its own, being £20 for the first fifty wagons leaving the Natal railhead with supplies and arriving in Johannesburg. The Cape said it was short of rolling stock, and could offer only sympathy.

The Chamber's exertions, supported by the Government, induced an extraordinary flow of supplies, and famine was averted. Nature weighed in with copious rains towards the end of October which fell over a wide area including all along the transport routes from Natal and Kimberley.

The Chamber was soon to assert itself in a different way. In December the Chamber received a request from Ralph Charles Williams, British Agent at Pretoria, for information about the labour market. The information was supplied and produced on 19 December a letter criticizing the industry. Williams wrote, *inter alia*:

> Month after month passes and no sign is given that the mines are contributing anything approaching to their fair share of the cost entailed in supporting the wants of the great mining, trading, and agricultural population. Many companies are so overloaded with capital that even in the event of a greater production little hope can be entertained of their paying a dividend; while vast sums are subscribed, for the ostensible development of properties, on which there is no reasonable prospect of finding a single shilling's worth of gold.

> The newly founded organisation of the Chamber of Mines has, I believe, the genuine welfare of this country at heart, and I venture to think that straightforward reports dealing with the root of the matter, and issued by it … will do more towards establishing the industry than will greater or lesser booms that bring only evanescent prosperity.
>
> Up to the present your valuable mines have existed in great part on speculative hopes – on promotion schemes, and on a bulling and bearing of mining properties, and land companies; with the result that public expectations have been unfulfilled.
>
> A legitimate statement of the actual resources of the great companies, and a wholesome exposure of the gross frauds so plausibly imposed upon the public whether in mining or land schemes, a lesser promotion, and a greater production, can alone re-establish the Transvaal mines in the minds of the investing public of Europe.[14]

There can be little doubt that Williams was expressing the anger of those who had burnt fingers in some of the speculative promotions of the previous three years.

The Chamber's Secretary, J M Buckland,[15] replied with equal indignation two days later, stating that the Chamber felt it necessary to record its dissent from some portion of the Agent's communication.

> With your remarks concerning over-capitalisation, promotion and speculation, the views of the Chamber are to a great extent in accord. An eagerly speculative market, however, has been one result of the impression produced upon the public mind by the revealed wealth of the Witwatersrand Gold Fields. It has been no doubt often taken advantage of by unscrupulous persons, whose actions the Chamber sincerely joins with you in condemning. But speculation in shares, and schemes of promotion … spring from causes in the public temper which no Chamber of Mines, or other public body can control. The duty of such institutions is merely to advance the real prosperity of the industry, and to record and circulate the actual facts of its progress.…

Your characterisation of the position as 'the present crisis,' and your statement that 'vast sums are being subscribed for the ostensible development of properties upon which there is no reasonable prospect of finding a shilling's worth of gold,' are expressions to which ... the Chamber must take most emphatic exception. No facts are known to the Chamber calling for or justifying these expressions ....

The Chamber desires to record as its deliberate view that the results already attained by these fields are highly satisfactory; and indeed, in view of the difficulties by which they have been surrounded, may justly be considered brilliantly successful.

... Is it to be justly said that an industry does not contribute its share to the general cost, which even in its infancy, and from one district only, contributes annually over £500 000[16] to the public revenue – a contribution which, in the absence of public works, constitutes an annual absolute loss?[17]

Buckland wound up by inviting Williams to visit the fields and see it all at first hand. Williams, in reply, maintained that some points admitted of argument, but declined further 'paper discussion'. He graciously accepted the invitation to visit the mines, and did so two months later.

The Chamber followed this up by inviting members of the Volksraad to visit the industry in May. Merriman, who was soon to return to the Cape, acted as host for the Chamber. Speaking in Dutch, he urged the Raad to extend transport and grant municipal rights to Johannesburg.[18] The Members of the Volksraad and Williams were the forerunners of the host of armchair critics who would visit the mines to see for themselves at the invitation of the Chamber.

[1] First Annual Report of the Witwatersrand Chamber of Mines, 1889, p 8.

[2] Etheredge, p 3, citing *Standard and Transvaal Mining Chronicle*, 7 March 1888.

[3] Taylor, *Recollections of the Discovery of Gold on the Witwatersrand*, pp 11-12.

[4] He was managing the Langlaagte gold mine at the time.

[5] R R Hollins, 'Johannesburg's Oldest Resident', *Pioneer Number* of *The Star*, 20 September 1926, p 83.

[6] *The Star*, 7 June 1889.

[7] J B Taylor, *A Pioneer Looks Back*, p 165.

[8] *The Diggers' News*, 15 August 1889.

[9] Circular signed by Campbell and quoted in *The Diggers' News*, 3 October 1889.

[10] *The Star*, 11 October 1889.

[11] Nederlandsche Zuid-Afrikaansche Spoorweg-Maatskappij.

[12] Second Annual Report of the Witwatersrand Chamber of Mines, 1890, p 5.

[13] 1 Muid equalled 3 bushels (24 gallons).

[14] Annual Report of the Witwatersrand Chamber of Mines, 1889, p 24.

[15] J M Buckland: a financier, who was first Secretary of the Chamber, served until February 1892. He was later for many years Chairman of the Rand Club.

[16] In 1886 the gross revenue of the State was £308 387 6s 2d; it rose to £722 331 2s 7d in 1887, to £881 275 17s 0d in 1888, and to £1 577 445 7s 11d in 1889. (From the Second Annual Report of the Witwatersrand Chamber of Mines for the year 1890, p 91.)

[17] *Ibid*, pp 25-26.

[18] Lewsen, *Merriman: Paradoxical South African Statesman*, p 137.

CHAPTER FOUR

Humbly Sheweth

The Chamber's staff in the early years was minimal. They got through an astonishing work load, the Secretary and his assistant writing all letters by hand. Buckland resigned in February 1892 and H E Green acted as secretary for a while. Meanwhile the post was advertised and A R Goldring was selected from ninety candidates and appointed in May. He had been at one time Editor of *The Daily Independent* of Kimberley, and more recently a broker on the Rand. Green was second on the short list and was appointed Assistant Secretary.

Until 1891 the Chamber was without permanent accommodation. It held its meetings in the Stock Exchange, in City Chambers and in Barnato's Buildings, all in the centre of the town on Commissioner Street. Then, in April 1891, it leased 'roomy' offices in Bettelheim's Buildings, a block away on the corner of Simmonds and Fox Streets, which it used for the next four years. They housed not only the Chamber's offices, but also its library and museum. The accommodation soon proved to be not so roomy and many members had to stand during the monthly meetings. Chamber staff coped by hiring additional rooms and arranging for building extensions. Eventually the Chamber bought a site on the Market Square adjoining the National Bank and erected the first Chamber of Mines Building at a total cost of £18 500. The three-storey building, with the imposing posture of a Victorian bank, was to meet the Chamber's needs for many years. It was opened by the President, Lionel Phillips, on 20 November 1895, in a speech which reflected that resentment of government policy on the gold-field was reaching flash-point.

Over the first six years of its life the growth of Chamber membership was rapid. In 1890 there were seventy-six members representing fifty-three gold mining companies and the first coal mining member, the Coal Trust. Numbers dropped in 1891 and only thirty-two companies were represented. Membership returned to its previous level the following year. During 1894 the membership increased greatly, there being 109 members for seventy-one companies by the year-end. At this stage Phillips was able to declare that the companies represented in the Chamber contributed ninety-six per cent of the total output of gold. At the end of 1895, a total of 141 members represented ninety-three companies. Ahead lay the secession of a quarter of the membership in the turmoil and division following the Jameson Raid and the abortive Uitlander rising.

There were at first rumbles of dissatisfaction with the membership system and in particular with the weight which the larger mining houses were able to pull. This arose in part from a lack of understanding of the nature of the Chamber. *The South African Mining Journal*, which at the time was often critical of the Chamber, set the situation properly in perspective:

> ... the Chamber ... will ... necessarily remain an association of representatives of capital. Such being the case, it almost inevitably follows that the representatives of the greater interests will carry the greater weight.[1]

In more modern times, this situation has been tempered by a sense of history among those associated in the Chamber. As the early giants were surpassed in money power by younger, more aggressive mining houses, they did not lose comparable weight in the decision-making process. The Chamber has increasingly operated through a carefully nurtured consensus rule.

Unobtrusively in 1894 there occurred an event of great future significance. Three gold mines established the Rand Mutual Assurance Company, later to fall under the umbrella of the Chamber, to act as a 'captive' non-profit mutual insurance company. It was the world pioneer in workmen's compensation, preceding the British Workmen's Compensation Act of 1897 and the Transvaal Workmen's Compensation Act of 1907.

In the early days there was some press criticism of the Chamber by journals supporting the Transvaal Government for displaying an uncompromising hostility towards the authorities, for being abrupt and dictatorial, and for 'an unhappy tendency towards querulousness and impatience'.[2]

This is not borne out by the Chamber documents of the day. In all official dealings the Chamber seems to have adopted a dignified stance and shown courtesy and respect towards the representatives of Government. When Kruger visited Johannesburg on 4 March 1890, he addressed a big crowd at the Wanderers' Club Pavilion at a time when feeling was running high in the town over what was seen as a callous disregard of its interests. Kruger's speech was not well received (he was often rough and ready of tongue) and public disturbances followed. The mob tore down the Transvaal flag, the *Vierkleur*, on the Market Square. A demonstration outside Von Brandis's home, where Kruger was spending the evening, had to be broken up by the police. The Chamber at once dissociated itself from the unruly behaviour. It telegraphed the State Secretary:

> This Chamber desires to record its extreme regret at the unseemly behaviour of a comparatively small section of the population ... and its emphatic opinion that such conduct is distinctly prejudicial to the best interests both of the country in general and of the inhabitants of Johannesburg.[3]

The Chamber undoubtedly owed much to the tone set by its first President, Hermann Eckstein. Cartwright has described him as immaculate in dress on the dustiest days.[4] His neatly trimmed beard, his short stout figure and dignified manner combined to give him a remarkable resemblance to the Prince of Wales, afterwards King Edward VII. Most importantly, he was a man of integrity – a quality in short supply around mining camps – and was highly respected in the community. He kept the Chamber, like the Corner House, detached from politics. Unhappily, he was destined to leave Johannesburg through ill-health in 1892 and to die suddenly of a heart attack in January the following year on a visit to Stuttgart, near which he had been born forty-five years before. His monument is the Hermann Eckstein Park, containing the Johannesburg Zoo, in all 200 acres, donated to the city in his memory by Wernher, Beit in 1903.

The Government came quickly to recognize the authoritative standing of the Chamber and to respect its advice on legal and technical matters. But when the proposals were at variance with the ethos of the Government, the Chamber cut no more ice than it would with the successive twentieth-century administrations which would govern South Africa in accordance with similar tenets of Afrikaner hegemony.

L V Praagh,[5] writing on the Transvaal shortly after the turn of the century, gave this picture of the Chamber's struggle to improve the industrial environment:

Tolerated and disliked, bullied and feared, the mining community insisted upon its rights and asserted its position, in season and out of season, entirely regardless of its unpopularity throughout the country, and the enormous increase of revenue accruing to the bare coffers of the State induced a grudging concession as to the usefulness of industrial enterprise, the while it was earmarked for ceaseless and irritating extortions.

A part of this dislike and fear was reflected in the persistent refusal of the Government to grant corporate status to the Chamber. The Volksraad saw the requests for incorporation as a sinister attempt to establish an *imperium in imperio*. Today the Chamber's legal status is that of an employers' organization, registered as such with the Department of Labour under the Labour Relations Act. Such registration makes it a body corporate capable of suing or being sued, or acquiring property – or doing anything which its Constitution permits it to do. In the old republican days the Chamber had to rub along as best it could without legal standing.

Soon after its founding the Chamber began the stream of memorials to the Government and the Volksraad by which it was to present the pleas of the mining industry. The memorials typically began:

To the Honourable the Volksraad of the South African Republic.
THE MEMORIAL OF THE UNDERSIGNED INHABITANTS OF

THE STATE HUMBLY SHEWETH:

That the contentment and prosperity of your Memorialists, in common with those of the rest of the inhabitants of the State, are bound up in the prosperity of the great Mining Industry, which has been developed within the last three or four years …

And typically ended:

Wherefore, your Memorialists urgently pray that your Honourable House will give earnest consideration to their representations, and take such steps as in your wisdom, under Divine guidance, you may deem expedient to avert the grave perils to which the Government and people are exposed.
And your Memorialists, as in duty bound, will ever pray, etc.

In its Annual Report for 1890, the Chamber recorded that it had submitted memorials to the Volksraad on Railway Construction, Amendment of the Gold Law, Special Duties on Flour, Theft of Amalgam, Theft of Concentrates, Taxation, Public Works, Tenure of Mining Property, and Subordinate Officials. The Chamber noted optimistically:

There is great matter for congratulation in the more sympathetic and appreciative spirit which was evidenced by the Raad last year in dealing with the requests of the mining community. The practice of granting Industrial Concessions or Monopolies which has always received the Chamber's strenuous opposition was entirely discontinued.

The Chamber indicated the open field for concessions which had previously existed by listing twenty-six applications for monopoly rights refused during 1890, ranging from the supply of water and electricity to the manufacture of 'Jams, Biscuits, etc'. The change in policy did not, of course, affect the most notorious concessions, the dynamite, railways, and liquor monopolies granted in the previous decade, which continued very much in being.

No matter was of more importance to the inhabitants of the gold-fields than the provision of railway links with the coastal ports. The Chamber wrote to the Government in November 1889 asking that it should receive a delegation to discuss the question. C van Boeschoten, the Acting State Secretary, replied on 31 December that the Executive Council had had an extraordinary pressure of work. After that, there had been no quorum on account of the absence of the President. The Chamber's request would be considered, after the return of the President, as soon as there was a quorum of the Executive.

While the delegation waited not-so-patiently for an audience, the Chamber organized a memorial to the Volksraad, stressing the benefits that railways would bring to industry and State. It was circulated throughout the gold-fields and signed by 5 000. The memorial pointed out, *inter alia*:

That the Railway from Cape Town *via* Kimberley to Warrenton is now completed to within 270 miles of Johannesburg. The Railway through the Cape Colony and Orange Free State is constructed to within about 250 miles .... The Natal Railway will, in a few months, be completed to Charleston, which is within about 160 miles .... These Railways have from these points to travel only across the high veldt on which Railway construction is cheap ... and easy.

That the Delagoa Bay Railway has still about 325 miles to be constructed to reach Johannesburg, and before this Railway reaches the high veldt very mountainous country has to be crossed, over which Railway construction must necessarily be costly and expensive and difficult.[6]

The Chamber was moving in an area of fundamental importance not only to the revenues of the several states and colonies, but to the cherished aspirations of Paul Kruger.

At the close of the 1880s the states and colonies of South Africa were more prosperous than they had ever been. As Dr Jean van der Poel, the historian of railway and customs policies, wrote, they were

... drinking deeply at the fountainhead of the Rand. They were absorbed in a fury of railway construction, the maritime colonies seeking to attach themselves to the very centre of nourishment and the Transvaal trying to ward them off and direct the flow of trade over 240 miles of her own territory, out towards the east coast and perhaps to a harbour of her own. Customs duties and the receipts of railway traffic, which kept pace with them, became the mainstay ... of all the states and colonies alike.[7]

Dr van der Poel goes on to point out that no unified power existed to control this riotous expansion of the transport system of South Africa.[8]

Kruger was basically opposed to any kind of co-operation with the British colonies, whether commercial or political. Fearing that the Cape's grip on the traffic would not easily be loosed, he refused to sanction railway connection with the Cape until the long hoped for line from Delagoa Bay in Moçambique had reached Pretoria.[9]

At the heart of Kruger's policies lay his determination to maintain the independence of the Transvaal. He saw that total security called for an expanding republic with access to the sea on its own eastern seaboard. He sought the closest relationship with the sister republic of the Orange Free State to the south, and the avoidance of British encroachment and encirclement on the west, north and east. And he sought *lebensraum* for land-hungry burghers who faced impoverishment as the frontiers closed.

In pursuit of these aims he participated in the scramble for Africa, then getting into its full swing. The Portuguese were dreaming of a return to ancient glories and an African empire linking Angola on the west with Moçambique on the east through the lands of the Shona whom they claimed as vassals. And they disputed the British presence in Nyasaland and the valley of the Shiré. The Johnny-come-lately of colonial powers, Bismarck's Germany, had annexed South West Africa in 1884 and also contemplated linkage across the hinterland with the east coast. And Rhodes did more than dream of African empire but moved purposefully to paint the map red from Cape to Cairo, and to link the two by rail.

The Republic, its independence newly restored, first came head on with Rhodes in 1882 when Boer freebooters moved west across the imprecisely-defined western boundaries of the Transvaal into disputed tribal territory, and set up the puppet republics of Stellaland and Goshen. Their presence challenged the British claim to the Great North Road, the trade route through Bechuanaland to the Zambesi, and heightened fears of German intervention in the region. By the end of 1884, Kruger's designs were frustrated, for Rhodes had won the support of the British Government for his view that the way to the Zambesi, and the path of the future railway, must be kept in British hands. An expedition was dispatched under Sir Charles Warren, and Kruger was forced to accept a western boundary that excluded the Road and wrote finis to short-lived Stellaland and Goshen.

Kruger then turned east and made a bid for possession of Zululand. Early in 1884 some three hundred Boers had found an opportunity to champion the cause of Dinizulu, son of the late Zulu king, Cetshwayo, against a rival faction, and took as their reward almost half of his kingdom. They called the territory the New Republic and included St Lucia Bay in their survey of prospective townships. This was too much for the British who once again feared German aspirations as well as Transvaal aggrandizement. They dug up a treaty made with the Zulu king, Mpande, in 1843, and on the strength of it annexed St Lucia Bay in 1884. Germany protested, but Britain and Germany reached an understanding in 1885 that Germany would withdraw her protest, and that the east coast south of Delagoa Bay would be regarded as a British sphere of influence in return for Britain's recognition of Germany's interest in the Cameroons. In 1887, Britain recognized the New Republic and annexed the rest of Zululand. Kruger in turn the following year incorporated the New Republic in the Transvaal.

In 1889 Rhodes obtained a charter for his British South Africa Company to exploit the mineral rights granted to Charles Rudd by Lobengula in Matabeleland. In due course, Rhodes's representative, Dr Jameson, at the head of Charter Company forces, turned back at the Limpopo the Adendorff Trek sponsored by Kruger's rival for the Presidency, General Piet Joubert. Kruger, who had foreseen that Rhodes would seal off the north, had already switched his attention to Swaziland, as the route to the last possible harbour left unclaimed on the east coast – Kosi Bay.

Swaziland had long been a concession hunters' paradise, and an amazing variety of concessions had been extracted from its drunken king, Umbandine. Kruger had made it his business to buy up the more important of them, so that the Transvaal Government acquired the sole right to build railways, levy customs, conduct telegraph and postal services, and establish banks in Swaziland. Moreover, many Transvaal Boers had traditionally grazed their flocks over the border and had obtained grazing rights in the territory. Kruger's policy left Britain without any commercial advantage to be won by the incorporation of Swaziland, and in due course she would countenance its annexation by the Transvaal. She would also herself in due time annex Tongaland, the last unclaimed territory on the east coast, to block Kruger's wish to acquire Kosi Bay.

While Kruger pursued these objectives, he saw clearly enough that his only firm hope of harbour facilities independent of the Cape and Natal lay in treating with the Portuguese for traffic through Delagoa Bay. It would still be a foreign port, but at least it would not be British. Moreover, Moçambique was so economically dependent upon the Transvaal that the Republic could dictate terms. Rhodes had recently become Prime Minister of the Cape and thinking big, as ever, tried to circumvent Kruger by buying Delagoa Bay. Merriman, now Treasurer-General in the Cape Ministry, and strongly supporting acquisition of the port, was Rhodes's agent in secret London negotiations with the poverty-stricken Portuguese. Unfortunately for Rhodes and Merriman, Britain, mindful of her European relationship with Portugal, and of German sensitivity, was not playing this time. Nor were the Portuguese. Neither its port nor its railway was for sale or lease. Kruger was free to go ahead with his long-cherished plan for a railway linking Pretoria with Lourenço Marques at Delagoa Bay. He, too, had attempted to buy the port from the Portuguese, but had to be content with favoured nation facilities.

His Boers had not at first favoured a railway; many of them preferred transport riding to and from colonial railheads to farming. But Kruger knew that if the Transvaal did not build its own line, it would be drawn out of Republican seclusion and exposed to a British take-over. Accordingly, in 1883, the Transvaal and Portuguese Governments had set in train the survey of the route. As the material for building the line had to be shipped through Delagoa Bay, the Moçambique section would have to be finished ahead of construction in the Transvaal. It proceeded desperately slowly.

Meanwhile Kruger had granted in 1887 a monopoly concession to a Netherlands company with German financial participation to operate all Transvaal railways. The company, the Netherlands South African Railway Company, first constructed in 1891 the so-called Rand Tram, a light railway bringing passengers and goods, especially the all-important coal, from East Rand collieries, to Johannesburg and the gold mines along the Witwatersrand.

The Rand Tram was highly profitable and a valuable milch cow for the struggling company. It was a fruitful cause of dispute and an on-going wrangle with the mining companies, both because its rates were high and because it was reluctant to agree to sidings and bulk delivery of coal to reduce handling costs for the mines.

Despite this profitable venture on the Rand, the company was in its early years so unstable financially that there was a seemingly endless delay in completing its major task, the construction of the trunk line between Pretoria and the junction with the Moçambique line at Komatipoort.

> This delay, following upon the exasperating slowness with which the Portuguese section had been laid down, did nothing to calm the feelings of Kruger's opponents both in the Volksraad and among the mining population .... They and Joubert's[10] followers complained bitterly of the high cost of living caused by the ruinous tariffs and by the lack of railways through to the Rand. The Cape and Natal lines would have relieved their difficulties long ago but for Kruger's persistent obstruction of them in order to preserve the traffic monopoly for an easy-going and impecunious company. They looked upon the Netherlands Company as another of Kruger's Hollander institutions which they condemned as hangers-on of the Government and swindlers of the State.[11]

By the end of February 1890, Kruger had realized that he could not keep the Rand waiting any longer for a rail system and decided to give way. Eckstein interviewed him at the Presidential residence in Pretoria on 25 February on a number of important matters. Kruger told him, as politicians will who are about to reverse direction, that he was not departing from his stated policy. However, preparations for the extension of the Delagoa Bay trunk line were now advanced to the point where he was prepared to urge upon the Volksraad the desirability of bringing on quickly the Cape line from Bloemfontein. President Reitz, of the Orange Free State, he said, had already been informed that there would be no objection to the line's being pushed forward from Bloemfontein. In fact, Kruger declared, he had no objection to construction of the line from Bloemfontein to Johannesburg even before the great trunk line from Delagoa Bay was ready for traffic.

Kruger visited Johannesburg on 4 March and the Chamber's railway delegation at last got a hearing. He reiterated to its members the undertaking given to Eckstein and, in due course, this was endorsed by the Volksraad. Soon construction gangs on the Highveld were forging the iron links which, after another twenty troublous years, would impel colonies and republics at long last to economic and political union.

But the Rand would have to wait until 15 September 1892 for the first train to steam into Johannesburg. The line had been taken via Elandsfontein (Germiston) to preserve terminal status for Pretoria, and though Johannesburg got its train first, the town's celebratory committee, of which the Chamber's President was a member, felt obliged to cancel its celebration plans in deference to a Government request not to make too big a thing of it. The first train from the Cape puffed into Pretoria three-and-a-half months later, on 1 January 1893, but because the Volksraad had made no provision for such expenditure 'the greatest public work yet undertaken in this country took place without any of those demonstrations of public rejoicing which are usual on such occasions'.[12]

In 1889 the Cape and the Orange Free State had entered into a customs union, which the Transvaal and Natal refused to join, 'the former for political and the latter for economic reasons'.[13] The refusal of the Transvaal to participate meant that the mines must continue to pay the duties levied on imported commodities at the Cape harbours and at Durban, in addition to the general *ad valorem* rates and the special dues on a number of foodstuffs and beverages imposed by the Republic.[14]

Kruger attempted to counter the Cape-Free State customs union by granting favours to Natal. However, there were political difficulties in allowing the Natal line to 'come on' from Charlestown on the border, and the link-up was not completed until 1895.

The financial difficulties of the Netherlands Company became more acute than ever towards the end of 1891. Due to depression in the mining industry and in the world in general, it was not possible to raise money abroad. In order to obtain money to meet the importunities of its creditors, the company was obliged to accept a loan from the Cape Government and agreed in return to carry the Cape-Orange Free State line on to Johannesburg within a year. It was also compelled to agree that, from the completion of the line in September 1892, up to the end of 1894, the Cape should operate the whole line from her ports to Johannesburg and fix the rates on through traffic to that town.[15]

In the course of 1892 there was a resurgence of confidence in the future of the mining industry in the financial capitals of the world and a consequent improvement in the credit of the Republic. In June Kruger succeeded in obtaining funds from a loan floated by Rothschilds of London of £2 500 000 to finance the railway to Delagoa Bay.

Lord ('Natty') Rothschild was renowned for his caution. It would be said of him in later years that he refused to insure the ill-fated *Titanic* because, although he knew nothing of ships, it seemed to him 'too big to float'.[16] In the 1880s he had made a massive investment in De Beers to finance the amalgamation of diamond mining companies. This proved hugely profitable, but he regarded the deal as speculative, and a risk of a kind which he was never again prepared to take. In future he would stick to investing in governments. Rothschilds had confidence, the company wrote to Kruger, on 13 July 1892, in the 'wisdom of Your Honour's Government as well as in the future prospects of the Transvaal'. Rothschilds counselled the greatest prudence and economy in using 'the large sum ... raised', and spelt out what it considered proper measures of financial control (by Rothschilds!).[17] The company was promptly told, in reasonably diplomatic terms, to mind its own business. Leyds wrote in reply on 3 September 1892, *inter alia*:

> I have therefore the honour to communicate to you as the point of view of the Govt, that no control can be allowed, that the Govt, prior to the several drawings being made, cannot state for which purpose the money will be

used, and further that the Govt cannot consent to the money remaining deposited with you until it be required for the purposes for which it is borrowed.[18]

Rothschilds in their letter counselled a reasonable rates policy and the avoidance of 'ruinous competition with the Cape Railway'. They might well have saved their pen, ink and paper on that score as well. Ruinous railway competition was coming and would, on its own, prove almost fatal to the peace of South Africa.

Meanwhile, the Netherlands South African Railway Company, its financial worries removed, built at a great pace and completed its principal line by end 1894. As traffic at long last got under way in 1895, the Volksraad found £20 000 for a sumptuous official opening ceremony at Lourenço Marques.

[1] *The South African Mining Journal*, 8 July 1893, p 641.
[2] *The Diggers' News*, Editorial on 30 January 1896.
[3] Annual Report of the Witwatersrand Chamber of Mines, 1890, p 18.
[4] A P Cartwright, *The Corner House: The Early History of Johannesburg*, p 4.
[5] L V Praagh, ed, *The Transvaal and its Mines*, p 541 *et seq*.
[6] Annual Report of the Witwatersrand Chamber of Mines, 1890, p 22.
[7] J van der Poel, *Railway and Customs Policies in South Africa: 1885-1910*, pp 45–46.
[8] *Ibid*, p 47.
[9] *Ibid*, p 29.
[10] General Piet Joubert.
[11] *Ibid*, pp 54–55.
[12] Fourth Annual Report of the Witwatersrand Chamber of Mines, 1892, p 73.
[13] J S Marais, *The Fall of Kruger's Republic*, p 35.
[14] *Ibid*, pp 35–36.
[15] *Ibid*, p 36.
[16] A Jenkins, *The Rich Rich: The Story of the Big Spenders*, p 134.
[17] Transvaal Archives, Staatsekretaris (SS), Volume 8703: Brieweboek, N M Rothschild and Sons, London, to S J P Kruger, 13 July 1892.
[18] Transvaal Archives, Staatsekretaris (SS), Volume 8703: Brieweboek, W J Leyds to N M Rothschild and Sons, London, 3 September 1892. (Translation.)

CHAPTER FIVE

Confronting the Concessionaires

The gold mining industry on the Witwatersrand, destined soon to head the top league of world gold producers, continued to grow at a pace that created unending problems for industry and State alike. The Chamber applied itself vigorously, with varying success, to everything that impinged on the prosperity and well-being of the mines. It involved itself not only in mining matters, but in the wider issues affecting the industry's growth in the environment provided by a government that was sometimes sympathetic, sometimes obstructive, basically hostile.

In 1890, the Chamber had focused its endeavours on hastening the construction of railways. In 1891, its chief labour was to obtain amendments to the Gold Law. Early discoveries in the Transvaal had led to the enactment of what might be called the first Gold Law of the Transvaal – Law No 1 of 1871. Article 1 was reminiscent of the early feudal concept that gold and precious stones found within a kingdom belonged to the king, whereas the ownership and exploitation of other minerals, being ignoble or base, could be left to commoners. The Article set a precedent followed in every subsequent law of the Transvaal Republic, the Transvaal Colony and the Republic of South Africa itself on the subject of gold mining. It declared:

> *Het mijnrecht op alle edelgesteenten of edelmetalen behoort aan den Staat behoudens die reeds verkregene regte van private personen ....*

In these words, it reserved to the State the right of mining for, and disposing of, precious stones and precious metals, without prejudice to the vested rights of private persons. This sounds like a contradiction in terms which, of course, it was and is. Law No 1 was followed by a series of amending enactments which became longer and more detailed as the tempo of activities increased.[1]

Law No 8, 1885, introduced changes on the lines of Kimberley legislation, primarily to meet the needs of the alluvial fields of the north-eastern Transvaal. It provided for the proclamation of diggings, the maintenance of law and order, the issue of prospecting and diggers' licences and control over dealing in unwrought gold. It gave the State President the power, in consultation with the Executive Committee, to proclaim private land as public diggings on which claims might be pegged, but it gave the owner of the land the right to mine one-tenth of it, this portion to be held by him under mining lease, or *mynpachtbrief*.

As mining spread in the years following, the law was adapted to meet new and different circumstances. In June 1891 Christiaan Joubert, the Head of the Mines Department, responded to Chamber pressure and called a conference of mining commissioners to consider the amendments which should be proposed to the Volksraad. The Chamber was invited to send representatives and appointed George Goch, a Vice-President, and Charles Leonard, its solicitor. The conference, after deliberating for several weeks, accepted the Chamber's proposals, almost in their entirety. They were approved with some modification by the Raad, and incorporated in the law. The principal changes were important because they enabled owners of gold mining property to obtain title deeds, giving them indefeasible ownership which had previously been lacking. Scarcely less important was an enactment which gave a vested right of renewal to holders of a *mynpacht*. The effect of the changes was a substantial increase in the value of gold mining property. *The South African Mining Journal* commented that the amendments would prove of incalculable value to the industry and would:

> ... help to restore the confidence which these Fields have lost in the eyes of the English and Continental capitalist, owing to insecurity of tenure under which mining properties were held under the old law. If this were the only work achieved by the Chamber of Mines, it would more than justify the very large support which is being afforded to that Institution.

The Journal added that all doubts as to the security of the fields had been set at rest, making the jumping of claims a 'bugbear of the past'.[2]

Further amendments were proposed by the Chamber in 1892; some were accepted by the Raad which also empowered the Government to have the law codified. It was high time. The Gold Law was a jumble of clauses and amendments of which no proper arrangement or classification had been made. Joubert underlined the lack of administrative depth in the Government service by asking the Chamber to undertake the codification. It did so willingly and speedily, but legislative delay was such that the long-awaited codification did not appear on the Statute Book until 1895. However, in due course of time, there resulted from the co-operative attitude of the Raad a statute that one commentator described as a liberal, popular and well-considered piece of legislation.[3] It, of course, benefited property owners in general, and the industry's requirements were for once not seen as running counter to interests, such as agriculture, which provided the Government with its political power base. Both capitalist mine-owner and capitalist farmer had no problem in seeing the benefit of security of tenure and the protection of vested interest in land.

The accord between the Chamber and the Government over land was unhappily soon marred by a seemingly endless dispute over the right to mine under *bewaarplaatsen*, the portions of land reserved in the early days for surface installations or the exercise of water rights. They were usually located down dip to the south of the outcrop and the law prohibited mining under them, it not being appreciated at the time that deep-running reefs might lie underneath. Later it became clear that the *bewaarplaatsen* were overlying ground containing gold worth millions of pounds.

Obviously, someone should be allowed to mine the underlying orebody. The vital question was who? Easy, replied the Chamber, the surface rights holder must obviously have a priority right to mine the ground under them, particularly when the holder is already mining the adjacent area. There were others who saw these rights as being up for plunder. A syndicate in which that suave concessionaire, Lippert, was prominent, for example, campaigned to be given a concession to mine under *bewaarplaatsen*, irrespective of who held the surface right.

The Chamber was adamant in asserting the prior claim of the holders of the surface rights, and it devoted its energies to securing an amendment giving them the preferment of mining under it. The stakes were high, and the battle would be fought relentlessly, with allegations and counter-allegations of bribery by competing parties.

According to *The South African Mining Journal*, the Lippert syndicate distributed money freely in Pretoria in support of its venture.[4] In 1894, Lionel Phillips wrote to Beit:

> The Bewaarplaatsen question will, I think, be settled in our favour, but at a cost of about £25 000, and then only because Christiaan Joubert has stuck to us like a leech. The old man styles himself the 'father of the mines' and seems disposed to run absolutely straight.[5]

Phillips was being over-optimistic. The Volksraad did accept the validity of the Chamber's case, but, despite this, the Government succeeded in deferring a decision. The issue would be kept alive, with fluctuating fortune, but without resolution, through the years of life remaining to the Transvaal Republic.

Phillips initiated on 26 January 1893, on the completion of his first term as President of the Chamber, the tradition of the formal presidential review of the industry at the annual general meeting. He paid graceful tribute to Hermann Eckstein who had recently died, and commented aptly on the difficulty of succeeding 'a gentleman of such keen perceptions, and possessed of such an unusual amount of tact and good judgement'.

Phillips reported that gold production had doubled in the previous two calendar years. He was able to declare to applause that the 'pyrites bogy' had been laid to rest, a reference to the overcoming by the cyanide process of the problem of recovering gold from the more refractory pyritic ores found below the oxidized conglomerates of the outcrop mines. He commented on the industry's great good fortune in the discovery that the Transvaal abounded in excellent coal.

The industry, as ever, was deeply concerned with the level of working costs, but Phillips wound up in hopeful vein.

> ... With cheap coal, which I hope to see still cheaper by delivery in bulk, with a great reduction in the cost of native labour, and the gradual raising of the standard of its efficiency, with cheaper explosives, to which I think we are justified in looking forward, with improvements in mechanical appliances and chemical processes, with conglomerate beds proved to be phenomenally continuous, both in extent and value, the gold mines of the Witwatersrand will doubtless show results which no similar area on the globe has hitherto done.[6]

Phillips would be disappointed in his hopes for great reductions in the costs of labour and for cheaper explosives. However, the Chamber had better luck in challenging patents for new processes than it did in upsetting already well-entrenched concessions.

The scrutiny of applications for patents has remained a vital function of the Chamber ever since, bringing enduring, if usually unobtrusive, benefit. The Chamber's avowed policy has been not to oppose genuine innovation or to discourage inventors, but to prevent the granting of patents for alleged inventions which made use of processes which were already public property. Indeed, the mining industry has always sought, from obvious self-interest, to encourage research and development. Equally, it has been averse to being fleeced by those who seek to profit from patent rights on insubstantial grounds.

In its early days of opposing patents, it had one notable victory, its action against the African Gold Recovery Company which held two patents covering the famous McArthur–Forrest Cyanide Process for the extraction of gold. Patent No 47 gave it the right to extract gold from ore by means of a certain solution of cyanide, and Patent No 74 gave it the right to precipitate the gold from the cyanide solution by means of zinc shavings. The Chamber began negotiations with the company as early as November 1892, seeking a reduction in the tariffs covering the use of the two processes. The correspondence did not produce results and four months later the Chamber decided to test the validity of the patents before the High Court. The company, perhaps conscious of the patent's vulnerability, now showed an interest in coming to some 'fairer arrangement',[7] but the Chamber by then had made up its mind.

It would take the Chamber three years of persistent endeavour to bring the matter before the High Court. Kruger, in line with his inclination to support the monopolist as a counter-balance to the power of the magnate, appears to have facilitated delays that worked to the advantage of the patent holder. An attempt followed to protect the patent by establishing a State Cyanide Monopoly and by appointing W W Webster of the African Gold Recovery

Company as the Government's agent. The Chamber was vigorous in its opposition, and managed to extract an undertaking that would permit its case against the patent to be heard. However, the Chamber's position remained perilous, and there were attempts to undermine it further by bribery. On 16 June 1894 Phillips wrote to Beit:

> The Cyanide Monopoly ... suddenly comes up again and it is in a rather dangerous state. Fortunately Dr Leyds and Esselen[8] are dead against it and we may baulk it this year .... Next year however it will come up again – even if we succeed in postponing it. The other side is spending lots of money in bribes and we shall probably have to spend more next year than this [year] to oppose it.[9]

Sure enough, a bid was made in the Volksraad in 1895 to amend the law to provide that a challenge to a patent would lapse if not completed within eighteen months. The effect would have been to debar the Chamber's action which had been pending for more than two years. The Volksraad voted to defer consideration of the amendment for a year – but only by the narrow margin of the Chairman's casting vote. The case against the African Gold Recovery Company at last came before the Supreme Court, Pretoria, on 17 February 1896, in the name of James Hay, Chief Justice Kotzé presiding. Hay was then President of the Chamber, having succeeded Phillips, who coincidentally was under custody in a cottage a mile or two away at Sunnyside, on the outskirts of the town, awaiting trial on a charge of high treason.

Hay's case, in essence, was that when the patents were granted it was common scientific knowledge that gold could be separated from its ore by a solution of potassium cyanide. The African Gold Recovery Company contended that their process was uniquely advantageous in the extent to which the cyanide could be diluted. Before the case was heard, however, the strength of the Chamber's case was emphasized by judgements against the McArthur-Forrest patentees in England and Germany, declaring the patents invalid in those countries.[10]

Judgement in the case was given at last on 5 November 1896, in favour of the mining companies, with costs, the McArthur-Forrest patent being cancelled. The Chamber commented laconically:

> The effect of this judgment was to throw the cyanide process open for public use. Previously the mining companies had had to pay a heavy royalty, which constituted a considerable charge in connection with the recovery of gold from tailings. From this expense the judgment has freed them.[11]

Hay described the benefit as 'incalculable'.

Yet the McArthur-Forrest process had not only laid the pyrites bogy, it had made possible the extraction of a fortune in gold once thought for ever lost in

Nineteenth-century travellers to Pretoria admired the cascades that fell from the Ridge of White Waters (Die Witwatersrand).

Boer farmers, with wives, children and servants, were accustomed when winter came to trek from the Highveld to the warmer bushveld.

The road past Orange Grove, Johannesburg, trodden out by the rush to the gold-fields in 1886.

By mid–1889, the Witwatersrand was an established phenomenon.

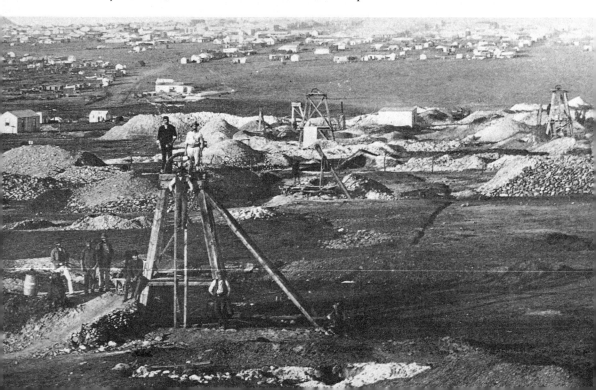

Black workers in the early days.

Herman Eckstein, the founder-President.

Minnie Eckstein, with her mother, and four children.

Left: Alois Hugo Nellmapius, who was granted a monopoly by Kruger to distil liquor. In the wrong hands it became fearsome stuff.

Right: Edward Lippert, the 'Prince of Concessionaires'.

President Kruger and President Reitz, of the Orange Free State, at the opening of the first railway bridge over the Vaal River in May 1892.

Lionel Phillips's house, Hohenheim, on Parktown Ridge - in 1895 the favoured venue of conspirators against the Kruger regime.

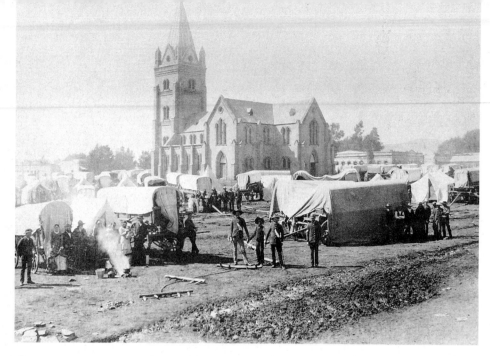

The conspirators who planned the Johannesburg rising at the end of 1895 overlooked that Boers from the country would flood into Pretoria at Christmas for the ceremony of *Nagmaal* (Communion). (Picture taken in 1888.)

Sir Jacobus de Wet, British Agent, from the balcony of the Rand Club, calls on the rebels to lay down their arms.

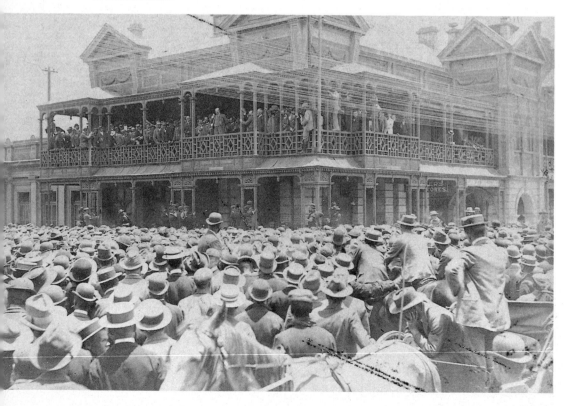

Left: Warrant signed by J C Juta, sheriff, committing Phillips, Farrar, Rhodes and Hammond to Pretoria Jail to await execution for high treason.

Right: The last vain bid for peace. President Steyn introduces the two men of iron, Kruger and Milner at Bloemfontein on 31 May 1899.

Boer commando passing up Commissioner Street, Johannesburg.

Leaders of the Reform Committee. Clockwise, from top left, with the Secretary, Percy Fitz-Patrick, in the centre, Colonel Frank Rhodes, DSO, George Farrar, John Hays Hammond and Lionel Phillips.

the discarded tailings of the Rand. Some seventy years later, a claimant attempting to fend off the Chamber's opposition to proposed patents, vainly recalled the McArthur-Forrest case to the Court as an example of the Chamber's propensity for quashing patents. We can be sure that John McArthur and brothers William and Robert Forrest, in the declining years remaining to them, felt no affection for the Chamber.

Kruger introduced the concessions policy soon after the Transvaal regained its independence in 1881 – well before the discovery of gold on the Rand. His aim was a modest incentive to industrialization based on the processing of farm surpluses.[12] This hopeful policy would soon be totally undermined with the emergence of mining as the economically dominant sector, but by then Kruger had charted his course and made commitments from which it would seem impolitic to depart.

Entrepreneurs, that is those who had themselves not been fortunate enough to win concessions in the free-and-easy early days, and their natural spokesman, the Chamber, attacked the policy because it artificially inflated the cost of living and the cost of mining. The mining interests were not alone in their opposition to the monopoly rights conferred by concession. They attracted critics from all sectors and from burghers whose mounting opposition found expression in the Volksraad, the approval of which was a prerequisite to the grant of a concession. By 1895 when the Volksraad investigated the industrial concessions, it found that most of those granted had lapsed. The following year the Raad proposed an alternative scheme which led to the establishment of soap and match factories with a measure of tariff protection.[13] The most controversial – and enduring – concessions, were those relating to railways, alcoholic liquor and explosives.

The Chamber's attitude to the liquor concession was not based so much on the monopoly advantage of the concessionaire as on the enormous scale of drunkenness among black mineworkers, which stemmed principally from illegal traffic and maladministration of the Liquor Act.

The first of the concessionaires was Alois Hugo Nellmapius, a flamboyant entrepreneur of Hungarian birth, who gained the reputation in the early days of being the 'evil genius' of the Republic.[14] He had qualified as a civil engineer in the Netherlands, emigrated to South Africa and rose to prominence on the gold–fields of Lydenburg and Pilgrim's Rest. He won the trust of President Kruger, and in 1881 was granted a monopoly concession to distil liquor. At the same time he was granted monopolies in the preservation of fruit and the manufacture of gunpowder and crockery. He established a distillery on what was formerly Sammy Marks's Hatherley Farm, about ten miles east of Pretoria. The factory included a glass manufactory and cooperage for which additional concessions were granted. It was called De Eerste Fabrieken in de Zuid-Afrikaansche Republiek. Kruger officially opened it, and named it 'Volkshoop' – the People's Hope,[15] giving expression to the wishful thought that homespun ventures of this sort would play a supportive role to the farm-based economy.

Nellmapius then formed a partnership with Sammy Marks, Isaac Lewis and Barnet Lewis to operate the concession. In 1892 the partners sold out to a company of which Marks became a director. Nellmapius died the following year on the model farm near Pretoria that he had named for his daughter Irene. Kruger attended the funeral of his friend, who had indeed done much to stimulate agriculture and general development in the Republic.[16]

The liquor appearing under brand names of the Hatherley Distillery was familiarly known as 'Mapius'. It was able to undercut Cape brandy, but was itself at a disadvantage in competing with spirits imported from Moçambique which entered the Transvaal duty-free, some of it being potato spirit of German origin re-shipped through Lisbon.[17] All of this liquor was bought by middlemen who sometimes adulterated it and sold it under forged labels.[18] Thus a recipe for 'Kaffir Brandy', price 16s 6d per dozen bottles in 1899, was said to be:

15 gals Delagoa proof spirit, 15 gals water, 1 gal cayenne pepper tincture, $1/2$ lb mashed prunes, $1 1/2$ oz sulphuric acid and 1 oz nitric acid.[19]

The Hatherley Distillery paid handsome dividends in 1895 and 1896, but after the completion of the Delagoa Bay Railway it lost market share and was unable to pay dividends in the three years before the outbreak of war. The purity of its product as it left the distillery is not clear as the Government failed to yield to pressure to appoint a Public Analyst. However, it is certain that in the wrong hands it became fearsome stuff.

The availability of liquor was as important to the miners of the Witwatersrand as it was to the sourdoughs of the Klondike, the Soviet peasants of the modern *artel* groups blasting gold from the permafrost of Siberia, or the *gampeiros* who pan the Brazilian Amazon. The black worker did not need to learn to drink from his white co-worker, but took readily to his kind of liquor; 'Cape Smoke' becoming one of the popular amenities of the diamond diggings. 'Mapius', and its derivatives and counterparts, were equally popular on the Rand. Charles van Onselen, the revisionist historian, has done impressive research and has cast much light into the dark places of the liquor trade. Some of his interpretations, however, are debatable.

He finds for example:

To their delight, the mining capitalists discovered that the black Mozambicans who formed the majority of the African labour force had an especially well-developed liking for alcohol. It was this liking, or partial addiction to alcohol that mine owners exploited to procure a labouring population from basically peasant economies.[20]

In short, says Van Onselen, alcohol was a distinct aid in proletarianizing African peasants. The essential basis for this judgement seems to be the initial reluctance of the Chamber to campaign for the prohibition of an amenity commonly available to workers the world over. It is reasonable to deduce that the Chamber did not so much see its availability as an attraction, as it did foresee that its prohibition would be a positive deterrent to recruitment.

Van Onselen also found:

> The mining industry, for its part, was quite content for its workers to spend their wages on Hatherley products if they so desired. For, the more money the mineworkers spent on liquor, the less they saved; and the less they saved, the longer they worked before returning to the peasant economies of their rural homelands. In other words, mine owners realised that wages spent on liquor helped lengthen the periods of migratory labour, and tended to produce a more stabilised labour force – in short, it facilitated the process of proletarianisation.[21]

However, a mine manager might as specially plead that a worker rendered inefficient by booze was likely to become increasingly so the longer he stayed on the mine; that a sober worker was likely to do more productive work on a short stay than a drunkard on a longer one. The Chamber was in no doubt that drink aggravated the labour shortage. A report presented by its Executive Committee at a meeting of the Chamber on 19 December 1895 declared:

> The shortness in the supply, as compared with the demand for labour, has been greatly accentuated by it. Where possible, more natives are kept in the compounds than are actually required for the work to be done, to make allowances for those who are disabled by drink. This not only puts the company to undue expense, but, at times of scarcity, bears hardly on the other companies who cannot get enough labour to enable them to carry on their ordinary operations. Were the efficiency of native labour not impaired by drink, less labourers would be wanted than is now the case, and the difference between supply and demand would not be so great.[22]

Van Onselen found linkage too in the fact that when the Hatherley Distillery went public in 1892, it attracted capital from the Rand as well as from investors abroad, and that mining capital was represented on its board. Nothing much has changed there. In modern times, investors and entrepreneurs still seek diversification and risk-spreading. Today, the mining houses have major holdings in, for example, the mighty South African Breweries.

Whatever the attitudes of individual magnates or mine managers may have been, the record shows indisputably that year in and year out, in memorial after memorial, the Chamber protested to the Government and the Raad at the vast and illicit liquor trade that enmeshed the Rand, battening on the black mineworker and incapacitating him with vile and poisonous liquor. It attributed many of the accidents in the mines to drunkenness and its aftermath.

For the first five or six years after its founding the Chamber chose to campaign for proper control of the liquor trade. When this failed, and the cost in terms of debauched and incapable workers became intolerable, the Chamber switched to a campaign for a total ban on the sale of liquor to black mine-workers. In 1896, as the result of the latest memorial from the Chamber, the Raad grasped the nettle and resolved on prohibition. The ban came into force on 1 January 1897. It would endure until 15 August 1962.

A dramatic reduction in drunkenness followed prohibition, but the illicit liquor dealers, though somewhat thinned in numbers, were quick to find ways through and round, and in defiance of, the law. Soon the mines were back to a situation in which around one quarter of the workforce could be incapacitated by drink. The problem was enforcement with inadequate policing resources.

In 1894, the Commandant of Police, D E Schutte, in an open letter, had admitted:

> I acknowledge the *rottenness* of the entire police force, but decline to accept the disgrace attached thereto, having striven to reorganise the same, but failed through lack of support.[23]

Despite improvements, the problem of enforcement with inadequate policing still remained.

A manuscript history, almost certainly written by Leyds in or about 1913,[24] reveals the distrust which the Government had of the mine-owners. It suggests that the Chamber was overstating the effects of the illicit trade as propaganda for the introduction of a closed compound system for black workers. Etheredge has pointed out that there is little to substantiate Leyds's allegation, there being no mention of the closed compound system in the Chamber's records of the times. In fact, what records exist, and recent research, tend to confirm that the Chamber's agitation was fully justified. Thus, Christiaan Joubert in his report for the year 1897 states

> To my regret I must report that the provisions of the Liquor Law have not succeeded in attaining the purpose in mind insofar as concerns the selling of strong drink to Native Labourers on the Mines. It appears to me from incoming reports that the evil, rather than diminishing, is increasing.[25]

Lobbying and pressure to win back the right to sell liquor to blacks on the mines would continue until the war of 1899. In that year a bill was introduced in the Raad to give retailers the right to supply two drams a day to blacks, but the bill was dropped on the intervention of Kruger's vital ally, President Steyn of the Orange Free State.

Back in 1881 Nellmapius had established a gunpowder factory in terms of the concession granted him, but it did not prosper and the Government took it over.[26] When mining began on the Rand the mining companies were at first allowed to import explosives under permit, but in 1887 Lippert, with the support of Sammy Marks, was successful in obtaining a monopoly concession which was ratified by the Raad the following year. Its terms gave him the exclusive right to manufacture gunpowder and explosives, and to trade in them. He was permitted to import machinery and materials free of duty. But the concession stipulated: 'The contracting party shall however not have the right to import from elsewhere gunpowder, cartridges, dynamite or other explosives or ammunition'. Lippert was also required to erect within one year 'one or more factories for the manufacture of dynamite and other explosives' and to produce explosives of a standard to meet Government requirements.[27]

Lippert first registered the explosives company, De Zuid-Afrikaansche Maatschappij van Ontplofbare Stoffen Beperk in London, and negotiated a deal with the 'Ring' of manufacturers operating on a monopoly basis, known as the French or Latin Trust. Early in 1899, the company set up a subsidiary in Pretoria, but nearly all the shares remained in French hands.

L G Vorstman, who was well-known to Leyds, became Managing Director in Pretoria. Lippert, now established as the 'Prince of Concessionaires', became salesman of the company's products at a commission of twelve and a half per cent.

The first complaints by the Chamber concerned the quality of the dynamite provided, but by 1891 the grounds for complaint seem largely, though never wholly, to have been resolved. During April of that year, the Chamber submitted a lengthy memorial to the Raad urging the free importation of dynamite. It pointed out that the so-called Transvaal dynamite supplied by the explosives company was really imported and only mixed in the Transvaal. Figures were supplied to show that the State was receiving less revenue from the monopolists than it would from import dues. Meanwhile, the Government had appointed a commission to investigate the matter. Its report, which favoured the concessionaires, was debated in the Volksraad, together with the memorial from the Chamber and other submissions, including one from the Barberton Mining and Commercial Chamber. Kruger backed the concessionaires and was opposed by the representatives of the mining areas, Meyer (Witwatersrand) and Loveday (Barberton). The Raad, after a long and lively debate, supported Kruger and the concessionaires by fourteen votes to nine. However, the Raad stipulated that the terms of the concession must be enforced strictly and that steps must be taken to ensure that explosives were manufactured from local materials as soon as possible. The company was ordered to pay import dues on the dynamite it was importing.[28]

The situation led W Y Campbell to declare in a Chamber report:

> The subservience by a Government of an entire industry to the profit of one individual is, as far as I know, without parallel in any civilized country at the present time.[29]

The situation was now complicated by the intervention of the great Anglo-German 'Ring', known as the Nobel Trust, which had earlier declined involvement in the explosives company. British and German dynamite companies protested to their respective governments that their dynamite was being denied entry. The British Agent in Pretoria duly lodged a formal complaint in September 1891, and in May the following year, after some preliminary negotiation, the German Consul followed suit. The Republican Government felt obliged to act and in August informed the explosives company that the contract had been cancelled because the company had not only failed to manufacture dynamite in the Transvaal, but was importing the finished product. This was followed in turn by a protest against the cancellation from the French Government through its Consul in Pretoria.[30]

For a while Kruger was inclined to allow events to unfold and to hope that an agreed solution would emerge. He issued permits to mine operators permitting the importation of dynamite from France, England and Germany in equal quantities. The Chamber worked hard to maintain this system of free trade, but in the end its endeavours were nullified by government action.

At a meeting of the Chamber on 8 August 1893, Lippert, still a member of the Executive Committee, argued, in typically eloquent fashion, the case for introducing a state monopoly to handle the dynamite business. However, he did not convince his colleagues who took a wholly contrary view. The Chamber resolved:

   (a) that it was alarmed at the dearth of dynamite and would urge the Government to speed up arbitration and the free importation of dynamite under a permit system;
   (b) that it should protest against the creation of a State Monopoly;
   (c) that it would be satisfied only with free competition;
   (d) that a deputation should inform the Government of the Chamber's firm attitude.[31]

Unhappily, the deputation which saw Kruger the next day received short shrift, being received, according to a contemporary account, 'with the greatest possible discourtesy'. He told them, in effect, to keep their noses out of his business, and accused them of disloyalty to the Republic.[32] All too obviously, Lippert had already had the presidential ear and, soon after, the Raad was ordered to debate draft regulations for a State monopoly. Kruger argued in support the need to ensure the independence of the Republic. After a debate, by no means all in his favour, the principle of a state monopoly was accepted by a margin of thirteen votes to ten.

The Chamber was unremitting in its efforts to offer alternatives, but to no avail. On 25 October 1893 the Government – incredibly – appointed as agents of a state monopoly (for fifteen years) the French Company, once again disguised as De Zuid-Afrikaansche Maatschappij van Ontplofbare Stoffen Beperk and represented in Pretoria by Vorstman.

There were further protests from the British and German Governments, and Nobel's agents got in touch with the Chamber, offering contracts at cut prices. The Chamber resolved to recommend acceptance to its member companies. In the debate in 1893 that preceded this, Lippert accused the Chamber of desiring merely to make a demonstration against the Government. He was rebuked by the Chairman, Hanau, who wound up by saying 'that the sooner the people at Pretoria were made to see that the Chamber were not going to be sat upon and have their life blood drained without remonstrance, the better it would be for all concerned'.[33] At the conclusion of the debate, Lippert at last resigned from the Chamber's Executive Committee. When he attempted to explain his position at a Chamber meeting on 14 December, members rudely shouted him down.

By the beginning of 1894, Nobels had decided to abandon the Chamber and its member companies, and come to a more profitable arrangement with the Government and the French Company. It opened negotiations accordingly and in February completed a deal. The rival rings now came together and agreed to form a company with equal shareholdings which would be managed by the Nobel Trust from Hamburg. Lippert got 25 000 shares and a sales commission which would bring him in £360 000 over five years. Sammy Marks got a royalty of two shillings a case sold.[34] The mining industry was now in the grip of a monopoly far stronger than the original one.

High duties were charged on any imported explosives and the explosives company exploited its enviable position by continually raising its prices. More than one million cases were consumed in the Republic from June 1894 to September 1899 and the profit was about forty shillings a case above Kimberley prices. The impact on the mines was heightened by a rapid decline in the consumption of dynamite on the deep-level mines in favour of the even more highly-priced blasting gelatine. Repeated requests by the Chamber and the British Government to open the explosives market to competition and thereby cheapen the price were ignored by the Government of the Transvaal. Explosives were an important element of working costs.[35] The artificial inflation of their cost, the threat that this might be raised higher still, and the intrigue which constantly surrounded the monopoly, did much to poison relations between industry and State.

Although the Chamber could not triumph, it won at least one important battle. The explosives company sought in the second half of 1894 an extension of the time in which it was required to establish a dynamite factory, with the obvious motive of continuing to enjoy the greater profits to be earned by simply importing dynamite rather than manufacturing it.[36] When the matter was debated, on 13 and 14 September 1894, the Raad for the first time showed itself hostile to the monopoly and, led by Carl Jeppe, refused the company's request by eighteen votes to four. The Government was instructed to see that the regulations were carried out and that the factory was completed within two years.[37]

However, it was October 1896 before the company at last got down to building the factory at Modderfontein, on the north-eastern outskirts of Johannesburg. It was completed two years later and acknowledged to be one of the finest in the world.

Despite the ready condonation by the Government of the many breaches of contract, it seems that the company lived in fear of the cancellation of its monopoly. Rightly or wrongly, it thought it necessary to spend more than £39 000 in Pretoria during 1897/98 with the intention of influencing Government officials, Members of the Volksraad and others. Among those who received gifts were Leyds (a bank credit to speculate with and some shares), J T Klimke, the State Mining Engineer (some gold shares) and J M A Wolmarans, Executive Council Member (at least £500).[38] The eminent historian of the period, J S Marais, found that the evidence quoted by the Transvaal Concessions Commission of Inquiry appointed by the British Government in 1900 did not justify its conclusion that the survival of the monopoly was the result of bribery by the Hamburg-based dynamite company. According to Marais, it could hardly be doubted that financial inducements played some part in the continuation of the monopoly in the face of the intense dislike it engendered. However, Marais was equally certain that neither a dedicated statesman like Kruger nor a public servant of integrity like Leyds could be influenced by considerations of personal gain.[39]

The concessions policy had been introduced to give a modest stimulus to industrialization. As time went by, the policy became more and more an assertion of republican enterprise against foreign encroachment.

The reason for Kruger and Leyds's defence, through thick and thin, of a monopoly regarded by President Steyn of the Orange Free State as indefensible, was the importance that they attached to '"capitalist" allies on whom the government could depend, as a counterpoise against those capitalists, including mining magnates, whom they regarded as enemies of the republic'.[40] The Government did in fact obtain direct assistance, financial or otherwise, from concessionaires.[41] Moreover, as the explosives company waxed fat on its enormous profits, its expropriation became beyond the financial capacity of the Government. But overriding all was Kruger's obsession with the independence of the Republic. He saw the explosives company supplying not only ammunition for the armed forces in emergency (in the end the Government was compelled to buy most of its munitions of war abroad), but as underpinning its viability as an economic entity free from Imperial suzerainty.

As Kruger was obsessed with independence, so Lionel Phillips became obsessed with the injustice of the dynamite monopoly. It has been suggested that this could have been a critical factor in his decision in mid–1895 to come down on the side of direct revolutionary action.[42]

[1] J W Shilling, 'Historical Review of Certain Aspects of the Taxation of Gold Mines in the Transvaal and Orange Free State', p 2.

[2] 'Amended Gold Law', *The South African Mining Journal*, 19 September 1891.

[3] Praagh, ed, p 544.

[4] For example, on 21 April 1894, p 437.

[5] M Fraser and A Jeeves, eds, *All That Glittered: Selected Correspondence of Lionel Phillips, 1890-1924*, p 78, letter dated 16 June 1894.

[6] Annual Report of the Witwatersrand Chamber of Mines, 1892, pp 19, 23.

[7] Leading article, 'The Cyanide Judgment', *The South African Mining Journal*, 7 November 1896, p 103.

[8] Ewald August Esselen, a progressive politician who served for a time as State Attorney.

[9] Fraser and Jeeves, eds, p 78, letter dated 16 June 1894.

[10] Seventh Annual Report of the Witwatersrand Chamber of Mines, 1895, p 147.

[11] Eighth Annual Report of the Witwatersrand Chamber of Mines, 1896, p 252.

[12] C van Onselen, 'Randlords and Rotgut: 1886-1903', *Studies in the Social and Economic History of the Witwatersrand: 1886-1914: 1 New Babylon*, p 94.

[13] Marais, p 23.

[14] M H Buys, 'Nellmapius' in *Dictionary of South African Biography*, IV, pp 404-405.

[15] *Ibid*, p 404.

[16] *Ibid*, p 405.

[17] Van Onselen, pp 54-55.

[18] *Ibid*, pp 55-56.

[19] *Ibid*, p 56.

[20] *Ibid*, p 94.

[21] *Ibid*, p 52.

[22] Annual Report of the Witwatersrand Chamber of Mines, 1895, p 77.

[23] Van Onselen, p 61, quoting a letter from D E Schutte to the Editor, *Standard and Diggers' News*, 11 October 1894.

[24] Etheredge, p 82, citing the Leyds Archives, 100.

[25] *Ibid*, p 83, quoting *Rapport van het Hoofd van Mijnwezen ... over het jaar 1897*.

[26] In 1886 Nellmapius was found guilty by a jury of embezzling funds belonging to the explosives factory and sentenced to eighteen months' imprisonment by Judge C J Brand. Nellmapius appealed to the Executive Council and was released through the intervention of Kruger. Brand resigned. Nellmapius was re-arrested but acquitted by a full judicial tribunal on the legal issue reserved for its consideration.

[27] Annual Report of the Witwatersrand Chamber of Mines, 1890, pp 55-56.

[28] Etheredge, p 49, citing First Raad, Article 1184 of 1891.

[29] Third Annual Report of the Witwatersrand Chamber of Mines, 1891, p 31.

[30] Marais, pp 28-29.

[31] Etheredge, p 60, summarizing part of an article from *The South African Mining Journal*, 12 August 1893.

[32] Fifth Annual Report of the Witwatersrand Chamber of Mines, 1893, p 86.

[33] 'Chamber of Mines: The Dynamite Debate', *The South African Mining Journal*, 25 November 1893, p 133.

[34] Marais, pp 29-30.

[35] Richardson and Van-Helten, p 33.

[36] *Report of the Transvaal Concessions Commission* dated 4 April 1901: 1 Dynamite Concession, p 72.

[37] Sixth Annual Report of the Witwatersrand Chamber of Mines, 1894, p 106.

[38] Marais, p 31.

[39] *Ibid*, pp 31-32.

[40] *Ibid*, p 32.

[41] *Idem*.

[42] Fraser and Jeeves, eds, pp 30-31.

CHAPTER SIX

Of Money and Men

By 1894 abundant proof was forthcoming that the Witwatersrand gold deposits persisted at depth, dipping southward from the outcrop. In the Presidential Address on 25 January of that year, Phillips drew attention to the development under way on the deep levels. He went on to point out the significance of the tapping of the Main Reef by borehole, the most dramatic being that on the Rand Victoria property:

The borehole is situated 4 100 feet south of the outcrop of the Main Reef, and upon June 3rd last the South Reef was intersected at a depth of 2 343 feet, 13 inches wide, and assaying 1 oz 3 dwts[1] 2 grains per ton. The Main Reef was struck at a depth of 2 391 feet, and proved to be 9 feet wide. The gold was mostly contained in the lower 4 feet, and the average result of nine assays was 1 oz 15 dwts, the value varying from 1 dwt to 10 ozs. A portion of this core showed visible gold freely, and according to tests ... the gold contained in the samples is as easily extracted as that contained in ore now being worked nearer the surface. The importance of this cannot be exaggerated.

There were other boreholes, such as those on the Henry Nourse Deep Level, Rand Deep Level and on some of the Gold Fields properties, to confirm the permanency and continued value of the reefs.[2]

Despite the proven potential, the financing and technological problems of the mines were legion and impelled the progressive development of the Group System to mobilize capital resources and mining expertise. This has continued to underpin the industry ever since. The majority of mines, while operating as public companies with separate shareholders and boards of directors, are associated with a mining finance corporation, or mining 'house', in the sense that the house has provided development capital, and has a contract to provide managerial, technical and other services. A mining house and its member mines constitutes in modern parlance a 'mining group'.

The mining houses often started as simple partnerships and evolved to meet the exigencies of mining under the unique conditions prevailing. Thus Wernher, Beit, the most important of the mine operators, and the firm representing it in Johannesburg, the Hermann Eckstein partnership, launched Rand Mines in 1893 to exploit deep-level mines. Rand Mines would continue to be known familiarly as 'the Corner House', reflecting the name of Eckstein (Corner Stone) and the position of its offices at the corner of Commissioner and Simmonds Streets.

Gold Fields was launched as a company from the outset, though it too had its origin in a partnership, the Rhodes-Rudd combination of Kimberley days. It was initially invested in De Beers and Rhodes's British South Africa Company (The Charter Company) to the extent that its gold mining interests represented no more than an insignificant part of the whole.[3] The Company was reconstructed in 1892, being renamed the Consolidated Gold Fields of South Africa, to enable it to develop deep-level mining interests. However, Corner House had been first in the field and held control of extensive blocks of deep-level claims immediately south of the major outcrop mines. Gold Fields, plagued in the early days by Rhodes's hesitancy and relative lack of interest in the Rand, had to make do with second-best pickings, further from the outcrop in less promising areas, but it also benefited from the policy followed by Rand Mines of offering participation in mining ventures to other houses and interests (with hopes of *quid pro quo* to come).[4]

Goertz and Co was formed in 1893 to take over the interests acquired by Adolf Goertz, a German mining engineer who had arrived in 1888 as the representative of the Deutsche Bank and the Berlin Handelgesellschaft. It was the forerunner of the powerful Union Corporation. Another German entrepreneur, George Albu, had acquired assets in the name of a private firm, G and L Albu. In December 1895 he formed from these and other assets the General Mining and Finance Corporation. Eighty years later the Corporation, by then a proud assertion of Afrikaner enterprise, would absorb Union Corporation.

Barney Barnato had established the Johannesburg Consolidated Investment Company, familiarly known as JCI or 'Johnnies', in 1889. In 1895 it, too, began buying deep-level properties. Originally a land company, it survived Barnato's speculative adventures and financial buccaneering to become a major mining and finance house.

There were a number of other important mining and investment groups which have not survived as separate entities. They never developed into mining houses as such and did not form part of the Group System in the full sense of the term. These included the financially powerful Robinson Group, which in the nineties was still concentrating on a big tract of outcrop property, principally the Langlaagte Estate and Block B Langlaagte properties. At the same time it was acquiring the claims which were to provide the assets of the Randfontein Estates, still a thriving mining company in 1986. Another company still operating in 1986 is The East Rand Proprietary Mines Ltd (ERPM) formed in the early days, from a combination of outcrop and deep-level claims, by the Farrar-Anglo French Group. S Neumann and Co, apart from ventures on its own account, had important participations, and the

Lewis and Marks and Abe Bailey Groups had highly diversified holdings in land and industrial ventures, in addition to gold mining interests on a relatively small scale. There were other small groups and fringe operators.

The mining finance houses made profits from share dealing as well as from mining, and engaged in market operations, sometimes in a manner that would not now be countenanced or contemplated. Industrial society the world over had still to evolve codes of ethical behaviour and to express them in law and regulation. It was an age in which few holds were barred to the financier, and all took advantage, though the degree of advantage taken differed widely.

In floating the early companies of the Rand, mining claims and other assets were transferred to the new companies in return for shares in them. It was easy for promoters to over-value assets in determining the so-called vendor's interest. It was equally easy for outsiders and critics to undervalue the enterprise, flair and risk-taking involved in acquiring the assets. The risks were all too real and large sums were lost as well as made by big-time promoters and speculators. It is certain however that the successful entrepreneur gained substantially more from flotations than the investing public, and on the part of certain financiers, outrageously so. There was also widespread and profitable 'insider' trading. Though the financial methods adopted by the mine controllers differed radically in propriety from house to house and financier to financier, the consequent notoriety tended to be apportioned to all. The 'robber baron' image would long persist and furnish the political enemies of the capitalists with a ready store of ammunition.

As gold mining became an established industry the houses increasingly turned from profiteering in the 'scrip industry' of share market operations, to concentrate on long-term, stable returns from mining.[5] It was after all the prudent – and surer – course to follow, for mining houses themselves did not always read the market aright and were sometimes left, in the inevitable bust that followed the boom time, with shares that would prove valueless.

Mining the deeps called for the attraction of capital on an unprecedented scale, just when many were licking the wounds sustained in the first rush for riches in Rand shares on the stock markets of the world. Initial development of mines along the outcrop had been undertaken with capital accumulated on the diamond fields. Despite the re-investment of profits from early outcrop mining, the funds available were now wholly inadequate to meet the needs of the hugely complex properties developed to open up the deep-running reefs. These mines would ever be greedy for capital. Moreover, investors would have to be prepared to wait long years before a modest flow of dividends could begin.

It was in the financing of the deep levels in the early nineties that the mining houses established their prime role in the future and demonstrated the critical service they could render through the access to capital markets abroad which their expertise commanded. The principal source of funds was the City of London, but there was strong participation from the money markets of Paris and Berlin, from international consortia like the Rothschilds and from banks like the Deutsche Bank and the Banque Française de l'Afrique du Sud. Such institutions were to play a vital role in placing shares on the stock markets of Europe. With these connections the mining houses, by endorsing the shares of individual companies, were able to channel speculative funds on a scale that could not have accrued to individual flotations. They could offer, too, shares in the mining houses themselves without, to be sure, the prospect of the huge dividends and capital profits for which small investors plunged so wildly in the booms of 1888/9 and 1895, but shorn, too, of the risk of buying shares in individual companies. Investment in mining houses provided the more prudent investors with a secure spread of interest in all the member companies of the group.

The quantum of investment from abroad which the mining houses raised was substantial enough to alter the pattern of international investment, and to lock the gold mines into the cycles of growth and recession of the world economy.[6] The mines in turn became increasingly important internationally and the cynosure of the eyes of the major powers in their aggressive competition for new economic resources.

The gold flowing from the Witwatersrand represented a huge accrual to a previously restricted supply, and came just in time to remove the threat to world trade contained in the inadequacy of gold supply in relation to currencies. Instead, it would make possible a lively expansion of trade. The most important currencies at that time were tied, by the gold standard, to national reserves of bullion in the vaults of central banks. Between 1890 and 1896 the value of gold reserves held by the Bank of England doubled to reach a record of £49 million – a direct reflection of the role of British financial institutions in expanding international trade, and also of the escalation of the quantum of bullion and of gold coin in circulation[7] as an indirect consequence of the soaring output of the Rand.

Capital formation apart, the technology involved in the mining of the Witwatersrand conglomerates was complex enough to warrant, on its own, the evolution of the Group System. Despite the size and regularity of the deposits, the Main Reef, which alone among the reefs of the Witwatersrand Geological System could be regarded as uniformly payable, was shown by international standards to be of low grade. Within the same properties and in the same reefs on the Rand wide variations in value were – and still are – the norm. This made it necessary to work on a selective basis, mining a mix of grades to ensure a profitable margin between working costs and the price paid for gold.

Because the price paid was immutably fixed, the level of costs was unarguably the decisive factor. Gold mining was thus both capital intensive and highly cost sensitive, a sensitivity which was to be accentuated by the proving of the deeps. As if this were not enough, it was labour intensive, too. While the shafts plunged, labour requirements soared.

Just as the need for capital and technology established the vital role of the mining houses, so the need for sensible control of labour consolidated the function of the Chamber as the centre of consultation and regulation. This situation was to provide the mining houses with powerful incentive to co-operative action, and to establish for the Chamber an overriding *raison d'être*.

If the great gold deposits of southern Africa had lain in a populated area, it would all have been so different. Unfortunately, the natural and human resources of the sub-continent are unevenly distributed. Minerals, in particular, tend to lie in areas remote from human habitation, without communications, fuel or water, and lacking the most rudimentary amenities. The Witwatersrand and surrounding areas, never closely settled by Bantu-speaking tribes, had been depopulated by the *Difaqane*.

The facts of geography compelled the entrepreneurs to import their labour, attracting by high wages from urban areas far away, usually abroad, the skilled workers who would make their homes on the Rand. Their huge needs of unskilled labour to shovel rock and push the cocopans of broken ore to the shaft they met through the migratory system. The only alternative, the large-scale resettlement of men and families along the Reef, was and would long remain economically suspect to mine-owners, and politically unacceptable to successive governments. Moreover, circumstances forced mining companies to look further and further afield for their labour. It is a common human characteristic not to choose to work down a mine when alternative employment is on offer in a more congenial situation, and the tribesmen of Africa proved no exception. Those who were settled relatively close at hand tended to take employment in the industries and services that sprang up to cater for the needs of the mines. They and migrant workers who opted against return to the distant homeland provided a nucleus of an increasingly de-tribalized urban population. The bulk of migrant labour however tended to retain their tribal allegiance and stayed on the mine or in town only for periods, usually brief, before returning to the tribal homeland. The migratory system would retard the opportunity of these men to progress up the ladder of skills, and would help to consolidate the acceptance of colour as a barrier to advancement.

Historian De Kiewiet has sagely told us that modern South Africa was not built on gold and diamonds alone, but on the availability of cheap black labour.[8] To the early gold mine operators, however, black labour was neither readily available nor cheap. It was scarce and expensive. Day in and day out, they held forth, to anyone who would listen, about the lack of it and the cost of it, and they readily expanded on its inefficiency. Nevertheless, they poached men from one another and bid up the wages with a reckless disregard for the consequences.

The Transvaal Government introduced a hut tax of 10s a year in 1895, in addition to the £2 poll tax, to induce men to work, but the measure was poorly administered and proved of little help.[9] The blacks themselves were not eager, being possessed of what the economists call a 'high leisure preference'. Despite this, the burgeoning desire to acquire consumer goods, the increasing need for ready cash, and severe epidemics of rinderpest and red-water fever which

78

ravaged the herds in the 1890s, impelled men to leave the tribal areas in search of work. This movement was accelerated by the aura of adventure surrounding the mines, purveyed in the tall stories of those returning, which was seen as offering a substitute for dwindling opportunities to test manhood in inter-tribal war.

The mines looked to the Chamber to produce somehow the rabbit from the tribal hat, while busily undermining any control measures that institution might devise in the common interest. This brief period of free competition for black labour has been described as 'a classical example of the free interaction of supply and demand'.[10] It was a costly failure from the point of view of the mining companies, and was often a time of bitter hardship for the tribesmen who made their way from distant kraals on foot, harassed and unaided across countless, inhospitable miles, to eGoli, the City of Gold, where conditions in mines and compounds in those early days could be bad enough to render the reality a nasty shock.

In 1890 the number employed was fourteen thousand. By the end of the decade the number had increased sevenfold. Men were sought all over southern Africa. In 1897, according to contemporary estimates, half of the labour force came from Moçambique, a fifth from territories to the north, and the rest from Bechuanaland, Swaziland, Natal, the Transkei and elsewhere in the Cape Colony. Of nearly forty-three thousand employed in and around Johannesburg in July 1896, less than a thousand were from the Transvaal Republic.[11]

From the outset, the cost of this labour was a major factor in the profitability of gold mining.[12] The mine-owners saw it as excessive, both in the South African context, and in relation to the wages paid to miners in Europe. According to the Consulting Engineer to the General Mining and Finance Corporation, the sudden demand from the Rand lifted wages for black workers to three or four times that paid to blacks in Natal in those frugal days.[13]

Out of a total of £4 500 000 spent by sixty companies in 1894, the cost of the salaries of managers, officials, miners and skilled craftsmen was £1 500 000. Unskilled black labour (including the cost of their food), cost as much again. Stores, including explosives and fuel, cost around £1 500 000.[14]

The cost of black labour, which was to loom so large in the councils of the industry, arose partly from cash wages, food and accommodation, and partly from the need to recruit far afield. The brisk demand led to the emergence of a corps of enterprising and often unscrupulous individuals who, on their own account, or on behalf of mining or other companies, travelled far and wide in the search for recruits, and charged handsomely for their services.[15]

They took on labour in the tribal territory, or 'poached' from the troops of men, marching to the mines, who had been engaged by others. Touts also tried to tempt workers in employment to move elsewhere, with promises of higher pay which were not always realized. Even when mines did their own recruiting, there was heavy cost involved with no guarantee that the worker would arrive and remain in employment thereafter.

It devolved on the Chamber therefore to develop ways to reduce both cash wages and the cost of recruiting, and, if possible, to introduce some order out of chaos, some stability into the pattern of employment. In doing so, it sometimes worked in association with – and at other times at odds with – the influential Association of Mine Managers, founded in 1892, which would continue to play an important role in industry affairs.

However, the attainment of these desired ends depended upon men coming forward in sufficient numbers for regular periods. Even in those hopeful days it was clearly understood that attempts to reduce black wages in periods of low supply and high demand were unlikely to succeed. Nor was the Chamber particularly successful in its attempts to stimulate flow, for the tribesmen usually hearkened to their own tribal impulse. Workers customarily went home when there were crops to be harvested, and only came out to work on the mines when there was little fun or feasting down on the farm. They left routine cultivation and cattle minding to the women and children. Their recruitment to the mines was inhibited, too, by the sterner imperatives of war. There were serious interruptions in flow caused by the Government's punitive expeditions against Chief Malaboch in the northern Transvaal in 1894, and, in the following year, by the operations against chiefs in the Woodbush in the north-east of the province, and the war between the Portuguese and Chief Gungunyana. There were further adverse effects from the Jameson Raid in 1896, and finally the absolute disruption occasioned by the South African War of 1899-1902. Other facts inhibiting or stimulating the flow were the alternation of drought and flood, and the incidence of good rains, leading to ample grazing and bumper harvests. The study of rainfall and the state of crops and cattle would henceforth become an essential part of the business of mining.

Black workers who sought work outside the tribal area were subject to a law requiring them to carry a valid pass, which the Transvaal Government had based partly on that in force in Natal.[16] This Pass Law should have regulated the numbers on the gold-fields and made it possible to trace a man who had broken his contract. However, the administration of the law was wholly ineffective. At that stage, too, the Chamber was unsure that the answer lay in a more efficient law which by increasing restrictions might deter men from seeking mine work.

The first successful measure introduced by the Chamber was a switch from a daily wage system to monthly pay.[17] This at least ensured some return for the trouble and expense incurred by a mine in engaging a worker in his tribal area and bringing him to Johannesburg.

In August 1890, the first attempt to reduce wages was made. A total of sixty-six companies agreed to enforce a nominal maximum wage of £2 for a twenty-eight-day month. The average wage, excluding the cost of food and accommodation provided at company expense, fell from £3 3s 4d in August to £2 8s 10d in October. The agreement worked well for only a short while, until the seasonal shortage of 1891 set mining companies once again to pursue the usual course of unenlightened self-interest. The following year was a difficult one throughout, in which rapidly increasing requirements coincided with inadequate supply. The wage agreement broke down completely. In his speech to the Annual General Meeting on 26 January 1893, Phillips declared that the average payment for four weeks had risen to £2 17s 6d, representing a cost of more than 8s 6d a worker per ton milled.

> When I tell you that in some countries this sum suffices to cover the entire cost of mining and milling, you will the better realise what an extravagant charge this is. The excessive rate of pay is not only disastrous to the interest of the shareholders, but pernicious to the native himself. It is but necessary to remember that the wages paid to natives exceed those earned by first class labourers in Europe, who support wives and families, to appreciate the wrong we are doing, which does not alone affect the industry, but the farmers, carriers, and townsmen.[18]

The Chamber attempted to meet the situation by establishing a Native Labour Department at the end of the year. The first Native Labour Commissioner, heading the new department, was William Grant. His duties were to organize the supply of labour, give his official sanction to contracts between employers and employees, and hear complaints from and, when necessary, obtain justice for black workers.

Increasing dependence on a supply of labour pointed up the necessity for a workable Pass Law to control the inflow from across the borders and in particular that from Moçambique. It was also deemed necessary to intervene in the chaotic situation in which workers brought to the Rand at the expense of one company could with impunity break their contracts and return home or take up service with another. In the end the Chamber was obliged to draft a new law and to present it to the Government which, in turn, passed it to a commission of inquiry. The commission recommended acceptance, and it was passed into law in October 1895, with only minimal alteration. The new Pass Law was at first applied only to De Kaap (Barberton area) and Johannesburg, but representatives from the Chamber obtained its extension to Krugersdorp and Boksburg. It did not work satisfactorily, even when further amended to the Chamber's requirement in 1897, largely because the Government did not vote the funds necessary for its proper administration.[19]

Meanwhile the supply continued to be inadequate, the wage agreement collapsed and in 1895 no two mines paid alike, wages being related to the assessment of the value of their work. According to the Native Labour Department the usual wage rates were from £2 to £3 a month, but skilful drillers might earn £3 10s.[20] A solution was sought in the formation of the Rand Native Labour Association which operated quite independently of the Chamber or any other organization. A reduction in wages of twenty to twenty-five per cent was effected from 1 October 1896. At the same time, standard arrangements were laid down for hours of work and food.[21] The workers generally accepted the reduction with the exception of those on the Crown Reef who went on strike for two days.[22]

The Chamber's Native Labour Department continued to operate independently of the Association, supplying considerable numbers of men to the Chamber's member mines, and reaching an important agreement with the Moçambique Government for the recruitment of workers in that territory. However, the Rand Native Labour Association seemed to be doing better, partly because it did not suffer from lack of funds as the Chamber's Native Labour Department did. At the end of 1896, the Chamber's Native Labour Department was dissolved, and its depots were handed over to the Association. Grant accepted the post of Manager of the Association, but resigned early in 1897.[23]

The new Association was soon in the same kind of difficulties as the Chamber's department had experienced. The supply again deteriorated, partly no doubt as a result of the wage reduction which had been accepted in hard times. Once again companies found it hard to hold the ring. Nevertheless, when the position improved a new wage reduction was introduced setting wages at a minimum of 28s and a maximum of 70s for four weeks. Seven-and-a-half per cent of workers might be paid more. This reduction led to large-scale departure of workers. In due course, however, the position again improved as the new wage scales became accepted. At the end of 1897 the mines, requiring between 80 000 and 100 000 workers, were in a better position than for years, but the situation was still unsatisfactory. The problem of attracting enough unskilled men, at wages which the mines regarded as affordable, would be a major preoccupation all the years of the Chamber's existence.

[1] One dwt (or pennyweight) equals twenty-four grains or one-twentieth of a troy ounce. A troy ounce equals 31,10 grams.

[2] Annual Report of the Witwatersrand Chamber of Mines, 1893, p 17.

[3] A P Cartwright, *Gold Paved the Way: The Story of the Gold Fields Group of Companies*, p 54.

[4] Fraser and Jeeves, eds, p 29.

[5] Richardson and Van-Helten, p 29.

[6] *Ibid*, pp 21-22.

[7] *Idem*.

[8] De Kiewiet, p 96.

[9] S T van der Horst, *Native Labour in South Africa*, p 152.

[10] F Wilson, *Labour in the South African Gold Mines, 1911-1969*, quoted by G A Fenske and T R N Main in 'Labour and the Gold Mines' (Review Note), *The South African Journal of Economics*, Volume 41, No 3, September 1973, p 299.

[11] Van der Horst, pp 136-137.

[12] *Ibid*, p 128.

[13] G A Denny, *The Deep-Level Mines of the Rand*, p 149.

[14] Van der Horst, p 128.

[15] *Ibid*, p 129.

[16] A Jeeves, 'The Control of Migratory Labour on the South African Gold Mines in the Era of Kruger and Milner', *Journal of Southern African Studies*, Vol 2, No 1, October 1975, p 11.

[17] Etheredge, p 72.

[18] Annual Report of the Witwatersrand Chamber of Mines, 1892, p 21.

[19] Etheredge, pp 77-79.

[20] Annual Report of the Witwatersrand Chamber of Mines, 1895, p 52.

[21] Annual Report of the Witwatersrand Chamber of Mines, 1896, pp 157, 163.

[22] *Ibid*, p 166.

[23] *The South African Mining Journal*, 20 February 1897.

CHAPTER SEVEN

Then Hey for Boot and Horse, Lad!

Lionel and Florence Phillips and their three children lived for a time in the four-roomed brick house which Hermann Eckstein had built at 27 Noord Street on the edge of Johannesburg and named 'Hohenheim' after his birth-place near Stuttgart. In Eckstein's time the comfortable dwelling with its shady verandah looked over open veld across the newly laid-out grounds of the Wanderers' Club to the Johannesburg Fort. The coming of the railway and the building of Park Station changed the scene. Florence began to look for a site for a home away from the alternate dust and quagmire of the streets, and the endemic typhoid and diphtheria of the insanitary town.

She was an enthusiastic horsewoman, riding far and wide in the 'wild country' of ridges and plantations to the north. One day she discovered a dramatic site on a rocky eminence in a location now submerged beneath the monstrous hulk of the Johannesburg General Hospital. There they built a mansion, completed in 1894, and transferred to it the name 'Hohenheim', which may be translated, appropriately, as 'Home on High'. It was 'perched like a Rhine residence in eery isolation upon its crag above the empty country-side'.[1] The view to the distant Magaliesberg was not unlike that once enjoyed by the primitive iron smelters of Melville Koppies a mile or two to the west. An architect described Hohenheim thus:

> Hohenheim, with its vast assemblage of rooms, its surface variety of bays, alcoves, verandah recesses and look-out turret; its intricacies of a vast roof-scape of valleys, hips and timbered gables, punctuated with its masses of chimneys; its applied decorations of tudor timberwork, decorative parapets and great, mullioned windows, projected an atavistic image of personal power.[2]

It was a home in keeping, perhaps extravagantly so, with Phillips's position of leadership on the Rand. It was in keeping, too, not so extravagantly, with the riches that flowed from his flair for successful risk-taking in both mining ventures and investment. He had made a major contribution to the organi-zation of mining, the strengthening of management and improving technology. He helped to lift the Witwatersrand from slump to boom in the early 1890s, and at Hohenheim he enjoyed some of the fruits. In Johannesburg at that time the impact of the huge house was stunning. Florence displayed her own individual flair in furnishing with antiques, oil paintings, rich carpets and other treasures from Europe. It was said of her that her intent was to establish in Johannesburg a home of such grace and style that it would prosper her husband's aims and instil an uplifting influence on the 'resident barbarians'.[3] It quickly became the centre of the exclusive end of Johannesburg's social whirl – and the favoured venue of conspirators against the Kruger regime.

Phillips at first held aloof from Uitlander agitation. He was conscious of his responsibility to the financial interests he represented. Indeed, he had no authority to step outside the Wernher, Beit policy of political detachment. The firm believed that direct consultation with the Government was likely to be more effective in advancing the mining interests. Like J B Taylor, who represented the Corner House in the capital, and other magnates, Phillips cultivated the Kruger connection.

> I was in the habit of visiting Pretoria about once a fortnight to discuss various problems affecting the mining industry, and on very many occasions had long interviews with President Kruger. Over cups of coffee, with his long pipe always in action and a waste paper basket as spittoon, he used to listen to my complaints and advice, interjecting a great many rather gruff 'ja's,' but never giving me any further indications of his thoughts …. I became gradually upon reasonably friendly, personal terms ….[4]

In 1892 the National Union was formed to provide a voice for Uitlander grievances. Mine-owners in general stayed aloof and the Union represented mainly professional, commercial and artisan classes. Its first President was the Hon John Tudhope, a former Cape Cabinet Minister, who had become General Manager of the Consolidated Investment Company formed in Johannesburg in 1889. The Union under his leadership sought change by constitutional means, vainly urging the claims of the Uitlanders to equal rights at mass meetings and by petition. Tudhope was a Representative Member of the Chamber of Mines and at the Annual General Meeting in January 1893, Lippert and Barnato backed him for the presidency in opposition to Phillips. Phillips held off the challenge and was re-elected by fifty-eight votes to twenty-six. Tudhope gained election to the Executive Committee but thereafter made little impact on the mining or political scene. The following year he gave way as President of the Union to Charles Leonard, the prominent solicitor, who was to prove a more ardent and active reformist.

However, Leonard, who was of 1820 Settler stock, always made it clear that his aim was for political reform within the framework of an independent Transvaal.

Phillips's 'hands off' stance was in accordance with the philosophy of the Chamber of Mines which continually asserted its non-involvement in politics.

In the letter which the Chamber wrote to the British Agent in Pretoria soon after its foundation, it had declared:

> ... any action of a political character is beyond the province of this Chamber, which, however, in its endeavour to secure relief from oppressive taxation, and to promote the execution of public works, can never fail to take the keenest interest in the circumstances of the South African Republic.[5]

It seems to have repeated the theme whenever occasion arose. For example, in March 1895 a letter was received from the *Burgermacht*, a political organization, inviting the Chamber to send one or two delegates to a meeting at the Good Templar's Hall. The Chamber thought representation would be 'rather a delicate matter'. However, the organization was a strong one which aimed to counter the activities of the *Volksmacht*, the progressive organization which provided the chief burgher opposition to Kruger. The Executive Committee decided, therefore, to send delegates solely to give factual information about mining. It later reported, *inter alia*:

> ... Mr [J] Ballot, one of the delegates, replying, recited [to the meeting] the circumstances under which the Chamber had appointed representatives, and strongly emphasised the fact that they were present to give information on any matters connected with the mining industry, but would take no part in the discussion of any political questions, the Chamber being a non-political body and holding rigidly aloof from politics.[6]

Phillips conformed with this policy for some years in exemplary fashion. However, under his leadership, Corner House supported the election of the progressive burghers who opposed Kruger, by contributing to their election expenses. Both as Wernher, Beit's representative and as President of the Chamber, he was caught up in a crescendo of activity. Florence called it 'the mad treadmill',[7] something which has been echoed down the years by a long succession of presidents' wives. Phillips, a gregarious man of exceptional vivacity, accepted every obligation, official, social and charitable. He was expected to take the lead in all these fields; no new enterprise was launched without first seeking his support.[8] A generous man, he gave freely of time and money, and appeared to enjoy every minute of it.

Florence did not support his political neutrality. She repeatedly urged him to take a stand on political grounds and show the Transvaal Government that it was no longer possible to endure a state of affairs which she thought intolerable. Lionel remained adamant that it was for others to 'take up the political cudgels'.[9] It could not have been easy to withstand the spirited and imperious Florence, who developed a talent for riding opposition underfoot, quite often to the substantial benefit of the community in matters cultural and artistic. By one of those strange South African turnabouts, the one-time State Attorney and commando leader under Kruger, General Jan Christiaan Smuts, would deliver the eulogy at her funeral in 1940. Smuts, who was then Prime Minister of the Union of South Africa, said on that occasion, among other things:

> ... She was a very remarkable woman outstanding in her day and genera-
> tion. She belonged indeed to a time, to a generation, when South Africa
> provided a number of very remarkable men and women. ... She was fit to
> occupy her place among the most remarkable personages of her time ....
> She was direct in speech and outspoken, sometimes overwhelmingly so ....
> She and her husband ... were among the most prominent and outstanding
> personalities who built up the Rand and the new South Africa ....[10]

With the passage of time Phillips became aware that the situation was building towards civil upheaval. The opposition Press voiced the growing criticism of his political inactivity, attacking him as head of the mining industry for standing aloof from the agitation.

Dissatisfaction over the cost of living, Government maladministration, the concessions policy, the insistence on Dutch as the medium of education and the language of the courts, found a focus and a unifying factor in resentment over the denial of the franchise. In the first years of the Republic, citizenship and franchise were obtainable after five years' residence, and the payment of the then substantial sum of £25 for naturalization. This was the norm accepted and expected by the often mobile population of the colonies and republics. When the Uitlander invasion came, Kruger feared that if he did not take action the burgher population would be swamped. The ratio of Uitlanders to Boers however seems to have been widely exaggerated. Uitlanders overstated the position to strengthen their claim to participate in the Government, and Kruger in turn over-estimated the threat that they constituted, in order to justify excluding them from the franchise.

Marais found that as late as 1899 there were probably more Boers (men, women and children) than Uitlanders, although there may have been more Uitlanders than Boer male adults because of the high proportion of men among the Uitlander population.[11] Nonetheless it is perhaps not surprising that Kruger should have tightened up the qualifications for the franchise to keep the newcomers off the voters' rolls. By 1894, after a series of amending laws, the position was reached when fourteen years was the minimum residential qualification and there were additional deterrents to exercising the franchise. The minimum qualifying age for an Uitlander was made forty. Uitlanders of British origin had to renounce their British citizenship before they could qualify. As a sop to the newcomers Kruger did establish the Second Volksraad for which it was possible to qualify in two years, but, though a useful sounding board, its measures had to be ratified by the First Volksraad and its area of competence was limited.

Carl Jeppe, one of the leading Progressives, who represented the Witwatersrand in the First Volksraad from 1893-1897, was inclined to discount certain of the alleged disabilities, but he campaigned for the reform of the franchise. Equity apart, he realized that the Kruger franchise policy was a tactical blunder that would lead inevitably to the destruction of the Republic. Soon after that had occurred he wrote in his memoirs:

> The inhabitants of the Rand at that time may be divided into two categories. There were the Britishers, who formed the majority. Of these ... very few, if indeed any, would have accepted the Franchise. The rest of the population had been gathered together from all corners of the earth .... By far the most of them were anxious to become Transvaalers, and their accession to the ranks of the Burghers would therefore have been a source of strength and not one of danger to the Republic.[12]

He pointed out that there were amongst them Americans, French, Hollanders and Germans, a very large contingent of Cape Dutch, and many Free State burghers. All these elements were driven 'into the camp of those who wished no good to the Republic'.[13]

It was unfortunate that at a time when the British were accustomed to demand, and enforce if need be, respect in the world, certain Members of the Volksraad adopted a contemptuous and provocative manner in rejecting petitions for the franchise.

By the beginning of 1894 it seems that Lionel Phillips was beginning to have doubts about the wisdom of non-involvement. He was not the man to take a back seat amid momentous events. In his Presidential Address on 25 January there was a discernible change of tone.

> ... The mining industry of this country ... contributes, according to a statement recently published, somewhere in the neighbourhood of nine-tenths to the revenue of the State, and we have a right therefore to demand, as we do demand, that the expenditure of State funds shall be well administered. So long as this is done, so long have we no right to interfere in politics; but our collective views on financial matters are entitled to be received with courteous consideration by Government, and if Government should fail or refuse to listen to our representations, and to give due weight and thought to them, the newcomers would be forced to become constitutional agitators in order that the people of the country might become conversant with our grievances. I can see no other possible means of obtaining redress.[14]

In June there were ructions in Pretoria and on the Rand. The Transvaal Government called up Uitlanders of British citizenship for commando service against the rebel Chief Malaboch who had refused to pay taxes. Some of those called up refused service on the grounds that they were neither citizens nor enfranchised. They were arrested and sent to the front. Sir Henry Loch, the British Governor at the Cape and High Commissioner for South Africa, came up to request exemption for British citizens from commando service (which he obtained), and to discuss the administration of Swaziland, soon to be taken over by the Transvaal. He found the Uitlander population in a ferment. There were disturbances on his arrival at Pretoria Station in which a coldly angry Kruger was subjected to a demonstration of pro-British sentiment.

The Chamber sent Phillips hurrying to Pretoria to express its support for the Government and to dissociate itself from the disturbances (while taking the opportunity to re-state the grievances of the industry). Kruger asked Phillips to use the Chamber's influence to calm down the population of Johannesburg, and to persuade Loch not to go there in the potentially explosive situation. Phillips did so and had two long talks with Loch, in which Loch questioned how many rifles Johannesburg could muster, and whether the town could hold out for six days if need be. Loch had become convinced that feeling among Uitlanders was such that a revolution was likely. The situation had an ugly look with armed burghers patrolling both towns, and sections of the Uitlander population spoiling for a fight. Florence insisted that Lionel buy and carry a rifle for personal protection on his journeys to Pretoria. Presumably, he checked his firearm with his hat before his meetings with Loch.

At their talks, Loch gave Phillips a clear impression that if a rising occurred the British Government would intervene to restore order and protect the lives of its subjects. Phillips was a restraining influence on Loch, who seems to have been tempted by the possibility of an immediate, personal coup in Johannesburg. After Loch's departure the tension subsided, but the High Commissioner had come to the conclusion that a military solution should be sought. He proposed accordingly to Lord Ripon, the Secretary of State for the Colonies in Rosebery's Liberal administration. Loch judged that a successful rising was likely and that if it was achieved without British assistance, the Uitlanders 'would probably maintain the independence of the Republic and pursue a policy hostile to Federation'.[15] Too many Uitlanders, for his taste, would have readily exchanged the Union Jack for full burgher rights under the *Vierkleur*. He worked out a plan for British intervention by an Imperial force from Mafeking, but Ripon would have none of it. Van der Poel, in her careful study of the events leading to the Jameson Raid, concluded that Loch's frustrated intention went beyond pure police action to protect lives and property and contemplated the encouragement of revolt and armed intervention.[16] Loch soon returned to England. Rhodes, who was developing plans of his own, and had no wish to be upstaged by the Queen's representative, engineered his replacement by the seventy-year-old Sir Hercules Robinson who had held the post from 1881 to 1889, and with whom Rhodes enjoyed a close rapport. A doubtful Queen Victoria required reassurance from her Ministers before sanctioning the re-appointment, which amounted to the recall from retirement, after an illustrious career, of an aged and ailing man.

Sir James Rose Innes, the distinguished jurist who served as Attorney-General in Rhodes's first Cape Cabinet, was close to events both in the Cape and the Transvaal. He has recorded that 1894 was a climactic year for Rhodes, whose great aim was a federation of the colonies and republics into a single South African state within the British Empire. He was then at the height of his prestige and power with an international reputation as a statesman of the British Empire, and was soon to be sworn a member of the Queen's Privy Council. Up to the beginning of 1894 Rhodes believed that time was on his side. Patience was the keynote of his activities. He was content to wait for customs conventions, trade agreements and other manifestations of common economic interest to pave the way for seemingly inevitable political association. On 6 January, on his return from a tour of Matabeleland, the Cape gave its Prime Minister a non-party banquet in Cape Town.

> ... he dwelt upon his favourite vision, an enlarged and united South Africa. But there was to be no hurry; he was prepared to wait. Like a man, who, in his old age, planted an avenue, he was content to know that none could alter his lines. 'I cannot expect to see more than shrubs, but with me rests the conception of the shade and the glory.' ... before the year was out, the stream of his energy was flowing in a new direction. He had decided on a more forceful policy, which led him to exchange the constitutionalism of the statesman for the lawlessness of the revolutionary.[17]

In the southern spring of that year, Rhodes visited Matabeleland again in the company of the brilliant and adventurous American consulting engineer, Hays Hammond, who helped to build the Consolidated Gold Fields on the Rand into a flourishing company. Hammond submitted a report on Charterland, the future Rhodesia, which, while not wholly discouraging, extinguished hopes of a second Rand in the north. It was clear to Rhodes that the fulcrum of economic power had shifted irrevocably to the Transvaal, providing Kruger with the financial muscle to maintain independence and to continue to block any move to closer association with the British colonies.

Perceiving an enduring threat to the ideal of a federation, Rhodes decided on a bid to get on terms with Kruger. He made the difficult journey overland to Beira, took ship for Delagoa Bay and the train to the Rand. It was to be his sixth meeting with Kruger – and his last. He found the President implacably opposed to economic union.

Rose Innes wrote in his memoirs:

> No record exists of the interview ... de Wet, the British Agent and Jameson were the only other persons present. But confidential proceedings are apt to leak out, and from a trustworthy source I heard, soon after, that Rhodes had attempted to conciliate and secure the co-operation of the President, and that he signally failed. Kruger declared on a later occasion that, though his schooldays had been necessarily few, he had learned in the school of life to know an enemy from a friend. ... The interview ended on a stormy note;

the two men parted 'shaking their fists at one another'. .... the die had been cast.... [18]

Rhodes's impatience was fed by the knowledge that his life would not be long. His strong face, now growing flabby, was often grey from heart disease. He became a man in a hurry, determined to have his way. The world, he declared, must judge his actions in the light of what he achieved. His achievements were astonishing, but the new direction he had chosen would lead him to disaster.

Kruger, too, blundered in choosing the path of provocation. He was flirting with Kaiser Wilhelm II and the warmth of the German response ruffled the imperial plumes in Whitehall. Britain was already past the zenith of her greatness and battling to maintain her share of world markets. An aggressive imperialism, wrote Van der Poel, was the outcome of commercial and financial necessities.[19] Britain could not afford to give ground before the *grosse Politik* of the Wilhelmstrasse. The Transvaal had ceased to be only a British colonial question and became increasingly one of international consequence.

Rhodes began actively to plan the downfall of the Republic. In June 1895 Rosebery's Liberal Government fell and was succeeded by Lord Salisbury's Unionists. Joseph Chamberlain, the key force in the party, chose the office of Colonial Secretary in succession to Ripon. Like Rhodes – and many other Englishmen of the day – he believed devoutly in the civilizing force of the Empire and that Britain's role and destiny lay in its expansion. (Unhappily for him, the Boer, too, had a sense of a divine destiny to rule in Africa.) Rhodes visited London and endeavoured to obtain from Chamberlain the fulfilment of a Liberal Government promise to hand over Bechuanaland to his Charter Company. Chamberlain would not play, but gave him a rail strip along the Transvaal border on which to extend the railway from Mafeking to the north. It provided Rhodes with a convenient jumping-off place from which to intervene on the Rand.

Chamberlain was careful to avoid official knowledge of what Rhodes was up to, but he was well aware that trouble was brewing, and wanted to be sure that he could turn it to advantage when it came. In late October, he asked Hercules Robinson for an appreciation of the situation. Robinson's response was drafted with the aid of Rhodes and Graham Bower, the Imperial Secretary at the Cape.[20] He told Chamberlain that a revolt would take place sooner or later and that an accident might bring it about any day. He proposed that if this occurred he should call on both parties to cease hostilities and submit to his arbitration. He should then go at once to Pretoria and order the election of a constituent assembly elected by every white male. He warned that it would be necessary to move fast to forestall the intervention of Germany. Speedy action on his part, backed by the British Government, could result in a revolution without loss of life or the firing of a shot.[21]

Chamberlain replied:

Agree generally with your idea.... I take for granted that no movement will

91

take place unless success is certain. A fiasco would be most disastrous.[22]

Rhodes had a powerhouse on the Rand in Consolidated Gold Fields and he sent his brother Frank there to make military preparations while ostensibly managing the company. He did not shine in either role. He was a professional soldier, both genial and gallant, but otherwise without ambition. He had no taste for conspiracy, or stomach for dying at some forgettable barricade with half-hearted revolutionaries.

It was clear to Cecil Rhodes that for a successful coup it was essential to involve the Corner House. For this he turned to his old associate, Alfred Beit, in London. Beit came out to South Africa in June 1895, and in talks at Groote Schuur agreed that the Corner House should support the Transvaal National Union, and that Wernher, Beit would share the cost of arming Johannesburg and bringing in an armed force from Pitsani in the Bechuanaland 'rail strip'. He visited the Rand to brief Phillips who had kept him informed about the situation and his own doubts about the right course of action. Phillips later recalled:

> Beit, although a German by birth, was a keen imperialist. To my surprise, I found that he thoroughly shared my opinion that revolution was coming. He told me that Rhodes held the same view and thought we should take a hand to ensure success, if possible. Generally speaking, I was invited to co-operate, and after Beit's return to England I went down to the Cape to stay with Rhodes.

> At that time Cecil Rhodes, his brother Frank, John Hays Hammond, Jameson, and one or two more, with myself, were the only persons involved in the movement.[23]

The five named have been described as gathering in mid–October on the verandah at Groote Schuur 'with its basket chairs, gate-legged table and superb views of the wooded slopes beneath Table Mountain'.[24] They spent two to three days in planning and endless discussion. From there the scene shifted to Hohenheim where the Johannesburg conspirators reputedly met in its Swiss-style wing.[25] At this juncture, Kruger almost rendered the plotting unnecessary. He created a *casus belli* over the bitter rivalry of the Transvaal and Cape railways for the lion's share of the traffic to the Rand.

In 1889, the Cape and the Orange Free State had signed a customs convention, in which the Transvaal and Natal had refused to participate, eventually coming to a bilateral agreement of their own. After extending its line to Johannesburg and Pretoria, the Cape had for two years enjoyed, in terms of the Sivewright Agreement, a monopoly of the traffic to the Rand. When the Delagoa Bay line reached Pretoria the agreement lapsed and a rates war developed. The Cape, which had invested heavily in the line, demanded two-thirds of the traffic. To enforce this unreasonable and unrealistic demand it threatened to undercut the Netherlands Company, which responded equally unreasonably by tripling the rates charged over the Transvaal section of the line from the Cape. Kruger's encouragement of the company's exploitation of its monopoly deprived the Cape of the source of half of all Government revenue, and antagonized both the Cape farmers and the *Afrikaner Bond* which formed the essential base of the Rhodes Administration.

The Cape railways met the challenge by unloading goods on the Free State side of the Vaal, and taking them to Johannesburg by ox-wagon through drifts (fords) over the Vaal, thus avoiding the high rates on the Transvaal section. Kruger now retaliated by closing the drifts on 1 October 1895. W P Schreiner, the Cape Attorney-General, declared their closing to be a breach of the London Convention of 1884 which forbade discriminatory treatment of British imports. The British Government Law Advisers upheld this claim. A secret bargain was struck between the British and Cape Cabinets that, if force became necessary, the Cape would give every assistance and bear half the cost. Chamberlain was on holiday in Spain. Salisbury without recalling him issued an ultimatum and Kruger climbed down, averting civil war in which Cape Afrikaner would have been ranged against Transvaal Boer. Thus, he got out of a tight corner with some saving of face, but he left the impression that he would not stand up to stern measures and might similarly climb down in the face of firmly-backed demands.

It is interesting to reflect how much shorter in those days were the fuses that separated peace from the explosions of war. Concurrently with the Drifts Crisis, Britain was in dispute with Venezuela about the boundary with the colony of British Guiana. The following month, President Cleveland of the United States entered the lists and threatened Britain with war, in an assertion of the Monroe Doctrine of paramountcy in the Americas a good deal more powerful than Britain's hitherto muted assertion of her suzerainty over the Transvaal. President Cleveland's action would add its own ingredient to a simmering pot, at a time when the label 'imperialist' was proudly worn.

The Chamber meanwhile was busy with the opening of its new building next to the National Bank on the Market Square. The three-storey building, which according to *The Star* looked tall enough for six, was ornamented externally by Anton van Wouw. On the first floor above the magnificent stairway was the Board Room, nineteen feet wide by thirty-one feet long and eighteen feet high, in which Chamber meetings would be held. The walls were clad with Japanese leather, the woodwork was of polished Kauri pine and the windows were of stained glass. There were offices for Goldring, the Secretary, and his assistant, Green, a reception office and a committee room. On the floor above were the library, the museum and the Labour Commissioner's office. Technical societies and other concerns were housed in the building as well.

Phillips opened the building on the evening of 20 November 1895, the month which marked the sixth anniversary of the Witwatersrand Chamber. About three hundred and fifty people attended the reception which *The Star* described as probably the most representative gathering in the history of the town. Phillips electrified his audience by choosing the occasion to throw down the gauntlet. He caused a sensation throughout South Africa.

> All we want in this country is purity of administration and an equitable share and voice in its affairs. I hope that wiser councils may prevail, and that the Government of this country may be induced to see that present policy will not do. Nothing is further from my heart than a desire to see an upheaval, which would be disastrous from every point of view, and which would probably end in the most horrible of all possible endings, in bloodshed, but I would say that it is a mistake to imagine that this much maligned community which consists anyhow of a majority of men born of freemen will consent indefinitely to remain subordinate to the minority in this country and that they will for ever allow their lives, their property, and their liberty to be subject to its arbitrary will.[26]

Next day, *The Star's* main leader headed 'The Capitalist's Conversion' applauded the speech and said that it was the most important political statement made from a Johannesburg platform. But *The Star* regretted that Phillips had not carried on to spell out the logical conclusion.

> … Mr Phillips did good work last night – better work, perhaps, than he was aware of. It has not often been our good fortune in Johannesburg to find any one of our great capitalists forgetting for a moment his own direct interests, and transcending the obligations of his trusteeships so far as to recognize the more imperative duties which are common to every man, be he millionaire or miner, who respects himself and the traditions of his race. … He is evidently under the impression that his weighty remonstrance will prove effective …. For the present, at least, we, too, are content to 'faintly trust the larger hope' – but very faintly.

Phillips could hardly have been expected to divulge the plot he was hatching with Jameson, now Resident Commissioner of the Bechuanaland Rail Strip and aglow with the euphoria instilled by a spectacular victory over the Matabele. The final plan was that Johannesburg, armed with rifles and maxim guns smuggled in with the help of De Beers, would rise on 29 December. A squad of picked men was then to surprise and rush the defenders of the Pretoria arsenal, thus seizing the Republic's reserve of arms and ammunition. The rising, in which many non-British elements would join, would be under the Republican *Vierkleur*, and not the Union Jack. Once the rising had taken place an appeal would be sent to Jameson to ride to the aid of the town. Jameson asked for a letter of appeal to justify his position and Leonard drafted a powerful one, calling on Jameson to hurry to the succour of the women and children. The letter was signed by Phillips, Frank Rhodes, Hays Hammond and George Farrar, leaving the date blank to be filled in by Jameson at the appropriate time. The letter was very nearly the death warrant of the signatories, for when it came into Boer hands it was enough to prove the capital offence of high treason. Clearly, the conspirators hoped that Jameson's force would merely confirm a *fait accompli*. They had nothing to gain from a drawn-out conflict that would disrupt the flow of profits from the mines. The conspirators thought they could do the trick by bluff, backed by a show of force.[27] There was indeed to come just a moment when Kruger was tempted to deal. At his request, the Transvaal Executive Committee removed the special duty on foodstuffs as the beginning of a process of concession. But the moment passed, as mishandling by the conspirators caused events to descend to a Gilbertian muddle. The arms build-up was far too slow for the date set for the rising. It had been overlooked that Boers from the rural areas would flood into Pretoria at Christmas for the ceremony of *Nagmaal* (Communion). Everyone seems to have known that a rebellion was in the offing. Kruger's agents were everywhere. Some of the townspeople were half-hearted; others totally opposed.

George Albu and some members of the Stock Exchange held a meeting and denounced plans for rebellion. The Mercantile Association, representing commercial interests, declared it would take no part in a revolt.[28] Nonetheless, on 26 December, Leonard issued a manifesto of grievances and called on the Government to reform or pay the consequences. From Cape Town the cause looked just and Merriman wrote approvingly to both Leonard and Phillips, something which he regretted when the details of the plot were published.

The final spanner in the works was mutual distrust between the Johannesburg leaders and Rhodes. Rhodes feared that a reformed but still independent Transvaal would continue to stand aloof from a British Federation. Abe Bailey, newly arrived from England (to attend the races in Johannesburg), came up from Groote Schuur with the news that Rhodes intended Jameson to come in under the Union Jack. The men on the spot realized that the British flag would rally to Kruger's side the burghers of the Republic, including the influential group of progressives who actively opposed Kruger's policies. The Union Jack would also alienate the Americans and the Continentals. Emissaries were sent to Rhodes to convince him that any attempt to annex the country would bring disaster, and to tell him categorically that the revolutionaries in any event were unready and must postpone the rising. Others were sent to Pitsani to hold back Jameson who had promised not to move until called in from Johannesburg. Rhodes equivocated, appearing to accept the pleas from Johannesburg while taking no effective steps to stop Jameson. For at this stage came an echo of the Venezuelan crisis in a telegram from London which Van der Poel saw as 'urgent exhortations ... to act at once before international circumstances made it impossible for the British Government to intervene decisively'.[29] Meanwhile at Pitsani, Jameson's raiders totalled only five hundred men, instead of the promised fifteen hundred and threatened to dwindle further if there were delay. But in those days, small bands of adventurous men, handled with dash, achieved incredible results. Jameson was impatient to be off and he decided, in the tradition of Robert Clive, to act boldly and trust that Fortune would come to his aid.

On 29 December 1895 the bewildered rebels heard that he was on his way. Hoping against hope, they quickly formed the Reform Committee and took over the town, the Republican Police withdrawing discreetly to the Johannesburg Fort. About sixty leading men joined the Committee, some because they liked to be on the ground floor of every promotion, others just caught up in the *élan* of the moment. Even members of the Mercantile Association and others formerly opposed to armed force tried to hedge their bets. The Reform Committee armed their men and for about ten days Johannesburg was a rebel town.

Lionel Phillips assumed the leadership and maintained law and order. Leonard had gone down to Cape Town, and stayed there. FitzPatrick, who had been in the plot all along, acted as secretary. The Committee held unofficial talks with the Government and succeeded in bluffing its representatives as to the real strength of the movement and the extent of its armaments. As evidence of the representative nature of the Committee Phillips handed over a list of its members. It was a cosmopolitan group.

> There were 23 Englishmen, 16 South Africans, 9 Scots, 6 Americans, 2 Welshmen, 2 Germans, 1 Irishman, 1 Australian, 1 Dutchman, 1 Canadian, 1 Swiss and 1 Turk. (Their occupations were: 10 mine owners, 9 solicitors, 9 dealers in shares, 7 company directors or managers, 7 doctors, 6 merchants, 3 stockbrokers, 3 engineers, 3 mine managers, 2 barristers, 2 soldiers, 1 sanitary inspector, 1 journalist, 1 secretary.)[30]

Soon came the news that Jameson had been trapped about seventeen miles west of Johannesburg by Boer commandos, who had had ample warning of his approach. He was forced to surrender with the loss of seventeen dead, fifty-five wounded and thirty-five missing. The Boers lost four men killed and three wounded.

Chamberlain, perceiving that the fears of fiasco he had earlier expressed to Hercules Robinson were taking dreadful shape, hastened to condemn the Raid, which Robinson had tried in vain to turn back. Robinson now hurried up to Johannesburg, not to impose reform, but to advise the rebels to surrender, and to seek clemency for the raiders.

Kruger, with all the good cards in his hands, reacted to the emergency with calm good sense. He handed over Jameson and the Raiders to the British for punishment. The Reform Committee was arrested and, in due course, brought to trial. Leonard evaded capture, but Phillips, Frank Rhodes, Hammond and Farrar pleaded guilty to high treason (on the understanding that they and the remainder of the Reform Committee would get off lightly). To the general outrage they were sentenced to hang. They spent an uncomfortable night in the condemned cell, listening to hammering which they took to be the erection of the gallows. The next day the sentences were commuted to fifteen years' imprisonment and six weeks later to fines of £25 000 apiece. The remaining members of the Reform Committee were convicted of a lesser offence and, after commutation of a jail sentence, were fined £2 000 apiece.

Rhodes, declaring that Jameson had upset 'his apple cart',[31] resigned as Prime Minister of the Cape. The Cape Parliament voted to condemn the Raid and to appoint a Select Committee of Inquiry. The Select Committee, under the chairmanship of Upington, the Attorney-General, and including Schreiner, Merriman and Rose Innes, found that Rhodes as head of Charter, De Beers and the Gold Fields had controlled the combination which made the Raid possible. His behaviour was not 'consistent with his duty as Prime Minister of the [Cape] Colony'.[32] A Select Committee of the British Parliament in turn confirmed Rhodes's complicity but exonerated Chamberlain. The fact that Chamberlain was a member of the Select Committee, which did not probe sensitive areas, led to its description as 'the lying in state[33] at Westminster'.[34]

The Jameson Raid had consequences way beyond the norm for a nineteenth century filibuster. The tendency in the Cape for political association across the English/Afrikaner boundary was aborted, and the Rhodes-*Afrikaner Bond* alliance fell apart. Polarization of English and Afrikaner throughout the country received an unholy impetus. Mutual distrust between Britain and the Republic was deepened, and the prospects for *rapprochement* and an orderly move to federation undermined. On the international scene, the Kaiser's cable of congratulations to Kruger produced an onrush of patriotic sentiment in Britain that turned Jameson's Raiders back from brigands into heroes in the public eye.

To what extent was the Chamber involved in the Rising and the Raid? By the actions of its President, from which it could not be dissociated, up to the neck. Phillips apart, S B Joel, a vice-president, was a last-minute reluctant adherent of the Reform Committee. However, Joel was not an intimate of Phillips nor among those welcomed socially at Hohenheim (Florence referred to his uncle as 'that brute Barnato').[35] Joel was clearly not of the inner circle. James Hay, the other vice-president, who did not represent a major group, was out of the country and not involved. Two members of the Executive Committee, J S Curtis (a Corner House consulting engineer), St John Carr and the Secretary, Goldring, joined the Reform Committee. Of the remaining nine members of the Executive Committee, Albu and Goertz were actively opposed to the conspiracy and so were the Groups they represented and those headed by J B Robinson and Barnato. Thirteen of the Chamber's more than one hundred Representative Members, including Abe Bailey, joined the Committee, but most were Johnnies-come-lately to the plot. Judge Gregorowski, in his report to the Transvaal Government, indicated that, in his view, many of the members of the Committee had been misled, and were the victims of circumstance.[36]

The fact was that the Chamber comprised so many conflicting elements that it was not a useful instrument of conspiracy. The meetings of the conspirators were principally held at Hohenheim and the Corner House, and the head-quarters of the Reform Committee was in the Gold Fields Buildings. There is no evidence to be found of the involvement of the Chamber as an institution and nobody at the time or since, in the contemporary Press or elsewhere, has seriously suggested that this occurred.[37]

In the aftermath, the division among Chamber members on the issue of the Rising crystallized the dissatisfaction of certain groups with a constitution that permitted, in their view, dominance of the Chamber by the Corner House and its associates.

The consequence was the hiving-off from the Chamber of twenty-three companies, of which eighteen belonged to the Robinson, Goertz and Albu groups, and the formation in April 1896 of the rival Association of Mines.

[1] T Gutsche, *No Ordinary Woman: The Life and Times of Florence Phillips*, p 97.

[2] P Bawcombe and T Scannel, *Philip Bawcombe's Johannesburg*, p 119, quoting the architect, Clive M Chipkin.

[3] Gutsche, p 95.

[4] L Phillips, *Some Reminiscences*, p 136.

[5] Annual Report of the Witwatersrand Chamber of Mines, 1889, p 26.

[6] Annual Report of the Witwatersrand Chamber of Mines, 1895, pp 147-149.

[7] Gutsche, p 86.

[8] *Idem.*

[9] *Ibid*, pp 99-100.

[10] *Ibid*, pp 393-394.

[11] Marais, pp 2-3.

[12] Jeppe, p 133.

[13] *Ibid*, p 134.

[14] Annual Report of the Witwatersrand Chamber of Mines, 1893, pp 19-20.

[15] J van der Poel, *The Jameson Raid*, p 17.

[16] *Ibid*, p 20.

[17] J Rose Innes (ed B A Tindall), *James Rose Innes: Chief Justice of South Africa, 1914-27: Autobiography*, p 108.

[18] Ibid, p 109.

[19] Van der Poel, *The Jameson Raid*, p 11.

[20] *Ibid*, p 54.

[21] *Ibid*, p 55.

[22] *Ibid*, p 56.

[23] Phillips, pp 141, 142.

[24] E Longford, *Jameson's Raid: The Prelude to the Boer War*, p 124.

[25] Bawcombe and Scannel, p 120.

[26] *The Star*, 21 November 1895.

[27] Van der Poel, *The Jameson Raid*, p 64.

[28] *Ibid*, p 80.

[29] *Ibid*, p 76.

[30] Longford, p 13.

[31] Rose Innes (ed Tindall), p 142.

[32] *Idem.*

[33] The Romans had a word for it: '*mendax gloriosa*'.

[34] Van der Poel, *The Jameson Raid*, p 230.

[35] Gutsche, p 57.

[36] D Rhoodie, *Conspirators in Conflict: A Study of the Johannesburg Reform Committee and its Role in the Conspiracy against the South African Republic*, p 101.

[37] Etheredge, p 115.

CHAPTER EIGHT

Lost Causes

Historians in many countries have brought formidable talents to bear on illuminating the causes of the Jameson Raid, the Johannesburg Rising and the South African War of 1899-1902. Some have seen the main push emanating from the imperial factor (with Joseph Chamberlain as the front man); others see the imperial factor responding to the pull of power politics at the South African periphery (Cecil Rhodes); others again believe that conspirators of international finance (the Randlords) are the true villains of the piece. Then there are those who point to the inevitability of a culture clash between Transvaal Boers, said to be eighteenth century in outlook, and *fin de siècle* Uit-landers.

As Donald Denoon found, by the early sixties there was fairly general agreement that these ethnic, economic and strategic forces had combined to produce a dramatic dénouement – but then came Blainey.

> The consensus was destroyed by an academic terrorist making a single sortie into a new terrain. Observing that not all mining capitalists took part in the plots which produced the Jameson Raid, Professor Geoffrey Blainey calculated that it was capitalists who owned deep-level gold mines who had led the revolutionary movement, and that they did so in the belief that 'it was the economic environment of Kruger's land that had failed'.[1]

The maverick Blainey wrote principally about Australian mining history and the brief 'Lost Causes of the Jameson Raid' was his only raid into the Transvaal. It was basic to his theme that the grievances of the mining industry were stronger than historians had recognized, and critically so for deep-level operators, whereas outcrop operators suffered substantially less.[2]

Thus, he saw the Jameson Raid as essentially the role of the two big companies, Rand Mines and Gold Fields, that were 'heirs to the treasures and problems of the deep-levels'.[3]

Blainey's general exposition of the role of the capitalists was of an indirect line of descent from J A Hobson who, writing immediately after the War, was concerned to show, on grounds subsequently shown to be insubstantial, that imperialism was designed to further the interests of monopoly capitalism, and that capitalists were monolithic and conspiratorial.[4] Like Hobson, Blainey inspired a deal of new research and writing and evoked a sophisticated response. Thus, Arthur Mawby has concluded that Blainey offered a hypothesis without attempting to prove it,[5] while Robert V Kubicek responded to Blainey by showing that while 'the Randlords dabbled in conspiracy they forged no united, monolithic front'. He went on to find:

… no commonly shared financial problem distinguished Randlords who participated in subversive politics from those who did not. Ironically the firm which had the least to gain, Wernher, Beit, was most involved. As Milner put it on another occasion when the Randlords were reluctant to throw in their lot with the imperial factor, 'moneybags are apt to be shortsighted'.[6]

Blainey's thesis was challenged also by Alan Jeeves, who found that economic motives played at most a secondary role. He pointed out that Wernher, Beit, the principal deep-level operator through Rand Mines, was also the principal outcrop operator through the H Eckstein partnership, retaining 'outcrop holdings which in both extent and profitability were unrivalled ….'[7] Only Consolidated Gold Fields was an exclusively deep-level company to the degree postulated by Blainey, but such companies were not significantly more burdened by tax exactions or high costs than any other.

Richard Mendelsohn in another dashing sortie paid tribute to Blainey for his challenge to those who attributed the origins of the Raid solely to the political and strategic factors, but pointed out that, contrary to Blainey's thesis, the Gold Fields company in 1895 was financially strong and well placed to ride out the collapse in the share market in the last quarter of that year. By contrast, J B Robinson and Barney Barnato, who were opposed to the uprising, 'commanded financial sandcastles'. However, he stressed that Blainey's critics had drawn too stark a contrast between the financial stability of the conspirators and the instability of the non–conspirators. The financial strength of Gold Fields and Wernher, Beit had to be evaluated in terms of their huge commitment to the fulfilment of their strategic objectives. In summation, Mendelsohn found 'Blainey's extended argument that economic necessity drove the Rand's deep-level companies to rebellion in 1895 has effectively been dismantled'. However, Blainey's basic technique might still provide the best means of uncovering the 'lost causes' of the Raid. Mendelsohn concluded:

The chief difference between firms inside and those outside the conspiracy was that the former were committed by 1895 to long-range mining programmes while the latter were either preoccupied by stock jobbing or were content with modest holding operations. This meant that the conspirators stood to gain far more over the long term than the rest from the replacement of a self-willed and frequently obstructive Boer government by one more easily manipulated by the mining industry.[8]

The debate continues, but whatever future interpretations may be proffered, it is at least clear that by 1895 Phillips had come to believe that the progressive failure of Kruger to make legislative and administrative changes made revolution inevitable. It was not hard then to convince Phillips that it would be prudent to take a hand in shaping the revolution to ensure that the Transvaal did not fall into irresponsible or even less competent hands than Kruger's. A belief in the certainty of spontaneous revolution was shared by British Government representatives in South Africa and accepted as the expert man-on-the-spot view by Joseph Chamberlain, who facilitated privily what he saw as inevitable so as to ensure that it redounded to British advantage, and did not leave the Transvaal open to German intervention. Rhodes, in turn, thought he discerned a golden opportunity to accelerate federation and strengthen British paramountcy in Africa, while incidentally advancing his business interests. Kruger, for his part, blundered along, on his chosen, provocative path, exacerbating tensions by fiercely quarrelling with the Cape over rail traffic, and by seeking alliances with Germany and Holland against Britain. In Johannesburg, as revolution budded, Phillips and other representatives of Rhodes and Beit sought prematurely to bring it to flower. Some capitalists, who were striking industrial roots in Africa, rallied to the conspirators. Other capitalists did not because they were content with the enormous profits they had made on the stock markets which they hoped to take back to Europe with them; or for a wide range of other reasons including French and German counter-loyalties, national rivalries and mistrust, or mere personal judgement or mis-judgement of what was best to do.

The diversity that characterized the capitalists soon found expression in the aftermath of the Raid, in a challenge to the leadership of the Chamber of Mines. During January 1896, a total of thirty-eight mining companies joined the Chamber and mustered between them forty-seven new representative votes, mainly in favour of the Robinson, Albu and Goerz groups. British houses, too, increased the representation of member mines to strengthen their voting power, apparently in preparation for a trial of strength.

A record number of 180 representative members attended the Annual General Meeting on 30 January 1896. There were notable absentees - those 'unavoidably detained' in Pretoria Gaol. Among them was Phillips. He would remain imprisoned until June that year, apart from a twenty-four-hour pass to enable him to be at Hohenheim to welcome Florence on her return home from medical treatment in Europe. For this indulgence he was required to lodge bail of £10 000 in gold. After his sentence had been reduced to a fine, he left South Africa to take up an appointment with Wernher, Beit in London and would not be involved personally in the affairs of the Rand for a decade.

Those attending the annual meeting for once did not hear a presidential review of the year's events. Nor was there any reference to the Raid and the

Rising in the published proceedings of the meeting or in the Executive Committee's Annual Report for 1895 which the meeting formally approved. The meeting then proceeded to elect office-bearers. Kruger was re-elected Honorary President (an honour which he subsequently declined). Phillips was proposed for re-election as President, but a message was read saying that he was not prepared to stand. James Hay was then elected unanimously.

Joel and Curtis, both Reform Committee members, were proposed as vice-presidents, and so was J W S Langerman who represented the Robinson interest. Joel and Curtis were elected, Langerman coming bottom of the poll. Langerman succeeded in winning election to the Executive Committee in a poll topped by Phillips and fellow-prisoner Sidney Farrar, who was an elder brother of George Farrar. But George Albu, Adolphe Wagner (A Goerz) and Edward Brochon were all defeated leaving the so-called 'cosmopolitan' interests without representation.

Hay proved a popular choice as President, but both *The Standard and Diggers' News* which was usually hostile to the Chamber, and *The Star* which usually supported it, expressed disappointment at the exclusion of the Goerz and Albu groups from the Executive Committee.[9]

About the middle of February the Chamber received a letter dated 31 January from twenty-three companies, asserting that the Chamber's Constitution did not provide adequate representation of the interests of all sections of the mining industry. It claimed that many of those at the annual meeting were nominees in minor positions who were unable to exercise an independent judgement.

> ... the representation at the Chamber is capable of manipulation to such an extent as to make the voting power practically become purchasable. As a consequence, the vote at the last meeting of the Chamber has eliminated from the governing body several important sections of the industry, and left the control of the Chamber practically in the hands of a few firms and corporations.[10]

The companies urged the amendment of the Constitution to limit company representation to one executive who should be a director or manager. They also argued that it should not be permissible for more than one member of a firm or corporation to hold office and that the President should not serve for more than two successive years.

The Chamber appointed a committee of six, three representing signatories of the letter and three representing the Executive Committee. Albu, Langerman and Wagner represented the signatories, and Hay, Farrar and A J King (S Neumann) the Executive Committee. They failed to agree. Towards the close of March, twenty-two companies withdrew from the Chamber.

The Chamber now proceeded tardily to repair its Constitution, taking the opportunity to treble the annual subscription of £25. It scrapped clauses 14, 15 and 16 and substituted:

> Article 14: Any mining Company or mining and finance Company carrying on business in the South African Republic, the shares of which are officially quoted on any European Stock Exchange or the Johannesburg Stock Exchange, and any mining Company or mining and finance Company registered in the South African Republic paying an annual subscription of seventy-five pounds shall be entitled to nominate a representative member to the Chamber. All other Companies, as well as Syndicates, and any owner or association of owners of claim or claims may, upon application, be elected to membership by the Executive Committee; and if elected shall pay an annual subscription of seventy-five pounds.
>
> Article 15: No one shall be eligible for nomination as a representative member except a Director or the Consulting Engineer, Manager, or Secretary; or, in the case of foreign Companies, the Accredited Agent of the Company making the nomination.
>
> Article 16: No representative member shall have more than one vote.[11]

The amendments were important contributions to a more equitable balance of power. They might largely have met the needs of the dissenters but they came too late to prevent the creation of the rival Association of Mines of the South African Republic, on 16 April 1896, with twenty-six founder members, representing the Robinson, Albu, Goerz and various smaller groups. Four more companies joined later in the year. The Constitution was similar to the Chamber's but specifically barred activities that had any reference to the 'general politics of the State'.[12] It also provided that nobody could be chairman for two succeeding years. The first Chairman was Langerman. The Executive Committee consisted of Brakhan, Brochon, Albu, Wagner, Dr Josef Magin, George Goch, A Epler and W H Adler.

In an address to the first monthly meeting on 31 May, Langerman gave reasons for the foundation of a separate association, but omitted any reference to the Raid or the Rising. Langerman declared that the Association was not formed in opposition to the Chamber, nor was it antagonistic to it. They would be glad if at any time they could join with the Chamber for the benefit of the mining industry.

In February 1897, George Albu succeeded Langerman as Chairman.

Jeeves has suggested that behind the denunciation of the Rising by the 'cosmopolitans' and their foundation of the Association of Mines lurked a lively self-interest.

> Behind their strident rhetoric it is possible to discern other motives. With the two largest mining houses seriously discomfited by the Raid, rival companies had economic motives for dissociating themselves from the conspirators. Whatever their allegiance to Germany, their love of Kruger or

their hatred of Rhodes, they could hope to take advantage of the much weakened position of the industry leaders. Amandhus Brakhan, Johannesburg manager of the A Goerz group, expressed just this view to Georges Rouliot.... According to Brakhan, the Association of Mines was formed in the hope of favoured treatment from the republic.... Untainted by involvement in the Raid and presenting themselves as the allies of the government, Brakhan and his associates expected substantial material reward for their loyalty, and the Association was their instrument for the achievement of this purpose.[13]

They were to be disappointed. The Association succeeded in winning Kruger's agreement to accept the office of Honorary President, and the Chairman of the Association replaced the President of the Chamber on the Liquor Licensing Board. That apart, the only important concessions were obtained from joint action with the Chamber.

In the absence of special government favour, there was nothing fundamental to keep the bodies apart, and the Government's appointment in 1897 of the Industrial Commission of Inquiry into the Mining Industry soon demonstrated the wisdom of consolidated action.

A serious depression had persisted since the stock market collapse at the end of 1895, signposting the need for an inquiry into the disabilities of the mines, about half of which were working at a loss. Clearly, Kruger hoped that inquiry would reveal that the problems of mining stemmed, not from State maladministration and oppression, but from the financial buccaneering of the Randlords. The Republic's official historian J F van Oordt, has confirmed that the Commission was appointed so as to astonish the world at the mismanagement and deceit prevalent on the Rand.[14] It did not work out that way.

The members appointed to the Commission were:

Schalk Burger, member of the Executive Council, generally regarded as a progressive. A year later he would stand against Kruger in the Presidential election.
J S Smit, Government Railway Commissioner.
Christiaan Joubert, Head of the Mines Department (the so–called 'Minister of Mines').
G Schmitz-Dumont, Acting State Mining Engineer.
J F de Beer, First Special Judicial Commissioner.
Thomas Hugo, General Manager, National Bank, as financial adviser.

There were at the outset three 'advisory' members as well. They were A Brakhan, E Brochon, of the Robinson Group, and A Pierce (Manager of the Natal Bank in Johannesburg). A week after the opening of the inquiry on 20 April, Hay and Albu in their respective capacities as President of the Chamber and Chairman of the Association were added to the advisory members. In all but name, the advisory members became full members of the

Commission. All of them, with the exception of Pierce, gave evidence as well, Brochon stating that he represented great French financiers.

In open proceedings, the Chairman said that all those interested in doing so would be given an opportunity of giving evidence. He said that the Commission was determined to probe the alleged grievances to the bottom.[15]

> What the Government and Commissioners wanted was a clear statement of fact, and if there was any blame or culpability ... on the side of the Government ... the Commission would promptly advise the Government .... On the other hand, they wanted clear and unreserved and honest statements from the other side as to what was the origin or cause of the present depression. The evidence would have to be given fully and boldly and without reserve, for the Commission wanted to know whether this depression ... was due to over-speculation or other causes.[16]

The Commission heard a mass of evidence from mining and commercial interests and from representatives of the railway and dynamite monopolies. It presented its report with the speed that the critical economic situation called for. To the shock and chagrin of the Government its conclusions were overwhelmingly in favour of the mining industry. In the Volksraad debate that followed, Kruger accused the Chairman, Schalk Burger, a man with the reputation of being 'honest and capable',[17] of playing the traitor.

It seems to have become part of the conventional historical wisdom, on insubstantial evidence, that the report was 'the work "of the mining industry"',[18] and by implication not the considered judgement of the official members or their financial advisers. Further, that these members were overpersuaded into accepting the industry's case and this, per *non sequitur*, was not a weighty one. Jeeves, for example, in a generally balanced review of the years between the Jameson Raid and the War, wrote:

> For the Transvaal, as for the *ancien régime* in France, it was the least attractive and least defensible aspects of its government which were often most on display. ... The hearings of the Industrial Commission, for example, were dominated by the Randlords, who were permitted to turn the proceedings into an uncompromising assault upon government policy root and branch.[19]

It is true that the Chamber provided the industry's witnesses with an information and statistical service of incomparable sophistication. It is also true that the Randlords were men of dominating personality, because only such could have created what they did in an infrastructural wilderness. However, it is by no means clear which 'Randlords' were dominating the Commission, and how. If Hay was a Randlord he was a minor one. He did not represent a Group and was not even chairman of a mine. He was a well-liked stockbroker with directorships on four companies of which two were paying their way.

Moreover, before the Commission presented its report, Hay resigned from the Commission and as President of the Chamber. This left Albu, Brakhan and Brochon, the 'cosmopolitans' to 'dominate' a commission of four Government officials and two bankers, with a leading member of Kruger's Executive in Schalk Burger in the chair.

Burger was a protagonist of reform whom some dismissed as young and inexperienced (a common fault at the time perhaps) but, though he emerges from the pages of history as a somewhat insubstantial figure, he was first and foremost a Boer patriot, and far from pro-Uitlander. He was a *bittereinder* in the Anglo-Boer War who, after Kruger's departure to Europe, became Acting President and remained in the field with the guerrilla forces to the bitter end.

Jeeves, pursuing the line that the Randlords dominated the Commission, wrote:

> At the time the commission was appointed, several of the magnates admitted privately to Conyngham Greene, the British Agent at Pretoria, that the depression was due ... to 'over capitalisation and initial excessive expenditure' on development. Yet no effort was made by the ... commission to make the industry itself share the blame for the depression.[20]

There was nothing particularly private about that admission to the British Agent (who seems to have become the principal historical witness for the prosecution of the Industrial Commission). The magnates' 'admission' was much closer to being common knowledge.

Thus one wordy witness before the Commission was C S Goldmann, a member of the Executive Committee of the Chamber of Mines, the Chairman of twelve mining companies and the author of a history of the fields. He volunteered in his voluminous evidence-in-chief that the causes of the depression were: withdrawal of capital; disappointed investors; over-estimates of the richness of the reef; under-estimates of the cost of equipping mines; unsatisfactory condition of the black labour market; extreme taxation of the mines; inefficient administration of laws; feelings of distrust and want of confidence on the part of the investing public; the industry's discouragement at its failure to enlist the necessary co-operation of the authorities.

Witnesses before the Commission were questioned on these points by the official members of the Commission. The witnesses, while denying responsibility for bogus or doubtful flotations over which they had no control, did not deny that speculation, inefficient management and faulty capitalization had been contributing factors.

For example, the published record of proceedings shows that Albu told the Commission in his evidence-in-chief:

> Now, you must further understand that we have been novices in working this industry. We could only gain our experience, if I may say so, by the capital which we have put into the mines. ... To earn experience costs a lot

of money, and it is still costing us a lot of money. We have not attained perfection in the working of our mines yet. I know that the European capitalist is perfectly willing to support us financially to earn this experience, provided that the Government will treat this industry in a fair and equitable manner.

And again, under cross-examination by the Chairman:

... I am not ashamed to say that there are mines which are over-capitalised, and there are also mines in existence which have no gold, although the property was reported to be very rich at the time of the flotation. We would have been a very extraordinary community if there had not been some of us who had taken advantage of the people who were ready to put in money from Home. This sort of thing you find when there is a boom. You have had this in America and Europe.

Again, under cross-examination by De Beer:

De Beer
Is it not a fact that too much money has gone into the pockets of the vendors and promoters? – That may have been the case years ago.

Joubert
Is it not a fact that the confidence of capitalists in Europe has been shaken? – Yes.
If the Government give a reduction in the railway tariffs; if the Government tries ... its utmost to get labour wages reduced, and make an arrangement about dynamite, will that confidence be restored, in your opinion? – Decidedly.

Joubert
And the confidence in Europe will be restored without proper proof being produced that companies are floated on an honest basis? – Well, the flotations which have not been done on an honest basis are finished with. They cannot get that money back.

Joubert
Don't you think it would be desirable for the Commission to point out to the investing public what has been done with the money in the past which has been lost? – They know themselves how it has been lost.
They don't know generally? – By Jove! I think they do.

Albu, under cross-examination by Brakhan about flotations when the mining industry was in its infancy:

108

I have explained to Mr de Beer that I consider capitalists are the people who put in capital in those days, and ran the risk of losing their money.... And to show you how uncertain we were of the quality of our mines, I may simply point out to you that in 1887 or 1888 a very eminent mining engineer, Mr Gardner Williams, ... [reported] that he did not think the conglomerate bed would be continuous and that it was only a surface wash. ... Does it not strike you as being very plucky for men to put in £50 000 or £5 000 at the time, and as the profit is always in proportion to the risk which a commercial man takes, that the money which these men in the early days made they were justly entitled to make?

And again, De Beer in cross-examination of FitzPatrick:

You speak a good deal about what is wrong on the side of the Government... is there no mismanagement or waste of material; is there not too much money spent on managers, engineers, &c, &c? Are you so perfectly satisfied with yourselves? – Certainly not! We are never satisfied – always trying to improve .... I never intend to give the idea that we claim to be perfect. It is impossible and absurd. Every year we find out something fresh in the way of reducing some of our costs and we hope to go on in that way.[21]

In its report the Commission found that, although mistakes had been made in the past, there existed in the present all the indications of an honest administration. Most of the mines were controlled and directed by financial and practical men who devoted their time, energy and knowledge to the mining industry, and who had not only introduced the most up-to-date machinery and mining appliances, but also the greatest perfection of method and process. The problem (of depression) could not be solved by probing the past of some mines. To avoid the calamity of mass closure of mines it behoved the Government to cooperate with the industry and to devise means to make it possible for lower grade mines to work at a profit.

The Commission expressed its total disapproval of concessions. Such concessions might have been expedient in the past but the country had arrived at a state of development that would only admit of free competition according to republican principles.

It urged further that the Government should take a hand in improving the flow of native labour, that it should improve the administration of the liquor and gold theft laws and reduce the cost of living at the mines as much as possible.

The Commission expressed its gratification at the wealth and detail of evidence submitted by the generality of witnesses. But it recorded its disapproval of the evidence tendered by the Explosives Company and said that despite persistent questionings, it had been able to elicit few facts about the cost of importation. It found that the price paid by the mines for explosives of all kinds was unreasonably high, and called for a considerable reduction. The Explosives Company was found to be making enormous profits at the expense of the mines. Ordinary dynamite costing 41s 6d delivered in the Republic ex Hamburg was sold to the mines for 85s a case. On blasting gelignite, which had come into more general use, the profit margin was far greater. The industry was bearing a burden which did not enrich the State.

The Commission recommended that the State consider taking over from the monopolists and itself import explosives for the mines, subject to a duty of not more than 20s a case.

In addition, the Commission recommended an average reduction in rail rates of twenty-five per cent, the largest reduction to be applied to coal traffic.

The Government sought to escape from its embarrassment over the Commission's findings by appointing a Volksraad Committee of politicians to report on the report of the experts. The Volksraad Committee took no further evidence other than from Vorstman of the Explosives Company, and presented a report which began with the introductory statement that it 'was not aware that any Industry in this country has ever, at any time, been opposed or hindered by Your Honourable Assembly or the Government'.[22] Its conclusions were received with dismay by the industry. There resulted only minor reductions in railway rates (mainly on coal), and in the cost of dynamite. There were reductions of certain duties on food, but other duties were raised so that the Government (in some trouble with falling revenues) gained on balance.

For the Chamber, a spin-off from the sittings of the Industrial Commission was the row that blew up between the Executive Committee and its President, Hay. The Chamber came to fear that Hay, far from 'dominating the Commission', was going to acquiesce in a compromise, and jeopardize the industry's long-term advantage for the immediate benefit of a unanimous report.

On 10 June, the Chamber met to pass a series of resolutions setting out its basic requirements and called on its President not to commit the Chamber by signing a report that did not meet them. Hay refused, and there followed a meeting in Johannesburg between him and a representative group of Chamber members. The discussion was set out in a letter to Hay eleven days later, containing some twenty-eight points of record. The letter asserted, *inter alia*:

> You definitely refused to endeavour to have the views of the Chamber of Mines embodied in the Report of the Commission, or to have them expressed in any report which you may sign, or to express them in a minority report of your own.
>
> We asked you to abstain from signing a report which would be in conflict with the views expressed by us, and you refused.

> You denied that you occupy a seat on the Commission as President of the Chamber of Mines, and stated that you were there as a private individual who is 'supposed to know something about the Industry,' and whose advice would be of some value to the official members; that you would not

accept the views of others even of the Chamber, and would act on your own judgment solely.[23]

Hay, in a long written reply, did not contest these points, and refused to accept that he was simply the official representative and recognized advocate of the Chamber. Presumably, he was encouraged by the Commission in his attitude.

The Chamber now requested Hay to resign as President and he did so with dignity, being succeeded by Rouliot. The *contretemps* may seem trifling in the light of the subsequent report of the Commission acceding largely to the Chamber's requests. But it was important in setting the precedent that the President is responsible to the Chamber's members; and that he must present the policy agreed by their Executive Committee under his chairmanship and cannot, without authority, depart from it. Hay's resignation also

> ... marked a significant victory for those magnates who were being forced to take a longer view of mining prospects on the Witwatersrand. With their expanding investments in new mines, they recognized that the speculative era was largely behind them.[24]

Or to put the last part another way, the robber baron was still around, but his heyday was over.

Meanwhile, increasing co-operation between the Chamber and the Association (particularly over black workers' wages) re-established the unity of the industry. Terms of amalgamation were agreed between the two executive committees on 11 November and ratified at a general meeting a week later. The Chamber's name was changed to the Chamber of Mines of the South African Republic and the Association was dissolved. The constitution of the renamed Chamber took over from the Association the phraseology that barred it from 'any action related to the general politics of the State' (unless the direct interests of the industry were affected thereby).

In the reshuffle, the Chamber's Executive Committee was increased from fourteen to fifteen members, and it was agreed that the president and vice-presidents be elected from this number. N J Scholtz of the former Association became a vice-president in place of Curtis. Albu, Brakhan, Brochon and Epler joined the Executive, replacing W H Rogers, F Lowrey, J J Lace and C S Goldmann. Kruger resumed the office of Honorary President.

While the industry closed its ranks the Transvaal Government contemplated the widening rift with the Uitlanders and with Britain. The years following the Jameson Raid were successive years of crisis in which war with Britain was at times a suspended breath away.

The foundation in 1896 of the South African League in the Cape, Natal and the Transvaal had provided a vociferous channel for pro-British, anti-Republican sentiment to which Chamberlain turned a ready ear. The League's public appeals for the extension of British supremacy, not surprisingly, evoked an equal and apposite reaction from republicans. In the Transvaal, the

League replaced the Transvaal National Union as the spokesman of the Uit-lander. There was a fundamental difference between the two organizations, for the Union was committed to a reformed Republic, and directed its appeals to the Volksraad, while the League was committed to British supremacy and addressed itself to the British Agent, Greene. It represented professionals, commercial classes and the working man. It tended, incidentally, to be anti-capitalist. The mine magnates, for their part, had withdrawn from the political fray to lick fingers burnt in the Raid, and would for the time being concern themselves only with mining matters.

In September 1896 the Volksraad enacted legislation providing for the summary expulsion of aliens deemed to be a danger to the public peace, and followed this with an act controlling immigration. Chamberlain declared both of these enactments to be contrary to the provisions of the London Convention protecting the rights of British subjects to enter, live and work in the Republic. Kruger rejected Britain's representations as foreign interference. Britain responded with a firm note in April 1897, backed by the dispatch of a naval unit to Delagoa Bay. Kruger then gave way, once again strengthening credence that he would yield before a threat of force.

The Government's subsequent failure to respond reasonably to the findings of the Industrial Commission was seen as the unacceptable face of Krugerism and even Boers protested about it. In Cape Town, Sir Alfred Milner, the Governor of the Cape and High Commissioner of South Africa, who arrived in May to succeed Sir Hercules Robinson (now Lord Rosmead), looked on reflectively and saw hopes of constitutional reform in Boer agitation. They were to be dashed by the Presidential elections of 10 February 1898.

Schalk Burger stood against Kruger on a platform of industrial reform, with the lukewarm assistance of mine-owners who saw his prospects of winning as a long shot. It was obvious to them that his platform was unlikely to succeed amid the deepening international tensions of the time. Commandant-General Piet Joubert renewed his past rivalry to Kruger and stood as well, disregarding appeals not to split the opposition vote. Kruger made rings around his opponents with the old and tried emotional appeal, rallying the burghers to the cause of independence. He polled 12 764 votes, Burger 3 716, Joubert 1 943.

There followed in February 1898 Kruger's dismissal of Chief Justice John G Kotzé who had sought to exercise a testing right on legislation and a measure of control on the tendency of the Volksraad to rule by sudden *Besluit* (resolution) rather than by the measured processes of *Wet* (law). Kotzé was a highly respected judge, but may himself have been precipitate in his challenge to the legislature (and the existing body of legislation). Milner, in transition from being watchfully hopeful to militantly aggressive, interpreted the dismissal as an attack on the independence of the judiciary and a further threat to the personal freedom of the Queen's subjects. He sought to make an issue of it, but the British Government, currently in serious conflict with France, Russia and Germany, for once met his proposals with rebuff.

Patriotism was dry tinder in those days. It was, coincidentally, in this same month that the USS *Maine* blew up in Havana Harbour. United States newspapers cooked up such a fire storm of national sentiment across the nation that President McKinley was obliged to declare war on Spain. The explosion, which brought long-standing issues to a head, was alleged to be the work of Spanish saboteurs, but, even at the time, it was thought much more likely that the cause was careless handling of munitions by American sailors.

At the end of 1898 there were again ructions in the Transvaal in protest against the shooting of an Uitlander called Tom Jackson Edgar by a Republican policeman (ZARP). In the absence from the country of Milner, the storm died down, but the final crisis was now only nine months away. The pity of it was that the mining prospects were again bright. As Rouliot said in his Presidential Address at the annual meeting on 20 January 1898, no one could fail to be impressed with the magnitude of the mining industry.

> The magnificent output declared for 1897, the steady progress made year by year, must convince anyone of the stability of our industry for the present, and the opinions of the eminent engineers who have visited these fields, and which have been so frequently quoted, must bring the same conviction as to the future.[25]

A year later, at the Annual General Meeting on 26 January 1899, Rouliot was able to announce that the year's work had hoisted the Transvaal to 'the proud position of being the first gold producer of the world'.[26] Moreover, the depression along the Reef had finally lifted. Alas! the political sands were running out. Rouliot's address also contained a new note of firm protest against continued extortion, reflecting the relationship that had been established recently with Chamberlain. A fortnight previously, Chamberlain had intervened on behalf of the mining industry with a dispatch expressing the view that the Government's proposed extension of the dynamite concession was in restraint of British trade, and contrary to the London Convention. The Kruger Government responded predictably by declaring this to be an unwarranted interference in the domestic affairs of the Republic.

The Chamber's next step was to offer the State a loan of £600 000 to enable it to cancel the monopoly and to compensate the concessionaires. The Government allowed this offer to lapse. In August, it renewed the monopoly. Meanwhile, unrest among Uitlanders reached such a pitch that the South African League organized a petition to the Queen for the redress of grievances. In a bid to calm the Rand, the Government of the Transvaal at last made a conciliatory move of apparent substance. It approached mining houses through intermediaries (initially Lippert), offering what came to be known as 'The Great Deal', providing for the redress of mining grievances and a five-year franchise (orchestrated to obviate any serious shift in the balance of voting power). In return, the mine-owners were to accept the dynamite monopoly, disown the South African League and abandon agitation in the

113

Press and elsewhere. Certain magnates now emerged from political obscurity and co-operated with Milner, serving as 'instruments of British policy'.[27] FitzPatrick, who had developed a rapport with Milner, was the chosen intermediary between him and the Transvaal Government, which was represented principally by the twenty-eight-year-old Smuts, newly appointed State Attorney, but also by Leyds, now the Republic's Chief Plenipotentiary in Europe (and continually exposed to the Republic's poor international image) and by F W Reitz, who had succeeded him as State Secretary.

It was soon apparent that there was no unanimity among the mining houses about what should be demanded from the Government. Not only A Goerz and General Mining but Gold Fields (under new British management) were unwilling to ask too much.[28] Other magnates were not convinced that the proposals were other than a ploy to win a cooling-off period. E S Birkenruth, the Gold Fields Manager, who had refused to join the Reform Committee in 1895, remained a confirmed non-interventionist and the London-based company bound its employees to abstain from politics. W Wybergh, a Gold Fields consulting engineer, who was Chairman of the South African League in Johannesburg, was sacked for chairing a political protest meeting.[29] Wernher, Beit and its Johannesburg subsidiaries were divided internally. In London, Wernher, the peacemaker, differed radically from his more adventurous partner Beit; in Johannesburg, Rouliot and Friedrich Eckstein shared Wernher's outlook and FitzPatrick that of Beit. The financial strategy of Wernher, Beit dictated peace and peaceful reconstruction rather than the resolution of war,[30] and Rouliot did what he could to bring about reconciliation between the industry and the Kruger Administration, but FitzPatrick, like Milner, doubted the value of such efforts and was inclined to bring matters to a head. The Chamber, 'imperfectly representative of Uitlander opinion and far from solid on the main issues'[31] could take no initiative. The mine-owners withdrew once more from the stage into the political wings. The path was cleared for Milner to conduct directly the business of detailed negotiation.

Last-minute attempts at mediation led to the conference between Milner and Kruger at Bloemfontein from 31 May to 5 June. The two men of iron were at last in direct confrontation. The ageing, ailing Voortrekker was the more skilful negotiator of the two, but they were equally matched in their strength of purpose. Kruger now offered concessions that might have resolved the conflict a year or two back, but his past procrastination was to prove fatal. Not by any means for the last time in Southern Africa, a Head of State was offering the disenfranchised too little, too late. The necessary mutual trust no longer existed. Milner saw Kruger as hedging whatever he offered on the franchise with precautionary provisos, and seeking endlessly the ungrantable *quid pro quo*. Kruger saw Milner as implacably resolved on the destruction of his independence, either through a ballot box swollen with Uitlander votes, or by the ruthless exercise of Imperial power.

The real reason for Britain's switching, with some reluctance, from diplomacy to the threat of armed force was not in order to deliver Uitlanders from oppression, though this was the declared *casus belli*. Nor did she do so to enrich Randlords whom she did not hold in particularly high regard. The underlying field of force was Britain's concern with her position of supremacy in Africa and her current loss of trade to competing powers. The sub-continent of southern Africa, long regarded as vital to Empire from the Cape's position on the sea routes, had gained substantially in importance from the premier position recently attained by the Rand gold-field. Increasing flows of monetary gold would buttress Britain's key position as the centre of the world's money market, nourish world trade and strengthen the sinews of military power in future wars with Germany that already cast shadows before. Nobody was better placed to grasp this than Milner with his background as a financial administrator and his access to the corridors of power. But Britain did not go to war in 1899 because she perceived the role the gold-field would play as a strategic counter. The threads of gold were among the many in the web of causation.

Britain was much more concerned with the possible loss of her position of supremacy to a competing power such as Germany, or by a process of erosion through the expanding assertion of Afrikaner nationalism. Milner perceived clearly the immediate political threat created by the emergence of the Transvaal Republic as an economic power, and he foresaw the Afrikaner republican government, independent of the Commonwealth, that would one day rule South Africa. Unhappily, in the immediate pre-war years, he came to believe that these perils could be averted by the enfranchisement of the Uitlanders, and managed to convince Chamberlain, too, that the Transvaal would become part of the Empire provided, as Marais put it, 'Britain obtained complete political equality for the new citizens without delay and at the same time mastered the republican will to independence'.[32] Milner was fatally wrong about the Uitlanders being numerous enough to shift the balance of power, and he was destined to fail in his bid to quench the Afrikaner will to independence.

In the absence of *rapprochement*, Chamberlain's determined assertion of British supremacy, transposed *en route* into Milner's hard line, carried the unhappy corollary that in the end there remained to Britain the sole options of climbdown or armed intervention. But there was a point beyond which Kruger would not – or could not – go. The negotiations at last came to that deadly end. Smuts, finally disillusioned, abandoned the struggle for compromise. Britain was saved from declaring war by an ultimatum from Kruger who, urged by the now militant Smuts, resolved to strike first while the combined Transvaal and Free State forces still outnumbered those available to the British. Boer commandos invaded Natal on 11 October.

On the world's greatest gold mining industry came the catastrophe of total shut-down. The sheave wheels ceased to turn and an unfamiliar quiet fell over Johannesburg as mine after mine hung up its stamps. Mining houses and mine staffs packed up and departed. The Chamber vacated the building on the

115

Market Square and set up office at 32 Mansion House Chambers, in Cape Town's Adderley Street. The mines were left to caretaker staffs of non-belligerent nationality, and to the mercy of the Republic, happily exercised in their favour.

Since the discovery of the Rand, the Transvaal had undergone a transformation from a rural backwater to a great mining country, a feat 'unrivalled in the annals of world history'.[33] But now all seemed in vain as the great tragedy of the War was unleashed upon South Africa.

[1] D J N Denoon, University of Papua New Guinea, 'Capital and Capitalists in the Transvaal in the 1890s and 1900s', *The Historical Journal*, 23, I (1980), p 111.

[2] G Blainey, University of Melbourne, 'Lost Causes of the Jameson Raid', *Economic History Review*, (1965), Vol 18.

[3] *Ibid*, p 364.

[4] J A Hobson, *Imperialism: A Study*.

[5] A A Mawby, University of Manchester, 'Capital, Government and Politics in the Transvaal, 1900-1907: A Revision and a Reversion', *The Historical Journal*, XVII, 2 (1974), p 415.

[6] R V Kubicek, University of British Columbia, 'The Randlords in 1895: A Reassessment', *Journal of British Studies*, XI, 1972, pp 85, 102-103.

[7] A Jeeves, Queen's University, Kingston, Ontario, 'Aftermath of Rebellion – The Randlords and Kruger's Republic after the Jameson Raid', *South African Historical Journal*, No 10, November 1978, p 105.

[8] R Mendelsohn, University of Cape Town, 'Blainey and the Jameson Raid: The Debate Renewed', *Journal of Southern African Studies*, Vol 6, 2 April 1980.

[9] Etheredge, p 121.

[10] Annual Report of the Witwatersrand Chamber of Mines, 1896, p 26.

[11] *Ibid*, p 28.

[12] Annual General Report of the Association of Mines of the South African Republic, 1896, p 9.

[13] Jeeves, 'Aftermath of Rebellion', pp 106-107.

[14] Etheredge, p 127.

[15] *The Mining Industry: Evidence and Report of the Industrial Commission of Enquiry*, pp 1-2. (Compiled and published by the Witwatersrand Chamber of Mines, 1897.)

[16] *Ibid*, p 2.

[17] Marais, p 186.

[18] Ibid, p 190, quoting Greene, the African (South) series of papers printed for the British Colonial Office.

[19] Jeeves, 'Aftermath of Rebellion', p 112.

[20] *Idem*.

[21] *The Mining Industry: Evidence and Report of the Industrial Commission of Enquiry*, 1897, pp 10, 12-13, 17, 18, 37-38, 73-74.

[22] Etheredge, p 129, quoting Report which was quoted in Parliamentary Paper C 9345, p 14 *et seq.*

[23] Ninth Annual Report of the Chamber of Mines of the South African Republic, 1897, pp 67-69.

[24] Jeeves, 'Aftermath of Rebellion', p 111.

[25] Annual Report of the Chamber of Mines of the South African Republic, 1897, p 31.

[26] Tenth Annual Report of the Chamber of Mines of the South African Republic, 1898, p 22.

[27] Marais, p 324.

[28] *Ibid*, p 325.

[29] P C Grey, 'The Development of the Gold Mining Industry on the Witwatersrand: 1902-1910', p 5.

[30] R V Kubicek, *Economic Imperialism in Theory and Practice: The Case of South African Gold Mining Finance: 1886-1914*, p 72.

[31] W K Hancock, *Smuts: 1. The Sanguine Years, 1870-1919*, p 89.

[32] Marais, p 329.

[33] J J Van-Helten, 'Empire and High Finance: South Africa and the International Gold Standard: 1890-1914', *Journal of African History*, 23 (1982), p 529.

PART TWO

Colonial Twilight

CHAPTER NINE

Exile and Return

As the remaining days of peace ran out, the mine-owners faced up to the closure of mines producing one-third of a million ounces of gold every month. So reluctant were they to accept the reality that war was at last upon them that a delegation from the Chamber interviewed Kruger and his Executive Council on 23 September 1899, and sought a *modus vivendi* that would permit mines to continue operating through the hostilities and to export gold. The Government, not surprisingly, refused. It was vitally interested in the continued mining of gold, but not its export for the profit of Uitlander companies.

From July onwards, people had been leaving the Rand in steadily increasing numbers. The mine-owners offered attractive bonuses to skilled and supervisory staffs to induce them to stay, but in vain. By the end of September the exodus had become a stampede. The Government now offered protection to those who remained at work. Most continued to vote with their feet. Almost every mine was forced into total shutdown as white workers packed their bags and queued at Park Station for trains to the south, while black workers scattered to kraals on the four points of the compass.

Seven thousand mineworkers from Natal, in desperate straits, were set marching by a man of compassion, J S Marwick, of the Natal Native Affairs Department, acting on his own initiative.

> There had been strange scenes in the great exodus from the Rand, but none stranger, perhaps, than the scene that followed. At the head of Marwick's procession of Africans were a couple of drunken Boer policemen. Behind them, marching thirty abreast, were a group of musicians, playing concertinas. They played popular African tunes. Behind the musicians marched an immense body of men, Zulus in African or European dress, all the tribes of Natal.[1]

Marwick led them to the border and through the forming battle lines to their homes 240 miles from the Rand.

At the end of September, the Chamber's Executive held the last meeting to be held in Johannesburg for more than a year and a half. Company managements did what they could before departure to mothball plants, to secure the safety of machinery and stores, and to keep pumps going to protect mines from flooding. The Government then took over control and appointed a State Board to run the industry. Its members included B J Kleynhans, the new Head of the Mines Department, and J H Munnik, the Acting State Mining Engineer. Apart from officials, the Government also appointed to the Board, presumably to represent foreign interests, E Boucher, a member of the Chamber's Executive Committee, and W D Gordon, the American Consul. The Government consented to the formation of the Mines Police Force to protect mine properties in the absence of the Zarps, the Transvaal Republican Police, who had been mobilized and sent to the front. The Mines Police, recruited from non–belligerents, were paid by the mining houses. The State Board managed to engage about six hundred Uitlander miners. To Milner's displeasure, many were British.

In January 1900 he informed Chamberlain that a number were

> ...actually assisting them against us by working in their coal and gold mines. Former is of direct military assistance to enemy and latter of equal assistance indirectly by providing them with funds ....

Chamberlain accepted the counsel of his legal advisers that no action should be taken against the miners.[2] The State Board progressively replaced them with burghers and Afrikaners from the Cape Colony.

By November 1899 the Board had got nine of the richest mines, all in the Johannesburg area, back in operation again. Their output, together with gold commandeered at the outbreak of hostilities, produced vital millions to nourish the sinews of war. Supplies for the forces were often paid for in raw, unrefined gold.

The Boer Government announced as a war measure taxes on the gold mines of from thirty to fifty per cent on gross production. Apparently it hoped thereby to stampede friendly powers whose nationals were heavily invested to intervene to stop the war. But the threat served only to alienate sympathy.

Then, as the Republican armies relinquished early gains in Natal and the Cape, and fell back to the Transvaal, State Secretary Reitz sent a *frisson* through international stock exchanges by letting it be known that the Republic at the last resort planned to stage its counterpart of the burning of Moscow. It was going to blow up the mines. Reitz's threat made headline news in Paris, Berlin, Vienna and cities across America in which gold mine shares were particularly strongly held. It may have been no more than a bluff. Nevertheless, in Kruger's Government and its Press there were those ready to urge that the British should find only scorched earth when they occupied the land.

The mining groups in Cape Town got early intelligence of such intentions, and urged Milner to warn the burghers that damage to private property would incur retaliation. There followed, on 26 March 1900, Proclamation VII:

Whereas, it is necessary that all State and private property in the South African Republic and the Orange Free State shall be protected from wanton destruction and damage:

Now therefore, I Frederick Sleigh Baron Roberts ..., do hereby give notice that all persons who, within the territories of the South African Republic or the Orange Free State, shall authorise or be guilty of the wanton destruction or damage, or the counselling, aiding, or assisting in the wanton destruction or damage of public or private property (such destruction or damage not being justified by the usages and customs of civilised warfare), will be held responsible in their persons and property for all such wanton destruction and damage.[3]

That same month the Mines Police, under Commandant L E van Diggelen, learned that blasting materials were being smuggled into the mines with sinister intent, and found that holes were being drilled for dynamite charges on various shafts. At one mine more than forty had been drilled at depths from 5 to 500 feet. The Mines Police moved in to halt the drilling. Giving evidence subsequently in a treason trial, Munnik disclosed that he had received instructions from higher authority to prepare shafts for destruction by blasting.[4] Protests were sent to the Head of the Mines Department, and the representatives of foreign powers sought and received official denial that destruction was contemplated. However, the Mines Police found that dynamite was still being conveyed clandestinely and in quantity to various places along the Rand. General Louis Botha, who had succeeded the ageing Piet Joubert as Commandant-General, now intervened and instructed the Commandant of Johannesburg, D E Schutte, that he would be held personally responsible for the safety of the mines. Schutte, with the Senior Magistrate, N van den Bergh, and the Senior Public Prosecutor, Dr F E T Krause, had been appointed as a triumvirate to rule Johannesburg, the so-called Commission for Peace and Order. However, Schutte was removed from his post and responsibility for overseeing the police seems to have devolved on Krause. At the eleventh hour he too played a key role by blocking an attempt to destroy the mines by Judge A F Kock, who was then arrested on Botha's orders.[5] When Lord Roberts, the British Commander-in-Chief, invested the town on 30 May 1900, and called for unconditional surrender, Krause persuaded him to allow a breathing space in which armed Boer groups could be encouraged to leave. Roberts agreed to a day's delay to avert street fighting and the destruction of property. He entered Johannesburg on 31 May and took possession of the keys of the town the day after at a ceremony which included hauling down the *Vierkleur*, and hoisting a silken Union Jack worked by Lady Roberts. The mines appeared intact. Mining house engineers were sent to the Rand and confirmed that there had been no wanton damage.

Roberts pressed on to Pretoria, but not quite fast enough. Kruger and Reitz had already slipped away to establish a new seat of government in the eastern Transvaal on the trunk line to Delagoa Bay. They left Smuts to do what he could to safeguard the Republic's reserves of gold and munitions. By a display of armed force, Smuts compelled the National Bank to disgorge its gold. He wrote later:

> It has ever after been some consolation to me that this paltry sum of less than half a million in gold and coins which I succeeded in removing through shot and shell from Pretoria on that eventful occasion held its own for two years against something like 200 million sterling from the British Treasury. Nay more, after having nobly done its work during the war ... it continued thereafter to spook in the minds of great British statesmen and to conjure up visions of millions hidden away on the veld or secretly despatched to Europe to supply the sinews of war in the future national campaign of the Boers.[6]

As Smuts rode away, the last Republican trains were steaming out of Pretoria laden with munitions and British prisoners-of-war.

It was the general belief in British Government and mining circles that the fall of Johannesburg and of Pretoria had heralded the end of the War, but it was not to be. Roberts and his Chief of Staff, Lord Kitchener, soon had their hands full with the unfolding guerrilla campaign as Boer generals in the Transvaal and Orange Free State launched the 'unorthodox, macabre, heroic counter-stroke of the Boer people'.[7] The mines that the Boers had worked shut down once again. For another year or more the stamps would remain hung up in idle silence. The Peace of Vereeniging was two years away. The occupying armies were soon overstretched across an area half the size of Europe, much of it wilderness. From Pretoria to the Cape seaboard, the lines of communication, including thousands of miles of railway, were vulnerable to the quick-thrusting mounted commandos, led by Botha, Smuts, Christiaan de Wet, J H de la Rey ('The Lion of the Western Transvaal'), C F Beyers, Manie Maritz, and J B M Hertzog.

Along the Rand the disbandment of the Mines Police in the first euphoric days of occupation left a vacuum which, as the bitter war of movement intensified, invited attack. In October 1900, the Boer guerrilla commanders meeting at Cyferfontein in the Magaliesberg made two bold decisions – to invade the Cape and to concentrate for an attack on the Rand mines. The Boer leaders who had protected the mines against saboteurs in April and May had now changed their minds, seeing in the mines a strategic counter that might bring a favourable peace. Sir Keith Hancock, in his biography of Smuts, has recorded:

> Smuts ... had been in close touch during the previous year with a number of pro-Boer, anti-capitalist liberals. J A Hobson in particular had encouraged him to believe that the British people would not be greatly in love with 'a mine-owner's war'. The mine-owners themselves, in Smuts's view, were not patriots but profit-seekers. Was it likely that they would still think the

war worth fighting if it destroyed their profits at the root? ...

Smuts no doubt deceived himself if he ever seriously imagined that sabotage on the Rand 'would detach the financial wing' of the jingo-capitalist alliance; indeed, the picture he painted of that alliance was something of a caricature.[8]

In the event the invasion of the Cape prospered, but the opportunity for concentrated attack on the mines never presented itself. Nevertheless, there were sporadic and damaging raids. On 31 December 1900 the Chamber's Executive Committee, still confined to Cape Town, had before it reports of attacks on the Modderfontein and New Kleinfontein mines on the East Rand, and of the destruction of plant and buildings. New Kleinfontein had been the target of a raid by a commando 350-strong, led by General Piet Viljoen. The Manager, E J Way, had been taken prisoner, but released the same day. The new Commander-in-Chief, Lord Kitchener, admitted that he did not have the resources to protect the mines.

The Chamber moved fast to obtain his authority, and that of Milner, for the establishment of a mine guard, to be mustered as the Rand Rifles Mines Division, to fill it with 1 500 of the former mine employees waiting on the coast for permission to return to the Rand, and to appoint former mine managers to officer them. By the end of January 1901 the unit was forming at Green Point Common, Cape Town, and at Stellenbosch. News was then received that raiders had damaged the property of the Rand Electric Company that powered pumps on the mines. There followed the burning of mills at Van Ryn and Modderfontein mines. The Mine Guard was hurriedly dispatched northwards, being sped on its way from Stellenbosch by members of the Executive Committee.

On the Rand, the Guard proved an effective deterrent, and repulsed a number of minor attacks on mine property over the months that followed. The mining companies met the full costs of £136 540, a trifle compared to the £173 000 000[9] capital investment at risk. In November 1901 the Rand was at last declared safe from attack and the Guard was disbanded, the men being absorbed onto the staffs of mines gearing up for a modest resumption of operations.

Earlier, on 4 May 1901, the roar of the stamps had been heard again as the first mine got under way, Kitchener being present at the starting-up of the mill at the Meyer and Charlton. Soon seven companies were at work again, but by the year-end the number had increased to only fifteen – less than one-quarter of the pre-war total. In January 1902 Kitchener at last felt secure enough about his rail communications to authorize mining houses to step up the re-starting of mines at the rate of a hundred stamps a week. A steady progression back to near-normality, co-ordinated by the Chamber, got under way, but it would take more than three years to return to pre-war production levels.

The limiting factor was manpower, white and black. A large number of white employees was still serving in various irregular corps. The Chamber had given them a pledge that their jobs would be kept for them. Permission to re-start was accordingly coupled with the proviso that the men signed on should not receive more than those still serving with the Colours. The colonial force rate of 5s a day, with rations, was accordingly laid down for the Rand mines. The Chamber set up the Mines Fund into which mining companies paid the difference between 5s a day and normal mine wages, and from which special allowances were paid to families and dependants of men on the mines and in the field.

Of even greater priority in bringing mines back to production was to re-assemble the 100 000 black workers scattered by the outbreak of war. To meet the problem the Chamber called meetings of mining house representatives in Cape Town in the latter half of 1900 and took decisions of far-reaching import-ance and consequence. One decision was to reconstitute the Rand Native Labour Association with wider powers and a larger sphere of action. The new organization was formed under Chamber auspices, its Board of Management being the Chamber's Executive Committee. It was to overcome endless difficulties and to flourish down to the present day. It was given the name of the Witwatersrand Native Labour Association – and became known as 'Wenela' to generations of black workers and their dependants. H F Strange, representing the Johannesburg Consolidated Investment Company on the Chamber Executive Committee, became the first Chairman.

Men and mines had long suffered the consequences of a free-for-all in the recruitment of black workers. Recruiters obtained men from distant kraals by misrepresenting pay and conditions of employment; passed them from hand to hand for commissions, without regard for their welfare during long periods in transit; enticed them from other recruiters; or induced them to desert one employer for the promise of additional benefits, often illusory, with another. The new Association, a non-profit organization, was created to stamp out this unholy traffic and to replace it with a controlled flow of migrant workers, at controlled rates of pay.

Less happily, the Executive Committee decided to alter the schedule of wages for blacks and to introduce reduced rates of pay to replace the average rate of 43s or 44s a month in force before the War. The war-time rate fixed by the Republic, and maintained by British military government, was 20s a month. The new minimum wage was set at 30s a month of thirty working days or 1s a day, and the maximum 35s a month or 1s 2d a day. It was agreed that up to seven and a half per cent of workers could be paid at higher rates. As before, board and lodging was provided free. The system of recovering the cost of passes and travelling expenses by deduction from workers' pay was abolished and it was agreed that all expenses of this kind would in future be met by the employer. The mine-owners hoped that the reduced wages would be accepted by prospective employees, both because they were 'reasonable', and because the worker would prefer a guaranteed wage, free of deductions. The hopes of willing acceptance proved unfounded. The decision, taken unanimously at a conference of Chamber members in Cape Town far removed from the scene of operations, took no account of the disruptive effects of the War on the black races, and the disillusionment that stemmed from war-time employment, often enforced, at low rates of pay, by the combatant white races. Nor was the decision based on a sound appraisal of circumstances likely to prevail on the Rand in the aftermath of war. In the years immediately ahead, it would serve to intensify the labour shortage and would contribute to events with consequences far beyond the Transvaal.

Despite its exile for much of the War, the Chamber from its Cape Town office in Mansion House Chambers managed to maintain continuity of action, and its Executive Committee met regularly there. Some members of the multinational committee had remained in Johannesburg,[10] and so had one of the joint assistant secretaries. Thus, both from Cape Town and Johannesburg the Chamber kept a watching brief on the interests of the industry.

In this way, it was able to assist in the driving of nails into the coffins of the concessionaires who had exercised so baleful an influence on Kruger. This influence seems to have continued for so long as Pretoria remained the Boer capital. At the last session of the Volksraad in the old Raadzaal in May 1900, almost in the cannon's mouth, Kruger suddenly introduced a motion to authorize the Government to sell underground mining rights at reasonable prices. According to Rouliot:

> Mr van Rensburg, one of the Progressive members, opposed it in most scathing terms, and said, according to the published proceedings of the session, that, whilst the burghers at the front were sacrificing their lives, their property was to be sold behind their backs to the mercenary speculator. He knew they were here, this speculating coterie; he had seen them with his own eyes that very day at Pretoria hanging about the hotels and the Raadzaal lobbies; he could not understand such action of the President in view of his statement that the mines bring in enough gold to cover war expenses, and he wound up by saying: 'I see, gentlemen of the Raad, the hand of the mercenary speculator, the person in the lobby, in this business. I protest most vehemently against such harpies dabbling in our misfortune and fattening on the noble sacrifices of life and blood that are being made.' On his proposal the authority to sell was refused ....[11]

The British Government was hot on the trail of the 'harpies'. The commission to inquire into the concessions granted by the Kruger Government landed in Cape Town in August 1900. Its members were the Hon Alfred Lyttelton, Q C, M P (Chairman), who would succeed Chamberlain as Colonial Secretary in 1903, A M Ashmore, C M G, a senior official of the British Colonial Service and a future Lieutenant-Governor of Ceylon, and R K Loveday. It opened its sittings in Cape Town on 1 October, and on 3 October the Chamber handed in admirably terse statements on its special *bêtes noirs* the Dynamite Monopoly, the Railway Concession, and the Liquor Concession.

The Commission's report, presented to the British Parliament on 19 April 1901, led to the nationalization of the Railways and cancellation of the explosives and liquor monopolies.

The Chamber moved back to its offices overlooking Johannesburg's Market Square in March/April of 1901. The first important action of its President and Executive was to hold a meeting in the Council Chamber with the High Commissioner, Sir Alfred Milner, prior to his departure to England for consultations and elevation to the peerage. Milner had already taken up residence in Johannesburg, to begin the work of reconstruction. After the peace agreement was signed on 31 May 1902, military government was replaced by crown colony rule. Milner became the supreme authority in both the Transvaal and Orange River Colonies, governing the Transvaal through a legislative council of officials under the chairmanship of Sir Arthur Lawley, the Lieutenant-Governor.

The Chamber representatives and Milner discussed problems encountered in re-starting the mines and departed amid mutual expressions of goodwill. He told the meeting that his Government 'though autocratic in form, ... will not be so in spirit'. He did not wish to be an autocrat, but desired that the people should govern themselves. He sought the co-operation and assistance of all the great interests of the country, and of these the Chamber, as representing the mining industry, was the chief.[12]

The Chamber had been able to publish its annual report for 1899, somewhat incomplete, in Cape Town, but no Annual General Meeting was possible until 3 April 1902, in the penultimate month of the War, by which time it was judged that the great majority of members was back in town. Until then, Rouliot and his Vice-Presidents, W Dalrymple and A Brakhan, had to remain in office. The triumvirate was multinational, being French, Scottish and German respectively.

The meeting authorized with acclamation their extended term and noted their proposal to change the name of the Chamber to the Transvaal Chamber of Mines. This change – the third since 1887 – was confirmed at a Special Meeting to revise the Constitution in the following month, and would endure for the next fifty years.

The Annual Meeting also noted that the Chamber had taken advantage of the break in operations to pioneer the declaration of results of gold mines in ounces of fine gold instead of in the unrefined ounces of varying fineness produced by mines. In course of time, other mining countries followed the Chamber's example and this became the standard international practice.

Rouliot, in the first Presidential Address of the twentieth century, given at the meeting, reviewed three years of uncertain peace, war and the beginnings of reconstruction. Great figures had passed from the stage since last the Chamber met. Queen Victoria had died the year before and the Colossus, Cecil Rhodes, the previous week at his cottage in Muizenberg. Each of these deaths had, in its way, marked the closing of an era. Adolf Goerz, founder of the great mining house, had died in 1900.

128

Rouliot told the meeting, optimistically, that about half the industry should be back at work within three months and that not many months thereafter the industry should have returned to the point reached in the dying days of Kruger's Republic. Those attending had a keen interest in discovering the fate of gold taken from the mines during hostilities. They heard that the Boer Government had seized 110 203 fine ounces in the mail train at the border just prior to the outbreak. They had seized in the banks and on the mines another 72 487 fine ounces of gold ready for shipment; and by working mines they had obtained 459 494 fine ounces. There was thus available to the Boer authorities a total of 642 184 ounces worth £2 697 173. A Government refinery was erected on the property of the Robinson Mining Company, where some of the bullion was treated before being sent to the Mint.

In all, the Government expended some £1 872 237, obtained from 445 771 ounces; losses in minting and smelting amounted to 4 912 ounces; 9 633 were under treatment at the Robinson Refinery when the British troops arrived and another 43 233 ounces were found in the Mint in Pretoria. And

> ...there is an amount of no less than 138 645 ounces, or £582 310, which has vanished, and of which no trace can be found. (Laughter.)[13]

The record does not reveal whether the laughter was jocular or pained, but the mysterious disappearance of gold aroused keen speculation, which received further impetus when the Republic's European banks handed over £34, all that remained in their possession of the Republic's liquid assets. It is perhaps not surprising that the myth of Kruger's Millions, cached somewhere in the tangled mass of the Drakensberg escarpment, should have survived into modern times, and that many should have sought to find them.

Rouliot reported that the amount of gold spent by the Boer Government had been assessed as follows: sundry creditors had been paid in raw gold to the extent of 57 182 ounces; 223 127 ounces had been minted into Republican pounds at the Pretoria Mint or in the field. The fate of 165 462 ounces was unknown. The Chamber lodged claims for the gold remaining in the Mint which could be directly traced as belonging to mining companies.

Rouliot essayed a preliminary estimate of the losses sustained by the mines as a result of the War, and proffered a figure of 'no less than £3 400 000'. These were actual cash disbursements, or losses, including the cost of Mines Police and Mines Guard, but exclusive of interest on debentures or overdrafts.[14] A committee of consulting engineers later put the figure at £6 667 442, a figure which included interest on debentures and overdrafts but excluded loss of profits.[15]

Rouliot wound up an inevitably long address by replying, also at length, to those who claimed that the War had been organized by the mine magnates to boost their profits. As a Frenchman who had worked hard to maintain peace between Boer and British, he was entitled to do so.

... the anti-capitalist cry was initiated years ago by the monopolists – dynamite, illicit liquor sellers and various classes of adventurers, in order to carry on their campaign against the industry; it has nothing to do with the economic relation of capital towards the State or the various classes of inhabitants, and the curious part is that it has been originated by capitalists in the very worst sense of the term. That the Boer Government should have encouraged this campaign is natural. Realising the constantly increasing gravity of the situation, they had every interest to represent the agitation going on here as inspired by sordid motives and resting on an artificial basis. ... Unfortunately it is a cry that is popular with the masses.[16]

Rouliot declared that the Chamber had always kept clear of political organizations, and political matters had never been discussed at Chamber meetings. Certain capitalists had participated in political agitation as individuals; and why not? There was no reason why the possession of wealth should debar a man from interesting himself in the events taking place in the country. Nor did the fact that he took part justify the imputation of base motives.

He asked what benefit could accrue to mine-owners from armed conflict.

... considering the vast sums that had been already sunk in machinery and works, would it have been sane reasoning to risk the loss of all that ... for the doubtful prospect of obtaining cheaper dynamite or lower railway tariffs? ... The people connected with the mines have already an enormous amount of work ahead of them, they have vast properties, many of which are awaiting development. They want enormous sums of money to open them up; would it have been [in] their interest to spread mistrust, frighten capital and possibly run the risk of losing all that had already been done. Is it, as it has been also said, for share market purposes? This, to my mind, is the most untenable argument of all. I have never heard of a capitalist, unless he was mad, that would spend all his time and energies in trying to surely damage nine-tenths of what he owns so that he may or may not pull off a doubtful coup on the remaining tenth![17]

Rouliot declared his willingness to leave the verdict to posterity, when passions would have cooled and temperate judgement could supervene,[18] a challenge which historians have accepted with alacrity and diligence without arriving at a simple or a common conclusion. What he could not have foreseen was that the Chamber, which had been accused of conniving, in the capitalist interest, to topple one government, would soon stand arraigned, by Boer politician and labour unionist alike, of being the grey eminence behind the throne of its successor.

[1] T Pakenham, *The Boer War*, p 120.

[2] S B Spies, *Methods of Barbarism? Roberts and Kitchener and Civilians in the Boer Republics: January 1900 - May 1902*, p 21.

[3] Quoted in Spies, *Methods of Barbarism*, pp 40-41.

[4] Grey, pp 20-21.

[5] Hancock, *Smuts: 1. The Sanguine Years*, p 121.

[6] *Ibid*, p 116.

[7] *Ibid*, p 119.

[8] *Ibid*, p 121.

[9] A Descriptive and Statistical Statement of the Gold Mining Industry of the Witwatersrand: Annexure to the Thirteenth Annual Report of the Transvaal Chamber of Mines, 1902, p 7.

[10] For example, Adolph Epler, an Austrian, served as a captain in the Mines Police.

[11] Twelfth Annual Report of the Transvaal Chamber of Mines, for the years 1900 and 1901, p LVI.

[12] *Ibid*, p 74.

[13] *Ibid*, p XXXVI.

[14] *Ibid*, p XXXVII.

[15] Annual Report of the Transvaal Chamber of Mines, 1902, p LVIII.

[16] *Ibid*, p XLIX.

[17] *Ibid*, p LI.

[18] *Ibid*, p LV.

CHAPTER TEN

Overspill

Rouliot's successor as President of the Chamber of Mines was that exuberant personality and notable raconteur, James Percy FitzPatrick, the son of an immigrant of a distinguished Irish family who had become a judge of the Supreme Court in the Cape Colony. The new president was the current Corner House occupant of Hohenheim where like Phillips he led a life of elegant splendour. There in the moments of leisure spared to him as a leader in business and society he set down his early experiences as a transport rider in the gold-fields of the eastern Transvaal in the classic *Jock of the Bushveld*, to be published in 1907. Earlier, he had written *Through Matabeleland with Pick and Pen*, the record of a tour with Lord Randolph Churchill, believed to be the first book printed and published on the Rand.[1] His polemic *The Transvaal from Within*, which revealed him as a politician to the fingertips, was written after the Jameson Raid and published in England in September 1899. It was an often well-documented, but over-heated attack on the Kruger regime which did much to rally British public opinion behind the war effort.

Milner, who regarded the leaders of the mining industry as the Transvaal *élite*, thought FitzPatrick and Farrar the outstanding personalities among them; both were appointed in 1902 to the Legislative Council when this was enlarged by the addition of unofficial members. Both were knighted during the year. Milner's influence may have been decisive, too, in persuading FitzPatrick to accept nomination as President of the Chamber. FitzPatrick, though a tough and well-seasoned thirty-nine, was in poor health at the time (he suffered from a duodenal ulcer) and might have been glad to defer the burden of office. Moreover, there was some resistance among Chamber members to extending the long occupancy of the chair by a representative of the Corner House. At the Annual General Meeting on 2 April 1902, Carl Hanau registered a formal objection on these grounds, but there were no other nominations and FitzPatrick was elected unanimously. It would be four years before a Corner House man was again elected to the chair.

Shortly after the outbreak of war, Milner had written to FitzPatrick: 'One thing is quite evident. The *ultimate* end is a self-governing white Community, supported by *well-treated* and *justly governed* black labour from Cape Town to Zambesi. There must be one flag, the Union Jack, but under it equality of races and languages.'[2] In FitzPatrick he had found a man who shared in many ways his particular view of the role of the Transvaal in the future South Africa. Despite this coincidence of ideas, there was a fundamental difference. Milner was essentially the loyal servant of Imperial Britain. FitzPatrick was first and foremost a South African particularly concerned with the interests of the English-speaking settler.

> ... [FitzPatrick] was no mere Milner-worshipper ... but was himself engaged in the race against time to create the basis of British-Progressive political solidarity north of the Vaal upon which a future British South Africa seemed to depend.[3]

In December 1900 Milner set down in a memorandum the principles he would follow:

> ... On the political side, I attach the greatest importance of all to the increase of the British population. British and Dutch have to live here on equal terms. If, ten years hence, there are three men of British race to two of Dutch, the country will be safe and prosperous. If there are three of Dutch to two of British, we shall have perpetual difficulty .... We not only want a majority of British, but we want a fair margin, because of the large proportion of 'cranks' that we British always generate, and who take particular pleasure in going against their own people.[4]

Milner believed that next to building up the British element of the population the most important area was that of education. Dutch should only be used to teach English, and English to teach everything else. Language was important, but the tone and spirit of teaching was even more so. He attached special importance to school history books. The political aim must be to work towards the federation of the colonies and former republics by making as many branches of government as possible common to two or more of them.

> I believe a great deal can be done to federate *practically and in detail*, before we embark on the discussion of a federal constitution, just as I believe in a lot of *virtual self-government* in the new Colonies, without letting the supreme control out of Imperial hands. We must be very sure of our ground before we part with executive authority.[5]

To secure the ends of an increasing British population, and economic progress, the country would depend on a rapid development of agriculture, industry and transport services. To supplement the loans and grants that might be coming from Britain he would depend on the 'overspill' from the country's one source of wealth, its mines.[6]

At the end of his ideological rainbow, Milner saw a South African federation or union, dominated by people of British allegiance, whose very existence would provide a surety of Empire. He was not consumed by lust for glory, by an obsessive drive to set Britain's bounds 'wider still and wider'. He was motivated by the practical need to defend existing interests in a real world peopled by hostile and acquisitive powers. The record shows that he consciously dedicated his life to 'working for the integrity and consolidation of the British Empire'.[7]

He upheld a brand of imperialism familiar enough in his day, but in a manner far from that of an archetypal Englishman. Milner was born in Germany, and had part of his education at Tübingen University, where his father was Reader in English Literature. On a walking tour with his father in 1870 he watched the Prussian armies lay siege to Strasbourg at the outbreak of the Franco-Prussian War. He was impressed by the panoply of military power, as he was later by Bismarckian socialism. He became 'both a doctrinaire and a passionate believer in the creative role of political power'.[8] He was impatient of what he styled 'drift' and sought always the clear-cut solution and the 'clean finish'.[9]

Against this philosophical background Milner became Governor of the Transvaal and of the Orange River Colony, relinquishing the Governorship of the Cape while remaining High Commissioner in South Africa with his official residence in Johannesburg. There he rolled out his plans for rebuilding the war-torn territories of the new Crown Colonies. The task was horrendous. The hoped-for lightning campaign had endured for thirty-one months.

> During the first phase of the war, as Winston Churchill put it, blood flowed freely but from a healthy wound; in the second phase the blood flowed sluggishly from a festering wound. Milner had not approved of farm burning or of concentration camps, but he was powerless to alter those policies as long as Roberts and subsequently Kitchener justified their actions on the grounds of military expediency. From February, 1901, Milner attempted to put into practice what he called 'reconstruction under arms' and although he made some progress he was constantly being hampered by military operations ....[10]

Milner was a dynamic administrator and he set in train all that had to be done with astonishing rapidity. The Boer prisoners-of-war, many of them in camps in Ceylon and St Helena, were brought home and resettled on the ravaged lands with the women and children returned from the concentration camps. Fifty thousand Uitlanders and one hundred thousand blacks were resettled too. The shattered economies were revived. The foundations were laid of a modern agriculture. New administrations were created in the former republics. He 'revolutionised all existing standards of government in South Africa'.[11]

However, hoped-for targets of recovery and expansion were by no means attained. A brief post-war boom soon gave way to slump. In addition to the labour problems that braked the rehabilitation of the mines, the beginnings of agricultural recovery were extinguished by the failure of the rains. As the dry cycle of the 1890s, against the meteorological odds, reasserted itself, 'the blight of a record drought was laid upon the land'.[12] With it came the familiar plagues of Africa: swarming locusts and the rinderpest.

It was vital to Milner's plans that the gold mines be restored to pre-war levels of production without delay, but he looked to the industry for more than the hoped-for overspill. He depended on mining houses for assistance in building the new state, particularly in the fields of public affairs and education. For example, the mining companies in 1902, at the request of the Chamber provided sites on properties along the Reef for the establishment of Government schools.[13] Similarly, mining entrepreneurs and engineers played a leading role in the process, set in train by Milner, of establishing facilities for technical and higher education. So heavily did he rely on the industry that it was not surprising that a special relationship should have developed between the Administration and the Chamber of Mines. The Chamber, in turn, expected much from the Administration, but Milner was always very much his own man and expectations often went unfulfilled.

It was written in a contemporary publication that his Administration attracted a storm of obloquy which did not cause him to depart one jot from his declared path.[14] FitzPatrick's role in tempering dislike of the new regime may have been critical, for some of its members were inefficient and others overbearing.

Milner was conscious of the importance of public opinion and when it seemed to him politic to placate it, he did so. He made full use of commissions of inquiry before bringing in changes, to enable all views to be aired. Commissions are a familiar instrument of government, often used to create a cooling-off period for an agitated public, or to avert the need for action. Milner used them to obtain quick results, and he got them down to work before the war was over. Thus in 1901 the Milner Administration proposed the extension of the municipal boundaries of Johannesburg and the inclusion of the mines of the Central Rand within them. The Chamber protested vigorously on the grounds of a divergence of interest between town and mines. Milner would have none of it, and told the Chamber that the mines would be incorporated.

He then appointed a commission under Patrick Duncan, Controller of the Treasury and one of the so-called Milner 'Kindergarten' (Lionel Curtis, the Town Clerk of Johannesburg, was another). FitzPatrick and Strange were appointed to represent the Chamber and Johannesburg's first mayor, W St John Carr, and H Lindsay were appointed to represent the Town. The commission's function was to examine two draft proclamations, one setting the new boundaries and the other granting power to levy rates in the enlarged municipality. In due course, it recommended, and the Administration accepted, that the Chamber should have the right to comment on draft by-laws that might affect the mining interest. The commission also noted that the draft proclamation exempted from rates land held under mining title unless it was occupied for residential or other purposes not relevant to mining operations. It reported:

> The exemption from Municipal taxation … appears to us in principle to be fair and equitable, and no representations have been made to us for or against it.[15]

At the end of 1901 Milner appointed a commission to 'prepare a scheme for the creation of an unfailing water supply for the Rand and the mines'[16] to replace the costly, erratic supply provided by private promoters. G V Fiddes, Secretary of the Administration, was the Chairman. The Chamber nominated its President, Rouliot, and Executive Committee members A Brakhan and B Kitzinger; and J W Quinn, W McCallùm and St John Carr represented the Town. Their recommendations led to the creation of an enduring institution, the Rand Water Board, charged with the duty of supplying water from Randfontein to Springs. The Board was to operate free from any private company interest.

> If an abundant water supply is necessary to the progress of the mines, and therefore to the prosperity of the country, it is even more necessary to the health of the community grouped round the mines, and there can be no abundance to the average consumer without cheapness. … every saving in the cost will tell its tale in the health returns. There is, therefore, no room for promoters' profits or companies' dividends.[17]

The consequence was that the Rand Water Board was established with representation balanced between municipalities and the Chamber, on behalf of the mines, under an independent chairman, and this continues today.

A commission to inquire into the Gold Law was less immediately productive of result. It produced in June 1902 a majority report signed by Sir Richard Solomon, the Attorney-General, Chairman, C A Wentzel, the Chief Magistrate of Johannesburg, Rouliot, and Brakhan. However, the three remaining members, W J Wybergh, Commissioner of Mines, R K Loveday, MLC, and a local businessman with mining interests, W Bleloch, signed a minority report reflecting serious disagreement with the majority. The conflict of opinion would not be resolved before the advent of a wholly elected legislature in 1907.

Milner soon had to look to the gold mines for additional revenue. On 5 June 1902 he issued a proclamation, repealing the tax of five per cent imposed (but not collected) by the Kruger Government on the net profits of gold mines, and levying in its place a tax of ten per cent. Not surprisingly, the Chamber at once sent a deputation, headed by FitzPatrick, to protest and to point out the practical difficulties in applying it. FitzPatrick declared that the tax was a 'bad tax' and the move 'a thoroughly bad departure'.[18] (He later changed his mind

136

and declared a profits tax preferable to a tax on dividends or production.[19])

Milner replied to the deputation, as governments are inclined to do on such occasions, to the effect that he had to have £500 000 to balance the budget, and the new tax was a reasonable way to raise it. He said soothingly that in his experience taxes always appeared to the taxpayer to be difficult and costly to apply, but in practice worked easily. His tax, he claimed, was simpler than most. He reminded them that the mines were benefiting from lower costs of explosives. They could look forward to lower customs duties as well, though relief on rail rates would have to wait a while. He told FitzPatrick that the principle of the tax was for the present irrevocable.[20]

The Chamber did in time succeed in obtaining agreement that the tax should be effective from proclamation rather than for accounting periods closing after that date; and that defence costs incurred by mines during the War would be assessed as capital expenditure. However, the effect of the tax was compounded by the efficiency of Milner's tax gatherers compared with those of Kruger's ill-managed administration.

Denoon has claimed that Milner's tax policy was fixed in August 1902 at a meeting between Beit and Chamberlain in London, in a ploy to benefit the deep-level companies which, he alleged, dominated the Chamber of Mines, at the expense of the outcrop companies.[21] In a devastating riposte, Mawby has shown Denoon's projection of a deep-level conspiracy to be without substance.[22] He has incidentally pointed out that the meeting between Beit and Chamberlain referred to by Denoon took place in August, two months after the proclamation of the tax in June. According to FitzPatrick, the tax was foreshadowed by British Treasury official Sir David Barbour, in a report to the British Houses of Parliament in April 1901. Nonetheless, writing to Wernher in July 1902, FitzPatrick referred to the 'unexpectedness' of the tax.[23] Leaving that aside, the distinction between outcropper and deep-leveller proved no more meaningful forced into a twentieth-century frame than it was when forced into a nineteenth. The mining Groups still embraced both outcrop and deep-level companies, and had interlocking interests in the mines of both categories belonging to other Groups.

The gold-bearing reefs plunged southwards from the outcrop at an incline of seventy-three degrees, flattening later to twenty-six or twenty-seven degrees. The outcrop companies sank shafts and followed the reef down from surface until they passed the boundaries of the mine area. At this point mining was regarded as having moved from the category of outcrop to that of deep-level. There was no standard mine area however. The distance from outcrop to the down-dip boundary on individual mines ranged from 400 to several thousands of feet, and the depths of workings were proportionate to that distance. South of the outcrop, mining proceeded through several rows of deep-level mines, the deepest stoping of ore taking place , in 1902, at 2 400 feet. At this vertical depth the reef was found to display the same characteristics as it did on the outcrop properties. The content of gold in the ore varied widely not just from mine to mine, but within the same mine. Some outcrops were rich and some poor, and the same applied to the deep levels, while poor mines could include rich patches and vice versa, and so on in endless variety.

Clearly, the future lay with the deeps. Clearly, too, the cost of developing at ever-increasing depth called for special consideration, in the common interest, but this was not a matter of contemporary controversy. While mines were as individual as human thumbprints, the similarities between outcrop and deep-level mines, both as to ownership and operation, remained greater than their differences. Examination of their supposed conflict of interest lends no credence to the economic rivalry, and even political schism, postulated by Denoon, and accepted by some other historians, beguiled perhaps by the rich tapestry of his studies of the period.[24]

An early point of friction between the Administration and the mining houses was the contribution to be levied on the Transvaal towards meeting the cost of the War. There were fears in the Transvaal that a crushing war debt as high as £100 million would be imposed. In terms of the peace agreement, this could not be levied on the Boer farms which, in fact, were in dire need of financial aid and subsidy. Yet the British voter expected a contribution and the only possible source was the mines, themselves struggling to get back to pre-war production. The importance of South Africa to the Empire, and of the decision to be taken, prompted Joseph Chamberlain to decide on a personal visit to the Colonies, an unprecedented form of ministerial activity. To prepare for the visit, the Chamber set up a committee of consulting engineers to compile a brief on the mining situation for presentation to him on his arrival. The Chairman of the committee was Hennen Jennings, the renowned American mining engineer, employed by Wernher, Beit, whose mansion Sunnyside, in Parktown, had been taken over as Milner's official residence.

The committee's report is a remarkable document, revealing in detail the progress made in the previous sixteen years in defining the nature of the Witwatersrand Geological Basin; and revealing both the complexities of mining it and the future prospects. The committee also identified the coal fields that were to help create the greatest industrial complex south of Milan. At that time the Middelburg-Belfast area, which would later become the most important producing field, was producing only twenty-five per cent of the output, the majority coming from the now defunct Springs-Brakpan field.

The consulting engineers reported that the Main Reef gold-bearing formation had been traced almost continuously from Randfontein on the west to Holfontein in the east, a distance of some sixty-two miles. Of this extent, the centre section of about twelve and a quarter miles had produced three-quarters of the gold won up to that time. Conglomerates had been traced over a far greater area, and correlated by geologists with the Witwatersrand gold-bearing beds. The committee could reveal that the beds stretched over some 308 miles of which rather more than half had been proved by outcrops and boring, 123 miles lay buried beneath other strata deposited in more recent geological times, while over another twenty-one miles the continuity was interrupted by faults (displacement of strata) and dykes (intrusions of lava).

Thus, there were already clear indications of the 300-mile 'golden arc' of mines which would one day extend into the Far West Rand, Klerksdorp and Free State fields.

> Gold-mining as a business in other parts of the world has been recognised as the acme of speculative investment. Here, though capricious as units, the mines are, as a whole, regular within certain fixed limits; and it is perfectly true that *greater* reliance can be placed on the continuance of the deposit than has ever before been known in gold-mining, and, therefore, large preparatory outlays on the basis of a staple industry are more justifiable.
>
> Up to the time of the discovery of the Witwatersrand deposits, no auriferous conglomerates had been worked on a large industrial basis in any part of the world.
>
> At the start, therefore, these fields were unique as to general experience, and consequently the engineer had to grope his way and the capitalist to follow cautiously, or risk rashly.[25]

The ultimate depths to which mining would be conducted would depend on the grade of ore met with and the working costs, the latter being influenced by the level of wages, the depth of hoisting and the temperatures and water encountered. Mining engineers were already discussing mining as possible at depths from 6 000 to 12 000 feet, setting a pattern for their successors who would take mining deeper into the earth's crust than Man had previously dared to venture.

In their study of working costs the committee named the labour factor as of dominating importance. An experiment had been conducted into the employment of unskilled whites in place of the black workers who had not yet returned after the War, but the consensus among managers had been that it had been costly, in that it had been necessary to pay more for the same work, and unsatisfactory because it had unsettled skilled white men, made them fearful of reductions in pay, and bred agitators.

The causes of the current shortage of black workers were the relatively large amounts which blacks were able to earn and save during the War; the high post-war demand for men for the purposes of reconstruction, resulting in higher wages on offer outside the mines, the abundant harvests at the turn of the century, insufficient socio-economic pressure on the black, compared with the white, to make him look for work, and the Chamber of Mines's decision to reduce the schedule of mine wages.

The members of the committee were divided as to the wisdom of the Chamber's decision. The advocates of low pay claimed that if food and housing were taken into account, the black workers got as much as certain workers in the mines of some European countries; that the more pay the black got the shorter the time he would remain at the mines; that the mines could not possibly continue to bid up the price of labour while higher pay could not increase the supply if blacks did not exist in sufficient numbers in the country.[26]

By contrast, the opponents of the reduction claimed that it was illogical to imagine that a worker could be obtained for less than the amount to which he was accustomed, especially when others were willing to employ him at higher wages. The opponents believed, too, that the 'length of stay' argument was a fallacy because some workers after completing mine contracts, took employment in Johannesburg at higher rates and remained for long periods.

> ... recent experience shows that any estimates of future saving in the matter of native pay are quite chimerical.
> ... in order to induce natives to remain at work, their wants must be cultivated ... higher pay naturally cultivates wants by giving means for their gratification.[27]

The consulting engineers reported that the only remedies to the burning question of an adequate labour force seemed to be more legal and moral pressure to compel a greater number of workers in British possessions to work; extension of the present recruiting areas with the utmost vigour; and, as a last resort, the importation of Asiatics under stringent Government control.

In concluding their study, the consulting engineers underlined the truths of mining on the Witwatersrand:

> The value of these fields as a producer of dividends, or as the foundation for the expansion of South Africa, depends on the amount of ore that can be treated at a profit.

> ... the lower the grade of ore worked, the greater will be the number of mines and men employed.

> Our great problem is the obtainment of an abundant coloured labour supply.[28]

The committee asked for the support and encouragement of the Government in the solution of this problem, because on its proper solution depended not only the dividends of the mines but the welfare of the whole country.

Chamberlain, accompanied by his wife, duly arrived in the Transvaal by train on 3 January 1903. They were met at Charlestown on the Natal border by Milner and Sir Arthur Lawley, the Lieutenant-Governor, who had passed time waiting for the train by riding over the battlefield of Majuba Hill.

They travelled together to Pretoria. Two days later, Lawley gave a garden party in their honour, to which was summoned the élite of the capital and of Johannesburg. The ladies paid the price of Edwardian elegance for they must have sweltered in the heat of high summer, despite the delicacy of the chosen fabrics, in their long skirts, tightly-fitting bodices, high collars and long sleeves. The men were elegant, too, none more so than the monocled

140

Chamberlain, with his ever-present orchid buttonhole.

To judge by the report of the *Rand Daily Mail* of 7 January, black and white were the colours favoured by the ladies. The lovely Mary Chamberlain wore black aeolian closely tucked over white silk, with a black and white hat. White kid gloves were worn, 'particularly adapted to Mrs Chamberlain's most exquisite of toilettes'.

The *Rand Daily Mail* tells us that the mining wives were not outshone. Mrs Friedrich Eckstein sported an 'exceptionally dainty toilette' in fine white muslin trimmed with medallions and insertions of lace, the skirt having a deep lace flounce. Her white hat was trimmed with chiffon and ostrich plumes. Mrs Harold Strange was most fashionably gowned in green floral muslin over white silk. Mrs Drummond Chaplin (her husband was Joint Manager of Gold Fields) wore blue and white foulard, with a standing collar and full-length bishop sleeves, and a hat trimmed with black lace and ostrich plume.

At a banquet in Pretoria that night, Chamberlain was brought abruptly back to earth by evidence of the dissatisfaction with the Government prevailing in the new colony. According to the *Rand Daily Mail* two days later:

> When Mr M R Greenlees [a Pretoria advocate] rose to propose the health of Lord Milner, the clock pointed to half-past ten, over two hours having been consumed in the exercises of the table.
>
> Mr Greenless said Lord Milner's political solvency was beyond all question. Although he had many creditors in the Transvaal, their only reason to complain was that he spent so little time in Pretoria. It would be idle to pretend that they were satisfied altogether with the form of Government under which they lived. (Applause.) That they ascribed to the form, not to Lord Milner. (Cheers.) They did not desire at present representative Government in its fullest form. They knew the time was not yet – the country not yet ripe; but they hoped it would come soon. The Crown Colony Government was a necessary expedient. As such they loyally and faithfully accepted it. They would like to see some slight change in form – more elasticity, less secrecy in its deliberations, more security that public opinion would find due weight and due attention. They did not mind Crown Colony Government if there were less of Crown and more of Colony. (Cheers.) The remedy was to enlarge the Legislative Council and render its deliberations public. (Cheers.)

In Natal, Chamberlain had received an undertaking from the Natal Government that it would contribute to the compensation of the Colony's war losses. He now sought an arrangement by which the Transvaal would contribute to the cost of the War by means of a loan to be guaranteed by interests independent of the Government.

On 7 January, Chamberlain addressed a banquet in Johannesburg and declared that he did not intend to exact payments that would hamper the recovery of the country, nor did he seek grudging concessions. In the days following he held a series of meetings with leading mining, professional and labour representatives on the Rand and obtained their agreement to the raising of a loan of £30 million over three years to provide funds additional to the promised Imperial loan of £35 million. The Chamber was not involved in the discussions, but its member mining houses (with the exception of J B Robinson's Group) agreed to guarantee the first third of the £30 million. In the event, economic conditions in the Transvaal continued to be so stringent that the loan was never raised.

The most important consequences of the visit were probably the partial defusing of the agitation against the Milner Administration and British rule, and the wide-ranging talks Chamberlain had with Milner during the two weeks in January he spent at Sunnyside. Immediately afterwards, Milner announced the creation of the Inter-Colonial Council to administer the Central South African Railways formed from the amalgamation of the rail systems of the former republics, and the South African Constabulary formed from the amalgamation of their police forces. The extensive programme of railway construction that resulted was 'one of Milner's more lasting contributions to the country'.[29] There followed, in March 1903, the Bloemfontein Conference of representatives from the Crown Colonies and Portugal, called in hopeful pursuance of Rhodes's long-cherished dream of a common customs tariff. After adjourning to allow a railway rates agreement to be cobbled together, the Bloemfontein Conference re-assembled and agreed on a convention which laid the basis of customs union. With copious amendments, it somehow survived much inter-colonial acrimony, and endured until the achievement of political union rendered it no longer necessary.

Milner and Chamberlain also agreed on the addition of sixteen unofficial members to the fourteen official members of the nominated Legislative Council of the Transvaal. Milner offered seats to the former Boer commando generals, Botha, Smuts and De la Rey. They were politically astute enough to see the hostility that would accrue to the reconstruction regime. With suitable courtesy they returned to Milner 'the poisoned chalice'.[30] Milner was obliged to appoint five 'respectable Dutchmen', of whom one was a *bittereinder* and all of whom could be dismissed as unrepresentative.

The enlarged council met for the first time in May 1903. Two were appointed to represent the mining industry: FitzPatrick who had completed his term of office as President of the Chamber in February, and Farrar, who had succeeded him. FitzPatrick had had quite a year as President. He spread himself in saying so at the Annual General Meeting on 26 February 1903, and his Presidential Address covered no less than thirty large book pages of dense type, of which more than half brooded over that burning question of the day – where were the mines to find the labour which alone could fructify that overspill of revenue on which everything else depended?

[1] L H Hugo, 'FitzPatrick' in *Dictionary of South African Biography*, I, p 292.

[2] C Headlam, ed, *The Milner Papers: South Africa: 1899-1905*, II, p 35.

[3] A H Duminy and W R Guest, eds, *FitzPatrick: South African Politician: Selected Papers, 1888-1906*, p 8.

[4] Headlam, ed, p 242.

[5] *Ibid*, p 244.

[6] *Idem*.

[7] A L Harington, 'Milner' in *Dictionary of South African Biography*, III, p 613.

[8] S E Katzenellenbogen, 'Reconstruction in the Transvaal', P Warwick and S B Spies, eds, *The South African War: The Anglo-Boer War 1899-1902*, p 341.

[9] E Stokes, 'III. Milnerism', *The Historical Journal*, V, I, (1962), p 52.

[10] S B Spies, 'Reconstruction and Unification, 1902-1910', C F J Muller, ed, *Five Hundred Years: A History of South Africa*, p 363.

[11] V R Markham, *The South African Scene*, quoted in S Marks and S Trapido, 'Lord Milner and the South African State', P Bonner, *Working Papers in Southern African Studies*, Volume 2, at p 53.

[12] Headlam, ed, p 456.

[13] Annual Report of the Transvaal Chamber of Mines, 1902, p LIV.

[14] Praagh, ed, p 32.

[15] Report of the Commission appointed to consider certain questions arising out of the proposed extension of the Municipal Area of Johannesburg, 1902. (Annual Report of the Transvaal Chamber of Mines, 1902, p 322.)

[16] Report of Witwatersrand Water Supply Commission, 1902. (Annual Report of the Transvaal Chamber of Mines, 1902, p 301.)

[17] *Ibid*, p 312.

[18] Report of the Chamber of Mines deputation, 16 June 1902, Transvaal Archives – Colonial Secretary: Volume 1078 No. 053/02, quoted in Mawby, 'Capital, Government and Politics in the Transvaal', at p 400.

[19] Annual Report of the Transvaal Chamber of Mines, 1902, pp LII-LIII.

[20] *Ibid*, pp 184-185.

[21] D N Denoon, *A Grand Illusion: The Failure of Imperial Policy in the Transvaal Colony during the period of Reconstruction 1900-05*, p 183.

[22] Mawby, 'Capital, Government and Politics in the Transvaal', pp 399-400.

[23] FitzPatrick to Wernher, 5 July 1902: Q2 A/LB XVII, quoted in A H Duminy, 'The Political Career of Sir Percy FitzPatrick, 1895-1906', at p 194.

[24] See for example Leonard Thompson in *The Oxford History of South Africa*, II. *South Africa: 1870-1966*, at p 335.

[25] A Descriptive and Statistical Statement of the Gold Mining Industry of the Witwatersrand: Annexure to the Annual Report of the Transvaal Chamber of Mines, 1902, p 6.

[26] *Ibid*, p 25.

[27] *Idem*.

[28] *Ibid*, p 33.

[29] Katzenellenbogen, p 359.

[30] G H L Le May, *British Supremacy in South Africa: 1899-1907*, p 159.

CHAPTER ELEVEN

The Chinese Alternative

The prosperity that had flowered in the first halcyon months of peace was soon over. The immediate problems of the gold mines, and of the Transvaal that depended wholly on them, were legion. After 1896, the price paid on world markets for mining supplies and equipment had risen steadily while the price of gold remained effectively fixed by the central banks which operated the International Gold Standard. The purchasing power of gold fell to its lowest level since 1886 at a time when the extension of deep-level mining had escalated requirements,[1] and the decline would continue right up to the outbreak of war in 1914.

The industry's plight was worsened by the sheer scale of the operations to which mining houses now committed themselves. It seemed to them that the only alternative to grasping the proffered nettle was to go small: to concentrate on the higher-grade areas, to neglect that large part of the Transvaal's inheritance of gold locked in lower-grade deposits, and to accept curtailed working for the mines, together with diminished revenues and profits. Measured against the expectations of State and public such a course was unthinkable.

Not the least important need was to satisfy dividend-hungry investors. In 1902, no less than 299 new mining companies were registered. But investor confidence had proved brittle in the past, and the reconstruction era was no exception as investors took fright in an atmosphere of impending crisis. Increasingly, the financial credibility of the mines was at stake. A forbidding picture presented itself to the controlling houses.

It was known that there was material for an enormous expansion. But this involved mining at greater depths and taking rock in larger quantities, and not the richer portions only. Thus, while the capital expenditure for the equipment of the average mine was perhaps doubled, the average return to be expected from the rock extracted became much less. ... Working costs thus became a matter of prime importance in all schemes for future development. Every item had to be carefully examined, and the cost of native labour was one of the most important .... To one of the older and richer outcrop mines, it might have been merely a question of a slight reduction in the dividend whether their native wages were £3 or £5 a month, but to new enterprises, which contemplated working low grade reef ... it was a question of life or death.[2]

The attempt to cut costs by reducing black wages was an immediate failure. In July 1903 the number of black workers on the mines was little more than half the figure of around 90 000 at work in July 1899. They were far too few to return mines to the pre-war scale of operation, let alone to meet the needs of the planned expansion. Wages were quickly raised to pre-war rates and then increased above that. Annual average rates in 1903-1904 were up 26,8 per cent on the previous year. It did not lessen the frustration of mine managers of operating mines that each vacant job was a measurable cost in terms of opportunity loss. For some mines it was soon not a matter of labour at lower cost, but labour at – almost – any price. In a situation that became increasingly desperate the Transvaal, like California, Western Australia and British Columbia in the previous century, turned to the teeming millions of China, accustomed to labouring for a penny or two per day.

> There can be no doubt that the prolonged inability to increase the African labour supply to meet even pre-war requirements, the rising costs of labour and the enforced adoption of a low-grade policy were the major factors which forced the industry into a pro-Chinese position.[3]

The Chamber at first opposed the introduction of Asiatics, but by the Annual General Meeting on 26 February 1903, it was clearly divided in its councils. FitzPatrick remained opposed and in his Presidential Address on that day he declared that Africa had not yet been exhausted as a source of labour. He stoutly defended the endeavours of the Witwatersrand Native Labour Association. The previous month F 'Peter' Perry, formerly Milner's Imperial Secretary, had taken over from Harold Strange, of Johannesburg Consolidated Investment Company, who had acted as Chairman on an honorary basis since the foundation of the Association. The 'silent and sphinx-like' Perry[4] was appointed full-time salaried Chairman and Managing Director. G A Goodwin was the General Manager. Their charge was to extend the area of recruiting in Africa as rapidly as possible.

In 1901, Milner had signed a *modus vivendi* with Portugal which gave the WNLA the sole right to recruit in the southern provinces of Moçambique which had been the principal source of labour for the mines before the War. In return, Portugal demanded that the British Government renew the preference granted by the Kruger regime in rail rates and customs duties. Milner, with nowhere else to go, could not do other than sign. In his haste, he may have been unaware that he was getting only the *southern* provinces. In terms of the agreement, through rail rates from Delagoa Bay to Johannesburg had to preserve the same relation to the rates from British ports as they did before the War. No higher duties were to be imposed on goods entering the Transvaal

145

from Moçambique than on goods entering through British ports. The only important change was that rot-gut spirits of Portuguese origin could no longer enter the Transvaal duty-free.[5]

Thus recruiting was renewed in Moçambique at the beginning of 1902 and two-thirds of those recruited by the WNLA in that year came from there, the second most important source being the Transvaal with around eighteen per cent, followed by the Cape with five per cent.

Natal, a country teeming with black tribes, had been importing Indian labour since 1860 and her Indian population would soon outnumber the white. The Natal Legislature had passed in 1901 the Labour Touts Act, closing the borders to recruiters of black labour from the Transvaal and elsewhere. Thus barred from Zululand, WNLA sought to spread recruiting into British Central Africa, British East Africa, the Congo Free State, Uganda, and Portuguese and German West Africa, but with little success. Blacks who did respond were often in poor physical shape and scorbutic from malnutrition. The mortality on the mines in that year was horrendous, particularly among blacks from tropical areas who did not acclimatize readily to the freezing Highveld winter, and who had little resistance to the pneumonia which raged in the compounds.

Shortly before the War the Chamber had intervened to improve living conditions on the mines. At the end of 1898 an outbreak of bubonic plague was reported at Delagoa Bay. The danger was perceived of the disease being brought to the mines, and spreading from the compounds outwards into the tribal areas. The Chamber acted at once and telegraphed the Plague Research Committee in Bombay.

> ... Can you send immediately sufficient material to inoculate at least 10 000 men, also serum for injection during disease, and means and directions for preparing both here? Could you send at same time competent medical man to organize preventive measures and train other medical men. Chamber will pay all expenses and any monthly fee required. Reply paid unlimited.[6]

This and following cables produced the prompt dispatch of materials and a cable from Dr R Hornabrook, who had worked in plague-stricken regions in India.

> Government consent. Willing organise plague. Reply Government Bombay.[7]

In the event, there was no plague to organize, but Dr Hornabrook streamlined measures of plague prevention at East Coast ports from Mombasa to Durban. He reached Johannesburg in May and was commissioned by the Chamber to inquire into the conditions prevailing in the compounds, and to advise how best to ensure a high standard of health. His report was summarized and published in pamphlet form for the guidance of the mines. He recommended

146

closer supervision and inspection, and swift measures to deal with epidemics; and he set out guide rules for the construction of compounds, the space to be allotted per man, and for proper ventilation and sanitation. He laid down the dietary precautions necessary to prevent scurvy, and he recommended that each mine should have its own small hospital with surgical, medical and isolation wards.[8]

Few of the proposals could be put into effect before the outbreak of war. When mining began again, many of the compounds were dilapidated. Sanitation was generally primitive and the diet inadequate. A report from Dr C L L Sansom, District Medical Officer for the Witwatersrand, in the first month of peace led Milner to call on the mining houses to bring about improvements.

There followed, in February 1903, a conference between Sir Geoffrey Lagden, Commissioner for Native Affairs, and the Chamber and mine medical officers, which appointed a committee of doctors to investigate the causes of deaths from disease among black workers. They found the principal causes, in the six months November 1902 – April 1903, the first period for which statistics were available, to be pneumonia, and diarrhoeal diseases, accounting for 41,7 per cent and 20,5 per cent of deaths respectively. Scurvy, 'entirely preventable', was at twelve per cent the third biggest killer, and was actually being contracted not only prior to engagement but during service on the mines.[9] The doctors recommended better supervision of clothing, care of those found on arrival to be temporarily unfit for work, better accommodation, a defined scale of diet, improved hospital administration, provision of change houses at shaft heads, and improved sanitation.[10] The Chamber's Executive Committee endorsed the report and declared that the recommendations had already been 'practically adopted'.[11] A grant of £1 000 was made for investigation into the cause and prevention of pneumonia, the first of a long series of endeavours to find an effective vaccine. The Commissioner of Native Affairs reported substantial improvements during 1903-1904.[12] In September 1904, Drs L G Irvine and D Macauley, who both had experience on the mines, testified in a statement to a government commission on the provision of adequate air space in compounds, that 'the factor of diet need no longer be regarded as contributory to the death rate. Indeed, all observers agree that the condition of the natives leaving the Rand is immeasurably superior to that on arrival.' Pneumonia in mid-winter and diarrhoeal diseases in mid-summer were still the main killers, and the biggest problems were those of acclimatization and adaptation to mine conditions.[13] The doctors were a little over-optimistic about scurvy because its cause was not yet fully understood, and total prevention lay still in the future. Nor did doctors yet understand how the flames of respiratory infection were fired by the constant influx of non-immunes from distant tribes.

In that year, Portuguese Government officials visited the mines and declared themselves 'favourably impressed by the living quarters, food and hospitals'.[14] From July 1904, the WNLA introduced a first medical examination of recruits in the recruiting district followed by another examination for

Moçambique natives on the border at Ressano Garcia. A central compound was established at Waterval Boven for men *en route* to the mines who were found to be temporarily unfit for work. The selection, care, and clothing of recruits travelling to the Rand were substantially improved.[15]

Conditions on some mines, however, continued to be bad. The Chamber had no executive control, and its suggestions and recommendations, and those of the Native Affairs Department, were sometimes disregarded. The Government accordingly took powers to enforce improved conditions by passing the Coloured Labourers Health Ordinance in 1905. Conditions were established which helped substantially to overcome the reluctance of black labour to seek work on the mines.

However, at the time of the labour crisis, in 1902-1903, there was little in compound life to attract the black tribesman. FitzPatrick for a time favoured the use of white unskilled labour and supported experiments conducted at Village Main Reef, under the management of F H P Creswell, and at Crown Reef, Witwatersrand, and East Rand Proprietary Mines. By early 1903, however, like almost everybody else, FitzPatrick had become convinced that white labour offered no present solution. In his Presidential Address he revealed his changed position, and declared his belief in the availability of black labour. Clearly, however, the protagonists of Chinese labour were gaining ground. FitzPatrick spelt out the pros and cons of the debate which was dividing Chamber committees. He proffered the example of a mine which was typical of a class.

> The reef is of good workable size .... It is not working, and cannot restart under present conditions, and it did not pay under the old conditions. It is claimed that with Chinese labour this mine could be worked at a profit, and would employ directly, say, two thousand Chinese and four hundred white workmen. Taking the average of conditions as far as they can be ascertained, it is urged that these four hundred white workmen directly employed would involve the presence in this country, reckoning in their families, the tradesmen, agriculturalists and others who form that nebulous fringe of collateral development which attaches itself to all creative enterprise, at the very least six hundred more, making a thousand persons .... Multiply this result by fifty and it will show you what Chinese labour would do for this country in the immediate future.

FitzPatrick declared this to be a good case. He emphasized, however, that it was precisely the case for the employment of African native labour.

> ... until we are satisfied ... and the people of this country are satisfied that Africa cannot provide us with a solution of our labour difficulties, it is unnecessary to turn to Asia.[16]

This might be labelled FitzPatrick's Last Stand. The Chamber had prepared

148

the ground for a volte-face if this should be proved necessary. Without committal, it had sent a 'shrewd, far-seeing Scot',[17] H Ross Skinner, the General
Manager of Durban Roodepoort Deep, to California, British Columbia,
Japan, Hong Kong, China and the Federated Malay States to inquire into the
availability of suitable Chinese or Japanese labour, and the conditions
necessary for its employment under indenture. It would subsequently send
one of Farrar's vice-presidents, and President of the WNLA, F H Hamilton,
to India to report similarly about Indian labour. The expenses of both missions
were paid by the WNLA.

FitzPatrick was soon to give way before the seemingly incontrovertible
logic of the case for indentured Chinese labour and to support the views of
George Farrar, the succeeding President, already a convinced advocate of the
Chinese alternative.

Farrar, who had made a fortune on the Rand in the 1890s, was now on the
threshold of a substantial political career. He was forty-two, a short, dapper
man of keen sporting interests. In his younger days he had set a South African
record for the mile. He had a passion for orderliness which, while he was in
custody for high treason after the Jameson Raid, led him to 'keep house' for
the other principal conspirators. Hays Hammond declared afterwards that he
was never as well cared for as by his millionaire valet.[18] In later years, Farrar,
at his home, Bedford Farm (now St Andrew's School for Girls), where he entertained lavishly, would dress for dinner early so that he could check the tidi-
ness of the drawing room before the guests arrived. A close associate once observed him 'coming into the room, pushing the chairs back into their places,
patting the cushions and even dusting the piano with his handkerchief'.[19] The
other side of this harmless eccentricity was a seemingly infinite capacity to
absorb the details of business and marshall the facts of high finance. Courage
was an almost essential attribute of top mining men in those turbulent days
and Farrar was no exception. In the War, he proved a gallant soldier, served
on the staff with distinction and was awarded the DSO. It has been suggested
recently that his preoccupations as soldier, politician and public figure led him
progressively in the post-war era to neglect the management of his mining
interests.[20] It was alleged that while his mines showed poor returns, he
continued to enrich himself personally through the share promotions of
associated financiers in London and Paris which gave his Anglo French
Exploration and ERPM an ill reputation.[21] This does not accord with the view
of his contemporaries. He was well-regarded by the people of the Rand, including those who were hostile to him politically, and was highly respected
by Milner who had no time for less scrupulous mining promoters whom he
dismissed contemptuously as 'gold bugs'.

At Milner's and Chamberlain's insistence the labour crisis was added to the
agenda for the Customs Conference at Bloemfontein in March 1903, in addition to the broad question of 'native affairs'.[22] Milner presided over the conference, attended by delegates from the Cape Colony, Natal, the Orange
River Colony, Rhodesia, and the Transvaal. Moçambique was also rep-

149

resented but its delegate did not vote. The conference was the first to involve all the British colonies of South Africa, and was intended to pave the way for federation. It did, indeed, contribute to the achievement of Union seven years later. In addition to the customs and railways agreement, the delegates agreed to set up a commission of inquiry to evolve a common South African policy for its black citizens.

In the course of the conference Farrar cabled the Chamber asking for an expression of views from the Chamber on the importation of indentured Indians. The Executive held a special and fully representative meeting under Hamilton's chairmanship on 12 March, and resolved to reply that it was of the unchanged view that it was 'undesirable to import foreign coloured labour until the resources of Africa … have been exhausted'.[23] However, in Bloemfontein after much long discussion, Farrar moved and the conference passed, possibly with some reluctance, the following resolution:

That this conference, after considering all available statistics, and hearing the reports of the highest official authorities of the several States, has come to the conclusion that the native population of Africa south of the Zambesi does not comprise a sufficient number of adult males capable of work to satisfy the normal requirements of the several Colonies, and at the same time furnish an adequate amount of labour for the large industrial and mining centres. Under these circumstances, it is evident to the conference that the opening of new sources of labour supply is requisite in the interest of all the South African States.[24]

The twenty-five delegates were élite public figures. They were headed by Sir Gordon Sprigg, Premier of the Cape, Sir Albert Hime, Premier of Natal, H F Wilson, Colonial Secretary of the Orange River Colony, and W H Milton, Administrator of Rhodesia. The moral effect of their unanimous vote was tremendous, for it could not be claimed, as it sometimes was of other deliberations at the time, that the proceedings were 'packed' by the mining interest.

Farrar followed up the conference by holding a public meeting at Boksburg. He received a mixed reception. A few days after, a meeting called by the recently-formed White League at the Wanderers' Ground voted 5 000 to two against Chinese labour. The Chamber did not back Farrar's attempt to arouse public opinion, electing to maintain a low profile for the time being. It also resisted pressure from certain Executive Committee members, led by Carl Hanau, to urge immediate action on the Government.

Outside the Chamber, the task of testing, or mobilizing, public opinion got under way. The Labour Importation Association (LIA) was formed. George Goch, long a prominent figure in mining and municipal affairs, was Chairman of its Executive and H F E Pistorious, a leading commercial man, was Vice-Chairman. The Reformer, J W Leonard, M R Greenlees, the Pretoria politician, and J A van Zyl, a company promoter who had fought for the Boers,

150

served on the Executive, and its membership included prominent suppliers of engineering materials and equipment.[25] Almost simultaneously, certain anti-Chinese interests, including the White League, combined to form the African Labour League under the presidency of J W Quinn, the prominent baker and public figure; with a committee largely representative of commerce. The League campaigned for white immigration.

The LIA was not connected with the Chamber which distanced itself from it and from the controversy at this time. However, the LIA is believed to have received financial aid from some mining houses. It launched a full-scale propaganda campaign in July and drafted an enabling ordinance which a deputation headed by Colonel R Bettington, the magnificently moustached pioneer and stockbroker, handed to the Chamber for comment. Later, the LIA advised that it proposed to publish its draft ordinance. The Chamber's Executive resolved on 10 September that the LIA be asked to leave the matter in abeyance, and proceeded to set up its own drafting sub-committee of Farrar, Drummond Chaplin, Samuel Evans, and J N de Jongh. G L Craik, who had recently been appointed Legal Adviser, was instructed in consultation with Chaplin to prepare a skeleton outline.[26]

The Government, for its part, reacted to the Bloemfontein Conference by appointing the Transvaal Labour Commission. The members of the Commission included five representatives of the mining interests. Farrar was a member. The Chairman was A Mackie Niven, a Johannesburg stockbroker and financier, who was a representative member of the Chamber. So were three others: Samuel Evans, a partner in Corner House, George Goch, and C F B Tainton, a Johannesburg pioneer and mining journalist. J C Brink, one of those appointed to the Legislative Council *vice* the Boer generals, represented the farming interest. E Perrow, until recently President of the Transvaal Miners' Association, and P Whiteside ('the People's Peter') represented labour. (A third nominee of labour refused to serve.) J W Quinn, Colonel J Donaldson, Jno W Phillip, and W Leslie Daniels represented commercial and other interests. The Commission began work in July and was to report at the end of November.

By the time Lieutenant-Governor Lawley announced the appointment of the Commission, Milner had already made up his mind. He had at first been attracted, like FitzPatrick, by Creswell's advocacy of unskilled white labour, for it fitted with his overall design of an increased flow of immigrants from Britain. However, he came gradually and reluctantly to believe that Asiatic labour offered the only hope of achieving the desired overspill from mining operations. Since the Indian Government would not accept South Africa's restrictions on Indian immigrants, the labour would have to come from China whose government was more amenable.

Milner was helped to make up his mind by the renewal of the drought in the first weeks of 1903. It was to persist for twelve searing months, bringing economic depression inevitably in its wake as crops failed and the volume of business shrank. Many left the country, and of those who did not, more and more pinned their hopes of recovery on the coming of the Chinese.

On 1 April, Milner wrote to a friend that indentured Asiatic labour was a necessary expedient.[27] 'Thereafter he never wavered.'[28] But he was never able to convince Chamberlain.

During his visit to South Africa Chamberlain had judged Transvaal opinion to be hostile to the importation of Chinese (as it certainly was at the time) and declared that he would not agree to importation until a substantial majority of the Transvaal population was positively in favour. He maintained this position until his resignation as Colonial Secretary in September 1905 in order to campaign for tariff reform outside the Conservative Unionist Party.[29] It is possible that Milner would have persuaded him in time, but by no means certain, because Chamberlain's background of provincial politics made him alive (which Milner was not) to the resurgence of the Non-Conformist conscience as a force in British political life. 1903 ??

The news of Chamberlain's resignation reached Milner at Carlsbad where he was spending a holiday, from 7 to 26 September 1905, and enjoying a quiet routine of walks, waters and mud baths. On 21 September the King's Messenger delivered to him a letter from the Prime Minister, A J Balfour, inviting him to succeed Chamberlain as Secretary of State for the Colonies. This was backed up by a message from the King at Balmoral expressing the Royal wish that he should accept.[30] Milner, high-minded and altruistic, and ever-devoted to what he conceived to be his duty, declined on the grounds that his work in South Africa was unfinished, and that he could best serve the Empire by returning there. He maintained his position through long hours of dialogue with Balfour in London. The job went to Alfred Lyttelton who regarded Milner as his chief, and continued to do so in their new relationship. Milner went back to South Africa to continue the work that would diminish his political reputation as it already had his personal finances.

Before returning from London, Milner took the opportunity to explain his views on Asiatic labour to the leaders of the opposition Liberal Party. He got no change out of the Leader of the Opposition, Sir Henry Campbell-Bannerman, and his close political associates.

> Swayed by an intense dislike and mistrust of 'capitalists' (other than them-selves), they were ready to oppose any project which was advocated by the mine-owners as necessary to the prosperity of the Rand. Opposition to the introduction of Asiatic labour offered the additional inducement of a tre-mendous political opportunity for agitation against any Government that sanctioned it. Such agitation had already begun.[31]

He had better luck with more moderate liberals like Sir Edward Grey, Robert Haldane and Herbert Asquith, but in the event their influence did not avail much.

At this time the Chamber took the decision to end the nine-year association with its London agent, A Barsdorf & Co. 'Owing to the enlarged scope of the

Chamber's duties and the increasingly important questions on which rep-
resentations may require to be made in Europe', it was decided that the
Chamber should be directly represented in London and open offices there.[32]
A R Goldring, Secretary of the Chamber since 1892, was appointed London
Secretary, and was succeeded in Johannesburg by the Assistant Secretary,
J Cowie.

The decision to send Goldring to London was far-seeing. Goldring, who
had once edited *The Daily Independent* in Kimberley, was to play a key role in
London in presenting the industry's position to Parliament, Press, and public.
He was to be the London representative for thirty-three years and to serve the
Chamber, in all, for forty-four. Long service and continuity were to become
traditions of the institution. (From 1940 to 1964, Goldring's daughter, Mrs
Doris Jackson, was in charge of the typing pool, popularly known to staff as
'Jackson's Drift', after the ford of that name on the Klip River, south of
Johannesburg.)

As the labour crisis developed in the Transvaal in the latter half of 1903,
Lawley agreed to a joint request from the Chambers of Mines, Commerce,
and Trade for a major postponement of railway construction to make
labourers available for the mines.

In September, Ross Skinner, recently home from China, submitted his
carefully thought-out proposals. He reported that men from both southern
and northern China would be suitable. Necessary restrictions on their
movement and employment, and compulsory repatriation at the end of indenture, would deter many, but would not affect the influx of sufficient numbers
to meet requirements. Taking into account the cost of return passage money,
wages, food, and recruiting costs, the Chinese labourer on, say, a three years'
indenture, would in no sense be cheap.

> ... I have never lost sight of the serious undertaking it is to bring into a
> country a large number of people of an alien race, whose whole idea of
> civilisation and manner of living is entirely at variance with that existing in
> the land ....
> Only with unceasing care and watchfulness is the task to be accom-
> plished ....[33]

The Executive Committee now decided that the importation of Chinese
labour should be handled separately from the WNLA and arranged for this to
be undertaken initially by the Committee of Agents, a loose association of
mining houses. At a special meeting on 15 October, Farrar reported that Sir
Richard Solomon, the Attorney-General, had handed him, confidentially, a
draft ordinance prepared by his department, providing for Asiatic importation and this was passed to the Chamber's drafting sub-committee. At that
meeting it was decided to decline an invitation to attend a meeting, with the
LIA and other bodies, to discuss a possible referendum on the labour issue and
to call on the Government for a meeting of the Legislative Council. However,

the Chamber subsequently agreed to a meeting between its drafting sub-committee and the LIA.

The Transvaal Labour Commission reported on 19 November. A total of ninety-two witnesses had given evidence at its hearings which were open to the Press and public. The witnesses included twenty government officials, seventeen farmers, twenty-three representatives of the mining industry (of whom twenty were specifically deputed by the Chamber) and nineteen labour organizers, agents and recruiters (of whom eleven were deputed by WNLA). Among the farmers were Generals Botha and De Wet who had declared their opposition to the importation of Chinese at public meetings. Botha warned that Chinese labour would result in political cleavage between the mines and the rest of the Transvaal.

The Commission produced a majority report, signed by ten commissioners, and a minority report from Quinn and Whiteside who as members of the African Labour League were declared antagonists of Chinese labour.

The majority found that historically there had been a constant shortage of labour in South Africa wherever industry had made considerable demands on the supply. Industry had sought to attract workers from among pastoral and nomadic peoples who were ignorant of the uses of money and could not be dragged suddenly into the labour market by the ordinary law of supply and demand. The tribesmen's needs were few and obtained with little exertion, and there was as yet little pressure upon the means of subsistence. There was some evidence of a change, as contact with European civilization brought about increasing needs for manufactured goods. The commissioners rejected proposals for compulsion, or modifications of tribal systems or of land tenure. The consequences of compulsory labour would be prejudicial to both employer and employee and would create social problems of the utmost magnitude. The effectiveness of taxing blacks to make them work had been overvalued. The maintenance of relations between black and white was of greater importance than a full supply of labour for local industry.

The Commission heard evidence from W Wybergh, Commissioner of Mines, and F H P Creswell that the shortage could be solved by the large-scale introduction of white labourers. The majority found however that all the evidence supported the view that white unskilled labour could not profitably compete with black. White labour had been condemned by past and present experience as impracticable.

The majority summed up as follows:

(1) That the demand for native labour for agriculture in the Transvaal is largely in excess of the present supply, and as the development of the country proceeds, this demand will greatly increase.
(2) That the demand for native labour for the Transvaal mining industry is in excess of the present supply by about 129 000 labourers, and, whilst no complete data of the future requirements of the whole industry are

obtainable, it is estimated that the mines of the Witwatersrand alone will require, within the next five years, an additional supply of 196 000 labourers.

(3) That the demand for native labour for other Transvaal industries, including railways, is greatly in excess of the present supply, and will increase concurrently with the advancement of mining and agriculture.

(4) That there is no adequate supply of labour in Central and Southern Africa to meet the above requirements.[34]

In their minority report, Quinn and Whiteside challenged the majority report on the grounds of exaggeration and bias.

> ... a figure representing the net requirements of native labour is not to be arrived at by accepting, without scrutiny, the statements of interested parties, and especially of persons who have no permanent interest in the country, but desire an immediate expansion, regardless of future consequences or the permanent prosperity of this Colony.[35]

They concluded that there was sufficient labour in central and southern Africa for the present and the future, although efforts would be required to obtain it; that the shortage was temporary and preventable; and that in many ways black labour could be superseded by white.

They were not wrong in claiming that the Chamber's estimate of future requirements would prove to have been exaggerated, nor that future needs could be met locally. However, they were pinning hopes on blacks from central Africa and on white labour, as postulated by Wybergh and Creswell, that were to prove illusory. And their critics could claim that they were content to allow the pace of development to slow down to match the availability of black labour. They had no solution to the situation posed by Milner's friend, Henry Birchenough, Special Commissioner of the United Kingdom Board of Trade, who had recently completed a mission to the Transvaal.

> The real danger ... lies in the prolongation of the present situation. ... it is a race against time, and that is why experiments, however well meaning, which take years to show results, are impracticable.[36]

The Chamber finally declared publicly its support of Chinese importation on 2 December 1903. At a special meeting, it resolved unanimously to ask for immediate enabling legislation. On 28 December Farrar, at Lyttelton's suggestion, introduced a motion in the Legislative Council, calling for the required ordinance to be introduced by the Government. He was no great speaker but he marshalled impressively all the arguments in favour of recruitment in China.

He castigated those who were prepared to stand still, hoping for African

155

labour that showed no signs of materializing. On the hopes of Central African labour, he declared:

> ... There is on the Rand a mine called the Turf Club Mine. They have got to sink for four years before they get down to the reef, and with the cost of the shaft and the cost of the equipment they have got to spend a million and a half of money. It is on such deep level propositions that the expansion of the country, the future policy of the Government, and every inhabitant depends; it is only one of a number. Let me put the question: If you go to those people and say, 'You sink your shaft, you put up your million and a half of money, and when you have sunk your shaft, your future working has got to depend on the supply from Central Africa and Uganda' – what would they say? I think they would say, 'Good afternoon; we prefer to keep the money in the bank.'[37]

After considerable debate, Farrar's motion was accepted by twenty-six votes to four, with one abstention, the officials being allowed a free vote. It was after midnight, but Milner was immediately informed by telephone. Lyttelton now required of him satisfactory assurances that the great majority of the Transvaal supported the coming of the Chinese. In the absence of elected representatives, or any electoral machinery for a referendum, there was no way that this could be accurately judged. There was certainly strong support among the business community and among some farmers. At the same time, traders feared the competition from Asiatics that had resulted from Indian immigration to Natal. There was influential opposition among white labour and among Boers both of whom had genuine fears allied to a lively sense of political opportunity.

A clear indication of a shift in public opinion had come in November with a meeting of 400 members of the scientific and technical societies. They resolved with only six dissentients that black labour was inadequate, unskilled white labour too costly and Chinese labour immediately necessary.[38] The Chamber's declaration of support in December brought the resignation of W F Monypenny, Editor of *The Star*, a supporter of Creswell and an opponent of Chinese labour. He had long been following a line independent of the owners of the newspaper, the Argus Printing and Publishing Company. He had let it be known privately that he would resign as soon as active steps in favour of Chinese labour were taken by the mines. He now explained publicly that he did not wish to place the proprietors of *The Star* 'in a false position by continuing to oppose them from a platform with which they themselves have provided me'.[39] *The Star* at once switched to active support of Chinese labour. There followed declarations of support from the Chamber of Trade and the Stock Exchange. The LIA organized a monster petition of 45 000 signatures in favour and Farrar laid it on the table of the Legislative Council. Some questioned the validity of the signatures but Milner was now satisfied. As late as March his view seemed to be confirmed when the Johannesburg Chamber of

Commerce voted overwhelmingly to revoke its long-sustained opposition and to call for urgent importation.

The Government published the Labour Importation Ordinance on 6 January 1904, and this duly passed the Legislative Council on 10 February. It has been suggested that the Ordinance was 'in essence the work of the Chamber of Mines',[40] but this phraseology is too simplistic. It obscures the input that flowed from the Transvaal, British and Chinese Governments, and the need to frame the Ordinance to meet so far as possible the fears expressed about Chinese importation in Britain and elsewhere in the British Empire, notably the Cape Colony, Australia and New Zealand. Nor does the assertion pay adequate regard to the official studies of existing ordinances permitting indentured labour. Lyttelton made detailed stipulations about the Ordinance, and the all-important regulations to be made in terms of it.

For its part, the Chinese Government was in no way prepared to deal directly with the Transvaal and insisted on long negotiations with Whitehall, aimed at preventing any recurrence of abuses which had arisen in Chinese immigration over the previous seventy years.[41] Importantly, the Chinese Government insisted on stringent conditions to control the transfer of employees from one employer to another, banned speculative importation and limited engagements to those effected with *bona fide* employers, and required assurances in regard to the manner of engagement in China, proper explanation of the terms of contract, hours and nature of work and rates of pay, and the care of workers on board ship and in the Transvaal.

As a result of in-depth study and negotiation in three continents, the Ordinance was an advance on previous enactments covering indentured labour. It was also cumbersome and in Perry's words 'a confusion of the functions of Government, and private enterprise'.[42] The magnitude of the operation, moreover, was a guarantee of problems that no care in drafting could obviate. The Ordinance provided for a three-year contract with provision for renewal by mutual agreement. Chinese workers were restricted to unskilled work and, despite objections from the Chamber to including a list of 'prohibited trades' in the Ordinance, the Government, to still the fears of skilled white workers, accepted in the Legislative Council the addition of a schedule which spelt out fifty-five categories of mine work from which Chinese were excluded. The Ordinance thus provided an ominous precedent for a legal colour bar.[43]

Labourers were restricted to mine property, in definition a relatively large area which could include shopping and other facilities adjacent to the mines. There was provision for leave for up to forty-eight hours to visit specified destinations outside the Rand. Penalties were provided for refusal to work and for desertion. At the end of the contract period the worker was to be repatriated at the employer's expense. The living and working conditions on mines were essentially the same as, or rather better than, those applying to black workers. However, unlike migrant blacks, the Chinese were permitted to bring their wives, and children under ten, with them at the employer's expense. Few availed themselves of the opportunity, it not being customary for

Chinese wives to accompany migrant husbands.

The British team which conducted negotiations with the Chinese Government included the former British Governor of the Straits Settlements, Sir Frank Swettenham, and O W Warner, former Emigration Agent for Trinidad at Calcutta. The Colonial Office recommended the Indian Emigration Act of 1883 and the Trinidad Emigration Ordinance of 1893 as models on which regulations should be framed. A maze of legal enactment and regulation of Indian indentured emigration to British colonies had actual force in Natal at this time.

> For the Chinese Government, the position was even clearer. Indentured labour had in the past been subject to every form of exploitation, and nothing short of the most stringent and far-reaching regulations would induce them, albeit reluctantly, to agree to any legal form of contract emigration. To this, had been added the insults of exclusion in the United States, Canada and Australasia, and the anomalies of the so-called 'free' emigrant traffic. The request by the Transvaal for labour therefore presented the authorities in Peking and elsewhere with their best chance in almost forty years to rectify this situation. All aspects of the chequered history of those years may be found in the Regulations which made up the Emigration Convention of May 1904.[44]

The Ordinance came into force in the Transvaal on 19 May with the notification of the approval of the British Government. The Transvaal Government established the Foreign Labour Department to supervise the administration of the Ordinance under an official designated the Superintendent of Foreign Labour, a job given to 'Chinese' William Evans, formerly Protector of Chinese in the Straits Settlements. He controlled the emigration agencies in China, officials at the disembarkation port in Durban, and inspectors on the Rand. To replace the Committee of Agents the Chamber formed the Chamber of Mines Labour Importation Agency, on similar lines to the WNLA, with the Executive Committee as the Board of Directors. The CMLIA acquired property in China, that at Tientsin being still nominally in Chamber ownership. Perry became Chairman of the new Agency, in addition to his chairmanship of WNLA. Major the Hon W L Bagot, who like Perry had experience in the British Government service, became General Manager. Professional consular representation and liaison were established in Johannesburg by the Chinese Government.

At the Annual General Meeting of the Chamber on 18 February 1904, Farrar summed up the position by declaring that the interest of the whole community had been taken into consideration, and especially those of skilled artisans and traders. The dangers of competition from an industrious and intelligent race of people had been very real to the miner and the trader. They had both been reassured, the task of overcoming the prejudice of the trader against Asiatic competition having proved the more difficult.

Looking back over his Presidential year, and being unable to see what lay ahead, Farrar must have felt a sense of satisfaction with what had been achieved. But he showed some prescience when, in replying to the customary vote of thanks, he remarked jocularly that it was right that he should be replaced if his character was as black as painted by the Opposition in the British House of Commons. He passed the Chinese baby to Harold Strange, the General Manager of the JCI, who succeeded him as President.

The first contingent of 1 055 Chinese sailed from Hong Kong aboard the SS *Tweeddale* on 25 May and arrived in Durban on 18 June. After accommodation at the depot established by the CMLIA at Durban, the Chinese entrained for the Rand. They had all been engaged for the New Comet mine, part of Farrar's ERPM. Strange and Lady Farrar were there to meet them. The New Comet was the first to begin crushing again as the result of the advent of the Chinese. It was quickly clear that the industry's investment in the Chinese alternative would be handsomely recouped. The political bill was still to be presented.

[1] P Richardson, *Chinese Mine Labour in the Transvaal*, p 16.

[2] *Ibid*, p 17, quoting a Memorandum on the Unskilled Labour Question, 27 May 1907: Records of H Eckstein & Co, Barlow Rand Archives.

[3] *Ibid*, p 18.

[4] J A Reeves, 'Chinese Labour in South Africa: 1901–1910', p 20.

[5] Van der Poel, *Railway and Customs Policies in South Africa*, p 109.

[6] Eleventh Annual Report of the Chamber of Mines of the South African Republic, 1899, p 150.

[7] *Ibid*, p 151.

[8] *Ibid*, pp 168–173.

[9] Report on the Mortality amongst Natives employed on the Mines of the Witwatersrand. (Fourteenth Annual Report of the Transvaal Chamber of Mines, 1903, pp 122-123, 127.)

[10] Grey, p 177.

[11] Memorandum by the Executive Committee of the Transvaal Chamber of Mines on the subject of a Report to the Commissioner of Native Affairs on the Mortality amongst Natives on the Mines of the Witwatersrand, compiled by a Committee of Medical Officers of Mines. (Annual Report of the Transvaal Chamber of Mines, 1903, p 119.)

[12] Grey, p 179.

[13] Supplementary Statement on the Causes of Native Mortality on the Mines of the Witwatersrand. (Fifteenth Annual Report of the Transvaal Chamber of Mines, 1904, pp 89, 84.)

[14] Grey, pp 179-180.

[15] *Ibid*, pp 183-184.

[16] Annual Report of the Transvaal Chamber of Mines, 1902, pp XLVIII-XLIX.

[17] Reeves, p 68.

[18] J Hays Hammond, *The Autobiography of J Hays Hammond*, Volume I, p 360.

[19] H O'Kelly Webber, *The Grip of Gold: A Life Story of A Dominion*, pp 89-90.

[20] Kubicek, *Economic Imperialism in Theory and Practice*, p 140.

[21] *Idem.*

[22] Reeves, p 84.

[23] Chamber of Mines Archives: Executive Committee Minutes, Transvaal Chamber of Mines, 12 March 1903. (Minute Book covering the period 6 November 1902, to 25 February 1904, p 73.)

[24] Annual Report of the Transvaal Chamber of Mines, 1903, Report of the Executive Committee, p XXXI.

[25] Reeves, pp 92-93.

[26] Chamber of Mines Archives: Executive Committee Minutes, Transvaal Chamber of Mines, 10 September 1903. (Minute Book covering the period 6 November 1902, to 25 February 1904, p 167.)

[27] Reeves, p 72.

[28] *Idem.*

[29] Chamberlain, who had been seriously injured in a cab accident the previous year, was not in good health.

[30] Headlam, ed, pp 471–472.

[31] *Ibid*, pp 476–477.

[32] Annual Report of the Transvaal Chamber of Mines, 1903, Report of the Executive Committee, p. XXIII.

[33] Annual Report of the Transvaal Chamber of Mines, 1903, p 168.

[34] Majority Report of the Transvaal Labour Commission. (Appendix to the Annual Report of the Transvaal Chamber of Mines, 1903, p CLXV

[35] Minority Report of the Transvaal Labour Commission. (Appendix to the Annual Report of the Transvaal Chamber of Mines, 1903, p CXC.)

[36] Transvaal Labour Importation Ordinance: Speech by Sir George Farrar, DSO, 28 December 1903, on the occasion of the introduction of the Labour Importation Ordinance in the Legislative Council of the Transvaal Colony. (Appendix to the Annual Report of the Transvaal Chamber of Mines, 1903, p CCXXIX.)

[37] *Ibid*, p CCV.

[38] A A Mawby, 'The Political Behaviour of the British Population of the Transvaal, 1902 to 1907', p 133.

[39] Neame, p 139.

[40] Richardson, p 29.

[41] *Ibid*, p 46.

[42] *Ibid*, p 36.

[43] Chamber of Mines Archives: File 137 Ch 16: 'Chinese Labour No 1':

> Letter dated 11 January 1904, to Sir Richard Solomon, Attorney-General of the Transvaal, Pretoria, from J Cowie, Secretary, Transvaal Chamber of Mines, Johannesburg.

> Letter dated 13 January 1904, to J Cowie, Secretary, Transvaal Chamber of Mines, Johannesburg, from Sir Richard Solomon, Attorney-General of the Transvaal, Pretoria.

The Transvaal Labour Importation Ordinance, 1904, p 32.

[44] Richardson, p 35.

Boers leave for the front.

The panoply of power. Five British men-of-war lie at anchor in Lourenço Marques in April 1900, in company with a French and a Dutch warship.

Left: Georges Rouliot, the Frenchman who was President of the Chamber of Mines 1898–1902.

Right: Drummond Chaplin, who was President during the peak of public protests against Chinese labour.

Lord Milner is driven by an *aide* through the streets of Johannesburg. He took up residence at Sunnyside, Parktown, in 1901, to begin the work of reconstruction.

Lord Milner (centre) at a garden party given by Sir Percy FitzPatrick.

Joseph Chamberlain and his wife, Mary, were fêted by Johannesburg when they visited South Africa in 1903.

Strange and Lady Farrar were among those at the station to meet the first of the Chinese when they arrived at ERPM's New Comet mine.

By 1904 a quiet metallurgical revolution was under way as the result of the introduction of the tube mill in the winning of gold from the mined ore.

Sir George Farrar, a Progressive Party candidate in the Transvaal General Election of 1907, is welcomed in Johannesburg by supporters. This was the first election in South Africa in which motor cars played a part.

After the 1907 Strike Afrikaners began to replace British immigrants as miners. (Frank Holland: 'The Star'.)

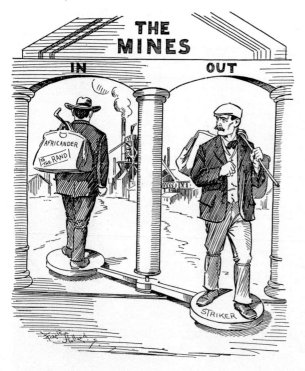

Sir Percy FitzPatrick addresses enthusiastic supporters at the Stock Exchange, Johannesburg, after his sensational defeat of General Louis Botha, the Prime Minister, in the first General Election after Union.

The General Strike of 1913: police start to disperse the mass meeting on the Market Square, Johannesburg, on 4th July.

Police charging on the Market Square.

Women played a leading role in inflaming mob violence.

The unions bury their dead after the 1913 Strike.

The South African Institute of Medical Research, completed in 1914, has made a major contribution to protecting black mineworkers against disease.

CHAPTER TWELVE

The Pay-Off

The first of the Chinese came mainly from Kwangtung Province in South China and were not a great success. It was sturdy peasants from Chihli, Shantung and Honan, driven by the grinding poverty endemic to China and barred from their usual migration to Manchuria by the Russo-Japanese War, who signed on for work in the Transvaal and gave the gold mines the post-war lift-off so urgently awaited. Production in 1898, the last full year of peace before the Anglo-Boer War, had established a record for the field of 3 564 581 fine ounces. In 1903 production was only 2 859 482 ounces, but with the coming of the Chinese in 1904 a new peak of 3 653 794 was attained. Output thereafter rose spectacularly year by year and reached 6 220 227 ounces in 1907.[1] The growth of mining was reflected in a general increase in economic activity in the Colony.

However, it seemed that there was no end to the problems of employing Chinese. In China, bribery or 'squeeze', and fraud were endemic to the social system and much money allotted to families never reached them. Even if the explanations of the contract given before embarkation were as adequate as the Transvaal Ordinance and Anglo-Chinese Convention required, it was not easy for simple peasants to grasp the conditions of employment or to visualize the work they would be expected to perform underground. There were initial disturbances on mines. A criminal element among the workers and a quota of 'won't-works' were the cause of continuing friction. A proportion were addicted to opium. Gambling was the national passion, and the failure to pay a gambling debt the unforgivable sin – involving unbearable loss of face.

> … the great predisposing cause of all Chinese crime … is gambling and its resultant debt, to a lesser degree supplemented by illicit traffic in opium. [The coolie deserts and] … after days of wandering becomes desperate through starvation, and robs in order to live.[2]

However, unfamiliarity, communication and control were the main problems and these were largely overcome. The Chinese settled down to work. They proved to be more resistant to disease than black workers although more liable to accident, as a result of being mainly employed at the sharp end of mining,

161

breaking out ore in the narrow stopes. The Chinese mortality rate in 1905, the first full year of employment, was less than half that of the black worker, and though the black rate fell steadily, the Chinese health record was comparatively good throughout their stay.

Mine-owners benefited by the relatively long contract period which tended to build a better-trained labour force. Moreover, the piecework increasingly offered appealed to the intelligence and willingness to work of the Chinese. Employing them turned out to be simply good business, and would have been more so if not cut short by the political shock waves engendered.

At end-1904 however the full implications were not apparent and the Chinese had become part of the scene on the Rand. Returning prosperity had helped to bring at least a general acceptance of the *fait accompli*. The early tumult died down. Harold Strange in his Presidential Address on 23 February 1905 could report favourably on the results of importation. In all nineteen ships carrying some 35 000 men had left China for South Africa.

> The behaviour of the Chinese coolies has been closely observed both here and abroad, and I can only repeat … that we have no cause whatever for complaint or alarm. The men came here to work, and seem much more anxious to work than to give any cause for complaint. I have been told that the fear of being sent back to China before completion of the contract term of service has a great restraining effect.[3]

Strange, born at Kingston-on-Thames, came to South Africa in 1887 at the age of twenty-six, and became a stockbroker in Pretoria. He was one of the few Uitlanders who managed to become a burgher of the Republic, and the only burgher to be imprisoned with the Reformers. In 1892 he became Manager of the Henry Nourse mine on the Rand and thereafter was appointed General Manager of JCI. In 1898, he was present at the meeting at which Woolf Joel was shot dead by Von Veltheim. A man remarkable for intellectual ability, he is remembered as an important collector of Africana, and as a donor of books to the public library. His own collection, purchased from his widow, formed the nucleus of the Strange Library of the Africana Museum in Johannesburg. The resource and helpfulness of 'The Strange' is remembered gratefully by innumerable students of the history of the Rand.

Strange's presidential year may seem, in retrospect at least, uneventful compared to those of his predecessors, but it was a year of progress in diverse fields. The Chamber at last achieved incorporation, giving it the legal status which it had sought in vain under the Kruger regime.

In July the WNLA established a compound in Johannesburg which was to become a familiar rendezvous for millions of black workers in the years ahead. It also established a hospital to care for those unfit to work on arrival.

That year saw, too, a new focus of attention on miners' phthisis. Mining men on the Rand had been made dramatically aware of the previously unsuspected disease among underground workers by the alarming proportion

162

found to have died when the industry sought to reassemble the miners employed pre-war. According to the Annual Report of the Government Mining Engineer for 1901, 16,5 per cent of white miners formerly employed on drilling machines on the Rand from Krugersdorp to Germiston were known to have died between October 1899 and December 1901.

It was soon realized that the disease was caused by work over a period of years in the dusty atmosphere that was the aftermath of drilling and blasting. Black workers who stayed for only short contracts were less exposed to the danger.

Mining companies imported thousands of respirators, but in the heat and *Phthisis* sweat of underground work such devices have never proved acceptable to workers. More successfully, water jets and sprays were used to wet down working places. The Chamber sponsored a competition with prizes of £500, £250 and £100 for the best practical suggestions and devices to prevent the disease. The competition was widely advertised at home and abroad and 229 entries were received. The judges decided that the best method of prevention would be the use of a drill with an integral water jet, together with the use of an atomizer for allaying dust and gases during blasting and shovelling. Trials proved their recommendation to be practicable. T J Britten, a pioneer who had become Consulting Engineer to the Abe Bailey interests, submitted the atomizer which was considered the most nearly perfect mechanically, and he was awarded the first prize and a gold medal. None of the water drills submitted had been perfected sufficiently to enable the judges to recommend its general use. The Leyner drill did the best work of its class in the trials, and its inventor was awarded the second prize for its theoretical value.

Earlier in 1902, Milner had appointed the Miners' Phthisis Commission. The Commission examined 1 210 white miners of whom 15 per cent were found to have phthisis and another 7,3 per cent were considered suspect. These were mostly men with a history of previous employment in mining, mainly in Cornwall. There were no radiographic facilities and the incidence could well have been higher, especially as many miners refused to be examined for fear that they would lose their jobs.[4] The Commission recommended improvements in working conditions, including improved ventilation of working places. The Government took immediate action and the Mines, Works and Machinery Regulations Ordinance of August 1903 laid down the beginnings of standard ventilation practice. The Chamber began the first scientific investigations. However, it would take time for the real importance of preventive measures to be understood, both by the managements of mines and by the miners themselves, often reluctant to take the simplest precautions. Water installations erected at considerable expense were 'cast aside as nuisances and hindrances by the men whose lives they were intended to save'.[5] Though the first effective precautions were introduced at this time, the disease would constitute a major problem and a mounting political issue for years to come.

The opening of the Transvaal Technical Institute to provide the beginnings of higher education was another notable event of 1904. The history of the Institute's development into the University of the Witwatersrand in 1922 has been authoritatively described by the university's historian, Bruce K Murray.[6]

The South African School of Mines had been established at Kimberley in 1896 where it did useful pioneering work, but it soon became evident that the Rand was the more suitable location. There the Witwatersrand Council of Education, founded by prominent Uitlanders in 1895, had started evening classes in physics, chemistry and assaying in 1897. However, the major pre-occupation of the Council was the desperate need of schools for English-speaking children. The Council launched a drive for funds to support a large-scale programme of school-building, and by 1899 had raised £100 000 from the mining houses. With the coming of colonial administration after the War the Council's original *raison d'être* disappeared and it henceforth saw its role as the promotion of higher education. It was to make an important contribution to the new Institute.[7]

From the outset, the Institute offered a three-year course in engineering and a fourth year of specialization in mining, mechanical, electrical, and civil engineering. It awarded its own certificates and diplomas; those desiring degrees had to sit the examinations of the University of the Cape of Good Hope.

The Institute began classes in March in premises at the corner of Gold and Kerk Streets that had been used as a cigar factory, and in a building on Von Brandis Square used to store lost property found after the War, and more recently occupied by the Government High School for Boys, the forerunner of King Edward VII School. The School of Mines at Kimberley was closed and the thirty students there moved up to Johannesburg.[8] Strange and Farrar were appointed to the Board of the Institute in addition to mining engineers already appointed in their personal capacities. Henry Hele-Shaw, formerly first Professor of Engineering at Liverpool University College, was appointed senior professor.

Evening classes in association with the Institute were made available at Johannesburg, Pretoria and Reef towns, an important objective being to build up a stable workforce of skilled white craftsmen. A total of 426, principally mine apprentices, enrolled in the first year.

Early in 1905 the Institute was moved to Plein Square. The following year the Institute was renamed the Transvaal University College. Courses in law, the arts and pure science were added successively. Imposing buildings, now part of the Witwatersrand Technikon, were erected, and occupied in 1908. The Government contributed £30 000 to the initial capital expenditure on buildings and would later grant another £30 000. The Council of Education gave £60 000 from the funds subscribed by mining houses.

Murray has recorded that the mining houses, in the years of depression and labour difficulties that followed the War, showed little enthusiasm for financing higher education, despite urging by Chamberlain and Milner. However, at the end of 1904, Alfred Beit sought to give impetus to the pro-

164

vision of facilities by donating 1 600 acres of magnificent land at Frankenwald, north-east of Johannesburg. Beit was also persuaded by FitzPatrick, then a key figure in the Council of Education, to make provision in his will for the bequest of £200 000 towards the building of a University of Johannesburg. Beit died in 1906 but the use of the bequest was first delayed, and then diverted to the University of Cape Town in 1916[9] by an Act of Parliament that reflected Smuts's implacable opposition to the location of a university in Johannesburg. Smuts's justification was that the University of Cape Town should become a national university. Murray writes:

> ... Smuts himself had no lingering hostility to Johannesburg as a town of Uitlanders, Randlords, and Progressives, and he entertained no narrow Afrikaner objection to a university that might promote a genuine assimilation of Boer and Briton. Rather his hostility to Johannesburg as the seat of a university was academic and puritan. As a product of the Victoria College, Stellenbosch, and Cambridge University, he associated university education with relatively quiet provincial towns, and found incongruous the idea of locating a university in a bustling industrial and commercial centre. When that centre happened to be Johannesburg, he found the idea positively obnoxious.[10]

Smuts, who was Minister of Education as well as Colonial Secretary in the Transvaal Government, was determined that Pretoria should be the centre for higher education in the Transvaal, and his view was to hold sway and determine the course of events. Separate Pretoria and Johannesburg Divisions of the Transvaal University College were created in 1908. The teaching of the liberal arts and pure science were then transferred to Pretoria. Finally, in 1910, the Pretoria Division shed its Johannesburg affiliation and retained the title Transvaal University College. It would become the University of Pretoria in 1930. Johannesburg was left with the School of Mines and Technology. It began a separate existence as a technical institution which was to develop into the University of the Witwatersrand.

Smuts's creation of separate seats of learning at Pretoria and Johannesburg was not achieved without vigorous opposition, partly because it ran counter to Milner's hopes of anglicizing the Afrikaner through education; and partly because it set an unhappy precedent by separating higher education into racial streams. This danger was emphasized in September 1907 by a Departmental Committee which clear-sightedly pointed out that Smuts's scheme (which it supported reluctantly and under pressure) had a cardinal weakness.[11]

> This effect of the proposed organisation is to be profoundly regretted. The students will represent the future aristocracy of the professional, agricultural, and industrial sections of the inhabitants. From their ranks the leaders of social and political life will be recruited. But they will not meet during their most impressionable years. They will have no opportunity to develop

mutual understanding, toleration, and respect through the discipline of common fields, common class-rooms, a common hall, and a common chapel. The organisation proposed will indeed fail in respect of one of the highest of university functions, namely, the cultivation of social magnanimity.[12]

Strange's successor as President was Francis Percy Drummond Chaplin, the Joint General Manager of Consolidated Gold Fields. He would have been Strange's predecessor but was seriously ill with typhoid, a not uncommon fate in Johannesburg in 1904. Chaplin was educated at Harrow and University College, Oxford, and called to the Bar at Lincoln's Inn in 1891. He came to South Africa in 1895 and was for a time Johannesburg correspondent of the London *Times*. The historian Reeves described Chaplin as something of an idealist who was 'reserved in manner, cold in speech, aristocratic in his political views and an extreme Imperialist with a very clear mind'.[13] A monocle accentuated the appearance of aloofness, but time and experience seem to have mellowed his personality.[14] He was destined to play a leading role in both mining and political affairs in the Transvaal and South Africa before becoming Administrator of Rhodesia in 1914. He and his wife played a leading role in the social life of the time and entertained in some style at their home Marienhof below the Parktown Ridge. It would later become the home of Sir Ernest Oppenheimer and his son, Harry. The name was changed to Brenthurst because of the hostility to all things German engendered by the Great War.

Clearly, Chaplin had a rough time over the Chinese affair, and this glimmers through the measured terms of his review of the year, presented on 22 February 1906. The industry, he remarked with sorrow, had certainly not apprehended that all the arguments advanced in support of Chinese labour two years previously were going to have 'to be arrayed afresh'.[15] Nor that the murderous outrages, committed by rioters on mines or by bands of deserters on lonely farms, would be invested with an undue amount of importance simply because they were committed by Chinese.

> ... the total number of persons who are known to have been killed by Chinese coolies through such outrages, from the arrival of the first batch of coolies in June 1904, to the present time, when there are 49 100 coolies on the fields, is 19, all of whom were men. Of this number, eight were white men, including the victim of the disturbance at the Consolidated Langlaagte Mine in June last, and including two men whose murder has been attributed to Chinese but not proved to have been due to them, and eleven natives, Indians, or Chinese; figures which, after all, do not compare at all unfavourably with the criminal returns either of the white or native population of the Rand.[16]

Despite the problems, the increased availability of labour enabled the mining houses to concentrate afresh on technical improvements. In Chaplin's review there is the first such reference to the quiet metallurgical revolution that was under way as the result of the introduction of the tube mill in the winning of gold from the mined ore.

The tube mill was introduced as an accessory to the stamp mill and made possible a finer grinding of material and a higher recovery of gold. An early tube mill, made by Krupps, was twenty-five feet long and five feet in diameter, fitted with iron linings and containing a quantity of flints as grinding agent.[17] Experience confirmed that tube mills increased extraction at little cost and that it was cheaper to step up production with tube mills than by extra stamps. The tube mills improved in particular the position of the low-grade property operating close to the margin of profit. They quickly caught the imagination of mining companies and were rapidly introduced throughout the industry. The use of heavier stamps was also introduced in pursuit of the crushing of higher tonnages. Chaplin pointed out that every advance in recovery technique enlarged the field of economic mining and enabled ore of a lower grade to be crushed.[18]

The year 1905 was notable for events of political and administrative consequence.

Two years previously Milner had appointed the South African Native Affairs Commission, under the chairmanship of Sir Geoffrey Lagden, to draft a common policy for the administration of blacks in the colonies and protectorates that might contribute to closer union. Lagden was a dedicated official of the Colonial Service who had spent twenty-five years in Africa, and was Resident Commissioner of Basutoland before becoming Commissioner for Native Affairs in the Milner Administration. The Commission now presented its report, recommending territorial segregation and political separation between blacks and whites, and approving the establishment of locations for urban blacks. This has led Martin Legassick, the revisionist historian, to claim that 'it was during the reconstruction period that many of the guidelines of twentieth-century segregationist policies were set out in relation to the town and countryside'.[19]

However, what the Commission set out was not the product of original thought, establishing fresh points of departure in policy. On the contrary, the proposals reflected accepted white thinking in the four colonies, and far beyond, on the problems of finding a *modus vivendi* with fellow-citizens regarded as being lower on the cultural ladder. The Commission, following its conventional course, was displaying none of the singularity of vision of latter-day Afrikaner nationalists who dressed up segregation in new philosophical and theological clothes, at a time when the rest of the world was moving decisively, if regretfully, away from it on political, diplomatic and humane grounds.

In March 1905 Milner's long term of office came to an end at his own wish. Balfour confirmed the importance of South Africa in the British Government's eyes by sending Lord Selborne to succeed him. Selborne was First Lord of the Admiralty and had done important work with Admiral Lord Fisher in strengthening the Royal Navy. Before that, Selborne was Under-Secretary of State for the Colonies and was thus Chamberlain's deputy through the crucial years between 1895 and 1900. Milner regarded him as his great stand-by. 'No less ardent an imperialist than Milner, his methods were, however, less precipitate and forceful.'[20]

It seemed clear to Milner as he took passage homeward that his grand design had failed. There was no prospect of British immigration on a scale that would tip the balance of power in favour of the imperial interest as he saw it. The 1904 census had shown that the Boers were in a majority and that this was likely to increase. The white population of the Rand had grown from a few scattered families in 1886 to 117 000, or rather more than one-third of the total white population of the Transvaal and Swaziland. The Boers were growing faster for they married young and had large families while the British settlers were often single, there being only sixty-one women to every one hundred men in Johannesburg.[21]

The Transvaal had not been transformed into an outpost of England. The Boers had neither been cowed nor persuaded into acceptance of the Empire; indeed they were better organized and more subtly led than ever before. He had failed either to consolidate or to inspire the British. The enthusiasm which he evoked from his colleagues did not extend far beyond the small circle of the administration. He could point to remarkable achievements – to new railways built and planned, to improvements in irrigation and agriculture, to the foundations of local government, on the English pattern, in the towns, to telegraphs and telephones, to better police and prisons – but these represented only the beginning of the grand design.[22]

The historian of Union, Professor L M Thompson, wrote:

On balance … there can be little doubt that Lord Milner and the Unionist Government wrought harm in South Africa. Encouraging unattainable aspirations among British South Africans, increasing anglophobia amongst Afrikaners and doing little to improve the prospects of the non-Whites they made it immeasurably more difficult for the people of South Africa to establish for themselves a stable and humane society.[23]

Thompson's summing up has long been generally accepted among historians. More recently Milner's role has been re-examined, not only in terms of short-term achievement but within the broad framework of the imperial interest which was his prime allegiance. The revisionist historians Shula Marks and Stanley Trapido have argued cogently that in this context Milner succeeded better than he realized, for he and his associate officials laid the foundations of a state which not only 'reflected the demands of twentieth-century British imperialism but also fulfilled them'.[24]

168

Unquestionably, his aggressive attempts at anglicization not only ignored the opportunities of winning allies among the Afrikaner people but actually served to re-unite them, and to stoke the fires of a new nationalism.

Yet, though he failed to impose what he saw as the best solution, he did set a stamp, in only three short years of peace-time rule, that would endure. On that base, the alternative policy of conciliation that was now followed by Whitehall would secure for Britain for fifty years an ally with the administrative and economic strength, including, in particular, a thriving gold mining industry of unique strategical importance, that would make that relationship highly advantageous. When finally there did emerge the independent Afrikaner republic which Milner feared, South Africa nonetheless remained an integral part of the West and, as the dominant regional power, would continue to fill a vital link in the global defence chain.

Selborne would by personal choice have extended what has come to be called Milnerism, but it was not to be except in diluted form, for he would almost immediately have to conform to a different political philosophy. It was already clear when he arrived in April that the long reign of the Unionist Government in Britain was coming to an end. It had incurred odium over war and taxes, had split over the issue of imperial preference or free trade, antagonized Non-Conformist and trade union opinion. The Chinese controversy provided the Liberal Opposition with a useful cudgel with which to belabour Balfour's failing administration, and to rally to Campbell-Bannerman's side all the disparate liberal and labour elements who sought to bring down the Government.

On 21 March 1904, Campbell-Bannerman had moved in the British Parliament an unsuccessful motion of censure on the Unionist Government for approving the Labour Importation Ordinance. The debate revealed what was to become a main line of attack, the suggestion that the terms of the Ordinance were 'uncommonly like slave laws'. The debate saw too what was to become a classic line of Unionist defence – that other ordinances permitting similar labour, often under stricter conditions, had been approved by the Liberals when they were last in power. There followed, on 26 March, a monster procession in Hyde Park in which 50 000 trade unionists and other supporters took part carrying banners. There was strong white labour advocacy involved in the campaign of protest.[25]

In his September letter that year, the Bishop of Hereford put the view of the more extreme opposition to the employment of 'serfs' under conditions 'which partake of slavery',[26] while the spokesmen of labour asserted that Chinese were filling jobs which belonged properly to workmen unemployed in the depression that had Britain in its grip. Among those who went to England to speak for British labour on Liberal platforms was the Australian R L Outhwaite, now a trade union leader on the Rand, and F H P Creswell. Outhwaite had a nice line in vituperation – 'The mine owners of the Transvaal have waded through slaughter to a throne – They have shut the gate of mercy on mankind'.[27] Creswell was much more temperate. But as a former mine

169

manager who had employed black labour under the same conditions as the Chinese Creswell was forced into verbal gymnastics on the issue of slavery.

The only essential difference between the slave and the indentured worker, he declared, was that the slave was the actual property of his master for life, and received no pay, while the indentured Chinaman was the master's property for only three years and was paid. This was an essential difference from the indentured labourer's point of view, but he declared that there was no such essential difference in the degrading effect on those who depended for their prosperity on the labours of the indentured. However, he admitted that so far as the slavery cry was founded on the notion that Chinese or black labourers were brutally housed, fed and generally maltreated, it was a mistaken one.

> The mine owners want the first lot, at all events, to send good reports to their friends, and as Mr Dalrymple ... [of Farrar's Anglo French Company] said when the first batch arrived, 'they will have everything they want except dry champagne.' Personally, I think they would have got that, too, if they had expressed any particular desire for it. At present, at all events, and I speak from personal inspection, I should say that both natives and Chinese are, on all the best mines, in greater material comfort than they have ever been in their lives.[28]

The opposition in England had many strands:

> There was in England a well-established humanitarian tradition of safeguarding the interests of non-European peoples, a tradition largely submerged towards the end of the nineteenth century, but now resurgent. These were the days of a new criticism of 'capitalist' Imperialism, largely intellectual in origin, but filtering down in a debased form to the mass of the people. Campbell-Bannerman ... the Liberal leader, admired the writings of J A Hobson and the whole attack had much to do with the 'pro-Boer' feelings of left-wing Liberals, which engendered a hatred of Milner and the capitalists, whom they held to be guilty of the war and now of Chinese labour.[29]

Trade unionists were easily aroused by orators like Creswell and Outhwaite. One candidate went so far as to organize a parade of pig-tailed Chinese with handcuffs. Another organized a company of workmen supposedly deprived of jobs by Chinese indentured labour.

> ... there seems, indeed, good ground for saying that much of the opposition to the Chinese was totally illogical – the face of a leering Chinaman had an irresistible emotional appeal.[30]

On the eve of the General Election that was to bring him a landslide victory Campbell-Bannerman announced that importation of Chinese would be suspended pending an investigation. However, he was embarrassed to discover that it would be far too costly for the Liberal Government to abrogate licences already granted to mining companies to sign on for three years specified quotas of Chinese workers, numbers of which had just been issued. The Unionist Opposition now charged the new Liberal Government with gross inconsistency. Either the Chinese were slaves and should be repatriated, or they were not. Lord Elgin, formerly Viceroy of India, had become Colonial Secretary with the young and radical Winston Churchill, who had earlier crossed the floor of Parliament, as Parliamentary Under-Secretary. Campbell-Bannerman and Elgin now denied that they had ever said the Chinese were slaves while Churchill coined a famous phrase when he admitted that to call Chinese mineworkers slaves was a 'terminological inexactitude'.[31]

Campbell-Bannerman however responded to those who believed that the Chinese had been forced or tricked into service by offering state-aided repatriation to any Chinese mineworker who wished to terminate his service. Only 1,25 per cent availed themselves of the offer. (Some of those who did, re-engaged soon after their return to China and a few slipped through the net and arrived back on the mines.)

The Chamber, which had enjoyed a few years of close rapport with the Government of the Transvaal, now entered upon a new phase. The rapport with the Administration continued for a time but behind it was a government in Whitehall whose hostility was described at the Chamber's Annual General Meeting on 28 February 1907, as 'naked and unashamed'.[32] Moreover, the Chinese controversy which had helped the Liberals to power in Britain, had simultaneously 'reactivated the Transvaal British population politically and sharply divided it'.[33]

[1] Eighteenth Annual Report of the Transvaal Chamber of Mines, 1907, p 341.
[2] Report of the Superintendent of Foreign Labour, 1905-1906, quoted in the Seventeenth Annual Report of the Transvaal Chamber of Mines, 1906, at p XXIX.
[3] Annual Report of the Transvaal Chamber of Mines, 1904, p XLIX.
[4] A P Cartwright, *Doctors on the Mines: A History of the Mine Medical Officers' Association of South Africa: 1921-1971*, p 136.
[5] Grey, p 310, quoting the Commissioner of Mines, Colony of the Transvaal, 3676/1906, G M E Minute to the Secretary for Mines, Pretoria, 24 September 1906.
[6] B K Murray, *Wits: The Early Years: A History of the University of the Witwatersrand Johannesburg and its Precursors: 1896-1939*, p 3 et seq.
[7] *Ibid*, pp 13-14.
[8] Annual Report of the Transvaal Chamber of Mines, 1904, p 251.
[9] The equivalent of R8 million in 1984 terms, it was added to £200 000 donated by his partner Wernher in 1910. Beit also bequeathed £25 000 to Rhodes University, Grahamstown.

[10] B K Murray, p 28.

[11] *Ibid*, p 29.

[12] *Idem*.

[13] Reeves, pp 110, 228.

[14] Fraser and Jeeves, eds, pp 314–315, letter from Sir Lionel Phillips, London, to H R Skinner, Johannesburg, dated 12 July 1918.

[15] Sixteenth Annual Report of the Transvaal Chamber of Mines, 1905, p LXII.

[16] *Ibid*, p LVII.

[17] Grey, p 412.

[18] Annual Report of the Transvaal Chamber of Mines, 1905, p LXVIII.

[19] M Legassick, 'Ideology and Social Structure in Twentieth Century South Africa', quoted in Marks and Trapido, p 79.

[20] S B Spies, 'Palmer' in *Dictionary of South African Biography*, II, p 532.

[21] Le May, p 168.

[22] *Ibid*, pp 175–176.

[23] L M Thompson, *The Unification of South Africa: 1902-1910*, quoted by Spies in C F J Muller, ed, *Five Hundred Years*, at p 366.

[24] Marks and Trapido, p 56.

[25] Reeves, pp 146, 148.

[26] Mawby, 'The Political Behaviour of the British Population of the Transvaal', p 286.

[27] Reeves, p 234.

[28] F H P Creswell, Pamphlet: *The Chinese Labour Question from Within: Facts, Criticisms, and Suggestions: Impeachment of a Disastrous Policy*, p 83.

[29] Reeves, p 135.

[30] *Ibid*, p 239.

[31] *Hansard*, 22 February 1906, quoted in V Bonham Carter, *Winston Churchill as I knew him*, p 137.

[32] Annual Report of the Transvaal Chamber of Mines, 1906, p LXXIII.

[33] Mawby, 'The Political Behaviour of the British Population of the Transvaal', p 87.

CHAPTER THIRTEEN

The Generals Strike Back

'... we have got the Government of the country .... We are in for ever now!' declared Smuts in March 1907 in the aftermath of the General Election that swept Louis Botha's *Het Volk* (The People) to power in the Transvaal. He was speaking to Sir Percy FitzPatrick, whose defeat of Sir Richard Solomon in Pretoria South Central had been the only fly in the ointment for *Het Volk* (and when you looked close enough the fly vanished).

FitzPatrick riposted: 'For five years, perhaps.' Smuts came back instantly and almost fiercely: 'No, that's where you keep on making the old mistake! Not five years, fifty years! For ever!'[1]

Forever is a long time, but so far Smuts has not been proved wrong.

The thirty-seven-year-old Smuts could be forgiven his moment of jubilation for he was the architect of Afrikaner victory. It was he who had discerned the opportunities created by the often ugly face of nineteenth-century capitalism, by the war guilt of the liberals in Britain, by the political divisions that arose among the British settlers in the Transvaal. He perceived that if he could exacerbate the divisions and re-unite and reactivate the Boers, *Het Volk* would be in with a chance. He and Botha bound, where they could not heal, the wounds of Afrikanerdom, bringing back into the fold of the *Volk* the *hensoppers* who had surrendered after the fall of Pretoria, and even the National Scouts who had thereafter borne arms for the British. They personally assured Campbell-Bannerman of the new-found loyalty of the Afrikaner to Crown and Empire (a promise that Botha and Smuts would do their utmost to honour), encouraged the British Liberal Party in their distaste for magnates, and won the battle of words before the committee, under Sir Joseph West Ridgeway, which would give *Het Volk* the vital edge by its drawing of electoral divisions. From this firm base, Smuts sought allies among former foes, and from the embryonic white labour movement. And he encouraged Botha to enter into an agreement with English-speaking allies that, in the event of their joint victory, *Het Volk* would serve under the prime ministership of Sir Richard Solomon, the brilliant barrister who had held the office of Attorney-General in the Cape and Transvaal Governments successively.

FitzPatrick's upset victory over Solomon in Pretoria put paid to that arrangement, and Solomon moved off-stage to become the Transvaal's agent in London (and later South African High Commissioner). Botha became Prime Minister. With Solomon went the prospects of the more liberal Cape's ascendancy in the Union that would follow three years after, and of John X Merriman's becoming the first Prime Minister of the Union of South Africa. Instead, Boer generals would share office across a span of forty years, until succeeded by more ardent apostles of the basic dictum that 'The Nationalist Afrikaner must rule in South Africa'.

Capitalism had entered the twentieth century with its image tarnished by the behaviour of the big American trusts, and by big corporations in Europe and the British Empire, including the questionable activities of certain mining entrepreneurs in South Africa. Rand millionaires who lorded it in mansions in London's Park Lane and Johannesburg's Parktown had been caricatured since the Jameson Raid. In November 1902 the stereotype was given satirical life by the character 'Hoggenheimer of Park Lane' in the London comedy 'The Girl from Kays' by Owen Hall. The Cape cartoonist Boonzaier adopted the character with relish. The picture of Hoggenheimer, swollen with profits and rich living, would be exploited to influence the political unfoldment in South Africa for many years to come. Sir Keith Hancock, the distinguished historian and biographer of Smuts, gives a lively picture:

> The creature first appears in the Smuts Papers in a letter from Merriman dated 4 June 1904; he reappears in a letter from Outhwaite, a radical Australian journalist, dated 27 March 1905; thereafter he becomes a frequent and, indeed, a welcome visitant. One feels quite sorry to lose him after 1907, when Smuts took responsibility under Botha for the good government of his country, and quickly learnt that the resources of the Rand were the indispensable foundation of South African economic life, and that men like Farrar and FitzPatrick bore no close resemblance to Hoggenheimer and Co.[2]

Coincidentally, as the new century began, Marxist philosophy, socialism, syndicalism and trade unionism were coming to the ascendant.

> The turn of the century was thus a critical time for working men throughout the Western world, and especially the English-speaking world, for it saw the rapid growth of social and political consciousness and agitation on class lines amongst them. Within the British Empire, that growth was accompanied by a most significant extension of their organised political strength.[3]

Capitalism became a useful dirty word to the whole Marxist-trade union spectrum, and indeed to any politician (including capitalist politicians) short of a stick to beat an enemy or rally support for a cause.

Smuts was one of those quick to attack capitalist conspiracy. (He was even quicker to drop his attacks once *Het Volk* was in power.) In June 1903 he wrote

174

to *The Times* stigmatizing 'the utter and naked selfishness' of the financiers and their 'general interference in the politics of the Transvaal from the days of the Jameson Raid up to the present ....'[4] He declared the existing Government of the Transvaal to be almost completely dictated by the mining magnates. Setting sights on responsible government, Botha and Smuts operated closely with British liberals like Emily Hobhouse and Hobson, and took every opportunity for political advantage offered by the behaviour of the Chinese on the mines. In February 1905 the Generals founded *Het Volk* as a sectional Afrikaner movement and began to organize openly.

The party concentrated power in the Head Committee which could dissolve subordinate bodies which did not follow its dictates. It 'exercised a discipline over its members and commanded an obedience which resembled conditions in the commandos of 1902 rather than in the Republic of 1899'.[5]

The Afrikaner political revival that followed was in part a response to Milner's emphasis on anglicization. It was accompanied by a cultural revival based on the establishment of Christian National Education schools for Afrikaans children under the wing of the Dutch Reformed Church, and financed partially from the republican funds acquired by the generals,[6] and from other sources in the Netherlands. Botha and Smuts shrewdly combined the refusal of any co-operation with the Transvaal Administration, and of any responsibility for it, with loyal and conciliatory professions to the Liberal leaders in London. Towards them, they adopted a posture of reasonableness, and were careful to suppress among their supporters agitation for the revival of the old republics.[7]

Political division among the British was first focused on the constitutional future of the Transvaal. Clearly official rule could not long endure in a society with democratic roots, and responsible government would have to be granted before long. The majority of the British believed however that a too precipitate introduction of responsible government would hand power back to the Boer. They sought an interim arrangement that would allow the British population and electorate time to grow. They accordingly opted for representative government, that is a legislative chamber with nominated officials who would retain executive power, and with elected members who would give expression to the views of the electorate. The Progressive Association (or 'Progressives') was formed in November 1904 in support of this policy. The Transvaal Responsible Government Association (the TRGA or 'Responsibles') was formed in the same month to campaign for immediate responsible government. Both groups drew from similar levels of British Transvaal society, including mining, commerce and the professions, but the Progressives had by far the greater support. Both supported the importation of Chinese labour on economic grounds.

Through the Kruger years the mine-owners were chary of involvement in politics because they were dependent on direct and cordial relations with the regime which would be damaged by sustained public opposition. When the British Administration took over, those inhibitions were removed. Entry into

175

public life was open to all, and in a mining community it was natural that some mine-owners should emerge as political leaders. Farrar, FitzPatrick and Chaplin became prominent in the Progressive Association because they were the outstanding English-speaking personalities of the reconstruction era, and not because they represented mining houses. The houses were often critical of the Milner Administration, none more so, FitzPatrick apart, than the partners of the Corner House.[8]

The Responsibles were at first in the happy position of opposition parties elsewhere in that they could concentrate on destructive tactics, even using them to conceal the lack of alternative policies. They could join with *Het Volk* in writing off promotion of English-speaking interests by the Progressives as the work of jingos and racialists. For their part, the Progressives found that resistance to popular government inevitably involved them in defence of the unpopular Crown Colony Administration. They led with their political chins, encouraging their opponents to declare the Progressives to be 'the party of the magnates' and by derivation of the Chamber of Mines which, by derivation again, was alleged to have an unholy influence on the Milner/Selborne Administrations.

In truth, the Progressive Association was the only conventional and democratic political party of the reconstruction era. After the first annual congress in February 1905 it expanded its organization over the whole Transvaal. By September Farrar, who had been elected President at the congress, could report that there were forty-three branches and thirty-two thousand members. The Association was a mass party with branches and members who controlled an annual council of delegates. Each branch was entitled to one delegate for twenty-five members with a maximum of six. As Johannesburg always constituted a single branch it was never entitled to more than six delegates.

> Even assuming that the mining leaders wished to dominate the Association and that the Rand branches of the Association were prepared to be dominated – an extremely unlikely eventuality, when one considers the composition of the Johannesburg branch – no such domination of the whole Association could have been achieved under this Constitution.[9]

The charge that the Chamber of Mines dominated the Progressive Association has been propagated so vigorously that even illustrious historians have fallen into the trap of accepting it. Thus, Hancock wrote:

> ... the Smuts-Merriman assault upon the big capitalists, despite its lamentable demagogic lapses, was sound not merely in tactics but in principle. For it was the Chamber of Mines which financed and controlled the Progressive party, and it was the Progressive party which whipped up jingoistic and 'racialist' emotions among the English-speaking community.[10]

Hancock gives no authority, quotes no source. He seems to have absorbed this assumption through the pores, as it were, in his study of the voluminous papers stemming from Smuts's demagogic days in the bitter aftermath of defeat. Hancock and other historians who have accepted this assumption are mistaken.

In fact, the fundamental nature of the Chamber precluded it from controlling or financing a political party. All parties were represented among its members, whose fees provided its only source of income. The members included the powerful Robinson and Albu Groups whose heads were not supporters of the Progressive Party. On the contrary, Robinson and his local representative J W S Langerman were hostile, and not only to the Progressive Party. In February 1906 Robinson took his companies out of the Chamber in a dispute over black recruiting. (Although, oddly, his companies remained for a time thereafter members of the WNLA). Politically, Robinson supported the Responsibles and later *Het Volk*, and would have been delighted to expose any political jerrymandering in the Chamber. So would H C Hull, who represented the Pullinger gold mining interests, and was to serve as Treasurer in Botha's Transvaal Ministry and as the Minister of Finance in his first Union Cabinet. T M Cullinan, the founder of the Premier diamond mines, and R Goldmann were among Chamber members opposed to the Progressive Party. Strange, of JCI, who was President of the Chamber at the time of the foundation of the Progressive Party, did not support it, which is perhaps why Milner, otherwise an admirer of his, thought Strange 'politically unreliable'.[11] Neither did De Jongh, representing the Sammy Marks Group, who succeeded Chaplin as President in 1906, support the Progressives, nor Louis Reyersbach of the Corner House who succeeded in turn as President in 1907. Reyersbach was indeed an often bitter critic of the Transvaal Administration. A study of the Archives of the Chamber of Mines revealed no hint of any link with the Progressive Party. The historian Mawby found, too, that the FitzPatrick Papers, particularly revealing historical documents in their record of frank and private communications between colleagues, do not 'reveal or suggest any political activity involving the Chamber as a corporate body'.[12] Mining houses were free to support the party of their choice financially; there would have been no sense in even trying to do so through the Chamber, because it would have been impossible to obtain the consensus of opinion which is the essential base of action through that institution.

Nor in fact did mining houses control the Progressive Association financially. 'Late in 1906 ... [its] finances were in a poor state'.[13] Farrar and FitzPatrick tried to raise funds in London from gold mining companies there. According to Mawby, Farrar failed 'to get "a bob"' from anyone.

FitzPatrick, through one of the Wernher, Beit & Co partners, F Eckstein, managed with considerable difficulty to get £10 000 from the Rhodes Trustees. Eckstein was quite emphatic that if the Progressive Association wanted any further money it would have to get it in the Transvaal. Clearly neither Wernher, Beit & Co nor anyone else in London controlled the Progressive Association through its finances, as *Het Volk* and the TRGA alleged in 1906.[14]

The opposition British party in the Transvaal, the TRGA, unlike the Progressive Association, was never a conventional political party. It did not enjoy mass support and soon gave up the attempt to enrol members and form branches. The Association's President, E P Solomon, two vice-presidents and its committee were elected at the inaugural meeting and continued to hold office indefinitely.

> In practice the control of the Association appears to have fallen into the hands of an even smaller group of men, as J W Quinn discovered in April 1905 over the most crucial decision the TRGA ever took, that to ally with *Het Volk*.[15]

The TRGA was in essence a group of independent and dissident politicians of British origin.

> In the parlance of political science, the TRGA was ... a cadre party and a caucus party, decentralised, weakly knit, and without membership. In contrast, the Progressive Association was a mass party, with membership and branches, centralised and firmly knit. The two Associations are almost classic examples of these two types of party. The latter is identified with the modern popular and democratic party. The former is identified with the older patronage party under the control of a powerful clique. It is of the greatest significance that the realities of the party structures were the exact reverse of the images cultivated by many of the Progressive Association's opponents, above all Smuts, and still accepted by historians as accurate.[16]

The accession to power of the Liberal Party in Britain, and the announcement that it would grant responsible government to the Transvaal, removed the main *raison d'être* of the Responsibles, for the Progressives at once dropped their opposition to self-government and began to organize for the coming election. The Responsibles were forced to seek political allies because they lacked popular support or any alternative policy of substance. They were in consequence pushed into the arms of those who denounced mining capitalists. Embarrassingly, the Responsibles were themselves capitalist in character. Their President, E P Solomon, was a director of Barnato's for 1905 and 1906, while almost all leaders of the diamond industry supported them, Cullinan becoming a vice-president. The Responsibles endeavoured to draw a line between foreign magnates who battened on the Transvaal and decent, homegrown magnates who supported the TRGA. But

> Of all the heads of these houses, the one who most fully accorded to the TRGA's image of a 'bad' capitalist – the absentee Park Lane magnate of

178

flamboyant vulgarity and shady exploitation – was its friend J B Robinson.[17]

Robinson would become a supporter of *Het Volk*, too, and be rewarded by Botha with a baronetcy in 1908.

The TRGA was also in the difficult position of supporting Chinese labour which its potential ally vigorously opposed. It resolved the problem by means of a compromise agreement with *Het Volk* whereby the Labour Importation Ordinance was to be left operative for five years. The alliance cost the TRGA support. J W Quinn, the former anti-Chinese campaigner, broke with the party, warning that supporters would not 'allow themselves to be marched under the attractive banner of Responsible Government into a political ambush'.[18] However, the compromise was only of temporary worth as the fear aroused by outrages in the countryside led to renewed *Het Volk* attacks on Chinese labour and gave a new focus to its attack on mine magnates. These attacks were paralleled by those of the nascent labour movement.

The Transvaal Miners' Association (TMA) had been formed in April 1902 following a strike on Crown Reef over the introduction of piece-work for artisans. It received impetus from a strike on Creswell's Village Main Reef later in the year in opposition to experiments with the use of unskilled whites in place of blacks. The miners saw this white labour policy, as they would later see the use of Chinese, to be aimed at cheapening white jobs. They struck in protest at the extra work involved for members of their Association, and compelled changes in working arrangements.[19]

The tradesmen involved in the strike at Crown Reef formed a joint strike committee with the miners, out of which grew at the strike's end the Johannesburg Trades and Labour Council. It at once widened its scope to become the Witwatersrand Trades and Labour Council. For the next eight years, the WT & LC would be the leading labour organization in South Africa. Headed by Peter Whiteside and W H Andrews of the Amalgamated Society of Engineers, it soon became the political voice of white labour.[20]

The spokesman of the WT & LC attacked mine-owners and the Milner Administration and demanded responsible government. However, the political voice was not a strong one, the membership of the Council being only about 3 000. Most of the 15 500 miners and artisans did not support them,[21] nor did they feel threatened by the arrival of the Chinese which resulted in the creation of 4 700 new jobs for skilled whites in some eighteen months. Nevertheless, the labour leaders provided a further divisive element in the English-speaking electorate. Various groups formed the Independent Labour Party to prepare for the elections and a labour representation committee was formed to provide further co-ordination.

Another development was the formation in mid-1906 of the Reform Club, giving expression from outside the main political parties to renewed hostility to Chinese labour which was encouraged by the victory of the Liberal Party in Britain. Creswell was prominent among the membership which was small but vocal. As *Het Volk*, the Reform Club and the labour movement led a new hard line of opposition to Chinese labour, the TRGA tended to drift into political isolation. It sought escape from its predicament by a political reshuffle which freed it from past political commitments. It was announced that the TRGA would dissolve and be absorbed in a new Association with wider scope. The formation of the Transvaal National Association (The 'Nationalists') followed on 20 September 1906. It absorbed the TRGA, the Reform Club and the Transvaal Political Association of Pretoria. E P Solomon became President. Creswell joined its executive and Hull became prominent among leading members. The Association adopted the policy of the Reform Club on Chinese labour – no further importation and repatriation at the end of existing contracts.[22] The TRGA had given in to *Het Volk* pressure. Once again a political manoeuvre cost the Association influential friends and failed to win new ones. Labour was not enticed, and organized separately for the coming election.[23] However, the leaders of the new Association were able to draw the political rewards of a closer accord with Botha and Smuts. It also provided the Liberal Party in Britain with a British party in the Transvaal to which it could look hopefully as a bridge between the British and Afrikaner races, and a potential holder of the balance of power in a Transvaal Parliament.

In April 1906, the new British Government had sent out a committee under Sir Joseph West Ridgeway, an unsuccessful candidate in the British General Election, to draft an electoral plan for the Transvaal. Ridgeway and his colleagues examined nearly five hundred witnesses and received more than seventy deputations across nine weeks.[24] They did so in private so that witnesses could not be cross-examined by people of different view, or possessing the political understanding of the Transvaal which the Committee wholly lacked. Ridgeway and his colleagues were hostile to the Progressives but charmed with Botha and Smuts. They lent a ready ear to Smuts's written declaration that the central issue was not the hostility between Briton and Boer, but the relationship between the mining industry and the rest of the country. The Committee also accepted *Het Volk's* statement that it did not aim at or expect a position of prominence in the new Government, despite a warning to the contrary from Selborne.

The Committee duly reported:

> Their leaders do not desire a Boer majority in this, the first Parliament. ... They have, therefore, throughout these negotiations admitted that there should be a British majority, but they claim that that majority should not be so overwhelming as to reduce the Boer parliamentary party to impotence, and above all, that it should not be a Rand majority, fulfilling the dictates and carrying out the policy of absentee and other capitalists.[25]

There was a voters roll available which had been drawn up under the so-called Lyttelton Constitution, an earlier proposal for representative government abandoned by the British Government. *Het Volk* objected to this roll being taken as an authentic record, claiming that the figure of 46 000 voters for the Rand was 3 000 voters higher than that given by the census. (The election showed the actual number of voters on the Rand to be 54 972.[26]) Ridgeway set aside the roll on the grounds that justice must not only be done but be seen to be done. On the census figures he used to delimit constituencies the Rand and the country districts were counterbalanced and a possible British majority transferred into a certain minority. This lesson in what can be achieved by winning the delimitation debate has not been lost in South Africa.

The Ridgeway Committee, it is believed, was searching for a formula that would lead to a broad-based administration under the control neither of *Het Volk* nor of the Progressive Association, it being left to the National Association to provide the balancing element. If this was indeed what the Committee set out to achieve, it botched the job. The results of the General Election were:

Het Volk	37
Progressives	21
National Association	6
Labour	3
Independents	2

Het Volk polled 24 123 votes, the Progressives 17 635 and all others 19 496. The house divided had fallen with a crash that shocked the British population of the Transvaal.

Not for the last time, the allegedly magnate-dominated Press had failed to swing an election for the English-speaking interest. *The Star, The Transvaal Leader* and the *Rand Daily Mail*, the principal dailies, gave solid support to the Progressives. Much political capital was, and would be, made out of the fact that Barnato's and Eckstein's had interests in the Argus Group which owned *The Star*, and that Eckstein's had interests in *The Leader* through its shareholdings in *The Cape Times*. The *Rand Daily Mail* was founded in September 1902 by H Freeman Cohen who had extensive mining interests. It ran into financial difficulties and was acquired by Abe Bailey in a rescue operation in 1905. He soon leased the paper to an independent syndicate of which he was not a member.

In fact, mining houses acquired interests in newspapers, but did not interfere in the running of them. The Boards, on which they were represented, chose editors with the greatest care, and thereafter gave them a free hand so long as their newspapers yielded a reasonable return on investment, and this approach is current today.

Mawby has pointed out that the degree of subjectivity normal in political reporting today was offset in 1907 by the contemporary practice of reporting major speeches, regardless of political tone, verbatim, sometimes at eight-column length.[27]

After carefully researching the role of newspapers in the run-down to the 1907 election, Mawby concluded:

Rand mining men thus held a considerable shareholding in the main Johannesburg papers. Their influence over the editors of the papers was only indirect and slight, however. The editors, furthermore, confined the expression of subjective views (whether their own or imposed upon them) to their editorial columns and cartoons. Outside these columns, the Johannesburg papers were remarkably open-minded and objective. Mining house influence over their actual news coverage and news reports was in practice non-existent. The Progressive Association's advantageous position with regard to the press was a consequence of the editorial support it enjoyed, and not of unfair reporting. The Johannesburg papers are, as a result, a most valuable historical record of this period.[28]

Both Botha and the British Liberal Party were probably surprised at the scope of the election victory, and some of the Liberals may have been disappointed too. But the power passed to Botha and Smuts by Campbell-Bannerman was in part a genuine gesture of magnanimity, and in part a clear-sighted appreciation that it was the most effective way, in the circumstances of the time, to strengthen the British Empire. Campbell-Bannerman died the following year. Though he did not live to see the fruits of his decision, Churchill did and throughout a long life never doubted the worth of it.

The grant of responsible government to the Transvaal, and the Act of Union which followed three years after, left many South African problems unsolved, especially those related to black, Indian and Coloured citizens. However, these constitutional changes did serve to build bridges between Afrikaner and British; Botha and Smuts did serve the cause of reconciliation and fight off those who wanted to wreck it; and they did contribute to the building of South Africa as a stable capitalist state of great economic strength, in ways that most effectively safeguarded the British Imperial interest.

[1] Mawby, 'The Political Behaviour of the British Population of the Transvaal', p 409, quoting FitzPatrick, 'The Solomon Election' in *Scraps of History*: FitzPatrick Papers A/MSS VII.

[2] Hancock, *Smuts: 1. The Sanguine Years*, p 202.

[3] Mawby, 'The Political Behaviour of the British Population of the Transvaal, p 230.

[4] *Ibid*, p 247, quoting Botha to L Hobhouse, 13 June 1903: Smuts Papers Vol II, No 226, pp 100–106.

[5] Le May, p 173.

[6] T Cameron and S B Spies, eds, *An Illustrated History of South Africa*, p 223.

[7] Mawby, 'The Political Behaviour of the British Population of the Transvaal', pp 212–213.

[8] *Ibid*, pp 262-264, 269-270, 271, 276.

[9] *Ibid*, p 269.

[10] Hancock, *Smuts: 1. The Sanguine Years*, p 202.

[11] Mawby, 'The Political Behaviour of the British Population of the Transvaal', p 273, quoting Milner to Selborne, 14 to 18 April 1905: Milner Papers, Volume 1194.

[12] *Ibid*, p 273.

[13] *Ibid*, p 272.

[14] *Idem*.

[15] *Ibid*, p 280.

[16] *Idem*.

[17] *Ibid*, p 279.

[18] *Ibid*, p 221.

[19] E Katz, *A Trade Union Aristocracy: A History of White Workers in the Transvaal and the General Strike of 1913*, pp 47–48, 54, 79, 80–82.

[20] Mawby, 'The Political Behaviour of the British Population of the Transvaal', p 239.

[21] *Ibid*, p 246.

[22] *Ibid*, pp 293, 299-300.

[23] *Ibid*, pp 301–302.

[24] Le May, p 197.

[25] *Ibid*, pp 197–198, quoting Ridgeway Report, I, para 27.

[26] *Ibid*, pp 199, 211.

[27] Mawby, 'The Political Behaviour of the British Population of the Transvaal', p 364.

[28] *Ibid*, p 365.

CHAPTER FOURTEEN

Topsy-Turvy

The new Transvaal Government was sworn in on 4 March 1907, at a time when economic depression reigned in British South Africa. It was at once confronted with a crisis of unemployment and poverty among whites on the Reef. Two months later the Rand was struck by the first serious strike by white miners, the forerunner of much worse upheavals to come in 1913, 1914 and 1922. Immigrants, especially from Britain and Australia, had laid the foundation of trade unionism on the Rand, and evolved the policy which would establish 'the trade union aristocracy' of white skilled labour, that came to characterize the movement.[1] The drive to labour élitism had some roots in the successful campaign to keep Australia white, but stemmed more importantly from the South African situation. It was to prove increasingly attractive to Afrikaners forced into urban slums by a shortage of farm land and rural depression, creating the 'poor white' problem that was to plague South Africa for thirty years.

> In the early stages of mining in South Africa it had been possible for the white miners to maintain their position through their scarcity value. As the nature of mining altered, through increased mechanization and with the consequent development of semi-skilled jobs, the situation changed considerably, and there were now an increasing variety of jobs which could be performed by non-whites. Scarcity was thus no longer enough, and to maintain their supremacy something more was needed: organization through trade unions provided part of the answer and political pressure the other.[2]

Not surprisingly, the views of the mine-owners were diametrically opposed to those of the white unions. By 1906, the cost of underground operations in the new deep-running mines had reached critical levels, and ore was yielding lower values. The narrow profit margin attainable made it difficult to attract the investment capital needed for development and shaft sinking.

Thus, mine-owners were not sympathetic to union attempts to preserve artificially the scarcity of skilled and semi-skilled labour. They were already paying more for skills than in other mining fields, and inadequate training and inefficiency were undeniably a serious problem.[3] Moreover, the increasing availability of races other than whites able to perform semi-skilled work seemed to justify reduction in rates paid to whites, especially where the work done was largely to boss gangs of blacks or Chinese who needed less supervision as they gained in experience. The mine-owners, too, had watched the disruptive effects of trade unionism and syndicalism elsewhere, and were determined to be uncompromising in the face of aggressive industrial action.

Thus it was a drive to increase the productivity of highly-paid skilled and supervisory workers that was the crux of the confrontation of 1907. Early in that year there was public and perhaps provocative criticism of white output by mine-owners and managers. Unemployed whites, many of them encamped on the open veld, lent a ready ear when the radical Australian Outhwaite warned a mass meeting on the Market Square on 25 April that mine-owners intended to reduce the number of white employees. In the same month, hundreds of unemployed marched to Pretoria, and a deputation met Smuts. He could offer only road construction work at Louis Trichardt at 2s a day. He expressed the hope that unskilled work on the mines might be opened to them.[4]

At the beginning of May, Knights Deep, of the Gold Fields Group, gave notice of a reduction of the rate paid to white miners for breaking out rock in the stopes. It was claimed that high rates had been granted because of excessive water in the mine, but that pumping had since much improved working conditions. The reduction now sought to bring wages back in line with those on other mines.[5] At the same time, the mine management ordered the white miners to increase from two to three the number of rock drills operated under their supervision. This practice was in operation on other mines. It is an interesting sidelight that the Creswell experiment on Village Main Reef in 1902 had involved the operation of three or more machines by unskilled white labourers, supervised by a single skilled white miner.[6] It was open to the miners on Knights Deep to offset the rate reduction by breaking more rock with the additional machine, and even possible for them to earn more money than before.[7] Knights Deep has been dubbed an unlucky mine which, one way or another, encountered every misfortune a gold mine could be expected to encounter.[8] On this occasion its attempt to get a better return from wages paid certainly sparked a chain of unhappy events. On 1 May, the miners on Knights Deep, encouraged by Mathew Trewick, General Secretary of the Transvaal Miners' Association (TMA), came out on strike.

The TMA set a pattern of union practice when, within a few days, a deputation called on the Minister of Mines, Jacob (Japie) de Villiers. The deputation argued that it was not possible to work safely and control the handling of explosives while supervising three machines; and that the increased exposure to dust would increase the already high risk of silicosis. De Villiers, like his successors in office, tried to reassure the miners, promising justice and telling them that a commission would be appointed to investigate mining practice.

The deputation did not complain to him about the reduction in stoping rates, presumably because they realised that their case was not strong. Stoping contractors were the élite of the workforce, earning far more than the average white wage which at the time was £30 5s 0d a month. Gold Fields published figures showing that the Knights Deep stopers were earning from £80 to £120 per month, and up to £150 a month, amounts which astonished the public of the day, although there was sympathy for the rugged and hazardous conditions under which the miners worked. An investigation by the Government Mining Engineer showed that the Knights Deep miners on the reduced rates would still be better off than those on neighbouring mines.[9]

The TMA began to drum up support and the strike spread to other mines where there were no real grievances. Mine managers countered by replacing strikers from the unemployed in the tents on the veld, some of them Afrikaners finally forced off the farms as the locusts ravaged the crops. (On one occasion locusts even held up traffic in the streets of Johannesburg.) The strikers responded with picketing, assaults on scabs and general unrest and violence. All affected mines were given police protection. On 10 May Outhwaite declared at a meeting at Village Main Reef:

A strike is like a war and that party succeeds which strikes quickest and with most effect. Now war has been declared on the part of the miners against the financiers who control these mines.[10]

At a further meeting the next day the Union called on the Chamber to agree to arbitration, failing which a general strike would be called.

Arbitration by an impartial outsider has always appealed to trade unions, because it is in the nature of arbitrators to 'slice the cake down the middle', while unions, which for tactical reasons tend to inflate demands, have only to put forward a big enough cake to assure themselves of a satisfying slice. Trotsky indeed urged workers always to put their demands so high that any concessions by employers would appear trifling. Not surprisingly, employers in 1907 and since have tended to reject arbitration at any price. Nor could the Chamber intervene. It was not then an 'employers' organization', and was not empowered by statute, or by decision of its members, to act for mines. Industrial relations were conducted at mine level.

The TMA, as threatened, called a general strike from 22 May, but the workers, including the key hoist drivers, did not respond. However, the strike continued to spread among miners in haphazard fashion, and within a few days more than 4 000 were on strike. On 24 May, the Government, alarmed by mounting violence, called in the British garrison, and 200 miners, who had marched on the Croesus mine, were dispersed by a cavalry charge of the 2nd Dragoon Guards.[11]

The number of mines affected soon reached forty-nine. A miners' deputation set another union tradition when they appealed to the Prime Minister, and interviewed him on 1 June, the day after his return from the Imperial Conference in Britain, the first of five such interviews during the strike. The depu-

186

tation presented a petition with 3 271 signatures calling for the formation of an arbitration court. They also protested against the Government's use of troops. Botha pointed out that, bearing in mind the large number of blacks and Chinese accommodated on the mines, it was the Government's clear duty to prevent violence and maintain law and order.

Botha promised the miners nothing, but on 4 June he wrote to Reyersbach, the current President of the Chamber:

> I am very loth to interfere in questions between employers and employed until the last means of conciliation as between themselves has been exhausted. There is, besides, the further difficulty that no legislation exists at present to authorise the Government to act as I am asked to do.
>
> At the same time, it is admittedly neither in the interest of the State nor of the mining industry that the strike shall continue indefinitely. Besides the financial loss incurred, bitterness is created between employer and employed which may continue to react adversely to the tranquillity and settlement of industrial conditions generally.
>
> I would, therefore, ask you and the groups represented on your Chamber whether it is not possible even at this late hour to meet your late employees to discuss the situation frankly with them and to see whether, at any rate, some temporary arrangement cannot be made until the Government commissions now inquiring into the various aspects of the industrial situation have reported to the Government.[12]

Reyersbach replied that the Chamber had no authority to act, and suggested that Botha receive a deputation from the mining houses. This meeting, which Reyersbach attended for the Corner House, took place on 7 June. The mine-owners made it clear that they were not interested in arbitration, and did not recognize the union leaders' right to negotiate for the men. They suggested that the Mining Regulations Commission, which the Government had just appointed, should investigate the question of the number of machines that could properly be supervised by a miner. The strike dragged on until the end of July and then fizzled out after sporadic violence and outrage.

At the monthly meeting of the Chamber on 18 July, Reyersbach commented:

> I believe that the strike may be considered over. I have every reason to think that the men are heartily sick of it, and that they have decided wherever possible to go back to work. I am afraid that some of them might find some difficulty in obtaining employment, merely for the reason that their places have been taken by other men, but I can assure all those men who have gone out that with very few exceptions they will all be reinstated wherever possible – wherever an opening can be found. Naturally the mine managers will be loth to take back those men who have taken an active part in the campaign. I am referring to the agitators and to the principal leaders, but I hope

that even these men will see that though the managements of the various mines will not employ them again there is no bitterness against them. ... the men who have agitated and who in many cases have committed assaults against other men would not be safe of their lives if they did go back, as those men would retaliate. ... we hope that the men have learnt a lesson and that they will be less foolish in the future.[13]

The pious hope expressed in the final sentence would not be realized. The lessons the miners learned were about organizing strikes, and about challenging the legitimacy of the State. They would be put to use in the future. After the strike, trade unions throughout South Africa gained members. The Labour Party received a boost which would help it win seats in 1910.[14]

Lionel Phillips, now back in Johannesburg and again at the head of the Corner House, had written to Wernher during the strike:

The whole position is really getting topsy-turvy; a Boer Government calling out British troops to keep English miners in order while the Dutchmen are replacing them in the mines. ... You may rest assured that we are taking every advantage of the strike to reduce working costs as far as possible.[15]

His attempts at reconciliation with the *Het Volk* Government had already featured in his letters, because he had launched a sustained effort to reach a rapport with Botha and Smuts. With the return of a Boer Government former political associations had become an embarrassment to the Corner House.

Steps were ... undertaken to detach the firm from public controversy .... Without much loss to the business, FitzPatrick was eased into retirement ....[16]

The mining industry had come to realize, through past and bitter experience, that it could not win a challenge to the government of the day, and that it must seek an accord in matters mining and economic, whatever the political differences might be. However, Chaplin and Farrar, together with FitzPatrick, took their seats in the Transvaal Legislative Assembly and continued in active opposition to the Government. Nor did Phillips win as much influence as he believed; to an extent Botha and Smuts used him as a useful counterweight to Chaplin, Farrar and other supporters of the Opposition.[17] Botha and Smuts were prepared to 'sup with the devil', but 'we do our best to use long spoons'.[18]

The economic historian, David Yudelman, in a study of the relationship between State and mining industry in South Africa since 1902, has concluded that it quickly became one of mutual dependence or symbiosis, even in times of overt conflict.

The state-capital relationship in South Africa, then, was not characterized by the dominance of Afrikaner nationalism, as the liberal, nationalist, and pluralist schools of thought have all argued. Nor was it characterized by the dominance of capital, as the Marxists and neo-Marxists suggest. Rather, it was (and is) characterized by symbiosis. Individually, neither the state nor big business could attain hegemony in South Africa; combined, they very early established an effective dominance. The dominance has endured until the present, surviving important changes in the composition of both the state and capital.[19]

Yudelman in his lively re-interpretation of past events, takes his conclusion a step too far, for though the industry achieved much from co-operative action, it would never be able to divert the basic political thrusts of successive governments sufficiently to enable it to reach a position of dominance.

At the outset, also, Yudelman in his enthusiasm for his thesis, paints an over-coloured picture of the degree of state support won by the mine-owners in the Strike of 1907 – 'the explicit sacrifice of white labour on the altar of this new relationship'.[20]

Once in power, Botha and Smuts could hardly not have grasped the Transvaal's critical dependence on mining revenue, nor have failed to discern the importance of overseas investment to develop the country, and the need to create an atmosphere attractive to it. It was clearly in the interest of the new and somewhat shaky administration to keep the sheave wheels turning, and not to lend encouragement to wildcat strikes and disruptive stoppages.

It was incidentally important to Botha to find work for unemployed Afrikaners, a factor which made it politically unwise to insist on the re-employment of strikers. Politically wise above all, Botha chose to sit on the fence, encourage the parties to the dispute to conciliate, while he endeavoured to keep the peace on the picket lines. In this he was helped neither by the intransigence of the mine-owners, nor the reckless behaviour of the miners which cost the Union public sympathy. The miners' case was not only ill-conducted, it was not strong. The TMA had not yet won recognition from the employers. Nor was there yet state machinery to intervene in disputes and bring about a settlement.

This gap Botha endeavoured to bridge with the Industrial Disputes Prevention Act of 1909, which prohibited strikes or lockouts without prior reference to a board. The Act, modelled on Canadian legislation, laid down negotiating procedures for employers and employees involved in a dispute which it was hoped would buy time for tempers to cool, and for the forces of public opinion to encourage conciliation. It was introduced with the support of the mining industry, and with opposition from labour only on points of detail. However, the effectiveness of the Act was diminished by the absence of machinery of compulsion, and by the reluctance of the employers to recognize the right of unions to negotiate for their members. Importantly, the Act established a Department of Labour and revised the duties of the Inspector of White

Labour, a post created immediately after the strike and filled, for the few months remaining before his death, by the prominent and respected labour leader, A S Raitt.[21]

Botha also appointed the Mining Industry Commission and the Mining Regulations Commission with the intention of enhancing the efficiency of the mining industry, and improving working conditions on the mines. The Mining Industry Commission was appointed on 2 May 1907, under the chairmanship of Andries Stockenström, MLA, an advocate who was the scion of a distinguished Afrikaner family. Its members were the labour leader, Peter Whiteside, MLA, J A Hamilton, who had been Joint Manager of JCI in Johannesburg from 1896 to 1905, Creswell, and C H Spencer, a prominent consulting engineer. The Commission was directed to inquire into the means best calculated to increase the employment of white labour. It was given other functions as well, but Stockenström, Whiteside, Hamilton and Creswell chose to concentrate on the white labour issue. In their report dated 10 March 1908, known as the Creswell Report, they recommended, in the teeth of the expert evidence, that the employment of white manual labour in place of black should be forced on the industry.[22] This, they recommended, should be achieved principally by setting a limit on the number of blacks engaged outside British South Africa (mainly Moçambicans) which should be extended to a total ban within three years; by making a legal requirement the employment of a skilled white miner for every machine drill operated; and by requiring the owners of mining ground to find continuing employment for a given number of white men, or to relinquish their rights to it.

The remaining member, C H Spencer, had investigated the 1902 white labour experiment on Village Main Reef and reported that there was scope for the employment of whites in selected unskilled jobs. This may explain why Botha appointed him as a member of the Mining Industry Commission of 1907. However, Spencer, in his Minority Report, stated that the majority of commissioners had misinterpreted the expert evidence. He commented

> ... the whole of the calculations ... seem to me to be much too academic and hypothetical to give grounds for recommending the Government to take measures which it is admitted mean a revolution in the whole labour system, and the effect of which would be disastrous to the mining industry, and to the country as a whole, if the calculations of the Report turned out to be wrong.[23]

He recommended instead, as the best way of employing more whites, the development of the mining industry and the opening of new mines; the establishment by the Government of a miners' training school; housing assistance, and reducing the cost of living by lower taxation.[24]

The Majority Report reflected Creswell's perception that 'under the conditions imposed by civilization and modern principles of government the people who do the work of a country will in the end inherit it'.[25] He was not wrong, but no amount of wishful thinking was going to create the conditions of the Californian or Australian gold-fields on the Rand. This report from an influential ally came as an embarrassment to Botha, for no responsible government in power could contemplate the gamble with its principal revenue source involved in the white labour proposals. Creswell's report was doomed to be deferred, referred and finally given its quietus by a select committee of the Union Parliament. Disillusioned with *Het Volk* and his former political allies, Creswell resigned from the National Association in 1909. There lay ahead for him a tumultuous political career as leader of the South African Labour Party.

One important result which flowed from the Minority Report of the Mining Commission, and support for it from the industry, was the establishment of the Government Miners' Training School (now College) which would become an enduring joint venture of the Government and the Chamber. This was inaugurated in 1910 by setting aside a whole level of the Wolhuter mine as a training area in which white trainees performed all the tasks of mining without the assistance of black labour. Another result was a general improvement in the standard and availability of housing for white workers.[26]

The change wrought by the strike in the racial composition of the white labour force had come to stay. From now on the proportion of Afrikaners on the mines would steadily increase and the proportion of Cousin Jacks and other immigrants decrease. Mine-owners also co-operated with the Government in providing increased opportunities for unskilled whites, who might later become skilled, and many of these were Afrikaners.

After the strike, the mine-owners were successful in reducing the contract rates earned by white stopers. As a result average white wages fell steadily from £363 a year during the strike to £333 in July-December 1908.[27] Working costs per ton milled fell by 16,2 per cent, contributing substantially to the prosperity that now returned to the Rand.[28]

The Mining Regulations Commission was appointed in May 1907 under the chairmanship of Dr F E T Krause to make recommendations for the better protection of the health and safety of men working in mines, and to examine such matters as the measuring of contract work and the certification of engine drivers. It did a thorough job and only finally reported in 1910, although certain legislation, the Mines, Works, Machinery and Certificates Bill, was recommended in an interim report and passed by the Transvaal Parliament in 1909. It was concerned particularly with proper management and government inspection of mining operations. In its final report the Commission published some 320 proposed regulations embodying its recommendations. It found for the miners in the 1907 dispute by recommending, solely on health grounds, that no miner should be required to supervise more than two machines. In fact, changes in working conditions would make practical an increase in the number of machines supervised. It also recommended an eight-hour day. The proposals were referred to the Union Government for consideration with the proposed Mines, Works and Machinery Bill, which did not come before Parliament until 1911.

Most importantly, the draft regulations also contained the structure of a statutory colour bar to which the Chamber objected. As long ago as 1896 it had suggested in vain the use of the word 'competent' instead of 'white' in regulations so as to permit the employment of Coloured men in certain occupations.[29] In response to the draft regulations the Chamber again raised the issue. On 19 November 1910, it wrote to the Secretary for Mines:

> ... my Chamber desires to call the attention of the Minister to the frequent recurrence throughout the regulations of the term 'white person.' In its opinion either the word 'competent' or 'reliable' in each case should be substituted for the word 'white.'[30]

In the political climate then prevailing, its representations would be unavailing in the application of the regulations in the Transvaal.

Meanwhile, as the number of Chinese workers fell from its peak in 1907, the WNLA absorbed the Chamber of Mines Labour Importation Agency. At the Annual General Meeting of the WNLA, on 9 April 1908, the Chairman, Perry, gave the following assessment of the achievement of the CMLIA:

> It is not a small matter for a private company to enlist an army of 50 000 men, to collect them at sea-ports, to transport them over 8 000 miles of sea and many hundred miles of rail, and at the expiration of a certain time to transport them back again, without a single mishap. Powerful Governments, with all the resources of a country behind them, have carried out smaller undertakings less successfully.[31]

Richardson, the historian of Chinese labour on the mines, has commented that this 'was a succinct summary of the flavour of this aspect of the exercise'.[32] The last Chinaman returned home in March 1910.

Adventure and high drama, as well as routine care, marked the journeys of the Chinese miners. Perry went on to recall:

> Though the voyage is certainly a difficult one, we have only had one shipwreck – I mean that of the 'Swanley' at the end of 1904, and in that case, although there were over two thousand men on board, and, I think, less than a dozen Europeans, though the ship was disabled far from any port, and the whole of the passengers had to be landed and kept for four weeks on an uninhabited island, they were eventually brought to their destination with the loss of only a single life.[33]

[1] Katz, pp 1–13.

[2] Doxey, pp 116–117.

[3] Grey, pp 262–263.

[4] *Ibid*, p 248, quoting the *Rand Daily Mail*, 2 May 1907, p 5.

[5] *Ibid*, p 268.

[6] *The Transvaal Leader*, 23 May 1907.

[7] Grey, p 265.

[8] Cartwright, *Gold Paved the Way*, pp 109–110.

[9] Grey, pp 267, 288.

[10] *Ibid*, p 271.

[11] 'The Miners' Strike', *The Star*, 25 May 1907.

[12] Annual Report of the Transvaal Chamber of Mines, 1907, p 33.

[13] *Ibid*, p 433.

[14] D Yudelman, *The Emergence of Modern South Africa: State, Capital and the Incorporation of Organized Labour on the South African Gold Fields, 1902-1939*, p 76.

[15] Fraser and Jeeves, eds, p 179.

[16] *Ibid*, p 144.

[17] *Ibid*, p 145.

[18] W K Hancock and J van der Poel, eds, *Selections from the Smuts Papers, June 1902-May 1910*, Volume II, p 292.

[19] Yudelman, p 7.

[20] *Ibid*, p 71.

[21] Annual Report of the Transvaal Chamber of Mines, 1907, p XLVII.

[22] Extracts from the Majority Report of the Mining Industry Commission, 1907. (Annual Report of the Transvaal Chamber of Mines, 1907, pp 150-158.)
Chamber of Mines Archives: File: M4 1908, C VI 4: 'Mining Industry Commission'.

[23] Extracts from the Minority Report of the Mining Industry Commission, 1907. (Annual Report of the Transvaal Chamber of Mines, 1907, pp 158-163.)

[24] *Ibid*, p 162.

[25] Extracts from the Majority Report of the Mining Industry Commission, 1907. (Annual Report of the Transvaal Chamber of Mines, 1907, paragraph 91, p 158.)

[26] Grey, pp 294–295.

[27] *Ibid*, pp 287-288, quoting the Annual Report of the Government Mining Engineer, 30 June 1910, p 38.

[28] *Ibid*, p 287, quoting M.M. 1227/1908: Memorandum by R N Kotzé, Government Mining Engineer, 29 July 1908.

[29] Annual Report of the Witwatersrand Chamber of Mines, 1896, p 61 *et seq.*

[30] Twenty-First Annual Report of the Transvaal Chamber of Mines, 1910, p 43.

[31] WNLA Limited, Chairman's Speech at the Sixth Annual Meeting, 9 April 1908. (Annual Report of the Transvaal Chamber of Mines, 1907, p 541.)

[32] Richardson, p 165.

[33] WNLA Limited, Chairman's Speech at the Sixth Annual Meeting, 9 April 1908. (Annual Report of the Transvaal Chamber of Mines, 1907, p 541.)

CHAPTER FIFTEEN

The Coming of Age

The decision taken by the Campbell–Bannerman Government in 1906 to end the importation of Chinese labourers into the Transvaal came at a time when black workers were again hard to come by. Intensive competition erupted, collapsing the co-operative arrangements carefully put together by the WNLA in the British colonies. Mines bid against each other at wages above the agreed scales and began to poach labour as they had in the bad old days. As a consequence, the Chamber was compelled progressively to release mines from the controls imposed by WNLA membership on recruitment in British South Africa.

The Chamber was soon in difficulties in Moçambique as well, for J B Robinson was quick to sense an opportunity to fish in troubled waters.[1] He had been close to Kruger in the pre-war period, and was perhaps smarting at the positive distaste shown towards him by the British Colonial Administration. Nor was he a man who could work happily in partnership with others. In particular, he nursed a long-standing grudge against Wernher, Beit and the Corner House. Alfred Beit had given him his initial stake – and the basis of his fortune – on the Rand, but to Robinson's chagrin Beit proved the more far-sighted in evaluation of mining land. When the two quarrelled and dissolved their partnership, Robinson sold to Beit the Robinson mine at what proved to be a bargain-basement price when the mine's fabulous riches were proved.[2] Robinson was easily embittered, and he developed a lively antagonism for other mining leaders as well.

As the labour war hotted up, Robinson from 'his mansion in Park Lane … moved to destroy WNLA'.[3] He perceived the advantage that might lie in the hostility between the new Liberal Government and the mining magnates. He complained that the WNLA exercised its *de facto* monopoly in the allocation of Moçambican labourers in a manner that discriminated against his Group – and was inefficient to boot. He did so in terms well calculated to appeal to Lord Elgin, the new Secretary of State for the Colonies, who was noted for his hostility to all forms of monopoly.[4] Elgin's young radical Parliamentary Under-Secretary, Winston Churchill, was a receptive listener, too. Robinson succeeded in winning the support of the Imperial Government. To the fury of Selborne's Colonial Administration, Churchill announced in the House of

Commons that Robinson would undertake independent recruiting in Moçambique, and that the Imperial Government would assist in obtaining the necessary authority. Selborne pointed out in vain that competitive recruiting in Moçambique would jeopardize the controls built up to protect black workers. He warned Elgin: '... the experience of the Native Affairs Department is that the mines of the Robinson group will take no measures involving any expense for the welfare of their coloured labourers which cannot be enforced by law'.[5]

Despite this, the Imperial Government continued to give support to Robinson. As a result, he succeeded in obtaining from the Portuguese the grant of a licence to recruit in Moçambique. Now clearly in breach of the constitution of the WNLA, Robinson Group companies were compelled to resign from that organization in October 1906. However, the Moçambique Government, recalling past unhappy days of blackbirding, continued to be opposed basically to competitive recruiting. They refused to grant Robinson the right to sub-agents and African runners without which the licence to recruit in the vast hinterland of Delagoa Bay was of little practical value.

The *Het Volk* Government now grasped what the Imperial Government would not, that to unleash the recruitment free-for-all of British South Africa on Moçambique would be highly disruptive of the mining industry and disastrous for the struggling Transvaal. No doubt, too, Botha was conscious of the pickle in which his ally Robinson had landed himself through his inability to recruit effectively for his mines in Moçambique. In any event, Botha broke the deadlock by advising Elgin that recruiting in Moçambique must be carried on 'through a single organised body [and] the Witwatersrand Native Labour Association must be kept in existence for this purpose'.[6]

The organization built up by the WNLA in Moçambique was substantial. It covered an area of 50 000 square miles, half of it too arid to sustain population. Some eight hundred thousand people lived in the remaining 25 000 square miles, a density only exceeded in southern Africa in Basutoland. The WNLA operated eighty-three stations, in addition to offices in Lourenço Marques and Ressano Garcia, and employed a permanent staff of 24 whites and 1 450 blacks. Runners were sent to tour the kraals and invite men to engage for work on the mines. Those who agreed were guided to the nearest WNLA resthouse.

Thence they are taken on from station to station, being supplied free of charge with food for the journey, and with guides if required, until they come to the nearest European camp. Here they receive rations of meat and wine, as well as mealie meal, and are given a blanket apiece. ... the native is given the choice of returning to any mine on which he may have worked before, or of going forward for general allotment. ... any friends of his coming from the same kraal are allowed to enlist for the same mine if they wish. Twice a week a travelling gang leaves the camp, and proceeds, generally in charge of a European, either to the nearest point on the line of railway, or to the nearest port of embarkation on the coast.

The natives are thus finally collected in the Association's Depot at Ressano Garcia, which is capable of holding two thousand men. Here they are medically examined, and any who are found to be unfit for work are either sent back to their kraals or kept in the Depot for rest and feeding; or, if necessary, treated in the hospital attached to the Depot. At Ressano Garcia the natives enter into their contracts of service before the Portuguese Fiscal. They are each supplied, by way of advance, with a complete suit of clothing, suitable for the colder climate of the Transvaal.

Twice a week a special train is despatched from Ressano Garcia, which brings the natives to the Witwatersrand.

> ... from the day that he steps out of his kraal until he reaches the Witwatersrand the native is lodged and fed without any expense to himself....[7]

In the belief that the Transvaal's best interests required the continuance of these arrangements, Smuts, the Colonial Secretary, set to work to heal the breach within the mining industry, and to draft terms of settlement. As a result, the Robinson Group rejoined the Chamber in September 1907 and the WNLA subsequently. Co-operative recruiting was restored in Moçambique. The Government undertook a general control over the WNLA and its articles were amended to provide for Government arbitration which would be binding in disputes among members.

The historian Jeeves after a close study of the period, concluded that it highlighted the extent to which the mining industry was dependent on the State for assistance in obtaining labour for the mines. While the leaders of the mining industry were substantially united in the formation of policy, they did not necessarily possess the power to impose its implementation on individual mines.

> ... The mining industry was brought into close association with government not because it was strong, united and able to impose its will but because it was divided in its councils and (at frequent intervals) crippled by destructive competition. For the Randlords, the relationship was rather one of dependence than of domination.[8]

Internal divisions and competition apart, no enterprise so all-embracing as the engaging of huge numbers of men across an ill-developed sub-continent could be hopefully contemplated without state assistance and co-operation. There was additionally a special onus on the Transvaal Government, which had backed repatriation of the Chinese, to help find the labour to replace them.

While the Government was able to restore the WNLA's pre-eminence in Moçambique, the renewal of co-operative recruiting in British South Africa would have to await the formation, under the aegis of the Chamber, of the Native Recruiting Corporation in 1912, an organization which the Robinson Group did not join until 1919.

In the interim, the Transvaal Government actively intervened to assist the mines. The Government Native Labour Bureau was established in May 1907 to popularize the Transvaal mines as a field of employment. H M Taberer was appointed its first director. Taberer, who had been Secretary to the Native Affairs Commission in 1903, was to become prominent in the Native Recruiting Corporation and famed among blacks in South Africa. The Corporation would become known to them as KwaTEBA, the house of Taberer, and the modern recruiting association perpetuates his name as TEBA (The Employment Bureau of Africa).

The Transvaal Government also succeeded in persuading the Natal Government to amend the Natal Touts Act in October 1907, thus opening its territory to recruiting from the Transvaal. The Transvaal Government then negotiated a new ten-year agreement with the Moçambique Government to replace the *modus vivendi* of 1901, renewing the labour agreement and guaranteeing the Portuguese a substantial share of rail and harbour traffic in its South African hinterland. The agreement became applicable to Union the following year, and was indeed a necessary preliminary to its foundation.

In total, the efforts made to improve recruiting and enhance working and living conditions on the mines led to a steady increase in the black labour force. The mine-owners' fears of disaster as a result of the repatriation of Chinese were not realized. In the years 1907 to 1909 the inflow of black workers more than balanced the outflow of Chinese, as a result of big increases from Moçambique and from the Transvaal and, especially, from the Cape, partly as a result of the depression in diamond mining and in the general economy of that colony.

An important legislative milestone in the first year of the new Transvaal Government was the passage of the Workmen's Compensation Act which became effective in April 1908. The insurance of mineworkers at work on a voluntary basis had been pioneered by the formation of the Rand Mutual Assurance Company in 1894, the original membership providing cover for the employees of three neighbouring companies. By 1900 membership had increased to forty-two mines, but a voluntary scheme had obvious drawbacks. The advent of compulsory insurance was welcomed by Reyersbach, on behalf of the Chamber, in his Presidential Address on 27 February 1908. The Act provided half-pay for workmen recovering from injuries at work and for lump sums payable on death or permanent disablement, the amount being related to earnings, subject to laid-down ceilings. The provisions applied only to white workers, and a separate, voluntary, and far less beneficial compensation scheme, introduced in 1905, was continued for black workers. However, provision for compensation for black workers would be made by the Union Parliament in the Native Labour Regulation Act of 1911. With the passage of time the Rand Mutual, acting under the aegis of the Chamber, would provide insurance for workers of all races in accordance with, or higher than, the statutory scale of benefits.

Reyersbach was succeeded by Lionel Phillips, back in the chair for the fifth time after a ten-year gap during his absence from the Transvaal. He too would be able to welcome a legislative milestone though he did so in somewhat muted tones. The event was the passage of the long-debated Precious and Base Metals Act of 1908, to be known, like its predecessors, as The Gold Law. Although it would be substantially amended over the years, it would continue in force until 1967.[9]

The Gold Law reasserted the traditional private ownership of rights to minerals and the vesting in the Crown of the right to mine for precious metals and dispose of them. The exploitation of base minerals was left to the owner of the mineral rights (who might or might not also own the land in which they were found). It retained the system by which the holder of mineral rights was entitled to a *mynpacht* or lease over a portion of private land on which gold had been discovered.

Most importantly, the Act introduced the system whereby the State could lease to any person the exclusive right to mine gold on land proclaimed as a public diggings. The effect was to secure for the State a share of the profits in gold mining operations undertaken to exploit the enormously valuable mining rights awaiting disposal. The new policy, incidentally, settled the long-standing controversy about *bewaarplaatsen*, or land set aside in pioneer days for surface plants, tailings dumps and water rights before it was realized that rich reefs ran under them. The Act vested the right of disposing of such land in the State. A Mining Leases Board was established in 1909, under the chairmanship of the Government Mining Engineer, R N Kotzé, and in the following year agreement was reached on the allocation of the first of the disputed areas.

The new Gold Law reflected the Government's acknowledgement that mining on the Rand was a massive operation involving the complex aggregation of capital funds. The throwing open of proclaimed areas for public pegging gave way to one by which the Government invited tenders for mining under lease.

Kotzé described the advantages of the new system as he saw them:

> Not only will the State be able to share, to a larger extent than hitherto, the profits to be derived from the exploitation of its minerals, but the security in title and the absence of the necessity for satisfying vendors' interests will tend to encourage capital, and will offer advantages which have not been present in the past.[10]

The system has been more cynically described as one in which the State takes none of the risk, but assures for itself a lion's share of the profits. However, the mining historian Cartwright puts the Gold Law of 1908 in a more kindly light:

> ... it marked a turning-point in South African history for, from that day to this, the State has been a partner in most gold mining enterprises, to the

immense benefit of successive Ministers of Finance and the taxpayers.[11]

The most spectacular, early result was the flotation of the Government Gold Mining Areas (Modderfontein) Consolidated Ltd on the East Rand in 1914. The lease was obtained by JCI and the shares were eagerly subscribed by the public. After a difficult start, the mine would produce profits amounting to £80 million over forty-five years, the major portion of which went to the State.[12] The proportion of such lease mines would grow steadily in the years ahead.

At the beginning of 1909 the outlook of the industry seemed to be set fair. The gold production of the Transvaal had risen the previous year by 600 000 ounces to 7 000 000 ounces. Phillips in his Presidential Review on 25 February 1909, was able to report encouraging evidence of values persisting at depth and to declare that current indications pointed to the possibility of mining being continued on the Rand in the twenty-first century. He concluded:

> Never before in our history has the outlook been brighter. No mining industry can be absolutely described as permanent, but all the indications point to the life of the Rand being almost entitled to that description.[13]

However, Phillips ended on a sombre note, commenting on a disaster fresh in the public mind. In the previous month, the Transvaal had experienced un-precedented floods. As dams overflowed, the May Consolidated Dam at Knights collapsed and its water poured into the Witwatersrand mine, trapping 152 men in the workings with huge loss of life. By an incredible rescue oper-ation the water-level was lowered and twenty-three men brought to the surface alive eight days after the flood. Phillips paid tribute to the heroism and self-sacrifice displayed in rescuing fellow-workers that was to become a cherished tradition on South African mines.

Phillips was succeeded as President by J W S Langerman, J B Robinson's deputy, who represented *Het Volk* in the Transvaal Legislative Assembly. His year of office was notable for the reduction of costs through the amalgamation of mine properties, and the centralization of crushing plant, a trend evident for several years. A memorable event in mining history was the formation of Crown Mines, to be one of the great mines of the world, from a string of smaller properties on the central Rand.

At the Annual General Meeting on 24 February 1910, Langerman digressed from the record of economic progress to refer to the coming of Union as 'the brightest and happiest page in the history of South Africa, a country which for hundreds of years has been the scene of racial animosity, discord, suspicion and warfare'.[14]

When the Inter-Colonial Customs and Railway Conference met in Pretoria in May 1908, the agreements cobbled together five years before were in tatters.[15] Instead of tinkering with the fiscal patchwork, the Conference adopted a motion calling for closer union of the colonies. It was proposed by

Smuts and seconded by John X Merriman, who had become Prime Minister of the Cape. These two were to emerge as the principal architects of Union. Thirty delegates from the four colonies were appointed to a National Convention to draft a constitution. The Transvaal delegation consisted of Botha, Smuts, Schalk Burger, De la Rey and Hull, and three Progressive Party members, Farrar, who was Leader of the Opposition, FitzPatrick and H L Lindsay, a Johannesburg attorney who represented the Troyeville constituency. There was general accord in the Transvaal about the benefits of Union, and amity in bringing it about. Farrar declared that on the issue there was no division between the political parties.

Remarkably, the constitution of the Union was settled between the colonies in less than a year and approved by the British Parliament in August 1909. It was agreed that Union would come into being on 31 May 1910. Lord Gladstone was appointed Governor-General of the new state, and it fell to him to select the political leader to head the new Government. Botha and Merriman were the possible selections, but Botha emerged clearly as the more acceptable politically.

For a while Botha toyed with the idea of a 'Best Man', or coalition government, suggested by Jameson, the Leader of the Opposition in the Cape. Botha discussed the idea with Phillips and FitzPatrick at Bad Kissinger in Germany in 1909, where they met as fellow-patients 'taking the waters'. Afterwards he discussed the idea further with Jameson on a fishing holiday they took together in Scotland.

At the same time he was negotiating with Afrikaner political leaders in the Cape and the Free State, and no doubt it was the political realities that led Botha to abandon the concept of coalition. He set about promoting the amalgamation of the Transvaal's *Het Volk* with the Free State's *Orangia Unie*, led by General J B M Hertzog, and with Merriman's South African Party-*Afrikaner Bond* alliance. He wrote to the leading Cape Afrikaner, F S Malan, on 29 December 1909:

> I ... have come to the conclusion that it is in the interests of the Afrikaners to open our arms wide ... to ensure that we will control the Government of South Africa forever .... If we miss this chance now, it will never occur again.[16]

Botha duly took office on 31 May 1910, and formed a cabinet of political allies, plus two former Natal ministers. Smuts became Minister of the Interior, Mines and Defence, Hull Minister of Finance, F S Malan Minister of Education, and Hertzog Minister of Justice. Merriman was offered a cabinet post but declined to serve under Botha. Botha set 15 September as General Election Day and campaigned as a leader of a loose alliance of *Het Volk*, *Orangia Unie* and the South African Party-*Afrikaner Bond*. His principal opponents, the Cape Unionists, the Free State Constitutional Party, and the Transvaal Progressives, merged formally to become the Unionist Party. Their leader was

Jameson. The policies of the opposing parties in the election did not differ radically. Both favoured one South African nation, ties with Britain and immigration from Europe. Both shared a lack of policy towards Indians, Coloureds and blacks. Their manifestos were thus remarkably similar. The principal difference was that the supporters of Botha were in the main Afrikaans-speaking and those of Jameson English. They found a focus of controversy in the fiery personality of Hertzog whose particular vision of 'South Africa first' seemed to many English-speaking people to mean Afrikaner domination. The accord of the National Convention dissolved as the election degenerated into a racial clash between Afrikaners and English South Africans.[17]

In the event the Botha alliance was returned to power but with a majority less overwhelming than Botha had hoped for.

Predictably, the Unionists were attacked during the campaign for being the party of the mining magnates. Phillips, standing in Yeoville, pointed out that only five of forty-nine Unionist candidates were financiers. Presumably he counted himself, Farrar, Chaplin, Abe Bailey and Jameson, and omitted FitzPatrick who had retired from business. The six were certainly leading lights of the Unionist Party, and, with the exception of Bailey, were all elected to Parliament. FitzPatrick brought off yet another sensational upset by defeating Botha in Pretoria East by ninety-five votes. Likewise Farrar triumphed over the Minister of Finance, Hull, by a large majority at Georgetown, Germiston.

For their part in bringing about Union Jameson and Farrar were created baronets in 1911, and FitzPatrick KCMG, but none of the magnates figured significantly in Parliament. Phillips saw his function in Parliament to be the education of his own party to the importance of the gold mines; to guard against Government attempts to plunder the industry, and to counteract the propaganda of Labour members.[18] For the next five years, he made a useful contribution to debate but is remembered best for promoting legislation that established the National Botanic Gardens at Kirstenbosch. It is hard to imagine a more splendid memorial to public spirit. Phillips was created a baronet in 1912 for this and other public service. In the following year, while walking to the Rand Club, he was shot three times by a crazed assassin. FitzPatrick happened on the scene and saved Phillips's life by whisking him to hospital in his car.

Farrar resigned from Parliament at the end of 1911 to attend to the affairs of the ailing ERPM. Jameson resigned from the Unionist leadership and from Parliament in 1912, partly for health reasons, and returned to England, where he became Chairman of the Charter Company. Chaplin resigned in 1914 to become Administrator of Southern Rhodesia and was made KCMG in 1917. In 1920 he was made Administrator of Northern Rhodesia in addition. He retired from office in 1923 and returned to Parliament in 1924. By then the Unionist Party had ceased to be, its members being generally absorbed into Smuts's South African Party.

FitzPatrick was a Member for ten years after 1910, but, as often happens, he did not make the impact on Parliament that he did on the hustings. Johannesburg is indebted to him for the founding of its zoo in 1904 on land donated earlier in memory of Hermann Eckstein, and as its enthusiastic patron thereafter; ex-servicemen remembered him for his purchase after the Great War of Delville Wood, scene of the heroic fight to the death of the South African Brigade in 1916, which he presented to the nation. He was credited by some with the idea of the two-minute silence long observed on Armistice Day. Thereafter, his major distinction was his pioneering work for the citrus industry.[19]

In a parliament which, like the colonial parliaments that preceded it, was heavily representative of the farming interest, the mining industry would not exert influence by the eloquence of its representatives or their seats on government benches. It would have to do so by the weight of its argument and by the persistence with which it was presented; and by pointing to the flood of mining revenue 'plundered' by the Government and diverted to the extension of agriculture, railways, state infrastructure and other industries generally.

On 4 November 1910 J G Hamilton, of the Consolidated Mines Selection Company, who had succeeded Langerman as President of the Chamber, represented the industry at the opening of the First Union Parliament. It was just twenty-one years since the formation of the Chamber of Mines. In that time it had come of age in experience as well as in years. The Chamber had helped to create a great industry, a city, and a modern state, in a rural wilderness. It had helped to build a body of laws, to set in train a migration of men across seas and continents. It had spoken for mining in forceful, measured terms that could never wholly be denied. It had witnessed its President sentenced to death for leading a revolution, and seen all it had helped to build go down to war and seeming ruin. It had helped to rebuild industry, city and State, and to create Union from the vortex of that war. Against this kaleidoscope of history the Chamber was destined to play a momentous role in the cavalcade of events that now unfolded.

[1] Jeeves, 'The Control of Migratory Labour on the South African Gold Mines', p 22.
[2] R Ovendale, 'Robinson' in *Dictionary of South African Biography*, III, p 718.
[3] Jeeves, 'The Control of Migratory Labour on the South African Gold Mines', p 22.
[4] R Hyam, *Elgin and Churchill at the Colonial Office: 1905-1908: The Watershed of the Empire-Commonwealth*, p 532 and Note 4.
[5] Jeeves, 'The Control of Migratory Labour on the South African Gold Mines', p 25, quoting SNA, 60/989/1906, Governor, Johannesburg, to Secretary of State, 1 December 1906 (telegram, confidential).

[6] *Ibid*, p 27, quoting TAD, Union Native Affairs Department Archive (UNAD), 191/596, J C Smuts to L Reyersbach, 29 May 1907. CO 879/94/866 Selborne to Elgin, 17 June 1907 (separate, confidential).

[7] Annual Report of the Transvaal Chamber of Mines, 1906, pp 4–7.

[8] Jeeves, 'The Control of Migratory Labour on the South African Mines', p 28.

[9] Shilling, p 11.

[10] Grey, p 104, quoting Annual Report of the Government Mining Engineer, 30 June 1909, p V.

[11] A P Cartwright, *Golden Age: The Story of the Industrialization of South Africa and the part played in it by the Corner House Group of Companies: 1910-1967*, p 24.

[12] Grey, pp 108–109.

[13] Nineteenth Annual Report of the Transvaal Chamber of Mines, 1908, pp LXII, LXXVIII.

[14] Twentieth Annual Report of the Transvaal Chamber of Mines, 1909, p LXIV.

[15] Cameron and Spies, eds, p 226.

[16] Lewsen, *John X Merriman: Paradoxical South African Statesman*, pp 335–336, quoting A H Marais, ed, *Politieke Briewe, 1909-1910*, Vol. 1, Botha to Malan, 29th December, 1909, 1:56-57.

[17] B J Liebenberg, 'Botha and Smuts in Power: 1910-1924', C F J Muller, ed, *Five Hundred Years: A History of South Africa*, p 386.

[18] Fraser and Jeeves, eds, pp 5, 224.

[19] Hugo, 'Fitzpatrick' in *Dictionary of South African Biography*, I, p 293.

PART THREE

The Struggle for Survival

CHAPTER SIXTEEN

Confrontation and the Colour Bar

As the euphoria of 'closer-union' subsided, the new South Africa stood revealed as a nation bitterly divided. Whites regarded fearfully the mass of black, Coloured and Indian fellow-citizens, for the most part submissive, or sullenly biding their time. Citizens of British origin moved closer together in opposing their Afrikaner compatriots. Afrikanerdom was itself sundered by *broedertwis*. While some sought reconciliation, others turned to a separate nationalism. An influential few plotted the return of the old republics. Against this background, Capital and White Labour met in a confrontation of rare violence. Within five years the fledgling State would face successive revolutionary assaults on its right to govern.

In the year after Union, Parliament passed the Mines and Works Act, the statutory base of the mining operation. Its purpose was to control general working conditions and to ensure the safety and health of mineworkers.

Botha also employed regulations framed under the Act to fulfil his commitment to White Labour, by giving legislative sanction to the conventional colour bar evolved in the regimes of Kruger and Milner. The regulations specifically reserved to whites in the Transvaal and Orange Free State jobs in the management hierarchy, in the operation and maintenance of machinery, and in the general supervision of manual workers. In particular, regulations reserved the all-important right to hold a blasting certificate and the work of ganger, banksman and onsetter.

The definitions in the Act included:

'Manager' shall mean the white person appointed to be responsible for the control, management, and direction of a mine or portion of a mine or of works.

'Ganger' shall mean a white person in charge of workmen in one or more working places in or at a mine.

'Banksman' shall mean a white person stationed at the shaft-top, duly appointed by the manager to supervise the loading and unloading of persons in the cage, skip or other means of conveyance, and to give the necessary signals to the engine driver and to the onsetter.

'Onsetter' shall mean a white person appointed by the manager to have charge of the cage or skip underground in which persons are being raised or lowered and to communicate the necessary signals to the banksman or engine driver.

Regulations included:

(99) (1) (a) No person other than a white person shall conduct blasting operations in or about a mine in the Transvaal or Orange Free State.

179. The operation of or attendance on machinery shall be in charge of a competent shiftsman, and in the Transvaal and Orange Free State Provinces such shiftsman shall be a white man.

285. Certificates shall not be granted to any coloured person in the Transvaal and Orange Free State and certificates granted to any coloured person in any other Province shall not be available outside such Province.

The colour bar thus introduced effectively reserved all truly skilled mining and artisan work in the Transvaal for the white worker. In the clashes that followed, up to the great strike of 1922 and beyond, this area of skilled white employment would never be challenged seriously. The fierce contention that erupted was centred on the critical grey zone of employment in which whites, and, increasingly, blacks, performed unskilled and semi-skilled work. The lifting of the statutory colour bar introduced in the Mines and Works Act would remain a matter of occasional academic discussion but would not be regarded as a practical option.

However, Farrar's associate, H O'K Webber, who was President of the Chamber in 1911, pointed out the Government's inconsistency in permitting some relaxation of the colour bar in the Cape and Natal, but not in the Transvaal:

> The Act, with its regulations, is now in force. The latter deals with every conceivable subject connected with mining, but mainly with the protection of health and the safety of the employees, both white and coloured. There are regulations also dealing with the rights of the worker. In this particular I would warn the Government against legislation tending to militate against healthy competition amongst white workers. I would also warn the Government that the omission of disabilities upon coloured men in certain districts and the enforcement of them in others shows a vacillating spirit of inconsistency and a disinclination to face a difficult problem bristling with legal points.[1]

Webber had rightly indicated the element of political expediency involved by his reference to the anomalous substitution of the phrase 'competent person' for 'white person' in the application of the regulations to Natal and the Cape, thus acknowledging the important share of skilled work won by workers other than whites in these provinces. The Chamber already suspected that the Government's racial discrimination against the Transvaal mines was *ultra vires* but the matter was of such little practical moment that it would be more than a decade before it came before the courts. Challenging the statutory colour bar was simply not practical politics, and this situation, unhappily, would long endure.

The statutory colour bar introduced in 1911 was explained away at the time on the grounds that it was essential to safety in mining, and there was substantial support for the contention in the social circumstances of the day. The lifting of the colour bar would in fact have brought no more than a minor change in the composition of the labour force. The earning of the requisite certificate of competency for skilled work required not only literacy, in which blacks were almost totally lacking, but at least some measure of schooling at secondary level, and periods of training or apprenticeship which migrant tribesmen mostly did not work long enough to acquire. However, some had adopted mine work as a career and, advancing rapidly in skill and experience, outstripped the least skilful of the whites. For them, the colour bar was a cruel deprivation of the right to develop industrial skills and to earn a commensurate wage.

The Act included an important advance in the introduction of a statutory limitation on working hours. It laid down a maximum working day of eight hours at the face or working place, that is 'from face to face', excluding time spent *en route* to and from the shaft bank on surface, rather than 'bank to bank'.

This legislative limitation on working hours was approved in March 1911 by Lionel Phillips and his Unionist colleagues in Parliament, Farrar and Chaplin, giving ground under fiery attack by South African Labour Party leaders, Creswell and Walter Madeley. Their unauthorized committal of the industry caused a flare of schism in the Chamber's Executive Committee. Past-President Hamilton had to be restrained from moving an angry motion that the Executive Committee debate the justification for the continued existence of the Chamber.[2] Phillips commented calmly in a letter from Cape Town to R W Schumacher at the Corner House:

> I hear rumours of the Chamber expressing its disapproval of our conduct here in regard to the eight hours. I think such a course would be regrettable. The concurrence with the eight hours all round is going a long way towards knocking out the absurd proposals of the Labour people.[3]

Hamilton did cool down, withdraw his motion, and accept one declaring that steps should be taken to make clear to the Government and the public that the Chamber was the only official representative of the Transvaal mining industry.[4] Hamilton would be elected President for a second time in February 1912, only to die in office in the following July. He was succeeded for the remaining part of the presidential year by Max Elkan of A Goerz and Company.

The white miners who came to the Rand from Britain and Australia in the early days brought with them a tradition of all-round competence. Unhappily, with the passage of time, the tradition was weakened. The white miner was too often inadequately trained and content to do the minimum personally, leaving the maximum to the more experienced of the black workers in his charge.

At the time of the passing of the Mines and Works Act, around 25 000 white men were employed on the gold mines, or nearly double the number at work in 1904 when the Chinese were introduced. Of these about one-half were employed on surface in mill, cyanide plant, offices, mechanical workshops and the like. The 12 500 working underground included officials, that is mine overseers, section managers, shift bosses, foremen, and others in the line of management. Of the 11 000 workmen employed underground, some 3 000 were engaged in supervision of the breaking out of rock in the stopes by gangs of black workers in their charge. These were the super-aristocrats, paid by results on a contract basis and earning high wages when the ground was rich and easy. The remainder of the underground workforce were craftsmen or those engaged in a wide variety of tasks along transport ways or at the shafts. They included whites of a low educational standard in charge of black gangs.

By 1913, relations between management and its white labour force were abysmal. Partly as a result of the contract system then in vogue, the white labour force was highly mobile and workmen had not developed the loyalties to individual mines that prevail today. This was especially true of immigrant miners who came to the Rand to make quick money before returning to their homes abroad. They regularly changed their jobs in pursuit of more lucrative contracts, and relatively junior officials had the power to fire them, so that high turnover depressed productivity. Earnings were substantial but working conditions bad, with high risks of injury and of contracting miners' phthisis. Mine-owners displayed paternalistic and detached attitudes to the lot of the workers that were typical of the age, and shared with their counterparts in other mining countries a determination to restrain the growing power and recklessness of the trade unions. The militant response of the trade unions was equally typical and mirrored the industrial unrest of America, Australia and Europe. In South Africa however underlying fear of the black masses, and agitation about unfair competition in the workplace, added a cutting edge to the clash of management and labour.

During the 1907 Strike the union leaders had expressed fears that the mine-owners were trying to rid themselves of immigrant miners, with their tradition of trade unionism. By 1913, however, the South African unions were still firmly in immigrant hands. Their thinking had been greatly influenced by the visit of Tom Mann in 1910. Mann was the first Secretary of the British Independent Labour Party and one of the pioneers of the union movement in Britain.[5] Mann preached a militant industrial unionism with overtones of syndicalism, the concept of the right of the worker to control industry and to dominate the State. Syndicalism had found its full expression in the doctrine expounded in France in 1906 by the *Confédération Générale du Travail (CGT)* that 'it was a revolutionary organization which aimed at the seizure of economic power by means of direct action culminating in a general strike'.[6] In

South Africa, the trade union movement was greatly attracted by the potential of the general strike and of 'strikes in sympathy' by workers not involved in the dispute at issue. The labour historian, Elaine Katz, has demonstrated that the majority of trade union leaders did not seek to use the strike weapon to overthrow Capitalism and the State, but simply to better the position of workers.[7] Equally clearly, there was a militant minority that did have re-volutionary aims, and which was vocal enough to alarm mine-owners and the Government alike. Not only Smuts but Merriman, who could take a detached view in distant Cape Town, saw syndicalism on the Rand as a real threat to the security of the State.

Mann had emphasized that if trade unions were to be effective they must group together for common action. In particular, there was a need for a federation of unions that could wield effectively the weapon of the general strike. The Witwatersrand Trades and Labour Council had lost support after its failure to intervene effectively in the 1907 Strike. Thomas Mathews, Organizing Secretary of the Transvaal Miners' Association, Bill Andrews, organizer of the Amalgamated Society of Engineers (ASE), and other trade unionists accordingly established the Transvaal Federation of Trade Unions ('the Federation') in April 1911. It was to play a leading role in the industrial upheavals to follow. However, the South African Engine Drivers' and Fire-men's Association (SAEDFA), to which hoist drivers belonged, refused to join the Federation.

The Federation was composed solely of craft unions of skilled workers and did not represent the mass of semi-skilled and unskilled workers. It was not therefore a 'syndicalist' organization as such. Even though committed to the doctrine of the general strike, it had no means to compel constituent unions to comply with its decisions.[8] Nor was socialism a dominating philosophy within the trade union movement.[9]

By the end of 1912 industrial unrest among white workers in South Africa had reached the pitch where little would be required to precipitate strike action. Nowhere was this more likely to occur than on the mines which have a high propensity for strikes the world over. However, the trade union movement on the mines was weak in numbers. No more than half the qualified craftsmen had joined the ASE, and no more than thirty per cent of qualified miners belonged to the TMA whose members hardly exceeded 1 000 in number.[10] The unions could do little to attract members by promises of higher pay, because pay was already high. Membership had therefore to be whipped up along other avenues. Workmen, however, often feared to incur the hostility of management by joining a union, while the weakness of the unions encouraged management to refuse recognition to the unions on the grounds that they were not sufficiently representative of the men on the mine, an attitude that caused increasing bitterness towards management among union leaders.

The spark that fired the General Strike of 1913 was a minor dispute over the hours of work of five mechanics at the New Kleinfontein mine. It lit a slow fuse that would two months later culminate in a violent explosion.

[1] Twenty-Second Annual Report of the Transvaal Chamber of Mines, 1911, p LXII.

[2] Chamber of Mines Archives: Executive Committee Minutes, Transvaal Chamber of Mines, 2 March 1911. (Minute book covering the period 1907-1912, pp 384-385.)

[3] Fraser and Jeeves, eds, p 235, letter from Lionel Phillips, writing from Cape Town, to R W Schumacher, Johannesburg, dated 24 February 1911.

[4] Chamber of Mines Archives: Executive Committee Minutes, Transvaal Chamber of Mines, 2 and 9 March 1911. (Minute book covering the period 1907-1912, pp 384-385, 388-389.)

[5] Katz, pp 219-220.

[6] *Ibid*, p 255.

[7] *Ibid*, pp 6, 255-256.

[8] *Ibid*, pp 262-263.

[9] *Ibid*, pp 6, 263-267.

[10] *Ibid*, pp 246, 252.

CHAPTER SEVENTEEN

The Trade Unions Grab for Power

In 1913, as part of the incessant, inescapable struggle to preserve a margin between cost and revenue, the mining houses pursued the policy of amalgamation of properties and strove to increase the efficiency of labour. Production on the Rand the previous year had reached record levels, and average profits had risen, but this was offset by the rise in costs. A major cause was a fall in the productivity of white labour underground, arising in part from its scarcity. Elkan declared in his Presidential Address on 27 February 1913:

> ... every man knows very well, whether he is highly competent or only fairly so, that he need only walk a short distance along the Reef to obtain another job, with the result that, as soon as he imagines he has the slightest cause for complaint, he obtains his cheque and goes elsewhere for employment. The deplorable consequences of this constant migration cannot be over-estimated. ... How can we expect efficiency from a native labourer when his master is constantly changing? How can we expect efficiency from the white man when he is continually moving from mine to mine? ... No wonder the accident rate does not show that decrease we should like to see, that the efficiency of the white man tends to diminish, and that the efficiency of the native, although admittedly somewhat better than it used to be, is still lamentably low ....[1]

On 1 May, Edward Hensley Bulman, former manager of the Apex mine, was appointed to manage New Kleinfontein, with a directive to improve efficiency. He had earned the reputation of being a hard taskmaster on the New Goch mine. In 1910 when mine managers were reducing hours of work without qualification Bulman would only do so if the men in turn agreed to reduced wages. Chaplin wrote to Merriman:

> The Kleinfontein Company had allowed the mine to become a hotbed of 'Labour'. The miners were allowed to earn an exorbitant amount of money, and the result was that they subscribed more in 1912 to the Miners' Association than was subscribed by the men of any individual mine. The management at last arrived at the fact that they were losing a good deal of

profit and appointed a new manager to 'cleanse the stable'.[2]

Bulman brought a new underground manager with him, and made a minor re-organization. He discharged two mechanics and transferred the remaining five underground mechanics from the charge of the Resident Engineer to that of the new Underground Manager. Seeking to correlate their employment more closely to the miners whose machines they serviced he changed their hours of work to conform. The underground mechanics had previously worked eight-and-a-half hours daily and five-and-a-half hours on Saturday, giving them a half-day off. On 10 May Bulman reduced their working day to the statutory eight hours, but required them to work eight hours on Saturday as well, as the miners did. The five men resented the loss of their half-day on Saturday and refused to accept the new hours. They were dismissed and re-placed by non-union members.[3]

On 11 May the ASE posted a notice ordering its members on the mine not to go underground. On the following day, George Kendall, organizer of the ASE, together with Mathews and James Forrester Brown of the TMA, inter-viewed Bulman who declined to alter the conditions of employment, but arranged for the three union representatives to interview William Dalrymple, of Anglo French Exploration, who was Chairman of the mine, together with members of the Board. Dalrymple sympathized with the men and referred the deputation back to Bulman to do what he could to resolve the matter.[4] The Board had in fact set a precedent by interviewing trade unionists who were not their employees and soon came under pressure from other mining houses not to repeat the error. The Chamber remained aloof, for participation in industrial disputes was still outside its function.

Back at the mine, the union called off the strike, but there was no unanimity among the men on a compromise solution, and a series of discussions with Bulman proved abortive. Workers at New Kleinfontein became incensed at the prolongation of the dispute, and the Federation decided to take charge. A strike committee of delegates from the various trade unions was appointed, including Tommy Tole, Vice-President, and James Bain, organizer of the Federation, with Harry Haynes of the TMA as Chairman. Other prominent members were George Mason, of the Amalgamated Society of Carpenters and Joiners, and Kendall of the ASE.[5] Work at New Kleinfontein came to a standstill on 27 May.[6] A particular shock to the mine-owners was the partici-pation of the SAEDFA, the one union that had a working agreement with the Chamber. Its Organizing Secretary, Robert Burns Waterston, was appointed to the Strike Committee despite the fact that his union was not a member of the Federation.[7] The Committee demanded reinstatement of all men con-cerned, abolition of Saturday afternoon work, an eight-and-a-half-hour working day on week-days and five-and-a-half hours on Saturday ending at 12 30 pm.

Both the Government and the mine-owners thought that Bulman had in-fringed the law by introducing changes without giving the month's notice stipulated in the Industrial Disputes Prevention Act. In fact, because the number of men involved was less than ten, the change may well have been legally within managerial prerogative. Nonetheless, new broom Bulman, in too much of a hurry to sweep clean, had put his company morally in the wrong, thus giving the Strike Committee an initial advantage which they made the most of. The Minister of Mines, F S Malan, blamed the Kleinfontein Company for the dispute and urged it to revert to the status quo ante. Dalrymple was anxious to settle, and agreed that the hours should revert to what they were before Bulman's arrival, and that all employees should be reinstated. However, he was reluctant to recognize the Strike Committee by communicating with it, and passed the information to it through the Deputy Mayor of Benoni, who had earlier intervened in an attempt to act as mediator. The Strike Committee was 'incensed that it had been by-passed in this summary fashion'.[8] The company's offer to revert to the status quo ante was then posted on noticeboards on the mine, but the Strike Committee refused to modify its demands unless there were direct negotiations with the Board. This Dalrymple refused to concede and the strike continued. From then on the Strike Committee's attitude was one of disregard of the Industrial Disputes Act. Moreover, it now shifted ground and demanded that Parliament pass a law imposing an eight-hour day 'bank to bank'.

The Minister of Mines, in distant Cape Town, resisted all entreaties to come to the Rand. He took up the attitude that the Kleinfontein Company was morally responsible for the dispute, that it should reinstate the men and meet their representatives without making this a precedent, and that the Government should remain absolutely impartial. On 7 June a notice was posted at the mine that the company was prepared to reinstate all strikers, to revert to the working hours before the dispute, to see if the Saturday shift could be started earlier, and to meet the committee on employees, but not trade union representatives. The company also announced that those who did not return by 11 June would be paid off, and replaced by strike-breakers. The response of the strikers was to hold a mass meeting and urge a general strike. On 9 June the men were paid off, and on 11 June the company took on strike-breakers and reopened the mine. The Federation now indicated its willingness to accept the company's offer, provided that all the men were reinstated and the strike-breakers engaged in their places dismissed. This the company would not accept, on the grounds that it had moral obligations to the strike-breakers. The Federation decided that unless the dispute was resolved by 25 June affiliated unions would be asked to hold ballots on the issue of a general strike. Before then, negotiations between the New Kleinfontein mine and its employees had ended in deadlock.[9]

The industry, with the exception of the J B Robinson Group which stood apart, now rallied behind the New Kleinfontein Company, while the Federation decided as a preliminary phase to extend the strike to other mines in the Benoni district. On 19 June a secret ballot was taken among mineworkers on the Van Ryn Estates. They voted 126 to 80 against going on strike. Katz has recorded:

> The strike committee realised that the ballot was indicative of the sentiments of the majority of the men on the Van Ryn and thereupon resorted to different and dubious tactics.
>
> Tommy Tole, Mason and Crawford harangued the crowd and declared that all who opposed striking were 'scabs'. An open ballot was then called for by a show of hands. Men were asked to raise their hands not if they wished to strike but to indicate whether they sympathised with their fellow-workmen. The mineworkers unanimously voted in sympathy with the New Kleinfontein men and, acting on this vote, a strike was declared by the strike committee.[10]

A similar procedure was followed two days later at New Modder. Attempts were now made to regularize the ballot for a general strike, but events moved quickly out of control of the Federation. The introduction of strike-breakers provided an explosive element, and striking miners roamed the streets assaulting 'scabs' or 'blacklegs'. As violence spread the Johannesburg Chamber of Commerce asked for protection as merchants were having difficulty in supplying goods to Benoni.[11] The famous 'Pickhandle Mary' Fitzgerald wrote at this time in the *Strike Herald*, which appeared throughout the strike

> A visit to Benoni these days is, as a rule, most enjoyable, and yesterday was no exception. I went, of course, chiefly on business bent, but no one can do business – even for a strike paper – when a game of scab-beating is on.[12]

At this time, Mason was prosecuted for incitement to violence for his infamous statement:

> As for blacklegs they have no right to live, as long as there was a pool of water deep enough to drown them, or ropes long enough to hang them.[13]

The whole messy business was swamped in a tidal wave of violence. The Strike Committee took control, in disregard of the Federation, and a procession of strikers went from mine to mine pulling the men out on strike. On 1 July, the TMA announced that it had assumed control and declared a general strike on 4 July. The Federation, to stay in the picture, found itself obliged to back the strike call, even though the wild-cat strike, declared without exhausting conciliation procedures, was both illegal and contrary to the Federation's powers and constitution. The miners responded, some caught up in the frenzy of the moment, others spurred by fears of violent assault on themselves and their families. By 5 July every mine and power station on the Rand had shut down.

From 11 June onwards the mine-owners urged in vain the prosecution of men who went on strike without fulfilling the prior requirements of the Industrial Disputes Act. On 20 June the Government invoked the Unlawful Assemblies Act to ban public meetings in the streets and squares of Benoni, but otherwise followed a hands-off policy. General Smuts, who was now Minister of both Defence and Finance, and Acting Minister of Justice, responsible for law and order, took charge on the Government side in disregard of the Minister of Mines, who tended to grapple ineffectually with the problems of the Rand from his office in distant Cape Town. Smuts came to the Rand, to the relief of despairing Government officials, and met representatives of the strikers on 22 June in a vain bid to end the strike.

On 24 June large red handbills were issued by the Strike Committee calling on all miners on the Reef to assemble in the Market Square at Benoni on Sunday, 29 June, and 'to come armed'. Publication of the handbill was a clear committal of the public law offence of incitement to public violence, and was probably seditious as well. The Strike Committee was beginning openly to defy the law.[14]

The Police informed the strike leaders that the meeting would not be allowed to take place. Bain, the Secretary of the Strike Committee, told H J Kirkpatrick, Commandant of Police, that they would take no notice of the warning and that they would hold the meeting at all costs.

However, Madeley, who was the Member of Parliament for the Springs constituency, in which Benoni fell, interviewed Smuts at Pretoria and urged that the meeting be allowed. He promised, on behalf of the strike leaders, and strikers, that the meeting would pass off peacefully and that there would be no violence. At a subsequent interview between the Magistrate, W J Thompson, Kirkpatrick and the Strike Committee similar guarantees were given. The Police were particularly concerned to prevent the meeting going to the Kleinfontein mine, which was nearby the square and visible from it. Smuts then agreed to the meeting against the advice of the Commissioner of Police, Colonel Theo G Truter, that the real object of the meeting was to rush the Kleinfontein mine, to destroy the property and pull out the so-called scabs.

Truter said that the feeling of the strikers were directed particularly against New Kleinfontein which was running successfully again, despite their efforts. He claimed that they would stop at nothing in order to bring about the destruction of the property and the ill-treatment of the men who were working the mine.

However, the meeting was given the go-ahead by Smuts and the Railways ran special trains to bring miners to it from other parts of the Reef.

Kirkpatrick decided to attend the meeting with six men, and to station the majority of the police force out of sight at the mine. The crowd was visibly armed with sticks and staves and 'there is little or no doubt that many possessed revolvers as well'.[15]

Speeches were made and resolutions were passed, but before the last resolutions had been put the strikers' band struck up *Dixie* (the opening words of the chorus being 'We want to go') and the bulk of the crowd rushed as a body towards the mine. Several of the more responsible strike leaders tried in vain to halt them.

According to Kirkpatrick, Bain incited the mob to go for the Kleinfontein mine.

> The crowd was led on by Mr Bain, who told them to go on, not once, but several times. I spoke to Mr Bain and told him he was breaking his contract; he said to me, 'Be damned, I am going,' and he shouted to the men to go on and have a look at the Kleinfontein.[16]

However, when the mob reached the mine fence, they found the main force of the Police guarding it. The crowd hung around in an ugly mood, but they realized the Police were too strong for them and drifted away at dusk. However, the effect of the meeting was disastrous, for after it the spirit of lawlessness spread like wildfire. The subsequent enquiry found:

> The strikers and the mob lost all self-restraint, and within a few days after this fateful meeting they perpetrated repulsive acts of cowardice, cruelty, and barbarism.
>
> The scum of the Benoni population gained the upper hand, and lawlessness and ruffianism reached such a pitch that the town was in a state of anarchy.
>
> The Strike Committee assumed to itself, unchallenged, some of the functions of government. It gave its 'placet' to persons whose property it thought should be respected, and inferentially therefore the absence of a permit left men at the mercy of the mob. The owners of property went to the Strike Committee for protection and even men in the position of clerks of the National Bank preferred a permit of the Strike Committee to police protection ....[17]

The unrest quickly spread along the Reef to Johannesburg. On the morning of 4 July, the *Rand Daily Mail* published an announcement of a public meeting to be held on that day in the Market Square, Johannesburg. The intention to hold the meeting had up to that time been kept secret from the authorities, and no permission had been asked to hold it.

The previous day an article had appeared in *The Worker*, the official organ of the South African Labour Party.

> The war has now got to be fought not 'to a finish,' as the phrase goes, but to victory, neither death nor any other alternative being accepted. And it can be done; though it will need more than a Rand strike to do it. For victory means bringing the South African public, and in particular the Union Parliament, to its senses and its knees, and extorting substantial legislation in the workers' interest.

218

... really, once it is war, the things usually called murder, arson, destruction of property, and so on, become the principal occupation of armies, and there is no reason in principle, but only in tactics, why these should not be included in the various forms of acute pressure which have to be exercised in industrial war.[18]

Fearing a repetition in Johannesburg of the Benoni débâcle, the Government sent Colonel Truter to prevent the meeting. Truter arrived on the Market Square shortly after noon, but it was effectively too late to stop it. Truter had at his disposal 264 Police, with a body of the Royal Dragoons drawn up in support on the south-west corner of the square. The meeting deteriorated into an organized stoning of the Police, who suffered eighty-eight casualies, mostly cuts about the face and head, but themselves acted with restraint. Four civilians and a police sergeant were taken to hospital by ambulance. The Dragoons, employed to clear a portion of the square, did so by showing only the flats of their sabres and the crowd moved away.

The presence of British cavalry reflected the inadequacy of the Police Force and the vulnerability of a government that lacked military resources of its own. In the emergency, Smuts was compelled to call on the Imperial garrison for help. Despite the impeccable behaviour of the Dragoons, in the face of riot and under fire, their use to maintain order caused a furore in Britain, where it would be asserted that workers had been shot at the behest of a Boer government.[19]

As the meeting on the Market Square ended the mob spread across the town. A portion of the crowd, many of them women, made its way to the Municipal Power Station, and temporarily forced it to shut down. As darkness fell, other mobs, many armed with revolvers, fired the goods shed at Park Station, burnt down *The Star* premises and attacked the Corner House where the military opened fire in support of the Police for the first time. The mob now looted the gun shops and swelled its armoury with firearms of all descriptions.

Colonel C F Stallard, who would serve in Smuts's Cabinet twenty-six years later and live to be 100, was staying at the Rand Club and gave to the subsequent inquiry his impressions of that night:

... I was at Pretoria in the afternoon attending the Provincial Council. I came back by the 5 20 train and the train was stopped at Jeppes ... I got out there and walked into town. The town was quite crowded and in a state of suppressed excitement ... I went to the theatre in the evening. After the theatre had come out the town was in a very much more excited condition. I saw the flames from Park Station and *The Star* office.

We walked through the streets. There was a most extraordinary crowd, a mixture of the criminal classes, the out of works, poor whites, and quite a sprinkling of the determined striker and also what struck me as being very extraordinary a very large number of peaceful citizens, men with their wives and children having tea on the Balcony. They were walking through the streets also and regarding the whole proceedings as a sort of glorified firework show. They were all mixed up together. When I got down by the Market Square, I suddenly became aware that a great proportion of the crowd was armed.[20]

Later, Stallard watched the looting of the gunsmith's opposite the Rand Club.

The man with the bicycle just smashed the window. He used his bicycle as a battering ram … Someone turned on the electric light and they lighted up the shop. They then distributed the arms and ammunition.[21]

Rioting continued sporadically through the night of 4/5 July and flared up again in the morning. Shortly after 1 pm at considerable personal risk Botha and Smuts came into Johannesburg. They had a meeting with Sir Percy FitzPatrick and the respected Johannesburg pioneer, Dr W T F Davies, and authorized the raising of a force of special constables, responsible to Colonel Truter. FitzPatrick feared, above all, that the 200 000 blacks in the Reef compounds might run amok, for it was known that they were being incited by strikers.[22] About two-hundred-and-fifty special constables were signed on immediately. Stallard was among a group of about twenty who were issued with rifles and bayonets and sent to assist in the defence of the Rand Club where serious trouble was brewing.

There was a woman leading them on with a red flag. She was shouting to them to come on for the Club.

We had a race for it with the mob and I got there first, just before the lady with the red flag. … I thought she must be stopped at all costs, so I caught hold of the flag. She was screaming, 'Shoot me, shoot me,' so I assured her no one wanted to shoot her and requested her to depart.[23]

A squadron of the Royal Dragoons arrived at this juncture. It was already clear to the overall military commander, General E D J O'Brien, that the position was extremely serious and the point at issue was now whether the Police and military were to control Johannesburg or whether the rioters were to do so. The Dragoons were under the command of Captain E B Leighton.

He had been through the turmoil the whole night, and had refrained from firing though often sorely tried. He, like most responsible people present, thought the crowd a mischievous, dangerous, and violent mob, and after having endeavoured to disperse them by every means at his command – persuasion, threats, hostile demonstrations, and charges – after having been subjected to showers of missiles and after an officer had been shot, a sergeant wounded, and other casualties, he ordered his men to fire.[24]

After this violent clash on the morning of 5 July it became clear to Botha and Smuts that they were losing control of Johannesburg to the strikers. The Union Defence Force, which had only begun its formation in the previous year, was still in an embryonic stage and, overall, the Government had to face the hard fact that it lacked the ability to restore law and order without shedding the blood, not only of rioters but of innocent citizens. They accordingly sought a meeting with the Federation. Subsequently that day, Botha and Smuts met the representatives of the major mining houses, Phillips, Farrar, Chaplin and Gustav Imroth (JCI), at the Orange Grove Hotel and told them that the Government could not guarantee protection to the mines and villages on the line of the Reef. They thus obtained reluctant agreement to make the best deal they could with the strikers. Botha and Smuts then signed a truce with the Federation at the Carlton Hotel at 4 00 pm in an atmosphere in which the threat of violence was ever present. The generals agreed that the strikers would be reinstated and that approximately a hundred-and-sixty strike-breakers employed in their place would be dismissed but compensated with a year's pay each at Government expense. This would cost the Government more than £45 000, a large sum of money in those times.[25] Botha and Smuts undertook to investigate miners' grievances. Smuts afterwards expressed his humiliation at having to sign an agreement with such as Bain – '... it was one of the hardest things I have done in my life ...'.[26] In fact the strikers might have driven a harder bargain. An uneasy peace returned to the Reef and the unions subsequently ratified the truce.

The rioting had cost twenty-four dead, of whom eleven were miners. The other dead included a municipal clerk, two commercial travellers, a shoe-black, the proprietor of the Carlton Theatre, a pianist, a railway worker, a black burnt to death at Park Station, a black sanitary worker, a dentist's apprentice. The hospital treated a further seventy-three casualties, mostly with bullet wounds, of whom sixteen were miners.[27] The Royal Dragoons reported that thirteen officers, NCOs and men had sustained shot and bullet wounds in the rioting at *The Star*, the Corner House and the Rand Club, the casualties being sustained at each of these places before firing was returned. Four of their horses were shot dead and fourteen wounded.[28]

The Government appointed two judges, Sir Johannes Wessels and the Hon Charles Ward, to conduct the Public Judicial Inquiry, known as 'The Disturbances Commission'. The Federation refused to recognize the Commission, apparently because the judges had found against them in an industrial case, and called on all workers not to give evidence. They thus lost an opportunity to state their case, but also escaped the skilful and searching cross-examination by learned counsel which was the lot of those who did give evidence.

The Chamber did not give evidence either, its position being that industrial disputes were a matter for individual mines. Katz has argued that 'the refusal of the Chamber of Mines or any of its affiliated companies to negotiate with the strike committee, which was acting on behalf of the Federation and trade unions, not only aggravated the situation, but turned a minor dispute into a major upheaval'.[29] This may be a valid criticism, as the subsequent official inquiry found, of the mine-owners involved. However, the Chamber had no option in the matter, as the mining groups responsible for its policy had not yet delegated to it the role of representing the mines in labour negotiations on an industry basis. A study of the minutes of the Chamber's Executive Committee for the relevant period shows that the only discussion on the strike took place on 26 June, a month after it had begun. The question that then came before the Executive Committee concerned the need to keep the London Office informed of what was happening so that it could in turn keep British newspapers in the picture. The Committee decided that, as the Chamber had no official part in the strike, it was inadvisable to send any official communications to London. However, the Chairman undertook to arrange for unofficial communications when it appeared desirable.[30] It appears that as a consequence information on the position was given to Reuters, resulting in the circulation of two articles on the strike.[31]

Despite the specific requirement that the Chamber should not be involved, its expanding staff was a close observer of events which were to find tragic echo in the future, none more so than William Gemmill, who had joined as Statistician in 1908 and had since been appointed Actuary as well. He would soon be made Joint Secretary of the Chamber with Edward L R Kelsey, the Legal Adviser, and would then add to his functions that of Labour Adviser. As such, he was destined to play a leading role in the events of 1922.

The President at the time of the 1913 General Strike was John Munro of JCI. He commented laconically on the findings of the Disturbances Commission:

> ... The Commission ... attached blame all round. It blamed the employers for not recognising the Trades Union leaders when the trouble arose at the New Kleinfontein Mine, it blamed the workmen's representatives for making a settlement difficult by constantly shifting their ground as they thought their power to extract concessions increased, and it blamed the Government for not realising the gravity of the position, and for leaving subordinate officials to carry on negotiations on behalf of the Mines Department. In that portion of the Report dealing with the suppression of the riots of the 4th and 5th July, the Commission vindicated the policy adopted by the Military and Police Authorities, and affirmed that they did their utmost to avoid a conflict.
>
> The reason the employers declined to recognise the strike leaders was that they represented only a minority of the employees on the mines, and had no mandate to represent the general body of workmen, the majority of whom did not belong to any Trades Union.[32]

The General Strike ushered in a new tempo of involvement in improving conditions on the mines, on the part of both mine-owners and Government. Only three weeks after the men had returned to work, on 31 July, *The Worker* published what it called the Workers' Charter, a long list of grievances and demands, together with the replies of both the Government and the mine-owners.[33]

The Federation demanded the repeal of the 1894 legislation under which public meetings had been banned during the General Strike. It asked the Government to legislate for an eight-hour day, including travelling time 'bank to bank'; for the repeal of the controversial Industrial Disputes Prevention Act; the amendment of the Workmen's Compensation Act; for minimum wages, for the abolition of Sunday work, for ten days' annual holiday in addition to public holidays, for overtime payments of time-and-a-half on weekdays and double time on Sundays, for weekly payment of wages 'in coin' (the popular wage being a sovereign a day). It also demanded the official recognition of trade unions, and much else besides.

The Government agreed to a new Riotous Assemblies Act (in fact, it would make the law more stringent); to draft an improved and uniform Workmen's Compensation Bill and to consider employees' representations on it; and undertook to appoint a commission (which would be known as the Economic Commission) to investigate other matters.

For their part, the employers agreed that the time of travel to working places underground should normally be limited to thirty minutes. They agreed to pay wages weekly, and that no official under the rank of mine captain should be entitled to discharge an employee. They made a major concession, for those days, in agreeing to grant ten days' leave annually on half-pay, after twelve months' service underground or two years on surface. This was the forerunner to the granting by the Chamber in 1915, on its own initiative, of holidays on full pay, subject to the maximum of a pound a day.

Most importantly, the employers guardedly agreed to the recognition of individual trade unions. They made this conditional on the constitutions being acceptable to them, on guarantees that union funds would not be used for political purposes, that recognized unions should consist solely of mine employees and that they undertook not to interfere in discipline or management on the mines.

Although the mine-owners accepted the need for the recognition of individual trade unions, subject to safeguards, they adamantly refused to recognize the Federation. The General Strike had confirmed the mining groups and the Chamber in their abhorrence of trade unions, and the members of the Federation were particularly disliked and mistrusted.

Interestingly, a general strike had broken out in the copper mines of Michigan immediately following the strike on the Rand. The employers' association, the Copper Country Commercial Club, reported:

On July 23 the Western Federation of Miners called a general strike of all its members employed in the mines of this district and within a few hours by forcible means and otherwise, every man employed in or about the mines,

223

whether a member of the Federation or not, was deprived of his work, thus throwing out of employment an immense body of men.

From the day of its inception, the strike has been attended with rioting and bloodshed. Every day riotous mobs roam through the streets of our communities and are held in check only by force of the National Guard of the State. Attacks on working men are of daily occurrence; our jails are filled with persons awaiting trial for violent acts during the strike; our children daily have before their eyes the spectacle of men acting in absolute disregard of law and order; all of which creates a deplorable and disgraceful condition which should not be tolerated in a civilized community.[34]

As the result of the Michigan strike, the Club agreed to introduce an eight-hour day from 1 January 1914, but declared resolutely that all managers would continue to refuse to recognize the Western Federation of Miners under any circumstances because every dispute in which the Western Federation had taken a part was accompanied by bloodshed and violence.[35]

Botha immediately followed up the promise of an investigation of workers' grievances with the appointment of the Economic Commission on 11 September 1913. The Chairman of the Commission, S J Chapman, Professor of Political Economy at Manchester University, and its members were highly respected, and acceptable to all concerned. The Chamber, the Federation and most of the trade unions gave evidence.[36] The Commission tendered its report on 17 January 1914.

The Commission declared that the State's imposition of a colour bar, preventing the advancement of workers other than white, was undesirable. This view was endorsed by the Dominions Royal Commission which visited South Africa the following month during a survey of conditions in the dominions of the Empire.

After a careful examination of available statistics of wages, and living costs in mining countries, the Economic Commission found that wages for whites on the Rand were nearly 40 per cent higher than in America and nearly 225 per cent higher than in Europe. When allowance had been made for the high cost of living, the Rand worker was better off than the worker in America and much better off than the worker in Europe. Miners earned more than any other worker in South Africa, but they laboured under so many disadvantages that their earnings were not unreasonably high.[37] The outstanding danger was miners' phthisis.

Of late great efforts have been made to cope with this disease, and marked improvements have been effected in the mines, which are expected to reduce largely the liability of the employees to contract it, and now that the matter has been taken up, particularly in view of the interest shown by the Government, further reform may be expected in the future. It is impossible as yet to demonstrate what the rate of improvement has been ... but the impression prevails amongst persons competent to judge that a great advance has been made in respect of the healthiness of mining on the Wit-watersrand.

... In addition to measures to reduce liability to miners' phthisis, much has been done to help those who have contracted the disease.[38]

The Commission noted that the Chamber had in 1908 initiated negotiations with the Government with a view to the establishment of a sanatorium for miners' phthisis patients. As a result the sanatorium was erected at a cost to the gold mining companies of £52 000, on a site donated by the Government, and opened in November 1911, providing accommodation for seventy patients. The annual maintenance cost was shared between the Government and the gold mining companies.[39] The Springkell Sanatorium has continued in operation ever since, under the administration of the Chamber, and with the steady decline in the incidence and severity of miners' phthisis has come to treat other disabilities as well.

Coincidentally, another important development in 1913 was the establishment by the Chamber, under the aegis of the associated Rand Mutual Assurance Company, of a mine safety committee. This body, soon to be known as the Prevention of Accidents Committee, was representative of all sections of the gold mining industry. It set out on the road of communication and enlightenment that was to make a substantial contribution to a growing trend towards fewer accidents with the passing of each year. In 1915, the Chamber launched its safety magazine, *The Reef*, due to become an institution on the mines. Among those who occupied the editor's chair was Harry Haynes, one-time Chairman of the 1913 Strike Committee at New Klein-fontein. Harry Haynes, who chained himself to the gallery rails of the parliamentary debating chamber in 1923, in a sustained vocal protest against the treatment of unemployed workers, was associated with *The Reef* for thirty-three years and Editor from 1936 to 1957.

The accident fatality rate which was 3,81 per thousand at work per year in 1913, would be halved over the next twenty-five years. This was achieved as a result of a concentrated drive for safer mining, despite a steady increase in the depth and extent of underground workings, and the continuation of the migratory labour system, characterized by high turnover and a regular influx of novice workmen without industrial training or skills.

The Economic Commission conducted its enquiry against a country-wide deterioration in industrial relations. Trade unions exulted in their July victory, and the recruiting of new members was brisk. On the mines, relations between man and mining company continued at high tension.

Discipline was dead, and no one dared to offer a word of criticism, no matter how inefficient or flagrantly indolent their workmen might be.[40]

The weapon of the general strike appealed more than ever and there were re-peated threats to use it. Certain trade union leaders openly declared their wish to take over and control the industries of the country, and there was talk of the Trades Hall at Fordsburg being the real centre of Government. Moderate union leaders were overshadowed by the flamboyant and aggressive. There was a strike of coal miners in December 1913 and a new eruption of militancy. The same month Henry Burton, Minister of Railways, heightened tension to snapping point with the announcement that some temporary employees would be retrenched.

Lionel Phillips, recovering in hospital after the attempt on his life, received a visit from General Smuts.

> General Smuts ... told me another strike was impending and timed to break out about the New Year. I asked him whether the Government had benefited by the experiences of the previous strike, and he said there need be no apprehensions on that account. And so it proved.[41]

Railwaymen in Pretoria struck on 6 January, and by 8 January the railway strike had spread to Johannesburg and Germiston. The Federation declared a general strike on 13 January.[42] But the Government was determined not to allow Labour to call the tune as it had in Australia, and Smuts was not to be caught napping again. He had already moved 10 000 troops to the Rand. He now called up another 50 000. Generals De la Rey and Beyers led the burgher commandos into Johannesburg. Martial law was declared. Hundreds of trade unionists and labour leaders were taken into custody, Creswell, leader of the SALP, among them. He was sentenced to a month's imprisonment. The Trades Hall in Fordsburg was besieged and De la Rey trained his field artillery on it. The entire Executive Committee of the Federation was arrested.

On this occasion, the miners did not respond to the general strike call in any numbers, partly because they were protected against coercion by unions. Most of the mines did not cease operations, and it was only in the Benoni area that there was serious disruption.[43]

With the Federation powerless and discredited, workers drifted back to work and the strike movement collapsed. The great bid by White Labour to seize power had failed.[44]

Smuts's victory was total, but he now overplayed his political hand by deporting nine strike leaders, including H J Poutsma, Organizing Secretary of the Amalgamated Society of Railway and Harbour Servants, and the mine strike leaders, Mason, Bain and Waterston, to Britain on the *Umgeni*. His action was undoubtedly illegal, Botha claiming that the safety of the State was the supreme law. The deportations were widely condemned, and not only in Labour circles.

The Chamber was not among the critics. The Executive Committee telegraphed the Prime Minister on 9 February 1914

> ... its great appreciation of the prompt and energetic steps taken ... to counteract the effects of the Strike among the Railway Servants and of the

subsequent General Strike called by the Federation of Trades, and views with extreme satisfaction the success achieved ... in defeating the recent attempts to paralyse the industries of the Union.[45]

The SALP, capitalizing on the revulsion against Smuts's strong-arm tactics, now came to the fore and achieved a brief peak of glory on the Rand by winning control of the Transvaal Provincial Council by a majority of one in the provincial elections on 18 March 1914. The Federation, however, had lost the quite fortuitous pre-eminence thrust upon it by the turn of events the previous year. It would take the exigencies of the world war that now impended to bring the Federation and the Chamber together for a few short years of co-operation.

[1] Twenty-Third Annual Report of the Transvaal Chamber of Mines, 1912, pp LXXXII–LXXXIII.

[2] Katz, p 382, quoting Merriman Papers, 1913 Correspondence, F D P Chaplin to J X Merriman, 15 July 1913.

[3] *Ibid*, pp 381–382.

[4] *Ibid*, p 383.

[5] *Ibid*, p 387.

[6] *Ibid*, p 385.

[7] *Ibid*, p 386.

[8] *Ibid*, p 389.

[9] Union of South Africa: Report of the Witwatersrand Disturbances Commission, September 1913 (UG No 55 - 1913), pp XIII, XV.
Katz, pp 391, 393–394, 399.

[10] Katz, pp 397–398.

[11] *Ibid*, pp 399–402.

[12] *Ibid*, p 402, quoting *Strike Herald*, 25 June 1913.

[13] Union of South Africa: Judicial Commission of Inquiry into Witwatersrand Disturbances: June - July 1913: Minutes of Evidence (UG No '56 - 1913), p 360.

[14] Report of the Witwatersrand Disturbances Commission, 1913, p XX.

[15] *Ibid*, p XXIV.

[16] *Ibid*, pp XXIV–XXV.

[17] *Ibid*, pp XXV, XXVI, XXVIII.

[18] *Ibid*, pp XXXII–XXXIII, quoting from *The Worker*, 3 July 1913.

[19] Cameron and Spies, eds, p 235.

[20] Judicial Commission of Inquiry into Witwatersrand Disturbances, 1913: Minutes of Evidence, p 215.

[21] *Idem*.

[22] *Ibid*, pp 304–305, Affidavit of Sir Percy FitzPatrick, dated 8 August 1913, presented to the members of the Judicial Commission of Inquiry.

[23] *Ibid*, p 216.

[24] Report of the Witwatersrand Disturbances Commission, 1913, p LXIV.

[25] Katz, p 419.

[26] Union of South Africa: Debates of the House of Assembly: Fourth Session, First Parliament: 30 January - 7 July 1914, Column 80. (Speech by J C Smuts.)

[27] Judicial Commission of Inquiry into Witwatersrand Disturbances, 1913: Minutes of Evidence: Annexures C 45 and C 46, pp 440-443.

[28] *Ibid*, Annexures C 10 and C 11, pp 422, 423.

[29] Katz, pp 394-395.

[30] Chamber of Mines Archives: Executive Committee Minutes, Transvaal Chamber of Mines, 26 June 1913. (Minute book covering the period May 1912 - September 1916, pp 169 - 170.)

[31] Chamber of Mines Archives: Executive Committee Minutes, Transvaal Chamber of Mines, 10 July 1913. (Minute book covering the period May 1912 - September 1916, p 172.)

[32] Twenty-Fourth Annual Report of the Transvaal Chamber of Mines, 1913, p LX.

[33] Katz, pp 321-322, 487-505.

[34] Annual Report of the Transvaal Chamber of Mines, 1913, p 434. (Statement No 12: Economic Commission: Evidence of the Transvaal Chamber of Mines: Report of Mining Conditions and Strike in the Copper Mines of Michigan, United States of America. [Reprinted from *The Daily Mining Gazette*, Houghton and Calumet, Michigan, 14 October 1913.])

[35] *Ibid*, pp 432, 437, 468.

[36] Katz, pp 321-324.
Union of South Africa: Report of the Economic Commission, January 1914 (UG No 12 '14), p 7.

[37] Report of the Economic Commission, 1914, pp 27, 28, 69.

[38] *Ibid*, pp 27-28.

[39] *Ibid*, p 28.

[40] Phillips, *Some Reminiscences*, p 221.

[41] *Ibid*, pp 221-222, 225.

[42] Twenty-Fifth Annual Report of the Transvaal Chamber of Mines, 1914, p L.

[43] Annual Report of the Transvaal Chamber of Mines, 1913, p LIX.

[44] Davenport, p 183.

[45] Chamber of Mines Archives: Executive Committee Minutes, Transvaal Chamber of Mines, 9 February 1914. (Minute book covering the period May 1912 - September 1916, p 224.)

CHAPTER EIGHTEEN

Patterns of Protest

The Government, having withstood the onslaught of White Labour, had now to face another from those Afrikaners who saw in the Great War an opportunity to regain, by force if necessary, their lost republican independence. 'The long fuse' of treason stretched back to 1902.[1]

> ... certain Boer notables claimed that some die-hards in 1902 at Vereeniging had only acquiesced in the peace settlement after it had been agreed that the struggle would be renewed at a future date when Britain was involved in another conflict. In 1912, [S G 'Manie'] Maritz, J C G Kemp and other former Boer Generals and Commandants had discussed using their positions in the Defence Force to restore the republics if suitable circumstances should arise.[2]

By 1914, there were others, not wishing to go so far as revolt, who had become restless under the reconciliation policies of Botha which gave no scope to the cherished ideal of independence from Britain, and seemed to condone the perceived dominance of the English language and of English-speakers in the public service and business. Many former burghers of the republics saw themselves, or were encouraged to see themselves, as robbed of their old freedoms. In particular, impoverished Boers and *bywoners* forced off the land to compete in the towns with skilled immigrants came to believe that they were 'politically and economically strangers in their own country'.[3]

Afrikaners holding these attitudes lent ready ears to the doctrine of 'South Africa First' expounded by General Hertzog who denied the right of English-speakers to a dual loyalty to South Africa and the British Empire. He advocated separate cultural streams for the development of the two groups, but preached 'South Africa for the Afrikaner', explaining only tardily that he included as Afrikaners all who unequivocally accepted South Africa as their country.[4]

Hertzog was a sincere protagonist of Afrikaner interests, and it was hard for Botha to gainsay his dictum of 'South Africa First'. Sadly, however, Hertzog's corrosive attacks on English settlers sowed division in the new Union, and set South African politics in an unhappy mould. He publicly castigated as 'foreign fortune-hunters' men like Sir Thomas Smartt, the Unionist Party leader, who had farmed in the Cape for thirty years and served South Africa well. It was not long before Hertzog's stance of contemptuous disregard for the Botha approach to nation-building made his exclusion from the Cabinet inevitable. However, he refused to tender the resignation Botha demanded. Botha himself was forced to resign in December 1912 and accept the Governor-General's invitation to form a new Cabinet, from which he would exclude Hertzog.

It was at once clear that Hertzog could count on strong support, particularly among rural Afrikaners, including some of those forced to seek work in the towns. A number of influential Afrikaners joined him, including former President Steyn and General C de Wet of the Free State, and Tielman Roos of the Transvaal, a man who was to play a pivotal role in coming political events. The National Party of the Free State was formed under Hertzog's leadership in July 1914, and there followed the formation of separate branches of the Party in the other provinces. A Federal Council was formed in 1916 and the Party has remained federal in organization.

The historian B J Liebenberg has concluded that Hertzog and Botha did not differ fundamentally in principle.

> Botha remained an Afrikaner, and the Afrikaner's rights were his first concern. His personal letters show clearly that his opinions on the Afrikaner language and culture, on the relations of South Africa with the British Empire and on the Unionists coincided with those of Hertzog. The differences between them were not so much differences of principle as tactical ones ....

> His mistake was that he over-estimated the Afrikaners' loyalty to him. He did not make sufficient allowance for the feeling of his own people.[5]

Many Afrikaners misunderstood Botha's demonstration of loyalty to the Crown and his eagerness to bury the past. They resented his donation of the huge Cullinan diamond to King Edward VII in 1907, his readiness to give financial assistance to the Royal Navy, and his unveiling of the magnificent memorial to Cecil Rhodes on the slopes of Devil's Peak on Cape Town's Table Mountain.[6]

The expiry of Britain's ultimatum to Germany on 4 August 1914 automatically involved the dominions in the war, for they were not yet wholly independent. However, the scale of involvement was a matter for their decision. Botha at once cabled Whitehall offering to take over the defence of the country from Imperial forces stationed there so as to release them for service elsewhere. Soon after, Britain asked the South African Government if it was prepared to invade German South West Africa so as to immobilize radio stations feeding information to German submarines in the Atlantic. Botha agreed to do so and his decision was ratified by Parliament with a large majority. However, this degree of involvement in Britain's war was resented by many in the constituencies and in the Government service, including the Defence Force. The former Boer general, C F Beyers, whom Smuts had appointed Commandant-General, resigned in protest.

As has so often happened at critical departure points in South Africa's history, a savage drought contributed its portion of embitterment and despair. Many of those who now saddled up to follow the dusty roads of revolt had little to lose. Yet perhaps there would have been no rebellion were it not for the charisma of the personalities who emerged to lead it. The patriarchal figure of the ageing 'Lion of the Western Transvaal', General Koos de la Rey, now a member of the Union Senate, was to have provided the lift-off, but fate intervened to remove him from the leadership. On 15 September he and General Beyers left Pretoria by car for Potchefstroom in the Western Transvaal. Nine months earlier they had ridden together to suppress the strikers in Johannesburg. Now they were *en route* to a council of dissident officers, and the evidence strongly suggests that they had an armed revolt of their own in mind.

On their way through Johannesburg De la Rey ordered the chauffeur of the grey Daimler to ignore successive police orders to halt at a series of road blocks. He was not to know that their purpose was to apprehend the murderous Foster gang, coincidentally on the run after shooting a policeman. As the Daimler sped through the fourth road block, in Langlaagte, a policeman fired at the right rear wheel. The car stopped. Beyers got out and said that De la Rey was dead. According to Kemp and other officers awaiting him at Potchefstroom, De la Rey's arrival was to have triggered the uprising.[7]

On 9 October Maritz, who commanded the North West District of the Cape, crossed the frontier of German South West Africa with more than a thousand Citizen Force men (and some prisoners) to join the Germans. In the Transvaal, rebel leadership devolved on Beyers and Kemp. Another Boer hero, General C R de Wet, roused the north-eastern Free State.

Once again the Government found itself obliged to declare martial law, this time to suppress rebellion among old friends and comrades-at-arms. Hertzog, with difficulty, managed not to commit himself to either side, while former President Steyn, when appealed to by Smuts, felt unable to call on the rebels to lay down their arms unless he were permitted to condemn the invasion of South West Africa at the same time.

Botha, always a man to rise to the occasion in a crisis, took the field himself, and employing only Afrikaners, some of them commandeered for service in much the old style, suppressed the rebellion after fierce fighting. He defeated De Wet at the farm Mushroom Valley, near Winburg in the Free State, on 11 November. De Wet was forced to surrender after skirmishing that showed the motor vehicle had written finis to the supremacy of armed horsemen in irregular warfare on South African terrain.

Beyers was drowned while swimming a river near Rustenburg to escape from Government forces. Kemp made an epic march to join Maritz who had invaded the north-west Cape, and, with him, was compelled to surrender his forces to General Jaap van Deventer. Maritz escaped to South West Africa. In all more than 11 400 joined the rebellion and Botha put 32 000 Afrikaners into the field to suppress them. A total of 190 of the rebel forces was killed, including De Wet's son, and 132 Government soldiers.[8] Among the *bittereinders* in hard fighting north of Pretoria was Jopie Fourie who had failed to resign his commission in the Citizen Force, and would be the only rebel to pay the supreme penalty before a firing squad. To some he would live on as an heroic martyr of a just protest in arms. The rest were treated with sensible leniency, but there was an enduring legacy of bitterness among some Afrikaners.

Thus within the short space of eighteen months the Government withstood powerful challenges to its authority from two forces quite distinct from one another – those of White Labour and of the advocates of an extreme republicanism. The distinctions however were blurring.

> Confrontation between the Government and the labour unions resulted in a growing polarisation of forces, in which English-speaking labour enjoyed support from rural as well as urban Afrikaners, whose anti–capitalist posture was at least as old as the Jameson Raid.[9]

The forces of labour and republicanism would move closer to one another in the head–on clash with the State that was to follow the war, during a period of rare historical importance in which the struggle for power 'clearly cut across the lines of racial division'.[10]

Meanwhile, the Coloured races of South Africa watched the internecine struggle of the white races in wonderment that men who enjoyed the franchise and a much-envied political voice should find it necessary to spill each other's blood in the furtherance of their separate interests.

The Indian population had developed its own form of protest under Mohandas Gandhi who inspired them to follow the non-violent path of *Satyaghra* to secure relief from discriminatory laws. In 1910 Tolstoy Farm near Johannesburg became the centre of *Satyaghra*. In October 1913 Gandhi led 2 000 Indian men and women from Natal to cross into the Transvaal in defiance of the law that limited Indian immigration and residence. Indian workers in the Natal coal-fields went on strike in sympathy. The *Satyaghris* were jailed, Gandhi being sentenced to a year's imprisonment.

Gandhi did not crusade for immediate equality nor did Indians ask for political rights. They sought freedom to trade, the right to own landed property, and relief from discriminatory laws. Under Imperial pressure, and the influence of the personal relationship formed between Gandhi and Smuts, Gandhi was released and the Government passed the Indian Relief Act which ameliorated some Indian disabilities. Gandhi soon returned to India. Smuts wrote: 'The saint has left our shores, I sincerely hope for ever.'[11]

The South African National Native Congress, later to become the African National Congress (ANC) was formed in Durban in 1912, to improve the situation of the black races. Leading roles were played by Pixley ka Izaka

Seme, a lawyer, and Walter Benson Rubusana, an ordained minister and journalist who represented Tembuland in the Cape Provincial Council. At this time as in the past

> 'Native policy' ... was often determined by white economic demands (particularly those relating to labour and land), by white fears and prejudices, rather than by black needs. White attitudes were conflations of insecurity and beliefs of black inferiority. Such attitudes were common amongst Europeans concerned with colonial rule in other parts of Africa in the second decade of the twentieth century. It would have been strange if it had been different in South Africa.[12]

The Native Labour Regulations Act of 1911 followed the pattern of the 'Masters' and Servants' laws of the former colonies, providing for the prosecution of blacks who broke their contracts with employers, and withholding the right to strike. A more profound protest among blacks was aroused by the Native Land Act which established territorial segregation by making it illegal for blacks to buy land outside the Native Reserves. The limitations on occupation of land on white farms caused hardship for numbers of blacks expelled from land on which they had settled, and blacks in the Orange Free State suffered in particular. However, while the Act lowered the status of some black farmers to that of labour tenants, the total numbers living on white farms soon rose higher than before. Nor did the Act significantly affect the flow of labour to the mines.

Surprisingly, Dr Francis Wilson in his thoughtful study of mine labour asserts that the Land Act played a decisive role:

> Although pressure for the legislation came primarily from farmers its effects were to prove even more beneficial to the Chamber of Mines which drew so large a proportion of its black labour force from the overcrowded 'reserves' created by the Act.[13]

This is puzzling. The Land Act did not apply to the Cape because the black vote, based on a property qualification, was entrenched in the South Africa Act. In 1912, the major source of labour for the mines was Moçambique, 47,93 per cent, and the Cape 26,17 per cent, while the provinces to which the Land Act would apply together supplied 16,58 per cent. Ten years later the figures were Moçambique 44,24, and the Cape 34,52, while the percentage from the provinces to which the Land Act applied was 8,64 per cent. In 1930, the figures were Moçambique 37,11, Cape 35,33, other South African 10,68.[14] The long-term trend thereafter was for the increasing use of foreign labour, particularly from Basutoland, and for the numbers recruited in South Africa to fall. The labour from the 'overcrowded' reserves created by the 1913 Act was important enough, but it was a small proportion of mine labour; and as

Dr Wilson himself shows, the actual numbers from South Africa (including the Cape) fell between 1936 and 1969.

> Although the total number of men employed by the Chamber of Mines rose from 318 000 to 371 000 between 1936 and 1969 the number of black South Africans fell from 166 000 to 131 000.[15]

Mrs Merle Lipton, in a critical study of the mine labour system published in 1980, concluded that coercive measures such as restrictions on the ownership of land and special taxes to force blacks to earn cash wages were channelled towards 'politically-powerful White farmers rather than the mainly foreign mine owners'.[16]

In the years after 1906, the industry was assisted in getting labour from the Eastern Cape by the depression in that Colony, but the major recruiting effort mounted by the competing mining groups became a much more important factor. Group recruiters made allies of country traders and local headmen, and poured huge sums into the tribal areas.

As a consequence of the impressive benefits provided in cash and cattle, more and more blacks from the Cape began to go regularly to the mines, and to make a career of mining. The proportion of experienced male workers who voluntarily made their way to Johannesburg, without the assistance of a recruiter, rose dramatically in the second decade of the century. The flow was strong enough to assist the Chamber to disregard the independent recruiters. It accordingly established the Native Recruiting Corporation (NRC) in 1912 to provide member mines with a recruiting service in South Africa and in the neighbouring British Protectorates on the same lines as that provided by WNLA in the Portuguese and tropical territories. The way was eased for the new organization by changes in the control of mines that formerly followed an independent role in recruiting. Thus ERPM had passed under the effective control of the Corner House by 1915 and JCI acquired the maverick J B Robinson's Far West Rand mines in 1916-1917.

Not surprisingly, black workers on the mines had been disturbed by the violent events of 1913. Striking white miners incited them to join the strike, and to demand an increase to 5s from the average of around 2s a shift. The strikers also threatened blacks with violence if they worked with scabs. There was trouble at half-a-dozen mines during the course of the General Strike, but H M Taberer, General Superintendent of the NRC, or KwaTEBA (The House of Taberer) as it was to become known, was able to calm them down by addressing them personally.[17] Taberer had won the confidence of blacks. He was a man of cool nerve and a linguist who could communicate his genuine concern for the welfare of black workers to an angry mob. As such he was a prototype of a long line of humane men who have played a key role in the administration of the labour force.

The culmination of the bewildering events going on around the black mine-workers in June and July of 1913 encouraged them to believe that violence and riot would bring results, and more serious trouble followed. Fortunately for the authorities this did not occur until 8 July when violent action by white miners had subsided. Black workers on four mines then refused to go to work without increase in pay. A compound manager was seriously injured by stone-throwing workers who showed themselves ready for a stand-up fight with the Police. At one mine they stoned the mounted Police. Peace was only restored by the arrival of a company of infantry. The workers were sufficiently subdued by the flash of fixed bayonets to permit the arrest of the ringleaders in each of the affected compounds. The workers then went quietly back to work. The industry had narrowly escaped a veld fire of riot running wild along the compounds of the Reef.[18]

The Government was prompt to appoint H O Buckle, Chief Magistrate of Johannesburg, to conduct an inquiry into the grievances of black mine-workers, and Buckle was quick to get down to work. He visited practically every compound on the Reef, so that black workers might have a full and fair hearing. In all, he examined 1 144 witnesses and held 87 sittings, and recorded a variety of complaints.[19] The long list of recommendations in his report of May 1914 covered recruiting procedures and the control of black workers in compounds, as well as conditions at work and in the compound, treatment in hospitals, and complaints about pay and compensation. He recommended that when workers considered a working place underground to be unsafe, contrary to the view of their supervisor, they should have the right to the independent opinion of another supervisor, preferably a shift boss. He recommended, too, measures to prevent assaults underground, stricter control over the issue of so-called 'loafer's tickets' to workers who did not complete a standard day's work, periodic medical inspection of men during the contract period, and that a higher proportion of workers be employed on piecework rates. Importantly, he recommended the cancellation of the 'maximum permissible average' system which set a limit to payments for piecework, and seemed to him to be operating to the disadvantage of both mine and man.[20]

Buckle commented on complaints about lack of opportunity for promotion:

> ... The real grievance of the native on this point is the colour bar, which blocks practically all his opportunities of promotion. He argues – and I can see no flaw in the reasoning – that if he can do the same work as white men, there is no reason why he should not receive the same remuneration. That in many cases he can do it and in some instances is actually doing it, admits of no doubt.[21]

Buckle pointed out that the wide-ranging nature of the listed grievances might give the idea that the black's lot was entirely composed of hardships, and that his treatment was very bad indeed.

I wish definitely to repudiate any such opinion. Since I entered upon this inquiry I have been astonished to learn how much care and thought is expended upon the native labourer's health and comfort; and all witnesses with any long experience of the mines – including every class and colour – are absolutely unanimous in the assertion that the improvement in the conditions of the native labourer on the Rand has been enormous and continuous.

> ... A considerable number of the complaints made to me have been remedied during the sitting of the Commission as a result of their being brought to the notice of the managements concerned.[22]

At the Corner House, Evelyn Ashley Wallers had taken over from Lionel Phillips who had returned to London to fill the gap left by the death of Sir Julius Wernher. Wallers was made President of the Chamber for 1914 – 1915 and it fell to him to give the industry's views on the Buckle Report. In his address to the Annual General Meeting on 29 March 1915 he declared that to his mind it was

> ... the most valuable document we have ever had to help us in studying this subject. ... We have given to the recommendations made by Mr Buckle the most careful consideration, and as a result all the members of your Executive advised the Government that, with the exception of one Group, we agreed with the whole of Mr Buckle's report, with a few comparatively unimportant exceptions.

Wallers then went on to say that the Government felt that the present time of war was not opportune to make changes in the Native Labour Regulations to give effect to proposed changes in recruiting methods. However, the bulk of Buckle's recommendations, he said, did not require changes in regulations and were a matter of voluntary adoption.[23]

Ahead lay long years of war and an aftermath of depression in which prices and wages would fall the world over. Some of the recommended changes, including the removal of the 'maximum permissible average', would not be effected for many years to come.

Wallers was also able to announce the completion in 1914 of the beautiful building on Hospital Hill to house the South African Institute of Medical Research, founded in 1912. The building was designed by Sir Herbert Baker, architect of the magnificent Union Buildings in Pretoria, of Cecil Rhodes's Groote Schuur in Cape Town, and of the stately homes of Phillips, Chaplin, Farrar, and Dalrymple on the Rand. The Institute still occupies the building today. Its capital cost, largely financed by the Chamber, was £42 000. The Government and the mining industry shared the running costs. The unfolding of the Institute's work, like much else, was to be held up by the shortages and demands of the war, the priority being given after the outbreak to the urgent production of 87 000 doses of anti-typhoid vaccine for the armed forces. The

Institute has since played a priceless role in medical research and in the search for vaccines and their production.

Despite the efforts of the industry and the Institute, the Government came to the conclusion in 1913 that the mortality rate among tropical workers from north of twenty-two degrees latitude, with their particular vulnerability to pneumonia, was unacceptable, and it ended their recruitment, a ban that was to last for twenty years.

However, the mortality rate among all black workers on the mines fell from 22,1 per thousand at work per year in 1913, to a new low of 14,9 in 1914. Wallers declared that the figures reflected a steady and very great diminution in the death rate.[24] The diminution was to continue until in the 1960s, with 400 000 men employed, the figure was below two per thousand per year.

A fresh impetus to attaining a high standard of health care came from Samuel Evans, an Executive Committee member, and the Chairman of Corner House's Crown Mines. It arose from his study of events in Panama where America was cutting the canal that was to link the Pacific and Atlantic Oceans through a region notorious as a death-trap of disease.

The great Frenchman, Ferdinand de Lesseps, who had built the Suez Canal, had earlier tried and failed to build the Panama Canal in the face of the appalling mortality from yellow fever and other diseases, estimated to have reached 240 per thousand in the years between 1881 and 1889. France abandoned the project and ceded it to the United States by treaty.

While the Transvaal was bringing Chinese labourers to work on the mines in 1904, the United States was beginning the transportation of thousands of indentured black workers from the West Indies, mainly Jamaica and Barbados, to construct the canal and its associated railway. Colonel (later Surgeon-General) William C Gorgas of the United States Army Medical Corps was appointed Chief Sanitary Officer in 1906, with a wide brief to reduce the mortality from disease. As a result of the measures he took, mortality fell from 38,98 per thousand in 1906 to 6,37 by 1912, a year before the workforce reached its peak of 46 000 blacks and 12 500 whites.[25] Sir William Osler, a medical man of world renown, described in an article the work done to protect the workers, and declared it to be the outstanding achievement of preventive medicine of the twentieth century. Others agreed. Gorgas would later receive the Nobel Prize.[26]

Evans happened to read the article by Osler. It impressed him so much that he travelled to the Isthmus, made Panama City his headquarters, and spent an adventurous month studying the system of public health in the wild country between the two oceans. He met Gorgas, now world famous, and was handed over to a young assistant, Dr A J Orenstein, who had been on Gorgas's staff since 1905. Orenstein showed him all that was being achieved on the Canal. Evans returned to the Rand, deeply impressed, and utilized all his powers of persuasion on the Chamber. The Chamber responded and invited Gorgas to visit the Rand and advise how the health services of the mines could be improved. Gorgas duly arrived in December 1913, accompanied by distinguished medical advisers.

On 25 February 1914 Gorgas presented his recommendations. They were aimed in particular at combating pneumonia. He reported that experience at Panama showed, and this was confirmed on the Rand, that incidence was highest among men from primitive backgrounds with little immunity, and in the early months of their contracts. In 1907, the black workers in Panama had been allowed to scatter along the line of the Canal, and to build their own huts and bring over their families. He was satisfied that reduction of density of sleeping quarters through scattering of the workforce was the chief cause of the sudden and permanent drop in pneumonia on the Isthmus.[27]

He recommended a reduction in the density of accommodation on the Rand, preferably through the adoption of a village hut system, in which workers' families could be accommodated. The Dominions Royal Commission was to recommend something similar later that year, but the policy of the South African Government and its successors was diametrically opposed to the transfer of tribal workers to live in specially created mine settlements on the Rand. Nor was it favoured by the foreign governments or the tribal chieftains in whose countries men were recruited for the mines.

Gorgas also recommended the centralization of health services under the Chamber of Mines, which in practice lacked the direct executive authority necessary for this function. However, the Corner House proceeded to centralize its services, to follow the paths indicated by the Gorgas Report, and to set an example that other Groups followed. Orenstein was appointed medical superintendent to the Corner House, on Gorgas's recommendation, responsible directly to Wallers. In this way, Orenstein began a remarkable career which contributed to the development in the mining industry of an industrial system of medical care second to none. During the War, the Government appointed him Director of Medical Services to the South African Defence Force, but he continued to perform a dual function. From his office in Pretoria he sent out a stream of directives to his staff at the Corner House in Johannesburg, and took week-end leave to visit mine hospitals.[28] The War over, he could concentrate his remarkable talent on the Rand. In all, he worked at the Corner House for fifty-eight years, and died in his sleep after his day's work at the office in his ninety-third year.

Evans and Orenstein, both men of exceptional energy, were given the backing they needed by Evelyn Wallers, himself seemingly indefatigable. Wallers was to become increasingly influential in the direction of industry affairs. After his first Presidential year, he served as Vice-President in 1915-1916 to another President from the Corner House, W H Dawe. Wallers was elected President again in 1916-1917, in 1917-1918, and in 1918-1919. Thus it would fall largely to him to steer the Chamber through the five years between the invasion of Belgium and the Peace of Versailles.

[1] Cameron and Spies, eds, p 236.

[2] *Idem.*

[3] A G Oberholster, *Die Mynwerkerstaking: Witwatersrand, 1922*, p 35. (Translation from Afrikaans.)

[4] Cameron and Spies, eds p 233.

[5] Liebenberg, 'Botha and Smuts in Power: 1910-1924', p 392.

[6] *Ibid*, p 393.

[7] Cameron and Spies, eds, p 237.

[8] *Ibid*, pp 238.

[9] Davenport, p 183.

[10] *Ibid*, p 175.

[11] Hancock, *Smuts: 1. The Sanguine Years*, p 345, quoting the Smuts Papers, Volume 12, No 139. To Sir Benjamin Robertson (21 August 1914).

[12] Cameron and Spies, eds, p 234.

[13] F Wilson, *Labour in the South African Gold Mines: 1911-1969*, p 3.

[14] Van der Horst, pp 216-217.

[15] Wilson, p 71.

[16] M Lipton, 'Men of Two Worlds: Migrant Labour in South Africa', *Optima*, Volume 29, Number Two/Three, 28 November 1980, pp 75, 97.

[17] Judicial Commission of Inquiry into Witwatersrand Disturbances, 1913: Minutes of Evidence, pp 235-237, 319.

[18] Union of South Africa: Report of the Native Grievances Inquiry, 1913-1914 (UG 37-'14), p 64.

[19] *Ibid*, pp 1-2.

[20] *Ibid*, pp 90-94.

[21] *Ibid*, pp 38-39.

[22] *Ibid*, p 2.

[23] Annual Report of the Transvaal Chamber of Mines, 1914, p LXI.

[24] *Ibid*, p LX.

[25] Cartwright, *Doctors on the Mines*, p 28.
Annual Report of the Transvaal Chamber of Mines, 1914, p 338.

[26] Cartwright, *Doctors on the Mines*, p 28, 45.

[27] Annual Report of the Transvaal Chamber of Mines 1914, pp 335-341, 355.

[28] Cartwright, *Doctors on the Mines*, pp 36-38, 44-45.

CHAPTER NINETEEN

The Chamber at War

The outbreak of war marked the end of the high noon of the International Gold Standard, in which gold coins were everyday currency, along with banknotes, their interchangeability being guaranteed by gold reserves of an appropriate ratio in central banks.[1] Britain at once replaced sovereigns by notes which were dubbed 'Bradburys' after the Joint Permanent Secretary to the Treasury who signed them. However, the gold standard's decline was not immediately apparent, especially in South Africa where gold coins would circulate throughout the War, and black mineworkers receive their wages in sovereigns until 1920. A much more immediate and vital problem faced the Chamber and the mining houses – the transport by ship of the gold of the Rand through seas on which German surface raiders, and later submarines, ranged widely in search of prey.

Since the discovery of the Main Reef raw, unrefined gold had been sent to London on ships of the South African Shipping Conference for refining and smelting into bars of so-called standard ounces, containing twenty-two carats of fine gold, the balance being of copper alloy. The bars were then sold on the London Bullion Market where the Bank of England was obliged to buy gold on offer at close to £3 17s 9d a standard ounce[2] (the equivalent of £4 4s 11d a fine ounce). Shipping, insurance, refining and handling reduced the amount received by the mines to about £3 10s an ounce, a sufficient reduction on occasion to wipe out the profit margin to a mining company. These costs would inevitably increase during the War.

By 1914, the Transvaal was producing thirty-eight per cent of the world's gold, nearly double that of the United States which was the second biggest producer. For twenty-eight years, the knowledge that gold was flowing continuously from the Rand to the London Market had been an important element in international confidence in the ability of the Bank of England to meet its due obligations in gold, and to maintain its position of dominance in world trade and finance.[3]

In the run-down to war, Germany had mobilized financially and increased substantially its gold reserve. Its store in the Reichsbank had risen in value from £30 000 000 in 1910 to £68 000 000 in July 1914 and in the first quarter of 1915 reached £106 000 000. The payment of notes in gold was prohibited.[4]

Britain was quick, too, to secure her wartime needs, and at once offered to buy the total output of the Rand for the duration of hostilities. The South African Government called a conference of banks, mining houses and merchants, and after further consultations in London, it was arranged that South African gold should be sold to the Bank of England, ownership being transferred at the moment of its deposit in South African banks. At that moment, mining companies would be credited with ninety-seven (later ninety-eight and three quarter) per cent of the proceeds, and able to draw upon them for the payment of wages and dividends. The arrangement continued in force until 1919. Britain's reserves of gold were continually replenished without the risk of bullion ending up on the Atlantic sea-bed, and the receipts from gold sales, on which South Africa depended for much of its revenue, were assured for all of the War. No wonder Wallers described it as 'one of the most interesting' of the financial arrangements evolved to meet the exigencies of war. No wonder, either, that he opened his address to the Annual General Meeting on 29 March 1915, by saying:

> ... during the last seven or eight months we must all have happily obtained a clearer vision as to what it really means to be a member of the British Empire ... This relationship with the British Empire has meant to us our very existence ....[5]

The benefit of the agreement to Britain became clear too as she bought huge supplies of war materials from the United States of America and elsewhere at a time in which restrictions on exports set the balance of trade against her. It became more than ever important as the war years passed to maintain her credit position, and an important factor in doing so was the City's control over the gold output of the world.

Another vital issue for the Chamber was to assure the continuance of supplies to the mines. It was found in consultation with merchants that most supplies were likely to come forward in the ordinary way, except for cyanide, mercury and zinc, three chemicals essential to the processes of gold recovery. It was decided that the Chamber should take direct responsibility for these items, excepting for two Groups who chose to go it alone. There was accordingly established the Central Buying Department in the Chamber which, working under the Chamber's Central Buying Committee and in association with a London Committee of the Groups, entered into large contracts, and successfully maintained supplies. In time, as the war years lengthened, and the difficulty of maintaining supplies from abroad increased, a general pooling of mining supplies would be centralized under the control of the Chamber.[6]

As a consequence of the passing of the Union Defence Act in 1912 some men on the mines were being called up for short training periods in army camps even before the outbreak of war. It was agreed in the Chamber in June 1914 that these men should have their army pay made up to their mine pay while they were in camp.

After the outbreak, the Chamber evolved by stages a spread of payments and undertakings to ease the path of those called up for war service, including British Army reservists recalled to the Colours in Britain. It was agreed that all men called up, or volunteering with their employer's consent, would have their jobs kept open for them. Married men were granted half their mine pay in addition to their army pay; single men without dependants received quarter-pay, while those with dependants received an additional amount. The period of active service counted as service with their mine for the purpose of assessing leave entitlement. It was agreed, too, that on discharge each man should be given one month's leave in addition to any leave to which he was entitled by war and mine service. By the end of 1916, about twenty per cent of white employees were on active service. So was one-third of the staff of the Chamber.

Many more men would have volunteered, but were debarred from doing so because mining was regarded as essential to the war effort, and because South Africa was anxious to avoid the situation in France where men had to be released from the Colours to keep her industries going. In response to protests from gold mine employees who were refused managerial permission to volunteer, the question was referred by the Governor-General to the Imperial Government which replied by cable that 'in the opinion of His Majesty's Government the production of gold from British territory is of the utmost importance, and the maintenance of the gold output is in Imperial interests'.[7] Despite this, men volunteered in disregard of managerial objections. The Chamber was sympathetic. It was agreed that these men would be reinstated in their former situations on discharge from military service, their period of active service counting as time with the company for the purpose of assessing leave entitlement. They were also granted a month's leave in addition to their entitlement under the leave regulations.

Miners used to earning a sovereign a day or more would have found it hard to exist on army rates of pay without the supplement from their mine. One pound was a lieutenant-colonel's pay in the Union Defence Force, and the scale ranged down to 3s a day for 'gunners, privates, trumpeters and buglers'. Those who volunteered for the South African Brigade sent to France had even more reason to be thankful for mine pay. The Brigade formed a component of the British Army and was subject to British rates of pay. It was found that the rate applicable to unmarried men was 1s a day, the 'Queen's shilling' of long-days-gone-by. The Imperial rate for the South African contingent overseas was raised to 3s a day at the beginning of 1917.

Throughout the War the Chamber gave patriotic support to the war effort. In 1914, it decided to make a direct contribution of £30 000 towards the care of war casualties, on behalf of its members, other than the Robinson Group which made a separate contribution. A hospital ship was commissioned and in service by March 1915. The collieries made an important contribution as well, donating 100 000 tons of coal to the Admiralty in that year. In each of the years from 1916 to 1919, the Chamber made regular grants to the

Governor-General's War Fund, amounting in total to £104 000.

In 1916 the Government, at the request of the Imperial Government, formed labour contingents of blacks from South Africa and adjacent British protectorates, for service in the European theatre of war. Some of those who would have come to the mines signed on for war service instead. However, blacks were often reluctant to sign on for war service, largely because the wage offered was only ten per cent above mining rates. According to the *Cape Times*, some argued that the wage offered for military service 'was not enough in France where bullets were flying about, seeing that a similar wage was obtainable on the mines in Johannesburg without the fear of bullets'.[8] The Chamber helped in the recruitment for the War, through the WNLA, by training the hospital orderlies required by the contingents. It had helped, too, as early as 1915 in supplying black labour for the forces operating in German South West Africa. They included blacks from Moçambique, which had become a belligerent when Portugal, Britain's oldest ally, confirmed her allegiance on 7 August 1914. She began operations against German possessions in Africa the same year.[9]

An involuntary contribution was made by the mining industry in the shape of a Special War Levy of £500 000 on gold mining companies imposed soon after the outbreak of war. Wallers at the Chamber's Annual General Meeting on 29 March 1915 was reasonably complacent, saying that the industry, with the exception of one Group, had not protested, because it had been made perfectly clear that the levy was abnormal and would not recur. He thought it a reasonable view that the industry, which had been but lightly disturbed by the War, should contribute towards the abnormal needs of the Treasury. Waller's confidence and his optimism were misplaced, for the Government again took the levy in 1915, and yearly thereafter.

On 4 March 1916 the Chamber at last protested and at length, proving substantial discrimination against the mines. To which the Government replied, as governments will, that, seeing the national emergency existed, it had no alternative but to reimpose the levy.[10]

Certainly the Government had much to contend with at the time, and Botha's problems were compounded by the absence of Smuts, his right-hand man. Smuts was in that year sent to East Africa to command the Allied forces in the campaign against General von Lettow-Vorbeck. At the beginning of 1917 he would be summoned to London to serve in the Imperial War Cabinet. This body had been created, on the suggestion of Lord Milner, to conduct the global war effort. Milner became Secretary of State for War in April 1918, and the two old enemies sat together around the Imperial council table.

The Chamber had also to give some attention to a new development in South Africa, the introduction of Income Tax for which the Government legislated in 1914. It provided for a scale of tax ranging from 6d in the £ of taxable income to 1s 6d for those earning £24 000 a year and above. The only direct problem for the Chamber's thirty-man income tax committee was to ensure the avoidance of double taxation of already heavily-taxed gold mines.

In 1915, the Chamber took a pioneering step by introducing annual holidays for all white mine employees on full pay, up to a maximum of £1 a day. At the time leave for black workers was not considered because mostly they worked, and would long continue to work, for no more than four months to a year before returning home for a spell of at least several months in the home territory.

The introduction of paid leave for permanent white employees was sparked by C D Leslie, Superintending Engineer of the Gold Fields of South Africa, in a proposal to the Chamber's Sub-Committee of Consulting Engineers, later to be known as the Technical Advisory Committee. The motivation for the scheme was that workers, especially those underground, would benefit in health from an annual holiday at the coast and a complete change of scene. It was thought, too, that this would help the fight against miners' phthisis.

After the strike of 1913 the Chamber had reluctantly agreed to grant ten days annually on half-pay after one year's service underground or two years on surface. Now it decided, on its own initiative, to grant twelve days of paid leave to underground employees after one year's service, rising to eighteen days in the second year, and twenty-four days in the third. Reduction workers were granted a fortnight's paid holiday after one year's service and other surface employees were granted ten days after two years' service.

The new arrangements came into effect on 1 December 1915, and took previous service into account in assessing entitlement. It was also declared that for this purpose the strikers of 1913 and 1914 would not be regarded as having broken service. Among those who benefited greatly were the men on active service. They received a bonus of paid leave at the end of the War for, in terms of the scheme, their time in the army was counted as mine employment.

By 1917, all employees, surface and underground, with one year's service were enjoying at least a clear fortnight's annual holiday and Wallers was able to declare that he believed the industry was ahead of any other industry in the world in the granting of paid leave to daily-paid workers, something which leaders of industry elsewhere tended to regard as no more than a doubtful possibility for the future.

Apart from the grant of paid leave, there were other milestones in the improvement of conditions on the mines in 1915. The Chamber expanded its independent dust sampling of mines, introduced the previous year, and official dust samplers were appointed by the mines. Moreover, mines installed equipment that ushered in a new era of constant improvement in the quality of mine air. By the end of the year, electric fans in place on the mines had a capacity of four and-a-half million cubic feet of air a minute. Millions of gallons of water, pumped through many hundreds of miles of piping, were being used underground monthly, much of it in the suppression of dust. The adoption of a single-shift system had by that time become general practice, ensuring that adequate time was allowed after blasting for dust to settle, and haulage ways to clear of poisonous gases generated by explosives.[11]

Mining men debarred from volunteering for battle continued to distinguish themselves in the rescue of fellow-workers underground. In 1915, the Chamber announced that it would take over the recognition of bravery, formerly the province of the Rand Mutual Assurance Company. Its award for outstanding courage would be the Bronze Medal, soon to be known as the 'miner's Victoria Cross'. The first awards were made the following year to J M Bennett, of Crown Mines, who gave his life endeavouring to rescue a black miner from a gas-filled tunnel, and to F W Butler, of the same mine, who in turn put his own life at hazard in a valiant attempt to rescue Bennett. In 1917, there were no less than eleven awards, one of them posthumously, on Rose Deep, Crown Mines, Jupiter and Geldenhuis Deep. Wallers commented that such acts

> ... carried out without the stimulus of any excitement, deliberately and with a full and considered knowledge of the risks involved, must be numbered amongst the most gallant actions which it is possible to perform.[12]

In all, in the years since the inauguration of the Bronze Medal, more than eighty awards have been made to workers of all races, and other awards for bravery of a lesser order have been introduced.

The War also brought advances in the training of miners, mechanics and apprentices. In 1916, the Government Miners' Training Schools, largely financed by the Chamber, began an expansion that would gradually increase the number of schools on the Reef.

A feature of the gold mining industry during the twentieth century was to be a series of dramatic expansions into new fields. Throughout the war years, the first of these was under way – the development of the Far East Rand Field, the great gold basin to the east and south-east of Johannesburg. The mines established there would mine gold from a continuation of the Main Reef, characterized by rich pay shoots.

The Corner House had acquired the farm Modderfontein to the north-east of Benoni in the early days. It proved to be one of the most bountiful gold-bearing areas in the world. Much of the remaining land in the Basin was Government property, and its mining dependent on the negotiation of work-able lease arrangements. The first of these lease mines was JCI's Government Gold Mining Areas Ltd, founded in 1910. It was dubbed 'State Mines'. After initial difficulties, it would prove one of the most profitable propositions on the Rand.

Earlier, A Goerz and Company pioneered exploration to the east and was a member of the syndicate that acquired an option on President Kruger's farm Geduld, north of Springs.[13] By 1914 A Goerz, which had been founded by German capital in the 1890s, had become considerably anglicized. It was registered in South Africa and resident in Britain for tax purposes, and had acquired many British shareholders. However, more than half the shares were still held in Germany, and were regarded as enemy property when war broke out. (In all, some £3 000 000 in dividends was due to be paid to German shareholders of mining companies of the various Groups in August. Payment was cancelled at the last moment and the money passed into the possession of the Custodian of Enemy Property in South Africa.) A Goerz adapted to the situation by appointing a new Board of Directors in London. The company was then permitted to buy the shares taken over by the Custodian of Enemy Property and Britain's Public Trustee. It became completely British, and in 1918 would change its name to Union Corporation.[14] Thereafter, the company would found its prosperity on the interests it had acquired in the Far East Rand Basin. Modderfontein Deep Levels, Geduld Proprietary Mines, and later East Geduld would become the mainstays of the Group.

In 1916 Sir Henry Strakosch, the company's Managing Director in South Africa, appointed a young South African mining engineer, Peter Maltitz Anderson, as consulting engineer. The appointment 'caused some surprise',[15] but he was destined to play a major role in the Group and in the Chamber of Mines at a critical time in the fortunes of the mining industry. He would serve as President of the Chamber on five occasions and found a minor dynasty. After the Second World War his son Colin, also representing Union Corporation, would become President of the Chamber on four occasions and another son, Peter, who became Chairman of Rand Mines, on two. Their cousin, Adrian 'Attie' von Maltitz, representing Anglo-Transvaal Consolidated Investment Company Limited, would also serve twice.

By 1917, the Basin was getting into its stride and the mines there were paying more than forty per cent of the industry's dividends. It was against this background that Ernest Oppenheimer formed the Anglo American Corporation. Born near Frankfurt in Germany in 1880, the son of a cigar merchant, he went to London at the age of sixteen to join A Dunkelsbuhler and Company, one of the smaller of the diamond firms which made up the syndicate through which De Beers marketed its production. His cousin Gustav Imroth, also employed at one time by Dunkelsbuhler, later became Managing Director of JCI. A Dunkelsbuhler had an association with A Goerz and other interests on the Rand, including large holdings in the Transvaal Coal Trust, and in the Consolidated Mines Selection Company (CMS), which much later would be merged in Charter Consolidated of London. In 1902, when just twenty-two, Oppenheimer was sent to Kimberley to represent the firm. He stayed for thirteen years, marrying in 1906. His son Harry Frederick, who would one day succeed him as the head of the Anglo American Corporation, was born there. Ernest Oppenheimer travelled widely in Southern Africa, acquainting himself with the burgeoning mineral resources of the sub-continent.

By 1916, at the age of thirty-six, he had become a world authority on diamonds and was looking for fresh fields to conquer. While retaining his interests in diamonds (he would become Chairman of De Beers in 1929), he moved to the Rand as the special representative of CMS, on the Board of which A Dunkelsbuhler was strongly represented. CMS held mining interests which positioned it well strategically to play a major part in unlocking the vast gold deposits of the Far East Rand Basin. A year after Oppenheimer's arrival, the company acquired the deep-level lease of the Brakpan mine. Oppenheimer then entered into a reciprocal agreement with CMS, giving him the right to participate to the extent of fifty per cent, during a period of seven years from 8 June 1917, in interests acquired by the CMS in any part of the Transvaal east of the present property of the ERPM and south of Heidelberg. This was the basis on which the Anglo American Corporation was formed.

Oppenheimer was ahead of his time in his realization that the major mining houses should be managed and controlled in South Africa. The London-based CMS would not do. Moreover, it lacked the vigour he believed essential. He decided to establish a major new and powerful mining house, with which CMS and the Rand Selection Trust (formerly the Transvaal Coal Trust) might amalgamate and enjoy a fair share of the business now offering on the Far East Rand.

To raise the necessary capital Oppenheimer enlisted the aid of W L Honnold, an American consulting engineer who had been Managing Director of the CMS and Chairman of the Coal Trust until 1915, and who was now associated in relief work in Belgium with the American mining engineer, and future President of the United States, Herbert Hoover. Honnold arranged a meeting between Hoover and Oppenheimer in London on 17 April 1917, and in due course the Newmont Mining Company of the United States, with which was associated J P Morgan & Company, became shareholders of Anglo American on its formation on 25 September 1917. The new corporation was launched with an initial capital of £1 million, of which half was subscribed in America and half in England and South Africa. The capital was substantial for those days and Anglo American quickly became one of the important financial houses on the Rand. But this was only the beginning, for:

> ... while the going was good and De Beers hesitated Ernest Oppenheimer acted. He bought the former German diamond mines in South-West Africa and formed another company, Consolidated Diamond Mines of South-West Africa, one of the best investments he ever made.
>
> There is no story in mining history quite as exciting as this. In the short six years between 1915 and 1921 Oppenheimer had achieved the imposs- ible. He had followed the trail blazed by Rhodes, Alfred Beit and Robinson from Kimberley to the Rand and, without any of the advantages they enjoyed as pioneers, had laid the foundations of a financial empire that was to be bigger even than Rhodes's dreams.[16]

Ernest Oppenheimer was lucky to survive the War, for he was one of only 150 saved of the 1 000 people on board the *Galway Castle* torpedoed off Land's End on 10 September 1918. (Among those rescued was Henry Burton, Minister of Railways and Harbours, and later Minister of Finance.) Through- out his life Oppenheimer enjoyed a fair share of good fortune, which he was able to turn brilliantly to account. He was always in the forefront of his contemporaries in the discernment of opportunities, and he usually contrived to be ahead of rivals in the speed with which he moved to grasp them. Despite the gentle and courteous manner, he could be hard when the advancement of ambition demanded. Like the men who built the great mediaeval cathedrals, he had the ability to visualize the completed structure, and the strength of purpose that would give the dream reality.

The war years of 1914–1918 brought progressive expansion in the functions of the Chamber. In 1917 it was decided to take a step forward of enduring importance by providing a service to the coal industry, similar to that provided for the gold mines. The centre of coal mining had by now switched to the Middelburg area, where there were eighteen collieries, but four were still operating in the Brakpan–Springs district. There was already in existence the important Transvaal Coal Owners' Association which has continued to be responsible for the marketing of coal while the Chamber has handled matters related to production.

In 1917 a few coal mines were members of the Chamber, but the industry as a whole was not represented, something which resulted in lack of co-ordination between the two mining sectors. Henceforth, all collieries would be encouraged to join the Chamber and many would do so. A Collieries Committee was appointed to deal with coal matters, and provision was made for joint meetings with the Chamber's Executive when matters affecting both sectors required discussion. The Committee first met on 11 June 1918, and would soon have a membership of sixteen, each representing a colliery member. Like its gold mining counterpart, it was at once involved in negotiations with trade unions on behalf of the industry.

Alex Aiken was the first Chairman of the Collieries Executive Committee. He was one of the country's leading accountants and economists and, leadership of the coal industry apart, was a public figure in his own right. After he had served as an assistant to J Emrys Evans, financial adviser to Kitchener and Lord Milner at the turn of the century, he reorganized the finances of the newly-formed municipality of Johannesburg, and was for a time Town Treasurer. He subsequently played an important role in clearing the city's slums. He was prominent in the organization of higher education, and it was 'largely due to his untiring efforts' that the funds were raised to establish the University of the Witwatersrand. His work would be recognized by the award of an honorary degree of Doctor of Laws in 1929. Both he and subsequently his son, Arthur Stephen, would serve as Chairman of the University's Finance Committee.[17]

The decision to enlarge the Chamber's scope came at a propitious moment, for the coal industry produced its highest ever tonnage of coal in 1917, largely as a result of the big demand for the bunkers of ships calling at South African ports in wartime.

On the gold mines, the War taxed in many ways the ingenuity of mining engineers, metallurgists and other officials, faced with shortages of labour, an increasingly erratic supply position and rapid cost inflation. However, the industry pursued with dedication what it perceived to be its main wartime role – maintenance of full production. Remarkably, it succeeded. The value of production rose slightly from £35 656 814 in 1914 to £35 758 636 in 1918. Unfortunately, this was only achieved by substantial increases in the wage bill for skilled workers, and in the expenditure on stores. Profits fell sharply. In 1918 mines, other than those on the Far East Rand, paid less than one-third of the dividends they had paid in 1914 – 'a hopelessly inadequate return on the capital invested in them'.[18]

The War left the industry with an increased cost structure, and a legacy of greater significance. Trade unionism had been given a powerful stimulus, boding ill for the mining companies in the depression years that would follow soon after the Peace.

[1] Van-Helten, p 533-534.

[2] Ibid, pp 537-539.

[3] Ibid, pp 534, 547-548.

[4] Annual Report of the Transvaal Chamber of Mines, 1914, p LXVI.

[5] Ibid, pp LXV, LVIII.

[6] Ibid, p LXIV-LXV.
 Twenty-Eighth Annual Report of the Transvaal Chamber of Mines, 1917, p 69.

[7] Annual Report of the Transvaal Chamber of Mines, 1917, pp 190-191, quoting a letter dated 7 May 1917, from the Secretary to the Prime Minister, Cape Town, to the President, Transvaal Chamber of Mines, Johannesburg.

[8] A M Grundlingh, 'Black Men in a White Man's War: The Impact of the First World War on South African Blacks', War and Society, Volume III, No 1, May 1985, pp 56-57.
 A M Grundlingh, 'Die Suid-Afrikaanse Gekleurdes en die Eerste Wêreldoorlog', pp 200-201.

[9] 'Portugal, History of' in The New Encyclopaedia Brittanica, Macropaedia, Volume 14, Knowledge in Depth, 15th edition, p 872.

[10] Twenty-Seventh Annual Report of the Transvaal Chamber of Mines, 1916, pp 179-180.

[11] Twenty-Sixth Annual Report of the Transvaal Chamber of Mines, 1915, pp LXII-LXIII, LXV-LXVI.

[12] Annual Report of the Transvaal Chamber of Mines, 1917, p 72.

[13] Cartwright, The Gold Miners, p 177.

[14] Ibid, pp 187-188.

[15] Ibid, p 188.

[16] Ibid, p 194.

[17] I Isaacson, 'Aiken' in Dictionary of South African Biography, III, pp 5-6.
 Rand Daily Mail, 25 July 1945, p 9: Obituary of Dr Alexander Aiken.

[18] Twenty-Ninth Annual Report of the Transvaal Chamber of Mines, 1918, pp 68, 393.

CHAPTER TWENTY

The Bid for Industrial Peace

As the War progressed the Chamber was assigned for the first time the function of negotiating with employee associations on matters affecting the industry as a whole. It was increasingly an unenviable role in a time of rapid inflation, and of shortage of both men and materials, for the overriding need to maintain output dictated a quick settlement of disputes likely to lead to strikes. And there were other good reasons why the prevailing mood should be one of compromise.

In the pre-war world it had seemed to almost everyone that industrial strife was inevitable, that mutual suspicion, born of hostility and lack of trust between Capital and Labour, could be resolved only by a showdown of climactic magnitude. They were not wrong, but the War postponed the upheaval in the industrial countries. Some now feared that when it came it would rival the War itself in its damage to society. Wallers was among those who foresaw the danger to South Africa, and he would return again and again to the theme during his years of office. He was prepared to admit faults on the part of management in the past and to accept the shared responsibility of maintaining industrial peace through mutual discussion.

The first war-time demand of significance from the unions came from the former Transvaal Miners' Association, which had changed its name to the South African Mine Workers' Union (MWU). In May of 1915, the MWU wrote to the Chamber demanding an increase in wages of twenty to twenty-five per cent to match the rising cost of living. The Chamber suggested to the Government that a joint committee of employers and employees under a Government chairman be appointed to resolve the issue. The Government responded by appointing Buckle as Chairman, and extending the inquiry to cover certain other classes of employee.[1]

The Chamber agreed to this, but continued to refuse to have dealings with the umbrella South African Industrial Federation, the name adopted by the former Federation of Trades. Gemmill, the Chamber's Joint-Secretary and Actuary, wrote to Archie Crawford, the Secretary of the Federation, on 11 June, saying that the Chamber, while quite willing to hold discussions with trade unions representing the employees concerned, saw no reason 'for the interposition of your Federation as a third party'. Crawford replied tartly and cogently:

> Your Chamber reduced the multiplicity of mines to one co-ordinating body; our Federation does exactly the same thing for the Unions. Surely your Chamber, which is, after all, a Federation of Mine *Employers*, is not disposed to press its objection to our Federation of Mine *Employees*? It would indeed be a pity should such unreasonable prejudice lead to the slightest rupture.

> This Federation is not disposed to allow a mere whim or quibble on the part of your Chamber to again become a strike germ.[2]

Gemmill answered that the Chamber's Executive Committee had nothing to add to its previous reply. However, the Chamber began to use the Federation as a post office in communication with mechanics' unions. No objection seems to have been made to Crawford's nomination to serve on the Joint Committee on behalf of the Amalgamated Society of Engineers, which represented mechanics. There were two MWU representatives, two from the mechanics' union and one from the Boilermakers, Iron and Steel Shipbuilders' Union. The Chamber's five members were its President, Dawe, Wallers, James H Crosby, of the Robinson Group, Frank G Roberts, who had been appointed the first Technical Adviser of the Chamber, and Gemmill.

The Joint Committee agreed to the payment of special war bonuses to married men, and to improved working hours and overtime rates for mechanics.

Crosby did not support the higher pay or improvements in working hours proposed, on the grounds that workmen on the Rand were better paid than in any other part of the world. He said that the Robinson Group could afford neither an increase in wages nor reduction in time at work. Two representatives of the mining unions opposed the increases as inadequate. Nevertheless, they were put into operation on all mines other than the Randfontein and Langlaagte mines of the Robinson Group.[3] However, the maverick Robinson Group was soon to disappear from the scene, its mines being absorbed into the JCI.

In the years following, war bonuses, rates of pay and overtime, would be regularly reviewed and improved in the light of the impact of the rising cost of living on the married man, the aim being to reduce hardship rather than to meet fully the fall in the purchasing power of the pound. Interestingly, food prices in South Africa rose by a relatively low thirty-eight per cent during the War, reflecting in part the country's ability to feed itself. Food prices in the United States rose twice as fast, and in Britain three-and-a-half times.[4]

Rapprochement between the Chamber and the South African Industrial Federation developed, and there was a much improved atmosphere as management and men co-operated to keep production going in the face of the common enemy. Mine employees contributed generously to war funds. The Chamber, led by Wallers, worked hard to improve relations on a new basis of mutual respect and reasonableness, and the trade unions responded. The Whitley Commission in Britain had recommended that employer and employed should work closely together at every level of industry, a special place being given to joint consultative committees. Wallers seems to have arrived separately at similar conclusions and his personal involvement achieved much.[5] It was said of him that he had the gift of endless patience and courtesy in the discussion of all matters of business, however wearisome they might become. He was always willing to listen to 'the other fellow's point of view'.[6] This approach was extended to the class of employee categorized as officials, who did not belong to unions but to associations of their own. The Underground Officials' Association of South Africa was formed in 1918, and the Mine Surface Officials' Association of South Africa in the following year. The Underground Association included in its ranks the all-important shift bosses and those in more senior posts. The Chamber was careful to recognize the pivotal role the official played in the management hierarchy, and uniform conditions of employment were evolved in the period 1917-1919 with the two associations, and with the Colliery Officials' Association as the Chamber extended its role to cover member collieries. Officials formed a corps who, it was hoped, could be relied on to keep mines in good order in times of work stoppage and strike.

The concessions granted to the unions by the Chamber under Wallers were arrived at after round-table discussion in joint committees. They served for a time to create good industrial relations, but they also helped to entrench the power of the unions. Some of the concessions made would have been unthinkable only a few years previously, and the Chamber and Wallers were criticized for being weak in the face of union demands.

The Chamber agreed to minimum rates of pay for mechanics and miners. It accepted the 'bank to bank' principle on working hours for members of the MWU, agreeing that underground hours should be fixed at forty-eight-and-a-half hours 'bank to bank' instead of forty-eight hours in the working place. The daily hours were later adjusted to give a shorter working day on a Saturday. The reduced hours meant a diminution of the productivity of black workers, already impeded from working a full shift underground by the colour bar regulations which required a white overseer to declare a working place safe before black workers could enter it, and which required them to vacate the working place before the shift end to enable whites to carry out charging up and blasting. The effective shift of black workers was estimated at as little as five hours.

A more radical change was the agreement that trade union dues could be deducted from men's pay with their consent. A fillip was given to union recruiting and the collection of dues. More radical still was the agreement that shop-stewards might be appointed to represent men on individual mines in disputes with management. These men were to occupy pivotal positions in post-war unrest.

Of even greater importance for the future was the on-going conflict over the colour bar. While skilled jobs calling for trained and competent workers were generally reserved for whites, there were many jobs in the grey area between unskilled and semi-skilled that might be filled by either whites or Coloureds (the term including Indians, blacks and people of mixed race), the choice often depending on local circumstances. As the mining industry expanded into new areas, and went deeper, and as its technology developed, old jobs changed in character and new ones emerged. In jobs like track laying and pump and pipe fitting, the packing of waste rock to support the workings, the installation of timber supports, the operation of small winches, and attendance on simple machinery, the mining companies took such opportunities as offered to increase the employment of men other than whites. The process led to a slow but steady movement of these workers into unskilled and semi-skilled work once done by whites. However, the process of change was not enough to alter significantly the ratio of other races to whites. The ratio moved from 7,6 to 1 in 1910, peaked at 9,1 to 1 in 1916, and fell back to 7,4 to 1 in 1919.[7]

Sensing the threat to the protected status of the white worker implicit in the impending cost crisis, the trade unions became increasingly sensitive to any change in the colour line. On one mine, the stopers refused to work with a fellow stoper who had married a respectable Cape woman of mixed race. On another, the men protested against the employment of men of mixed race in jobs formerly done by blacks. To complicate the situation further, unemployed whites were signed on as unskilled labourers in work usually done by blacks, as an act of charity. There was nothing simple about the labour problems facing the Chamber. Out of the inevitable conflict with the unions developed the so-called Status Quo Agreement.

The origin of the Agreement was a demand by the Federation in 1916 that only whites should be employed as drill sharpeners and that men of other races should be dismissed. The Chamber, reluctant to turn back the modest advancement that had taken place, refused but, after considering a variety of alternative ways to defuse the situation, offered to maintain the status quo. The Federation, in turn, refused to accept this in 1916, and again when the argument was renewed in 1917. Despite the refusal of the unions to be bound by the status quo, they were quick to attack employers for alleged infringements of it. However, on 20 June 1918 the dispute was brought to a head.

The first item in a long list of demands submitted by the Federation on that date was a request that the unions be freed of their undertaking not to ask for higher wages until three months after the War. The Chamber refused and the miners accepted the refusal. The second demand read:

Coloured drill sharpeners on the Witwatersrand Mines to be dismissed, failing which, after 30 days from receipt by the Chamber of Mines of this

253

demand, federated unions will refuse to co-operate with coloured drill sharpeners.[8]

In the face of this threat from the unions, the affected workers at once protested and passed a resolution at a public meeting at the Pilkington Hall on 24 June 1918, earnestly requesting 'the Union Government and the Chamber to protect us, by not acceding to the demand'.[9]

The Chamber duly refused to meet the demand from the Federation, but again offered to maintain the status quo.

The Federation replied on 29 July 1918:

The reply of the Chamber in respect to this demand is disappointing to the Unions. Although only 73 coloured men, including natives, are working as drill sharpeners, there are 73 less supporters of a white standard of life on the mines.[10]

The Federation reminded the Chamber that it had warned employer representatives at a recent conference of 'the seriousness of the question'. It called on the Chamber to reconsider.[11]

The Chamber replied on 2 August 1918:

The Chamber cannot help thinking that the Unions have not appreciated the great importance to their members of accepting the Chamber's offer, which has universal application to all classes of mine work. The Chamber would point out that it is impossible for the Unions to reject the offer, and yet expect it to be acted upon in the future.[12]

The penny now dropped and the Federation accepted the thrice-proffered compromise, though this did not end union endeavours to make drill sharpening a white job and to extend the boundaries of the colour bar. The Agreement provided:

... the *status quo* as existing on each mine with regard to the relative scope of employment of European and Coloured employees should be maintained; that is to say, no billets which are held by European workmen should be given to Coloured [which included black] workmen, and *vice versa*.[13]

It applied only to unskilled and semi-skilled work (the so-called conventional colour bar) and not to skilled whites whose employment was protected by the regulations to the Mines and Works Act (the statutory colour bar). However, it would be widely invoked by the unions in the difficult post-war years effectively to prevent reorganization underground in the interests of improving productivity.[14] In retrospect, the Chamber must have regretted offering the Status Quo Agreement, as a war-time expedient, intended both to hold the colour line and to avert strike action. The Agreement only came into effect on

1 September 1918, less than two-and-a-half months before the Armistice.

Black workers were much less fortunate than the white. They received no increase in basic rates until 1919. There were sporadic strikes of short duration on mines, chiefly over pay, during the War. In February 1918 there was unrest along the Reef, paticularly among black municipal workers, which spread to the mines as well. Many Reef stores, alleged to be profiteering, were boycotted, and there were complaints among mineworkers about inadequate pay and lack of opportunity for advancement. The Government appointed J B Moffat, Chief Magistrate of the Transkei, and soon to become Secretary for Native Affairs, as Commissioner to investigate the grievances. He showed scant sympathy with the black mineworkers, who were provided with food, accommodation and medical treatment at no cost to themselves.

> So far as the mine native is concerned, the increase in the cost of living is practically limited to the cost of clothing. He is fed on a liberal scale, and all the natives who gave evidence were perfectly satisfied with their treatment in the compounds, where everything possible is done for their health and comfort. His position cannot be compared with that of the white workers, to some of whom increases of wages have been granted. ... The native's standard of subsistence at his home, excepting the comparatively few who have adopted European style of living, is not seriously affected by the War.
>
> ... the rise in cost of clothing ... is an inconvenience that everyone has to put up with, and cannot be regarded as a real hardship. ... If after four years of world-wide war people have nothing worse to complain of, they are fortunate. The average rate of pay earned by natives on the mines is, roughly, 2s per shift. Those engaged on drilling, tramming, etc, can earn considerably more.[15]

Moffat drew attention to the fact that since 1914 the number of blacks who made their own way to the Rand to work on the mines, without seeking the assistance of a recruiting agency, had increased from 32,5 per cent in 1914 to 58,4 per cent in the second quarter of 1918. Moffat deduced that they would not have done so if they did not find the wages adequate.[16] However, Moffat did recommend the repeal of the statutory colour bar.[17]

Wallers was more sympathetic, but he was clearly opposed to increases in black wages without provision for a corresponding increase in productivity. Productivity of all workers had in fact seriously declined through the war years.

He told the Chamber's Annual Meeting on 24 March 1919 that the one most important point of dissatisfaction among black workers on the mines was their inability to rise in earnings.

> It is true that we have on the mines a number of 'piecework' systems for natives, under which somewhat higher earnings can be made by the more efficient natives, but I feel very strongly that we must advance considerably

before this real grievance of the native is removed. In order to assist in this direction, your Executive Committee has decided to collate the information on such methods of payment to the natives, and to consider their extension where possible. To expect that the natives will be for ever content with their present position and limitations is absurd; to attempt to repress their legitimate aspirations, even if such repression were possible, is surely wrong; therefore, it behoves us to endeavour to remove, before they become acute, but with due regard to the position of the white workmen, the real grievances from which the natives are suffering ....[18]

However, the Chamber made it clear on another occasion that there was a point beyond which it was not yet prepared to go.

It is impossible to deny that the colour bar as laid down in the Government Mining Regulations imposes an artificial restriction on the advancement of the coloured and native population. But much more important than the Government Mining Regulations is the force of custom. Public opinion is not prepared to see the substitution of coloured or native workers for white skilled and semi-skilled workers, and any attempt to employ the non-white workman in mining work at present occupied by white men would cause a strike of the white employees on the mines, who would be supported by the great bulk of the white population of the Witwatersrand.[19]

Looking back over the war years in 1919, Wallers (recently created KBE) re-iterated his past condemnation of extremists among both employers and employees. These he saw as the real danger to industrial peace. He was quite ready to admit as perfectly legitimate workers' aspirations towards reasonable working hours and a definite status, and to concede that Capital had in the past been wanting in this responsibility.[20]

However, perhaps with a growing realization of the perils of following a conciliatory path, he cracked down on the extremists among workers who persisted in discrediting the employer beyond all reason, and who urged on fellow-workers that salvation was to be found only in extreme and revolutionary methods, regardless of discipline, or of law and order. He stressed the danger of workers acting as if there were an unlimited margin in any industry, or in the wealth of the community, from which increases in wages and reduction in production through shorter hours could be met. In support of this he reminded workers that the British Labour MP and leader of British railway men, J H Thomas, had warned his followers:

... People who tell you there is unlimited wealth somewhere, which you will collect if you can only find the key, are leading you on a false path. The truth is that the only wealth is the wealth we produce, and unless we keep that fact clearly in mind, we are going headlong to disaster.[21]

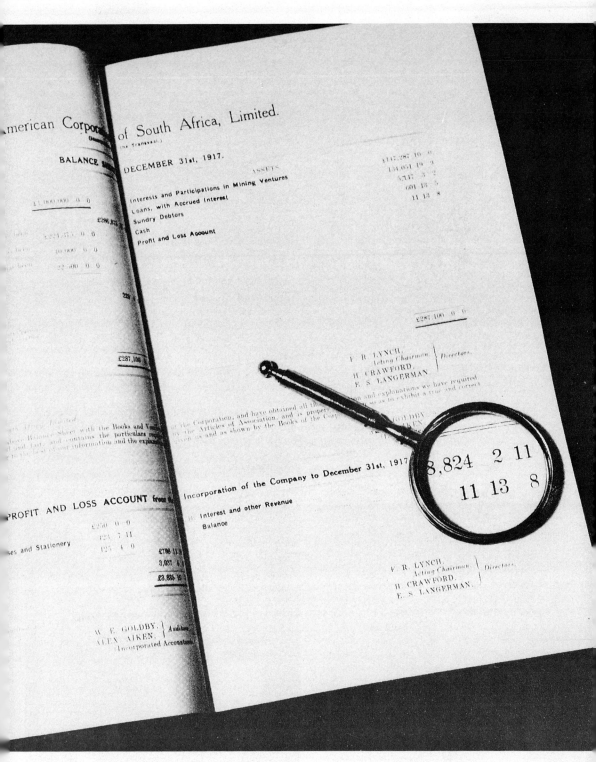

Anglo American Corporation was launched in 1917 with an initial capital of £1 million. The balance sheet and profit and loss account in its first report showed a profit of £11.13s.8d.

A conference of seven-a-side was charged with the purpose of resolving the industrial disputes of January 1922. The chairman, Judge Curlewis, did his best, 'but the conference drowned in an ocean of words'.

Sitting in the front row are (left to right): W Gemmill, Sir Evelyn Wallers, H O Buckle, Curlewis, and the strike leaders, Joe Thompson, James George and W A Butler. John Roy, representing the coal industry, is second on the left in the back row.

Sir Evelyn Wallers   P M Anderson

Strike commando on the march headed by its own brass band. They are carrying the strike banner 'Workers of the world fight and unite for a White South Africa'.

Arrest of strike leaders at the Trades Hall, Rissik Street.

Murder scene at Brakpan mine offices. Officials were shot and clubbed to death.

Casualties mount. Comrades fire a salute over the grave of Trooper H J Coetzee, victim of a Fordsburg sniper.

Boonzaier cartoon has Smuts hesitant to grasp the weapon of martial law, while Hoggenheimer watches expectantly from the background.

Smuts counter-attacks, using artillery and aircraft to bombard the positions of the commandos.

Aftermath of bombardment of Fordsburg.

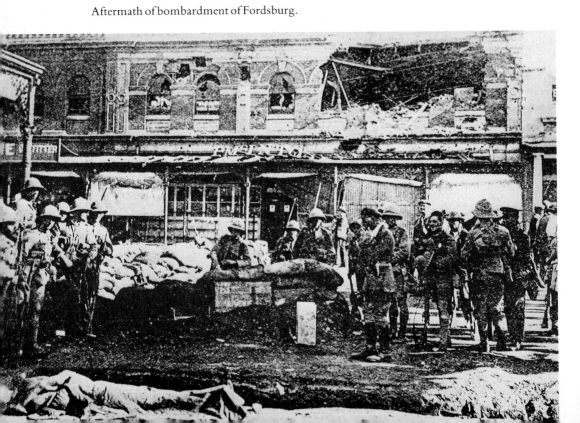

Aerial photograph of The Battle of Fordsburg at the moment of capitulation on 16th March, 1922, shows at top right the trenches in front of the rebel headquarters, and the barricade across Main Street. At bottom left, cars of the motorized volunteers surge up Main Street. The picture was one of the first to be taken by the newly-formed South African Air Force.

John Martin

Guy Carleton Jones

Rudolf Krahmann, who pioneered the magnetometer in the discovery of the West Wits Line.

Wallers would not, in the end, succeed in preserving industrial accord, for the underlying conflict between Management and White Labour was too strong. Wallers, and the Chamber, were aware, not only of the need to meet the reasonable aspirations of White Labour but that Black Labour had aspirations as well. However, black advancement pre-supposed the opening of more rewarding occupations to them. To this the unions were fundamentally opposed, and their members already resented the modest advances into the more simple tasks which some blacks had made while white labour was scarce. Tension over the colour bar, and the awful economic conditions that followed the War, would wreck Wallers's hopes. As elsewhere in the industrial world, the Peace would bring that showdown between Capital and Labour which Wallers foresaw and strove so hard and long to avert.

However, he did succeed in ameliorating the atmosphere of mutual hostility for a time, and in creating, with the help of trade union leaders, the custom of a free and frank exchange of views. They established together habits of negotiation that would survive the catharsis of 1922.

[1] Annual Report of the Transvaal Chamber of Mines, 1915, pp 10-17, LXVI.

[2] *Ibid*, pp 16-18.

[3] *Ibid*, pp 20-27, XLVI.

[4] Henry Strakosch, *The South African Currency and Exchange Problem*, graph entitled 'Increase of Retail Prices of Food over July 1914'.

[5] Annual Report of the Transvaal Chamber of Mines, 1917, pp 76-78.

[6] *Ibid*, p 77.

[7] Chamber of Mines Archives: File 75 1920, '*Status Quo*': Unemployment Commission: Preliminary Statement by the Transvaal Chamber of Mines, Johannesburg, 12 October 1920, p 2.

[8] Annual Report of the Transvaal Chamber of Mines, 1918, pp 116-119, 126.

[9] *Ibid*, p 117.

[10] *Ibid*, pp 126-128.

[11] *Ibid*, p 128.

[12] *Ibid*, pp 129, 131.

[13] *Ibid*, pp 122-123, 126-136.

[14] Doxey, p 125.

[15] Thirtieth Annual Report of the Transvaal Chamber of Mines, 1919, p 226. (Extract from Report of J B Moffat, the Commissioner appointed to Enquire into and Report upon the Causes which led up to the Partial Cessation of the Municipal Sanitary Services at Johannesburg, 6-8 June 1918, and the Threatened Strike on 1 July 1918.)

[16] *Ibid*, p 227. (Extract from the Report of the Moffat Commission, 1918.)

[17] Union of South Africa: Report of the Low Grade Mines Commission, 1920 (UG 34-'20), p 29, quoting from the Report of the Moffat Commission, 1918.

[18] Annual Report of the Transvaal Chamber of Mines, 1918, pp 70-71.

[19] *Ibid*, p 92.

[20] *Ibid*, pp 61-62.

[21] *Ibid*, pp 61, 63.

CHAPTER TWENTY-ONE

The Crumbling of Accord

As mining men in the services came back from the War to wives, families and their jobs on the mines, they found the industry so crippled by rising costs that nearly half of its mines faced the threat of closure. In April 1918 a Select Committee of Parliament had reported that the profits of fourteen mines had fallen to an average of only 9d for every ton of ore milled. A year later the Government appointed the Low Grade Mines Commission, under the chairmanship of Sir Robert Kotzé, the Government Mining Engineer. The Chamber was represented on the Commission by Wallers, Gemmill and Roberts, and the unions by Crawford of the Federation, and by James Forrester Brown and Bouwer Pohl of the MWU. There were two other members, J G van der Horst, a Cape businessman and economist, who resigned before the final report, and W T Welsh, a senior official of the Native Affairs Department in the Transkei.

The Commission speedily produced a unanimous Interim Report to meet the fast-deepening crisis. The report showed that of the fourteen mines under pressure the previous year, three had closed and the remaining eleven were showing an average profit of one-seventh of a penny on each ton of ore milled. The number of marginal mines had now risen to twenty-one. In the quarter preceding the Interim Report they were worked at an average *loss* of six-tenths of a penny for every ton they milled. In other words, they were being kept alive on little but hope of better times. These mines employed 10 500 whites and 80 000 blacks. They produced gold worth more than £1 million a month, and spent nearly all of it in wages and stores. The Commissioners were at one that some of these mines faced imminent closure and, once closed, might never be re-opened. For the Government, already facing deepening depression and rising unemployment, the prospect was unthinkable.

The problems of the mines stemmed from a rise of thirty per cent in the cost of production as a result of the War, due mainly to the high cost of stores and of white wages. There was, further, a shortage in the availability of blacks for unskilled work underground. In 1915 black labour was so plentiful that mines were able to employ virtually all the labour required (the so-called complement). Thereafter the labour force declined to 82,9 per cent of complement in 1916, to 72,6 per cent in 1917 and 61,1 per cent in 1918.[1] By then, the industry's position was probably worse than it had ever been. A factor was the epidemic of Spanish influenza that hit the world from 1918-1920, killing two-and-a-half times as many people as died in the War. In South Africa alone, nearly 140 000 people of all races died, according to official figures at the time, and recent research suggests that the total may have been much higher.[2] Fortunately, the type of the disease on the mines was comparatively mild, and proper measures were taken on mines and in mine hospitals to combat the epidemic. As a result, the death rate was less than elsewhere in the country. There were nonetheless 52 489 cases among the black workforce on the mines at the epidemic's height between 20 September and 31 October 1918, of whom 1 082 died, 421 of them from Moçambique.[3]

The main reasons for the persistent shortage of labour that developed during the War were the expansion of the industry into the Far East Rand, and the increased demand from other employers. Manufacturing industry had expanded dramatically under the stimulus of wartime demand. Moreover, productivity on the mines fell, largely as a result of the reduction in working hours. In gold mines on the Rand, with their large initial and running costs, a relatively high level of production had to be reached before profits could be earned. Similarly, a fall in output had a disproportionate effect on profits.

> ... the loss of profit from a reduced output far exceeds the proportion of output lost, since all the profit arises only from that part of the output exceeding the critical percentage. Thus, in the case of a mine whose critical percentage is 80 per cent, a reduction of 10 per cent in tonnage means a loss not of a tenth but of a half of its profit.[4]

The Interim Report proposed three immediate steps: greater co-operation between management and labour through works and joint committees, the re-arrangement of underground work so as to increase the effective working hours of unskilled black labour, and the lifting of the ban on the recruitment of labour from north of latitude twenty-two degrees south. Works and joint committees were already well-established on the mines and there was no apparent problem in implementing the proposal for closer co-operation. However, despite the concurrence of Commissioners representing labour in the more effective employment of blacks underground, their unions rejected at branch level the changes in regulations necessary to bring this about. Nor was Government agreement forthcoming to the re-introduction of tropical labour with its record of high mortality on the Rand.

Its interim report issued, the Commission continued with its deliberations, but the urgency evaporated as the mines were saved by one of those twists of economic fate that characterize the industry's history. The arrangements by which the Bank of England purchased the Transvaal gold output, taking delivery in South Africa, came to an end on 23 July 1919. From then on, all gold mined, other than that required for local currency or manufacture, was consigned to the Bank of England, processed by London refiners and sold on the open market by Rothschilds, as the agents of the producers. The free sale of Rand gold began at once to attract a premium above the previous fixed price, bringing great benefits to the mines.

Prior to the War the important industrial countries had currencies established on a gold basis and the exchanges between them were controlled largely by the practical freedom that existed in the transmission of gold from the one to the other. The War brought restrictions on the free movement of gold, which ceased to be the general basis of currency. Huge quantities of paper money were created, currencies were inflated and their values depreciated in relation to gold. The United States, however, owing mainly to the abnormal increase of its exports, and the excess over its imports, succeeded in maintaining its currency on a gold standard, so that English currency in relation to American showed a depreciation that exactly accorded with its inflation in terms of gold. As the adverse movement of the American exchange against the United Kingdom became marked in 1919, it was increasingly clear that free marketing of gold in London would result in a sterling price equivalent to that offering for gold in America. However, the extent of the premium that would be obtained was not at first appreciated. In the event, the premium from 24 July to 31 December 1919, averaged twenty-four per cent above the pevious price and went as high as forty-four per cent.[5] In March 1920 the premium was still thirty-three per cent, and at the Chamber's Annual General Meeting on the 22nd of that month, Wallers could announce that the average premium earned up to that date was twenty-six and-one-quarter per cent.

As a consequence, the industry had not only been able to avert disaster, but to increase dividends at long last. It was able to improve conditions of employment as well, perhaps unwisely in view of the hard times ahead, already writ large by economic forecasters. The Chamber granted paid public holidays on 16 December (Dingaan's Day, now known as the Day of the Vow) and 1 May (May Day); and gave increases in pay to help all categories of workers to meet still-rising living costs, and other benefits. The Chamber took the precaution however of stipulating during the negotiations that wages might have to be cut if conditions changed, and this was accepted by the Federation. Wallers warned that the premium was necessarily of ephemeral benefit and stressed that the same circumstances that created a premium increased costs as well.

> Before 1914, for longer than any of us can remember, 'one pound' meant the equivalent of one golden sovereign; in the last six years that phrase has come, by imperceptible stages, to mean 'the equivalent of one depreciated Bradbury.'
>
> The effect of this depreciation of currency is therefore to increase not only the price of gold but the price of everything else as well; so that what we receive at one end we pay out at the other in increased and increasing costs of stores and of living. In fact, ... we suffered the loss of this situation for five years before we began to gain any profit therefrom.

Furthermore, it is of no use to delude ourselves or others with the idea that this premium on gold is going to be permanent. Sooner or later, ... gold will return to its permanent standard value. When that time comes, we shall be faced with the necessity of adopting one of two alternative policies. Either half the Industry must be closed down, with the resulting unemployment ... or the costs of production, including the cost of labour, must be reduced.

As soon as it becomes clear that the cost to any mine of producing one sovereign will be, for any serious period, more than 20s, that mine must inevitably shut down.[6]

The Chamber was at once industrious in obtaining the best price for its gold while the buoyancy of the free market lasted. The War and its aftermath bred a distrust for the less substantial forms of wealth and encouraged men everywhere to convert savings into gold. More than one-half of South Africa's gold was finding its way to the East and, particularly, to gold-hungry India, where the premium obtainable was substantially higher than in the West. Unfortunately for the mines, they did not benefit because the Indian Government reserved the right of legal gold sales to itself, buying at the American price and taking a profit on domestic sales for the national benefit.

It became apparent to the Chamber that it had not, under wartime arrangements, got the best possible price for Rand gold at the lowest possible handling charge. It found to its chagrin that Canada and distant Australia had got a more favourable deal from the Bank of England.[7] Part of the Chamber's response was to urge on the Government the establishment in South Africa of a gold refinery and a mint. It was hoped initially that the two institutions would be set up side by side on the Rand, and might be jointly controlled by the State. However, the Government was insistent that its mint should be located in the administrative capital, Pretoria. The upshot was that the Government established a branch of the Royal Mint there, while the Chamber created a subsidiary company to build and operate a refinery at India Junction, Germiston.

The Rand Refinery was registered as a company with a capital of £50 000 on 27 November 1920, and was in operation by June 1922, refining the whole of South Africa's gold, a function which made it the largest gold refinery in the world. Its role ever since has been to process into refined bars of gold, and of silver, the bullion sent to it by the mines. The unrefined mine bars contain roughly 88 per cent gold, 10 per cent of silver which is an important by-product of gold mining on the Rand, and 2 per cent of other minerals. The Refinery operates on a non-profit basis, levying a refining charge and re-turning any resultant profit to the mines.

Since 1910, the Chamber had operated the Witwatersrand Co-operative Smelting Works Ltd, located on the Robinson mine, to handle waste materials from mine smelting houses, which contained residual gold and silver. It was later to be known as By-Products Ltd. The smelting works and the refinery continued a separate existence for nearly fifty years, but today are operated as a joint enterprise, producing refined gold and silver, as well as some osmiridium and base metals.

South Africa's international trading position post-war was further complicated by the strength of her currency which for a time earned a premium over sterling to which the South African pound was closely linked. South African banks built up large balances of depreciated sterling, and gold sovereigns began to disappear from circulation as they were illegally moved abroad to take advantage of the premium prices on offer. Some of them went through Moçambique to play their part in the thriving smuggling trade with India out of Arab ports. The situation brought an end to the payment of Moçambican mineworkers in sovereigns.

In 1919 Henry Strakosch, the London-based Managing Director of Union Corporation, began to play a leading role as an expert in international monetary affairs. In that year he was invited by the Union Government to advise it on banking and currency problems. He recommended the establishment of a central bank with the sole right to issue notes, to control the country's gold reserves, to manage credit in the country, and act as the 'banker of banks'. These proposals were given effect to in the South African Currency and Banking Act of 1920 which established the South African Reserve Bank.[8]

The Low Grade Mines Commission was still sitting in February 1920 when a major strike among black mineworkers broke out on the Rand. The form it took was new in that it was the first time that black workers simply withheld their labour to express discontent, instead of erupting in riot. About 71 000 workers, representing some forty per cent of the workforce, took part, demanding higher wages to meet the increased cost of living resulting from the War, recently accentuated by drought and famine in tribal areas. The men also demanded opportunities for advancement, and complained of profiteering by Reef traders. The work stoppage, which began on 17 February, was over on 27 February when the strikers returned to work unconditionally.[9] The event aroused fears that a new pattern of industrial action was developing among black workers, for they seemed to be copying the tactics of white unions. In fact, it was to prove an isolated occurrence. There would be no major black strike again until 1946.

Nevertheless, the strike was an event of major significance. In numbers involved and mines affected, it was not to be surpassed until the 1970s. The historian P L Bonner has pointed out that the trouble did not flare up out of the blue, for its roots went back to the black miners' strike of 1913, as a result of which the Buckle Commission recommended 'a wide range of reforms, which the industry by and large put into effect'. Nor were the improvements insignificant. They covered food, accommodation, medical facilities, working conditions and piecework pay, thus demonstrating the efficacy of collective action. The unrest built up through the war years in association with agitation in urban areas close to the mines. Nor did the unrest subside when the strike was over.[10]

The Chamber reacted to the stoppage by setting up trading stores where blacks could buy at fair prices. This aroused the fury of the Reef traders, but also brought about a general lowering of store prices, and dampened black militancy and demands for more pay, as did the general deflation over the next twenty years. The Chamber remained conscious of the need to satisfy black aspirations for advancement. It asserted the injustice of the colour bar, and the Native Recruiting Corporation urged on the Low Grade Mines Commission the need for white workers to yield certain categories of work to allow blacks to satisfy 'their justifiable aspirations in industrial life'.[11] The Chamber, however, sought to reassure white workers by reaffirming its intention not to seek abolition of the statutory colour bar so long as it was upheld by the majority of the white residents of the Rand.[12]

The Low Grade Mines Commission in its final report went a mite further, recommending that the legal basis of the colour bar be abolished. However, the Commission proposed to abolish the bar in law and not in practice. It was, in essence, expressing the view that:

> If there were no legal colour bar, the boundary line of the employment of natives would be more elastic and could be altered, by mutual agreement between employers and workmen, to meet the circumstances of the case. Such variation is rendered very difficult when the colour bar is prescribed by statute or by regulation. In the case of a low grade mine, the continued existence of the mine may be only possible by extending the scope of the employment of natives to a wider extent than is necessary or customary elsewhere.[13]

The trade union representatives on the Commission did not accept the majority view of the colour bar, and set out their reservations in a memorandum, published as an addendum to the main report. It was generally accepted at the time that the removal of the statutory bar would not improve the position of the mass of black workers because they lacked the educational qualifications to perform skilled work. Crawford, Forrester Brown and Pohl in their memorandum endorsed this view, and went further:

> The removal of the legal colour bar could not in any way improve the position of the natives, whereas it certainly would disturb public opinion unnecessarily, to the detriment of the industry. Indeed, in all probability, the effect of such removal would preclude the possibility of changes being introduced for the benefit of Low Grade Mines such as are recommended in the Commission's Interim Report and would, therefore, injure, rather than aid the Low Grade Mines.
>
> For instance the splendid relationship which has been established and which the Commission hopes to see developed through the extended

functions of Joint Works Committees would be destroyed, and the Commission's recommendation in favour of a rearrangement of underground work with a view to economy would be regarded with suspicion and aversion by the Unions since the absence of such fancied security as is afforded by the legal colour bar would suggest an inevitable pitfall in the path of any new departure from existing methods and customs.[14]

The labour commissioners reflected exactly the fears of the white working man that any advance accorded the black on a low-grade mine would inevitably come to be applied on higher-grade mines as well. It was becoming increasingly evident that trade union leaders, in the current state of politics and industrial relations, were quite unable to give an inch on the colour line. Of much more immediate concern to them was the drive to establish a larger say in the control of the labour force on the mines through the activities of shop- and shaft-stewards. And some leaders would increasingly identify themselves with a world trend towards demanding a say in management as well, an attitude that was guaranteed to bring a strong counter-reaction from mine-owners.

On 27 August 1919 Louis Botha died of heart failure and was succeeded as Prime Minister by Smuts. The following year Smuts went to the country. The Chamber's attitude to the former Parliament might have been summed up in Oliver Cromwell's *congé* of the Long Parliament: '... Depart, I say, and let us have done with you. In the name of God, go.' Wallers, smarting from Government imposts, referred to South Africa's Second Parliament as 'late' and 'unlamented'.[15] Mining representation there had dwindled with the departure of Farrar, Jameson, Chaplin and Phillips. Only FitzPatrick remained and he decided not to stand again. Phillips, out on a visit from England, commented at a Chamber meeting:

> ... isn't it rather an anomalous situation that this great gold mining industry should have no one representing it directly in the House of Parliament – ... who could speak with authority as to the conditions of the industry and as to the effects of anything that may be done in regard to it? It seems to me a monstrous condition ... a good many things are done in the House of Parliament rather in a hurry, and they are done not out of *malice prepense* at all, but with insufficient knowledge ....[16]

However, worse was to come in the years ahead. It had been clear that Hertzog was gaining ground since the Rebellion of 1914. Capitalizing on the emotional backwash, his National Party made an impressive advance in 1915, taking sixteen of the seventeen Free State seats as well as seven in the Cape and four in the Transvaal. The strength of its appeal to Afrikaners to unite in striving for a republican South Africa was reflected in Hertzog's mission to the Peace Conference at Versailles. His ostensible purpose was to convince the Allies that their promise to restore the rights of conquered peoples should not exclude the Boers. It is probable that he did not expect success but regarded the mission as good for home politics in the present, while preparing the way for constitutional development in the future.[17] In any event, the National Party continued to prosper, winning forty-four seats in the General Election of March 1920 and becoming the largest single party in the Assembly. Smuts's South African Party lost twelve seats and now held only forty-one, his majority depending on the Unionists who had lost thirteen and held twenty-five. The Labour Party, profiting from the post-war depression, and some split voting, had gained fifteen seats, mainly from Unionists, and now had twenty-one.

In the aftermath of this catastrophic defeat, Smuts purposefully sought to give expression to the desire of Afrikaners in the South African Party to be reconciled with those in the National Party. The two parties conferred in private, and thereafter met publicly at Bloemfontein. However, Smuts found it impossible to accept the Nationalists' insistence on South Africa's right to secede from the Empire. He had now, perforce, to turn to the Unionists and, at the end of the year, that party dissolved. Smuts made it clear that the Unionist Party was not being amalgamated with the South African Party, but that its members were joining 'unconditionally and without bargaining'.[18]

According to Smuts's biographer, Sir Keith Hancock, he confided in the young J H Hofmeyr that the dissolution of the party of Rhodes and Jameson was a glorious landmark on the road of South Africanism. However, he was uncertain whether his own Afrikaner supporters would see it that way.[19] Many did not, seeing in the Unionists the Imperialist/capitalist enemies of old, and in their absorption into the South African Party Smuts's capitulation to them. However, there had been little difference in the policies of the two parties and fusion was dictated by the growing power of the National Party.

Smuts went to the country again in February 1921 and was returned with seventy-nine seats, many of them formerly held by the Unionist Party. He also won twelve seats from Labour, who lost Afrikaner support through Creswell's rejection of republicanism. The Nationalists increased their holding by one seat to forty-five. Smuts's majority looked safe, but it was to prove not strong enough to sustain him in the wake of storms now gathering along the Rand.

There were many elements shaping the impending confrontation. One was the growth in the number of Afrikaners in the workforce since 1907. Many of those engaged as strike-breakers in that year had remained on the mines. With the outbreak of the War many more moved into jobs vacated by volunteers, and made semi-skilled work their particular province. These workers were peculiarly sensitive to any advance by blacks. They responded readily to the propaganda of the National Party and, while slow to participate in union affairs, imparted a fresh militancy to industrial relations. This militancy contained 'a distinctly nationalist, revolutionary strain because of the fervent desire among a large number of them for the restoration of a Boer republic'.[20]

During the War the Government had increasing cause for concern. In 1917, whites at the Van Ryn Deep struck over the engagement of men of mixed blood as waste packers under white supervision. In line with the wartime policy of appeasement, both mine-owners and the Government backed off and restored the previous position. However, the Secretary for Mines and Industries, H Warington Smyth, reported confidentially that the unrest was indicative that the large number of Afrikaners entering the industry constituted a new factor on the industrial and labour scene.

> These do not, as a rule, join the Miners' Union very readily, but there is reason to think that some organisation, more or less of a political character, is being carried on amongst them. It would appear that the greater part of the talking and agitating during the past few days has been due to these younger Afrikanders [sic] .... This is entirely a new danger.[21]

The Secretary warned of a new rebellion, 'started on industrial lines instead of having its origin in the country districts'.[22] His report was passed to the Commissioner of Police who confirmed that around two thousand five hundred Afrikaners had obtained work on the East Rand in place of those on active service. These workers were quick to agitate against the employment of non-whites in semi-skilled jobs, and feared loss of employment when the War was over.

> ... they would seize any pretext to jeopardize the position of the Government and with it the British regime in South Africa. ... there is little doubt that any industrial trouble will have the support of an element with less respect for Law and Order than was the case in Strikes of July, 1913 and January, 1914.[23]

Thus, the Afrikaner worker was seen as a new threat to industrial peace both because of his reactionary attitude to the colour bar, his very real fear of displacement and unemployment, and his political motivation to further the defeat of any government that obstructed the republican ideal. This threat was enhanced both by recurrent economic crises that came with the Peace, and by the seeming strength of Smuts's Parliamentary position after the election of 1921.

The historian Oberholster, in his review of events in *Die Mynwerkerstaking 1922*, concluded that it was not possible to define the extent to which the results of the election revived the idea of winning back republican freedom by armed uprising. He found that Smuts's resounding majority 'decidedly led many Nationalists to doubt whether they could ever realize their political ideals along a constitutional path'. However, Oberholster saw the republican struggle as only one of a number of factors that would bring the country to the brink of the revolutionary abyss. Socialism was also to play its part.[24]

Union leadership was still in the hands of immigrant craftsmen from Britain and Australia and they included revolutionary socialists like W H Andrews

('Comrade Bill'). In 1909, Andrews was elected Chairman of the Labour Party, and in 1912 he won the Georgetown seat at Germiston. However, the War broke the Labour Party apart, the moderate element under Creswell supporting the war effort, while Andrews and others opposed it, establishing the War on War League. Creswell succeeded in getting the upper hand and driving Andrews and his associates out of the party. Andrews then created the International Socialist League (ISL).[25]

The Bolshevik Revolution in Russia in 1917 provided fresh inspiration for revolutionary socialists everywhere. In 1918 the ISL affiliated with the Third International of the Communist Party. The creation of the South African Communist Party followed on 30 July 1921, with C B Tyler as Chairman, S P Bunting as Treasurer and Andrews as Secretary.[26] Previously, in 1918, Andrews had spent several months in England. There he grasped the power of the shop-steward movement and the potential it offered for decentralized industrial action, independent of, and often in conflict with, recognized union organizations.[27] On his return to South Africa, Andrews perceived the opportunity offered by the simmering discontent on the mines over the still-rising cost of living.

> He saw in this an opportunity to undermine the influence of the South African Industrial Federation which since the outbreak of the First World War had co-operated closely with the Chamber of Mines ... Andrews visited workers throughout the Witwatersrand and encouraged them to set up shop-stewards' committees at every workshop and on every shaft.[28]

The Chamber observed with concern the success of these tactics as the recognized trade union organizations found themselves progressively undermined by independent and wildcat action by shop- and shaft-stewards on individual mines.

> The shop-stewards' committees gave the International Socialist League a foothold among Witwatersrand miners in particular, and in this way enabled the communists to play an important role in the 1922 strike. The shop-stewards' committees were the forerunners of the Council of Action which embarrassed the South African Mine Workers' Union in the course of 1921 and dominated the South African Industrial Federation which was supposed to control the strike.[29]

Despite rises in pay, industrial unrest on the Rand proliferated in 1919 and 1920 as the inability of unions to control their branches contributed to continual turbulence. The civilized world faced similar problems and employers everywhere consulted one another on the best means to win the co-operation of workers, and restore stability. The signatories to the Treaty of Versailles had declared that there would be no durable peace without social justice. There followed the founding of the International Labour Organization, to further urgently improvements in pay, working hours and the conditions of labour generally. As a result, the first International Labour Conference, under the auspices of the League of Nations, was held in Washington in October and November 1919. William Gemmill, the Chamber's Actuary and Labour Adviser, was chosen by the Government to represent employers in South Africa; Warington Smyth, the Secretary for Mines and Industries, represented the Government; and Crawford of the Federation represented the workers.

Gemmill was by now a leading figure in the industry. He was tall in stature and dominating in personality, with a compelling eye and a fair portion of Victorian arrogance. It was said of him that 'he loved a fight'.[30] He sailed from Cape Town on 30 September 1919, and did not return until March 1920. It was a particularly propitious moment for a conference about labour matters because the 'entire relationship of labour and capital was being reviewed, and measures that still sound radical today, such as joint control and profit sharing, were being freely discussed'.[31]

While Gemmill was away, in November and December 1919, the South African Government called a National Conference of Employers and Employees. Union representatives could command a majority and they carried the following by forty-four votes to forty:

Industrial Unrest

That this Conference is of opinion that the private ownership of the industries of South Africa is against the best interests of the people of South Africa, and is the cause of industrial unrest.

The Conference is further of opinion that the national welfare demands that the industries shall be taken over by the State and shall, therefore, be managed and controlled by Local, District and National Boards, composed of equal numbers of representatives of the Unions concerned and the State.[32]

In Washington, Gemmill was able to consider the labour problems of England, Europe and America and discuss them with delegates. He had ample time, too, to ponder the lessons he learned, being particularly impressed by the similarity between the situation in South Africa and America, and by the manner in which the American Government dealt with the coal strike there.

He wrote to Wallers from Washington on 18 November 1919:

It is true, of course, that in labour matters we appear to be much in advance of other countries, so far as the co-operation with the employees is concerned, but the ease with which the extreme revolutionary sections of the labour party were dealt with by a strong capitalistic but nominally democratic government is an excellent object lesson.[33]

He was impressed by the way in which American employers gave good conditions and high wages (though hours were long), and encouraged suggestions and initiative, but demanded strenuous work and high efficiency in return. Scientific management, works committees, payment by results, and any scheme that promised results were tried out. But attempts to compel employers to employ only union men, or to retain inefficient workmen, were met and defeated. He wrote again to Wallers from London on 22 December, saying 'My American experience has made me more convinced than ever that employers in South Africa have the upper hand of labour, if they care to recognise that fact, and act accordingly.'[34]

In London, before sailing for South Africa, Gemmill compiled two reports: Report 'A' for publication, and Report 'B', which was marked 'Strictly Private and Confidential'. Gemmill distributed several hundreds of copies of this confidential report to the employers' organizations of South Africa which he had represented at the Washington Conference, and to Government officials. He properly reported to all associations, large and small, including those of master bakers, butchers and painters, as well as the chambers of commerce and industry.

The report ended by drawing attention to the formation of an International Federation of Employers at Brussels. Gemmill suggested for consideration that the time had come to form a central employers' body in South Africa, similar to those in existence in Britain, the United States and elsewhere. The suggestion evoked some interest, and dialogue, but nothing eventuated, except that Gemmill, representing South African employers, was to play a distinguished role in the management of the International Labour Organization, which established its office in Geneva.

Gemmill's Report 'B' was, in essence, what would have been expected of a Chamber official sent to a major international conference. He contrasted the realities of the situation in South Africa with the separate experience of Continental Europe, Britain, and the United States and Canada. However, the labour historian, David Yudelman, who has a *penchant* for vivid phraseology, saw deeper implications:

> Gemmill's 'Report B' and activities generally constitute, to some degree, a blueprint for an attack on organized labour, an evaluation of its strategic strength, and the types of alliance needed to defeat it.[35]

Report 'B' was published in *The South African Quarterly*,[36] of June 1920, three months after Gemmill's return, with the exception of three sentences and two paragraphs, which Yudelman describes in a note as having been 'censored'.[37]

However, a study of the complete Report 'B' shows that, with or without the three 'censored' sentences and the two 'censored' paragraphs, it did not in any way advocate the 'subjugation' of labour on the Rand, as Yudelman suggests. The first of the blue-pencilled sentences argued the need to avoid a predominance of members from Europe on the ILO's governing body, because the influence of communists on them was likely to be strong. The second dismissed the 'Red' element in South Africa as not important enough

to warrant serious consideration. The third noted that Pittsburgh steel manufacturers were prepared to close their plants indefinitely rather than concede
union demands.

The first 'censored' paragraph pointed to the mistaken hypothesis, prevalent in South Africa, that the granting of concessions (reasonable and otherwise) to the influential labour movement in Britain involved, necessarily, the
same concessions in South Africa, where labour's influence was relatively
small.

Yudelman relies heavily on the second 'censored' paragraph for his subjugation theory, but quotes from it only in part.[38] The full paragraph is as
follows:

> It will be noticed that the position of labour in South Africa is in many
> respects similar to its position in the United States. It is decidedly a minority
> of the population. Wages, conditions of work, and standard of comfort are
> high. There is a large body of unskilled labour antagonistic to the skilled.
> There is no great cohesion in labour. It cannot sustain a really prolonged
> strike, and so on. But in appreciating this, and realising that demands which
> the employers decide are unreasonable – such, for example, as demands in-
> volving control or part management of industry by employees or their rep-
> resentatives – cannot be forced upon South African industries which are
> prepared to fight, South African employers can continue to be in the
> forefront in providing good wages and conditions of employment in return
> for good work, and in co-operating to that end with the employees and
> their Unions and Federations.[39]

Thus, the conclusion reached by Gemmill was simply that American experience showed that it was possible to be a good employer, co-operating with
unions to give workers a fair deal on pay and conditions of work, while at the
same time resisting radical union demands for, say, a share in the management
of industry. Interestingly, he also noted that the British way of evolving
gradually to a less individualistic basis might be the best way, after all, of
securing the greatest good for the greatest number.[40]

Report 'B' was in fact focused on the defence of Capital at a time when it
was under heavy attack by Labour. Yudelman, however, having mistakenly
discerned in it a blueprint for the subjugation of Labour in 1922, was trapped
further into error.

The Chamber, as it moved to the front line of labour relations during the
War, evolved an arrangement whereby members shared the standing charges
of individual mines halted by strike action in disputes which involved points
of principle agreed to be relevant to the industry as a whole. Although in
practice rarely accorded, this support strengthened the hands of managers,
particularly those in charge of mines close to the margin of profitability, who
were faced by wildcat strike action. Yudelman, noting that Chamber
members contributed £846 18s 10d[41] to the standing charges of the Meyer and

Charlton mine, briefly halted by a strike in 1917, links this with the Chamber's establishment of a Reserve Fund at the beginning of 1920.

Yudelman then arrives at the following:

> The conclusion seems inescapable: the £50 000 Reserve Fund was, at the very least, an insurance policy imposed by mining capital on itself to face an anticipated wide-scale confrontation between labour and capital.
>
> Its purpose was to ensure that a prolonged strike would not result in compromise by the individual companies affected, only in the breaking of the trade unions. Ironically, the TCM Executive Committee decided later in 1920 to raise debentures to repay the contributions by its members to the Reserve Fund. Basically, this means that the trade unions were broken in 1922, at least partially, by borrowed money.[42]

This is wholly erroneous. The Reserve Fund was in fact raised to meet the domestic capital needs of the Chamber, in particular the provision of housing loans to thirty members of the staff.[43] It was when more such funds were required to finance the new Chamber building at the corner of Main and Hollard Streets that the issue of debentures to mines and groups – and not to the general public – was proposed. As Gemmill stated in a memorandum dated 28 April 1920:

> This reserve fund has been utilised to the extent of £33 000 for the Housing Scheme for the staffs of the Chamber and allied bodies, and £10 000 in the loan on second mortgage to the Technical Societies, leaving £7 000 unexpended.
>
> It would appear advisable to consolidate these liabilities of the Chamber into an issue of £100 000 Debentures secured on the new building, on the houses on which money has been advanced, and on the second mortgage on the Technical Societies' new building, and also on the Chamber's assets generally ....[44]

In the event, the debentures were issued to member mines and groups to finance a new company, the Chamber of Mines Building Company.

There duly appeared in the Chamber of Mines Annual Report for 1920 the following:

CHAMBER'S NEW BUILDING

It has been decided to form a Private Company with limited liability, to be registered under the Transvaal Companies Act, to provide (a) the capital cost of the new building, (b) the amount of loans made to employees under the housing scheme, (c) the amount of the loan of £10 000 on second mortgage to the Associated Scientific and Technical Societies of South Africa.

Under the scheme decided upon, the Reserve Fund of £50 000 created by contributions from members will be refunded.[45]

The building which the Chamber had occupied since 1895 had become too small for its expanding needs, and too exposed to the cacophony of the Market Square which it overlooked. At the Annual General Meeting on 22 March 1920, Lionel Phillips, out from England once again, sympathized with Wallers for having to give his annual address with 'the horrible complication – the horrible competition, perhaps I should say – of the tramcars, and some musical instrument going outside, no doubt accompanied by a monkey!'

The Chamber had already bought a site for a new building at the corner of Main and Hollard Streets from the General Mining and Finance Corporation, and sold the old, subject to a tenancy agreement, for £16 850. The courtly old building, which had seen so much of the personalities and the events of mining, would house the Chamber for only two years more. They would be years of high drama, as challenging as any yet.

[1] F A Johnstone, *Class, Race and Gold: A Study of Class Relations and Racial Discrimination in South Africa*, p 97, quoting from the Evidence of the Association of Mine Managers (J J Wessels, President of the Association of Mine Managers) to the Low Grade Mines Commission, p 2 079, paragraph 15 370.

[2] B Grun, '1918' in *The Timetables of History: A Chronology of World Events from 5000 BC to the Present Day*, p 473.
'World Wars' in *The New Encyclopaedia Britannica, Macropaedia*, Volume 19, *Knowledge in Depth*, 15th edition, p 966.
Union of South Africa: Report of the Influenza Epidemic Commission, 1919 (UG 15-'19), p 23.
A M Grundlingh, 'Die Suid-Afrikaanse Gekleurdes en die Eerste Wêreldoorlog', referring to the recent researches of H Phillips, p 399.

[3] Annual Report of the Transvaal Chamber of Mines, 1918, pp 71, 95, 98, 99.

[4] Thirty-Seventh Annual Report of the Transvaal Chamber of Mines, 1926, p 58.

[5] Report of the Low Grade Mines Commission, 1920, p 12, paragraph 53.
Annual Report of the Transvaal Chamber of Mines, 1919, p 60.

[6] Annual Report of the Transvaal Chamber of Mines, 1919, pp 60-62.

[7] Chamber of Mines Archives: Executive Committee Minutes, Transvaal Chamber of Mines, 14 April 1919. (Minute book covering the period 1916-1920, p 347.)
Annual Report of the Transvaal Chamber of Mines, 1919, pp 221, 290-291, 299, 543.

[8] A J Lamont Smith, 'Strakosch' in *Dictionary of South African Biography*, III, p 765.
Strakosch, pp 33-34.

[9] Thirty-First Annual Report of the Transvaal Chamber of Mines, 1920, pp 67-68, 91, 219.
Annual Report of the Transvaal Chamber of Mines, 1919, p 69.

[10] P L Bonner, '8. The 1920 Black Mineworkers' Strike: A Preliminary Account', B Bozzoli, ed, *Labour, Townships and Protest Studies in the Social History of the Witwatersrand*, pp 274, 275.

[11] *Ibid*, p 288, quoting from the Low Grade Mines Commission, 1919, Minutes of Evidence.

[12] Annual Report of the Transvaal Chamber of Mines, 1919, p 69.

[13] Report of the Low Grade Mines Commission, 1920, p 29.

[14] *Ibid*, pp 37, 38.

[15] Annual Report of the Transvaal Chamber of Mines, 1919, p 75.

[16] *Ibid*, p 81.

[17] O Pirow, *James Barry Munnik Hertzog*, p 79.

[18] Davenport, pp 187–188.

[19] W K Hancock, *Smuts: 2. The Fields of Force: 1919-1950*, p 33.

[20] Yudelman, p 129.

[21] Johnstone, p 116, quoting confidential minute of the Secretary of Mines to the Minister of Mines and Industries, 10 January 1917, paragraphs 1, 3 and 5, Archives of the Department of Justice, File 3/20/17/232, National Archives.

[22] *Idem, ibid*, paragraph 9.

[23] Yudelman, p 130, quoting from Secretary for Mines Archives (in South African State Archives), 1212/17, Volume 372, 30 January 1917.

[24] Oberholster, pp 48–49. (Translation from Afrikaans.)

[25] *Ibid*, p 50.

[26] *Ibid*, p 51.

[27] *Ibid*, p 54.

[28] *Idem*. (Translation from Afrikaans.)

[29] *Ibid*, pp 54–55. (Translation from Afrikaans.)

[30] Interview with J A Gemmill, son of W Gemmill, at Boschkop, Transvaal, on 22 February 1983.

[31] Yudelman, p 152, quoting *The Observer*, London, 8 February 1919.

[32] Annual Report of the Transvaal Chamber of Mines, 1919, pp 48–49, 211.

[33] Chamber of Mines Archives: File 23 1919: 'Gemmill, W (Private)'.

[34] Chamber of Mines Archives: File 33(1) 1920: 'International Labour Conference, Washington, USA'.

[35] Yudelman, p 154.

[36] *The South African Quarterly* was published by the Central News Agency, Johannesburg, etc., under the honorary editorship of J D Rheinallt Jones.

[37] Yudelman, pp 153, 163 (Note 82).

[38] *Ibid*, p 153.

[39] Chamber of Mines Archives: File 33 (1) 1920: 'International Labour Conference, Washington, USA', W Gemmill's Report 'B', London, 23 December 1919, p 3.

[40] *Idem*.

[41] Yudelman, pp 154–155.

[42] *Ibid*, p 155.

[43] Chamber of Mines Archives: Executive Committee Minutes, Transvaal Chamber of Mines, 22 December 1919, 9 February 1920, 23 February 1920, 22 March 1920, 12 April 1920, and 26 April 1920. (Minute book covering the period 1916-1920, pp 476, 500, 514, 527-528, 535 and 546, respectively.)

[44] Chamber of Mines Archives: File F4 (b), 'Finance: 1916 to 1920 inclusive'.

[45] Annual Report of the Transvaal Chamber of Mines, 1920, p 239.

CHAPTER TWENTY-TWO

Seconds out of the Ring ...

By 1920, the Chamber's involvement in labour relations had grown to the point where it was absorbing three-quarters of the President's working day, and the demands of the office had gone beyond the capacity of an honorary and part-time incumbent. The truth was that the Chamber's function in mediating between the mines and the unions had expanded beyond the limits of the sensible. The custom had evolved of submitting to conciliation boards, or Chamber boards of reference, quite trivial grievances on individual mines. The consequence was that the all-important role of management in settling disputes at the earliest possible stage was undermined, and boards of directors, which had earlier served as mediators when required, were being largely by-passed.

In the year 1 April 1919 to 31 March 1920 there were nine conciliation boards, on four of which Wallers served. There were twenty-seven boards of reference, six of them involving Wallers. In addition there were 431 meetings of various Chamber committees, more than double the number of three years before.

Wallers (or, more probably, Central Mining which controlled the Corner House from London) now decided that he would serve as President no more. It is likely that none of the other mining houses had the resources at the time to free an executive of other duties sufficiently to permit him to dedicate himself to Chamber business. The stop-gap solution was to appoint a full-time salaried president to succeed Wallers at the end of his marathon term. H O Buckle accepted a four-year appointment, at a salary of £5 000 a year. His two honorary vice-presidents were D Christopherson, CBE, of New Consolidated Gold Fields, who followed a strongly individual line, and F R Lynch, of Consolidated Mines Selection. Wallers remained on the Executive.

Buckle, the son of a Canon of Wells, was a barrister of Inner Temple, London, who served with distinction in the City Imperial Volunteers during the South African War. He settled in South Africa and became Chief Magistrate of Johannesburg, Chairman of the Miners' Phthisis Board, and, latterly, Chairman of the Industrial Advisory Board. The Government had appointed the Board to reconcile the differences of Capital and Labour, and had high hopes that it would close the gap growing between them. Their hopes were wrecked on the failure of union leaders to win the effective support of their membership even for those changes which they themselves found acceptable.

Buckle, precise and authoritative in manner, dapper in dress with pince-nez and buttonhole, was an experienced chairman, but could act only as a figurehead and a spokesman. Inevitably, the real power remained with the mining houses, and in particular with Corner House, still by far the strongest of them. When the chips of debate were down, it was Wallers's will which was most likely to prevail, and behind him stood Lionel Phillips, the last of the pioneering generation, now sixty six but, as ever, indomitable. Phillips was becoming more and more perturbed at the trend of affairs on the Rand, and more and more out of patience with the obstructive attitude of union committees at mine level. He expressed his dissatisfaction both in his private correspondence and on public occasions.

You will never have success in mine management without discipline ... I understand that in recent years a mine manager has to consult various committees upon almost every imaginable thing that he may want to do. You cannot work a mine under such conditions with success. Your manager has got to be the master in the mine. And although it is quite possible and quite proper to have certain committees established to consult with the mine manager, to advise him in certain directions ... you must have someone in authority who can in the matters of ordinary conduct of operations on the mine have his will performed.[1]

Concern over indiscipline was reflected, too, in reports by an outspoken Inspector of Mines at Krugersdorp, M Fergusson. In 1918 he had reported that on some mines there was a condition of chaos, shift bosses and other mine officials being unable to exercise discipline owing to the independent and aggressive attitude of the workmen. There was little wonder, he reported, that it was hard to find men willing to act as shift bosses.[2] In 1921 he declared that any relaxation of the regulations in order to increase black productivity was jealously resisted by the unions 'who dread the least suspicion of a native being permitted to lift a hand without the formality of a white supervisor's authority'.[3] Fergusson went on:

It does not appear logical that because a man is white he should be able to become a skilled miner within a few weeks or months, and if he is a black man a lifetime's experience in the mines does not enable him to gain sufficient knowledge to form an opinion as to the safety of himself and his fellow-workmen.[4]

He said that there was little doubt that many whites had been attracted to the mines by the high wages easily gained without the necessity for any preliminary knowledge or training.

It certainly seems unreasonable that because a man has once obtained an engagement in a mine he should expect to be clothed, housed, fed, and have his pockets kept filled with money for the rest of his life, irrespective of what he gives in return. Some of them seem to forget that there are two sides to every bargain ....[5]

Buckle's first annual report, delivered on 21 March 1921, was sombre in tone. As the premium on the gold price fluctuated and fell it seemed clear that a return to the old standard price was but a matter of time. Simmer Deep, Knights Deep, Jupiter, New Heriot and Princess Estate, all mines which could have been kept going at a higher price or a lower production cost, were closed down. Of the remaining thirty-nine mines, six made a loss in January 1921 and thirteen in February. It had to be recognized, declared Buckle, that the gold mines of the Transvaal constituted a shrinking industry. Production had been falling year by year since 1916, and the output in 1920 had been the lowest since 1910. The shrinkage was to an extent the natural result of mines coming to the end of their life, but the life of a mine was lengthened by every increase in efficiency, and shortened by every increase in costs. Buckle predicted that the cost of stores would fall as the price of gold fell. The other important factor – the cost of labour – must also be reduced if the rapid closing of several more mines was to be averted.[6]

Buckle pointed out that an increase in the real value of wages was taking place automatically with the fall in the cost of living that had begun. Prices in Johannesburg in October 1920 were fifty-seven per cent above those in 1914. By February this was down to forty-three per cent. It was apparent that the tide of inflation had turned and prices were on the downgrade.

South Africa was deep in the doldrums. Agricultural exports slumped and the income of farmers was at pitiful levels. Diamonds slumped, too, and 2 000 diamond miners were out of work. Retrenchment and wage cuts had come to stay.

The day after Buckle's address, the new Minister of Finance, Henry Burton, told Parliament that the financial position of the country gave cause for serious concern, and required the curtailment of expenditure. He announced a reduction in the cost-of-living allowances of the public service.[7] It was already clear that the Government's chances at the next election would depend on its ability to restore prosperity. Burton bore the brunt of administering corrective medicine. Fortunately he was a man of stature, and of principle, who did not court popularity. It was to be his lot as Minister of Finance to attract public opprobrium as the constant bearer of unhappy economic tidings.[8]

The whole world groaned under the burdens born of total war, and the economic emphasis on deflation that followed it. In the United States, President Harding had begun a term of office in economic conditions of the utmost gloom. Business failures, bad trading reports, poor earnings and dividend suspensions were the order of the day. Millions were out of work and wage cuts the familiar lot of those in employment. A similar picture was reflected in

Great Britain where the country was facing a national emergency reported to be the most serious since 1914. A bitter coal strike led to the defeat of the coal miners and the imposition of regional wage agreements and pay cuts, in all but the rich Yorkshire field. In Europe, still in part torn by war and revolution, the economic, and political, picture was more dreadful still.

A vital element in the unfolding drama on the Rand was the frequency with which trade unionists acted in disregard of agreements by which unions had bound themselves to refer disputes to boards of reference and conciliation, before resorting to strike action. There was a disturbing tendency for these disputes, which involved mines in heavy losses, to go beyond matters of wages and working hours.

In November 1920 the MWU wished to punish one of its members on the City Deep by suspension from a day's work, with the resultant loss of pay. The Manager refused to agree to this interruption to normal working. The men then struck, without the authority of the Union leadership. Their leaders, Ernest Shaw and Percy Fisher, who served as Chairman and Secretary respectively of the Strike Committee, had close links with the communist ISL.

The strike ended after seven days with acceptance by the Chamber of the Union's right to discipline its members, a concession seen by the men as a victory for local strike action, independent of the Union headquarters. In a subsequent arbitration, the strike was found to have been a breach of the Chamber/Union agreement. As a result it was agreed the Union should discipline its members by fines rather than suspension from work. However, Percy Fisher got enough kudos from the wild-cat strike to stand and win an election for General Secretary of the MWU. Fisher's term of office was, however, short. The election was quashed because the name of a candidate had inadvertently been omitted from the voting papers. A new election was held and this time Forrester Brown defeated Fisher to become Secretary once again. It may be that Fisher's activities had roused the MWU hierarchy into organizing against him.[9]

Fisher from his independent position continued to undermine the Union's authority. He was quick to take advantage of the unrest that erupted into strike on the Consolidated Langlaagte on 29 January 1921.

The cause of the work stoppage was the refusal of the mine manager to suspend a shift boss, T Langley, summarily and without inquiry. Their complaint against Langley was that he had told a miner named Botha, in brutal terms, that it was not necessary to take two days off to bury a dead child. The subsequent Board of Reference found that Langley had not used the words complained of, but recommended his transfer to another position in the interests of good relations. The angry miners did not await the inquiry. Spurred on by Fisher and Shaw, they formed a strike committee.

The General Council of the MWU, despite the breach of agreement, bowed to sentiment and passed a reluctant endorsement of the strike. Fisher, Shaw and others on the Strike Committee now called for a general strike to which the men of twenty-three mines responded.

As Fisher's involvement became evident, the General Council distanced itself from the strike, and ordered all members, other than those at Consolidated Langlaagte, back to work. However, Fisher and his supporters continued to rouse the mineworkers at a series of meetings along the Reef. On 16 February the Chamber informed the MWU that, because of its repeated failure to control its branches, mines would no longer collect Union subscriptions.[10]

The men had drifted back to work by 18 February, and a subsequent ballot did not reveal enough support for further strike action. The MWU eventually conducted an inquiry into who was responsible for calling the men out without proper authority. The Chamber now demanded disciplinary steps against the ringleaders, and made it plain that any condonation of the break in service of the strikers would depend upon proper disciplining of the instigators. In due course, after much shifting of ground, the MWU complied and fines of between £15 and £60 were imposed. The Chamber accordingly restored partially the leave forfeited by the strikers.

The Union also barred some of the strike leaders from office in the Union of varying periods, including Fisher, Shaw, J Wordingham, H Spendiff and A McDermid.[11] The strike leaders refused to accept the fines imposed on them, and called a meeting in the Johannesburg Town Hall on 24 July 1921, to found an organization to be known, and notorious, as the Council of Action.

The Chairman and Secretary of the Council were Pate and McDermid, and the communist, Andrews, was closely involved in its activities. Its manifesto urged workers to 'support direct industrial organisation, which would be used to institute a Republic of Industrial Workers'.[12]

> All indications were that it (the Council) was preparing itself to turn in due course to direct, and, if necessary, violent action on behalf of the envisaged workers' republic.[13]

The Council was to play a fateful role in the Revolution that followed the Strike of 1922. And, at the end of it, Fisher and Spendiff would die, by their own hands, in the Council's headquarters in Market Buildings, Fordsburg.

In a year characterized by disputes, there occurred a strike on a matter of lasting significance. On 7 November the MWU objected to the dismissal of a shift boss named Walthew by Crown Mines and called on the Chamber for a board of reference to inquire into the circumstances. The Chamber refused on the grounds that it could not recognize the right of workers' unions to represent, or act for, mine officials. On 9 November, the men on 5 Shaft of the mine struck. Despite various conferences the strike persisted and on 25 November the remaining members of the MWU on the mine came out as well. F S Malan, Minister of Mines, held a conference with the parties to the dispute on 28 November, and the Executive of the mining union finally accepted terms of settlement on 3 December. These established for the Chamber the important principle that officials should not be represented by workmen's unions in any dispute. The 'two-stream' policy was established by which white mine employees were either day's pay workers or officials. Day's pay workers could, if they so wished, join workers' unions, while officials could join officials' associations. The associations, though technically unions, did not operate as such, their members being regarded as a part of the management structure.

The arrangement made it possible for management, when union labour was withdrawn, to keep mines safe and free from flooding, and to administer the black labour force.

Parallel with such disturbances, negotiations over pay were almost continuous throughout 1921. In November 1920 the Federation, on behalf of affiliated unions, had presented a demand for an increase. The Chamber refused on the grounds of the altered position of the industry, coupled with the decrease in the cost of living. There followed a demand from the Amalgamated Engineering Union (AEU) for an increase of eighty-three per cent on pre-war pay and a reduction of from forty-eight to forty-four in working hours. This was in turn rejected, and at end January 1921 the AEU held a ballot among its members which resulted in a vote in favour of a strike. Smuts now called on the leaders of the Federation to act responsibly. The Federation responded. At a meeting of the Joint Executives of the unions concerned on 11 February, it was decided to accept the Chamber's rejection of the demand. The AEU on 13 February announced it would not proceed with the planned strike.[14] The Chamber, for its part, agreed that, as mechanics had done less well than other classes of employees in the past, their pay would not be reduced in the course of 1921.

It was becoming clearer every day to the Chamber that the time was approaching when it should take up the Federation on its acceptance a year previously that wages might have to be reduced if conditions changed materially. However, the Chamber did not immediately follow the lead given by the Government in its announcement at end March of reduced cost-of-living allowances for the public service. In May, the gold price fell to more than seventeen per cent below that reigning when increased wages were negotiated the previous year, and to only about twenty-one per cent above the standard price received prior to July 1919. Moreover, in the six months October 1920 to April 1921 figures issued by the Director of Census showed a fall in the cost of living of about eighteen per cent.[15] Accordingly on 28 May the Chamber met representatives of the Federation and proposed a reduction in wages. After extended negotiations, it was finally agreed in August that future adjustments in wages would be based on the rise and fall in the cost of living. In accordance with this arrangement, a reduction in the pay of gold mine employees, other than officials, mechanics and certificated winding engine drivers, of 1s 6d a shift, was made from 1 August. A further reduction of 1s a shift was made from 1 October. Reductions in the wages of officials, mechanics and winding engine drivers were deferred until 1 January 1922. (At the last moment, the mechanics' unions would try and abrogate their agreement to lower wages.)

Meanwhile, conditions in the coal industry were going from bad to worse. The world was flooded with cheap coal, in part because the peacemakers, by agreeing to Germany paying in coal a proportion of its war reparations due to the Allies, had dealt a stunning blow to the British coal trade. It became obvious to the South African coal industry that if it were to retain its export trade, it would have to lower both the price of coal and the cost of producing it. The Collieries Committee accordingly proposed in September that wages on collieries should be based on a sliding scale linked to the cost of living, such as that introduced the previous month on the gold mines. The Committee pointed out that the economic circumstances of the coal trade were on their own sufficient to justify a reduction. The necessary adjustment would, moreover, be eased by the fact that the cost of living had been steadily and materially declining for nearly twelve months.

The unions would have none of it. In a new mood of intransigence the Federation declared roundly that the colliery workers had never had a rise of wages commensurate with the inflation caused by the War, and that because other sections of workers had accepted a reduction on a false basis, was no reason for colliery workers to follow suit.

Negotiations dragged on until 24 November when Crawford wrote notifying the Chamber that the Federation had decided to call a strike ballot on the issue. The Government was now bound to take a hand, because a coal strike threatened the supply to the power stations and the maintenance of essential public services. The Secretary of Mines and Industries, on behalf of the Minister, wrote to the Federation warning it against ill-advised and unconsidered action, and pointing out that the proposed reduction would still leave wages on the coal mines higher than on the gold mines.

> The world price of coal has fallen during the last twelve months in a manner which has totally altered the prospects of the South African coal export and bunker trades. Welsh export coal, which cost about £4 per ton, is now selling at 24s per ton. A similar fall has taken place in every producing country in the world. At present costs of production the Transvaal mines cannot compete in the markets which were open to them when British coal prices soared after the war. ... If the Transvaal loses her export trade, the price of inland coal for industrial purposes must rise owing to the reduced tonnage to be worked, while a considerable portion of the industry will have to close down....
>
> ... During the period of rising cost of living the wages of the men employed on these coal mines were increased to a larger extent than in other industries generally, and no reduction whatever has taken place so far in the colliery wages, although other industries, including the gold mines, have accepted reductions below those which the colliers are now asked to accept, and have been working on that basis for several months past.[16]

The miners reacted angrily to ministerial intervention. The ballot proceeded and revealed a majority of 18 to 1 against accepting the Chamber's offer. A conference was held between the Chamber and the Federation but no agreement resulted. The Federation now appealed to the Prime Minister to intervene.[17] At this critical juncture Smuts fell ill with gastric influenza. In his place, Patrick Duncan, Minister of the Interior, met the Federation on 28 December and subsequently suggested to the Chamber that the matters in dispute be submitted to arbitration. The Chamber was not to be enticed into the spider's web of a binding arbitration. It pointed out that:

> ... the Federation did not avail itself of the provisions of the Industrial Disputes Prevention Act, under which it could have called for a board of conciliation to investigate the dispute before the reduction of wages became operative. The colliery owners gave three months' notice of their intention to reduce wages, and there was ample opportunity for conciliation and investigation during that time. ... For some of the collieries to have agreed to be bound by an arbitration, when they knew only too well that they could not carry on and continue those rates of pay, would have been a dishonest procedure. No one will agree to be bound by arbitration when it is possible that the decision of that arbitration may destroy his existence.[18]

The Government now appealed again to the colliery workers. It pointed out that the cuts in the wages of English miners as a result of the great strike earlier in the year went far beyond anything proposed in South Africa. If the country's coal markets were lost, it was the coal miners who would be the principal sufferers from the resultant retrenchment of colliery workers. Coal miners with the proposed reduction would still be better off than the gold miners. What the gold miners had accepted was surely not a matter for the coal miners to strike on.

Unhappily, the breakdown of negotiations that followed coincided with a breakdown of negotiations with the gold miners for quite different reasons.

In mid-1921 the recommendations of the Low Grade Mines Commission had, at long last, eventuated in amendments to the Mining Regulations aimed at increasing the productivity of black workers on gold mines. However, the changes made by the Mines Department had been so watered down to accord with union sensitivity that they actually involved the appointment of additional white supervisors. Phillips had visited South Africa earlier in the year and endeavoured to alert the Government to the catastrophe that loomed large on the Reef, without apparent success. Back in London, he learnt that Smuts, and Smartt, who had been attending the 1921 Imperial Conference there, would be returning to South Africa in August on the *Saxon*. He at once made arrangements to join the ship himself. On the voyage, protracted as a result of a fire in the coal bunkers, he endeavoured to inform Smuts in more depth of the problems of the industry.

Phillips may have succeeded in focusing Smuts's attention on the immediacy of the crisis, but Smuts did not have to rely on the mining houses to spell out the implications. As he later emphasized to the unions, he had his own impartial experts in the Government service, including Robert Kotzé, who had been Government Mining Engineer since 1908. Kotzé was not only a highly-qualified judge of the mining situation, he was an old friend of Smuts, who had edged him out of the Ebden Scholarship to Cambridge in 1891. Kotzé went instead to the Royal School of Mines and the Academy of Mining in Clausthal, Germany. He had pioneered legislation on safety and silicosis in mining, and invented the konimeter for measuring the dust in mine air. He was destined to give distinguished service as Vice-Chancellor of the new University of the Witwatersrand.

In 1921 Kotzé represented 'the most intelligent and knowledgeable part of the state bureaucracy'.[19] He estimated, independently of the Chamber, that if the gold price fell to parity, it would mean production at a loss for twenty-seven of the thirty-eight mines remaining on the Rand.

Kotzé had in earlier years consistently rejected, in public and in private, the concept of subsidizing marginally profitable gold mines, and had followed the conventional political thinking of regarding the mines as a golden goose or a milch cow for State revenue to the maximum the industry could bear. Now, in the face of incontrovertible evidence, he altered direction and advised strongly that the State attitude to mining had to change. He wrote to the Minister of Mines: 'The time is coming when it will be as necessary in the national interest to support and stimulate mining as any other industry.'[20]

Smuts was thus confronted with a traumatic change in the circumstances of the industry – and with an insoluble political dilemma. He knew already that if he was to retain power beyond the next election he had to steer the country out of the current depression, and away from mass unemployment and economic despair. His hopes of doing so rested on a continuance of the mining industry on the current scale. Yet its costs could not be reduced without cutting the earnings of white labour and increasing the productivity of black. And Smuts, for all his philosophy, was a politician to the fingertips. He was only too aware that the Rand was an area of high political sensitivity, critical to the maintenance of his position of power in terms of seats held against the mounting assaults of the National and Labour Parties. To back radical demands on the unions by the mine-owners, either overtly or covertly, would court certain political disaster. The only clear course for him to follow as a politician was to sit firmly on the fence and await an opportunity to bring the parties together in a compromise situation. Smuts did his best to do just that.

His immediate response to the worsening situation was to invite a deputation from the MWU to meet him on 4 November. At that meeting he was exposed at first hand to the belligerent mood of the Union. He appealed for the Union's assistance in the face of the crisis, and declared that he asked only for the amendment to the regulations recommended by the Low Grade Mines Commission, and specifically supported by Forrester Brown and Pohl, the MWU's nominees on the Commission. He stressed that the purpose of the change was to increase the productivity of blacks without altering the status of the whites, except to better it. F S Hendrikz, Acting General Secretary of the MWU, emphatically repudiated Forrester Brown and Pohl. The MWU had never agreed with their proposal. He accused the Prime Minister of complicity with the Chamber of Mines, claimed that the proposed amendment was the thin edge of the wedge aimed at removing the colour bar, and said that the gazetting of the amendment would be met within forty-eight hours by a general strike. In reply, Smuts denied that he was arguing the Chamber's case, and pointed to the advice of Government experts. He protested that his appeal for assistance had been met only with the threat of a general strike.[21] It was then agreed that a round-table conference should be held between the Government, the Chamber and the Federation.[22]

The conference followed on 10 November. There Smuts spelt out the position of the mines. The Chamber's representatives, headed by Buckle and Wallers, gave an assurance that no general assault was intended on the position of the white worker. The discussion then centred on the Chamber's wish for an amendment to the regulations that would increase the productivity of blacks by lessening, in a meaningful way, the degree of white supervision. The conference eventually arrived at a compromise proposed by the MWU, providing for a system of prior examination of working places during the night, so that blacks could start work without delay the succeeding day. In the course of the discussion Wallers spelt out the realities – and by so doing clearly defined the widening gulf between the employers and the workers. The amendment was useful but only marginally so. It did not go nearly far enough, nor carry with it 'more than the germ of a solution for the present grave situation'.[23]

Even with the premium that still remained, two huge mines employing 3 000 whites had run at a loss the previous month.[24] There were issues that had to be faced, such as the revision of excessively high rates earned by miners on contract, trade union restrictions on the productive employment of the workforce, and the Status Quo Agreement. 'We believe it will be necessary in the men's interests, as well as our own, to abandon that status quo agreement.'[25]

Wallers declared that the term 'colour bar' was being loosely applied to convey the impression that the whole of the white workforce was to be swept out.

That is quite wrong, but to meet that point ... we would be prepared to consider ... some ratio as between the number of natives and Europeans throughout the industry, in order that a considerable measure of protection should be afforded to efficient white workmen.[26]

Smuts neatly side-stepped these critical issues, and suggested that they be left to a conference between the Chamber and the unions.

On 24 October Wallers had raised in the Executive Committee the question of the Chamber's policy vis-à-vis trade unions. On the motion of Sir Ernest Oppenheimer, recently knighted for services during the War, it was agreed to form a committee representing the gold-producing groups to plan what the industry's strategy should be. This committee was the precursor of the Gold Producers' Committee which, formally constituted after the 1922 strike, was to be the major policy-making committee of the Chamber for nearly fifty years. It met on 6 December 1921 with Buckle in the chair. Its members were the two Vice-Presidents, Christopherson (New Consolidated Gold Fields), Lynch (CMS), with P M Anderson (Union Corporation), Sir William Dalrymple (Anglo French), G E Farquharson (General Mining), Professor J G Lawn (JCI), Sir Ernest Oppenheimer (Anglo American) and Sir Evelyn Wallers (Corner House). Gemmill was not present, and the senior Chamber officials attending were F G A Roberts, the Technical Adviser, and E L R Kelsey, the Secretary and Legal Adviser.

The dimensions of the crisis were by now fully revealed, and undisputed, and so was the imperative for urgent action. It seemed equally clear to the Chamber that its bid over the previous seven years to win the white workers' committal to co-operative endeavour had ended in failure. Productivity had declined in tandem with the improvement of working conditions, and the Chamber found itself faced with a workforce whose mood was one of discontent and truculent rejection of the employer. In response, the Chamber turned decisively from the path of appeasement. In the lives of nations, industries and individuals, there are a few critical points of departure. The leaders of the mining industry had reached one. Characteristically, they chose the bold course from the options available.

[1] Annual Report of the Transvaal Chamber of Mines, 1920, pp 80–81.

[2] Chamber of Mines Archives: File 61, 1919: 'White Labour – Miscellaneous': No 187 (a), letter dated 17 October 1919, from the Association of Mine Managers – Transvaal, Johannesburg, to the Secretary and Legal Adviser, Transvaal Chamber of Mines, Johannesburg, p 1, quoting from the Report of the Government Mining Engineer for the period ending 31 December 1918, p 104.

[3] 'Anomalous State of Labour Conditions on the Rand', *The South African Mining and Engineering Journal*, 17 September 1921, p 57, quoting from the Report of the Inspector of Mines, Krugersdorp, to the Government Mining Engineer, 1921.

[4] *Idem.*

[5] *Ibid*, p 58.

[6] Annual Report of the Transvaal Chamber of Mines, 1920, pp 60–61.

[7] 'Salaries in Civil Service', *The Star*, Johannesburg, 22 March 1921.

[8] N G Garson, 'Burton' in *Dictionary of South African Biography*, I, p 139.

[9] Oberholster, pp 67–68.

[10] Thirty-Second Annual Report of the Transvaal Chamber of Mines, 1921, p 46.

[11] Oberholster, pp 70–71.

[12] R K Cope, *Comrade Bill: The Life and Times of W H Andrews, Workers' Leader*, p 225.

[13] Oberholster, p 71. (Translation from Afrikaans.)

[14] *Ibid*, pp 60–61.

[15] *Ibid*, p 61.

[16] Annual Report of the Transvaal Chamber of Mines, 1921, pp 178–179.

[17] Oberholster, pp 73–74.

[18] Annual Report of the Transvaal Chamber of Mines, 1921, pp 179–180.

[19] Yudelman, p 143.

[20] *Ibid*, pp 142–143. (Yudelman quotes from State Archives, Prime Minister's Papers, PM 1/1/394, No 204/19, 'Closing of Low Grade Mines'.)

[21] Oberholster, p 78.
'The Rand's Low Grade Tonnages', and the Editorial, *The South African Mining and Engineering Journal*, 12 November 1921, pp 357–358, and 371–372.

[22] 'The Rand's Low Grade Tonnages', and the Editorial, *The South African Mining and Engineering Journal*, 12 November 1921, pp 358, 372.

[23] Editorial, *The South African Mining and Engineering Journal*, 12 November 1921, p 372.
'Result of the Mining Conference', *The South African Mining and Engineering Journal*, 19 November 1921, pp 392–396.

[24] 'Result of the Mining Conference', *The South African Mining and Engineering Journal*, 19 November 1921, p 395.

[25] *Idem.*

[26] *Idem.*

CHAPTER TWENTY-THREE

Showdown

The entrepreneurs who founded the gold mining industry were both dominating and indomitable, and those who succeeded them were of the same stamp. In the aftermath of the South African War, the industry's leaders could have settled for the lesser option, the exploitation only of the higher-grade ores, in fewer mines; and thereby enriched, without risk, those who had invested in them. They chose instead to build a vast low-grade industry, and spread the profits across a long span of years. In the process, the shareholders received returns that overall were no more than modest,[1] but the decision to go for growth long-term gave South Africa the promise of future greatness as the industrial giant of the African continent. Now in 1921 their successors, in turn, declined to opt for the easy way, and the lesser risk. They could have settled for the shrinking industry, profitable enough but of increasingly smaller size, with a dwindling workforce. They chose instead the hard road that sign-posted an industry that would constantly renew itself and expand.

It was clear to them by December 1921 that the industry could be preserved in being only if discipline and orderly management were returned to the mines; and if inefficient and redundant whites, sheltered by the Status Quo Agreement, were retrenched and replaced, if need be, by efficient blacks; and if the earnings of whites were related more closely to their true, and less to their scarcity value. It was, at the same time, just as clear that there was little prospect of the union leadership, already under fire for countenancing wage cuts, now agreeing to the restructuring of the labour force. Even if the union leaders could be brought to grasp the nettle, there was no hope of their carrying with them a workforce that was truculent in its resistance to change, the ready recipient of propaganda from Communist Left, Nationalist Right, or both, and surrounded by the stark reality of a poverty-stricken army of the workless. Nevertheless, the industry leaders decided on negotiation, with the implicit understanding that if the unions would not, or could not, see that the selective retrenchment of 2 000 was better than the inevitable erosion of five times as many jobs through mine closure, then so be it. The time of showdown would be, inescapably, upon them.

Phillips, who was personally involved, if at a remove, set out the background to events in private letters to colleagues. Thus, he wrote from

Johannesburg on 23 November to R S Holland, a director, and later Chairman, of Central Mining, in London:

> We are having a strenuous, anxious time. It is impossible to predict whether we shall get through without a big upheaval or not. If only Smuts and his Government will be strong, I think we may get radical reforms without all the disorganisation and loss which a general strike would involve, but we are quite determined to see the necessary changes effected. Smuts accused me of *wanting* a strike. This is, of course, furthest from my *desire*, but there are worse things than a strike (deplorable as it might be) viz: – to sit supinely by and watch ruin overtake half the industry with all its disastrous effects.

> Smuts' argument against a strike is that it is impossible to foresee its course or its end. This is moral cowardice (with an eye to the ballot box, perhaps, thrown in!), but our experience warns us that, unless our case is so overwhelming and so clearly popular, the Government would step in at the crucial moment and insist on some sort of weak compromise. Wallers has a very intimate experience in this connection and is a steadying influence where I might force the pace. Signs are not absent of serious differences among the Unions and, generally speaking, the outlook for getting back to control, discipline, and efficiency is better than it has been for years. ... All this is to pave the way for the serious battle with the men's leaders on the status quo agreement, ... modifications of contract system, etc.[2]

A more closely involved participant and observer of the troubled scene was P M Anderson, now taking over as the senior executive of Union Corporation in Johannesburg, following the sudden death of Major Michael McCormack, OBE, MC. The Corporation's head office was in London, under Sir Henry Strakosch as Managing Director. In the Johannesburg offices of most mining houses in those days, the preparation of the weekly London letter, in time to catch the mailtrain to Cape Town and the mailboat to Southampton, was a solemn ritual. (So was the annual journey by the director resident in Johannesburg to attend the AGM in the City, an odyssey taking in all around three months of each working year.) It became Anderson's duty to keep Strakosch informed of events on the Rand, and he did so in impeccable style. His private and wholly frank *rapportage* provided, week by week, a cool, immediate reflection of the white heat that developed at the interface of Capital and Labour. In this way, he bequeathed a unique contemporary record of the view of events taken by the leaders of the industry in the innermost councils of the Chamber, and of the motivation for their most crucial decisions.

Thus he wrote on 19 October 1921, revealing the stiffening resolve of the Chamber as the gold price fell dramatically in the last quarter of the year:

> There is a general feeling among the Groups that we are still a long way from having control of the mines and that, sooner or later, there must be a

trial of strength in the form of a general strike or a general lock-out, so as to clear up the position. In either event, it is felt that the condition of re-employment after an upheaval would have to be on a very different basis to that existing at present, both as regards wages and discipline.

While the atmosphere is, at present, highly charged, our own views are that the men will not go to the extreme length of a general strike, as they rather fear that they will be playing into the hands of the employers. Should a strike on a large scale take place, it would probably come suddenly as a result of some indiscretion, not as part of a pre-conceived policy.[3]

On 9 November he wrote about the proposed amendments to the mining regulations, scheduled for discussion at the Prime Minister's conference the next day.

... a much more important factor would be to break the domination of the Unions from which we at present suffer, the present position being that the technical administrators of the mines have no power to carry into effect any reforms for the reduction of working costs which affect the European employee without the previous consent of the Unions, and, in this connec-tion, the Unions have been most obstinate in resisting any change of condi-tions and have, in fact, been following a definite policy of attempting to enforce the employment of additional Europeans wherever possible.[4]

It was only now that Anderson had begun to doubt whether a strike of serious proportions could be avoided. He pointed out that if this came about the mines should be ready, in its aftermath, to introduce all desirable reforms. Dis-cussions were taking place in the Chamber on the possibility of obtaining union agreement to a ratio between the numbers of whites and the numbers of blacks employed. Even in the unlikely event of the mining companies being given a free hand, they would not, Anderson reported, wish on economic grounds to reduce the white labour force by more than twenty-five per cent.[5]

When he wrote again on 30 November, the strike at Crown Mines was dragging towards its end, despite a union attempt to extend the dispute by demanding that the area of supervision of white stopers be reduced (and more whites employed). Anderson expressed the view that a general strike would be 'rather welcomed' by employers, as it would afford an opportunity for the settlement of a number of matters which would have to be dealt with in the immediate future.

Should the Crown Mines strike be settled within the next few days, the Chamber proposes to immediately take up these outstanding matters with the Federation and attempt to arrive at a settlement by negotiation. Should negotiations fail, it is proposed to simply announce to the Unions what steps the Chamber proposes to take in connection with these matters.[6]

At the meeting of the gold producers on 6 December, Christopherson added an important consideration. It was necessary to help not only the struggling mines, but profitable mines as well, to enable the people who put money into them to get a reasonable return on their investment, and so encourage others to supply future capital.[7]

It was generally overlooked by public and Parliament alike that the lifespan of the industry, as opposed to that of individual mines, depended on the opening of new mines to replace those that came naturally to the end of their lives. If investment in mines was not shown to be rewarding, the required capital would not be put at venture and potential new mines would remain undeveloped. Moreover, as Wallers emphasized to the unions later in the month, the gold mines of the Rand constituted, as a whole, a low-grade industry. In other words, there were substantial quantities of low-grade ore even in the richer mines which would become unpayable at high costs or a low gold price, and would remain unmined to the disadvantage of the shareholders and the country as a whole.

Two days after the meeting on 6 December, J Boyd, the Assistant Secretary of the Chamber's Labour Department, wrote to the Federation, following up the Prime Minister's suggestion that the Chamber and the unions meet to discuss outstanding issues. In the letter, the Chamber identified these issues as a reduction in the earnings of highly-paid contractors; limitation of the Status Quo Agreement, and re-organization of working arrangements underground. The contractors, who were the élite of the underground labour force, were paid in proportion to the ore broken under their supervision, less the cost of stores and black labour involved.

> ... the prices paid for this work are out of all proportion to the value of the work done, and are so high as to cause discontent among other employees ....[8]

The Chamber proposed instead a 'no cost' form of contract, based on a day's pay plus bonus, a reform which had been under discussion for many years.

Turning to the Status Quo Agreement, the Chamber said that the time had come when the Agreement should be limited to skilled occupations only, and that the mines should make greater use of experienced blacks in semi-skilled occupations.

> It is not the intention of the Chamber to suggest that natives should replace Europeans in skilled trades and occupations, such, for example as those of mechanics, miners, etc, but that they should be employed instead of white men in those semi-skilled or unskilled occupations which natives are well able to, and in some cases actually do, perform, such, for example, as those of pump attendants, cleaners, greasers, rough pipe-fitting, sanitary service, wastepacking, and so on.[9]

The Chamber reiterated that it was not the intention to affect in any way the employment of tradesmen and skilled whites, but rather to secure for them wider opportunities by ensuring that the mines would continue to work when the gold price fell.

> I am desired to emphasise most strongly that it is only by some very drastic reduction in the cost of production that the mines can be kept going, and to urge on your Federation and the Unions the necessity of accepting the Chamber's suggestions, unless disaster is to overcome the Witwatersrand.[10]

The Chamber stated that the modifications proposed would involve the reduction over a period of months, if not years, of at most 2 000 in the number of unskilled and semi-skilled Europeans, not necessarily all of them by retrenchment. The alternative was the loss of employment to over 10 000 whites, or nearly half the total white labour force.

> Further, unless working costs can be reduced to a figure which will show a reasonable return on capital even when gold has dropped to its normal price, the ordinary process by which exhausted mines are replaced by the opening of new ones will entirely cease.[11]

The letter closed by proposing a conference a week later on 15 December, to which the Federation agreed.

Chamber representatives at the conference included all the members of the committee of gold producers, and Roberts, Kelsey and Boyd from the Chamber staff. The Federation was represented by its President, Joe Thompson, and twenty-six union delegates. At the outset, Buckle rolled out the case for the Chamber. The mines were currently receiving, after realization charges, £4 16s 0d for every ounce of gold. At that price there were eight mines producing at a loss, including the once-rich Robinson mine, and the presently-huge ERPM. The price was dropping, and if it dropped another 2s or 3s, four more mines would become unpayable. If gold dropped to its normal price of £4 4s 11d, the unprofitable mines would be joined by another twelve, spanning the Rand from west to east, including Krugersdorp's West Rand Consolidated, the Consolidated Main Reef, the Village Deep, the Simmer and Jack, and the Modder East.[12]

He appealed to the unions to give up the Status Quo Agreement. This involved no threat to skilled craftsmen or efficient miners, but there was a considerable amount of white labour which was redundant and inefficient and the mines could not afford to carry that labour any longer. It was also necessary for managements to have a free hand to utilize labour to the best advantage. It was not possible, for example, to employ one man to supervise jack hammers and another to supervise the installation of supports in the same stope, where both of these jobs could be done perfectly well by the same man.

290

E S Hendrikz, recently-elected General Secretary of the MWU, acting as a principal spokesman, rejected the abandonment of the Status Quo Agreement out of hand.

> ... I have no hesitation in saying that my rank and file will turn that down holus bolus and I am going to support them. [13]

He demanded from the Chamber that it spell out exactly what it had in mind in a further letter so that its other proposals could be clearly understood and put to the men. There could be no committal without the fullest explanation.

The Chamber refused. It was resolved not to be delayed by a long filibuster by union spokesmen; and equally determined not to assist in the fashioning of a new union strait-jacket on mining operations. It asked instead that the unions co-operate with individual mine managements to keep each mine going as long as it could be kept going, with as many or as few employees as were necessary.

Thompson responded for the Federation by saying that the seriousness of the position of the low-grade mines was fully realized. However, the workers were already being paid less than they should be to offset the rise in the cost of living. Moreover, the Chamber's proposals were far-reaching, and they were very vague. Thompson continued:

> We realize that we have large numbers of unemployed and we have a duty to these men and if there are to be more unemployed ... we realise also we have a duty to them.
>
> Sir Evelyn Wallers: Quite so. You have to find a method by which there is the least amount of unemployment possible.
>
> Mr Thompson: That is what we shall try to do. [14]

Thompson asked for further details and an opportunity of going fully into the Chamber's proposals, and on that note the conference was adjourned.

The Chamber gave further information in a letter dated 23 December, which incorporated tables showing the costs of individual mines, the main constituents of costs, a list of seventeen mines which had closed since 1915, and details of the earnings of contractors.

The letter showed that the number of mineworkers employed on contract, whose high wages it was proposed to reduce, numbered a little over 2 000, or ten per cent of the white labour force. On average, these contractors in June 1921 earned 50s a shift, or around sixty-six per cent above the usual white workman's wage on the mines. More than one half of the contractors received amounts varying from 45s to over 80s a shift, and the earnings of a few went as high as £200 a month, an extraordinarily high wage for the times.

The Chamber's letter gave additional examples of the categories of semi-skilled workers that might be affected by abrogation of the Status Quo Agreement. In all, the number of whites employed in the affected categories totalled

4 200, of whom 3 100 were employed underground. The Chamber pointed out that many of these men were so experienced in their work as to be able to hold their jobs against any competition.

The letter ended by proposing a further conference on 28 December, but the Federation indicated that more time would be required. On that date the Chamber, impelled into keeping up the pressure, gave the required statutory notice of one month, without prejudice to the negotiations in progress, of its intention to change working conditions and abrogate the Status Quo Agreement.

The postponed conference was re-scheduled for 4 January 1922, at the Federation's request, and then again deferred to 9 January. It was not to take place. The reforms proposed by the Chamber found the Federation in disarray. In no way comparable with the broadly-based Triple Alliance of British miners, dockers and railwaymen, it had recently declined in both membership and influence, in part because its moderate approach in negotiation with employers was unacceptable to many in the prevailing industrial climate. The Federation 'was a regionally cramped and racially exclusive organization of the aristocrats of labour' without funds of its own.[15] In the face of the critical situation that now arose, it could no longer represent the interests of all workers involved in the burgeoning dispute. At a meeting on 30 December the principal mining unions conferred and formed an *ad hoc* body to be known as the Joint Executives. The meeting authorized colliery workers to strike on New Year's Day, and decided to hold a strike ballot on other current disputes, not only on the gold mines, but in the Victoria Falls Power Company's plants in the Transvaal, and in engineering workshops in Johannesburg. The same meeting took the decision to enlarge the Executive of the Federation by appointing to it representatives of non-affiliated unions. The Augmented Executive, as it became known, embraced a wide spectrum, including the separate associations representing workers such as shop assistants, slaughtermen, clerks, warehousemen, power station employees and tramwaymen, the more extreme of whom tended to take a radical stance in discussions on the mine dispute. The Joint Executive now became the power behind the developing situation, and the Augmented Executive its puppet.

In terms of the Industrial Disputes Act it was open to the unions to call on the Government to appoint a conciliation board to resolve the dispute with the employers. The proposed changes could not have been introduced by the employers until the conciliation process had taken its measured course. This option, however, would have involved the unions in presenting some alternative solution to the crisis facing the industry, something which it had consistently failed to do. Moreover, to the unions conciliation meant sacrificing what they believed to be their most effective weapon, the lightning strike, unleashed without warning on the employer. They chose this option in its most deadly form – general strike – but the employers had already had enough and were ready to withstand it.

The strike on the coal mines began on 1 January 1922. On Saturday

7 January, the Federation met with the Prime Minister, who urged them to continue discussions with the Chamber. He also called on the Federation to co-operate in the maintenance of essential services. The Federation replied that they would do so on condition that the Federation was given complete control of coal stocks, of the collieries that continued to produce, and the distribution of coal. The General was not pleased.[16]

Meanwhile, the strike ballot was already nearing completion. The ballot paper embraced the dispute on the coal mines, the Chamber's 'threat to substitute cheap black labour for white' on the gold mines, and the proposed alteration of the contract system. It brought in for good measure the two matters outside the Chamber's jurisdiction, the refusal by the Victoria Falls Power Company to increase minimum wages, and a proposed reduction of the wages of men employed in engineering works. The ballot paper asked: 'Are you prepared to strike until these ultimatums are withdrawn? Mark X under Yes or No.' It then added the recommendation of the Joint Executives that union members should vote for a strike. Despite a low poll, the loaded questions posed on the ballot paper guaranteed a resounding 'Yes' from union members.

Events now moved fast. The Federation declared the result of the ballot on Sunday, 8 January, and next morning told the Chamber that the strike would be put into effect that night unless all the notices complained of were withdrawn. A hurried meeting was called between the Chamber's Executive and the Federation, when the Chamber was asked to withdraw its 'ultimatum'. The Chamber pointed out that it had not issued an ultimatum, but a notice in accordance with the requirements of the Industrial Disputes Act, and that there was ample time to arrive at an agreement before expiry of the notice. However, it offered to extend the effective date until 9 February to allow a full thirty days more for negotiation. The Federation decided, after consideration, to insist on withdrawal of the notice.

Smuts now intervened, meeting the Chamber's Executive at 5 pm and urging them to withdraw the notice, which he thought had been ill-advised.[17] If they would agree to do so, he would undertake to ask the Federation to withdraw the strike vote, thus clearing the ground for further negotiations. The Executive however was strongly of the opinion that withdrawal of the notice would be interpreted as a retreat in the face of a strike threat and would place the employers in a hopelessly weak position in further negotiation. The Chamber gained the impression, wrote Anderson, that the Prime Minister was 'not in the least surprised' at its refusal to withdraw.[18]

The strike duly came into operation next morning, and along the seventy-mile arc of the Rand from Randfontein to Springs the sheave wheels were still and the stamps silent. In all 22 000 men stopped work on mines, in power stations and engineering works. The Federation wrote to the Prime Minister spelling out its terms of settlement – the withdrawal of notices, and departure from the 'policy of eliminating white workers', and the fixing of a definite ratio of Coloured to white[19] (it had in mind a ratio quite different from the ratio under discussion within the Chamber).

Smuts continued his endeavours to bring the parties to compromise, but first he issued a message to the blacks on the mines:

Greeting.

I am sending this message to you to assure you that you need in no way be alarmed or disturbed about these conditions. The matter in dispute between the white workers and their employers will be settled without any necessity for anxiety on your part. Remain quietly in your compounds ....

I feel sure that this message will find you ready listeners and that your conduct will remain law-abiding and obedient until work is resumed on the mines.[20]

The black labour force responded to the appeal in exemplary fashion, even in the face of brutal assaults as the deteriorating strike situation created opportunities of licence for the vicious, criminal element on the Rand.

Smuts next backed a proposal for a conference of seven from each side meeting without pre-stated conditions. The conference assembled on Saturday, 14 January, and was charged with the purpose of resolving the disputes in the engineering shops and power stations as well as on the gold and coal mines. The independent Chairman was Mr Justice Curlewis. He did his best, but the conference drowned in an ocean of words, more than a quarter of a million being recorded by the shorthand writers. The coal dispute was taken first, the Chamber's team being led by John Roy, Chairman of the Collieries Executive Committee. The gold mines dispute did not come under discussion until 24 January. The union delegates concentrated on the issue of the Status Quo Agreement and it was clear that they would make the colour bar the crux of the confrontation. At the end, a union delegate summed it up well.

What is the use, we have met here for 12 days, and on any dispute we have dealt with, we are in exactly the same position as when we started – not the slightest improvement in the position of any dispute under consideration.[21]

The President of the MWU, W S Lewis, declared that the arguments put forward by the other side would in no way convince him any more than he expected his own arguments to convince the other side.[22] Buckle and Thompson agreed that the conference was a total failure.

Meanwhile, the strike continued. Its advent on 10 January had taken the mine-owners by surprise because they did not expect labour to be withheld until the changes objected to had been introduced after 1 February. The unions had got themselves a good rallying cry in the call for 'ultimatums' to be withdrawn, and a strong emotional appeal in the call to defend the colour bar, but they had also committed themselves to a no-win situation, for the Chamber was left with little room for manoeuvre. Any move to compromise would be interpreted as a victory for precipitate strike action, and the Chamber – and indeed the country – had had quite enough of that. Bodies as diverse in stand-point as the Federated Chamber of Industries and the Transvaal Agricultural Union wrote to Smuts, in support of the Chamber, declaring that no single sector should have power to paralyse the country, and calling for a lasting solution to the recurrent industrial unrest.[23] As the conference closed, Buckle warned that the strike had already done so much damage that the reforms proposed by the Chamber in December would no longer meet the case; it would now require additional measures to save the industry. Moreover, because black recruiting had been suspended, and time-expired blacks were being repatriated in escalating numbers, it would not be possible to resume operations at the pre-strike level, and there would be no guarantee that strikers would be re-employed at the strike's end.

The unions were in tough mood too. The withholding of essential services threatened to halt maintenance of shafts and tunnels, and worse, result in the flooding of mines. The mine-owners were presented with a daunting prospect – the stopping of underground pumping, causing subterranean water flowing into the workings to rise to levels high enough to drown the pumps. There-after, the mines themselves would be in danger of drowning, with the further threat of water spilling into neighbouring mines to start a chain reaction of perhaps irreparable destruction. The fears of the mine-owners were heighten-ed by uncertainty about what mine officials would do. Anderson wrote on 11 January that the general attitude of underground and surface officials was 'very wobbly' and it was not clear exactly how far they were prepared to stand by the management.[24] However, when pumpmen and engine drivers were directed to leave their posts by the Federation on Saturday, 14 January, their positions were nearly all filled by surface and underground officials. 'These Officials have completely changed their attitude and are now rendering very loyal service without demur.'[25] Many of them had been union members not long previously, and had to suffer 'that greatest of moral trials, the disapproval of their action by their relatives and intimate associates'.[26] Worse, they had to face the threat of violent attack and their attempts to protect mines from damage due to flood and other causes were not always successful.

There was vital help from another direction. The Association of Scientific and Technical Societies of South Africa, under the presidency of Dr Oren-stein, manned the power stations, so that Johannesburg in the dreadful days ahead 'did not have darkness added to the other horrors of the situation'.[27]

While officials decided, after initial hesitation, on co-operation with management, union members were swept up willy-nilly by the strike call, many of them being respectable, hardworking men, with no stomach for the rough stuff of emergent trade unionism. Ironically, among the less than ardent strikers were two future presidents of the Chamber. Calvin Stowe McLean (President, 1945-1946, 1948-1949 and 1952-1953) was a graduate of mining engineering at McGill University in Canada. He had come to South Africa on 10 October 1910. In the post-war period he had been quick to realize that rock-breakers on contract could earn far more than shift bosses, who were nominally above them, and sometimes more even than mine captains. So lucrative were the promised pickings that he sacrificed his official and graduate status and became a contract mineworker, and a member of the MWU. He soon earned enough to buy himself a motor car. As the 1922 Strike entered its violent phase, McLean, to avoid either upsetting his mine manager or being dubbed 'scab', displayed the shrewdness that was to mark his subsequent career. He arranged for the military authorities to commandeer his car with himself as driver.[28] The other presidential striker, Spencer Richard Fleischer (1951-1952), who had won the DSO and MC for gallantry in the War, was beginning his climb to the top of Gold Fields in a lowly job at New Modder. Though not in sympathy with the strike, he too had no option but to obey the union's call. To the gallant ex-soldier, the clash between military and strikers that lay ahead was a painful experience.[29]

[1] S H Frankel, *Investment and the Return to Equity Capital in the South African Gold Mining Industry: 1887-1965: An International Comparison,* p 27.

Frankel found that the internal rate of return of capital and dividends in the period 1887 to 1920 was 2,6 per cent, one of the lowest in the history of the industry. The figure given is the return over the whole industry after taking all capital losses into account.

[2] Fraser and Jeeves, eds, pp 330-331.

[3] Gencor Limited, Johannesburg: Union Corporation Archives: Letters to London, 1921-1922 (J to L PMA): Letter dated 19 October 1921, pp 3-4.

[4] Gencor Limited, Johannesburg: Union Corporation Archives: Letters to London, 1921-1922 (J to L PMA): Letter dated 9 November 1921, pp 1-5.

[5] *Ibid,* pp 5-6.

[6] Gencor Limited, Johannesburg: Union Corporation Archives: Letters to London, 1921-1922 (J to L PMA): Letter dated 30 November 1921, p 4.

[7] Chamber of Mines Archives: File 'Position of the Industry – General', 1921: Transvaal Chamber of Mines: Report of Meeting of Special Committee on the Chamber's Policy vis-à-vis Trades Unions, held on 6 December 1921, p 7 (No 15).

[8] Chamber of Mines Archives: File 'Position of the Industry – General', 1921: Letter dated 8 December 1921, from J Boyd, Assistant Secretary of Labour Department, Transvaal Chamber of Mines, Johannesburg, to Acting General Secretary, South African Industrial Federation, Johannesburg, p 1 (No 18).

Annual Report of the Transvaal Chamber of Mines, 1921, pp 145-146.

[9] Chamber of Mines Archives: File 'Position of the Industry – General', 1921: Letter dated 8 December 1921, from J Boyd, Assistant Secretary of Labour Department, Transvaal Chamber of Mines, Johannesburg, to Acting General Secretary, South African Industrial Federation, Johannesburg, pp 1-2 (Nos 18 and 19).

Annual Report of the Transvaal Chamber of Mines, 1921, p 146.

[10] Chamber of Mines Archives: File 'Position of the Industry – General', 1921: Letter dated 8 December 1921, from J Boyd, Assistant Secretary of the Labour Department, Transvaal Chamber of Mines, Johannesburg, to Acting General Secretary, South African Industrial Federation, Johannesburg, p 2 (No 19).

Annual Report of the Transvaal Chamber of Mines, 1921, p 146.

[11] Chamber of Mines Archives: File 'Position of the Industry – General', 1921: Letter dated 8 December, 1921, from J Boyd, Assistant Secretary of Labour Department, Transvaal Chamber of Mines, Johannesburg, to Acting General Secretary, South African Industrial Federation, Johannesburg, p 2 (No 19).

Annual Report of the Transvaal Chamber of Mines, 1921, p 146.

[12] Chamber of Mines Archives: File 'Position of the Industry – General', 1921: Report entitled 'The Gold Mining Industry: Conference between the Chamber of Mines, the SA Mine Workers' Union and the SA Industrial Federation regarding the following proposals of the Chamber ...', 15 December 1921, pp 1-3 (No 36).

[13] *Ibid*, p 10.

[14] *Ibid*, pp 33-34, 39.

[15] Hancock, *Smuts: 2. The Fields of Force*, p 67.

[16] Oberholster, pp 83-85.

[17] Gencor Limited, Johannesburg: Union Corporation Archives: Letters to London, 1921-1922 (J to L PMA): Letter dated 11 January 1922, p 2.

Oberholster, p 84.

[18] *Ibid*, pp 2-3.

[19] 'The Great Strike', *The South African Mining and Engineering Journal*, 14 January 1922, pp 671-672.

[20] *Ibid*, p 672.

[21] Johnstone, p 132.

[22] 'The Strike', *The South African Mining and Engineering Journal*, 28 January 1922, p 741.

[23] Yudelman, p 180.

[24] Gencor Limited, Johannesburg: Union Corporation Archives: Letters to London, 1921-1922 (J to L PMA): Letter dated 11 January 1922, pp 3-4.

[25] Gencor Limited, Johannesburg: Union Corporation Archives: Letters to London, 1921-1922 (J to L PMA): Letter dated 18 January 1922, pp 2-3.

[26] Annual Report of the Transvaal Chamber of Mines, 1921, p 69.

[27] 'The Strike', *The South African Mining and Engineering Journal*, 28 January 1922, p 737.

Editorial, *The South African Mining and Engineering Journal*, 4 March, 1922, p 919.

Annual Report of the Transvaal Chamber of Mines, 1921, p 69.

[28] 'Presidents of Private Enterprise – the Men who have led the Chamber of Mines', *Mining Survey*, No 3/4, 1982, pp 15-16.

Interview with Mrs Olive McLean, widow of C S McLean, at Johannesburg on 25 February 1983.

[29] Letter dated 22 March 1985, from Dr Roy Macnab, Johannesburg, to the author.

CHAPTER TWENTY-FOUR

To the Bitter End

The Chamber was determined not to have imposed on it a patched-up settlement which failed to meet the harsh imperatives of the economic equation. Anderson wrote to reassure his anxious head office in London that the employers fully realized that the consequences of retreat would be an immediate and serious contraction of the industry, bringing ruin to large numbers of people directly and indirectly dependent on it, and reacting most detrimentally on the Union's finances.

> Having stood very firm up to the present, at considerable expense, in order to secure the future of the industry, it is very unlikely that the employers will be stampeded by the Government into an unsatisfactory compromise, though such a contingency is never outside the scope of possibility when politicians meddle with industrial matters.[1]

Smuts, however, showed himself bent on getting the men back to work, even if that meant leaving key issues unresolved. He took the unusual step of postponing the Opening of Parliament, due on 20 January, until 17 February, partly to enable him to stay where the action was, and partly because he shrewdly assessed that the Opposition in Parliament was likely to exacerbate sensitivities and hinder *rapprochement*.

On the collapse of the Curlewis Conference on Friday, 27 January, Smuts wrote to both Federation and Chamber saying that the issue was not about the colour bar, but about how to save the low-grade mines. At the least, special and exceptional arrangements would be necessary to prevent disaster, and these called for calm and fair consideration.

The Chamber, following up the line foreshadowed by Buckle at the breakdown of the Curlewis Conference, proposed the next day that the average ratio of white to black be fixed for two years at not less than 1 white to every 10,5 blacks employed (replacing an existing ratio of round 1 white to 8,2 blacks). Within these limits the industry should be entitled to rearrange work as it thought fit, subject to statutory limitations and existing agreements. The Chamber further proposed that men re-employed after the strike be taken on at the rate of pay prevailing in December, but with the cost-of-living element reduced by one-half, this addition to continue until 30 June 1922, and then disappear. The Chamber also announced that men who took days off on May Day and Dingaan's Day would no longer be paid for them because these concessions had proved a distinct handicap to the poorer mines since their granting two years before. It added that, because of the inevitable curtailment of operations flowing, in particular, from the dispersal of black labour and the flooding of mines, a considerable number of men could not be re-employed at once after the strike. The Chamber stressed that the situation was not of the industry's making; it had been brought about by the pressure of economic circumstances, aggravated by the prolongation of the strike. The Chamber hoped that the industry would steadily recover, permitting the absorption of men not immediately re-employed.

The Joint Executives met the same day and passed a series of resolutions, which were duly endorsed by the Federation. F Hicks, President of the Tramwaymen's Union, then presented the resolutions on behalf of the Federation, to a meeting of union and Labour Party representatives in the Johannesburg Town Hall, which accepted them with acclaim. The resolutions declared that the Prime Minister's attitude showed that the Government was backing the employers in their attack on white workers, both in reducing their standard of living and curtailing their opportunity of employment.

> We therefore request the workers, and also all sympathisers, to take the necessary steps in conjunction with ourselves to defeat the present Government and substitute one calculated to protect the interests of the white race in South Africa. That with this end in view a conference be arranged at once with representatives of the opposition parties in Parliament to investigate what immediate steps can be taken to remedy the present situation ....

The resolutions then went on to authorize strike committees to stop scabs going to work.[2] In so doing the Joint Executives and the Federation, unwittingly perhaps, set in train the violence on the picket lines which would, as time went on, provide an unhappy hunting ground for the ruffians of the Rand.

Smuts wrote to a friend: 'The strikers now simply look to the collapse of the Government in Parliament for their salvation. Poor deluded people.'[3] He was correct, for no conceivable government could have imposed the strikers' demands on the mine-owners.[4]

The National Party was quick to express noisy sympathy with the strikers who were, after all, mostly Afrikaners, Nationalist voters, and seen as acting in defence of the cherished colour bar. The Labour Party was even more strident in support. However, the Opposition was to prove a paper tiger whose ready roar of rhetoric concealed a dearth of leadership and inability to offer a sensible solution to the impasse. Both Opposition parties were officially committed to the constitutional path of reform, and warned the strikers off illegal action. Nonetheless, individual party members did not seem to take this seriously, and did immeasurable harm by failing to keep 'their demagogic impulses under control'.[5] Robert Waterston, one of the deportees of 1914, was now the Labour MP for Brakpan. He plunged into the mêlée boots and all, becoming for a time the General commanding the Brakpan Commando, 800-strong and complete with brass band, duly dubbed 'Waterston's Army'. The Chamber of Mines, Waterston declared, in typically reckless vein, was plotting to eliminate ninety per cent of the white labour force.

Tielman Roos, the head of the National Party in the Transvaal, incited Afrikaners in the Active Citizen Force not to take part in the suppression of a strike if called up for the purpose. And he accused the Government of trying to create conditions that would justify martial law. At the end of January he summoned ten Nationalist and five Labour MPs to a meeting in Pretoria (which became known as the Pretoria or Roos 'Parliament') with the ostensible purpose of settling the industrial strife. Instead, they inflamed it.[6]

There followed on 5 February a mass meeting of strikers on the East Rand which called on the Roos 'Parliament' to set up a Provisional Government and proclaim a republic. The next day the resolution, presented by Waterston, was enthusiastically adopted by a turbulent crowd of 2 000 in the Johannesburg Town Hall. It read:

> That this mass meeting of citizens is of the opinion that the time has arrived when the domination of the Chamber of Mines and other financiers should cease, and to that end we ask the members of Parliament assembled in Pretoria tomorrow to proclaim a South African Republic, and immediately to form a Provisional Government for this country.[7]

A Government commission later found:

> It is indeed a striking commentary on the situation as it then existed in the Transvaal, that this treasonable resolution was openly submitted for the consideration of a body of politicians hostile to the Government, many of them avowed Republicans, who were assembled in a Government building in the Administrative Capital of the Union.[8]

The politicians now back-pedalled fast. The Roos 'Parliament' tamely resolved that a change of system could be reached only by obtaining a majority of the people in favour thereof, such majority to be reflected in the House of Assembly and Senate. Waterston, more tamely still, pretended that he had not moved the revolutionary motion in the Johannesburg Town Hall, but only 'presented it' on somebody's behalf. He soon returned to the safety of Parliament, leaving another 'general' to command his 'army'. The Roos 'Parliament' did however pass resolutions with a socialist stamp, including a call for the nationalization of mines and power stations. Hancock commented:

> The damage might have been less serious if their demagogic bubble had

been pricked just a day or two earlier; but, by an unlucky accident of timing, their mischief-making reached its climax – or anti-climax – just when Smuts was making his most determined bid for a negotiated peace.[9]

The Federation's Augmented Executive, appointed to run the strike as a front for the joint executives of the mining unions, had begun to regret its earlier decision to rebuff the Prime Minister and to call for a change of government. Both Thompson and Crawford, at one time or another, had doubts about the wisdom of continuing the strike. Crawford, just back from a meeting of the International Labour Organization in Geneva, was particularly lukewarm. He commented that a strike over wage cuts in the prevailing economic climate was 'a proper King Canute stunt'.[10] The Federation asked for a meeting with Smuts, who met its representatives on 4 February and recommended that the men return to work on the best terms they could get. If no better could be obtained, they should return on the latest terms offered by the Chamber. The all-important step was an immediate return to work. He stressed that the terms on which they returned were not material, because he guaranteed that these would be provisional only, and subject to change and adjustment. To arrive at a generally acceptable solution, he undertook that the Government would 'immediately appoint an impartial board to inquire into all the matters raised in the present dispute by both sides'. The Board would be required to report as soon as possible, its findings would be laid before Parliament, and if fair and workable, the Government would see that they were given effect to. If necessary a ballot of the men could be taken on the terms of settlement.[11]

Smuts then persuaded the Chamber to concede the retention of the Status Quo Agreement on the higher-grade mines. The Chamber accordingly announced on 6 February that the Status Quo Agreement would be terminated only on those mines which could no longer be profitably worked under previous arrangements at the standard price of gold, the decision in case of dispute being left to the Government Mining Engineer. To trade union commentators Ivan Walker and Ben Weinbren it seemed that the Chamber's compromise offered the possibility of a fair settlement to the dispute.[12]

The Federation however responded by refusing to accept any terms but the unconditional withdrawal of the proposal to abandon the Status Quo Agreement. It seems, at least, doubtful whether they would have refused the mediation of Parliament, rebuffed the Prime Minister and rejected the Chamber's offer, if it were not for the false hopes engendered by the Roos 'Parliament' in Pretoria. The leaders of the Federation 'threw away their last chance of an honourable and workable compromise'.[13]

The Chamber at once withdrew its concession. There seemed little left for Smuts to do. He did not have the constitutional machinery either to force the men to return to work or to compel the mines to operate at a loss. Yet, the continuation of the strike had disastrous implications for the ailing economy. He made a final effort on 11 February, calling on the Federation to end the strike, and on the industry to resume operations.

He told the men that continued disruption of the mines could only result in greatly reduced work opportunities and sacrifices many times greater than those originally called for. 'Under such circumstances victory itself becomes meaningless.' He appealed to them to leave the settlement to Parliament after impartial inquiry. He assured them of the Government's concern about the unemployment that was sure to follow, and announced that schemes were in hand to employ thousands on public works.[14]

In conclusion, Smuts assured the workers that those who returned to work would receive police protection on the picket lines. To the unions, this was a highly provocative step – the protecting by the Government of scabs and strike-breakers. Encouraged by Opposition politicians to see Smuts as the agent of the Chamber, the Joint Executives reacted aggressively the next day, calling on the workers to stand fast until the strike ended on their own terms.

For its part, the Chamber endeavoured to get the sheave wheels turning, but at first with little success. The uneasy peace on the mines crumbled and serious clashes began between strikers and Police. Immediately after the collapse of the Curlewis Conference the Federation had resolved:

> That all strike committees are instructed to take any necessary steps they may deem fit to stop all scabs continuing to work, and from now onwards they have full powers to do anything they desire to bring the present strike to a successful issue.[15]

Before this, the strike committees had begun to organize the men into strike commandos. At first they operated responsibly enough, providing a measure of occupation and discipline for the idle men, but as conditions deteriorated they assumed a para-military function. In the first week of February the Police were ordered to protect men going to work against assaults by strikers. On 8 February the Police arrested Fisher, Shaw, Wordingham, Spendiff and McDermid of the Council of Action on charges of inciting to public violence. Unhappily, prior to the declaration of martial law, the courts had no power to refuse bail[16] and the arrested men were all released on 22 February to continue a campaign in which they not only preached revolution but organized sabotage and violence.[17] On the evening after his release, Shaw told a meeting outside the Johannesburg Town Hall that the Council of Action favoured violence and that all great reform was brought about by force.[18] The Secretary of the Labour Party, C J McCann, later commented that the decision to let them go was disastrous. 'When I heard they were in gaol, I said "Thank God, I hope they will have sufficient sense to keep them there."'[19]

By unbridled eloquence and reckless incitement the Council of Action was enabled to expand its authority at the expense of the Federation. The alliance of the two bodies was a strange one indeed, because the Council's communist leadership was committed to the destruction of the colour bar in support of which the Federation and commandos were striking. This uneasy partnership against capitalism resulted in such absurd convolutions as banners with the

302

strange device: 'Workers of the world fight and unite for a White South Africa'. The Council provided some of the leaders of the Revolution that now followed, particularly in Fordsburg. It is easy, however, to exaggerate its role, for it lacked broadly-based support. The real thrust to revolt came from the commandos.

The Federation itself had become no more than a cipher in the power struggle. Not only were decisions of its Augmented Executive subject to the Joint Executives, but it had to take account of strike committees which became more and more subservient only to their own stern laws. These local committees were co-ordinated by yet another autonomous body, the Central Strike Committee in Johannesburg, which commanded powerful influence. The Augmented Executive's shaky authority was even further undermined by the strike commandos, those offshoots of the strike committees, which appointed 'generals', and liaised loosely through the so-called Co-ordinating Committee, yet another group of self-appointed leaders, who acted independently of other strike bodies, and who usually met in secret.

The historian Oberholster has commented that two of the most important requisites for a successful strike are union leaders of integrity who are at one on the policy to be followed, and public support strong enough to influence the authorities. During the 1922 Strike the Nationalists and socialists undermined the authority of the recognized trade union leadership, and eventually destroyed it, while the violence of the strikers lost progressively the sympathy of the public.[20]

The division of leadership between recognized trade union leaders, strike committees, socialists and commando 'generals' proved disastrous. On 2 February the Central Strike Committee had instructed strike committees to put out all scabs by 'force, friction or persuasion'.[21] With powerful commandos roaming the Reef from Springs to Randfontein, threatening, intimidating and assaulting workers and pulling out scabs, a collision between strikers and Police became inevitable. The War and the Rebellion of 1914 had familiarized large numbers of men with the use of weapons and tactics in armed combat. Among such men the commando movement spread like a flame, and commando members gradually acquired firearms to supplement the traditional pickhandle of the scab-beaters.

Taking all factors into account, the maintenance of reasonable order in January and February was remarkable. However, as the numbers of men at work grew, the die-hards of the strike became progressively more reckless. By Monday, 13 February, there were 4 000 whites at work, including officials, and there was a steady drift back of between 60 and 110 a day. However, intimidation and violence stopped the flow by 21 February.[22] On 27 February there were clashes between the Police and strikers at Brakpan, and the Civic Guard was mobilized. On the 28th the first serious clash occurred when the Police opened fire at Boksburg, killing three men and injuring several. A police officer was seriously wounded. A subsequent inquest, after examining sixty-three witnesses, exonerated the Police, but the incident was used by agitators to embitter the strikers.[23] By then, attempts to derail goods and passenger trains had become commonplace, and the long series of outrages reached its peak with the derailment of the mailtrain from the Cape in March.[24] Vituperative attacks on the Government and the Chamber continued in full spate as the strike moved to its violent and tragic climax.

By Saturday, 4 March, the Augmented Executive had lost direction and purpose, and was driven to re-open negotiations with the Chamber. On the morning of that day, after an all-night sitting, Crawford sent a letter to the Chamber by hand proposing a conference to discuss possible terms on which the strike might be called off. The Federation wished to know what modifications might be agreed, and offered to meet the Chamber at once.

The proposal was considered by the Chamber with equal dispatch. The Executive Committee was summoned and, after discussion the same morning, agreed to inform the Federation that it had already announced the terms on which the mines could be re-started, and that no useful purpose would be served by re-opening negotiations, the effect of which would only be to brake the back-to-work movement. The Executive decided that it would not, in future, deal with the Federation, chiefly on the grounds that it had come to represent very large interests wholly unconnected with mining. Anderson explained that the attitude of the Chamber was based, for example, on the fact that the union representing municipal power station workers, known for its extremism, had come practically to dominate the councils of the Federation. Anderson went on to say that the wording of the Chamber's reply was left to Buckle and the Chamber officials, and not revised by the Executive, because of the urgent need to reply to the Federation.

> The President's phraseology, as a rule, leaves nothing to be desired, but, unfortunately, on this occasion whoever drafted the letter did not maintain the usual standard of dignity and … it has unnecessarily given offence ….[25]

In this letter to the Federation, signed by Gemmill, the Chamber pointed out that, as the Federation had not proffered any fresh proposals or suggestions, a conference would obviously be futile.

> A fortnight was wasted in such discussions immediately after the beginning of the strike; and at the end of that time it was evident that, in spite of the full and convincing case brought forward by the Chamber, the representatives of the Federation were either incompetent or unwilling to grasp even the elementary fact that the industry was in a very critical position. Far less had they any remedy to propose. The Chamber will not waste further time in attempting to convince persons of that mental calibre.
> The urgent necessity now is not to hold debating society meetings, but to get the mines working without delay.[26]

The Chamber announced further that it would not deal with the Federation in

future, although it was quite prepared to deal with the unions really representative of the trades to which mine employees belonged.

> Whatever may have been the case in the past, when the Federation was
> under different control, it is evident that it no longer represents the bulk of
> the employees in the gold and coal industries, many of whom have returned
> to work in defiance of the orders of the Federation, while many more resent
> bitterly the intimidation exercised by your Augmented Executive in pre-
> venting them from returning. If the Federation continues to exist after the
> disaster into which it has led its deluded members, it will probably consist
> mainly of unions in no way concerned with the industry. The members of
> the Chamber are occupied with the winning of coal or gold, and they see no
> reason why they should discuss that business with representatives of
> slaughtermen and tramwaymen.[27]

In Parliament Smuts referred, quite rightly, to the 'deplorable tone' of the
Chamber's letter.[28] He was infuriated by its arrogant rejection of the Federation's approach because he believed that the Chamber had lost an opportunity to settle the strike peacefully. He was mistaken because, in truth, the
Federation had lost the power to mediate; nonetheless, the Buckle-Gemmill
brush-off was a blunder which did nothing whatsoever to advance the cause
of peaceful settlement.

The subsequent Martial Law Inquiry Judicial Commission commented that
the Chamber's letter was indisputably a frank and brutal expression of its
views, which had exasperated the rank and file. However, the leaders of the
Federation had displayed an equally frank and brutal tone in their dealings
with the Chamber. The Commission pointed out, moreover, that on receipt
of the Chamber's reply, the Federation's immediate reaction was to pass a
resolution that a ballot be taken to ascertain whether the men were willing to
return to work, pending the findings of a Board (as promised by Smuts) on
the terms offered by the employers. The Commission went on to say that it
was difficult to understand how the Federation 'could have failed to realize
that long prior to the 4th March any control they ever had exercised over the
strikers had vanished. They had sown the wind, they were about to reap the
whirlwind.'[29]

It was the attempt to organize a ballot on a return to work that culminated
in the Federation's final surrender to revolutionary force. The Federation and
the Joint Executives met in the Trades Hall, Rissik Street, at 10 00 am on
6 March to consider the proposed ballot. About a hundred and twenty attended, representing unions affiliated to the Federation. Soon after the
meeting began, armed commandos, several thousand strong, surrounded the
hall and took possession of the stairs and entrances to the building. They insisted, with much show of force, that no ballot be taken on the mines, and
demanded instead that a general strike throughout South Africa be called at
once. During the meeting, Fisher and Andrews addressed the commandos

from the balcony of the Trades Hall. The delegates of the Federation held out until 5 30 pm when Joe Thompson informed the massed commandos that a general strike had been declared.

There was no response to the general strike call outside the Rand, but on 10 March the commandos went over to full-scale revolution, and the Government responded with martial law. Smuts secured a supportive vote of Parliament and hurried to the Rand. An attempt was made to derail the train that brought him and he came under fire as he entered Johannesburg. The situation, however, never produced so direct a threat to the survival of the State as in 1913, although the loss of life was much larger. Smuts soon counterattacked, using artillery and aircraft to bombard the positions of the commandos.

Anderson set down on 15 March the view from the Chamber's new building in Hollard Street of the Rebellion raging on the Rand.

> Since writing last week ... the Rand has passed through one of the most fateful periods in its history. On Thursday morning rioting took place in Benoni and shooting at sight became general. Disturbances were also in progress in other parts of the Rand. ... On Friday a Commando of about 700 mounted and armed men who were on their way to Benoni took possession of the Brakpan Mines. The officials ... put up a resistance lasting at least one hour. Unfortunately, no police appeared on the scene and the mine officials had to surrender for the want of ammunition. ... a body of revolutionaries, among whom were many well-known strikers, thereupon submitted the 31 defenders to the most brutal treatment. A number of them were clubbed to death after receiving gunshot wounds and nearly all the rest were severely wounded or injured. By Friday afternoon all the Towns of the Far East Rand were in the hands of the revolutionaries .... On Saturday this position was general throughout the whole of the Witwatersrand. Such Police Forces as were scattered along the Reef practically became prisoners within their own barracks.[30]

Now, however, the situation began to change. Units of the Citizen Force went into action, supported by burgher commandos from the rural areas. Heavy fighting followed and sniping was general. However, the Government soon won control, and its armed forces rapidly mopped up the rebel commandos and captured the strikers' headquarters in Fordsburg. The strike was called off on 16 March and the strikers returned unconditionally to work. The cost in human life and suffering, and in damage to property, had been high. Casualties exceeded one thousand, including more than two hundred dead. About five thousand were arrested, and eighteen sentenced to death. Four of those were hanged, including 'Taffy' Long, convicted after a re-trial, of the 'execution' of a Fordsburg shopkeeper for passing information to the Police. As a consequence of riot and battle, public distress was widespread. A public assistance fund was created by Smuts, under the Hon A G Robertson, Administrator of the Transvaal, and an appeal for funds was launched, to which the Chamber contributed £20 000.

Smuts immediately appointed the Martial Law Inquiry Judicial Commission, with two Cape judges, Sir Thomas Lynedoch Graham, and Sir John H Lange, as members, to inquire into 'the causes, circumstances, character, and aims of the revolutionary movement, in which the recent strike culminated'.[31] Their findings, published on 16 September 1922, illuminated the mix of forces which combined to escalate industrial unrest into full-scale revolution. The judges blamed the strikers' commandos, and the leaders of the trade unions and of the Labour Party who encouraged them. They found responsible, too, those National Party members who sought to make political capital from the strike, and they pointed to the desire of the Nationalist element to use the industrial disturbance to bring about a republic in South Africa, the preponderance of such men in the commandos, the encouragement given by Waterston, and the belief of many strikers that rural Afrikaners would give them armed assistance, or at least accept Tielman Roos's suggestion to decline the call-up.[32]

Other principal factors named by the Commission were the intrigues of the Communist Party; the widespread belief that the Chamber intended to remove the colour bar; the ignorance of many mineworkers of the true functions of trade unionism; and the deplorable weakness of the Augmented Executive in allowing the dispute to become a political issue, and in relinquishing control to the armed commandos. The Commission also found that the revolutionary movement was caused, 'in a lesser degree', by the clash between Police and commandos at Boksburg on 28 February, by the Chamber's letter to the Federation of 4 March, and the release on bail of Shaw, Fisher, Wordingham, McDermid and Spendiff, who were known to be exponents of violent measures.[33]

The 1922 Strike and succeeding Revolution have since become the stuff of myth and self-perpetuating legend, and much has been made of the sinister forces that allegedly planned it all and then manipulated events and participants alike. In truth, the Strike was due neither to republican treason, Bolshevik plot nor a capitalist conspiracy to subjugate the unions. It arose from a tough pragmatism on the part of mine-owners and trade union leaders alike who, from their separate vantage points, saw the issue starkly as one of survival, and who reacted to events as they arose in ways which conformed to the mores of the time.

In Britain, where the condition of the comparable working class was much worse, a similar hard-nosed pragmatism was displayed in bitter and sometimes violent confrontation during the coal strike of 1921 and in the great general strike that followed five years later, without eventuating in loss of life. In South Africa, the circumstances were different. The young nation was still too close to the Frontier and to civil war to have evolved the moderation that comes with maturity. There persisted in its society those of disparate origin and purpose who were willing to seek political solutions along the barrel of a gun. These were melded by the heat of the confrontation between Capital and Labour in a bid to bring down the structure of the State.

The inquiry into the causes of armed revolt was followed by the appointment of the Mining Industry Board to conduct a measured and in-depth inquiry into the dispute and strike that preceded it. The Board's unanimous report generally exonerated the Chamber and found no substance in the case for the miners. Nonetheless, in the handling of the dispute and the strike the Chamber made mistakes and learnt lessons which it never forgot. And so did the unions. The grievous consequences of unresolved dispute brought home to both parties the virtues of endless patience in negotiation and in the search for mutually acceptable solutions. The trauma of 1922 left its stamp indelibly on the pattern of industrial relations.

For his handling of the Government's role in the affair, Smuts was criticized for taking sides with the employers and not doing all in his power to effect a compromise. These criticisms were both unfair and unjust, but the political mud stuck. He was criticized, too, with more justification perhaps, for delaying intervention by armed force. However, he had unhappy memories of earlier civil unrest. Eight years previously, he had been pilloried for being too ruthless in quelling the General Strike of 1914, and so had Botha for the manner in which he put down the Boer Rebellion which followed the outbreak of war. In mobilizing the army to restore order in 1922, Smuts could not be wholly confident that the burgher forces would answer the call-up. He tarried long enough for the ugly underside of South African society to be wholly exposed, and then crushed it in a manner which terminated the traditional resort to protest-at-arms of white settlers in South Africa. Ahead lay a period of internal stability, interrupted sporadically during the Second World War, and a unique record of industrial peace.

[1] Gencor Limited, Johannesburg: Union Corporation Archives: Letters to London, 1921-1922 (J to L PMA): Letter dated 15 February 1922, pp 1-4.

[2] 'The Great Strike', *The South African Mining and Engineering Journal,* 4 February, 1922, pp 773-774.
Union of South Africa: Report of the Martial Law Inquiry Judicial Commission, 1922 (U G No 35, '22), p 20, paragraph 111.

[3] Yudelman, pp 180-181, quoting a letter dated 3 February 1922, Secretary to the Prime Minister Archives (in South African State Archives), 1/1/422, 3/22, Vol 3.

[4] *Ibid*, p 181.

[5] Hancock, *Smuts: 2. The Fields of Force,* pp 69, 71, 72.

[6] *Ibid*, p 71.

[7] *Idem.*

[8] Report of the Martial Law Inquiry Judicial Commission, 1922, p 34, paragraph 169.

[9] Hancock, *Smuts: 2. The Fields of Force*, p 72.

[10] Shorten, p 313.
Hancock, *Smuts: 2. The Fields of Force*, p 72.

[11] Hancock, *Smuts: 2. The Fields of Force*, p 72.
'Continuation of the Strike: The Week's Developments', *The South African Mining and Engineering Journal*, 11 February 1922, p 805.

[12] I L Walker and B Weinbren, *2 000 Casualties: A History of the Trade Unions and the Labour Movement in the Union of South Africa*, p 110.

[13] Hancock, *Smuts: 2. The Fields of Force,* pp 72-73.

[14] 'The Great Strike', *The South African Mining and Engineering Journal*, 18 February 1922, pp 843-844.

[15] 'The Great Strike', *The South African Mining and Engineering Journal*, 4 February 1922, p 774.

[16] Shorten, p 318.

[17] Oberholster, p 118.

[18] *Idem.*

[19] Report of the Martial Law Inquiry Judicial Commission, 1922, pp 13-14, paragraph 68.

[20] Oberholster, pp 112-113.

[21] Report of the Martial Law Inquiry Judicial Commission, 1922, p 19, paragraph 103.

[22] Gencor Limited, Johannesburg: Union Corporation Archives: Letters to London, 1921-1922 (J to L PMA): Letter dated 22 February 1922, p 1.

[23] Report of the Martial Law Inquiry Judicial Commission, 1922, p 19, paragraphs 104 and 105.

[24] Report of the Martial Law Inquiry Judicial Commission, 1922, pp 12-13, paragraphs 63 and 65, and pp 70-74 (Schedule of Attempted Damage, Actual Damage, Suspicious Behaviour, and Interfering Generally with Railway Property during Industrial Disturbances, January-March 1922).
'The Red Revolution', *The South African Mining and Engineering Journal*, 18 March 1922, p 961.

[25] Gencor Limited, Johannesburg: Union Corporation Archives: Letters to London, 1921-1922 (J to L PMA): Letter dated 8 March 1922, pp 1-3.

[26] Annual Report of the Transvaal Chamber of Mines, 1921, pp 162-163.

[27] *Ibid*, p 163.

[28] Gencor Limited, Johannesburg: Union Corporation Archives: Letters to London, 1921-1922 (J to L PMA): Letter dated 8 March, 1922, p 3.

[29] Report of the Martial Law Inquiry Judicial Commission, 1922, pp 19-20, paragraphs 107-109.

[30] Gencor Limited, Johannesburg: Union Corporation Archives: Letters to London, 1921-1922 (J to L PMA): Letter dated 15 March 1922, pp 1-2.

[31] Report of the Martial Law Inquiry Judicial Commission, 1922, p 1.

[32] *Ibid*, p 32.

[33] *Idem.*

CHAPTER TWENTY-FIVE

Winners and Losers

While the Strike was at its height, the staff of the Chamber, and of its associated companies, moved into the handsome six-storey building of white stone with its entrance on Main Street opposite the Johannesburg Stock Exchange. The Stock Exchange has moved west to Diagonal Street, but the Chamber has stayed, the original building long since enlarged to cover the entire area bounded by Main, Hollard, Marshall and Sauer Streets. Its tower block rises seventeen storeys. A graceful embellishment in 1961 was the closing to traffic of Hollard Street and its transformation to a small park in the centre of the city's financial district. The first Council Chamber on the second floor remains, now a private dining room with a special ambience, seeming to hold between its panelled walls a whisper of days and deals gone by. There on 27 March 1922, as something like normality returned to the Rand, the industry's leaders gathered for the Chamber's thirty second annual meeting.

From the Presidential rostrum Buckle spelt out to the unions and their members the terms of their unconditional surrender ten days before. The cost to the country had still to be computed, but the gold producers were painfully aware of a fall in gold production of more than one million ounces. Not surprisingly, Buckle was uncompromising on major issues.

> Previous agreements have, of course, ceased to exist, but the Chamber has undertaken that it will continue for the present the arrangements as to hours and basic wages which obtained before the strike.[1]

The Chamber, he declared, would no longer be party to the system of shop- and shaft-stewards which in the years preceding the Strike had come to constitute a 'second management' on the mines. In the state of education in trade unionism then existing, the system had proved 'an entirely premature addition to the mining industrial fabric'. Shaft-stewards had actually gone so far as to issue instructions to employees in regard to their work, and in some glaring instances had held up whole shafts in defiance of the agreements between the Chamber and the MWU.[2]

The Chamber had ceased to recognize the Federation; it would however continue to recognize unions which included in their membership a substantial proportion of the particular class of employee which they purported to represent. Such unions must include in their constitutions proper provision for a secret ballot of members before the declaration of a strike. They must outlaw strikes to force non-union members to join them.

However, every facility would be given to employees to approach managers with grievances, and the Chamber was prepared to meet with accredited representatives of unions without waiting for formal changes to unions' rules necessary to provide for secret strike ballots.

Douglas Christopherson of Gold Fields then signalled a radical change of direction in the handling of labour relations. He declared that a situation had developed which enabled unions to deal directly with the Chamber in disputes affecting individual employees, often before discussing the matter with the mine manager. While the Chamber was made up of ordinary human beings, it seemed to workmen on the mines a remote machine without personality, something which could not elicit from them any feeling of personal loyalty or devotion.

> I can imagine no condition of affairs more favourable to the unimpeded progress of the activities of those who make it their business to create unrest among our workmen than the condition of affairs which has resulted from the present system. ... We must, by common consent, restore to the fullest possible extent the authority of the manager upon his own mine, and we must strive to restore to the fullest possible extent the close personal relations which must exist between a mine manager, who really manages his mine, and his officials and workmen. It is the personal touch in human relations that counts, and it is to the personal touch that we must try to get back.

Christopherson stressed that it would still be necessary for the Chamber and the unions to meet to discuss important questions of principle at top level. But once agreements had been reached, the Chamber's executive duties must cease. Mine managers, in harmony with their chairmen and boards of directors, must take over from then on and implement agreements.[3]

Christopherson was going his individual way and had not sought the prior approval of his colleagues on the Chamber's Executive. There was some umbrage, but applause as well, and he was forecasting very much the shape of things to come in labour relations on the mines.

The Mining Industry Board was appointed on 15 April to investigate the dispute that had led to the Strike, the first term of reference being concerned with the Status Quo Agreement. In choosing members the Government was careful to pre-empt accusations of bias. It appointed as Chairman Sir William Solomon, a Judge of Appeal, and future Chief Justice. He was the youngest brother of Sir Richard Solomon who had played a leading role in the politics of the Transvaal Colony in earlier years. It has been written of William Solomon: 'Without fear or favour he was fair to all the parties appearing before him'.[4] The Members of the Board were Sir Robert Kotzé; Sir John Carruthers Beattie, the distinguished scientist who had been appointed the first Principal and Vice-Chancellor of the University of Cape Town, and who was known as a man of wide sympathies;[5] and the Rt Hon William Brace, a former working miner and President of the South Wales Miners' Federation, and a British Labour MP, who had been appointed Chief Labour Adviser to the British Government. Smuts told Parliament that he had asked Whitehall to recommend a member whose ability and knowledge in the field would be beyond question.[6] As a consequence, Brace had been recommended as the man best qualified to deal with labour and mining problems. The Commission became generally known as the Brace Commission.

The Chamber was concerned at the omission of representatives of the mine-owners, and assessed the Commission's attitude initially as hostile. It sought to remedy the position by the weight and cogency of evidence submitted for consideration, with great success. The truth was that, however reluctant one might be to heed the arguments of the Chamber, the case it presented was, so often, indisputable. The whole country depended on the mines and therefore on the cutting of their costs to maintain output and to impart momentum to the entire economy. Henry Burton, the Minister of Finance, in presenting the Budget in 1923, could only prescribe 'the unpleasant medicines of economic orthodoxy'.[7] The Brace Commission, in its turn, would find itself obliged to bow to the economic imperatives.

The Chamber's Gold Producers' Committee (GPC) was formally constituted on Monday, 26 June 1922, and took over from the Executive Committee the function of setting policy for the gold mines, while the Collieries Committee continued its parallel role for the coal industry. Sir Evelyn Wallers, representing Central Mining (Corner House) was the first Chairman of the GPC, and Buckle, who had nineteen months of office to serve as professional President, did not at first attend meetings. He did so later, but as an adviser and not as a member. The Groups represented, in addition to Corner House, were Anglo French Exploration, Consolidated Mines Selection, General Mining, Johannesburg Consolidated Investment Company, Gold Fields and Union Corporation. The agreed constitution provided that gold mining companies must report to Group head offices on labour matters and not to the Chamber. The Groups would decide what should be referred to the GPC, but agreed that members would keep one another informed of any disputes with employees likely to prejudice the interests of other members. A technical advisory committee of consulting engineers was appointed to work under the direction of the GPC.

The GPC was at once involved in approving the comprehensive evidence prepared for submission to the Brace Commission, and in conferring with that body on the establishment of conciliation procedures. The Commission had examined the possibility of making compulsory by law the reference of industrial disputes in the mining industry to arbitration, and concluded that this was neither the best nor the most practical instrument for their settlement.

312

It also found that all witnesses appearing before it were determinedly opposed to compulsory arbitration. It found, too, that the previous system involving Boards of Reference, Works or Grievance Committees, and shaft- and shop-stewards, had developed in a way that made its continuance impossible, leaving an undesirable vacuum. At an early stage the Commission broke off its inquiry to hold a joint conference of employers and workers, beginning on 14 August. Over the following week it overcame the GPC's reluctance, and obtained its co-operation in drafting a conciliation scheme, published as a schedule to the Commission's report. The temporarily chastened unions, which had learned finally that they could bend neither Government nor Chamber to their will in a power struggle, fell into line. The scheme, which came into force on 1 October 1922, set up a permanent Conciliation Board, representing employers and unions, with the function of resolving disputes without resort to strikes or lock-outs. The scheme was no more than a stop-gap pending the passage of new legislation to extend state regulation of industrial disputes.

The Brace Commission completed its full inquiry in September, and its findings were made public in December in a unanimous report which the Chamber could claim completely vindicated its attitude on the strike issues. The Chamber did so claim, and with a brash eagerness which Christopherson and others feared would rub salt into wounds better left to heal.[8]

Reviewing the crisis that had faced the industry, the Commission concluded that 'drastic measures were needed to cope with the emergency'.[9] It declared that there was no necessity for the continuance of the Status Quo Agreement and that the Chamber's cancellation of it after the Strike was fully justified. The Status Quo Agreement was something entirely separate and distinct from the statutory regulations establishing the colour bar. It was a purely voluntary agreement between the Chamber and the Mine Workers' Union, arrived at during the War, when it was of the utmost importance that the mines should be kept going, and was no more than a makeshift. It could hardly have been contemplated that it should continue indefinitely after the War.[10]

The position of the white man in skilled operations was well entrenched. Those in semi-skilled operations were faced with the danger of encroachment by blacks, but the real remedy lay in extending the field of industrial employment, not in hampering managers by artificial restrictions.

The Commission found moreover that the effect of the abolition of the Status Quo Agreement upon the number of white men employed on the mines had been exaggerated. There was a divergence of opinion among mine managers as to whether from a purely economic point of view it was better to employ blacks or whites on semi-skilled work such as drill-sharpening.

It may be asked why, if the abolition of the *status quo* agreement has had so little effect in replacing white labour by black, the Chamber of Mines was so insistent upon its being rescinded. One answer is that an interpretation

313

was placed upon it by the Unions which it was never intended that it should bear. ... prior to the strike there was a considerable number of redundant and inefficient men employed on the mines.

> ... the evidence satisfies us that on the whole attempts by managers to dispense with the services of men, whom they did not require, were resisted by the Unions, and that their opposition was frequently based upon the allegation that the *status quo* agreement was being infringed. It was mainly on this account that it was deemed desirable to put an end to it once and for all.[11]

The Commission had hard words to say about the activities of shaft- and shop-stewards.

> Interference ... was carried to such an extent that the men frequently looked to the stewards rather than to the managers for directions regarding their work. They interfered with the appointment and dismissal of workmen and even of officials, claiming the right to be consulted in these matters ... The result was that under such threats managers have often, for the sake of peace, found it expedient to retain redundant or inefficient men, or have given way rather than face the annoyance and waste of time involved in an appeal to a Board of Reference. Workmen, realizing that they owed their retention in their jobs to the stewards, were led to pay greater regard to their instructions than to those of their officials. Men have been ordered to go slow in their work, to reduce the speed of a machine, to observe strictly the 'one man one job' principle. Lightning strikes have been called on slight provocation, and the work of the mines seriously hampered.
>   This is a formidable indictment, but it was amply proved by the evidence laid before us ... It was satisfactory indeed to find that on some mines the relations between the management and the stewards had been of a perfectly friendly character, but these, unfortunately, were exceptions to the general rule.[12]

The Chamber, in announcing the basis on which mines were prepared to resume operations after the Strike, had stated that it would pay a cost-of-living allowance until 30 June, after which the allowance would wholly fall away. This had duly taken place and had been much resented by the men who had claimed that they were worse off than in 1914 when the cost of living had been lower. The Commission pointed out however that the Economic Commission of 1913 had found that workmen on the Rand were better off than their counterparts in America, and much better off than those in Europe. That being so, there was a margin left for an increase in the cost of living, especially if account were taken of other improvements in the conditions of work such as holiday leave, 'a very liberal concession ... far in excess of anything that is given to labouring men in the mines in Great Britain'.[13]

The Commission however did not agree with the view that the wages were extravagantly high. Underground work was essentially more trying than work on the surface, and was aggravated on the gold mines by the risk of phthisis. It recommended neither increase nor decrease in the wages paid to whites since the Strike.

The position of the coal industry in South Africa was seen by the Commission as a simple one. In Great Britain the average export price per ton of coal had sunk from £4 1s 2d in December 1920 to £1 4s 10d in December 1921. In January, the minimum wage of British colliers was 20s 10d a day and this fell gradually month by month until in December it had sunk to 8s 9d. In the Transvaal the pithead price dropped from 7s 0,11d in January 1921 to 6s 0,73d in December and it was anticipated by coal owners that it would continue to fall. It in fact did so and stood at 5s 5,59d in August 1922. The collieries were dealing with profits measured not in shillings per ton, but in pence.[14]

In these economic conditions the Commission found that the Chamber was justified in reducing colliery wages, and that the reductions should have been accepted by the men. It considered however that not enough trouble was taken to put the facts before them.

William Brace, in finding against the men on the collieries, could draw on his personal experience of the mining valleys of Wales. He wrote to a friend in Cardiff at the time:

> Even now, after the events which have taken place, the coal miners of South Africa are receiving 24s 6d per shift of eight hours, with a guaranteed 48 hours weekly wage, in addition to 17 holidays per year with pay. If our miners had such a wage as that, I am sure they would think themselves well blessed. I do not think that the cost of living in South Africa is very much higher, if anything, than at home.[15]

In considering black wages as an element of mining costs, the Commission found that the pay of the ordinary black worker doing rough work compared favourably with that paid in other industries. Any increase in their pay would lay a burden on low-grade mines which some of them would find hard to bear. However, the Commission concluded that the bonus paid to experienced men might well be substantially increased, and so might the pay of those engaged on semi-skilled work, to close the wide gap between their pay and that of white men doing the same work.

In reviewing the year 1922, Buckle demonstrated the effect of the changes made after the Strike by comparing the situation in December of that year with that in December 1921. In that month before the Strike fifteen mines had shown either a profit per ton of ore milled of less than one shilling, or an actual loss. In December 1922, the number in that category was reduced to five.

> If the former working costs had continued, the loss of 7s 6d in the price of gold, which has since occurred, would have increased the number of mines

in that position in December, 1922, to something like twenty-four – if, which is improbable, they had all continued working. In fact, about nineteen of them would in all probability, have closed down permanently .... Their shutting down would have meant the dismissal of 7,573 white men ....[16]

The number of whites signed on when operations were restarted was on a sharply reduced scale, but increased steadily thereafter, as men qualified for leave and replacements were required while they were away. At 30 April 1924, two years after the Strike, the number employed was 18 567, compared with 20 511 in November 1921, a reduction of just under 2 000 men.[17] The numbers continued to rise but it would be 1928 before the average number employed returned to that of 1921. White wages were substantially reduced, and workers did not wholly recover their former wage levels for a decade.[18]

In January 1923 the Government published an Industrial Conciliation Bill, incorporating the recommendations of the Brace Commission. The Bill was referred to a select committee, and emerged in entirely different shape, containing, as the Chamber saw it, 'some fantastic provisions, under which Conciliation Boards could be called whenever the terms of a single individual were altered by his employer'.[19] The Bill made no provision for prior discussion of the grievance with the employer. The Chamber led the employers of the country in protesting against the Bill, which was substantially changed, and held over for a year.[20] Finally, after further amendment, the Industrial Conciliation Act passed into law on 31 March 1924. Its basic purpose was to provide machinery for the orderly settlement of disputes between whites and their employers in all industries, and to avert the violence that had characterized the major strikes of the past. It did not, in general, apply to blacks, for those required to carry passes were excluded, and so were those subject to certain other legislation applying to black workers. In essential public services such as power stations strike action was banned altogether and provision was made for compulsory arbitration. In all other organized industries the Act provided for permanent industrial councils in industries in which both employer and employee opted for their establishment; and it gave the agreements drawn up all the force of law. Employers and employees in the mining industry did not so opt, and chose instead a voluntary negotiating procedure. Most importantly, the Act made compulsory, for the first time, the reference of deadlocked disputes to a conciliation board before resort to strike or lockout.

The principle of the State's right to intervene in the bargaining process was accepted with reluctance by the unions, for, by accepting the measure, the unions were agreeing to statutory delays which would weaken what they regarded as their most effective weapon, the wildcat or lightning strike called without warning to the employer. They gave way partly because they were divided and demoralized after the 1922 Strike, but principally because the Act placed wide powers in the hands of the responsible Minister whom they hoped

316

would intervene when necessary to redress the balance in their struggle with employers.[21]

Their trust was not misplaced. Successive Ministers of Labour would sit on the fence for as long as they could when trade unions and employers were locked in dispute; but the contesting parties would be at all times aware that the Government could use its weight to enforce a settlement, and would do so whenever there were issues at stake which impinged on political policy or economic expectations. The Act moreover did not stop wildcat strikes, particularly when the political or emotional content of disputes made calling out the men a fair risk to take; and once such strikes were over the official tendency was to condone their illegality. Nor did the Act, as has been claimed, 'depoliticize' white labour.[22] White trade unions, and particularly mining unions, have remained a potent political force right down to modern times. The labour vote has continued to be a significant factor in electoral calculations, and the miners' vote, rightly or wrongly, has been regarded as holding the balance of power in marginal constituencies along the Rand. In consequence, organizations such as the Mine Workers' Union have enjoyed unrivalled access to Ministerial and even Prime Ministerial offices, and were enabled to maintain a status as the last bastion of white privilege in the workplace when all others had crumbled.

The Chamber showed no enthusiasm at the passage of the Industrial Conciliation Act which was to mean so much to the mines in terms of industrial peace. It had done its best to help create workable legislation, and when this was at last achieved, dismissed it with faint praise, declaring it harmless and shorn of the worst features of earlier draft bills. That was the most the Chamber could find to say in favour of 'this type of one-sided legislation, which appears to be chiefly designed to catch votes by harassing employers'.[23] Wallers, once again elected President on 31 March 1924, after the conclusion of Buckle's four-year term, still hankered after the Brace Commission plan; he declared that conciliation enforced by legislation could never be as effective as conciliation achieved voluntarily by free discussion between employer and employee.[24] When the Chamber sought registration as an employers' organization under the Act, the Secretary of Labour called for changes in its constitution, which the Chamber declined to make as it was 'difficult to find any advantage in being registered'. In May 1925 the Secretary waived the amendments,[25] and the Chamber has been registered as such ever since.

Smuts, in passing the conciliation legislation through Parliament, had tried hard to satisfy the unions, for, politically speaking, he had his back to the wall. Before the 1922 Strike he had been denounced for the manner in which the Government had put down unrest among black Israelites, members of a separatist church, at Bulhoek in the eastern Cape. And after the Strike he was attacked again for the force used against the rebellious Bondelzwarts tribe in South West Africa.[26] From then on nothing went right for him.

In October 1922 white Rhodesians were given the option either of joining the Union or of continuing as a British colony. Smuts dearly wished to bring

317

them in, and offered favourable terms, including provincial status with ten representatives in the Assembly and the prospect of more in the future. As luck would have it, delegates from Rhodesia were in the Visitors' Gallery of the House of Assembly during debate on the Rand Rebellion to hear Hertzog denounce Smuts, in words that would ring round the hustings, as the man whose 'footsteps dripped with blood'. Smuts still held high hopes, and Rhodesians who favoured incorporation found a leader in the former Administrator of Rhodesia and Chamber President, Drummond Chaplin. Milner and Churchill, successive Colonial Secretaries in the British Cabinet, put their weight behind incorporation, but it was not to be. White Rhodesians, deterred by Afrikaner nationalism and the unitary constitution of South Africa, voted to follow a lonely and fateful road as a separate self-governing colony. There was to be no assistance from that direction for the South African Party which since its victory in February 1921 had been steadily shedding seats at by-elections.[27]

In July 1922 Colonel F H P Creswell, the leader of the Labour Party, defeated a strong South African Party candidate by thirteen votes in a Durban by-election. Smuts wrote:

> That stupid elector, Hard Times, is all the time against me. My majority of 22 in 1921 has dropped to 13, which is not a very promising number.[28]

In the month of Creswell's election he and Hertzog took the essential first steps towards an electoral pact. Some common political ground, and mutual regard, had been evident for some time, and was consolidated in the community of interest, or advantage, that developed in opposition to Smuts during the 1922 Strike. By April 1923 they were ready to announce heads of agreement. Hertzog promised not to change the constitutional status of South Africa, while Creswell undertook to lay to rest the Bolshevik bogey. They found a common focus of policy in opposition to 'big financial interests'. These, they claimed, were jeopardizing the future of South Africans 'as a civilized people'.[29]

The following year, after defeat in a by-election at Wakkerstroom in the eastern Transvaal, Smuts decided to go to the country. His Government still had a year of office to run, and some supporters considered his action precipitate. However, Smuts regarded the defeat as critical because the South African Party candidate, A G Robertson, had resigned as Administrator of the Transvaal to fight against an unknown Nationalist who won the seat with the support of Railway workers and other Labour voters. Smuts called a General Election on 19 June 1924, and went down to defeat.

The roots of the Pact victory were unquestionably economic. Smuts had governed through three years of slump.

> Some people said that he and his capitalist masters had made the slump, but by a more plausible diagnosis its origins were overseas. Its effects on South

Africa's national income, public finance, economic activity and employment were catastrophic. They were aggravated by three successive years of drought which accelerated and dramatized the flight of Afrikaners from farming. The ruined farmers and *bywoners* – 'poor whites', as people called them – had to try to find city jobs at a time when industrial and commercial employment was everywhere contracting.[30]

It is not possible to assess to what extent the 1922 Strike contributed to the Pact victory of 1924. Undoubtedly the slump and the Strike together provided the Pact with all it needed to win the propaganda battle, but the really important gains were made by the Nationalists in the rural areas. The Labour Party, with the power of the Pact behind it, gained five seats on the Rand, but polled a marginally smaller proportion of the total vote than in 1920. The South African Party, which won most of its seats in urban constituencies, polled 46,5 per cent of the votes compared with 34,9 per cent by the Nationalists, 13,4 per cent by Labour, and 4,3 per cent by independents and small parties. It was the heavy weighting of rural seats that gave the Pact its twenty-seven-seat majority.

The Chamber had had its differences with the Smuts Government. It considered the taxation of the mines extortionate; that the levels of phthisis compensation, which the mines had to fund, were the highest in the world; and that the industry was charged high rail rates to permit lower charges on the requirements and products of farmers and other specialist interests. The Chamber clashed particularly with F S Malan, the Minister of Education and Mines and Industries, and acting Prime Minister when Smuts was overseas, over the restrictions he imposed on recruiting black labour in Moçambique, in the belief, subsequently found to be mistaken, that this would counter black unemployment in South Africa. Buckle, a man of mordant wit, publicly complained at the Chamber's quarterly meeting on 24 September 1923 of interference and Ministerial incompetence on the part of the South African Party Government. He declared that he longed for the Arcadian state of affairs depicted in *Iolanthe* –

> When noble statesmen do not itch
> To interfere with matters which
> They do not understand.

It would ever be the industry's lot when elections approached to be the target of the hopeful at the hustings. At the same meeting Buckle complained of Nationalist misrepresentation of the profits of mining by quoting working profits as though they were *net* profits, the far smaller amount that remained to shareholders after tax, Government's share of profits and other statutory charges had been deducted. He also drew attention to a letter published in several Nationalist newspapers claiming that the Chamber had bought 40 000 morgen to grow macaroni with which to feed black mineworkers, the purpose being to ruin the maize farmers. The writer, one Hendrik van der Walt, stated that the macaroni could be seen growing on the farms Uitkyk and Honeybos.[31]

While the Chamber entertained many reservations about the South African Party Government, it had none in its dread of a Hertzog-Creswell coalition. The industry had experienced such an administration in the Transvaal Provincial Council during the war years and immediately after, and had to fight off its attempt to add its own taxes to those exacted on the industry by the central Government. The GPC's hostility was so aroused by that Council that it contributed £200 to an organization known as the Provincial Council Abolition League. It also broke with custom by voting £7 000 to support the South African Party's unsuccessful bid to win control of the Province in 1923.[32] Nevertheless, despite some financial support from mining houses, the South African Party, 'the supposed mouthpiece of the mining magnates, continued to suffer from poor financial backing'.[33]

In an endeavour to counter propaganda against the industry after the Strike, Gemmill pioneered public relations in South African industry. Benefiting from American experience, he set up the South African Industrial News Service, under Owen Letcher, the Editor of *The South African Mining and Engineering Journal*, to provide positive news about the industry to the Press. The Chamber also took advantage of the advent of radio broadcasts from Johannesburg to give a series of talks on mining. And seventeen days before the General Election of 1924, the Chamber distributed a pamphlet, claimed to be unbiased and non-political, entitled *Party Programmes and the Mines: A Business Statement*. The pamphlet was a restrained analysis of the economic policies of all three parties; though not uncritical of the South African Party, it showed that its programme would be the least damaging. However, the Nationalists and their Labour allies, riding the crest of the political wave, won easily; and the electoral pact was carried over into the so-called Pact Government. Creswell was appointed Minister of Defence and, additionally, became South Africa's first Minister of Labour, and Thomas Boydell became Minister of Posts and Telegraphs and of Public Works. As leaders of the 1914 Strike, Creswell had been sentenced to a month's imprisonment, and Boydell held in custody for five days. Two other Ministers in the new Cabinet, J C G Kemp, the Minister for Agriculture, and P G W Grobler, Minister of Lands, had served terms of imprisonment for their part in the 1914 Rebellion. Other notable Cabinet appointments included a future Prime Minister, Dr D F Malan, as Minister of Internal Affairs, Education and Public Health, and N C Havenga as Minister of Finance.

Once the shock of the Pact victory had been absorbed, the Chamber got down to a policy of constructive engagement with the country's new administrators. The new Pact Government soon responded. It did not take long at all for the new ministers, Creswell excepted, to appreciate the country's dependence on a thriving gold mining industry. Nor could they fail to perceive that increasing the wages of miners had a far less feasible look to a government in power than to a party in opposition. The wages paid on the mines set the pattern for the country at large, including the public service, and the inflation of mining costs would have a multiplier effect on wages generally and the cost of living, and increase the charge on state revenue.

The change of government has been widely interpreted as a major turning-point in South African history, in which the miners, having 'lost the battle' in 1922, 'won the war' in 1924. However, Yudelman has contested this interpretation, in a sortie as dashing as Blainey's assault on the accepted causes of the Jameson Raid. Yudelman challenges the turning-point theorists from left to right of the ideological spectrum, and declares that the advent of the Pact Government was neither a defeat for mining capital nor a victory for white miners.[34]

In his book, *The Emergence of Modern South Africa*, a detailed re-interpretation of the years 1902-1939, published in 1983, Yudelman argues that South Africa, like similar modern capitalist countries, is subject to imperatives of 'legitimation' and 'accumulation', which are partially contradictory. Legitimation concerns the State's accountability to the electorate, and its role in politically sensitive areas such as job creation and the control of conflict between Capital and Labour. However, legitimation clashes with accumulation, for while legitimation can indicate the restraint of the capitalist's pursuit of profits, accumulation demands their continuance to protect state revenue.[35]

Yudelman finds that after 1924 the Pact Government, in spite of its intention to do well by white Labour, in fact entrenched the order established as a result of the 1922 Strike. It did so because the viability of gold mining had to be ensured as long as it remained the heart of the economy. Had the Pact taken its anti-capitalist rhetoric seriously, the economy would have been the main casualty.[36]

> ... the point is that any government, given the structure of the state and society, would have operated roughly within the same broad constraints at the time. Individual governments and new policies obviously do make some difference, but it is easy to forget the imperatives and structures that limit them all.
>
> No non-revolutionary, white-elected government in the Pact's situation would have been able to create a viable white workers' state, ignore the cost imperatives of the gold mines, or fail to intervene to stabilize labour relations on the gold mines and keep down mining costs. The Pact continued to face the legitimation and accumulation problems of previous governments, and it continued to respond to them in notably similar ways.[37]

Thus, Yudelman finds that the outcome of 1922 was far from being a defeat for the mine-owners. He emphasizes, too, that the nine years of the Pact Government were years of relative industrial peace. From 1919 to the Rand Strike of 1922 a total of 2,8 million man-days were lost to all South African industries as a result of disputes, the bulk being on the gold mines. By

321

contrast, from 1924 to 1932, only 114 000 man-days were lost.[38]

However, as Yudelman himself points out, industrial and race relations would be influenced for the next fifty years by the programme which the Pact activated.[39] Whether one opts for the theory of the turning-point or, like Yudelman, for an inevitable continuity of development, the truth is that the so-called 'unholy alliance'[40] of hardline nationalists and militant labourites was fateful, for it entrenched the privileged position of white workers in South Africa, encouraged their militant defence of the colour bar, ensured that the black mine labour force would long continue to be largely unskilled, lowly-paid and migratory, and set South Africa firmly in the mould of racial segregation.

[1] Annual Report of the Transvaal Chamber of Mines, 1922, p 11.
   Annual Report of the Transvaal Chamber of Mines, 1921, pp 69-70.
[2] Annual Report of the Transvaal Chamber of Mines, 1921, p 70.
[3] *Ibid*, pp 80-81.
[4] M J Swart, 'Solomon' in *Dictionary of South African Biography*, II, pp 683-685.
[5] M Boucher, 'Beattie' in *Dictionary of South African Biography*, IV, pp 23-25.
[6] 'The Industrial Commission', *The South African Mining and Engineering Journal*, 1 April 1922, p 1033.
[7] Hancock, *Smuts: 2. The Fields of Force,* pp 158-159.
[8] Chamber of Mines Archives: Minutes of a Special Meeting of the Gold Producers' Committee, Transvaal Chamber of Mines, 4 December 1922. (Minute book covering the period 1922-1925, pp 47-48.)
[9] Union of South Africa: Report of the Mining Industry Board, 1922 (UG No 39-'22), p 4, paragraph 10.
[10] *Ibid*, pp 5-6, paragraphs 17, 19 and 20.
[11] *Ibid*, p 7, paragraphs 24 and 25.
[12] *Ibid*, p 21, paragraphs 102 and 103.
[13] *Ibid*, p 15, paragraphs 66-68 and 71.
[14] *Ibid*, p 35, paragraphs 186-188.
[15] 'Notes and News', *The South African Mining and Engineering Journal*, 30 September 1922, p 43.
[16] Annual Report of the Transvaal Chamber of Mines, 1922, p 62.
[17] Report of the Mining Industry Board, 1922, p 11, paragraph 46.
   Chamber of Mines Publications: Gold Producers' Committee of the Transvaal Chamber of Mines: Pamphlet entitled *Party Programmes and the Mines: A Business Statement*, p 5.
[18] Yudelman, pp 25 and 26 (Table 1).
   Fiftieth Annual Report of the Transvaal Chamber of Mines, 1939, p 114.
[19] Thirty-Fourth Annual Report of the Transvaal Chamber of Mines, 1923, p 45.
[20] *Ibid*, pp 45, 62.
[21] Yudelman, pp 202-203.
[22] *Ibid*, p 209.
[23] Annual Report of the Transvaal Chamber of Mines, 1923, p 62.
[24] Thirty-Fifth Annual Report of the Transvaal Chamber of Mines, 1924, p 55.
[25] Annual Report of the Transvaal Chamber of Mines, 1924, p 43.
   Annual Report of the Transvaal Chamber of Mines, 1925, p 37.

[26] Hancock, *Smuts: 2. The Fields of Force*, p 89, *et seq.*

[27] Hancock, *Smuts: 2. The Fields of Force*, pp 151–154. Davenport, pp 189 and 196.

[28] Hancock, *Smuts: 2. The Fields of Force*, p 156.

[29] *Ibid*, pp 155–156.

[30] *Ibid*, p 157.

[31] Annual Report of the Transvaal Chamber of Mines, 1923, pp 193–194.

[32] Chamber of Mines Archives: Minutes of the Gold Producers' Committee, Transvaal Chamber of Mines, 8 and 22 January, and 5 and 12 February, 1923. (Minute book covering the period 1922–1925, pp 56, 60, 64 and 68, respectively.)

[33] Yudelman, p 217.

[34] *Ibid*, pp 24–30, 233.

[35] *Ibid*, p 10.

[36] H Kenney, Review Note, *The Emergence of Modern South Africa: State, Capital, and the Incorporation of Organized Labour on the South African Gold Fields, 1902-1939*, by David Yudelman, *The South African Journal of Economics*, Vol 52, No 4, December 1984, pp 429–430.

[37] Yudelman, p 243.

[38] *Ibid*, pp 233, 158 (Table 4).

[39] *Ibid*, p 217.

[40] D W Krüger, *The Making of a Nation*, p 137.

CHAPTER TWENTY-SIX

The Chamber and the 'Unholy Alliance'

The gold price fell as far, though not as fast, as the Chamber had feared. Gold sales continued to be at a premium, averaging yearly between five and ten per cent above the standard price of £4 4s 11d until the end of 1924. From January to July of that year the Chamber was able to announce a bonus to white mine employees of between four and six per cent, but there was little premium to be had thereafter. The premium disappeared altogether when Britain returned to the gold standard on 28 April 1925, an example which South Africa followed shortly after.[1] By then the mines had recovered from the upheavals of 1922. Cushioned by the premium, they had benefited materially from the cut in white wages, and had reorganized to increase productivity, a process which received a powerful boost from the ceaseless search for improved technology. Working costs were reduced by nearly twenty-five per cent, and there was a rapid increase in the productivity of both whites and blacks.

The change-over from hand drilling to the use of new, light jackhammers was now reaching a peak, and producing an amazing improvement in the rate at which rock was broken. On the mines of the Corner House Group during 1920 the jackhammer drill employed was biting sixteen foot into the rockface per shift. The switch to improved machines and harder, smaller bits increased the footage drilled in a shift to thirty. Then amendments to the Mining Regulations, introduced at the end of 1921, extended materially the time available per shift in which black machine drillers could operate. The footage rose again, from thirty to forty-two feet. Further improvements in machines and in drill steels then increased the footage to fifty-three. Finally, yet another new jackhammer was introduced, stepping up the penetration rate still further. In the space of three to four years, the capacity of the machine had been increased from sixteen feet per shift to sixty-three feet.

By 1924, Corner House mines were breaking out eighty-six per cent of the rock stoped with jackhammers. Across a two-year span black workers' output rose from 4,79 to 7,32 tons per shift. As a result there were great economies in the use of explosives. There were improvements in metallurgical procedures as well, the most important being the introduction of corduroy concentrating tables, in place of the traditional gold recovery process of amalgamation on copper plates. Gold production in 1924, more than 9,5 million ounces, eclipsed the record set in 1916, and was 1,4 million ounces up on 1921.

The Chamber re-organized, too, to unify its diverse operations, and reduce costs. From 1 January, 1924, Gemmill became General Manager of the Chamber, and of the WNLA and NRC. Taberer became Native Labour Adviser, Roberts Technical Consultant and Kelsey Legal Adviser. Buckle, at the end of his four-year term as professional president, became Consultant. The Chamber now reverted to its former practice of appointing an honorary president, and the GPC agreed that the president of the day should be its chairman. And as the office of president has remained an honorary one ever since, despite an ever-increasing work-load, it may be assumed that the mining houses did not regard the experiment of a professional president as an unqualified success.

To succeed Buckle, the Chamber on 31 March 1924 elected Wallers to be President one more time. His Vice-Presidents were Anderson and Openheimer. However, Oppenheimer was elected to Parliament as the South African Party Member for Kimberley, and it was as a parliamentary spokesman, and an increasingly influential link with the new government that he would play a key role in Chamber affairs in the immediate future. His inevitable absences in Cape Town would keep him from the office of president and meant that Anglo American would be represented in the Chamber by other people. The mantle of Wallers would fall on Anderson.

A colleague of Anderson's, M W Richards, has written that Anderson's 'peers and underlings throughout his distinguished life called him "PM" with respectful admiration but seldom to his face'. He wrote, too, that 'PM' was a hard taskmaster not only to himself but to all who came in touch with him. General managers and consulting engineers approached meetings with 'PM' with 'a schoolboy's mixture of fascination and dread when visiting the headmaster .... Sometimes there was praise and then it was a day to remember.' Mixed with the toughness there was, however, a human and kindly approach when people struck difficulties.[2]

Richard noted shrewdly that Anderson's rise marked a transition from the tycoons who had laid the industry's foundations.

> With P M Anderson's generation there came in a new breed of managers who took the best from the past and superimposed their own professional codes of ethics and behaviour, though inevitably some of the spirit of adventure of the tycoon was lost.[3]

The Pact Government came to power committed to resolving the problem of the workless 'poor white' and to strengthening the position of 'civilized' labour. The former was particularly the aim of the Nationalists, and the latter that of the Labour Party. They would find these aims to be somewhat incompatible, since the creation of sub-economic jobs would shave the slice of the national cake available to higher-paid, skilled posts. However, the new cabinet ministers at once summoned Wallers to ask what the mining industry was prepared to do towards finding jobs for the workless. Wallers was forthright in his refusal to create sub-economic employment. He later told the Chamber's Quarterly Meeting:

> ... the Mining Industry is employing on good terms a very large number of white workmen and a steadily increasing number. It will continue to employ every white man who can be employed advantageously, but it will not take on a number of superfluous men .... Our Government and we ourselves must have it clearly in mind ... that the remedy, the only remedy, for unemployment is to extend production upon economic lines.[4]

As part of its endeavour to improve the position of white labour, the Pact passed the Wage Act which created the Wage Board with the prime function of settling rates of pay for lowly-paid or sweated labour in industries lacking representative unions and employers' organizations. The first Chairman was F A W Lucas, the brilliant advocate and one-time leader of the Labour Party in the Transvaal Provincial Council. It was the Government's intention that the Board should concentrate on the position of poor whites, largely landless Afrikaners. However, the Board soon found that it had no power to fix wages according to race or colour. In its first investigation the Board decided that it could no more single out black or white workers for special attention than it could single out 'red-haired or blue-eyed employees'.[5]

Clearly, poor whites constituted an increasingly critical social problem. Their numbers in 1923 had been estimated to number 160 000, or ten per cent of the white population, and they would be found to be much higher than that during the depression at the close of the twenties.[6]

Fortunately, the Pact came quite quickly to accept that the country had nothing to gain by forcing expensive white labour on the mines, but stood to lose a great deal in lower taxes and share of profits, and from a shortening of the lives of mines. The Government chose instead to apply its civilized labour policy in the Public Service, on the Railways and in manufacturing industry, which was enjoying the benefits of the Pact's new protection policy. The number of white labourers employed on the Railways rose from 4 705 in 1921 to 15 878 in 1928.[7] The employment of Coloureds was also increased, while the numbers of blacks and Indians fell. The new men taken on by the Railways, 'following upon the Government policy of extending as far as practical the employment of Europeans', were paid a minimum of 3s a day at age eighteen and of 5s at age twenty-one and over, plus free quarters or a housing allowance ranging from 6d a day to a married rate of 1s 9d.[8] Many of these men 'discovered new reserves of initiative and advanced into the upper ranks of semi-skilled or even skilled labour'. The Government also, in terms of its protection policy, took powers to reduce the protective tariffs accorded manufacturers if they did not co-operate in the extension of white employment.[9]

Encouraged by the advent of the Pact, the hitherto quiescent Mine Workers'

Union lodged a demand for a twenty per cent increase in minimum rates of pay. The dispute deadlocked in a Conciliation Board, and the Union accepted a proposal by the Chamber that Mr Justice J de Villiers should act as mediator. To the Chamber's annoyance, De Villiers disagreed with the Brace Commission's finding that there was a margin in mineworkers' wages to cover the increase in the cost of living, and reported:

> The establishment of an 8-hour day, ... better facilities for recreation, the money spent in improving underground conditions, increased compensation for miners' phthisis, holidays on full pay, are all so much to the good. But to my mind it is not permissible to allow any or all of these to affect the basic wage, which is required by the miner to provide for himself and his family. [10]

He accordingly found that the Union's demand that rates should be adjusted from time to time, as the cost of living went up or down, was reasonable. He recommended a cost-of-living allowance of twenty per cent, to be added to those on minimum rates. Members of the MWU promptly assumed that the De Villiers Award meant a twenty per cent increase to all miners, whether or not they were already being paid above the minimum. It took a special clarification from the Mediator, distributed to the mines as a poster, to convince them otherwise.

Meanwhile, the recommendation led to a fine old row between the Chamber and Creswell. The Chamber asserted its emphatic disenchantment with cost-of-living allowances, and refused to have anything to do with them. Pointing this out to C W Cousins, the Secretary for Labour, Gemmill wrote that average pay was, in fact, already higher than the rates laid down in the 1918 agreement by, practically, the twenty per cent suggested by the Mediator. [11]

Creswell was furious. He and F W Beyers, the Minister of Mines and Industries, raised the issue with Wallers, Anderson, Oppenheimer and J H Crosby (since 1921 General Manager of JCI in Johannesburg) on 10 March, 1925, when they were in Cape Town for discussions on Government bills. At the discussion, Wallers stated that the amount involved in granting the increase was not large, but a principle was involved which could not be conceded. Creswell retorted that the Chamber was striking a blow at the whole conciliation machinery, and urged the industry to agree to an increase in minimum wages as recommended. Anderson replied that the Chamber could not give its assent, and Wallers urged instead a general investigation into wages (which the Government itself had in mind). However, Wallers wrote later to Creswell, offering to assist the Government by raising the minimum wages of shift workers in the lowest-paid categories. The proposed increases, varying on a sliding scale that gave 2s 6d to the lowest paid and 1s to certain of the more highly paid, would apply not just to miners, but to other classes of shift workers as well, and were to operate pending the appointment of a commission of inquiry into wages countrywide.

Creswell replied angrily to Wallers on 31 March 1925:

> A very brief conversation ... with responsible officials of the Mine Workers Union ... was sufficient to convince me that the Gold Producers Committee's offer does not furnish a basis of discussion acceptable to the other party of the dispute. And, I fear, that the hope I entertained of a voluntary concession by the Gold Producers Committee which would have established confidence in the Conciliation Act machinery must now be abandoned. [12]

Creswell followed up his letter by informing Parliament in reply to a question on 8 April 1925 that 'the only remedy now left to the miners is a strike'. [13] To some his remarks seemed close to incitement. He went on to announce that the Government would enforce the De Villiers proposals by law. And duly introduced soon afterwards the Mineworkers (Minimum Rates of Pay) Bill.

Anderson, then President, at once wrote pointing out that it had never been suggested by the Mediator or the Conciliation Board that his recommendation should be binding. By making it so the Minister himself was striking a fatal blow at the conciliation machinery. The findings of conciliation boards in the past had not always been accepted by the unions. Employers took part in all conciliation procedures on the basis that the boards had no power of compulsion. If awards in favour of the men were to be made binding by special legislation, the employers would have no alternative but to refuse to have anything to do with conciliation boards.

Anderson made it clear as well that the ripple effect of legislating to increase the minimum wages of one class of employee would be damaging not only to the mining industry but across the country. His letter was printed by the Chamber and circulated to Members of Parliament. Creswell was glad to back off and leave the Chamber and the MWU to sort out their differences, which they did by agreeing on a slightly more liberal sliding scale than the Chamber's earlier offer. The increases applied to all categories of shift workers, and were to continue in force pending publication of the report of the Economics and Wages Commission. When that happened, the Minister promised the miners the dispute would be referred to the Wage Board.

However, when in due course the Commission did report, the Government found itself precluded from referring the dispute to the Wage Board by that body's colour blindness. It was agreed instead that a conciliation board be appointed on which F A W Lucas, J F Malherbe and A T Roberts, the Chairman and members of the Wage Board, would act as mediators. Its investigation embraced a demand from the South African Association of Reduction Workers as well as the MWU. [14] In April 1927 the so-called Mining Industry Arbitration Board issued its award, the net result of which was to stabilize the average annual income of mine employees overall at £374, or about the amount prevailing before the award. In general, the Board accepted the employers' contention that rates were reasonable and higher than those in comparable occupations, a view which seemed somewhat in conflict with that expressed by Lucas as a member of the Economic and Wage Commission. However, small increases were made in the minimum rates of whites paid on a daily shift rate. The Lucas Award, as it became known, would establish an enduring structure of wages, hours and working conditions on the mines.

By 1930 the average wage of white shift workers (ie excluding contractors, who earned much more) would be 22s 6d, compared with 30s 3d in 1921, 20s 11d in 1923, and 21s 9d in 1926. The increase since 1923 was small, but better than it looked because workers benefited from a steady fall in the cost of living throughout the decade. By 1930 the retail price index on the Rand was thirty per cent less than it was in 1921. By 1932, as the depression bottomed, the cost of living was only two per cent above that in 1914.

Creswell, after establishing the Department of Labour, had handed over the Labour portfolio to Boydell in 1925. Creswell continued to press his cherished policy of replacing black labourers on the mines with white, but his insistence became increasingly a political embarrassment to the Pact. In deference to him, the Pact continued the policy of restricting labour from Moçambique pursued, for different reasons, by the Smuts Government.[15] However, South Africa could not manage without the Moçambicans, and for the Pact it became a case of 'We too, but not so loud'. In due course its Ministers would re-negotiate a labour agreement with Portugal in Lisbon, though not yet on a scale that satisfied the mining industry.

The Chamber also clashed briefly with F W Beyers, the Minister of Mines and Industries. Beyers, a former Attorney-General of the Transvaal, had quit the public service for the Bar and politics a decade before. He attracted the scorn of the public and of senior officials of the Mines Department by seeking to secure the appointment of a 'Government Director' on the boards of mining companies. P M Anderson declared that the appointee would not be a director at all, since he would have no vote, have no power to direct anything, and have no responsibility to the shareholders. The only function he would have was to report to the Minister of Mines, who would have a monopoly of publishing private information or not as he deemed fit.[16] The Government was glad to allow the Bill (The Government Representation and Investigation Bill, 1925) to disappear from the order paper, and to pass a revised Companies Act without 'the absurd and offensive chapter' appointing Government directors.[17]

Creswell dealt a particularly damaging blow to mining when, as Acting Minister of Mines in Beyers's absence overseas, he quarrelled with Kotzé, the Government Mining Engineer, over the appointment of a Ministerial nominee as Chief Inspector of Machinery.[18] Kotzé, who had a brilliant record in the reduction of accidents and the combating of phthisis, and was no man's lackey, duly resigned, only shortly after receiving the Gold Medal of the Institute of Mining and Metallurgy. Smuts described the affair as a 'gross and outrageous injustice'.[19] Kotzé was replaced by Dr Hans Pirow, who, after a brilliant academic career, had been acting as an assistant consultant engineer to

Union Corporation. He was a brother of Oswald Pirow, who would become Minister of Justice in Hertzog's Cabinet in 1929. Despite being a political appointee Hans Pirow proved an admirable successor.

The promised Economic and Wage Commission, appointed by the Pact in August 1925, was under the chairmanship of Stephen Mills, CMG, an economist from Melbourne. He was supported by another overseas expert, Professor Henry Clay of the University of Manchester. Stephen Mills and Henry Clay were reputed at the time to be two of the most noted economists in the world. The South African members were a mixed bag indeed. They were W H Andrews ('Comrade Bill'), the Communist General Secretary of the South African Association of Employees' Organizations (SAAEO), Willem Hendrik Rood, a Nelspruit farmer and Nationalist MP for Barberton, and John Martin, the Chairman and Managing Director of the Argus Printing and Publishing Company. No doubt the Pact hoped that the overseas experts would find enough credence in Pact policies to join in consensus with Andrews and Rood, and it sought to make assurance doubly sure by adding Lucas, Creswell's appointee as Chairman of the Wage Board, to the mix, but it was not to be. The only result was to split the Commission into two equal halves, with Mills, the Chairman, Clay and Martin presenting findings which for reasons of convenience came to be known as the majority report. Mills published some minor reservations on aspects of the majority report, and Andrews a major reservation to the minority. He wrote:

> In signing this report ... I desire to say that I am not in agreement with the theory that the gross inequalities and injustices in South African Society can be removed by measures such as those recommended therein, but that I am merely expressing the view that some partial, though perhaps only temporary, improvement may be made in the living conditions of a number of the poorer and more helpless members of the population if the suggestions therein contained are carried out.[20]

Martin's appointment to the Commission was, in part, a result of his involvement in the formation of the highly successful National Industrial Council of the Newspaper and Printing Industry. Martin was the first President (1919-1923) of the Council, which was the model taken by the drafters of the Industrial Conciliation Act of 1924. Tall and charismatic, he proved a notable negotiator with labour unions. His interest in employees and employee relations apart, Martin was a brilliant entrepreneur who was to play a leading role in the mining industry and in national affairs.

Martin was born in Scotland and never lost his soft Scottish burr, but had part of his schooling in Chicago. There he had his first contact with newspapers, selling them on street corners for pocket money. As a result of ill-health, he was sent to stay with an uncle in Australia where he worked as a reporter on the *Ballarat Star*. When poor eyesight compelled him to give that up, he joined another uncle in South Africa and worked as assistant secretary on a mine in the Germiston area. He turned to canvassing advertising space and became advertising manager of *The Star* in Johannesburg. After other newspaper posts, he was appointed General Manager of the Argus group of newspapers in 1915 at the age of thirty-one. He was made Chairman and Managing Director as well in 1922.

Martin built the Argus Group into the giant of South Africa's newspaper world, and would remain Chairman of the Group until his death in 1949. However, in 1926 he was destined to become Resident Director of Central Mining in Johannesburg as well, and take over as head of the Corner House interests, despite a minimal practical knowledge of mining. As successor to Wallers at the Corner House, he would play a leading role in the Chamber of Mines. His joint position as a leader of the mining industry and Chairman of the Argus Group gave him great influence in public affairs, and made him at times a controversial figure. It also led to a close rapport with Smuts.[21]

Mills, Clay and Martin, in their report, found that the rates of pay for skilled work in South Africa were far higher, in relation to the comparative size and strength of industries, than those in any other country. The explanation was to be found in the wide disparity between skilled and unskilled. The rates of mechanics, building artisans, miners and printers were the rates of a small skilled class of urban white labour. The level of white wages was due to and dependent on the level of black and other wages; and neither could be increased except at the expense of the other unless there was an increase in production per head.[22]

They found too that if the number of unemployed whites, reflected in available statistics, were trebled they would probably still represent a smaller percentage of unemployment than any other industrial country at that time. Misgivings about competition to whites from blacks would be falsified if South Africa continued to develop her natural resources on economic principles.[23]

The majority commissioners stated that the gold mining industry showed a higher average level of wages, both white and black, than any other branch of economic activity of comparable importance in South Africa. Dr C T Loram, a member of the Native Affairs Commission, had said in evidence: 'I only wish we could have as good conditions for natives elsewhere as on the mines.'[24]

Mills, Clay and Martin urged a complete survey of the economic position of blacks and that the black worker could and should increase his economic usefulness by widening the range of his occupations and raising the level of his skill.[25]

Lucas, Rood and Andrews considered that the massive evidence gathered (a digest covered more than 600 pages) was weighted in favour of the employers. They thought too that it was often misleading to make comparisons with other countries because of South Africa's heterogeneous population.

The minority commissioners remarked:

There was a tendency in some centres to let questions affecting the gold mining industry overshadow all other issues. Claims for special protection and consideration for that industry were based on the argument that a quarter of a million whites and one million natives were directly and indirectly dependent for their livelihood on the Witwatersrand mines. This may be true, but it must be taken only in its proper relationship to other industries.

Again, the representatives of the gold mining industry frequently laid stress on the contention that wages and conditions of labour on the Witwatersrand gold mines were a determining influence on conditions in other industries in South Africa, and therefore any attempt to raise wages and better conditions in gold mining would inevitably react in the same direction in every other important industry. In our opinion this contention is unsound. In some other highly organized industries in the Union the wages and working conditions of the employees, even on the Witwatersrand, are better than in the mining industry and the determining factor in the development of the wage conditions in those industries appears to have been the degree of organization of the employees rather than the influence of the mining industry.[26]

They pointed out that about thirty per cent of the blacks on the mines were on piecework and in exceptional cases earned up to 7s 6d a shift. Apart from piecework, the rates paid to the blacks did not exceed by much – when they exceeded them at all – the rates paid on the sugar plantations and by farmers in Natal. They declared that a choice would soon have to be made between importing large numbers of low-paid blacks from abroad and requiring expansion of industry to be on the basis of employment of larger numbers of reasonably well-paid white workers.

Public reception of the report tended to be severely critical because of its inevitable diversity. However, S Herbert Frankel, the economist, found the report to be probably the most valuable ever written on South African affairs. He claimed that comparison of the majority and minority reports revealed the points of agreement in them to be far more considerable than those of disagreement.[27] And *The Star* pointed out in a leading article that the commissioners were at least virtually unanimous on one important point. Nowhere did they make a recommendation or suggestion that justified the colour bar legislation which the Government had introduced into Parliament ahead of the publication of the Commission's findings.[28]

The Star said that the majority commissioners had opposed the exclusion from economic opportunities at present open to them of those unrepresented in Parliament for the benefit of those who were. They had warned that in the special circumstances of South Africa the policy of restricting opportunities of low-paid non-white workers was particularly dangerous; the white man had less to fear from improvement than from a deterioration in the economic status of blacks.

The Star found broadly the same line in the minority report. Lucas, Rood and Andrews had urged that there should be very sympathetic and generous consideration of the grievances of black workers, and declared that: 'Natives should not be forced out of the locations to work, but those who go out to seek work should be given full scope.'[29]

The colour bar legislation referred to by *The Star* was the Mines and Works Amendment Bill which sought to restore the statutory colour bar invalidated in the judgement in a case brought in 1923 against Gavin Hildick-Smith, Manager of the Eastern Section of Crown Mines. The Mines Department had become increasingly concerned that aspects of the post-1922 re-organization on the mines were in conflict with the colour bar regulations. In May, the Government Mining Engineer warned Crown Mines against employing blacks on driving electric locomotives underground. The GPC was informed and recommended that the company should disclaim any infringement of the law. It also resolved that Buckle should warn Kotzé, then Government Mining Engineer, informally that if the case was brought to court the validity of the regulations imposing the colour bar would inevitably be brought into question. Kotzé however had decided that a test case was necessary to clarify the law and was awaiting the first clear case of infringement to do so. The prosecution of Crown Mines was considered such a clear case, and the Government proceeded to prosecute Hildick-Smith on the grounds that he permitted an electric locomotive to be in charge of one Stephen, 'a native who is not a competent white shiftsman and who was not under the effective control of a competent white shiftsman'.[30]

The magistrate found that Stephen was a competent driver and had been carefully taught, but was not a competent person as prescribed by regulation, nor under the effective control of a white shiftsman, as claimed by the company. However, he held that because the regulation did not apply to all alike, it was therefore *ultra vires* the Mines and Works Act of 1911, which did not empower discrimination between races. The Supreme Court on appeal confirmed his view.

The Government, employers and unions had long been aware that the statutory colour bar was unlikely to withstand a challenge in the courts, but the Chamber had refrained from acting on the knowledge because it realized that it was not politically feasible at that time to assail the colour bar. The Chamber at once advised mines not to take advantage of the judgement, and gave an undertaking in that respect to the Pact Government.

The Pact however was committed to strengthening the position of skilled white labour and considered the verdict of the court unacceptable. It introduced a 'single-clause, high-explosive bill'.

It specifically named Natives and Asiatics as persons who could be excluded by regulation from receiving certificates of competency in certain trades, and it specifically empowered managements to apply a racial classification of their employees when apportioning work among them 'in respect of mines, works or machinery'.[31]

Beyers declared on introducing the second reading on 25 February 1925 that it concerned a great national question: the preservation and perpetuation of the white race. The Government was not prepared to allow matters on the mines to rest on the favours and good graces of the Chamber of Mines. He did not doubt its goodwill, but the matter must be put on a proper footing.[32]

The principle of job reservation on grounds of colour, thus given explicit legislative form, was bitterly attacked by the Chamber, which campaigned against it, and by the Opposition in Parliament.

Smuts, who was prepared to re-establish the validity of the old Mines and Works Regulations, saw a grave threat to South Africa in the new legislation. He rose in the House soon after the Minister's speech, and declared:

> While the Minister of the Interior is declaring every Native a South African, his colleague is bringing in a Bill under which we are going to declare to the Natives: 'You shall in future be debarred from rising above the level of hewers of wood and drawers of water.' I am all for the white man, but there is something in my breast that cannot stand this.[33]

In the adjourned debate on 6 April 1925 Oppenheimer, too, declared that it was wrong in principle to reserve jobs on grounds of colour.

> It is an evil to impose class legislation, and the curse of an evil deed is that one must continue to do evil. ... This is not the means to protect the European worker. It is only by efficiency and application to work that the Europeans can maintain the position which we now occupy in South Africa.[34]

The Bill was passed twice by the Assembly but each time subsequently rejected in the Senate, where the Opposition was in the majority. Finally, Hertzog invoked the South Africa Act to call a joint session of the two Houses on 12 May 1926. By a majority of sixteen votes the industrial colour bar became an established principle in South Africa.[35]

Smuts and Hertzog would clash often in the Assembly and there were crises which rent the country. In the end however they did reach some common ground. They agreed on a Flag Act which gave South Africa two official flags, the national flag and the Union Jack. And Hertzog made a major contribution to the Balfour Declaration of November 1926 which declared Great Britain and the Dominions to be autonomous communities and of equal status, and which paved the way for the enabling Statute of Westminster in 1931. In doing so, Hertzog built on the work done by Smuts at previous Imperial Conferences, and in particular on a memorandum prepared for the 1921 Conference, but withheld for tactical reasons. However, Hertzog and Smuts continued to disagree on a political dispensation for the black citizens of South Africa. At one stage, they held exploratory talks at which Smuts suggested examination of a common franchise for blacks and whites, based on occupation, education and income, not high enough to exclude the whites, but high enough to exclude the bulk of the blacks. Hertzog did carefully consider the proposal, but told Smuts that the time was not yet ripe.[36]

While political debates raged in Parliament, the mining industry steadily improved its relations with the Government from their rock bottom start. Thus, on 29 June 1925, a year after Pact came to power, Anderson was still complaining bitterly:

> The attitude of the Government towards the Mining Industry is strikingly shown in the whole tendency of its legislation …. One cannot help a feeling of grave misgiving as to the future of our Industry and those dependent upon it if this attitude is continued.[37]

However, by the end of his Presidential year on 29 March 1926, Anderson could discern a turn of the tide.

> … when the present Government came into office there was evidently a certain prejudice against the mining industry apparently based on the erroneous assumption that this Chamber was some sort of political organisation whose interests were inimical to those of the Government. We have been at some pains to dispel this erroneous idea, and we believe that we have made some progress. … This Chamber, as such, has no politics, and its desire is to work amicably with the Government in power, whatever its political complexion, unless compelled by hostile legislation to take up an attitude of opposition.[38]

His successors would echo his optimism. Thus Arthur French (General Mining) in his Presidential Address on 28 March 1927:

> … the attitude of suspicion towards this Chamber and all its works, which was very apparent in our legislators in the early days of the present Parliament, has given place to a much pleasanter atmosphere. … our relations with Ministers on the various occasions during the past year on which we have met them on Chamber matters, have been of the pleasantest description.[39]

Douglas Christopherson (Gold Fields) took up the theme at the Annual General Meeting on 26 March 1928:

> … I would in the first place like to be permitted to express appreciation … for the courteous manner in which they have received us and the free access

they have always given to discuss with them various matters of importance to this Industry. Although they were unable at times to agree with our representations, we have had the satisfaction of knowing these would be given full consideration.[40]

And A W Rogers (Corner House), wryly, on 25 March 1929:

The year under review was marked by the absence of legislation specially affecting the Industry, an omission for which we are duly grateful. I may add that this novel and pleasing feature bids fair to be repeated in the current session.[41]

The Pact had had the luck that deserted Smuts. The economic upsurge began with its advent in power. Diamonds flourished and diamond mining boomed. The value of gold production was a record for each year of the five years of the Pact's term of office. The proving of the vast platinum deposits of the Transvaal bushveld increased confidence in the future. The Government stimulated manufacturing industry and established the South African Iron and Steel Industrial Corporation Limited (Iscor). Hertzog benefited too from rains that broke the drought that had long plagued the thirsty farmlands of the interior and intensified the post-war depression. However, he was not content to stand on his record of achievement. The General Election of 1929 was characterized by a naked appeal to white prejudice through the 'Black Manifesto', largely the work of Tielman Roos, which depicted Smuts as the 'apostle of the black Kaffir state'. Its publication was backed by the trumpeting by Pact candidates of *Die Swart Gevaar* (the Black Peril). Despite the splitting of the Labour Party into two hostile halves, headed by Creswell and Walter Madeley, the country opted for Hertzog's brand of statutory segregation, economic, political, territorial. The Pact was returned to power with more Nationalist, fewer Labour, seats. But Hertzog's luck was at last running out. Ahead lay the Great Depression, the saddest yet to strike the civilized world.

---

[1] Thirty-Sixth Annual Report of the Transvaal Chamber of Mines, 1925, p 103. Information on the return of Britain and South Africa to the gold standard in 1925 was obtained from the Archives of the South African Reserve Bank, Pretoria.

[2] M W Richards, 'Mining: P M Anderson' in R M de Villiers, ed, *Better than they knew*, pp 100, 118–119.

[3] *Ibid*, p 120.

[4] Annual Report of the Transvaal Chamber of Mines, 1924, p 187. (Quarterly meeting held on 29 September 1924.)

[5] De Kiewiet, p 274.

[6] *Ibid*, p 181.

[7] *Ibid*, p 224.

[8] Union of South Africa: Report of the Economic and Wage Commission (1925) (UG 14-'26), p 91.

[9] De Kiewiet, pp 224, 263.
Davenport, p 361.

[10] Annual Report of the Transvaal Chamber of Mines, 1924, p 89, quoting from the Report of the Mediator, Industrial Conciliation Board, 1924.

[11] Chamber of Mines Archives: File 28a 1925: 'Conciliation Board – SA Mine Workers' Union and Mineworkers (Minimum Rates of Pay) Bill (de Villiers Award)': Letter dated 25 February 1925, from the General Manager, Transvaal Chamber of Mines (Gold Producers' Committee), Johannesburg, to the Secretary for Labour, Department of Labour, Cape Town, p 2 (No 250).

[12] Chamber of Mines Archives: File 28a 1925: 'Conciliation Board – SA Mine Workers' Union and Mineworkers (Minimum Rates of Pay) Bill (de Villiers Award)': Letter dated 31 March 1925, from F H P Creswell, Minister of Labour, Cape Town, to Sir Evelyn Wallers, KBE, President, Transvaal Chamber of Mines, Johannesburg, p 2 (No 286).

[13] 'Mines & Workers', *Rand Daily Mail*, 8 April 1925.

[14] Chamber of Mines Archives: File 88 1927: 'Mining Industry Arbitration Board: Arbitrator's Report': Award of the Arbitrators in Certain Matters in Dispute between The Gold Mining Companies, Members of The Transvaal Chamber of Mines and Certain of their Employees (No 2 *et seq*).

[15] Yudelman, pp 220, 230-231.

[16] Annual Report of the Transvaal Chamber of Mines, 1925, p 152. (Ordinary meeting held on 29 June 1925).

[17] Annual Report of the Transvaal Chamber of Mines, 1925, pp 59, 152.

[18] 'Topics of the Week', *The South African Mining and Engineering Journal*, 2 October 1926, p 133.

[19] *Idem.*

[20] Report of the Economic and Wage Commission, 1925, p 358.

[21] F R Metrowich, 'Martin' in *Dictionary of South African Biography*, II, pp 449-450.

[22] Report of the Economic and Wage Commission, 1925, pp 187, 188, 193.

[23] *Ibid*, p 103, paragraph 176, and p 195, paragraph 57.

[24] *Ibid*, p 138, paragraph 247.

[25] *Ibid*, p 187, paragraph 1, p 198, paragraph 80.

[26] *Ibid*, pp 254-255.

[27] 'Wage Commission', *The Star*, 4 September 1925.

[28] Editorial, *The Star*, 20 February 1926.

[29] *Idem.*

[30] Chamber of Mines Archives: File 43 1923: 'Mining Regulations – Crown Mines Case': Record of Evidence, Rex vs Gavin Hildick-Smith, p 1 (No 22).
Johnstone, pp 145-148.

[31] Hancock, *Smuts: 2. The Fields of Force*, p 208.

[32] Union of South Africa: Debates of the House of Assembly: Second Session, Fifth Parliament: 13 February – 25 July 1925, Volumes 3 to 5, Columns 267 and 273.

[33] Hancock, *Smuts: 2. The Fields of Force*, p 209.

[34] Debates of the House of Assembly: 13 February – 25 July 1925, Column 1922.

[35] Hancock, *Smuts: 2. The Fields of Force*, pp 209-210.

[36] *Ibid*, p 213.

[37] Annual Report of the Transvaal Chamber of Mines, 1925, p 152. (Quarterly meeting held on 29 June 1925).

[38] Annual Report of the Transvaal Chamber of Mines, 1925, p 66.

[39] Annual Report of the Transvaal Chamber of Mines, 1926, p 59.

[40] Thirty-Eighth Annual Report of the Transvaal Chamber of Mines, 1927, p 67.

[41] Thirty-Ninth Annual Report of the Transvaal Chamber of Mines, 1928, p 59.

CHAPTER TWENTY-SEVEN

The Turning-Point

Any lingering doubts about the central economic importance of the gold mines evaporated in the Great Depression which was signalled by the Wall Street crash at the end of 1929. World markets for major South African exports other than gold collapsed. The value of diamonds exported fell calamitously; and by 1934 earnings had been reduced to less than one-fifteenth of the £16,5 million earned in 1928, diminishing sharply an important source of state revenue. The prices of South Africa's staple agricultural commodities fell to levels that spelt ruin for many farmers. Wool which had fetched 16d a pound on the world market in 1927/1928 was down to 4,4d a pound in 1931/32. At a sheep sale at Harrismith in the Orange Free State in 1932, 800 merinos, carrying sixteen months' growth of wool, were sold for 3d each.[1] Maize fell from 15s 4d a bag to 9s 4d. With the deepening of the Depression, the number of whites on relief work rose seven-fold, and included men formerly in well-paid jobs, and even from the professions, ready to labour for 5s a day. The bankruptcy rate soared. In 1932 the old arch-enemy, drought, reappeared and added to the general misery.[2]

In this scenario of economic tragedy, gold mining staved off total disaster. The standard price of £4 4s 11$\frac{1}{2}$d an ounce, that had prevailed for over two hundred years, was not a great sum, but the demand for gold at that price was infinite. From 1929 to 1932, tons milled, gold output, and value received, continued to register record figures year by year, while profits and working costs marginally fell. Revenue earned by Rand gold mines at £46 671 258 in 1932 was £13 000 000 higher than in 1921.[3]

The gold mines actually drew advantage from the Depression in the abundance of blacks seeking employment, and the white labour force was expanded to supervise them. The number of blacks on Transvaal gold mines had exceeded 200 000 in 1928 for the first time since the War; in 1930 the number was 211 751, and it rose in each of the Depression years. In 1928, the number of white workers at last overtook the 1921 figure, and the total employed rose year by year thereafter.[4]

As the numbers of blacks engaged reached a new peak in 1932, the founder director of the Native Recruiting Corporation, and Native Labour Adviser to the Chamber, H M Taberer, died. The President, John Martin, at the quarterly meeting of the Chamber on 27 June 1932 commented:

> The Mining Industry, our recruiting organization and the Native employees of the mines have all suffered a heavy loss by the death of Mr H M Taberer. It was his duty as Native Labour Adviser primarily to represent the interests and the point of view of the Natives, and in that capacity, by reason of his wide experience, his knowledge and his character, he possessed the trust and confidence of the Natives and the Mining Industry as a whole. The late Mr Taberer will be greatly missed throughout South Africa, for his interests were manifold and his friends were legion.[5]

The black mineworkers had come to know the NRC as KwaTEBA (the House of Taberer) and the name, adopted by the modern recruiting organization, recalls Taberer and men like him, who did so much to open up the remote regions of Southern Africa. The quality of their service to mines and tribesmen alike is accorded today far less than its due.

The sharp focus of South Africa's dependence on the gold mines in the Depression years aroused fears for the country's future, for mineable reserves at the standard price were being rapidly exhausted. Dr Pirow, the Government Mining Engineer, in the Union Government Year Book, published in 1930, estimated, at the working costs and gold prices then prevailing, that the annual value of gold produced would be halved in twelve years and halved again in the following seven. He advised however that a reduction in costs of 2s a ton milled would avert a diminution of output for eight to ten years, while a fully adequate black labour supply would have a similar effect.[6] The picture he portrayed of an industry already past its prime and heading for early decline placed pressure on the Government to assist the industry to reduce its costs. Its response was to play for time, in the time-honoured governmental way, by appointing the Low-Grade Ore Commission of 1930. Events would justify the wisdom, from the Government's point of view, of delaying action.

C I Pienaar, the Secretary for Justice, was appointed Chairman, but after presenting an interim report recommending lifting the ban on black recruiting into tropical areas, Pienaar died, and was replaced by R J van Reenen, a civil engineer highly regarded by the Government who had been Chairman of the Irrigation Commission since 1926. He was supported by E H Farrer, CMG, Secretary for Finance, and A C Sutherland, a technical expert. The Chamber had recommended that there should be neither Chamber nor union representatives, but the Government insisted. Gemmill represented the employers and Donald Reich, a former official of the MWU, the employees.

The Commission duly echoed the general gloom about the future of the industry. It stated that there remained 335 000 000 tons of ore to be milled under conditions of cost then existing. As extraction was running at nearly one-tenth of that figure annually,

> ... the desirability and urgency of a reduction in costs, with the object of

rendering more tonnage available for mining, will be recognized.

Further, if consideration be given to the uncertainty that exists as to the mining possibilities of the eastern and western extensions of the Witwatersrand gold fields, and to the difficulties to be encountered in the mining of ore at depths below 7 500 feet, one cannot but be impressed by the fact that, if present conditions continue, the end of the gold mining industry on the scale that the country has known it for the last decade is already appearing over the horizon. Other avenues of employment for the people will have to be found ....[7]

Fortunately for South Africa what lay in reality over the horizon was a dramatic change of fortune in the form of increases in the gold price. The report of the Commission, eighteen months in the making, was cold turkey before it was published. Most of its recommendations could safely be ignored by the Government, including the proposal (Reich dissenting) that trained blacks should be permitted to perform such operations underground as they were capable of without detrimental effect on the safety and health of other workers. However, the Commission did serve to draw public attention anew to the high costs imposed on the mines by the State's discriminatory Railway policy, and by legislation laying on the mines the onus of compensation for silicosis, or miners' phthisis, on a scale unparalleled in the world.

The state railway policy had been highlighted in a wide-ranging study conducted at the instance of the GPC by the economist, Dr S H Frankel. He found that the rates charged were the result of the 'quite indefensible practice' of charging what someone in Government or the Railway thought the traffic ought to bear, with little reference to the reasonableness and justice of the rate or the cost of service. An analysis in 1926 had shown that 65,1 per cent of stores transported for the gold mines had been charged at the three highest rates in the tariff book, and 37,8 per cent at the two highest class rates. This would 'pass comprehension' if the rates policy were based on economic considerations, but the tariff was a political tariff designed to tax some industries in order to grant protection or bounties to others. Taking into account increases in working costs and increases in cost of living on the Rand, the total annual burden on the industry amounted to over £1 million. Frankel declared:

For years it has been the traffic directly and indirectly connected with the mining zone of the Transvaal which has been the mainstay of the revenue of the railways and has enabled the granting of the low rates on SA agricultural products and exports.

Yet the present suicidal and uneconomic rate policy, instead of doing everything possible to foster, actually restricts the development, shortens the life, and hinders the activities of this vitally important area.[8]

The need for a revision of the Railways' rating policy, thus exposed, would be deferred, then referred to yet another commission of inquiry. The anomalies would continue and rail costs would rise again. And so would the cost of funding compensation for silicosis.

Advances in combating silicosis, or miners' phthisis, on the Rand were highlighted by the International Silicosis Conference held in Johannesburg from 13 to 27 August 1932, under the auspices of the International Labour Office, Geneva.[9] The Chamber had played an important role in caring for victims of the disease through the foundation of the Springkell Sanatorium in 1911 and the Wedge Farm Sanatorium in 1918. (In 1934, Springkell would be enlarged, and Wedge Farm handed over to the Rand Aid Association for use as an old age home.) In 1916, too, the Chamber had established the Silicotic Employment Office, under the aegis of the Association of Mine Managers, to supplement the role of mining companies in finding surface work for miners who contracted silicosis. It had also co-ordinated the watch on dust levels on the mines since 1914, and was able to report a vast improvement in mine air.[10] Confident that the industry had a good report to make on research and prevention in both the engineering and medical fields, the Chamber followed up a visit to South Africa by a representative of the ILO in 1928, by offering to co-operate in the holding of a conference and to contribute to its cost. Experts from Australia, Canada, the Continent, Great Britain and the United States of America attended.

Between 1902 and 1925 silicosis on the Rand had been the subject of five Government commissions, ten parliamentary select committees, and nine Acts of Parliament. While sharing in public sympathy for silicosis sufferers, it had fallen to the Chamber's lot to endeavour to curb the eagerness of politicians to vote away 'other people's money without any regard for what is fair and just'. In particular, the Chamber resisted the award of compensation on levels way above that accorded other industrial diseases, and the requirement, declared to be inequitable by a Government commission, that existing companies should fund the compensation of silicosis resulting from service in mines long since extinct.[11] It did not succeed. The legislation became an extraordinary maze of 'sage provisos, sub-intents and saving clauses',[12] but in general, each successive Act resulted in an increase in the awards payable to sufferers and their dependants. By 1930 the burden of funding the awards had reached critical levels, despite considerable advances in the prevention of the disease.

The Act of 1916 had led to the institution of the Miners' Medical Bureau, a central body of full-time Government medical officers to conduct or control all examinations for silicosis. The introduction at the same time of an initial examination and periodical examinations, aimed specifically at the detection of silicosis, brought a big step forward in its prevention, by setting physical standards that would exclude men considered likely to prove prone to the disease, and by ensuring early diagnosis of the disease in those who contracted it. In the three years prior to the Conference the Chamber had introduced an annual radiographic examination of all blacks who had worked on any mine for five years or more. The results showed that no large number of undetected cases existed, but the examination contributed to a preventative system which drew 'round the mine native labourers a serviceably close net of opportunities for the detection of silicosis and tuberculosis'.[13] In 1955, as a result of pioneering work for nearly thirty years in the development of mass miniature radiography by Captain K G Collender of the WNLA, the Chamber introduced the radiographic examination of all workers at the start of each period of service.

Dr L G Irvine, the Chairman of the Miners' Medical Bureau, was elected Chairman of the 1932 International Silicosis Conference. He had served with distinction as a mine doctor before joining the Bureau, and had grappled with the problem of silicosis for twenty-eight years, regarding himself, he told the gathered world experts, as 'but a humble musket-bearer in the army of the Lord'. In his chairman's address, he outlined the progress that had evolved into a large and complicated system of prevention. As well as medical methods of detection, there were the provision of adequate ventilation, and the regulation of shifts and blasting. Success had undoubtedly been great.

> One may claim, I think, with truth, that the number of cases of silicosis which are arising annually today is only about one-third of the number which were arising fourteen or sixteen years ago. During the past three years there has been a continuous drop in the production rates of the disease. … The improvement attained … has been substantial, and there is reasoned hope for further improvement in the future. But, although we are satisfied so far, we are also disappointed. We have scotched the snake, but we have not killed it.[14]

Irvine also co-operated in a paper with Hans Pirow, the Government Mining Engineer, and Dr A Mavrogordato of the Chamber-funded South African Institute for Medical Research. Together, they traced the forty-year history of silicosis through the initial years of ignorance, of partial realization, hesitation and tentative improvement, and, through the thirteen years that followed, of increasingly energetic effort to prevent the disease.[15] They pointed out that the problem had been larger on the Rand, because of its magnitude, than in other countries, and the deaths and suffering caused by the disease more clearly apparent. They noted successive steps formulated in the control of working conditions, including the prevention of blasting more than once in twenty-four hours, and the regulation of work to prevent exposure to fumes and dust from the blast.

> As a mining field the Witwatersrand to-day stands unequalled as regards the scale on which operations are carried on, the depth the workings have attained, the organisation involved, and the extent of the precautions taken to prevent miners' phthisis. Visible dust underground is as rare as it once was common, exposure to fumes from blasting if occurring at all is accidental, and sustained efforts are being made to provide improved ventilation.[16]

342

The results of improvements in mine air and the working environment were reflected in the reduced attack rate of the disease. However, the engineers and scientists had still to battle with the hazard presented by minute particles of silica dust invisible to the naked eye, and the difficulty in adequately ventilating old mines laid out before the perils of dust-laden air were recognized. At further international conferences in Johannesburg in 1959 and 1969, they would be able to report fresh advances based on the expansion and modernization of the industry that was now close at hand.

On 21 September 1931, Britain, herself battling in the depths of the Depression, announced without warning her decision to abandon the gold standard and devalue sterling. A startled Smuts, who was in England, declared that the 'ark of the Covenant, the pound sterling' had fallen. He at once cabled home to call on South Africa to do likewise and join the new sterling area.[17] The South African Government responded with the declaration that the Union would remain on the gold standard, and, though it did not consult the Chamber, received its ready backing. Arthur French, then President, told the quarterly meeting on 28 September that the Government's stance was wise, because it was not possible to measure all the implications of Britain's radical departure from traditional financial policy. However, the GPC at once got down to studying them, and quickly came to the conclusion that South Africa must follow Britain's example.

On 13 November John Martin, Vice-President, told a special meeting of the Chamber that the net benefit to the industry and to the country of leaving the gold standard would be immediate and great. The alternative of adherence to the gold standard would necessitate a scaling-down by industries and public authorities of all expenditure on stores, wages and administration; cheapening of interest rates; effective reduction in the cost of living; and a lowering of taxation. The country, however, was not following a policy consistent with adherence to the gold standard.

Martin pointed out that the state of agriculture was a national calamity which the Government was seeking to alleviate by fiscal measures. It would be an unhappy outlook for agriculture if its ability to market its products abroad were to be limited by the availability of state subsidies. There could be no real prosperity for agriculture unless international action or external influences resulted in a lifting of the low level of commodity prices. So far as the gold mining industry was concerned, devaluation by as little as ten per cent would increase the average life of mines by at least fifty per cent.

He warned that, apart from its detrimental effect on the gold mines, adherence to the gold standard could lead to a serious slow-down in internal trade and industrial activity, and prevent a resumption of the export of agricultural products. The resultant reaction upon credits and investments of all descriptions would be far more serious than a measure of currency devaluation, especially as inflation of internal prices would not result in the reigning circumstances.

The Government would have none of it, thus causing an over-valuation of the South African pound, and preventing prices from adjusting to world levels.

> Was it fitting that a sovereign and independent State such as South Africa had become by the Statute of Westminster should compromise its political status by too servile a dependence on the British pound? On the more real and immediate grounds of economic expediency the debate was hottest. Argument faced argument while capital seeped out of the country.[18]

On 20 November N C Havenga, Minister of Finance, full of the confidence engendered by the fat years of the first Pact Government, told a special session of Parliament that leaving the gold standard would result in inflation on a grand scale and a vast increase in costs. He proclaimed: 'South Africa is on the gold basis and will remain on a gold basis.'[19] Measures were taken to control the flood of money leaving the country and to set up a pattern of restrictions to protect the currency. What Martin had so powerfully predicted duly followed. None suffered more than Hertzog's loyal supporters in the rural areas.

> At the end of the year and in early 1932, £100 sterling bought £125 Australian but only between £70 and £75 South African. With the South African pound valued at nearly double the Australian, competition on the world wool markets became almost impossible for South African growers.[20]

By January 1932 the Government, faced by mounting crisis, appointed a select committee to inquire into what course was in the best interest of the country. The Government also let it be known in advance that it was not going to change its mind anyway. In consequence, the Opposition refused to serve on the Committee.

The Chamber gave evidence. It emphasized that adherence to the gold standard would require, if the output of the industry was to be maintained, a reduction in wages, relaxation of the colour bar, reduction in railway rates and in other costs. In contrast, departure from the gold standard would increase the price of gold and open the possibility of a great expansion of the industry. Once again forecasting accurately, the Chamber declared

> Confidence would revive, new capital would flow into the country, and capital which has migrated would return; all mining and industrial activities would be stimulated, the internal markets for our agricultural products would be immensely increased, the Railways would become less unpayable, and the whole financial and economic position of the Union would be radically improved.[21]

The Government was unmoved and undaunted. Heeding their masters, the Select Committee gave its cachet to Havenga's policy of disaster, and the country was left to struggle on. The export coal business, except for the fulfilment of prior contracts, entirely ceased.

> Havenga clapped duties of up to 12.5 per cent on nearly all imports and offered a bounty of 10 per cent rising to 20 per cent on nearly all exports .... But fiscal measures could not stop a flight from the South African pound, if this looked like a promising speculative risk. People began to gamble on the possibility of the South African pound following sterling, and bought extensively on the London stock exchange, thus creating a currency famine in South Africa itself.[22]

As 1932 drew to an end the flight out of South African currency became a wild stampede. At last, in mid-December, the economic and political log jam was broken. Tielman Roos, languishing on the Bench of the Appeal Court, launched himself back into political life, rallying the country to demand de-valuation. The upsurge of public response raised speculation in the currency to a fever heat that forced Havenga's hand. On 28 December the South African pound was freed to find its level, and within four weeks reached parity with sterling.

By now economic disaster had fatally eroded the power base of the Hertzog regime. In Britain, a National Government had been formed to handle the crisis, and in South Africa, too, coalition was in the air. Roos made a bid for the leadership, seeking the premiership in a joint National Party/South African Party Cabinet. But Smuts, who thought him a charlatan, resolved the dilemma of his party by taking a personal decision not to deal with him.[23] However, according to Davenport, Smuts wanted a 'cessation of the orgy of racial politics which has been the stock-in-trade of our public life'.[24] Although he might have stood out for the premiership, he agreed to serve under Hertzog. After negotiations, a Coalition Government was announced with Hertzog as Prime Minister and Minister of External Affairs, and Smuts as Deputy Prime Minister and Minister of Justice. Havenga remained Minister of Finance. Jan Hofmeyr took the portfolio of Education and Public Health, and Patrick Duncan was given Mines and Industries. Oswald Pirow took over Defence and Railways from Creswell, who went out of office with his Labour colleague, H W Sampson, the former Minister of Posts and Telegraphs.

A General Election followed in May, the Coalition winning 144 seats to 14, and was followed in turn by fusion of the National and South African Parties in the United South African National Party (better known as the United Party). Dr Malan broke away to form the *Gesuiwerde Nasionale Party* (the Purified National Party). There was to be another breakaway. The new United Party's programme of principles declared that 'while the Party stands for the maintenance of the present constitutional position, no one will be denied the right to express his individual opinion about or advocate his honest convictions in connection with any change of our form of government'.[25] A few die-hard adherents of British Imperialism found this too much to stomach, and formed the Dominion Party, under Colonel Stallard.

As for Roos, he was left to form the short-lived Central Party, still hoping that political winds would blow his way. He was undoubtedly happier on the political platform than on the Bench. Boydell has recalled that when he asked Roos, while he was still a judge, how long the Appeal Court sat each year, Roos told him: 'Oh, about two months.'

Boydell asked: 'Only two months – don't you find the rest of the time boring?'

'No,' Roos said, 'It's the two months I find boring.'[26]

Concurrent with this period of political upheaval, the gold price was rising. In April, the United States devalued, and the price of gold rose, not only in terms of the South African pound, but in terms of the dollar and all other currencies as well. Within a year after devaluation in South Africa, the gold price had jumped by forty-five per cent.

> The ebb of money back to South Africa became a spring tide. Credit and confidence flowed again through the economic system. Withdrawals turned into deposits. Plentiful money lowered short-term rates of interest. The mines benefited from generous offerings of capital. The industries and occupations which were dependent upon them took heart as well. Not even the strongest advocates of an abandonment of the gold standard had expected such a powerful and energetic stimulus to be given to economic activity. Once again South Africa enjoyed a windfall, the greatest perhaps of its career.[27]

The prospects of the highly cost-sensitive gold mining industry were transfigured. Huge blocks of gold-bearing ore, previously 'not worth a pennyworth of capital expenditure',[28] became payable overnight. This ore was not only immediately to hand in existing mines, but in new fields that now beckoned the mining entrepreneur. The years of struggle to keep the mines in being would be handsomely rewarded.

On this foundation, South Africa would build a modern industrial state and attain the status of a regional power in Africa.

[1] Cartwright, *The Gold Miners*, p 254.
[2] B J Liebenberg, 'Hertzog in Power: 1924-1939', C F J Muller, ed., *Five Hundred Years: A History of South Africa*, p 423.
[3] Forty-Third Annual Report of the Transvaal Chamber of Mines, 1932, p 98.
[4] *Ibid*, p 116.
[5] Annual Report of the Transvaal Chamber of Mines, 1932, p 135. (Quarterly meeting held on 27 June 1932.)

[6] 'The Life of the Gold Mining Industry', *The South African Mining and Engineering Journal*, Johannesburg, 16 August 1930, p 699.

[7] Union of South Africa: Report of the Low Grade Ore Commission, 1930 (UG 16 '32), p 25.

[8] S H Frankel, *The Railway Policy of South Africa: An Analysis of the Effects of Railway Rates, Finance and Management on the Economic Development of the Union*, pp XIII, 26, 29, 37 and 46.
Paragraph 72 of the Synopsis of Conclusions (p 26) relates to paragraph 121 of the main text (pp 154–155).
Paragraphs 82 and 83 of the Synopsis of Conclusions (p 29) relate to paragraphs 132 and 133 of the main text (pp 169–172).
Paragraph 106 of the Synopsis of Conclusions (p 37) relates to paragraph 156 of the main text (pp 200–201).
Paragraphs 134 and 135 of the Synopsis of Conclusions (p 46) relate to paragraphs 187 and 189 of the main text (pp 232–234).

[9] Forty-First Annual Report of the Transvaal Chamber of Mines, 1930, pp 63–66.

[10] J Boyd, 'Methods for Determining the Dust in Mine Air, as practised on the Witwatersrand' (No 3, pp 9–12), International Labour Office, *International Silicosis Conference, Johannesburg, 13-27 August 1930: Reports*.

[11] Annual Report of the Transvaal Chamber of Mines, 1924, pp 58–60.

[12] Chamber of Mines Archives: File 33a 1930: 'ILO Silicosis Conference: Minutes and Reports': 'International Silicosis Conference: Appendix to the Minutes of the First Sitting: Chairman's Speech (Dr L G Irvine, 13 August 1930)', p 9.

[13] L G Irvine, 'The Functions of the Miners' Phthisis Medical Bureau and the General System of Medical Examinations conducted under the Miners' Phthisis Act' (No 15, pp 14–15), International Labour Office, *International Silicosis Conference, Johannesburg, 13-27 August 1930: Reports*.

[14] Chamber of Mines Archives: File 33a 1930: 'ILO Silicosis Conference: Minutes and Reports': 'International Silicosis Conference: Appendix to the Minutes of the First Sitting: Chairman's Speech', pp 1, 4–5.

[15] L G Irvine, A Mavrogordato and H Pirow, 'A Review of the History of Silicosis on the Witwatersrand Goldfields', (No 6, p 4), International Labour Office, *International Silicosis Conference, Johannesburg, 13-27 August 1930: Reports*.
Chamber of Mines Archives: File 33a 1930: 'ILO Silicosis Conference: Minutes and Reports': 'International Silicosis Conference: Appendix to the Minutes of the First Sitting: Chairman's Speech', p 3.

[16] Irvine, Mavrogordato and Pirow, p 1, p 6 *et seq*, for information on successive steps formulated in the control of working conditions, and p 25.

[17] Hancock, *Smuts: 2. The Fields of Force*, p 242.

[18] De Kiewiet, p 173.

[19] Union of South Africa: Debates of the House of Assembly: Fourth Session, Sixth Parliament: 18 November 1931 to 27 May 1932: Volumes 18 and 19: Column 20 *et seq*.

[20] Davenport, p 213.

[21] Annual Report of the Transvaal Chamber of Mines, 1932, pp 55–63. (Gold Standard Select Committee: Statement of the Gold Producers' Committee of the Transvaal Chamber of Mines.)

[22] Davenport, p 213.

[23] Hancock, *Smuts: 2. The Fields of Force*, p 245.

[24] Davenport, p 215.

[25] *Ibid*, p 217.

[26] T Boydell, *My Luck was in: With Spotlights on General Smuts*, p 216.

[27] De Kiewiet, p 174.

[28] Forty-Seventh Annual Report of the Transvaal Chamber of Mines, 1936, p 49.

PART FOUR

The Grand Advance

CHAPTER TWENTY-EIGHT

New Horizons

In the seven golden years that followed South Africa's departure from the gold standard, some £80 million was invested in gold mines. Huge sums went into the shares of mines previously on the point of closure but now granted an Indian summer of glorious life. Huge sums went, too, into the formation of new mining companies.

When, in September 1926, Johannesburg and the gold mines had celebrated, with notable enthusiasm, their fortieth anniversary, the Chamber's President, Arthur French, had gloomily remarked:

> Many people have asked, without receiving any satisfactory reply, 'Why the fortieth? The fiftieth we could understand.' I incline to think that the true answer, which, naturally, no one is anxious to give, is an unconfessed uneasiness as to whether, when the fiftieth anniversary arrives, there will be anything like so much left to celebrate.[1]

On 30 March 1936 W A Mackenzie, of Gold Fields, in his Presidential Address to the Annual Meeting of the Chamber could recall French's remarks and contrast their pessimism with the spirit of confidence and optimism that now abounded. Fifteen new mines were being opened up and twenty-three main vertical shafts were being sunk on them. Another thirteen new main vertical shafts were going down on existing mines. The bulk of the fifteen new mines were on the East Rand Basin, with Anglo American, Gold Fields and Union Corporation to the fore, but one, Venterspost, was being sunk by Gold Fields on a wholly new field, the West Wits Line. It was the first of eleven which would include among them some of the most profitable ever.

By 1930, the operations of the Gold Fields Group had dwindled, with only Sub Nigel, Simmer and Jack, and Robinson Deep in production, the last two being seemingly near the end of their lives. At this juncture, despite the discouragement of the world Depression, Gold Fields launched a search for the continuation of the Main Reef westwards toward Potchefstroom and the Mooi River. It was to prove fortunate for Gold Fields that the men at its head in London and Johannesburg were prepared, at a time when mining enterprise was at its lowest ebb, to back the opinion of their technical experts, and to take the calculated risks inseparable from large-scale mining ventures. Fortunately, too, those technical experts were men of exceptional judgement with courage to match. They were headed by Guy Carleton Jones, the Consulting Engineer, a Canadian and a graduate of McGill University, who had come to South Africa in 1914. He became a shift boss at the Sub Nigel where he worked for a time under mine captain C S McLean, a fellow-Canadian and life-long friend, who was also to play a leading role in mining affairs. In 1922 Carleton Jones became Manager of Sub Nigel, and in 1925 was transferred to Gold Fields in Johannesburg as Assistant Engineer. At head office his restless spirit chafed at the lack of opportunities for new ventures.

There had long been speculation and controversy about the possibility of a westward extension of the gold-bearing reefs. The outcrop of the Main Reef could be traced as far as JCI's great mine complex at Randfontein, but just to the west the reef disappeared and appeared to plunge deep beneath the rocks of the Transvaal System. There was some evidence to suggest their presence, but where did the reefs run? Was it possible to reach them through the water-filled fissures of the dolomitic overlay? And, once reached, would the reefs be payable? Now a new search for the lost reefs was sparked by Dr Rudolf Krahmann, an almost penniless German immigrant who was a pioneer of geophysical prospecting, employing an instrument known as the magnetometer, a type of compass which responds to the pull of magnetic strata far below the surface.

It was known that bands of magnetic shale ran at a fairly consistent depth below the Main Reef. Krahmann perceived that by magnetometric survey on the surface he could trace this shale 3 000 feet underground, and thereby define locations for a drilling programme that would intersect the reef running above it. He wrote later:

> My idea – it was the egg of Columbus – was to ignore the direct approach to the gold-bearing reef and to study the physical characteristics of the accompanying rocks; of these the magnetic content of certain horizons was the most obvious and appeared the most promising.
>
> These iron-rich shales of the Lower Witwatersrand System – occurring at reasonably constant intervals below the Main Reef – could then be used, indirectly, as markers to trace the continuation of the gold-bearing horizons of the Upper Witwatersrand System.[2]

Dr Leopold Reinecke, a consultant geologist to Gold Fields, listened and was impressed. A conference followed on 19 December 1930 with Christopherson, the Resident Director, and Carleton Jones. They agreed to back the survey despite the financial stringency of the times and the almost total lack of capital for new mining enterprise. Christopherson wrote apologetically to his head office in London:

> ... I have agreed to the engagement of Dr Krahmann for a period of three

The British Royal Family went underground at Crown Mines in 1947. Picture shows the Queen with the Princesses Elizabeth and Margaret.

Dr D F Malan, the Prime Minister, opened the country's first uranium plant at West Rand Cons on 8th October, 1952.

Stowe McLean who played a dominating role in the Chamber of Mines in the years after the Second World War.

Harry Oppenheimer, at the opening of President Steyn gold mine in the Orange Free State in April 1954.

Night scene at President Brand gold mine with the new town of Welkom in the background.

South African mining engineers are specialists in high-technology, high-speed shaft-sinking.

The Gold Producers' Committee in session in 1960. The President and Chairman, Dr Bill Busschau, sits on the right, with chair pulled back. Facing him as representatives of the mining houses are five past or future presidents. Clockwise from Busschau are: Tracey Milne, General Manager; Hugh Thomson, Assistant General Manager; Michael Falcon, Technical Adviser; Victor Robinson, Labour Adviser (left foreground); John Shilling, substituting on that day for

Hermie Koch (Anglo American); Colin Anderson (Union Corporation), W S 'Jock' Findlay (JCI); Stowe McLean (General Mining); 'Attie' von Maltitz (Anglo Vaal); Peter Anderson (Corner House); C Christie Taylor, Uranium Officer; James Gemmill, Native Labour Adviser; Angus Collie, Public Relations Officer; and B T 'Tanc' Tindall, Legal Adviser.

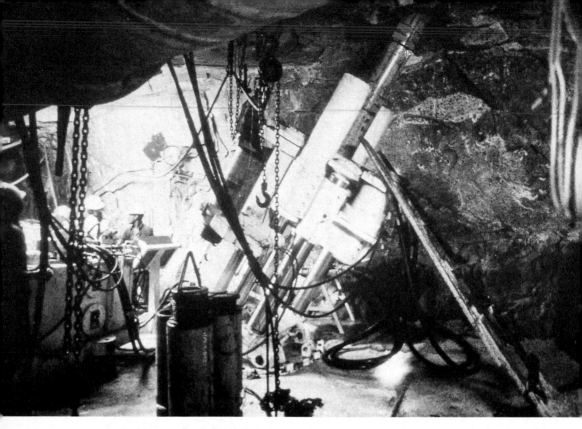

The raiseborer has played an increasingly important role in mining operations during the past twenty-five years.

A migratory worker bids farewell to his wife and child in remote Barotseland.

In the fifties WNLA used eight Dakota aircraft in an airlift between Francistown in Botswana, and Malawi; Zambia; the outlying districts of northern Botswana and the Caprivi Strip.

Homeward journey. By 1956, the WNLA was flying 32 million passenger miles yearly, cutting down travelling time to and from the Rand by up to fourteen days.

Western Deep Levels, the crowning achievement of Sir Ernest Oppenheimer's career, in the seventies.

Sir Ernest Oppenheimer

months at a salary of £100 a month, whilst other incidental expenses we shall have to bear will not exceed £200. I hope you will agree that it is worth expending £500 on a matter of this kind ....[3]

Krahmann duly took meticulous readings, a lonely trail that wound thirty-five miles westward across the grasslands of the Venterspost and Libanon farms, and of the Wonderfontein Valley, and produced a long series of readings which indicated the correctness of his theory. As Carleton Jones studied them, he became convinced that this was 'the discovery of the century'.[4] He laid his reputation on the line, and recommended expenditure of £90 000 on borehole drilling. Christopherson, who had moved, with some reluctance, to London Office, in turn proposed to the Board the formation of a company to continue exploration.

Other mining houses were invited to participate but not all were sure of the value of the geophysical survey. However, some saw the opportunities beyond the not inconsiderable risks. On 16 October 1932, F A Unger, then Manager and Consulting Engineer of Anglo American, reported to Sir Ernest Oppenheimer:

> The scheme as submitted to us has many attractions and it appeals to the imagination. The possibilities are immense, and if fortune favours the bold, the outlook for the Witwatersrand will undergo a complete change. ... My feeling is that a mining group could not very well afford to refuse participation at this stage, especially as the initial capital involved is not very great, certainly nothing compared with the magnitude of the prize.
>
> I must warn you, however, that the scheme submitted is a gamble, certainly a very attractive one, and of a type in which a mining house is absolutely justified in risking even a considerable sum of money.
>
> ... from a mining point of view the information is pretty scanty: the dolomite cover is bound to be thick, the sub-outcrop will mainly be at a depth of 3 000 feet or over and it will thus be an expensive business to get actual reef exposures .... As against this, the possibilities of the scheme are so great that one is inclined to waive all objections and to recommend participating ....[5]

Anglo was in and so was General Mining.

Gold Fields floated the Witwatersrand Areas Ltd on 12 November, with their participation. Gold Fields still had some difficulty in placing the shares and was obliged to take up more than it had bargained for. Six weeks later South Africa went off gold, and gold-linked shares soared in a wild boom on the Stock Exchange.

In the months that followed, the deep-probing drills one after another intersected the reef where Krahmann had specified. Not only were the borehole cores highly payable, but two new and unsuspected gold-bearing formations were discovered, the Ventersdorp Contact Reef and the deep-running Carbon Leader, which was to prove the richest ever. Gold Fields was careful not to make hasty predictions, but by 1935 John A Agnew, the Chairman, could permit himself to say guardedly: 'I find it very difficult to avoid the use of extravagant language in outlining the prospects.'[6] However, the new field would be greedy of resources and of time; and war, for the third time in a span of forty years, would hold back the advance of the industry. The shareholders who invested in West Wits at the outset would wait fourteen years for a dividend.

Once the new field had been proved, Carleton Jones had to develop the first mine in the face of technical challenges as extravagant as the prospects for the area. The new mines would one day stretch along the Gatsrand (the Ridge of Caves), but huge underground reservoirs of water at first barred access to their gold reefs. The problem of sinking shafts through this barrier was overcome by pioneering the use of cementation on a major scale, a process which involved the pumping of liquid cement under pressure to seal the water-filled fissures in the dolomite ahead of the sinking shaft. Venterspost cementation teams, in sinking its two shafts, had to battle floods which called for 500 000 pockets of cement and almost defeated them. Their success confirmed the practicality of mining through the dolomite and ensured the future of the field. Venterspost began milling in October 1939. Blyvooruitzicht, a mine located not far from the site of the new town to be called Carletonville, was brought to production by the Corner House in 1942. It was found to be astonishingly richer than the boreholes had promised. The development of other mines by Gold Fields would be held up by the outbreak of war in 1939.

As a logical step there followed the opening up of the Klerksdorp gold-field, long a centre of gold mining on a small scale. In the early days the field boasted 150 gold mining companies, a chamber of mines and a stock exchange. All it lacked, wrote Cartwright, was a steady source of gold.[7] The shallow, heavily faulted mines swallowed up capital and broke the hearts of the men who operated them. But some had faith in the future. Outstanding among them was Charles Scott, the owner of the farm Strathmore, and his civil engineer son, Jack. As news of Carleton Jones's success spread, and the price of gold passed £7 an ounce, Jack Scott would play a major role in the development of the area by the mining houses. Anglo American was there early, forming the Western Reefs Exploration and Development Company which would in 1941 give the area its first large mine, later to become part of Anglo's huge Vaal Reefs complex. General Mining played a major role and so did a new mining house, Anglo-Transvaal Consolidated Investment Company.

Anglo Vaal, as it is more familiarly known, was established on 1 June 1933, with a capital of £150 000, by a mining engineer, A S Hersov, a stockbroker, S G Menell, and the son of a pioneer, N S Erleigh. These three young men were the first to grasp the potential that existed in re-opening defunct mines at the new high gold price. They formed Rand Leases out of old mines and a lease agreement won from the Government, which entitled the public to participate in a share issue. The public did so with a will, over-subscribing the issue fifteen times. After four years Erleigh would leave Anglo Vaal, later to form New Union Goldfields. Anglo Vaal, under Hersov and Menell, grew into a powerful corporation that would play an important role in the Chamber of Mines.

The rise in the gold price immediately engendered expectations among shareholders which were as promptly dashed as the new coalition government, with Havenga in the van, moved in for the fiscal kill. Havenga, having fought to the last ditch to retain the gold standard, thought it intolerable that gold mining shareholders should now enjoy bonanza profits from what he regarded as debasement of the currency. In the words of John W Shilling, a future President of the Chamber:

The neck of the gold mining industry was thus bared to the guillotine ....[8]

In his Budget Speech in May, Havenga declared that the increase in the price of gold was due solely to state action, and that mining shareholders had no exclusive claim to the resultant profits. He conceded however that it was important to promote the mining of low-grade ore and to extend the life of the mines; and that the risks inherent in gold mining investment entitled the shareholder to some part of the windfall.[9] His Income Tax Act, generally mild in tone, carried 'a sting in the tail' in an excess profits duty on gold mining profits. Excess profits

... were defined, simply enough, as the excess of profits actually earned during a year of assessment over the 'standard profit' attributable to any mine. There any simplicity ended.[10]

The Government's intention was however quite clear. It had resolved to take half the profits arising from the increased gold price.[11]

The announcement shocked the industry and its shareholders; but alleviation soon came with the Government's willingness to settle for an agreed maximum amount from the industry. However, as the price of gold continued to rise, the arrangement proved too advantageous to the industry for the Treasury's liking.

For the gold mines there was no end to the punishment at the hands of the voracious Fiscus. By an enactment tamely called the Gold Mines Excess Profits Duty Amendment Act, 1935 (No 51 of 1935) a gold profits surtax was added to the excess profits duty.

The flow from the gold mines to the Fiscal blood bank continued unabated.[12]

The working profit of the gold mines (the profit before tax and other statutory charges) in the calendar year of 1932 was £13 770 296 of which £3 818 206 was paid in tax, State's share of profits and licences. In 1933 the working profit was £28 694 811 of which the State was able to gather in only £4 634 985. By 1934, the Fiscus was fully organized and the tax paid from a profit of £29 367 322 was £15 005 018.[13] By 1935, the revenue from gold mining constituted a full third of the Government's revenue from all sources. In that year, the Government appointed the Departmental Committee on Mining Taxation, to which the Chamber gave evidence. It pointed out that the State was taking forty-two per cent of taxable profits compared with nineteen per cent or less in Australia, Canada and the United States.

Havenga in his Budget Speech the following year admitted frankly that the basis of taxation of excess profits had been experimental, and had become unduly complicated. He introduced a new system of a single tax on the income of gold mines consisting of a flat rate tax and a formula tax, subject to a maximum percentage of profits. The structure then laid down still forms the basis of gold mining taxation today. The immediate effect was to maintain the unprecedented level of tax; in 1936, a year in which profits fell, it rose once again.

As a consequence of the gold bonanza Havenga was able to announce an incomparable series of Budget surpluses. Much of the revenue from mining was diverted to the support and encouragement of other sectors of the economy, including agriculture. The industrial diversification that followed virtually ended the poor white and unemployment problems.[14]

In 1939 the mining industry's position was summed up by the Chamber as follows:

> In 1931 the working profit per ton [of ore milled] was 8s 6d. The taxation in that year amounted to 11d per ton, and the lease share from certain mines (included in the working profit figure) was 1s 4d, so that the Industry retained a disposable profit of 6s 3d per ton.
>
> In 1938 the working profit was 11s 10d, but the total of taxation and lease share was 5s 3d so that the total disposable profit in the hands of the mines amounted only to 6s 7d per ton.
>
> In so far, therefore, as the shareholders' profit per ton is concerned, they have benefited to the extent of only 4d ....[15]

The shareholders' 'windfall' was therefore modest; they benefited principally from the increase in tonnage that had become economic to mine. There could be no doubt about the benefit to South Africa, nor indeed to world trade. South Africa became Britain's best customer as imports from there doubled between 1931 and 1937.

It has been argued by Yudelman that by the 1930s the mine-owners and the State had established so dominating a position over organized white labour that they were able to 'benefit fully from the gold price increase without passing on any significant share of the new prosperity to the white miners or to organized labour in general'.[16] This broad claim does not appear to take into account the advances in social and welfare benefits made by these workers.

The MWU reacted at once to the gold price increase by demanding in January 1933 a thirty-five per cent rise, arguing that the purchasing power of wages had fallen by that amount. The Chamber was able to turn this aside, pointing out that departure from the gold standard had not resulted in an increase in cost of living. Even if there were an increase in the future it was unlikely, the Chamber said, to neutralize the fall in the cost of living that had taken place since the Lucas Award of 1927. In terms of purchasing power there had been a steady increase in mine wages.

Later in 1933, unions representing the nine categories of mine employees formed the Mining Unions Joint Committee (MUJC) and put forward a pooled demand for a forty-hour working week plus a twenty per cent wage rise. After negotiation, this was remodelled as a demand for a share of profits in the form of a bonus. The Chamber in response took the positive stand against pay increases which it was to maintain throughout the 1930s. It argued that the ripple effect of increasing mine pay would lead to a general rise in the cost of living, to be followed by a request for still higher pay so as to maintain the level of real wages or the standard of living.[17]

The Chamber was mindful too of the difficulty it had encountered a decade before in reducing wages, granted in boom times, when the gold price fell. At the same time the Chamber conceded that employees should have a share in the enhanced prosperity of the industry, and turned to alternative methods of improving the lot of both officials and union members. It announced plans for the formation of a provident fund to give benefits on death, retirement or retrenchment, and appointed a mines' committee of representatives from the employees' medical benefit societies to work out a scheme. The result was the Witwatersrand Gold Mine Employees Provident Fund providing for lump sum benefits, to be run by the employees but funded by the employers. The mines' committee also proposed an additional scheme providing for improved benefits, based on contributions from the workers themselves. It was submitted to a referendum of all white employees and, unhappily, rejected by them. The consequence was that workers would have to wait for more than a decade for the increased benefits flowing from contributory pension funds. Meanwhile, the Provident Fund was established on 1 January 1934, with a contribution in 1933/1934 of £1 million from the gold mining companies. It was managed by a Board consisting of six employee representatives, one trade union and one Chamber representative and an independent chairman.

In 1934 officials and union men were given improved holiday leave. Many were granted an extra week's leave a year, and underground workers got up to four weeks' leave with thirty days' pay. In addition, the Chamber introduced for the first time an annual bonus, payable to an employee when going on leave. It agreed as well to make up to mine pay the army pay of men on gold mines and collieries who were called up in the new scheme for continuous training inaugurated by the Defence Force. Military training was counted as mine service for assessing leave entitlement.

The Chamber also announced its intention to build a specialist hospital, under the aegis of the Rand Mutual Assurance Company, to care for white workers injured at work. Black workers were already cared for in mine hospitals, as required by law, but white workers depended on the provincial hospitals and, in particular, the Johannesburg General Hospital to which a new wing had been added several years previously at the Chamber's expense. It now proceeded to build the new hospital on an eight-acre site at Cottesloe, Johannesburg. Cottesloe Hospital would establish an enviable reputation for the excellence of its surgical treatment and medical care.

The MUJC again sought pay rises in 1936. Once more the Chamber dug in its heels. It offered instead to establish a medical and dental service at the industry's expense to replace the current system of panel doctors and dentists provided by the medical benefit societies. The proposal was turned down by the unions, and instead the Chamber introduced medical benefit allowances and increased the holiday bonus. In due course it added a savings branch to the Provident Fund, again funded by the mining companies.

In the first financial year of the Savings Branch, up to 31 March 1939, employers deposited £491 549 on behalf of employees, of which £236 648 was withdrawn by them.

In the same month, after a ballot, most of the mines benefit societies amalgamated to form a single Mines Benefit Society. The Chamber donated £30 000 to assist its formation.[18]

In 1938 the men were allowed a day off on full pay to participate in the Voortrekker Centenary celebrations. The following year, 16 December, Dingaan's Day (now the Day of the Vow), became a paid holiday for those who could be spared, and those who could not were given an extra day's pay.

All in all, the benefits granted to trade union members were such that their unions gave an undertaking in 1934 that neither individually nor collectively would they make any claim for a general increase in wages unless conditions changed very materially. They did not keep wholly to the bargain, but they reiterated it in response to successive improvements in benefits. The Chamber, summing up the position of white employees in a letter to the MUJC on 22 May 1939, claimed:

> The expansion of the industry has not only benefited the shareholders but has been equally beneficial to the employees .... The total number employed has risen from 22 654 in 1931 to 40 793 in 1938 and the total white wages [including all benefits associated therewith] paid increased from £8 539 886 to £16 938 566 for the same year; further the employees benefit equally with the shareholders in the lengthened life of the Industry.[19]

Black employment increased dramatically as well, rising by more than 100 000. Their wages rose marginally, but because of the migratory nature of their employment, high turnovers, resultant breaks in service and the tendency to cease mine work at a relatively early age, these workers would have to wait many years for leave and provident schemes. The Chamber claimed, however, that the rapid increase in the numbers seeking employment, and the high percentage of former employees who re-engaged, confirmed that conditions of employment were competitive.

The Government, for its part, introduced in 1934 yet another Miners' Phthisis Act which increased the benefits to workers and dependants of all races at the cost of a rise of £900 000 in the total liability of gold mines. There would be further increases in both benefits and levies on the mines during the 1930s. The Government also passed into law the Workmen's Compensation Act, 1934, providing improved benefits for all races; and set in train the process that would lead in 1939 to the passing of legislation introducing unemployment pay for the first time in South Africa. It tried too, in effect, to expand the colour bar on the mines by securing, through the Minimum Wage Bill, the employment of whites in certain categories of unskilled and semi-skilled work done by blacks. However, the Chamber's counter-arguments, at a Government conference in Pretoria on 14 October 1935, prevailed and secured the withdrawal of the bill.

The relative calm that reigned in labour relations was dispelled by the formation on 7 April 1937 of the *Afrikanerbond van Mynwerkers* with the Christian National ethos of D F Malan's Purified National Party, its aim being a take-over from the MWU.[20] In a bid to avert the threatened unrest among miners the Chamber made an about face and withdrew its previous stern opposition to a 'closed shop' on the mines. It entered into an agreement with established unions, from 1 June 1937, providing that every employee (other than officials, apprentices and learners) should be a member of one of them. The nine unions were the Amalgamated Engineering Union, Amalgamated Society of Wood-workers, Building Workers' Industrial Union of South Africa, Ironmoulders' Union of South Africa, South African Boilermakers' Iron and Steelworkers' and Shipbuilders' Society, South African Electrical Workers' Association, South African Engine Drivers' and Firemen's Association, and the South African Reduction Workers' Association.[21]

The Chamber must often in after years have regretted its decision to concede the closed shop, because it did not succeed in its immediate purpose of curbing unrest within the MWU; while the fruits of the closed shop would include damaging strikes and the strengthening of the position of the unions, and especially the MWU, in defence of the colour bar.

The immediate effect of the Chamber's volte-face in 1937 was that the rival to the MWU, the *Afrikanerbond van Mynwerkers*, simply changed its name to *Die Hervormingsorganisasie* (The Reform Organization). The Reformers, as they came to be known, were backed with funds from the so-called National Council of Trustees, and were strongly under the influence of Hertzog's thirty-eight-year-old son, Albert, who was in the van of right-wing Afrikaner extremists. The Reformers worked within the MWU to gain control of it, directing their attack particularly against Charles Harris, the Organizing

Secretary since 1935. They called for cancellation of the wage agreement with the Chamber, and for an immediate increase in wages and other benefits. However, the *raison d'etre* for the movement was principally to establish in the ranks of organized labour a radical complement to the drives of militant Afrikanerdom.[22]

The initial upheaval within the MWU reached a peak on 13 February 1939, when the Reformers seized the offices of the Union and took possession of Harris's office. The Union was forced to obtain a court order to regain possession.[23] Harris in his annual report, published on 8 March, said that the year under review was 'fraught with attacks from either delinquent members or persons determined to sow racial hatred and discontent among their fellow-workers'. He claimed that, despite the subversive activity, more solid progress had been made than in any other period.[24]

The Reformers maintained their activity, circulating a leaflet urging 'away with Harris', and calling a mass meeting in the Boksburg Town Hall on 9 March.[25] Despite counter-attack and some setbacks the Reformers persisted and gained increasing support among MWU members on the mines.

The prevailing tension was soon to be heightened by a tragic event. On 15 June, Harris drove out of a garage in Kerk Street, Johannesburg. By chance, an unemployed and unbalanced miner of twenty-two named Jakob Moller Hugo, who had become intensely hostile to Harris, saw him leave and drew his attention. Harris stopped and leant forward to speak to him. Hugo drew a revolver and fired five shots, four of which struck Harris in the head and chest. He died instantly.[26]

Harris had long service in the trade union movement, having been an executive member of the old Federation of Trades back in 1922. His funeral at the Brixton Jewish Cemetery on 18 June was preceded by a march in procession through streets lined by silent sympathizers. The Chamber was represented by the President, G H Beatty (JCI), a Vice-President, W H Lawrence (Corner House) and by Gemmill. The *Rand Daily Mail* the next day described the crowd as the largest at a funeral since the death of Tielman Roos four years previously. Hugo's attorney challenged Press estimates of attendance as an attempt to create public feeling against his client, but there seems no doubt that the funeral was a major public occasion and a considerable expression of trade union solidarity with the Harris regime. Hugo duly appeared before Mr Justice Schreiner, charged with murder. He was defended by Dr T E Dönges, who would serve, successively, post-war, as Minister of the Interior and Minister of Finance. After a sensational trial, Hugo was found guilty of murder, but escaped the death penalty because of his mental state. He was sentenced to life imprisonment.[27]

Later in the year a bid was made to restore unity in the Union. On 7 November, *The Star* reported J A van den Bergh, the Union's President, as saying that a meeting had unanimously decided to support the policy of settling all differences between the rival groups. The accord was short-lived. A long period of dissension and discord lay ahead, but the Reformers would in the end achieve their aims as the MWU became aligned firmly to the right wing of Afrikaner nationalism.

As exploration and development of the West Wits Line and the Klerksdorp gold-fields proceeded after 1933, the attention of the mining houses was focused on the prospects of a major new gold-field in the Orange Free State. Exploration there received fresh stimulus from the results of drilling conducted by Anglo American's Western Reefs on the banks of the Vaal. Investigations were hampered however by a lack of scientific knowledge of the geology of the province. Krahmann's geophysical method was applied and contributed to a better understanding, but of more importance in Free State exploration was the torsion balance, pioneered by Union Corporation. This geophysical instrument enabled geologists to determine the specific gravity of underlying strata and estimate their thickness; they could then place borehole drills where they would avoid lava beds up to 5 000 feet thick which overlay much of the north-western Free State.

Investigation of the farms lying southward of Western Reefs did not reveal payable formations, but exploration continued across a widening area. By 1936 the mining houses had all the farms under option from the Vaal to the Sand River.

On 23 October 1933 a company called Wits Extensions had begun drilling on the farm Aandenk north of Odendaalsrus. This brave venture into the unknown was stopped in February 1935, as the company's funds ran out, with the drill at a depth of 4 064 feet. In the post-war years it would be extended 400 feet to intersect the Basal Reef, the main gold-producing formation in the Free State.

The most notable contribution to the proving of the field came, however, from the Western Holdings company floated in 1937 by Abe Bailey's South African Townships, Mining and Finance Corporation. Union Corporation took an important interest in Western Holdings, and made available the organization built up by Alfred Frost, Consulting Geologist, and Oscar Weiss, Consulting Geophysicist, to assist in exploring the huge area held under option by the company. In April 1939 a borehole drilled by Western Holdings on the farm St Helena struck the Basal Reef at a depth of 1 143 feet, giving an average yield of 34,62 dwt over 67,45 inches, more than fifteen times the minimum level of payability at the time. As exploration continued, the mining houses would soon be sure that a new gold-field had been discovered, but the outbreak of hostilities in Europe abruptly halted its development. And elsewhere around the industry's Golden Arc seven new mines, already shaft-sinking and developing, were summarily closed as South Africa opted for commitment to total war.

[1] Annual Report of the Transvaal Chamber of Mines, 1926, p 140. (Quarterly meeting held on 27 September 1926.)

[2] Cartwright, *Gold Paved the Way*, p 152.

[3] *Ibid*, p 157.

[4] *Ibid*, p 158.

[5] T Gregory, *Ernest Oppenheimer and the Economic Development of Southern Africa*, pp 514-515.

[6] Cartwright, *Gold Paved the Way*, p 167.

[7] Cartwright, *The Gold Miners*, p 247.

[8] Shilling, p 42.

[9] G W G Browne, 'Fifty Years of Public Finance', *The South African Journal of Economics*, Vol 51, No 1, March 1983, p 138.

[10] Shilling, p 42.

[11] Browne, p 139.

[12] Shilling, pp 51-52.

[13] *Ibid*, p 53.

[14] Yudelman, p 260.

[15] Annual Report of the Transvaal Chamber of Mines, 1939, p 73.

[16] Yudelman, p 261.

[17] Forty-Fourth Annual Report of the Transvaal Chamber of Mines, 1933, pp 44-45.

[18] Fifty-First Annual Report of the Transvaal Chamber of Mines, 1940, p 66.

[19] Annual Report of the Transvaal Chamber of Mines, 1939, p 73. See also reference to the Commission on Conditions of Employment in the Gold Mining Industry, 1948, in Chapter Thirty-One.

[20] Union of South Africa: Department of Labour: Findings and Recommendations of the Mine Workers' Union Commission (1941), p 6.

[21] Forty-Eighth Annual Report of the Transvaal Chamber of Mines, 1937, pp 33-34.

[22] Findings and Recommendations of the Mine Workers' Union Commission (1941), p 6.

[23] 'Mine Union Deadlock: Offices seized by "Reformers"', *The Star*, 13 February 1939. 'Miners' Union Executive will apply to Court today', *Rand Daily Mail*, 14 February 1939. 'Court restores Offices to Miners' Union'. *The Star*, 14 February 1939.

[24] 'Mine Workers' Solidarity', *The Star*, 8 March 1939.

[25] Chamber of Mines Archives: File 128 1939: 'SAMWU – Internal Dispute': Leaflet issued by the Reform Organization, No 47.

[26] 'Mr C Harris Killed in His Car', *Rand Daily Mail*, 16 June 1939.

[27] L Naudé, *Dr A Hertzog, Die Nasionale Party en Die Mynwerker*, pp 129-131.

CHAPTER TWENTY-NINE

The Sinews of War

The German annexation of Czechoslovakia in March 1939 left no doubt anywhere of Hitler's lust for conquest. Soon afterwards Oswald Pirow, the Minister of Defence and Commerce, summoned members of the GPC to discuss plans for the industry in the event of an emergency. It was agreed that gold mining should be regarded as an essential service, which would receive priority in the provision of materials, and in the maintenance of its labour force.[1]

The invasion of Poland followed on 1 September, and Britain and France declared war on Germany two days later. On the question whether South Africa should enter the War on the side of the Allies, Hertzog stood firmly for neutrality and Smuts equally firmly for war against Hitler. The Cabinet split 7-6 in Smuts's favour. By a strange co-incidence, Parliament was in session, having gathered the day before for the formal act of prolonging the life of the Senate. The war issue could thus be referred at once to the House of Assembly. Twenty-five years before, on 14 September 1914, the House had voted ninety-two to twelve for the invasion of German South West Africa. In 1939 the decision for war would turn on a handful of votes. After an all-day session on 4 September, a division was called at 9 00 pm in which eighty members voted for Smuts and sixty-seven for Hertzog. The United Party split down the middle. The Governor-General, Patrick Duncan, refused Hertzog's request for a General Election on the good grounds that Smuts had a clear majority in the House of Assembly. Hertzog resigned, and Smuts put together a coalition cabinet which included Walter Madeley of the Labour Party and Colonel Stallard of the Dominion Party. South Africa was fighting, Smuts declared, for the future of the human race and of Europe, the 'glorious mother continent of Western civilization – the proudest achievement of the human spirit ....'[2]

The Government would have to counter continual unrest engendered by elements opposed to the War, who carried out various acts of sabotage, including the blowing up of pylons carrying power to the gold mines. Davenport has commented:

... one of the outstanding characteristics of the Smuts wartime government was the coolness with which it handled threats to the security of the State. Like all belligerents, it armed itself under a War Measures Act of 1940, with the power to intern suspects and enemy aliens, and used them; it called in all firearms; and it helped itself to a range of arbitrary powers, including powers to control supplies and curb industrial unrest. But, profiting from the lessons of the First World War, Smuts pulled his punches in handling the most provocative opposition to his war policy, and refrained from the use of the death penalty even for blatant acts of treason.[3]

On 5 October 1939 the Chamber attained its Jubilee, but its celebration was not judged appropriate in a time of world crisis. A hopeful internal note recorded that Gold Fields had celebrated its Jubilee two years before by holding two dinners, giving each member of staff an engraved silver cigarette case plus a bonus, and giving junior typists a large box of chocolates valued at 25s. The note was laid before George Beatty. A Chamber official thereafter scrawled on it: 'Seen by President – rather cold glance.' The Jubilee did not even receive a mention in the Annual Report for 1939.

The Press however was more generous. *The Star* wrote that the increase in output from 306 167 ounces of gold in 1889 to nearly 12 000 000 in 1938 indicated the tremendous expansion in the scope of the Chamber's work for gold mining. But in recent times its interests had expanded far beyond the technical. Its leaders had shown that they had the welfare of the whole industry and its workers at heart.[4]

The *Rand Daily Mail* commented:

> Its leadership in the field of social insurance has been an inspiration not only to the Government of South Africa, but also to other parts of the world. Its long campaign against phthisis has earned the acknowledgement of scientists in every country, and its ventilation experiments and safety-first measures have altered the whole aspect of modern mining.
>
> It is as a great Rand institution, however, that the Chamber of Mines is most deserving of public gratitude. It has been identified, in very tangible form, with the progress of university and technical education throughout the Reef and has been a supporter of most of the public and charitable causes so near to the heart of this ever-generous community.[5]

An event much more dramatic than the Jubilee was the relinquishment of the post of General Manager by William Gemmill who had been on the staff for thirty-three years. On 5 July 1939 the Chamber announced that 'in view of the great increase in the scale of operations of the recruiting organisations serving the gold mining industry, Mr W Gemmill ... will relinquish the Chamber of Mines side of his duties at an early date and devote himself entirely to native labour matters'.[6]

However, behind the bland announcement lay the fact that the GPC had become dissatisfied with the Gemmill regime and had for some time contemplated a change. Undoubtedly, Gemmill through strength of personality had dominated the GPC in a way they did not always like. It is also said, and easy to believe, that having decided to remove Gemmill, no GPC member was anxious 'to bell the cat'. It fell to Beatty to ask for his resignation on the grounds of the need for organizational change. He did it by letter, dated 19 April 1939, to the Devonshire Club, St James's, London, where Gemmill was staying during leave overseas. In the event, the only important change made by the GPC was not to have a General Manager. A J Limebeer and D Smith, who was soon to retire, continued as Joint Secretaries. Limebeer, a mild man of courtly manner, who was the antithesis of Gemmill, was appointed Secretary to the GPC and became the quietly efficient co-ordinator of Chamber policy. The senior official was George Barry, the Legal Adviser. The Chamber would be without a manager for twelve years, a situation which enhanced the prestige and autonomy of departmental heads, and weakened management overall.

William Gemmill soon relinquished the office of General Manager of WNLA and the NRC as well, and departed northwards in April 1940 to become General Manager of the Tropical Areas Administration of the WNLA in Salisbury (Harare). In this capacity he would serve the Chamber for another twenty-one years. Covering remote tropical areas, he travelled and lived like royalty, and, after fifty-five years of service to the Chamber, died in 1961 at eighty-one from a stroke while lunching with the District Commissioner at Mongu in Barotseland.

Gemmill had his critics, but undoubtedly he made a major contribution to mining, and to the development of the Chamber of Mines with the multi-complex of services it provides today, including its extensive black labour organization. On his death, the then President, Hermie C Koch (Anglo American) flew to Salisbury to attend the funeral. Koch, a talented man with a gift for language, wrote of Gemmill in a published tribute:

> His physical stature and erect bearing were matched by the exceptional power of his highly trained and original mind, and by his commanding personality.
> It was in every way typical of him that, at an age when most men are in advanced retirement, he was carrying, more than adequately, a strenuous and responsible job, and that he died, so to speak, with his boots on.[7]

Gemmill's son James had joined the Native Labour Organizations before the War, but in truth grew up in them, accompanying his father on safari in remote tribal regions from an early age. He would rise to become General Manager of both WNLA and the NRC in 1952, and would carry the Gemmill tradition for the following twenty-two years.

William Gemmill's years in Central Africa were, coincidentally, marked by a progressive increase in the importance of the tropical areas as a source of black mine labour, for the obstacles to recruiting there were falling away. This was the result of the defeat by the mining industry of the scourge of pneumonia which in earlier years had proved deadly to the non-immune blacks of the tropics. The work of the South African Institute of Medical Research and of the industry's medical officers had gradually brought the disease under control, and it had been given its quietus as a rampant killer by the widespread use on the mines of the newly-discovered M&B sulfonamide drugs as these became available in 1938. In 1933 the South African Government had experimentally lifted its ban on recruitment north of latitude twenty–two degrees south, and the resumption of recruiting on a strictly limited scale had been successful. There followed an inquiry by the Rhodesia-Nyasaland Royal Commission which reported favourably in 1937 on the desirability of blacks from the Central African territories going south to work in the mines.

The labour historian, Dr Francis Wilson, has commented:

> The research initiated by the Chamber of Mines into the elimination of pneumonia is one of the most notable examples anywhere in the world of private investment in health leading directly to an increase in the supply of labour to a particular industry.[8]

With the approach of hostilities in 1939 the Government was quick to close in on the mining industry to fund the war effort. In June 1939 the total voted by Parliament for the running of the country was £68 717 014. Of this, a mere £2 504 920, or around 3,6 per cent, was allocated to Defence. By 1945 the vote would rise to £185 685 830 of which £101 250 000, or more than half, was expended on Defence.

Even before the outbreak of war Havenga sought to seize what he regarded as excess profits. As the gold price rose in August, in an atmosphere of world crisis, from £7 8s 6d to £7 18s 6d an ounce, the Hertzog Government announced that to curb undesirable speculation and to 'conserve such excess profits for national purposes', the Government proposed to appropriate in addition to existing taxation, all the proceeds from the sale of gold above £7 10s 0d an ounce. The Chamber reacted angrily against what it considered to be 'the most unfortunate and ill-advised measure of recent years'. Fortunately it was able to convince the new Government of the 'folly of a tax based on the quantity of gold produced, without reference to its cost of production'. The effect of such an expropriation would have been to limit artificially the grade of ore that could be profitably mined, thereby causing a contraction of mining operations.[9]

The measure introduced in its place was thought less destructive, but it was still punitive. The tax paid between 1939 and 1943 would double. Beatty stressed on 18 March 1940:

> ... disposable profit per ton in the hands of the mines is now only slightly greater than before the Union left the gold standard. Expansion has therefore been primarily responsible for the increase in total dividends dis-

366

tributed and investors have financed the expansion. ... This was not done by a stroke of the pen, nor was it entirely fortuitous.[10]

A year later P M Anderson returned again to the fray:

> The extent to which gold mining shareholders are contributing to the public purse, and the policy of differentiation between classes of tax-payers, are not fully appreciated in some quarters. ... As individuals in the State they are bearing their share of all forms of taxation, direct and indirect, according to their means, just as other individuals; but it is a mistake to assume that they are all rich people. The great majority of them indeed are not, yet they are singled out for differential treatment .... In taxing them as a class, rich and poor alike, at an exceedingly high rate, higher indeed than the Super Tax rate, there is complete departure from the principle of the individual's capacity to pay.[11]

However, neither at war nor in peace have the Chamber's pleas done more than ameliorate the State's propensity to plunder gold mining profits to finance a widening bureaucracy and escalating expenditure.

Early in 1939, the Chamber foresaw the coming of war, and made some provision for the procurement and stockpiling of the needs of mines. Its representatives established a liaison with the Department of Commerce and Industries. On the outbreak of hostilities the GPC appointed a Mines Stores Sub-Committee to watch over supplies to the mines, in collaboration with the National Supplies Control Board. An increasing emphasis was placed on the conservation of mining equipment and of economy in its use.

As soon as the 'phoney war' of the winter of 1939-1940 was over, and the fighting began in Western Europe, the Chamber was informed by the Government that gold was regarded as a munition of war and that its production should not only be maintained but if possible increased. The industry was placed on a war-time basis, and eliminated all services regarded as non-essential.[12] It also curtailed underground development where this could be done without affecting the maintenance of production.

In the 1914-1918 War Britain had decided that gold mining was of strategic importance to the Allies, and it had been appreciated that the mines would need to import equipment to maintain operations. The situation was by no means as clear in the 1939-1945 War. In particular, the American view on gold was being increasingly influenced by a new generation of economists who rejected the special importance of gold in the monetary system. The American Government was thus sceptical about the need to accord Allied shipping space to gold mining equipment. However, despite difficulties and shortages, the industry succeeded in keeping its mines in being. It was helped in maintaining some priority in supply by its role as a manufacturer of munitions.

In February 1940 the Government asked the Chamber if it could assist in producing weapons of war. The Chamber set up a Munitions Production

Committee under George Beatty to co-operate with the Director-General of War Supplies. A total of forty-five mine workshops was soon in production.

> Mine artisans ... turned out bombs of all sizes up to 1 000 lb. They made shells of all descriptions, parts for guns and howitzers and finally the guns themselves. When the crisis in the Middle East was at its height in 1941 they turned out millions of spare parts for tanks which were rushed to Cairo. In time the artisans in the mine workshops supervised some five hundred women employed in the manufacture of munitions.

> It was an invaluable contribution to the war effort. Tank spares and anti-tank guns made on the Witwatersrand played their part in the defeat of Rommel in the desert.[13]

It was decided by the GPC that the output of munitions from mine workshops would be on a non-profit basis. The Government paid only the wages of those employed, plus five per cent on overheads. All stores and materials were charged at cost, and no charge was made for administrative and secretarial work.

As in 1914, the mining companies were at once confronted with demands from employees to be allowed to volunteer for active service. It was agreed with the Department of Defence that the industry should retain enough men to maintain production, and that employees classified as 'key men' should not be called up for military service. With this proviso, it was agreed that as many as possible should be given military training. By the end of the War, between 11 000 and 12 000 officials and union men had served in the armed forces (though, fortunately, not all at the same time). More than 500 were killed or died on active service. Many blacks, who might have returned to the mines, opted instead to join military units which enlisted them in non-combatant, but sometimes hazardous, roles.

At the outset, the Chamber provided that officials released for training, or for active service, should receive full mine salaries for sixty days, in addition to army pay. Union men had their military pay made up to mine pay for the first sixty days. Thereafter, all married men, whether officials or union men, would receive an allowance of half mine salary or wages. Single men were paid a quarter, but those with dependants could get up to half. Military service was counted as pensionable service for the Provident Fund.[14]

Early in 1940 the Chamber was asked to form a voluntary engineering unit for mine employees who had been refused permission to volunteer for full-time military service. It was foreseen that the unit could have a vital role to play if there were a direct threat to South Africa.[15] In the event, many of its members would serve far beyond the country's borders. Colonel Spencer Fleischer, a Gold Fields manager and future Chamber President, a man of warm personality and a lively sense of humour, was appointed to raise and command the unit, designated the Mines Engineering Brigade of the South

African Engineering Corps.[16] In 1941, a company of the Brigade was established as the 61st Tunnelling Company and sent to Syria to complete the Chekka and Ras Bayada tunnels on the new strategic railway. It also constructed an irrigation tunnel. Thereafter, it was re-organized and sent to render distinguished service elsewhere in the Mediterranean theatre of war.[17]

In 1942 the South African forces suffered a crippling blow with the surrender of the 2nd South African Division in Tobruk to General Rommel. Smuts appealed for 7 000 fresh volunteers to 'avenge Tobruk'. In response a further 1 200 key men were released from the mines, as well as fifty-six mechanics in metal trades for posting to tank recovery and tank repair units in the North African Desert. Most of the new volunteers came from the Mines Engineering Brigade.[18] The industry additionally released men for work in war industries, including ship repairing; it also released men to work in Northern Rhodesia (Zambia), to boost war production in the copper mines there. The mines took on the repair of South African Railways trucks as well.[19]

As the War reached its nadir for the Allies in mid-1942, difficulties of procuring supplies overseas and obtaining shipping for them were intensified. The Union Government appointed Controllers of the various key commodities, and new burdens of coping with war-time controls were placed on the Chamber. The GPC appointed one of its members, C Stowe McLean, as the Chairman of the Stores Sub-Committee with A Tracey Milne, the Chief Buyer of Union Corporation, as Deputy-Chairman. At the same time, the Chamber set up a Mines Stores Department, and the mines agreed to pool supplies. New urgent directives, and guidance, were issued on the conservation of stores, and the reclamation of used material. As a result, substantial savings in consumption and in shipping space were achieved, particularly in the shipment and use of steel, oil and rubber. A stores committee for the collieries was formed, under the chairmanship of 'Kenny' Richardson of JCI, who was also to chair the Collieries Committee until 1948, and to serve as well on the GPC from 1946. Post-war, he would be twice President of the Chamber.[20] The collieries were to play an important war-time role in providing bunkering coal for ships, and boosting coal supplies to Allied war industries.

Throughout the War the mining industry and its employees were major contributors to war funds, the lists lengthening and the amounts escalating year by year. Top mining men played a major role in organizing fund drives. By end 1942 official donations by mining companies through the Chamber totalled £400 000.

Under conditions of war the Chamber at first maintained its opposition to cost-of-living allowances. But as living costs rose the precedent of granting allowances was conceded in other industries and accepted by the Government.[21] The Chamber accordingly agreed with the MUJC in May 1941 that an allowance should be paid and increased with the rise in the Retail Price Index. In September the allowance was extended to officials.[22]

As living costs rose, the wages of blacks in industries other than mining were raised in a series of determinations under the Wages Act. The Chamber did not follow suit, claiming that the fixed gold price made it impossible to pass these rises on to the consumer, as other industries could and did; and that it could not follow the example of other industries unless the scope of work the black worker was allowed to do was materially enlarged.[23]

However, dissatisfaction among black mineworkers was reflected in the emergence in 1941 of the African Mine Workers' Union, under the vigorous direction of the Chairman of the ANC in the Transvaal, S P Matseke, and two communist members of the ANC executive.[24] The Government responded by war-time decrees that strikes by black mineworkers were illegal, and by appointing, on 5 March 1943, a commission of inquiry under the Hon C W H Lansdown, Judge-President of the Eastern Districts Local Division of the Supreme Court, to inquire into black pay on the gold mines.[25] The Commission recommended an increase of 5d per shift plus 3d cost-of-living allowance and other benefits. The Commission also recommended the recognition of black trade unions in principle. However, it found against recognition of the African Mine Workers' Union because no movement had emanated from the mineworkers themselves, who had been manipulated by Communists.[26]

After considering its report, the Government directed that the wages of black mineworkers, then averaging about 2s 3d a day, plus free food, lodging and medical care, should be raised by 4d a shift for surface workers and 5d a shift for those employed underground. In future, black workers on overtime would be paid at time-and-a-half like white miners. The rise, which was less in money terms than Lansdown had recommended, seems insignificant in relation to black miners' pay today. However, in announcing the increase on 24 March 1944, Smuts accepted that the additional cost burden on the gold mines would have serious consequences, both for the industry and the country.[27] The wage bill for black mineworkers rose by twenty per cent between 1943 and 1945. The Government at first offset most of the cost by remitting the gold realization charges paid by the mines to the State. This, however, fell away when the gold price rose at the War's end.

The main burden of leadership of the Chamber during the War was shouldered by Beatty, Anderson, Carleton Jones, Unger, who played an important role in the rise of Anglo American, and W H A Lawrence, John Martin's right-hand man at the Corner House and his post-war successor. Lawrence was a man of retiring disposition who disliked public occasions and 'was not given to more words than were strictly necessary when called upon for speeches'.[28] His Presidential Addresses to the Chamber were models of brevity.

Inevitably, the draining away of employees, shortage of supplies, curtailment of development and other problems arising from the War, brought a downturn in mining operations. The peak was reached as early as 1941 when more than fourteen million ounces of gold were produced. Thereafter, production fell away, and the 1941 peak would not be attained again until 1955.

In reviewing 1943, Unger reflected that the industry's full committal to the prosecution of the War involved increasing embarrassment to the operations of the mines. Tons milled compared with the previous year fell by 7 million, and gold output was down by 1,3 million ounces. Revenue and profit were lower, working profit being down £6 million and dividends £2,25 million. 'In all the circumstances we were of course, prepared for this constriction of our fortunes ....'[29] The trend continued in 1944, with Lawrence reporting decline under all heads, except working costs, and commenting gloomily: 'A position of this kind is, of course, inseparable from a state of war. A nation at war grows steadily less prosperous ....'[30]

The final months of the War brought, very much behind the scenes, the events that signalled South Africa's entry into the nuclear era. Smuts telephoned Stowe McLean, who had just become President for the first time, to come to Pretoria on a matter of urgent national importance. McLean later recorded: ' ... I found that he wished to ascertain the magnitude of uranium deposits in the Witwatersrand ores and how these deposits could best be developed.'[31] Smuts gave him information of the utmost confidentiality.

The United States 'Manhattan Project', set up under top secret security wraps, had produced the atomic bomb that was soon to devastate Hiroshima and Nagasaki and bring the end of the war with Japan. The genie was out of the bottle. Its first presentation to mankind as death and destruction on a scale undreamed of, would long cloud its beneficial use as a new, abundant source of energy.

Enough uranium for the first atomic explosions was available in deposits in Canada and the Belgian Congo (Zaire). However, it suddenly became important to the West to locate overall availability, and the search focused on South Africa. It had long been known that radioactive minerals occurred there, and this was the subject of a paper to the Geological Society in 1915 by Dr A W Rodgers, the Director of the Geological Survey. At that time the first splitting of the atom was still to be achieved, but Robert Kotzé, then Government Mining Engineer, showed prescience in commenting on Rodgers's paper:

> In addition to the valuable scientific results obtained from such radioactive elements, results that appear likely in the course of time to revolutionize chemistry as well as the production of energy and indeed possibly the whole fabric of our present-day civilization, the application of these elements in medicine is of extreme interest and value.[32]

However, such minerals were dismissed as of no particular interest at the time. In the same academic vein, R A Cooper, a Corner House metallurgist, reported, in 1923, in a paper to the Chemical, Metallurgical and Mining Society of South Africa the presence of uraninite in Rand concentrates. Twenty years later Dr G W Bain, Professor of Geology at Amherst College, Massachusetts, visited South Africa and took back samples of Rand ores to add to his mineral collection. When America entered the War, Bain was asked to join the Manhattan Project. It became his task to describe possible sources of uranium in the world, and the routine cataloguing of all available information brought Cooper's paper on Rand concentrates to the surface. Bain then recalled the Rand ore samples in his mineral collection. A Geiger counter showed them to be radioactive.

As a consequence, an American geologist, Weston Bourret, was sent to South Africa on a top secret mission, and spent four months examining samples without revealing special interest or purpose. He has recorded in a letter to the author:

> I was sent to South Africa by the joint British-American uranium commission in mid 1943 to sample and evaluate the uranium tailings passing over Wilfley tables in the gravity circuits of the many old mills that employed stamp batteries instead of the standard all-slime ballmill circuits now in use.
>
>   I think the only South African privy to this study was Field Marshal Jan Smuts, who for security reasons was asked to hold this information 'top secret'.[33]

The next step in the proving of South Africa's uranium resources brought McLean hurrying to the Prime Minister's office. There he learned of an official approach to the Union by the United States Government for permission to investigate the extraction of uranium oxide from Rand gold mines. This would be followed by a second visit of geologists from the United States and the United Kingdom in 1945, headed by Bain and Dr C F Davidson, Chief Geologist of the Atomic Energy Division of the Geological Survey of Great Britain. The result was a sampling and ore-testing programme carried out jointly in the Government Metallurgical Laboratory in South Africa, and its counterparts in the United States and Britain. Davidson completed his report with the statement:

> Present evidence appears to indicate that the Rand may be one of the largest low-grade uranium fields in the world.[34]

Seven years later would follow inauguration of the first producer in what was soon to become a nuclear fuel industry vital to the West. It was based on the extraction of uranium oxide from materials formerly discarded as a waste product by the reduction plants of gold mines.

[1] Annual Report of the Transvaal Chamber of Mines, 1939, p 39.

[2] Davenport, p 232.

[3] *Ibid*, p 233.

[4] 'The Chamber of Mines: 50th Anniversary to-day', *The Star*, 10 October 1939.

[5] 'Fifty Years of Progress', *Rand Daily Mail*, 11 October 1939.

[6] Chamber of Mines Archives: File 49 1939: 'Internal', No 92. (Transvaal Chamber of Mines: Extract from Letter to London dated 5th July 1939.)

[7] 'William Gemmill "died with his boots on"', *The Star*, 30 October 1961.

[8] Wilson, p 95.

[9] Annual Report of the Transvaal Chamber of Mines, 1939, pp 52, 53-54.

[10] *Ibid*, p 54.

[11] Annual Report of the Transvaal Chamber of Mines, 1940, p 60.

[12] *Ibid*, p 35.

[13] Cartwright, *The Gold Miners*, pp 282-283.

[14] Annual Report of the Transvaal Chamber of Mines, 1939, pp 40, 41.

[15] Annual Report of the Transvaal Chamber of Mines, 1940, p 36.

[16] 'Spencer Richard Fleischer' in *Mining Men: 1910-1960*, p 38. (Transvaal and Orange Free State Chamber of Mines.)

[17] Fifty-Fourth Annual Report of the Transvaal Chamber of Mines, 1943, p 35.

[18] Fifty-Third Annual Report of the Transvaal Chamber of Mines, 1942, p 32.

[19] Annual Report of the Transvaal Chamber of Mines, 1942, pp 33, 34, 49. Annual Report of the Transvaal Chamber of Mines, 1943, p 37.

[20] Annual Report of the Transvaal Chamber of Mines, 1942, pp 38, 41.

[21] Annual Report of the Transvaal Chamber of Mines, 1940, pp 87-93.

[22] Fifty-Second Annual Report of the Transvaal Chamber of Mines, 1941, pp 28-29.

[23] Annual Report of the Transvaal Chamber of Mines, 1943, pp 53-54.

[24] Davenport, p 242.

[25] Wilson, pp 77-78.

[26] Davenport, p 242.

[27] Fifty-Fifth Annual Report of the Transvaal Chamber of Mines, 1944, p 25.

[28] Cartwright, *Golden Age*, p 305.

[29] Annual Report of the Transvaal Chamber of Mines, 1943, p 52.

[30] Annual Report of the Transvaal Chamber of Mines, 1944, p 56.

[31] C S McLean, 'The Uranium Industry of South Africa', *Journal of the Chemical, Metallurgical and Mining Society of South Africa*, Volume 54, No 10, April 1954, p 346.

[32] Cartwright, *The Gold Miners*, pp 285-286.

[33] Letter dated 13 January 1984, from Dr Weston Bourret, Pauma Valley, California, USA, to the author.

[34] Cartwright, *The Gold Miners*, p 289.

CHAPTER THIRTY

The Turmoil of Peace

South Africa emerged from the War in fairly good shape. Her territory had not been devastated like so many other Allied and enemy countries. Manufacturing industries had grasped the opportunities of war-time to begin the prodigious growth that would continue post-war. The increase in the public debt was modest, and foreign debt had been largely eliminated. Smuts was enabled to make an £80 million loan in gold to war-torn Britain at an interest of one-half per cent.[1] The loan would, incidentally, prove to be good business, for Britain, having spent nearly half of it on South African agricultural produce, would repay in three years. In 1947 the ailing J H Hofmeyr, Minister of Finance, who had borne much of the burden of wartime government, could declare that South Africa had met the financial revolution caused by the War with greater comparative success than any other belligerent. The change-over from war to peace was rapid, demobilization was reasonably smooth, and the economy soon resumed its pre-war momentum.[2] However, the gold mines were being inexorably squeezed between war-time inflation and a gold price that had fallen far behind its previous purchasing power. Moreover, the country faced momentous and daunting problems of human relations, poverty and housing. If the economic indicators, other than gold mining, were set relatively fair, the political outlook was stormy. Stowe McLean, in his review of the year that saw the transition from war to peace, declared that it was not possible to regard the post-war world as peaceful. 'There is a spirit of unrest abroad; this spirit ... is now manifesting itself in the Industry.'[3]

McLean was to be a dominating figure in the Chamber in the post-war years. He was a tough Canadian of bounding energy who enjoyed life to the full. He was also a man of vision who could make up his mind quickly and act immediately when the situation demanded. In reminiscent mood in later life, he would recall that when at school in Canada he won in his penultimate year the silver medal awarded for the best scholar. He was then in line for the gold medal given in the final year, but his teacher was a parson with a flaming temper. One day, the temper was irrevocably lost as the teacher seized a metal blind rod to belabour a recalcitrant pupil. 'As he raised the rod above his head,' McLean recalled, 'I could see that he was going to kill the boy. I stepped inside his guard with an uppercut and knocked him cold. I didn't get the gold medal.

It was very unfair. It put me off parsons for a long time.'[4]

Apart from being a shrewd businessman, McLean was a man who believed in luck, and was superstitious about following it. He would never pursue a course of action when the pricking of his thumbs dictated otherwise. He landed in South Africa on the tenth day of the tenth month of 1910, and found a good omen in this coincidence of numbers. Outside the business arena, he loved to gamble for lively stakes. After a spell on the Rand he got a job on the Lonely Mine in Rhodesia and won so much money at poker that he did not have to draw his pay for two years.[5] After the 1922 Strike, McLean, who had been working on the Rand as a highly-paid contract miner, switched back to official status. In 1923 he was sent to manage the struggling West Rand Consolidated Mines at Krugersdorp. His brief was simple – 'Close the mine within six months'. The senior officials were already looking for other jobs.

Soon after arrival the new Manager walked through an underground station and saw a group of whites sitting, drinking tea and chatting. When he returned some while later they were still there and he remarked: 'Funny time for a party.'

One of them said: 'Who the hell does he think he is?'

McLean said: 'Go to the Time Office and when you take your discharge you will find out who he is.'

Later the Chief Electrician came pleading that McLean had sacked his best electrician and he could not replace him.[6]

McLean became known as 'Mussolini' McLean to the men, but he took a keen interest in every person on the mine, including the children, and made it his business to find out about them.[7] Mine people came to regard him with respectful affection because though a demanding manager, who was determined to have his own way, he was fair, and understood every facet of the mining life from personal experience. These attributes he would carry into the policy councils of the Chamber, and into top-level negotiations with trade unions.

McLean revitalized West Rand Cons, and it has not closed yet. He remained Manager until 1936, and the mine would still be producing gold and uranium fifty years later. Krugersdorp regarded him as its saviour because the town depended for its economic life on the mine, and named a park after him in the main street. He took pride in making West Rand Cons a safe mine to work in and never lost his love of it. When he went to head office, even when he became Chairman of the General Mining and Finance Corporation, he kept in his office up-to-date plans of the mine in a detail usually only studied by subordinate underground officials.

H V Solomon, a post-war Manager of West Rand Cons, confessed to McLean's wife, Olive, that, faced with important decisions at his desk, he could always sense McLean peering over his shoulder, saying: 'Don't you bugger up my mine.'

The move to head office in 1936 did not change the essential McLean. He and Carleton Jones shook their less hardy colleagues by donning skates and turning out to play ice hockey with a visiting Canadian team during the Empire Exhibition of that year; and he would continue to be a keen tennis player into a vigorous old age. He never lost the love of gambling. During the War he was said to have raised huge sums for the war effort in many ways, including a high-powered roulette game with himself at the wheel. He was a keen and highly competent bridge player, often playing with equally tough top mining characters, including 'Peter' Carleton Jones, 'Kenny' Richardson, R Bein Hagart, a Deputy Chairman of Anglo American, and 'Slip' Menell, joint-chief of Anglo Vaal. Sometimes policy was 'hatched' over the bridge table. Chamber officials learned to watch warily, and to say to themselves: 'Hallo, what's up now!' as new ideas, coined at the bridge table, appeared 'out of the blue' at the huge oak table at which the GPC sat.

In March 1946 McLean found himself faced with a crippling strike by white miners, involving heavy loss to the mines. The strike resulted from an internal dispute in the MWU. McLean told the Chamber's Annual General Meeting:

> The fact that we who control the Industry were in no way responsible for this development is cold comfort indeed.[8]

The strike arose from the expulsion from the MWU of one of its members who had refused to pay arrear subscriptions. The MWU at once demanded that his employer, Durban Roodepoort Deep, should dismiss him on the grounds that he was not a member of a prescribed union, and the mine management, in terms of the closed shop agreement, had no option but to comply. The rank and file of the Union were incensed by the arbitrary action of their Executive, and within twenty-four hours 700 of them came out on strike. In the week that followed, increasing numbers of miners joined the movement until, finally, every mine was affected and ninety-five per cent had stopped work.[9]

The Chamber, in terms of its agreement with the MUJC, had no grounds on which to intervene. The Government, however, decided to do so and sent Ivan Walker, the former trade union leader who was Labour Adviser to the Prime Minister, accompanied by Brigadier F L A Buchanan, Secretary of Labour, to resolve the dispute. The background to the strike was widespread dissatisfaction among miners with the autocratic and unbusinesslike manner in which the MWU was run. Walker found it necessary to invoke war emergency legislation to stop the strike. He appealed successfully to the GPC to waive the penalties the men had incurred through their break in service. The strike settlement that followed provided for the appointment of a commission of inquiry into the administration of the MWU, and the holding of elections.[10]

In September 1944 the Chamber, under pressure to settle a long, drawn-out dispute over wages, had agreed, unwisely, to make available to the MWU the sum of £100 000 per annum for five years, plus an immediate £25 000, for assistance towards housing, co-operative or other schemes. The schemes were to be agreed to mutually by the Chamber and the Union, for the benefit of

376

members of the MWU. Members of the MUJC other than the MWU received a medical benefit allowance of equivalent cost.

The MWU had in operation a housing scheme, run in co-operation with building societies, but later introduced co-operative farming schemes with the intention of making farm produce available to members at cost price. In the event, neither scheme was effectively operated, and after the strike it was found that a great deal of the money made available to the Union up to that time had been frittered away, and a good portion lost through maladministration.[11]

The Commission of Inquiry reported on 27 May 1946 that there was obviously strong and bitter feeling among the members towards the Executive Committee and officials of the Union generally, and to the General Secretary, B B Brodrick, in particular. It also found that the Executive Committee was not functioning properly from an administrative point of view. Opposition to it culminated in the adoption of a resolution of 'no confidence' at a meeting of the General Council on 1 May 1946, and in the dismissal of Brodrick.[12]

The Commission then appointed an interim executive committee pending new elections. However, the troubles were by no means over. Six months later, elections were not complete and a dispute over which faction should take control led to a declaration of a strike by a contending group on 27 January 1947. The strike again spread rapidly, and in the course of a few days the operation of many mines was seriously impaired and all mines were affected to a greater or lesser degree. The Chamber declared that the strike, of a type known in the United States as 'jurisdictional', was a new development in South Africa, and estimated the cost of the strike, which endured for seven weeks, as running into millions.[13]

> ... the nine trade unions representing the views of the Industry's artisans and tradesmen and, in addition, the South African Trades and Labour Council, expressing the views of other trade union members, made it clear that they considered this essentially a union dispute calling for intervention by neither the Industry nor the Government. The Industry had to pay the piper without being able to call any sort of tune.
>
> But it must be clear that neither the country, nor the Industry, can afford repetitions of this internecine strife between opposing factions of a trade union.[14]

As strife continued, the Reformers finally won control of the Union in 1948 and Daan E Ellis became General Secretary. Ellis, an able man of strong personality, had been at one time a miner. From 1943 to 1949 he was a town councillor in Nigel, becoming mayor from 1945 to 1946. Prior to his appointment as General Secretary of the MWU, he was a so-called welfare officer employed by the *Nasionale Raad van Trustees*, which had financed the Reformers in the MWU. There he worked under the direction of Dr Albert Hertzog. Ellis, and others working for the *Nasionale Raad*, amalgamated with an action committee on the mines and succeeded in obtaining the election of their candidates. Ellis took over and appeared to have done a lot of good work in bringing the affairs of the Union into order out of 'something like chaos'. He became 'very much … of a dictator', ruling the Mine Workers' Union with an iron hand.[15]

However, Ellis and the new hierarchy would in turn have to face a commission of inquiry in 1951 resulting from criticism of the Union's conduct of the purchase, eighteen months previously, of Transafrika House in Harrison Street as a permanent headquarters for the Union. The Union had paid £176 000 which included, by agreement, the balance of £108 000 due by the Chamber to the Union. Dr Hertzog was co-opted on the Executive of the MWU which decided on an internal inquiry, which in turn recommended that the Government be asked to appoint a judicial commission of inquiry. The commission reported on 7 July 1951 that, after examining the negotiations to purchase, it was of the opinion that the building could probably have been purchased at a much lower figure than that which was paid if the matter had been dealt with in a more businesslike manner. On the other hand, the commission found that the building was worth more than had been paid for it.[16]

The commission recommended amendments to the Constitution to provide new controls on expenditure. Ellis survived the searching scrutiny of his role to play a major part in industrial relations. He is remembered as a convivial man whose remarkable capacity for Scotch whisky in no way hampered his shrewd management of union affairs. The Union benefited, too, from his seemingly instant access to ministerial offices in promoting the cause of the miners.

A positive development on the employment scene that followed the War was the establishment of an officials' pension fund. In publicly announcing the decision in March 1946, McLean recalled the referendum on the mines in 1934 which had resulted in the rejection of a proffered contributory scheme. He said that the GPC had become aware that the referendum result did not reflect the view of officials, who were in fact in favour of a contributory pension scheme. The Mine Officials Pension Fund was duly established on a basis of a contribution of five per cent of monthly salary from officials matched initially £ for £ by employers. Contribution rates would thereafter be substantially increased. A similar fund for union men was begun in September 1949. In addition to pensions from the funds, officials and union men would continue to receive lump sum retirement benefits from the Witwatersrand Gold Mine Employees Provident Fund. Collieries had joined the Provident Fund in 1940, and their employees were made eligible to join the new pension funds on their formation.

It is forgotten in modern times, when contributory pension funds are a commonplace fringe benefit of employment, that private pension and provident schemes were a comparative rarity before the War, and that the GPC's establishment of pension funds post-war was something of a pace-setter in industry. It is not always appreciated either that the amount of pension payable is a direct reflection of length of service and accumulated contributions, and that it takes time and unbroken membership before pension entitlements of appropriate amounts can be provided by a pension fund. It would be years before miners, even those who did not break service, could retire with significant pensions; and those with pre-war service would certainly get much less than would have been payable if a contributory scheme had been accepted in 1934. However, the Mine Officials Pension Fund and the Mine Employees Pension Fund, whose Boards are equally representative of the Chamber, officials' associations and the unions, would, with the passage of time, build up assets that would rival those of major insurance companies. In 1984-1985 the assets of the pension funds, and the benefits payable, would be increased by the transfer to them of the assets of the Provident Fund which would be phased out in 1986. In that year the market value of assets was expected to exceed R3 billion. The funds became large enough, in company with other financial institutions, to influence the day-by-day market in equities, and are substantial investors in property.

In 1946, less than a year after the Peace, the industry was faced with the first serious strike among the black labour force for more than twenty-five years. It occurred against a background of country-wide protest against the Pass Laws, threats of the mass burning of passes, and protest against the rising cost of living aggravated by food shortages and near-famine that plagued the country in the aftermath of war. Changes in the scale of food provided for mineworkers, and reductions in the maize and beer components, fuelled unrest on the mines. And so did losses from the failure of the maize crop through drought in the tribal territories, and increases in taxes in Basutoland (Lesotho).[17] The African Mine Workers' Union, in concert with the Communist Party, found ready listeners to their call for united protest against the low level of wages. However, the response was partial, and many blacks would be bewildered spectators or unwilling participants in the unrest that followed. Others left for home to avoid impending trouble.[18]

A meeting of 2 000 delegates of the Union at the Trades Hall in Johannesburg on 14 April 1946 called for a minimum wage of 10s a day, the minimum daily cash wage then paid being 2s 5d for underground work, and the average 2s 8,3d. The motion cited the 'almost superhuman labour performed by the African Miners, the high cost of living and the terribly low wages'.[19] It was submitted to the Chamber on 3 May 1946, and acknowledged by printed card saying the matter was receiving attention. The Chamber did not recognize the Union which it did not consider to be representative, and did not usually reply to its letters, it being the responsibility of mine managers, WNLA and NRC inspectors, and Native Commissioners, to respond directly by addressing black workers on the mines.

The men were duly informed that their wages could not be increased. They were reminded that they had contracted to work at current rates. When the contracts expired they would be free to return home but until then they were bound by them. The unrest continued with the Communist Party active in support of the Union. The Chamber continued to monitor the unfolding situation, while the Government and the Police followed, as far as possible, a hands-off policy. There was a rash of minor strikes, accompanied by some stoning of those who sought to go to work and some stoning of the police called to quell violence, or to protect those who wished to return to work.[20]

On 8 May the Chamber warned S F Waterson, the Minister of Mines, of the danger of serious disturbances. The idea had become prevalent among mineworkers that the Government supported the Union's demand, and that their increase was being blocked by the Chamber.[21] At the Chamber's request the Secretary for Native Affairs, G Mears, issued a denial that the Government favoured a further increase in wages following those recently granted by the Lansdown Commission.[22] There were further incidents in July; and sections of the workforce became truculent and an increasingly ugly mood was evident. However, a meeting of the Union in Benoni Market Square on 21 July attracted only a hundred blacks.[23] On 4 August about a thousand attended a meeting at Newtown Market Square in Johannesburg, and called for a general strike on all Reef mines on Monday, 12 August.[24] The Chamber estimated the number of mineworkers present as at around two hundred. J B Marks, the President of the Union, warned black mineworkers to hold their meetings quietly and not to attempt to break up the kitchens and the compound managers' offices as they had done on previous occasions. They must not start shouting their battle cry whenever they saw a policeman.[25]

The called-for strike duly followed on 12 August and lasted for four days. During that time, some 60 000 of the 300 000 blacks on the mines refused to work for varying periods, bringing nine mines to a standstill and partially affecting eight others.[26] At about 9 am on the first day police arrested three speakers for holding an illegal meeting on the New Kleinfontein mine. Soon after, 4 500 black workers surrounded the police station at Benoni and demanded the release of the prisoners. They were eventually dispersed by baton charge. On the Tuesday, the most serious incident so far took place when strikers attacked police at Sub Nigel who were escorting to shafts those who had offered to return to work.[27] Trouble had been brewing at the mine since the previous morning when police made arrests but were forced by threatening blacks to release their prisoners. A force of 100 police returned to the mine but withdrew at dark to avoid a clash with hostile workers. The next morning a force of 140 police returned, of whom sixteen of the most senior carried firearms. The force was confronted by strikers armed with whatever weapons they could lay their hands on. Eight policemen were injured by stones. The police fired twelve revolver shots and eight strikers were wounded, one of whom subsequently died. The strikers fled in panic, trampling four of their number to death in a stampede through the compound gates. The police then seized truckloads of weapons such as sticks, sledgehammers, steel balls, iron bars and knives.[28]

The same day 4 000 strikers, armed with a variety of weapons, attempted to march on Johannesburg from West Springs mine. They were intercepted

380

by the police at Brakpan, and after refusing to turn back, were forcibly dispersed, three of them being seriously injured. Similar columns of workers set off from Simmer and Jack mine and were dispersed by the police near the City Deep mine. Detectives from Marshall Square now arrested J B Marks, the President of the Union, under the Riotous Assemblies Act.[29]

The strike ended after four days, twenty-eight of the forty-five mines on the Reef having been unaffected by it. Nine strikers died, including the four trampled to death and one from gunshot wounds through the thighs. Three hundred and ten were admitted to hospital, and many more were treated for minor injuries in mine dressing stations.[30] It has been claimed that the response of the Government was to hit back at the strikers and that the Police were used to crush them.[31] The contemporary record suggests however that the Government was slow to intervene, while the inquest magistrate found that the Police acted with commendable restraint. The *Rand Daily Mail* commented:

> The people who come best out of the affair are the police. Their task was dangerous, tricky and arduous; and they did it extraordinarily well. The measure of their success can be judged by the relative smallness of the casualty list. Anyone could have suppressed this outbreak with heavy bloodshed; it took good policemen to protect the public at so small a cost in life and injury to the primitive tribesmen who have come under the 'guidance' of a western-model trade union.[32]

In similar vein, Carleton Jones paid a tribute to the compound managers and their staffs for their handling of a difficult and delicate situation.[33]

Otherwise comment on the strike was mixed. The National Party newspapers, *Die Burger* and *Die Transvaler*, predictably, blamed the strike on the Smuts Government's failure to suppress Communism. Equally predictably, the Labour Party protested against the Government's brutal suppression of the strike. The *Rand Daily Mail* on 13 August described the strike as a foolish one. It claimed that no newspaper in South Africa had regarded black aspirations more favourably than the *Rand Daily Mail* or been more insistent on a fair deal for the black population. It was precisely because of this sympathy, the desire that blacks should achieve a better position in the community, that it did not hesitate to condemn the strike.

> It was not to be supposed that South Africa could altogether escape her share of the industrial troubles which have been sweeping over the world after the war. ... It is strange, however, that it has taken just this form. For one thing, the mine workers are infinitely better off than most natives ... ... the natives' grievances about food, in so far as they are substantial at all ... are not due to any fault on the part of the Chamber of Mines but are the consequences of generally prevailing conditions which cannot be altered by anyone .... These are hard if unwelcome facts, which make success for the strikers out of the question.[34]

The Star however saw the failure to implement the Lansdown Commission's recommendations as the starting point of the trouble. On the subject of trade unionism *The Star* pointed out that operation of unions as practised elsewhere was difficult to apply to migrant labour. The Lansdown Commission had considered that black mineworkers had not reached the stage of development which would enable them safely and usefully to employ trade unionism; and it recommended other means of consultation and guidance. What was certain, *The Star* said, was that some alternative must be provided to the present hole-in-corner unionism which committed the cause of the black miners to the care of those perhaps least qualified to guide them. 'The whole history of industrialism shows that merely sitting on the safety valve can cause nothing but explosion.'[35] There were similar protests about the lack of channels of consultation from a group of leading liberals headed by Mrs Margaret Ballinger, one of the Native Representatives in Parliament, with a distinguished record as an advocate of black interests. The liberal group added that the workers had serious grievances to which the Government's only answer seemed to be the use of force.

The Chamber, for its part, strenuously denied that the recommendations of the Lansdown Commission had not been adequately implemented. It stressed that while the Commission had recommended an increase in minimum rates, the Government had decided that increases should be across the board at all wage levels.

> The Commission recommended a cost of living allowance ... and an increase in *minimum* wages at a total estimated cost of £2 642 000.

> The Government decided ... not that only minimum rates should be increased but that 'the wages of *all* Native surface workers will be increased by 4d a shift and of *all* Native underground workers by 5d a shift.'

> The increased cash benefit to the Native labour force ... is estimated at a total of £2 600 000, of which £2 300 000 represents the increase in wages.

> Contrary to the frequent allegations that conditions of employment on the mines have remained static, there have been constant and considerable improvements in the lot of the Native mine labourer and, so far as the recommendations of the Lansdown Commission can be measured in cash, they have been implemented by the Government and the Chamber of Mines nearly in full.[36]

Once the strike was over blacks resumed work without further demur. There would be industrial peace for more than twenty years. The Chamber improved pay somewhat by the introduction of service increments in 1948,[37] and a rise by about ten per cent in wages in October 1949.[38] The African Mine Workers' Union was broken by the failure of the strike and faded from the scene. Nor had violence and riot furthered the case for unionism among migratory workers. The Chamber declared trade unionism to be against the best interests of tribal blacks employed on the mines. These migratory workers, the Chamber argued, were not sufficiently advanced for trade unionism, and could not be expected to understand the responsibilities placed on workers by collective bargaining; nor did the majority of workers themselves want it. Moreover, the Lansdown Commission had found that the migrant workers, many of whom were domiciled in foreign countries, did not serve for long enough periods to facilitate union organization.[39] The Chamber was expressing the prevailing opinion of most whites, and undoubtedly their view was supported by the authorities, whether in South African, British or Portuguese territories.

In a pamphlet published on the subject, the Chamber posed the question: If trade unionism is unsuitable what is the alternative? Its answer was that avenues had existed for many years by which workers could represent their views to the management on traditional lines to which they were accustomed. The chain of communication in tribal hierarchy was the chief, the *induna*, the headman and the kraal head. In the mine compound, the pattern was the compound manager, the *induna*, and the tribal representative, called the *isibonda*. Each room elected one of the occupants as their spokesman and intermediary with the *isibonda*. This apart, any worker could go direct with grievances to his compound manager, a class of official described by the Lansdown Commission as experienced and having sympathetic consideration for the welfare and comfort of men in the compound. In addition, inspectors of the NRC regularly visited compounds, and so did Government inspectors. The Chamber did not suggest that the system could not be improved. The Lansdown Commission had recommended the appointment of special officials of the Native Affairs Department to meet regularly with chosen representatives of the workers, and this proposal was supported by the Chamber. The Government appointed these Labour Officers in 1947.

The strike had undoubtedly been ill-timed from a tactical point of view, for the mines were once again in a cost-price squeeze. The problem of increasing either black or white wages, which together constituted half of working costs, was underlined by a special meeting, called on 25 October 1946, to express alarm at the rapid deterioration of the industry's position and prospects. The gold mines were in a situation of deepening crisis not dissimilar to that of 1930. Carleton Jones told the meeting that the operations on many mines were being conducted with a slender margin of profit. If the steep upward trend of costs continued, a substantial part of the industry would soon disappear, while the effect of even moderate increases in black wage rates could only be the contraction of job opportunities. The meeting endorsed his diagnosis that 'the health of the gold mining industry, the heart of the country's activity and well-being, has been and is being seriously impaired by the excessive demands being made upon it'.[40]

Against the grim economic background pictured by Carleton Jones, Smuts faced critical political problems. He was sympathetic to the grievances of blacks, and expressed the view that policy would have to be liberalized, though at a pace that could accommodate white opinion.[41] He appointed the Native Laws Commission under Mr Justice Fagan to report on the operation of laws affecting the lives of blacks, including the Pass Laws, and on the future policy to be followed on migratory labour. Its report was published in February 1948. Davenport has pointed out that it came too late to influence policy before the General Election of May that year. It contained much that was acceptable to moderate black opinion, but it offered the white electorate 'a liberal aspiration rather than a policy, and if the choice for voters was between aspirations, the Sauer Report of the Nationalists, with its early spelling out of the gospel of *apartheid*, seemed to offer more security on more familiar lines'.[42] The hopeful plans of the Fagan Commission were doomed to be still-born.

Although the Smuts Government had successfully won the war to its credit, and demobilised its military volunteers efficiently, on the domestic front some resented the slow progress of its housing programme, others the lack of tax relief for wage-earners in Hofmeyr's budgets, others the irritations of wartime controls on food distribution. More seriously, its racial policies aroused opposition. Where they were illiberal, they came under pressure at the UN. In so far as they were either liberal or unsuccessful, the Nationalists knew how to capitalise on this, and set out to convince the electorate that the UP either consorted with or was not tough enough with the Communists, and that the Communists were a danger to South Africa.[43]

On 26 May the electorate took the fateful decision that was to set the country on an uncompromising road on black-white issues for more than thirty years. Malan's National Party won the General Election by seventy seats to the United Party's sixty-five. Havenga's Afrikaner Party, in an election alliance with the Nationalists, won nine seats; and the Labour Party, in alliance with Smuts, won six. The United Party recorded a thumping majority of votes cast, but the trend was now running strongly against the United Party. The era of the Philosopher–Statesman was over, and it was to be followed by the hey-day of the social engineers and of a new army of bureaucrats, many of whom had grown up in the depression years between the Wars, and had inherited fears of loss of identity and status. In a little more than two years Smuts would die at the age of eighty in his home at Doornkloof near Pretoria, and pass from the world scene he had dominated, and graced, for so many eventful years.

After the General Election, the Chamber had once again to establish relations with a governing party which it had not bothered overmuch to cultivate during the party's wilderness years. It set about the task in an economic climate that was even worse than in 1946. In March 1948 Unger, at the end of a third term as Chamber President, reported to the Annual Meeting that working profits had more than halved since the peak year of 1941. The alarming drop had materially affected the State which had seen its revenue from mining fall steeply over the same period from £27,3 million to an estimated £6,4 million. The aggregate of dividends paid by the gold mines was the lowest paid by the industry since the Union had abandoned the gold standard in 1932.

Unger died only two months later. His death was soon followed by that of other giants of a great mining era. Carleton Jones died in December 1948, A S Hersov, co-founder of Anglo Vaal, on 15 January 1949, and John Martin on 28 March. Sadly, they did not live long enough to see the full flowering of the new mining fields they had helped to prove.

At the Chamber's Annual Meeting on 27 June 1949 McLean was able to report that the downward trend in the industry appeared at long last to have been halted as the post-war expansion got under way. The trend of recovery was soon confirmed by a momentous event in September when Britain devalued sterling, and other countries, including South Africa, but not the United States, followed by revaluing their countries' currencies, too. On 19 September, the price of an ounce of gold rose from £8 12s 6d to £12 8s 3d, an increase of nearly fifty per cent in sterling terms.[44] Unhappily the devaluation occurred, unlike that of 1932, at a time of inflation, which the increase in the sterling gold price would help to fuel further. But the take-off in profitability was exciting enough to provide the initial momentum, when it was most needed, for the grand advance of the 1950s.

[1] E A Walker, *A History of Southern Africa*, p 767.
[2] Browne, pp 143-144.
[3] Fifty-Sixth Annual Report of the Transvaal Chamber of Mines, 1945, p 58.
[4] Told to the author by the late C S McLean.
[5] Interview with Mrs Olive McLean.
[6] *Ibid.*
[7] *Ibid.*
[8] Annual Report of the Transvaal Chamber of Mines, 1945, pp 58-59.
[9] Annual Report of the Transvaal Chamber of Mines, 1945, p 58.
Fifty-Seventh Annual Report of the Transvaal Chamber of Mines, 1946, p 35.
[10] Annual Report of the Transvaal Chamber of Mines, 1945, p 58.
Annual Report of the Transvaal Chamber of Mines, 1946, p 35.
[11] Union of South Africa: Report of The Mine Workers' Union Commission of Enquiry, 1951 (UG 52/1951), p 1, paragraph 8.
[12] Union of South Africa: Report of the Mine Workers' Union Commission of Enquiry, 1946

(UG No 36 - 1946) p 4, paragraphs 30 to 33, and p 6, paragraph 51.

[13] Annual Report of the Transvaal Chamber of Mines, 1946, p 57.

[14] *Idem.*

[15] Report of The Mine Workers' Union Commission of Enquiry, 1951, p 1, paragraphs 5 and 6.

[16] *Ibid*, p 7, paragraph 26.

[17] Wilson, p 78.

Chamber of Mines Archives: File 109a 1946: 'Native Labour – Native Trade Unions – Strike (1)': Extract from Minutes of the Gold Producers' Committee, Transvaal Chamber of Mines, 29 April 1946 (No 9).

[18] Annual Report of the Transvaal Chamber of Mines, 1946, p 58.

[19] Chamber of Mines Archives: File 109a 1946: 'Native Labour – Native Trade Unions – Strike (1)': Letter dated 3 May 1946, from the Secretary, African Mine Workers' Union, Johannesburg, to the Secretary, Gold Producers' Committee, Johannesburg enclosing Resolutions passed at a Conference of African mineworkers held on 14 April 1946 (Nos 15 and 16).

[20] Chamber of Mines Archives: File 109a 1946: 'Native Labour – Native Trade Unions – Strike (1)':

Note entitled 'Native Disturbances' (No 24).

Randfontein Estates Gold Mining Company, Witwatersrand, Limited, Randfontein, Record of Native Meeting held on 5 May 1946, pp 1-2 (Nos 40 and 41).

Randfontein Estates Gold Mining Company, Witwatersrand, Limited, Randfontein, Note entitled 'Attempted Strike: Natives: South Compound at 4 30 am on Monday, 6 May 1946', pp 1-2 (Nos 42 and 43).

'Police stoned by Native Mine Strikers', *Rand Daily Mail*, 4 May 1946.

[21] Chamber of Mines Archives: File 109a 1946: 'Native Labour – Native Trade Unions – Strike (1)': Letter from the President, Transvaal Chamber of Mines, Johannesburg, to the Hon S F Waterson, Minister of Mines, Cape Town, dated 8 May 1946, pp 1-2 (Nos 46 and 47).

[22] Chamber of Mines Archives: File 109a 1946: 'Native Labour - Native Trade Unions - Strike (1)': Notice dated 17 May 1946, issued by the Department of Native Affairs (No 73).

[23] Chamber of Mines Archives: File 109a 1946: 'Native Labour - Native Trade Unions - Strike (1)': Record of meeting of African Mine Workers' Union, Benoni Market Square, on 21 July 1946, pp 1-2 (Nos 115 and 116).

[24] 'Meeting plans Native Mine Strike', *Rand Daily Mail*, 5 August 1946.

[25] *Idem.*

[26] 'All Mines back to normal', *The Star*, 16 August 1946.

Chamber of Mines Archives: File 109a 1946: 'Native Labour - Native Trade Unions - Strike (1)': Minutes of a Special Meeting of the Gold Producers' Committee, Transvaal Chamber of Mines, held on 13 August 1946, p 1 (No 171).

Chamber of Mines Archives: File 109c 1946: 'Native Labour - Native Trade Unions - Strike (3)': Schedule of Total Casualties following Strike of Mine Labourers: 12-15 August 1946 (No 76).

[27] '45 000 Natives Strike at 11 Rand Mines', *Rand Daily Mail*, 13 August 1946.

'Eight Natives Wounded, Four Trampled to Death at Sub Nigel', *Rand Daily Mail*, 14 August 1946.

'32 of 45 Rand Mines not affected by Native Strike', *The Star*, 13 August 1946.

'Police Quell Attack at Sub Nigel', *The Star*, 13 August 1946.

[28] 'Eight Natives Wounded, Four Trampled to Death at Sub Nigel', *Rand Daily Mail*, 14 August 1946.

'Police Action at Native Mine Strike Justified says Inquest Magistrate', *Rand Daily Mail*, 24 October 1946.

[29] '4 000 Strikers try to march on Johannesburg', *Rand Daily Mail*, 14 August 1946.

'Strikers intercepted on way to City and dispersed', *The Star*, 14 August 1946.

[30] Chamber of Mines Archives: File 109c 1946: 'Native Labour - Native Trade Unions - Strike (3)':

                    August 1946 Strike: Summary of Hospital Admissions, etc dated 5.12.46 (No 75).
                    Schedule of Total Casualties following Strike of Mine Labourers: 12-15 August 1946 (No 76).

'Police Action at Native Mine Strike Justified says Inquest Magistrate', *Rand Daily Mail*, 24 October 1946.

[31] See, for example, Wilson, pp 78-79.

D O'Meara, 'The 1946 African Mine-Workers' Strike in the Political Economy of South Africa', P L Bonner, ed, *Working Papers in Southern African Studies: Papers presented at the ASI African Studies Seminar*, p 207.

[32] 'Total Defeat', *Rand Daily Mail*, 17 August 1946.

[33] Annual Report of the Transvaal Chamber of Mines, 1946, pp 56, 58.

(F A Unger delivered this speech in G Carleton Jones's absence, which was caused by illness.)

[34] 'A Foolish Strike', *Rand Daily Mail*, 13 August 1946.

[35] 'Native Mine Strike', *The Star*, 14 August 1946.

[36] Chamber of Mines Archives: File 106c 1946: 'Native Labour - Miscellaneous (3)' (Native Wages Section): Press Statement attached to a Transvaal Chamber of Mines memo dated 13 March 1946, pp 1-2.

[37] Sixtieth Annual Report of the Transvaal Chamber of Mines, 1949, p 71.

[38] *Idem*.

[39] Chamber of Mines Archives: File 108 1946: 'Native Labour - Native Trade Unions':

Transvaal Chamber of Mines - Statement of the Gold Producers' Committee's Views on Native Trade Unionism within the Mining Industry, pp 1-2 (Nos 43 and 44).

Extract from the Report of the Witwatersrand Mine Natives' Wages Commission, 1943, pp 1-4 (Nos 45-48).

[40] Chamber of Mines Archives: File 64b 1946: 'Meetings of Chamber and Reports (2): Special Meeting 25.10.46': Speech made by G Carleton Jones, President, Transvaal Chamber of Mines, at a Special Meeting of the Chamber held on 25 October 1946.

[41] Davenport, pp 243-244.

[42] *Ibid*, p 245.

[43] *Ibid*, p 252.

[44] Annual Report of the Transvaal Chamber of Mines, 1949, p 64.

CHAPTER THIRTY-ONE

Lift-Off

As exploration in the Orange Free State got under way after the War there came in April 1946 a borehole result so startling that financial editors did not want to believe the Press release. Nor were they singular in their disbelief. When the result was first communicated privately to top management at Anglo American head office in Johannesburg the result was thought 'too good to be true'; and it was feared that the sample had been 'salted'.[1] There would later be, among the myriad of published results from a variety of companies, one notorious, falsified result, but the Geduld borehole assay was professional and impeccable.

A programme of drilling, unprecedented in scale, was in progress along a seventy-mile belt. The exploration teams erected their derricks and their tin shanties amid the silent immensity of the maizelands, and resumed their seemingly endless, repetitive role. But now the drills could be placed with more hopeful expectation, based on the meticulous work of their pre-war counterparts in plotting the likely location of the principal gold-bearing horizon, the Basal Reef. Diamond drilling to great depths was as ever agonizingly slow, but by it the geological pattern of a new gold-field was progressively disclosed. And from time to time an assay of a borehole core would reveal an indication of exceptional richness, none more so than that of April 1946 on the farm Geduld (Patience).

In that month a charge-hand named 'Lucky' Hewitson, at work on his thirteenth borehole, extracted, from a depth of three-quarters of a mile, a core of reef, found to contain a little over one pennyweight of gold, worth about ten shillings. The implications in terms of grade at the point where the drill intersected the Basal Reef were staggering:

The Press release on 16 April read:

About five miles south-east of Odendaalsrust, Geduld Hole 1, on the boundary between Geduld No 697 and Friedesheim No 511, which is being drilled for joint account by the Blinkpoort Gold Syndicate Ltd and Western Holdings Ltd, has intersected the Basal Reef at a depth of 3 922 feet with a true width of 18,4 inches, assaying 1 252 dwt per ton, which is equivalent to 23 037 inch-dwt. ....

Neither the Press nor anyone else had ever heard of a borehole value of 23 037 inch–dwts before.

'Check and repeat' signals flashed back to Johannesburg. 'Borehole result given as 23 037 inch–dwt. This figure obviously incorrect. Check and repeat ....'

And back came the answer '... 23 037 inch–dwt repeat 23 037 inch–dwt correct. Mining houses concerned vouch accuracy of figure.'[2]

On 25 April Ernest Oppenheimer told shareholders of the Orange Free State Investment Trust that it was now certain that a continuous gold-bearing area ran north and south through the town of Odendaalsrus in which ten or eleven large gold mines would be established.[3]

By then, the most hectic boom in gold shares the world has ever seen was in full swing. Speculation became so fevered that warnings were issued that it was wrong to assume, on the basis of isolated borehole results, that the returns of mining in the new field would be exceptionally high. But the boom ran its course and, as booms will, ended with a bust. There followed a more sober appreciation of the difficulties to be overcome in bringing the gold-field to account in the bleak economic circumstances that prevailed. It was even suggested (though not by the industry) that the upward trend in taxation, costs and wages might prevent mines from ever being opened there.[4] Share values collapsed, but despite this, the focus of attention on the field's potential created an atmosphere in which it would prove possible to raise the huge capital sums entailed. The industry would back, with its reputation and re-sources, the achievement of its exploration teams.

Oppenheimer's son, Harry, had been with the Corporation since 1931, with the exception of war years as an intelligence officer with the 4th South African Armoured Car Regiment, a frontline reconaissance unit in the Western Desert of Libya. He joined the Executive Committee of the Chamber in 1946. The previous year he had become Managing Director of Anglo American, with special responsibilities for the new gold-field. He summed up the achievement there in 1950.

The discovery of the OFS gold field ranks in importance with the two pre-vious great mineral discoveries in South Africa, that of the diamond mines in Kimberley and that of the existing Witwatersrand gold field. But, unlike these two discoveries and so many other important mineral discoveries in South Africa and elsewhere, which were found by accident or good fortune only, the OFS field was located as the result of the application of modern scientific methods of drilling to geological theory based on study of the existing Witwatersrand field and its extensions to the West.

It appears probable that the average grade of ore to be worked in the OFS will be substantially higher than the average of the existing mines ... Since the new field will come into production far faster than the old mines will drop out … bearing in mind also that production from the West Witwatersrand Areas line of mines is going to increase substantially, we may look forward in a few years' time to a much higher total gold production with all the benefits which that connotes.[5]

The first mine to be opened was Union Corporation's St Helena. It took its name from the farm on which it was located, which in turn had taken its name from a lady. (It is said that an elderly member of the Corporation's Board in London had at first presumed the mine to be on the Atlantic island.) It was brought to production in November 1951.

By then, however, Anglo American were the clear leaders in the new field. Pre-war exploration by the Group and its associates had not been successful. By 1940 the Group had, perforce, allowed its options to lapse, and was virtually out of the Free State exploration scenario. Ernest Oppenheimer continued to be wide-awake however to the potential and when opportunities arose, as always he moved fast to grasp them. The Group had struggled to survive the collapse of the diamond and copper markets during the Great Depression, but since 1933 had moved steadily to the fore, and was now set to become the most powerful of the mining houses.

Following the death of Sir Abe Bailey in 1940, Oppenheimer secured control of South African Townships, and thereby the controlling interest in Western Holdings. Not unimportantly for the future, South African Townships held large coal interests as well. Oppenheimer followed this by obtaining control of the African and European Investment Corporation which held important options on farms south of Odendaalsrus. Anglo was back in the Free State.

From this strong base, Anglo American took a firm position in the complexity of companies with interests in the field. It was thus enabled to bring to production six large mines in the period between the end of 1951 and the beginning of 1956, and to participate in others. In the same period, the other mining houses added another five large mines. As on the West Wits Line there was much inter-Group participation in mobilizing the huge capital sums needed to finance the biggest shaft-sinking programme in mining history.

None of this development was easily achieved, for the new field would exemplify not only the rewards of mining investment, but its inherent risks. Some mines encountered vast inrushes of brackish water, and there were problems of methane gas in others. The progressive increase in the temperature of rock at depth, the geothermic gradient, was higher than on the Rand, complicating the ventilation of the workings and the cooling of mine air. There were huge dykes of igneous rock intruding where payable reef might have been expected, and inconsistencies in the payability of the reef; some grades were so persistently low as to dash the hopes aroused by borehole results. Not all mines floated thrived. One never produced gold, and others amalgamated to form economic units, or were absorbed by stronger partners.

But, in the main, the difficulties were overcome, often by technical innovation, and the new field flourished.

The development of the West Wits Line and Klerksdorp fields proceeded, *pari passu*, with that of the Free State. By 1949 there were three large mines in production on the West Wits Line and two more, including the fabulous West Driefontein, were shaft-sinking. At Klerksdorp, Western Reefs was in production and the first of the post-war mines was being opened up. To serve the two areas the mines created four towns, Westonaria, to the west of Randfontein, Carletonville, further to the west, which was named for Carleton Jones; and Stilfontein and Orkney near the old town of Klerksdorp. Everywhere the mines planted trees on the largely treeless veld. Between 1946 and 1951 more than a million trees had been planted on the West Wits Line and the Free State mines followed suit. Mining, traditionally the despoiler of the landscape, set out purposefully to improve it, and did so with dramatic success.

In developing the new mining areas, the mining industry was once again pioneering areas of remote farms lacking the infrastructure of modern enterprise, and this was particularly so in the Free State. It was clear to the industry that the situation there called for regional planning on a bold scale. The Government referred the matter to the Social, Economic and Planning Council which recommended a statutory administration on the lines of the Tennessee Valley Authority. However, the Government decided otherwise, and in 1947 passed through Parliament legislation to establish the Natural Resources Development Council (NRDC) which appointed a committee, with a mining industry representative, to co-ordinate the planning of the new field.

A year previously, Parliament had passed legislation authorizing a new branch railway line to Odendaalsrus, the gold mining companies concerned guaranteeing the line against losses for ten years. There followed the construction of a pipeline to bring water forty-five miles from the Vaal River to a reservoir on Koppie Alleen, the lonely eminence on the flat plain of the mining area. The Electricity Supply Commission (Escom) built new power lines and put in hand plans for a new power station at Vierfontein, just south of the Vaal. The NRDC decreed that there should be four new towns, Allanridge, named for the unlucky pioneer, Allan Roberts, Odendaalsrus, Welkom and Virginia. Welkom, however, at the strategic centre of the field, would be the most important, and would soon be second in size in the Free State only to the provincial capital of Bloemfontein. The planning of the gold-field towns and the speed at which they were brought to fruition would be regarded internationally as a model of achievement in town planning.

At Welkom, Anglo built the most modern hospital in Africa for the treatment of its black employees, and named it after Ernest Oppenheimer. On all mines the opportunity was taken to upgrade the facilities for black employees, and an attempt, which failed, was made by Anglo American to persuade the Minister of Native Affairs, Dr H F Verwoerd, to allow ten per cent of the black workforce to be housed permanently with their families in mine villages.

The hospital treatment of white employees raised a special problem, because this was urgently needed but was the responsibility of the Provincial authorities, which could not keep up with the pace of development. On 25 June 1951 Hagart, then President of the Chamber, announced that, by agreement, the problem would be solved by the mines providing most of the capital for three hospitals, building them and handing them over complete to be run by the Province. The three hospitals, the gift of the mines to the people of the Free State, were formally presented to the Administrator at a banquet in Bloemfontein on 20 January 1954.

With its hands full developing new gold-fields in the post-war decade, the mining industry had somehow to find the extra capacity to construct an entirely new industry vital to the West, that of uranium production. The existence of the system of joint consultation through the Chamber of Mines was to prove invaluable to the mining houses in bringing the new industry into being at a pace that would match the urgency of the strategic demand.

In November 1949 preliminary and highly secret negotiations were held in Johannesburg with a mission from the Combined Development Agency (CDA), set up as joint purchasing agency by the United States and Britain. The CDA's function was to ensure supplies for the expanding plants at which atomic bombs were being manufactured. The negotiations proved most complex.

South Africa had hoped that the Agency would offer a fixed price so that the industry could determine which mines could supply profitably. However, at the prices fixed in the United States and Canada, South African mines would not be able to produce at a profit. The Agency was prepared to deal only on the basis of the economic circumstances of individual producers, and this meant a separate price negotiation for each company involved. Negotiations did not get beyond a preliminary stage, but the CDA was able to obtain information on what South Africa could supply.

In the twelve months following, much progress was made towards determining the techniques which should be applied on mines and the probable costs. Pilot plant operations began.

In October 1950 the CDA returned to resume the discussions. A contract was drawn up between the Agency and the newly-created South African Atomic Energy Board, providing for the production of uranium at Blyvooruitzicht, Daggafontein, Western Reefs and West Rand Cons. These mines would pioneer uranium production in South Africa, the first in the field being West Rand Cons which would be formally opened by the Prime Minister, Dr D F Malan, on 8 October 1952.

Immediately after the signing of agreements with the British and Americans, a special sub-committee of consulting metallurgists and consulting electrical and mechanical engineers was formed by the Chamber, and a Chamber department was established, under the direction of a consulting metallurgist familiar with uranium plant design.

> For the first time in the history of the gold mining industry a committee of the Chamber of Mines, made up of representatives from the Groups concerned, collaborated in the design of plants for single mines.[6]

When the plant erection programme was started, structural steel, steel plant and reinforcing steel were in short supply everywhere. Bulk orders were immediately placed through the Chamber for the import of 64 000 tons of steel. Four months after the placing of the original orders, not only had the first consignments of steel arrived, but the first tanks were being erected on site. The Chamber was assisted in its drive to obtain supplies in a hurry by the decision of the British and American Governments to accord the highest priority to its needs. The Chamber's Mine Stores Department, which had played a key role during the war years, was assigned the co-ordination of purchase and delivery of urgently needed materials. It was also given a mandate to undertake the supply, under pooling arrangements, of the major raw material requirements.[7]

In October 1951 the representatives of the CDA returned to South Africa to ask for an expansion of uranium production to meet the need created by the escalation of the Cold War. Both America and Britain were fast stepping up the production of atomic bombs, and South Africa's gold mines were the best available source for the fissionable material required. The CDA mission came prepared to offer more favourable terms to all mines able to produce.

In the radically changed situation, it is certain that the CDA did not find the task confronting them in South Africa an easy one. The key South African negotiators were Hagart and McLean, men who had, perhaps, soft hearts, but who had, too, the toughest exteriors, and were the shrewdest negotiators in the mining world. Backed by J W Shilling, the Chamber's Legal Adviser at the time, they made a truly formidable team.

Hagart has recorded:

> When the first discussions were held in 1949, South Africa's main motive had been a desire to assist the Western World in the aim of securing an adequate number of atomic weapons. It had been emphasized that we would be contributing a great deal to this vital security need if we were to agree to produce uranium at prices showing only a moderate profit. We had been particularly asked not to take advantage of our strong position as uranium suppliers by holding out for unduly high prices. But when the Agency came back again in 1951 and wanted a very much larger quantity, we had to take stock of the internal position in South Africa and of the effect a vast programme of uranium production would have on the general economy of the country. We were at that time short of steel, power, cement and labour. If we had to go ahead with this large programme of building

and completing uranium plants within the time set, other sections of the country's activities would suffer, since priorities for supplies of all sorts, power, railway transport and labour would have to be given to the uranium industry.[8]

Put otherwise, the way had been cleared for the industry to drive a fair but highly profitable bargain. The agreement reached provided that each contract would run for ten years from the date of reaching full production. The CDA agreed to provide loan funds for the total capital costs of erecting the plants in South Africa, as well as the cost of numerous sulphuric acid plants to provide the acid essential to the recovery process. It provided the necessary capital loan for a central processing plant, established under the aegis of the Chamber, called, to disguise its then secret nuclear purpose, Calcined Products (Pty) Ltd. It made loans available to Escom, too, to boost the supply of power to the mines concerned. The loans were to be repaid, with interest, over ten years. The price paid was based on a formula which covered for each individual mine the cost of production and repayment of the loans, and provided a margin of profit.

Between January 1951 and April 1957 the construction of seventeen uranium plants around the Golden Arc constituted a major portion of the country's industrial activity. By 1956 gross profits amounted to £25 million and, even after allowing for loan repayments, were expected soon to double. The programme would be again expanded, and twenty-eight plants would be planned, but then there would be curtailment as the need for atomic stockpiles waned. The CDA returned to re-negotiate the contracts to provide for them to be extended over a longer contract period. By then the gold mines associated in the Chamber had established at record speed a new industry with incomparable reserves, and the prospects of long life as a supplier of nuclear fuel.

McLean in philosophic mood told the Chemical, Metallurgical and Mining Society of South Africa in April 1954:

> South Africa's own Atomic Energy Board was created in 1949 just when our planetary friend, Uranus, was completing its second known eighty-four-year revolution round the sun. Uranus is now on its third revolution and who dares to foretell what its patronymic, Uranium, will mean to this earthly civilisation during the period of this third and perhaps vital revolution.[9]

At the end of 1953 the Chamber duly recognized the expansion of the industry by adopting the comprehensive, if clumsy, title of Transvaal and Orange Free State Chamber of Mines. Other changes were under way. A J Limebeer had retired at the end of 1950 and A Tracey Milne was appointed Secretary in his place. Three years later he was appointed Manager. The choice was a narrow one, for there was support for John W Shilling, the able and ambitious Legal Adviser, who was senior official prior to the appointment. When the decision went against him, he decided to leave the Chamber after grooming B T Tindall to succeed him as Legal Adviser. He joined the management at Anglo American and rose to head first its Coal and then its Gold and Uranium Divisions. He became President of the Chamber in 1971.[10]

Milne, who was made General Manager in 1956, was the grandson of Perceval White Tracey, a Kimberley pioneer well known to Cecil Rhodes, who later discovered the diamondiferous pipe which became the Premier mine. The owner of the farm chased prospector Perceval Tracey off the property at the point of a rifle, but Tracey later formed a syndicate with Thomas Cullinan to buy it. Cullinan was the Chairman of the Premier mine and Perceval Tracey its Managing Director, when a black worker found the Cullinan diamond, glistening in a side wall.[11]

His daughter married Arnold Statham Milne, the holder of Mine Manager's Certificate No 3, and the manager and general manager of various mines between 1906 and 1934. Their son, Tracey Milne, began his working life with a degree in forestry from Downing College, Cambridge, and was for a spell employed planting trees, first in Northern Rhodesia and then in the eastern Transvaal. He was retrenched from both jobs, and in the aftermath of the Great Depression walked the streets of Johannesburg in search of any sort of a job, before finding one at Union Corporation. He rose to become the Group's Buyer and in this capacity began an association with the Chamber, representing the Group on the Buyers' Sub-Committee. When the role and scope of the war-time Stores Sub-Committee was increased he served as its Deputy Chairman under McLean. As such he played a distinguished role in obtaining vital supplies in the conditions of scarcity that arose. Milne, who could be both forceful and self-effacing, was to prove a sound choice as the man to head the Chamber, as its functions developed in concert with the grand advance of the industry. He would build a strong administrative and advisory team as the Chamber's departments were progressively expanded, and new ones added, to meet the demands of the industry, expressed through the GPC and the Collieries Committee.

Among the notable personalities in the Chamber of that time was Michael Falcon who had been appointed Technical Adviser in 1951. He was only the third incumbent of the post in the Chamber's history, for he succeeded J P Harding, who had taken over from Roberts in 1937. Falcon would die tragically in 1961 when, while recovering from a heart attack, the news was broken to him that his son-in-law had been killed in an air crash. Another leading figure was the talented Victor C Robinson, who became Labour Adviser in 1956, a post left vacant since W Gemmill was promoted General Manager in 1923. Robinson would become Chief Technical Adviser in 1964, with A B Daneel as Technical Adviser. A public relations official privately described Robinson as the 'lamb in lion's clothing', for his notoriously salty tongue belied his essential humanity.

The coal industry, in its own right an important contributor to mineral earnings, had been steadily expanding in parallel with the rapid industrial-

ization of the country. The advent of war in 1939, which re-asserted in no uncertain manner the vital strategic importance of the Cape shipping route,
created new opportunities for the collieries in the bunkering of the shipping
re-routed to South African ports. The collieries, too, played a key role in
developing an export trade to meet the needs of Allied war industries. However, post-war, the coal industry saw its export trade from the Transvaal decline and then come to a virtual standstill through the inability of the country's
transport system to cope with the demands upon it. However, domestic sales
continued to increase in response to the country's industrial growth. The coal
industry was laying the foundations of its own grand advance which would
follow the Opec-induced oil crisis of 1973.

Throughout the fifties the expansion of mining provided a special stimulus
for manufacturing and engineering, which in turn intensified the shortage of
skilled and scientific manpower in all categories. The competition forced the
mines to raise wages and salaries, thus increasing costs at a time when the
benefits of devaluation were rapidly being eroded by inflation. In 1948, a
dispute between the Chamber and the MUJC over the wages paid to union
men had been referred to a commission headed by the distinguished engineer
and economist, Dr H J van Eck. His function was to examine the costs of the
industry and the level of white workers' wages. The report of the Commission was made available to the Chamber in the immediate aftermath of the
rise in the gold price in September 1949.

The Commission found that union men on the mines had fallen behind
workers in other industries. In the light of the higher gold price, the Chamber
agreed to a fifteen per cent increase in wages, and other benefits, operating
from 19 September. Increases in pay and benefits of similar scale were accorded white officials.[12]

The MUJC in its submission had contended that although the Government
and the shareholders had participated in the industry's prosperity that
followed South Africa's abandonment of the gold standard in 1932, the
workers themselves had not done so. The Commission found, however, that
although the union men did not at first receive a proportionate share of the
increased prosperity, there was in later years a fairly rapid redistribution of
total revenue.

Moreover ... it was the Government and the shareholders, and not the
workers, who, during recent years, had had to bear the brunt of the Industry's declining fortunes.[13]

An examination was also made of the cost to the mines of the Chamber and
Group head offices. The Commission found that the cost of running the
Chamber in 1948 was a little over a penny-halfpenny per ton milled, out of an
overall cost per ton milled of £1 6s 2d, and that the saving possible was slight
and would probably harm the industry or its employees. Similarly, the Commission found the cost of Group administration to be less than fivepence per

ton milled and concluded this could not be much reduced without loss of efficiency.

Despite increases in wages the shortage of white miners became so acute that the Chamber set up a Directorate of Recruiting in 1955 under Hugh McLellan Husted, a former mining and finance editor, who had been appointed the Chamber's first public relations officer in 1944. Husted's function was to attract matriculants to the Learner Official Scheme conducted under the aegis of the Chamber since 1948, and to recruit miners in South Africa and overseas. There was at first a steady flow from overseas, and, despite initial language problems, some of the immigrant miners would make an important contribution to the industry and rise in its ranks. However, the high level of industrial activity in Europe would increasingly hamper recruiting there. The Directorate would soon be absorbed into the Public Relations Department under Husted and Angus Collie, another former journalist.

The Chamber had to contend with a shortage of black workers as well. The introduction of service increments in 1948, and improvements in wages in 1949 and thereafter, helped somewhat to increase the flow. In general, however, the mines would be compelled by the decline in the purchasing power of gold in the 1950s and 1960s to draw tight the purse-strings. Mine pay would become increasingly less attractive in South Africa, and the Chamber would solve the problem by extending the WNLA network to the north where the wages the Rand mines offered were superior to those paid locally.

With the agreement of Central African governments the WNLA set up stations in Nyasaland (Malawi) and in Northern Rhodesia (Zambia), including Barotseland, which was administered through a Resident Commissioner; and it built a web of roads which in northern Bechuanaland (Botswana) alone would extend for 1 300 miles, often through sandy, waterless wastelands. The opening up of the Kalahari and Okavango areas in northern Bechuanaland was undertaken at the same time.[14]

In Bechuanaland, roads were first made from Francistown, along the Southern Rhodesia border to Kazungula, at the junction of the Chobe and Zambesi Rivers; from Francistown to Maun and thence to Mohembo, on the Okavango River; from Mohembo to Runtu, in the Okavango Native Territory, and across the western Kalahari Desert to Grootfontein, in South West Africa. Through often appalling terrain, a regular road transport system ran from Francistown to Runtu, and from Francistown to Grootfontein, through Maun, the administrative centre of Ngamiland and the north-western districts of Bechuanaland.[15]

Motor barge transport was introduced in the Okavango Swamp. In Barotseland and the Zambesi area the paddle barges used for river transport, from time immemorial, were replaced by WNLA motor barges, running between Kazungula and Katima Mulilo. From Katima Mulilo, where rapids stretch along the Zambesi for 100 miles to Nangweshi, a road was cut to permit the ferrying of workers by lorry. Another 250 miles of road were added along the Northern Rhodesia/Angolan border to Sikongo. WNLA established its Barotseland headquarters at Mongu and built a chain of WNLA stations, running north to Nguvu, near the border of the Belgian Congo (Zaire) which was reached by diesel barges running twice weekly along an arm of the Zambesi. In Nyasaland a network of stations and sub-stations was created. By 1952 the opening up of road and river communications raised the tropical workforce to 40 000.[16]

The WNLA was careful not to designate its operations as 'recruiting' for this in terms of the ILO definition included 'all operations with the object of obtaining or supplying the labour of persons who do not spontaneously offer themselves at the place of employment, or ... at an office conducted by an employers' organization'. The WNLA had long been closely associated with the ILO, and operated within the guidelines set by that body. Only those who came to WNLA offices to offer their services were considered for engagement.[17] The numbers offering in this way grew rapidly and to accommodate them the WNLA introduced air services, cutting down the travelling time to and from the Rand by up to fourteen days. In 1956, more than half the industry's labour was coming from beyond South Africa's borders. The tropical areas north of latitude twenty-two degrees south were supplying 17,9 per cent, and another 47,4 per cent came from the areas of Moçambique and the British Protectorates south of this latitude. Operating out of Francistown, which was linked by rail with Johannesburg, the WNLA air service was flying 32 million passenger miles yearly over seven different routes.

In 1955, when the number of blacks at work on the mines reached an average of 327 000, the Chamber introduced the miniature radiographing, at its Johannesburg and Welkom reception centres, of all those entering the industry. The care of workers, which had become the norm, was reinforced by new drives to improve their productivity, employing modern techniques of management, aptitude testing, labour selection, training and incentive bonuses. However, B L Bernstein (Anglo Vaal) in his Presidential Address on 25 June 1956, warned: '... there is a limit to what can be done, because of the bounds imposed on us by law and by custom in the utilization of Non-European labour'.[18]

During Bernstein's year of office the industry at last surpassed the record output of 1941, marking up a total of 14 602 267 ounces for 1955, an achievement reflecting the contribution of the new mines in the Free State and on the Far West Rand. But the outlook was by no means altogether a happy one. Working costs had doubled since 1941, and the coming on stream at regular intervals of new, generally higher-grade mines, was accompanied by the closure of some old mines on the Rand, and a progressive decline in profits on others. More and more would be regarded as 'vulnerable', and candidates for closure.

The Minister of Mines called a round-table conference on vulnerable mines at the end of 1957. Hermie Koch reported to the Chamber's Annual General Meeting that at the outset the scope of the conference was limited so as to exclude any discussion of wages or the colour bar.[19] The scope that remained was restricted and produced nothing of moment.

Meanwhile, Union Corporation was making the moves that would complete the 300-mile sweep of gold-fields around the Golden Arc. The Group had been out-manoeuvred in the Free State, and somewhat stung by its inability to realize fully on the achievement of its exploration teams. It now discerned new openings in the eastern Transvaal. Aerial survey, including magnetometer readings, conducted on a huge scale in 1946, demarcated a possible extension of the Rand around Kinross and Trichardt. Union Corporation made sure that it would stay in the driving seat this time around.

> Then, in 1949, there appeared a number of young men representing Capital Mining Areas and authorized to take options over a number of farms where prospecting might be carried out. The farmers signed on the dotted line and pocketed the cash.
>
> And what was Capital Mining Areas? It was a subsidiary of Union Corporation. Very quietly it acquired the necessary options .... [20]

In due course three mines were proved by geophysical survey and by more than 250 boreholes plotting the course of the Kimberley Reef. The first of these, Winkelhaak, made its first return of gold in December 1958. The Bracken and Leslie mines would follow in August and October 1962; and a fourth mine, Kinross, in 1968. Union Corporation would enjoy complete control of the newest of the seven gold-fields and, appropriately, would name the new mining town which served it Evander, after P M Anderson's second wife, Evelyn Anderson. P M Anderson, however, did not live to see the culmination of the achievement. He died on 5 November 1954, at the age of seventy-five. Coincidentally, the President of the Chamber at the time was his son, Colin, who had succeeded his father on the GPC in 1948. He paid a tribute 'to the memory of a great South African' who, for a third of a century, had played a leading part in the direction of the industry's affairs. 'P M' had joined the Chamber's Executive Committee and GPC in 1922, and remained a member of the Executive Committee at his death.

Mining and other business interests apart, 'P M' was a deeply religious man, who played a leading role in education, and was for many years Chairman of the Council of Witwatersrand University, which 'with pomp and ceremony' accorded him a doctorate of science in 1930. He was also active in fostering the technical societies, and was one of those who promoted the idea of housing a number of related societies under one roof in Kelvin House, Hollard Street, opposite the Chamber. [21]

In this and other ways the Chamber contributed to the co-ordination of professional and scientific effort which was to underpin the industry's expansion into new fields. Appropriately 'P M', as President of the Chamber, officially opened Kelvin House in 1937, and his mining engineer nephew, Dr A A ('Attie') von Maltitz, would in turn perform the ceremony re-opening Kelvin House after its modernization in 1963.

399

The industry's technical advance was reflected in the sinking of shafts to depths not previously essayed by the world's engineers. The older mines along the Reef had reached 8 000 feet and more, and in the 1950s one of them, Rand Mines's huge ERPM, exceeded 11 000 feet to become indisputably the deepest mine in the world. Fantastic speeds were attained in sinking shafts and driving tunnels to exploit the deeper levels. On the West Wits Line a company, known as Western Ultra Deep Levels, had been formed by Anglo American in 1943 to explore the ground where the Ventersdorp Contact Reef and the Carbon Leader passed the southern boundaries of West Driefontein and Blyvooruitzicht. Western Ultra Deeps set out to investigate the sinking of shafts 6 000 and 10 000 feet in vertical depth to mine these reef extensions. The study revealed that at great depths there was a potential mine of huge dimensions, which could only be brought to production by venturing capital on a scale undreamed of. Once again Ernest Oppenheimer was prepared to take risks from which many younger men in Anglo American recoiled.[22] He expressed in action the philosophy that entrepreneurs must be ready to act on incomplete evidence and on what appears to be the balance of probabilities.

At the Western Deep Levels shaft-sinking ceremony on 24 July 1957, Sir Ernest said: 'This is the most important enterprise ever started in South Africa.' A little later he prophesied that the annual gold output from the new mine would one day exceed £15 million, which was then the monthly output figure for the entire industry.[23] It was an under-estimate that would be magnified by the rapid multiplication of the gold price that was to come after 1970. In 1984, the value of the annual gold output of Western Deep Levels would be in excess of R618 million (the gold price for that year averaging around ten times the 1957 figure). The working profit would be more than R361 million (plus another R1,5 million from uranium).

Oppenheimer did not live to see the mine produce its first gold. He died at the age of seventy-seven, only a few months after pressing the button to set in motion the sinking of the first shaft.

Western Deeps, the crowning achievement of his career, remained to symbolize the onward thrust of the industry. By 1985 the mine had reached a depth of 11 752 feet and a new R1 000 million South Shaft Complex operating at a vertical depth of from 12 470 to 12 840 feet was due to begin production in 1986.

Harry Oppenheimer, who succeeded his father as Chairman of Anglo American and of De Beers, had joined his father in the business twenty-six years previously, at a time when the 'Group … in its rapid assumption of leadership had bitten off a great deal more than it could comfortably chew'.[24] He had enjoyed his father's close confidence through those days of struggle, and had been involved in intimate detail in the rapid growth of the Corporation as the economic storms of the Great Depression blew themselves out. In a measured evaluation of his father's career, published in 1967, he recalled that he had remained in full control of policy up to his death, and retained an astonishingly detailed grip of affairs.

He had an essential youthfulness of spirit which remained with him till the end, so that it was difficult for those who knew him well to think of him as an old man. He achieved great success and he enjoyed success. He enjoyed money – both making it and spending it – but primarily he enjoyed it as a symbol and measure of achievement. He was often written of as an 'international financier', but this was quite wrong. There was nothing international in his thought or outlook, and he saw his financial success as a by-product of his part in building up South Africa.[25]

Harry Oppenheimer added thoughtfully that he doubted whether his father, had he lived on, would have easily or happily adapted to the fundamental changes that took place, in the decade after his death, in Africa and the Commonwealth.[26]

[1] Gregory, p 565 (Note 79).

[2] Cartwright, *The Gold Miners*, p 298.

[3] Gregory, pp 565-566.

[4] See Gregory, at p 566 (Note 81), quoting the Chairman of the Commercial Exchange of South Africa.

[5] H F Oppenheimer, 'The Orange Free State Gold Fields', *The South African Journal of Economics*, Volume 18, No 2, June 1950, pp 148, 156.

[6] McLean, p 348.

[7] D N Stuart, 'The Supply of the Raw Material Requirements of the Uranium Programme', *Journal of the South African Institute of Mining and Metallurgy*, Vol 57, No 6, January 1957, p 403.

[8] R B Hagart, 'National Aspects of the Uranium Industry', *Journal of the South African Institute of Mining and Metallurgy*, Vol 57, No 9, April 1957, pp 567-568.

[9] McLean, p 356.

[10] Interview with J W Shilling, at Sandton, Transvaal, on 9 March 1983.

[11] Letter from A T Milne, Johannesburg, to the Anglo American Corporation of South Africa, Limited, Johannesburg, dated 19 July 1963.

[12] Annual Report of the Transvaal Chamber of Mines, 1949, pp 40-41, 68-69.

[13] *Ibid*, p 68.

[14] W Gemmill, 'The Growing Reservoir of Native Labour for the Mines', *Optima*, June 1952, Volume II, No 2, p 18.

[15] *Idem*.

[16] *Ibid*, pp 18, 19.

[17] *Ibid*, pp 17-18.

[18] Sixty-Sixth Annual Report of the Transvaal and Orange Free State Chamber of Mines, 1955, pp 60, 64.

[19] Sixty-Eighth Annual Report of the Transvaal and Orange Free State Chamber of Mines, 1957, pp 43-44.

[20] Cartwright, *The Gold Miners*, p 315.

[21] Richards, pp 118-119.

[22] H F Oppenheimer, 'Sir Ernest Oppenheimer', *Optima*, Volume 17, No 3, September 1967, p 103.

[23] Cartwright, *The Gold Miners*, p 321.
[24] Oppenheimer, 'Sir Ernest Oppenheimer', p 100.
[25] *Ibid*, pp 95, 103.
[26] *Ibid*, p 103.

PART FIVE

Riding the Winds of Change

CHAPTER THIRTY-TWO

Verwoerdian Fantasy

The sixties, named 'swinging' in Britain, are remembered by South Africans for events, constitutional, political and monetary, of high drama and consequence. The decade's advent was at once attended by an escalation of the already endemic social unrest, bringing in train a crisis of confidence, the flight of capital and seeming economic disaster. There followed recovery and a remarkable boom, which was underpinned by gold, for through all these vicissitudes the new, expanded gold mining industry notched record returns with clockwork regularity. But haunting managements was the spectre that those record returns might mask a shortening of the life expectancy of their mines. The determination of the United States Government to hold down the price of gold to its 1934 level in disregard of rising costs and rising demand, come what may, impelled an extraction rate at a rising grade that by the decade's end would carry with it the threat of extinction for half the industry.

Changes in National Party leadership had brought to the country's helm ideologues of implacable resolve. Dr D F Malan had retired as Prime Minister in November 1954. To his bitter chagrin the National Party caucus on 30 November 1954 disregarded his advice, and chose Transvaal's 'Lion of the North', J G Strijdom, over the moderate N C Havenga, as the next Prime Minister. In personal relations, Strijdom was a man of gentle, almost old-world courtesy which contrasted oddly with his public image of belligerence. For the rest, he was an ardent republican, who was 'direct, averse to compromise, of limited intellectual capacity, and prone to frank statements about the white man's (ie the Afrikaner's) determination to stay on top'.[1] He enlarged the Senate to give the Government the necessary majority to rescind constitutional entrenchments, other than the protection of language rights, and removed Coloured voters from the common roll; he created the outward symbols of the coming republic, a single flag, 'The Union Flag', and a single national anthem, *Die Stem van Suid-Afrika* (*The Voice of South Africa*); and he applied the Group Areas Act to bring about residential apartheid. Strijdom did not dominate Parliament, like his predecessors or his successors, but he was a charismatic platform orator, and captured the imagination of his public. In 1958 he led the National Party to victory with an increased majority. After allowance for uncontested seats, the party could not yet be said to command a majority of votes, nor a large measure of English-speaking support. However, the win was decisive enough. Strijdom did not live long to savour the triumph, for only five months later he died. The caucus this time chose his Transvaal ally, Dr H F Verwoerd, as leader in preference to Justice Minister, C R Swart, and Interior Minister, Dr T E Dönges, who led the Party in the Free State and the Cape respectively.

Compared to Strijdom, Verwoerd was an intellectual giant. Unhappily, his exceptional talents enabled him to give a certain credibility to his fantasy of a South Africa unscrambled into separate states for black and white. Verwoerd made the watershed announcement of this departure from past apartheid policy in May 1959 when he accepted the principle, previously denied, of independence for the country's black areas. He did so at a time of rural unrest among blacks in the eastern and western Transvaal, and in Pondoland in the eastern Cape, motivated by a diversity of dissatisfactions, with a common denominator of opposition to controls imposed by a government seen as hostile to blacks. At the year-end the ANC and its break-away Africanist wing, the Pan African Congress (PAC), led by Robert Sobukwe, planned separate protest campaigns to precede the celebrations of the fiftieth anniversary of Union on 31 May 1960. Each was determined to excel the other in defiance of the Pass Laws.[2]

Jubilee Year, culminating in the Festival of Union in May, was expected to be the occasion for gestures of conciliation between, at least, the white races, and for the shelving of controversial issues. Verwoerd had other ideas. He was determined to hold a referendum on whether or not South Africa should become a republic. He had, it seems, decided that it was 'now or never'.[3] The opportunity might never again be repeated, and to improve the chances of success in the referendum, Verwoerd was prepared, initially at least, to accept a republic within the Commonwealth. Verwoerd's intent was not mentioned in the Governor-General's Speech from the Throne at the opening of Parliament on Friday, 15 January 1960, but it was revealed in the greatest secrecy to the Party caucus immediately afterwards. Sir De Villiers Graaff, the Leader of the Opposition, in moving the customary motion 'that this House has no confidence in the Government' on 19 January 1960, presumed that the republic was not at issue in 1960, and ignored it. Verwoerd, in reply to the debate the following day, caught him off balance by announcing that the referendum would be held after the celebrations of Union on 31 May, at a date to be announced. His statement occasioned

> ... one of the memorable scenes in South African parliamentary history. Verwoerd's statement was greeted with stormy applause by his own followers. The members of the Opposition sat as if stunned.[4]

Immediately following this dramatic event in Parliament came the dreadful news of the calamity at the Coalbrook North Colliery in the northern Free State. At 7 30 pm on Thursday, 21 January, the workings collapsed over a vast area in which 435 men were at work. It was by far the greatest disaster in the country's mining history and set in train the biggest rescue operation ever.

The scale of the rescue operation was not diminished by well-founded doubts of the men's chance of survival, nor by the fact that the operators of the mine, Clydesdale (Transvaal) Collieries, were not members of one of the major Groups associated with the Chamber. Soon after the cave-in, Dr W J Busschau, President of the Chamber and Chairman of Gold Fields, called a leading consulting engineer to his office and asked his view of the men's fate. The reply came without hesitation: 'They are all dead – killed instantly by the collapse of the workings.'[5] Despite the conviction that nobody could have survived the rockfall or the awful shock waves stemming from it, Busschau put the whole resources of the coal and gold mines at the disposal of Clydesdale. No effort or expense was spared in the bid to reach the entombed miners.

The frontline of the industry's effort was provided by 250 men of the Mines' Rescue Brigade, trained at the Chamber's Rescue Training Station in Johannesburg. The station had been started by Rand Mines in 1924. Thereafter, it took on the training of brigadesmen for other Groups as well. In course of time it became obvious that the training of brigadesmen in rescue work and fighting fires underground was best handled co-operatively for the industry. The Chamber took over in 1946. At the time of Coalbrook, the service was on the brink of an expansion programme to match the needs of the larger industry. Stations would be opened at Welkom in 1961, Witbank in 1966 (moved to Evander in 1982), and at Dundee in Natal in 1976, while the headquarters would be moved from Johannesburg in 1980 to a new station at Carletonville.

The brigadesmen are all volunteers from the ranks of mine employees who are hand-picked to become members of five-man teams, and rigorously trained in the use of oxygen-breathing apparatus in simulated but challenging situations of confinement, darkness, heat and smoke. After 1970, they were backed by support groups, also specially trained, from the ranks of unskilled black workers; in 1981 the men selected were redesignated rescue assistants. The brigadesmen's motto is '*Voluntate Serveo*' – 'Voluntarily I Serve'. Each mine has its own trained brigadesmen who can be called from their normal duties in emergency. In the event of a major disaster the mine can call on the central headquarters, and the brigadesmen of the industry can be mobilized in support of rescue and fire-fighting operations wherever the need may arise. In 1972 South African brigadesmen would volunteer to assist in the aftermath of the colliery disaster at Wankie in Rhodesia, and in 1976 and 1977 they would assist at separate disasters at the Moatize colliery near Tete in independent, Marxist Moçambique. Their mercy mission into Moçambique on the second occasion was made at unusual personal risk; for they knew that local workers had murdered all the white officials at the mine, mainly East Germans, whom they thought responsible for the loss of life that had occurred. But the taking of risks was in the tradition of the Brigade, for since its foundation more than twenty brigadesmen have given their lives in fighting fires or rescuing trapped workers.[6]

After the collapse of the workings at Coalbrook the brigadesmen battled with little rest or sleep, but vainly, for access was denied them by extent of the fall, and the ever-present risk of further falls or the explosion of methane gas released by the violent ground movements. The rescue drive was quickly channelled into sinking large boreholes to communicate with men who might be alive, and to provide them with the means of survival. The biggest available drills in South Africa were moved to the site, including a giant prospecting drill from Iscor at Thabazimbi; and for long days and longer nights the drills bit with agonizing slowness through the steel-like dolerite overlay.

On Monday, 1 February, Clydesdale announced:

> In the early hours of this morning the two 3" boreholes intersected the coal horizon in which the trapped men are known to have been working. No contact has been made with the men underground. Nothing has emerged to lessen the grave anxiety felt for the fate of the men trapped in the mine.[7]

Meanwhile, the management had decided to back up the drilling by sinking a new shaft to give access to the collapsed workings. On Sunday, 24 January, H MacConachie, Consulting Engineer to Anglo American, was called off the golf course by Busschau, who had visited the colliery the day before. He told MacConachie that Coalbrook had appealed for assistance in sinking an emergency shaft, and it was thought that equipment available at Welkom mine might be suitable.

MacConachie drove straight to Coalbrook, and summoned two gold mine managers to meet him there. By early the next day, the plans for the foundations of the stage and winding hoists, the headgear, shaft collar and ancillary buildings were on the site, and the necessary pegs and lines put in with the assistance of the colliery survey staff. That afternoon excavations started. Ten days after the call the selected area in an untouched maize field had been transformed into a full-scale sinking operation, work which at the normally hectic pace of shaft-sinking took six weeks. Sinking proceeded round the clock under a master sinker, who had recently set a world shaft-sinking record, with teams drawn from the President Brand and President Steyn gold mines. By mid-February the shaft was down 250 feet. Two weeks after that the concrete-lined, twelve-foot diameter shaft, served by a sixty-eight ton headgear from Welkom, had reached its planned level of 542 feet.

But this superb concentration of human will and expertise was in vain as well. On 5 February Dr Verwoerd read to Parliament a message from the directors of Clydesdale.

> It is with deep sorrow that we have to report to you that it is the grave and considered opinion of the technical management of the company that no further hope can be held out for the trapped men. This opinion has been

reached after considering all the information available and after consulting with the Government Mining Engineer and technical personnel connected with the drilling operations. It is accordingly intended that rescue operations should be discontinued, but the sinking of the shaft adjacent to the affected area is being continued with the object of reaching the mine workings ....

Verwoerd told the House that the long anguish of the rescue bid was at an end. The time had come for the nation to abandon hope and subject itself to the Will of the Almighty. He adjourned the House for the day as a demonstration of sympathy with the bereaved.[8]

The Coalbrook disaster brought many changes in the planning of supports and the methods of extracting coal. Up to then coal mining had relied essentially on accumulated experience. The subsequent inquiry revealed that no scientific basis was available for the design of pillar workings, and led to the mining industry and the Government establishing the Coal Mining Research Controlling Council to direct research into safety in coal mines. Subsequently, arrangements were made for a broader programme of research into coal mining problems to be undertaken under the aegis of the Chamber of Mines Research Organization, a decision that led to the establishment of the Collieries Research Laboratory of the Chamber in 1966. This slotted naturally into the expansion of the Chamber's research activity then under way, following the appointment of Dr W S Rapson, formerly a Vice-President of the Council for Scientific and Industrial Research, as Research Adviser to the Chamber in 1962. On Rapson's recommendation the Chamber of Mines Research Organization was established in 1964. It included a Mining Research Laboratory, an Environmental Services Division, a Physical Sciences Laboratory, and a Biological Sciences Division. The Organization would build on research, of earlier years, conducted by the Chamber and by the mining houses, in seeking those breakthroughs which would offset the cost of mining at increasing depths and temperatures and which would improve working conditions underground.

The uranium-producing members of the Chamber were also contributing half the cost of the massive research programme launched in 1959 by the Atomic Energy Board into uranium extraction and processing to the nuclear fuel stage, and into the use of nuclear power in South Africa.

Research work in the Collieries Research Laboratory produced a 'bible' of safe practice that enabled collieries to plan pillar working on sound engineering principles.[9] Added to this, the Chamber's Collieries Committee after Coalbrook bought a Wirth L10 rescue drill for man rescue from West Germany, and subsequently replaced it with a giant drill specially designed for South African conditions by Ingersoll-Rand of the United States. In tests the drill penetrated very hard dolerite rock at a rate of just over twelve feet an hour. It can drill a hole wide enough to accommodate a capsule, called the Dahlbusch bomb, large enough to rescue the heftiest miner. Its use in a rescue role has not been required, but it is maintained on call, and can be on the road in minutes.

On 24 January 1960, when the Coalbrook rescue drama was at its height, the British Prime Minister, Harold Macmillan, arrived in Johannesburg at the end of a 20 000-mile tour of Ghana, Nigeria, Southern and Northern Rhodesia, and Nyasaland. His years as Britain's Prime Minister were destined to be remembered for the decision purposefully to speed up the grant of independence to former colonies.[10] He was, in fact, swimming with the tide for, including British colonies, nineteen African territories were on the brink of independence. Before leaving for Africa he had decided on a public rejection of South Africa's racial policies: '... his countrymen could no longer afford to be seen as fellow-travellers of *apartheid* ....'[11] On the Rand, Macmillan held talks with political leaders and industrialists; and Dr Busschau took him on a tour of West Driefontein, a fitting representative of the great mines which capital from the City of London had helped to build.

References to Macmillan as a visiting personality obscure the fact that he had a considerable entourage, including a strong contingent from the British Press. It is recorded that the Manager of West Driefontein, the somewhat dour Stan Gibbs, was less than enthusiastic at the prospect of conducting this small army underground. He remained silent for some thirty minutes while a Chamber official gave him a run-down of the implications of the forthcoming visit; it was only when pressed to put questions that he responded with a laconic: 'Yes, I do have one question. Couldn't you take him to another mine?'[12] Despite the show of reluctance, the arrangements, in the event, were impressive.

Macmillan duly arrived, shook hands, murmuring 'Splendid! Splendid!' and toured the mine. He made a graceful speech at lunch, adding his sympathy over the Coalbrook disaster to that already received from Her Majesty Queen Elizabeth, and accepted the gift of a gold paper knife. However, he kept what was most on his mind for Cape Town. There he stayed with Verwoerd at the official residence, Groote Schuur, still keeping his own counsel. The speech he was to deliver to the combined Houses of Parliament had been drafted two months earlier by Sir John Maud, the British High Commissioner, after visiting Downing Street for briefing, and Macmillan had worked it up personally during his African tour. An attempt by Verwoerd's private secretary to obtain an advance copy of the speech was blandly ignored.[13] It was Macmillan's turn to deliver a shock to Parliament, and he did so on 3 February, in a speech in which he emphasized the spirit of nationalism throughout the world and in Africa.

> The wind of change is blowing through the continent. Whether we like it or not, this growth of national consciousness is a political fact. We must all accept it as a fact. Our national policies must take account of it.[14]

He went on to say that Britain, in the countries for which she bore responsibility, sought to create societies which respected the rights of individuals, and in which men were given the opportunity to grow to full stature, and to exercise an increasing share in political power. She regarded individual merit as the sole criterion for advancement.

Macmillan concluded with the warning that Britain could not support some of South Africa's policies, without being false to her own deep convictions about the political destinies of free men. He had signalled the parting of the ways, but so gracefully did he administer his admonition that its real import passed over the heads of some parliamentarians. The Press however at once fastened on to the sensational implications of Macmillan's statement, and it was well received throughout the Western world. President Eisenhower of the United States wrote to congratulate Macmillan on his masterful address and his analysis of the forces of nationalism in Africa.[15]

South Africa was soon gripped by an escalation of racial turmoil. In January an ominous event had taken place at Cato Manor in Durban. A mob of blacks attacked a squad of policemen in the aftermath of a liquor raid, and killed nine of them. In March, the rival ANC and PAC trod on one another's heels in their haste to capture the support of the black public for their separate campaigns against the Pass Laws. Sobukwe announced on 18 March that on 21 March, members and supporters of the PAC would leave their pass books at home, and offer themselves for arrest at the nearest police station. Sobukwe had informed the Commissioner of Police of his intention, and stressed that the protest would be non-violent. The slogan was 'no bail, no defence, no fine'; the aim: to bring about the collapse of the pass system by filling the country's jails with offenders.[16]

The protest in the Cape at first passed off peacefully, the police taking the names of those who presented themselves for arrest and warning them to appear in court the following week. At Sharpeville, near Vereeniging, however, when the police declined to arrest early arrivals, the crowd grew to some fifteen thousand to twenty thousand, and it grew steadily more truculent. Arrests followed and there was some stone-throwing in protest. Disaster then erupted as a lone policeman, perhaps recalling the Cato Manor massacre, lost his nerve and opened fire, and other policemen followed suit. The mob fled in panic, but too late; they left behind them sixty-nine dead and 180 wounded. Later in the day there were more shootings, and two were killed at Langa, near Cape Town.

The news went around the world like a shock wave, and condemnation of the South African authorities was universal. In South Africa there followed riots, the public burning of passes, and arson. The ANC called a day of mourning on 28 March, and many black workers heeded the call to stay away from work. The PAC now moved in, calling for an extension of the strike, and workers in some areas responded. Verwoerd retaliated with tough measures, declaring a State of Emergency, calling up the Active Citizen Force, and banning both the ANC and the PAC. On 30 March, when the State of Emergency was declared, 12 000 were detained in pre-dawn arrests, a figure that would eventually rise to 18 000.[17]

Apart from the absence of men called up for military service, the mines were unaffected by the unrest, and its black workers did not respond in any way to the calls to stay away from work. However, the mining houses were alarmed at the fall in the value of mining shares, and the likely effect on the flow of capital for the development of new mines. Moreover, the mining houses had by now diversified considerably and had taken an important position in manufacturing industry. Accordingly, the Chamber participated with other national employer organizations in joint analysis of the causes of unrest and in drawing up proposals to resolve them.[18]

On 9 April Verwoerd went to the Rand to perform the official opening of the Rand Show, held annually by the Witwatersrand Agricultural Society. The Society had received support from mining personalities since the days of Phillips and Farrar, and the Chamber had long been a principal exhibitor, erecting a large, new permanent pavilion in 1954. In 1960 it put on a particularly magnificent display to mark the Festival of Union, including goldware from the private collection of Her Majesty Queen Elizabeth. The pieces included two crystal decanters, with gilt embellishments, so rare that Buckingham Palace required them to travel on separate aircraft. Also included was South Africa's gift to the then Princess Elizabeth on her wedding to Prince Phillip. It was a tray, more substantial than pretty, stamped out of solid gold at the South African Mint. Jan Smuts is said to have remarked, with the simplicity that was part of his nature that, with thrones toppling in Europe, the gift would, if the worst came to the worst in Britain, provide something for the young couple to fall back on. Busschau showed the treasures to Verwoerd who appeared to show particular interest in the Royal Plate of the Sovereign he was soon officially to deny.

Busschau also took Verwoerd aside to tell him of the discussions on the unrest in which the Chamber was participating with leaders of the Afrikaanse Handelsinstituut, the Association of Chambers of Commerce, the Federated Chambers of Industries, and the Steel and Engineering Industries Federation of South Africa. Verwoerd promised that he would give their proposals consideration, but expressed concern at Press reports that business organizations were about to demand the overthrow of the Government. In fact, the participants were taking great care to avoid any suggestion of political intervention, and were focusing on means to ease racial tension.

Later that day Verwoerd went to the arena to make his official opening speech, and a tour of the cattle sheds. He had just taken his seat on the stand once more when a wealthy Transvaal farmer, David Pratt, approached, and fired two shots into Verwoerd's head at close range. Verwoerd was rushed to hospital where he made a recovery that owed much to superb medical attention and to his rugged determination to survive. To some, however, the recovery seemed miraculous. The event created a bond of sentiment, hitherto lacking, between the Netherlands-born Verwoerd and the Afrikaner people. He himself saw in his survival the hand of God, putting the stamp of divine authority on his mission as the architect of apartheid.[19]

By 12 May Verwoerd was well enough to receive Busschau in his private ward at the Pretoria General Hospital, and to accept from him a memorandum expressing the views of business leaders.[20] The document was mild in tone, recommending amelioration of the Pass Laws and the Influx Control Regulations to remove elements which were major causes of grievance; and urged restoration of the system of exemptions from carrying passes, which had been recently abolished. The document also recommended the abolition of curfew regulations; and the immediate lifting of the prohibition of liquor sales to blacks, which had become a major cause of crime and punishment. Verwoerd promised careful consideration. He reassumed the leadership on 18 May, in time to brush aside the prospects of reform that had been aroused by Paul Sauer, Minister of Lands, and Acting Prime Minister, in a speech at Humansdorp on 19 April, declaring that 'the old book of South African history was closed at Sharpeville'.[21] Verwoerd at once made it clear to his colleagues that nothing had occurred to turn him from the course he was set upon. The only change on any scale which followed was the lifting in 1961 of the ban on the sale of liquor to blacks, relieving the Police of a burden of law enforcement which policemen themselves considered to have lost all purpose.

Without pausing to draw political breath, Verwoerd launched himself into the campaign to win support for the forthcoming republican referendum, and even used the culminating ceremony of the Festival of Union at Bloemfontein on 31 May to appeal to whites to unite in support of the republican ideal. In August he announced that the referendum would be held on 5 October. He was not at all deterred by the threatened collapse of the economy.

> As capital fled the country, and gold and foreign reserves fell, South Africa faced its most serious balance of payments crisis since 1932. The Government's reaction was as tough as it had been in suppressing black dissent. It imposed stringent import and foreign exchange controls, which helped to reduce economic growth almost to zero.[22]

To the flight of capital was added a flight of some whites in the first of the 'chicken runs', seeking new and safer pastures. Most stayed, and few English-speakers among them were enticed by Verwoerd into voting for a republic at the referendum. However, events overall had played into Verwoerd's hand. Macmillan's appeasement of Black Africa, Sharpeville and its aftermath, and the attempted assassination, rallied sufficient support for Verwoerd to win the referendum with fifty-two per cent of the votes.

Thereafter he did his best, as he had promised, to keep South Africa in the Commonwealth. However if events in South Africa rallied support for Verwoerd at home, they had the reverse effect on Commonwealth members, who now demanded modification of South Africa's domestic policies as the price of continued membership. When Commonwealth prime ministers met in London in March 1961 to consider South Africa's application to remain a member, Macmillan worked hard to promote an acceptable formula. However, he was soon forced to the realization that he could not succeed without endangering the fabric of Commonwealth relations.

> The balance was finally tipped against South Africa by Verwoerd himself, who refused to accord the normal diplomatic courtesies to representatives of African Commonwealth countries.[23]

At the end, when it was clear that no compromise could be devised, and fearing that a vote on the matter would lead to the destruction of the Commonwealth, Macmillan persuaded Verwoerd to withdraw his application.

South Africa duly became a republic outside the Commonwealth on 31 May 1961. It did so amidst a renewal of internal turmoil. There were extensions of security legislation, large-scale police raids and arrests, cancellation of police leave and another call-up of the Active Citizen Force. More than 8 000 were arrested in pre-dawn raids. In mid-year there was a collapse of confidence and the recently introduced decimal rand faced the threat of devaluation.[24]

On 25 June Colin Anderson, at the end of the third of his four terms as President, commented that the abrupt loss of Commonwealth membership was an event of far-reaching consequence which the industry must regard with deep concern. It was, he declared, 'tragic' that affairs had come to such a pass that the Government had been forced earlier in the month to suspend the repatriation of overseas capital invested in securities to prevent a further outflow.

Anderson paid a fitting tribute to the participation of the City of London in the growth of the industry. Down the years the role of British investors had been of first importance. Their contribution to the grand advance of the post-war years had amounted to one-third of the capital required. Anderson added that the decline in favour of gold mining in South Africa as a sphere of investment was, on the economic facts, unwarranted. No less than thirty major new shafts were in process of sinking and the general picture was one of vigorous activity.

Exactly a year later, his successor, Hermie Koch of Anglo American, noted that the country's economy did not appear to have been seriously disturbed or impaired by constitutional severance from the Commonwealth.

> ... it is questionable whether this would be so if ... gold did not happen to command an assured export market, particularly in times of international uncertainty.[25]

South Africans generally, came quickly to accept their republican status. On 17 January 1963, responding to a request from the Speaker of the House of Assembly, H J Klopper, the Chamber's President, Peter H Anderson, presented to Parliament a mace fabricated of 18-carat gold, to serve as an appropriate symbol of the Speaker's authority in the republican Parliament.

By then the country was launched on its greatest economic boom. Manufacturing industry had taken off once more, imposing a strain on the balance of payments which the country was enabled to withstand by the flood of export revenue from new higher-grade gold mines. For the next three years, the growth rate consistently exceeded seven per cent. The new prosperity would attract 180 000 immigrants, mostly from Europe, in a decade, far overshadowing the drain after Sharpeville. Many South Africans who had faith in the country, and money to invest, became rich, and so did financial institutions.

Reviewing the economic scene in December 1963, George F D Palmer, Editor of the *Financial Mail*, Johannesburg, wrote in *Optima*:

> The fear of two-and-a-half years ago that South Africa, cut off from overseas sources of capital, would be able to advance economically only at a snail's pace has been countered. The gold mining industry, in effect, has stepped in where overseas investors feared to tread.[26]

One of the features of the recovery period was the greater role assumed by Afrikaner mining and finance houses. Afrikaners had for many years moved into the higher ranks of mine management. Now, with the assistance of Anglo American, Afrikaner capitalists took on a major entrepreneurial role. In 1963, as a result of an agreement between Federale Mynbou and Anglo, a new company was formed, Mainstraat Beleggings (Eiendoms) Beperk. The move led to the reconstitution of General Mining, which gave Afrikaner interests the majority shareholding. Tom F Muller, the Managing Director of Federale Mynbou, became Managing Director of General Mining, and in 1968/69 would become President of the Chamber. By 1967, Afrikaner capital would control about nine per cent of gold mining, thirty-seven per cent of uranium, twenty per cent of coal, and thirty-two per cent of asbestos mining.

In the years ahead General Mining would thrive and expand, absorbing Union Corporation, and in 1980 become General Mining Union Corporation (Gencor). Another major change came in 1971 with the entry of Thomas Barlow's into the mining field, absorbing the Corner House to form Barlow Rand. The mining division continued to operate as Rand Mines.

By then other structural changes within the industry had taken place. Mining shares were being distributed to an increasing extent among the general South African public, and large individual holdings had become rare. Most of the leaders of the industry were paid officials who were not large shareholders.[27]

Clearly, the Government's harsh determination to maintain law and order had helped in the restoration of confidence. With Verwoerd firmly in the saddle, there was no prospect of revolutionary upheaval. With this fear removed, there was nothing to prevent the resumption of the post-war trend of high economic growth, interrupted in 1958-1961.

In the prevailing prosperity, it was no surprise when Verwoerd was returned to power in March 1966 with a thumping majority, swollen by English-speaking voters who for the first time switched to support the National Party in significant numbers. Like Strijdom before him, Verwoerd did not live long to enjoy his triumph. On Tuesday, 6 September, shortly after taking his seat in Parliament for prayers at 2 15 pm, Verwoerd was stabbed in the neck and chest. He collapsed, and was rushed to hospital but died in the ambulance. His assailant was an immigrant, marked for deportation, named Demetrio Tsafendas, who was employed as a temporary parliamentary messenger. He was found to have acted on his own, and to be, indubitably, insane.

To succeed Verwoerd, the National Party caucus chose B J Vorster, the Minister of Justice, whose stern administration had done much to restore order in the years since Sharpeville. He declared that it was his intention to follow the Verwoerd road. In fact, he was to prove a deal more pragmatic, but he could not match the country's need as the winds of change blew colder.

[1] H Kenney, *Architect of Apartheid: H F Verwoerd - An Appraisal*, p 143.

[2] *Ibid*, pp 167-169.

[3] *Ibid*, p 170.

[4] *Ibid*, p 173.

[5] The author attended the discussion.

[6] 'When disaster threatens down below they stand ready', *The Chamber of Mines of South Africa: Ninety Years of Achievement*, pp 45, 49, 85. (Supplement to *The South African Mining and Engineering Journal*, July 1979.)

[7] Chamber of Mines Archives: File 'Coalbrook Disaster - General' 1960 (General Section): Official Statement issued at 11 45 am on Monday, 1 February 1960.

[8] Union of South Africa: Debates of the House of Assembly: Third Session, Twelfth Parliament: 15 January - 20 May 1960, Vols 103 to 105, Columns 1031-1032.

[9] 'Improving the Efficiency of Coal Mining', *Mining Survey*, No 68, April 1971, pp 3-5.

[10] N Fisher, *Harold Macmillan*, pp 231-235.

[11] Kenney, *Architect of Apartheid*, p 177.

[12] Author's recollection.

[13] Kenney, *Architect of Apartheid*, p 177.

[14] *Idem*.

[15] Fisher, pp 236-237.

[16] Kenney, *Architect of Apartheid*, p 181.

[17] *Ibid*, pp 183-184.

[18] Seventy-First Annual Report of the Transvaal and Orange Free State Chamber of Mines, 1960, p 32.

[19] Kenney, *Architect of Apartheid*, pp 194-195.

[20] 'Suggestions to end Unrest: Industry Leaders reveal what they told Verwoerd', and
'Industry's Plan to safeguard Future', *The Star*, 3 June 1960.

[21] Kenney, *Architect of Apartheid*, p 188.

[22] *Ibid*, p 197.

[23] Fisher, p 240.

[24] G F D Palmer, 'South Africa's continuing "boom" demands revised labour policies', *Optima*, December 1963, Volume 13, No 4, p 156.

[25] Seventy-Second Annual Report of the Transvaal and Orange Free State Chamber of Mines, 1961, p 5.

[26] Palmer, p 161.

[27] 'The Afrikaner's important Role in Mining Industry', *Mining Survey*, No 60, April 1967, pp 14-15.

CHAPTER THIRTY-THREE

Dark Days

The advent of the Vorster regime found the industry seemingly at the high point of prosperity. Since 1955 the mines had marked up a succession of record returns, the gold output in 1966 being double that of 1955. After a fall-off in 1967, output in each of the three following years would again be at a record level, 1970 being the historical peak year with production in excess of 1 000 metric tons of gold (or rather more than 32 million fine ounces). The high peaks, however, reflected a steady increase in the grade of ore mined, and a hectic rate of extraction, which together threatened to cut short the economic life of the industry. In all, seventeen mines closed down in the sixties, and, though there were nine replacements, Busschau was moved to exclaim in 1967: 'The Free State is being murdered, because it is producing too quickly.'[1] No doubt Busschau was resorting to hyperbole to drive home a point, for his statement served vividly to illuminate the extent to which new mines, as well as old, were being hard hit by the relentless pressure of rising costs against the millstone of a seemingly immovable gold price.

As early as 1963 Peter Anderson had warned that the spectacular achievements of the industry were distracting attention from the economic and other difficulties governing its middle- and long-term prospects. Seven mines had operated at a loss in 1962 and eight more had operated at a nominal profit in the hope of an increase in the price of gold. Yet all those marginal mines were of vital social and economic importance.[2] The Government, aware of the possible political backlash from diminishing job opportunities along the old Rand, announced a scheme of modest assistance to help marginal mines to cover the high cost of pumping out from their workings water overflowing from neighbouring mines already forced to close down. The following year state assistance was extended to certain mines to help to postpone their closure.

By 1964, costs were twice those of 1949. Black and white labour was costing eighty per cent more, expenditure on stores and materials had doubled and that on power and water had more than trebled. Appropriations from profits for capital purposes had increased sevenfold. Dividends to shareholders had increased two-and-a-half times, but this had been far outstripped by the increase in taxation and State's share of profits which was nearly four times greater than in 1949. Colin Anderson noted wryly that the State had shared lavishly in the profits without taking any of the risks that shareholders did in providing the capital to open up mines.[3]

The risks of unexpected loss or low returns were by no means academic, as had been demonstrated on the new gold-fields. Nor was mining free from unforeseen disaster. In the Free State field, Anglo Vaal's Merriespruit mine started with high hopes and, powerfully supported by United States capital, had drowned in 1956, and it would be many years thereafter before it could be de-watered and its reefs turned to account. But inrushes of water in the Free State were soon to be overshadowed in the public eye by sinkholes and surface subsidence on the West Wits Line. On the morning of 12 December 1962 a giant sinkhole, 150 feet wide by 150 feet deep, opened suddenly on the West Driefontein mine, engulfing a three-storey crusher plant with the loss of twenty-nine lives.

The Gatsrand of the West Wits Line had long been known to be riddled with natural cavities, among them the West Driefontein Caves which penetrate 500 feet down and are far deeper than the better-known Cango and Sterkfontein Caves. Under a certain combination of circumstances, sinkholes open with dramatic suddenness through the collapse of the roofs of dolomite caverns. This had occurred along the Gatsrand and elsewhere in South Africa since pre-historic times, but now on the West Wits Line twentieth-century mining had speeded up the process. Moreover, the dewatering of the area by pumping out water flowing into the mines from fissures in the dolomite caused subsidences and considerable damage to property. The first signs of this appeared at Carletonville in 1960/61 when waterpipes split, joints of electric cables pulled loose and houses cracked. Fortunately, the ground after a time tended to stabilize. By 1966, damage was estimated to total R14 million of which R9,7 million was to mine installations and R3,8 million to mine houses and facilities.

Safety and research measures costing R4 million were put in hand to protect people living there. There was continual physical and scientific surveillance of ground movement. In July 1964, after discussions chaired by Tommy L Gibbs, the Government Mining Engineer, the Far West Rand Dolomitic Water Association was created under the aegis of the Chamber to consider claims for compensation for loss of water flow in boreholes, or for damage to property. Thus, by the mid-1960s, the West Wits Line was adjusting to the threat of sinkholes and subsidences. Still ahead lay the major flood which threatened to drown West Driefontein, the world's most profitable mine.

Cartwright has recorded that the advent of the near-disaster at West Drie on 26 October 1968 bore 'some resemblance to that moment of horror at sea when, on a calm day, a liner strikes an uncharted reef'.[4] The first indication was a telephoned report from No 4 Shaft that 'a great deal of water' was coming down the shaft.[5] It was a cool description of a monstrous flood. For the next twenty-six days the mine staff would battle an inflow totalling some 2 000 million gallons of water. West Drie was narrowly saved by an incredible feat of off-the-cuff engineering. Battered by swirling floodwaters, the mine officials succeeded in first evacuating the workforce from underground, without loss of life, and then returning to build huge concrete plugs, and to seal off the flow. Asked to comment afterwards, the Manager, Ray Buley, said that in forty years of working underground he had never experienced, nor even heard of, anything like it. He said:

> No feat in the history of mining endeavour can surpass the work and the devotion of the men of West Driefontein, who successfully subdued the forces of Nature in the twenty-six days, October 26 to November 20, 1968.[6]

The post-war era had been one of remarkable technical progress, studded with world records in the speed of shaft-sinking and tunnelling. It was also one in which the industry could not fail to realize its increased dependence on scientific manpower. It had not only to encourage the training of technicians, graduate engineers and scientists, but to compete with other employers for a fair share of the trained men leaving technical colleges and universities in numbers wholly inadequate to the country's requirements. Institutions of higher education had long been supported financially by individual mining personalities, the mining houses and the Chamber. The sixties and seventies saw an extension of support through the Chamber for technical colleges in the Transvaal and Free State, and for universities countrywide.

But despite considerable advances in efficiency, the problem remained of American determination that gold should be held fast in the shackles of a pre-war dollar price, come what may. As a consequence, the industry found itself in mid-decade facing a daunting question: how to mine gold profitably at a price that had remained constant while the price of every other commodity had been free to soar. One answer lay in an increase in labour productivity, and the industry attempted 'some modification of traditional practices and attitudes',[7] or, to put it differently, the Chamber sought to engineer a bending of the colour bar.

The attempt at first gained momentum because it came in a package that offered the unions a *quid pro quo* of monthly pay, carrying improved and more stable earnings, better pension and leave benefits, and a new job status. Such changes had been successfully effected in other industries where the need was by no means so urgent.

The result was the so-called job experiment on twelve selected mines in 1964-1965. With the agreement of the Mine Workers' Union, the Government Mining Engineer relaxed regulations to permit experienced blacks, so-called competent non-scheduled persons (CNSPs), to take over some duties from white miners, notably the 'seeing in' of black gangs in areas where no blasting had taken place during the previous shift. This absolved the white miner from the time-consuming need to examine every working place personally before his gang could enter and start work, and eliminated many man-

420

hours wasted by black workers waiting for a white supervisor. The results were simple:

> ... the Bantu proved that they could do more responsible work, and safety on the mines was not affected. No employees were retrenched. The experiments showed that higher productivity could be achieved, enabling white miners and their Bantu assistants to enjoy higher earnings and improved status, and at the same time offering mines, especially older ones, the prospect of reduced working costs and longer lives.[8]

It was not to be. To the Chamber's chagrin the experiment was scotched by a break-away wing of the MWU, which created a sufficient rumpus to cause the Government to appoint a commission of inquiry. Having received the commission's report, the Minister of Mines and of Planning, J F W Haak, weakly backed off, stopping the scheme on the grounds that the commission had found it to have 'disadvantageous implications'. The upholding of the colour bar in the mining industry, he declared, was to continue.[9]

The Minister's announcement did not end the dispute that raged in the MWU, and there followed industrial unrest and sporadic strikes, which culminated in the capture of the Union by its right-wing rebels. In the seventies the same leadership would successfully block the advance of blacks in sampling and other spheres of employment which fell under the aegis of the Underground Officials' Association, and were not, *per se*, the concern of the MWU at all. The Union would constantly demonstrate that the spirit of militant white trade unionism was alive and well, and far from being subjugated.

Following the collapse of the experiment, the Chamber sought to improve its communication with employees in the hope that better understanding of proposed changes would facilitate their acceptance by union members. As part of this process, it established monthly newspapers, *Mining News* and *Die Mynblad*, circulated on the mines in English and Afrikaans respectively, to provide a bridge between employers and employees. However, for the time being, the Chamber could do no better than conclude monthly pay agreements with the unions in 1967, affecting both gold and coal mines, which contained some promise of increased productivity, at the cost of the biggest pay hike in the industry's history,[10] but with few of the gains which the Chamber had earlier hoped for.[11] The miners, moreover, proved reluctant to implement even the little that had been accepted by the Union. The Minister of Labour, Marais Viljoen, told Tom Reekie that the men did not like their security being 'chipped away'. Moreover, the employee benefits of the monthly pay agreements accrued solely to union members, and there was little in them for black workers.

Black labour was plentiful for most of the sixties, nearly two-thirds of the workers coming from beyond the country's borders. Their pay had been kept ahead of the modest rises in the Consumer Price Index through the decade, and a process was in train of encouraging their promotion to more productive mining jobs and better pay. However, average pay levels looked pitifully low in comparison to those offering in secondary industry, and were the cause of increasing concern in the mining houses, and of mounting public criticism. The labour historian, Francis Wilson, in his thought-provoking study of mine labour, argued that black wages had been so held down that, in real terms, black cash earnings in 1969 (that is, excluding benefits in kind) were no higher and possibly even lower than in 1911.[12]

The low level of pay to blacks reflected supply and demand. The men were willing to sign on at levels which were competitive with alternatives on offer; and the mines needed men at rates compatible with the low gold price and overall profitability. In fact, the profitability of gold mining was much lower than generally thought. S Herbert Frankel found that the average return to gold mining investment from 1935 to 1963 was only 4,3 per cent, compared with 7 per cent for United Kingdom equities.[13] Nor did the mining Groups ever wish that the right to progress to more skilled, better-paid jobs, should be denied to black mineworkers. This restriction was imposed by the colour bar.

Thus differences in earnings between blacks and whites, as Wilson recognized, lay deep within the social structure of South Africa. He considered that to narrow the gap between black and white earnings, and to increase the real level of black wages (without significantly reducing black jobs) at least five steps would have to be taken. These were the removal of the limitation on black wages imposed by the Chamber's 'maximum permissible average', the withdrawal of the legal barriers against black trade unionism; the abolition of the colour bar, both statutory and conventional; the alteration of the educational system to remove discrimination against those who were not white; and the withdrawal of legal barriers to a stabilized urban labour force.[14]

By 1969, the maximum permissible average was already of little force and effect, and was soon to be abolished. This apart, Wilson's list looked formidable, for the reforms advocated ran strongly counter to Government policy, and were beyond the power of the industry to further or influence; and this situation would remain unchanged for a decade. However, thereafter obstacles to advancement would crumble.

Fortunately for black workers they would not have to wait for rises until the reforms of the eighties. Wages were rapidly increased through the seventies as the United States's resistance to an increase in the gold price was crushed by economic pressures. Thereafter, job opportunities for blacks on the mines rapidly expanded. Mining houses were able to leave behind them the low wages of the past and to introduce unified remuneration structures that crossed the colour lines, so that those who did the same work got the same pay. And this would proceed *pari passu* with the erosion of the colour bar.

In 1966, however, the advances of the seventies and eighties could not be foreseen. The immediate economic outlook was gloomy and there seemed no weapons with which to combat the industry's decline. It is not surprising that

422

there were some in the mining houses who saw gold mining as a dying industry, and who began to press for meaningful subsidies to keep marginal mines in being. At the same time there were others who were opposed to subsidies in principle. They argued cogently that when a mine becomes unprofitable it was better to close it, and switch the available skilled manpower and resources to profitable enterprise. Subsidies as they saw them created artificial shortages and forced up remuneration. Two mining houses were convinced that the industry would have done better without subsidies. However, the majority of mining house opinion came down in favour of assistance to struggling mines. Dick S Cooke of JCI, President of the Chamber in 1966-1967, a man of tireless diligence, proved a formidable advocate of state assistance.

In 1960 Verwoerd had set up the Prime Minister's Economic Advisory Council to enable him to draw on the pooled wisdom of the Government, the Reserve Bank, the public utilities, and private enterprise. In 1966 the Council, reflecting general alarm at the threatened rapid decline of mining's contribution to revenue and foreign exchange, called on the Chamber for a fresh appraisal of the prospects for gold mining. Cooke, who was the industry's forceful delegate on the Council, presented a detailed study, which gave a sobering picture of the future of the industry, assuming that there was no increase in the price of gold and no discovery of new fields. The Chamber's appraisal showed that

> ... although gold production may continue to rise marginally for a few years, the turning point is in sight and when it is reached the drop will be alarmingly sharp. In twenty years' time output could well be only one–sixth of what it is today. Yet the tragedy is that there remains unmined within the Witwatersrand Geological Basin and extensions vast quantities of gold. At a higher price for gold this could become available to South Africa and to the world.[15]

The Council was impressed, and on its recommendation Dr N Diederichs, Minister of Finance, announced in his Budget Speech the following year the adoption of a comprehensive plan for state loans aimed at keeping vulnerable mines operating on a scale that would enable them to take the fullest advantage of a gold price increase. The Government was in effect betting on an increase in the price of gold; the called–for wager being no more than a negligible part of the total of mining's contribution to state revenues. Regarded in this way, the Government was about to pull off a spectacular gambling coup. But first the Chamber would have to endure the interregnum in which, in its most secret councils, it would be brought starkly to face with the prospect, of which public and Press were unaware, that it might be forced to sell the industry's output at prices in the dark depths below $35 an ounce.

[1] T Green, *The New World of Gold*, pp 54–55.

[2] Seventy-Third Annual Report of the Transvaal and Orange Free State Chamber of Mines, 1962, pp 8–10.

[3] Seventy-Fifth Annual Report of the Transvaal and Orange Free State Chamber of Mines, 1964, p 8.

[4] A P Cartwright, *West Driefontein - Ordeal by Water*, p 1.

[5] *Ibid*, p 2.

[6] *Ibid*, p 71.

[7] Seventy-Sixth Annual Report of the Transvaal and Orange Free State Chamber of Mines, 1965, p 9.

[8] *Ibid*, p 10.

[9] *Ibid*, pp 10, 31.

[10] Seventy-Eighth Annual Report of the Chamber of Mines of South Africa, 1967, p 9.

[11] Seventy-Ninth Annual Report of the Chamber of Mines of South Africa, 1968, p 9.

[12] Wilson, p 46.

[13] Frankel, *Investment and the Return to Equity Capital in the South African Gold Mining Industry: 1877-1965*, p 8.

[14] Wilson, pp 148–149.

[15] Seventy-Seventh Annual Report of the Transvaal and Orange Free State Chamber of Mines, 1966, pp 6–7.

CHAPTER THIRTY-FOUR

The Ides of March

While the older and less profitable gold mines faced the prospect that their future might be short, there was consolation for the country, and for the mining houses, in the performance of the total minerals industry. In the sixties the output of iron ore increased fourfold in value, that of copper fivefold and of platinum sevenfold.[1] The country had become, too, a leading world producer of antimony, asbestos, chrome and manganese. In all some fifty metals and minerals were exported. It was becoming apparent that South Africa was of major importance to the West, not only as a producer of gold, uranium and diamonds, but of a wide range of other minerals as well. South Africa, after the great territorial areas of America and Russia, ranked high as one of the major sources of strategic minerals.

Gold still dominated the scene, accounting for almost two-thirds in value of all mineral output, and would continue to do so for a long time to come. However, it was logical to recognize the advance of the mineral industries by changing and widening the scope of the Chamber. Accordingly, on 23 January 1968, the Chamber, which had been successively the Witwatersrand Chamber of Mines (1889-1896), the Chamber of Mines of the South African Republic (1897-1901), the Transvaal Chamber of Mines (1902-1952), and the Transvaal and Orange Free State Chamber of Mines, at last took its due place as the Chamber of Mines of South Africa. Its membership was opened to include, for the first time, mining companies in the Cape Province and Natal, and to embrace in its membership suitable applicant companies mining any type of mineral and metal.[2]

The new constitution provided for the creation of a Council, the first of which contained two representatives of each of the seven major mining houses.[3] In practice the Council would consist of the chairmen of the mining houses, together with another representative of each house, who would be appointed to the Executive Committee responsible for the general administration and management of the Chamber. Meetings of the Executive Committee were chaired by the President of the day, and it became customary for them to be attended by the Chairman of the Collieries Committee. The GPC, which had been the senior policy-making body since 1922, continued in being as the body specially responsible for the gold mining industry, but now, like the Collieries Committee, was ranged under the reconstituted Executive Committee.

The change in title and constitution was an overdue recognition of the national status of the Chamber, for it had been for many years the accepted spokesman on mining matters for the country as a whole; and all mining companies, and not just Chamber members, benefited from its activities. Of more importance for the future was the emergent international status of the Chamber. The Chamber had long been recognized in all mining countries as a clearing house for technical and expert information of all kinds. Its research organization was soon to be substantially expanded and to assume a leading role internationally; and it was to play key roles in the new dynamic markets that developed world-wide for gold and uranium.

The work of the Chamber had proliferated across its lifetime as mining houses widened the responsibilities assigned it. The workload on its office bearers and staff proliferated, too. Sir George Albu recalled in 1961 that in days not then so long past, the President of the Chamber was in the habit of arriving at the GPC meeting, held on Monday mornings, with no notes and no agenda; all this being carried in his head. The business of the week was quickly transacted, whereupon members adjourned for morning tea at a tearoom in nearby Simmonds Street 'which subsequently became a place of entertainment, the nature of which necessitated police intervention and its ultimate closure'.[4]

After the 1939-1945 War the work of the GPC so expanded that it required a full prior briefing of the President by the General Manager and half-a-dozen Chamber advisers. The weekly GPC meeting then lasted until after noon, the President occupying the chair on one side of the oval oak table dominating the panelled boardroom. He sat, flanked to the left and right by the General Manager and official advisers, with his six mining house colleagues opposite, facing them across the boxes of Havana cigars. After the meeting the members would depart for lunch at the Country Club a few miles away at Auckland Park (without the General Manager and officials). They would take their after-lunch coffee on the stoep shaded by the oak trees that grace that lovely estate. Sometimes, the more confidential or informal business of the GPC would be discussed at this time; the occasion providing an opportunity for an exchange of views between mining houses, without commitment. When decisions were taken, these were passed on later to the General Manager by the President. It became customary to refer to such decisions as having been taken 'under the oaks'. Later still when the agenda and the discussion of it became too full to allow of a leisurely lunch, a dining room was created out of the original Council Chamber of 1922, and a rather ugly, stylized, moulding of an oak tree was placed over the portal to preserve the tradition of more relaxed luncheon talk 'under the oaks'.

Tracey Milne, as Manager and General Manager, had established a new management pattern and orchestrated the Chamber's reconstitution as a national body. He now decided to retire at the end of June 1968. He handed over to his former deputy, Hugh D Thomson, who had joined the Chamber as a dispatch clerk in 1935. Thomson was particularly strong on the human relations side, it being said of him that he made many friends on his way up through the Chamber ranks, and lost none of them. He would prove a sound co-ordinator as the Chamber expanded and diversified, and would be ably assisted by the highly efficient David N Stuart who took over the deputy role and succeeded him as General Manager seven years later. The new management team was at once in the hot seat, for an atmosphere of crisis and international intrigue had been established a few months earlier as the United States mounted a bid to force down the gold price.

The International Monetary Fund was established at the United Nations Monetary and Financial Conference at Bretton Woods, in the United States, in 1944 as the basis of the future international monetary system, in which the currencies of member countries would be convertible into one another and into the dollar which the United States undertook would be convertible into gold at the current gold price of 1/35th of an ounce to the dollar.

In the early post-war years private transactions in gold were strictly controlled by the monetary authorities. As a result, black markets developed, chiefly in gold-hungry India and the Far East, where premiums above the official price could be obtained. In 1951, for example, South Africa was able to earn some £6,9 million above the official price. By 1954, however, the private demand for gold fell away and the premium disappeared.[5] The need of gold producers for a greater return on gold remained, and in 1955 the Chamber appointed a sub-committee of mining house experts, under Busschau's chairmanship, with the essential function of increasing mine earnings. It was given the bureaucratic title of the Sub-Committee for the Disposal of Gold. Chamber officials privately dubbed it the 'gold-is-good-for-you' committee. Its first concern was the presentation of learned contributions to the debate at international forums on the role of gold in the monetary system, advocating a revaluation of the metal, upwards of course, in terms of all currencies. Busschau played a leading role, travelling widely as an ambassador for gold. It was said of him that he was a formidable debater who firmly believed in never insulting anyone unintentionally. Under his chairmanship the 'gold-is-good-for-you' committee would also turn its attention to other ways of earning premiums, especially through the marketing of gold coins. In 1965, its stature and role was increased, and it was re-styled the Gold Study Committee, with Angus Collie as its full-time, world-travelling Secretary-General.

The Gold Study Committee was never to see the attainment of its goal of an orderly revaluation of gold, for the gold market would change in a most disorderly way through an explosion of demand. By 1961 this demand was already strong enough to force the price up to $40 an ounce. In response, a number of the principal trading nations formed the so-called gold pool, on the initiative of the United States which remained committed to trading at $35 an ounce, and was dedicated to upholding and enhancing the status of the dollar. Belgium, Britain, France, Italy, the Netherlands, Switzerland and West

Germany joined the United States as members of the pool, pledging their combined gold reserves in defence of the fixed gold price. A key role was played by the Bank of England which bought and sold on the London Market on behalf of the pool, in accordance with the movements of the daily London price fix. The Bank was also at that time the selling agent of the South African Reserve Bank, which was responsible for handling the country's gold sales.

The pool was effective in keeping the price within 20 US cents of $35 an ounce until 1968 but, despite the pool's massive backing, the economic forces acting counter to it became irresistible. First sterling, and then the dollar, came under speculative pressure, and there was a rush into gold. President de Gaulle took France out of the pool, but the remaining members believed they could maintain the price at $35 with the 24 000 tons of gold remaining in their reserves. They were mistaken. Devaluation of sterling in November 1967 triggered a demand that involved the unloading of $3 billion of gold from reserves onto the market within fourteen weeks in a vain bid to stop gold going above $35,20. William McChesney Martin of the United States Federal Reserve Board had declared that the United States would defend the price 'to the last ingot'. This rash promise involved the United States in airlifting to London in military aircraft nearly 1 000 tons of gold in a single week of March 1968. So much gold poured into the Bank of England that the floor of the weighing room collapsed. The gold pool collapsed, too, as pool members declined to unload their gold reserves further. The British Government was compelled to announce the closing of the London Market on 15 March 1968, 'at the request of the United States'.[6]

The IMF and the central banks had now to restructure the market, and chose to do so as a two-tier system, consisting of an official market on which gold was sold to central banks at the fixed official price for monetary purposes, and a free market on which gold for all other purposes was sold at prices fluctuating in accordance with supply and demand. At first sight, the so-called Washington Agreement of March 1968 seemed to signal the freeing of the gold price, but there was a 'sting in the tail' of the agreement reached between central banks and the IMF that had serious implications for South Africa. This was the declaration by central banks, at the instigation of the United States, that there was sufficient gold in the monetary system, backed by a pledge that they would not buy newly-mined gold in the future.[7] The pretext for this American device to force down the gold price (and enhance the role of the dollar) was the creation by the IMF of so-called Special Drawing Rights (SDR), dubbed 'paper gold', which former pool members decreed could replace either gold or dollars as a reserve asset of central banks.

To the dismay of South Africa, it soon became clear that central banks, and the IMF, were under strong pressure from the United States to observe this arrangement strictly, forcing South Africa to operate only on the free market, thus depressing the price. The IMF operated under a voting system weighted by the economic power of the country concerned, and was consequently dominated by the United States. And the United States was clearly determined to push down the price and re-establish the pre-eminence of the dollar, something which its financial advisers regarded as more important than any possible profit that might accrue from the revaluation of their country's own enormous gold reserves.[8] A senior official of the United States Treasury was reported at the time to have predicted that the free market price would soon drop below the official price and might even go as low as $6 an ounce.[9]

For twenty-one months after the Ides of March 1968, the fate of the economy of Southern Africa hung in the balance. Through this period the marketing of South Africa's gold was master-minded by the Reserve Bank, under the Governorship of Dr T W de Jongh, who played in the new ball park with remarkable skill. It was clear to the Bank that if South Africa openly entered into transactions on the free market, with the prospect of having to channel all gold sales there, the price would receive a serious set-back, which would have played into the hands of those who were bent on discrediting the role of gold in the monetary system.[10] The Bank thus operated under a cloak of confidentiality that shielded the public from the anxiety that robbed the country's administrators and mining leaders of their sleep.

In order to put South Africa's position fully to the test, the Treasury now asked the IMF to buy one million ounces of gold, a request to which the IMF was under an obligation to accede in terms of its Articles of Agreement, only to be fobbed off with the statement that 'no final decision had been taken on this offer'. Fortunately, it emerged from discussions with European bankers that they felt that the Americans had forced on them the card that restricted South African gold sales, and that the arrangement was unfair. Fortunately, too, South Africa was economically strong at that stage. It could afford to hold off selling gold on the free market for long enough to enable it to plot a careful course of action. However, it could not continue to hoard its massive production indefinitely. European banks now helped by lending money to South Africa to tide her over. Then certain monetary authorities, including an important one, indicated their willingness to buy clandestinely. The Reserve Bank also, acting as the agent of the mines, undertook the sale of gold to private dealers secretly in a manner that would not reveal the transactions to the market and influence the price.[11]

All this was done in close concert with the Chamber. The President for the critical three months following the Ides of March 1968, was Tom Reekie, a man of quiet manner and wit, who had advanced from office boy to Managing Director of Rand Mines. Reekie was a skilled administrator, but without intimate knowledge of the gold markets. He learned rapidly, for he found himself in an extraordinary position. He was brought into the picture under a top secret injunction that prevented him from disclosing details of transactions, even to his mining house colleagues on the GPC. He and his successors, Tom Muller and Dick Cooke, were obliged to consider and to endorse marketing proposals from the Reserve Bank on their sole responsibility. For nearly two years discussions with Dr de Jongh were recorded only in the handwriting of Tom Reekie and subsequently, Hugh Thomson. The record was kept locked in the Chamber's confidential strongroom. De Jongh and Reekie sought light relief from their heavy responsibilities by coining code names for each other such as '007'.

The American authorities were known to be watching the market closely to detect what sales South Africa might be making. They soon began to suspect that these were taking place, and did not like it at all. They went to great lengths to find out what was happening. The South African authorities in turn gave a top secret rating to the clandestine central bank deals and to the secret sales to private dealers that were now activated. Gold to meet the deals that De Jongh and Reekie forged were loaded on aircraft at Jan Smuts Airport at two o'clock in the morning.

However, the Reserve Bank was soon able to announce that countries had made rand drawings on the IMF and converted them into gold from South Africa, thereby providing an additional method by which gold could be channelled into official reserves, and the situation eased somewhat. In total, South Africa's sales to monetary authorities between the Ides of March 1968 and December 1969 amounted to more than 12 million ounces and, in addition, more than 28 million ounces were sold to private buyers. Partly as a result of the marketing expertise displayed, the free market price actually rose, and more than R65 million was paid out to gold mining companies in premiums above the official price.

Premiums apart, the skilful operation of gold marketing gave South Africa a breathing space in which to negotiate a considered agreement with the United States and to reject the initial American proposals. The final discussions took place in Rome from 12 to 16 December 1969, when South African and American delegates concluded an agreement which gave South Africa, in return for subscribing to certain rules to ensure orderly marketing, the right to sell gold to the IMF at $35 an ounce, thus effectively placing a floor under the price. This favourable arrangement came at a time when South Africa's balance of payments was under strong pressure and it was forced to sell substantial amounts of gold from its reserves. In addition, interest rates abroad rose steeply. The value of the new agreement was quickly proven, for the free market price came immediately under pressure; and on 8 January 1970, it fell below $35 for the first time. South Africa at once availed herself of the new agreement and sold gold to the IMF. The price soon strengthened again. In summation, it can be said that the gold market policy followed by South Africa at this critical time was to contribute importantly to the rapid rise in the price to above $100 an ounce on 14 May 1973. The price would soon thereafter go much higher than that, but then the major influences would be the Opec price hikes, high rates of inflation, the accompanying widespread loss of confidence in paper currencies, and general monetary uncertainty.[12]

De Jongh recalls that in the difficult days after March 1968 he found himself, on one of his journeys abroad, in a lift with Paul A Volcker, the United States banker and state financial adviser who was later to be described as 'the Henry A Kissinger of monetary diplomacy'.[13] Volcker looked down on De Jongh

430

from his six foot seven inches of height and said: 'Why don't you sell off that gold of yours while you can still get something for it?' Some years later, he met Volcker again and asked: 'What price our gold now?' Volcker offered no reply.[14]

It has to be remembered that in 1968 eminent economists in the United States and the West believed a monetary system dependent on gold to be a survival from the past that had no place in the modern industrial world. Great faith was placed in the SDR which they believed would, along with the dollar, largely take over from gold and provide a controlled growth in central bank reserves. However, some were sceptical. When the SDR was introduced a lunch was given for central bankers meeting in New York. An American banker speaking at the lunch produced a dollar bill and, pretending to scrutinize it, said that he had always believed that the words on the dollar bill were 'In Gold we trust'. Now he found that the words were actually 'In God we trust'. Similarly, it has been recorded that one Cambridge economist, near the end of a distinguished career, objected strongly that 'paper gold' was a contradiction in terms, but found his arguments dismissed in the Economics Faculty Common Room as a reflection of the old man's waning intellectual powers. When he burst out angrily: 'Try selling them to the Arabs', his younger colleagues shook wise heads. But the old man had the last laugh. By the end of the seventies, SDRs were estimated to account for some five per cent of the reserves of central banks, and currency about forty-five per cent, while gold provided around fifty per cent.[15]

When the London Market was closed for two weeks in 1968, the Swiss banks at once jumped in and established the Zurich Market. The Reserve Bank, in consultation with the Treasury, quickly grasped the advantages of the new market and most of South Africa's gold would henceforth be sold there. The consortium of Swiss banks who made the market were ready to give loans, and to buy from South Africa for their own account. These facilities the London Market could not match – there sellers had to rely on buyers coming forward to take gold at the price offering.[16] It was moreover difficult for South Africa after the collapse of the gold pool to deal with the London Market because of its close ties with the pool, the Bank of England, and the IMF.

The Chamber for its part quickly realized the need for more knowledge of the gold markets. One spin-off was the introduction of the portfolio system in the Executive Committee and the GPC, under which each member took on a special area of responsibility, acquired expertise in it, and created a greater continuity of knowledge. Another spin-off was the decision to conduct a study of research into the technical uses of gold, with a view to increasing its applications in the electronic and other industries. The Chamber decided to send its Research Adviser, Dr W S Rapson, to Europe and America to report on the possibilities. In a far-sighted review that went way beyond the technical, Rapson advised the gold producers unequivocally that they should prepare themselves to supply a market that would be increasingly industrial in character. He emphasized that the major and immediate opportunity lay in the promotion of gold jewellery. They should accordingly establish a gold marketing organization without delay.

At the same time, there had been set in train in London by Consolidated Goldfields and by Charter Consolidated, in separate surveys, the most careful scrutiny yet of the ultimate destination of the gold sold on official markets to meet requirements long assumed to be mainly monetary. The results of the surveys were astonishing, so much so that they were not readily believed. They showed that consumption of gold in jewellery alone had escalated to the point where it exceeded 1 000 tons a year, that is the equivalent of annual South African output which was then riding near its all-time peak. And they found that total absorption of gold in industry, including jewellery, exceeded world output.

For the first time there was demonstrated a strong incentive for gold mines to intervene in the market place, and the GPC moved at once to do so. Greg Cooper, a senior marketing executive with General Mining, was seconded as Gold Marketing Adviser, and a detailed study began of the role the Chamber might play in promoting gold sales. There followed the establishment of the International Gold Corporation, with the members of the GPC as its Board of Directors, and Cooper as its Chief Executive. The industry assigned to it the responsibility for establishing contacts with consumers, existing and potential, and in particular with the jewellery trade.

The Corporation, soon widely known as Intergold, was already operating in Europe when it was formally registered as a company in 1971. It was a propitious moment to launch for immediate events in the gold market operated in its favour. As European banks continued to trade dollars for gold with the US Federal Reserve at the bargain price of $35, the United States experienced a gold drain which forced it successively to eliminate the gold backing for Federal Reserve deposits and for its banknotes. Finally, in August 1971, the so-called gold window was slammed shut. The dollar was no longer convertible, no longer 'as good as gold'.

In the sixties financial writers had often dismissed the Chamber's predictions of an inevitable price rise as whistling in the dark that foreshadowed gold's inevitable decline. Events proved the writers to be poor prophets, and the Chamber an exceptionally conservative one. There lay ahead a new era of furious trading in gold, and a highly volatile price that would touch peaks undreamed of.

432

[1] Eightieth Annual Report of the Chamber of Mines of South Africa, 1969, p 12.

[2] 'Chamber establishes National Status', *Mining Survey*, No 62, April 1968, p 3, *et seq.*

[3] *Ibid*, pp 4-5.

[4] Annual Report of the Chamber of Mines of South Africa, 1961, pp 16-17. (Speech by Sir George Albu [second baronet] at Annual General Meeting held on 25 June 1962.)

[5] T W de Jongh, *The Marketing of South Africa's Gold*, pp 1-2. (Address delivered on 15 November 1974, on the occasion of the Annual Dinner of the Pretoria Branch of the Economic Society of South Africa.)

[6] Green, pp 114-115.

[7] Interview with Dr T W de Jongh, former Governor of the South African Reserve Bank, at the Strand, Cape, on 7 July 1983.

[8] Interview with Dr T W de Jongh.

[9] D G Franzsen, 'Monetary Policy in South Africa: 1932-82', *The South African Journal of Economics*, Vol 51, No 1, March 1983, p 112.

[10] Interview with Dr T W de Jongh.

[11] Interview with Dr T W de Jongh.
Dr T W de Jongh's address on 15 November 1974, p 4. (see [5] above.)

[12] Interview with Dr T W de Jongh.

[13] Interview with Dr T W de Jongh.
'Volcker, Paul A(dolph)' in *Current Biography 1973*, p 425.

[14] Interview with Dr T W de Jongh.

[15] J Forsyth (Morgan Grenfell & Co Ltd), *A Diversified Reserve Situation – The Role of Gold*, pp 123, 126. (Speech made at a Conference on World Gold in the 1980s, held in Montreux, Switzerland, on 12 and 13 June 1979.)

[16] Interview with Dr T W de Jongh.

CHAPTER THIRTY-FIVE

Renaissance of Gold

With the slamming of the United States gold window in 1971, there passed another crisis period in the history of South Africa's gold mines. For all of the seventies, the industry could plan once again for expansion and give the new International Gold Corporation the necessary resources to promote gold in jewellery, in a wide spectrum of industrial usage, in coinage and in investment. In the all-important jewellery field, Intergold gave special emphasis to sponsorship and participation in national jewellery associations, and other bodies concerned with promotion. It involved itself in the education of the trade, in exhibitions and trade fairs; and in influencing design and fashion. And the Chamber backed Intergold's operations by advocacy for gold in its new, expanding role. Chamber spokesmen such as Robin Plumbridge of Gold Fields and Tom R Main, the Chamber's Chief Economist and later Assistant General Manager, became acknowledged world experts on the role of gold and familiar figures at international forums.

Intergold focused its attention first on Europe, establishing a regional head office in Geneva, and then expanding to incorporate the principal European markets. Branches were opened in London, Munich, Paris, Barcelona and Milan. Gradually over the years the influence of these offices was extended to include Austria, Belgium, Denmark, Greece, Holland, Norway, Portugal, Sweden and beyond. Operations in the United States opened in 1975, a regional head office was established in New York in 1977 and activities extended to include Canada and Central and South America. In 1979, Intergold moved into the Far East, establishing its regional head office in Hong Kong, and developing important operations in Japan and elsewhere.[1]

At the end of 1972 Greg Cooper, having given Intergold its initial impetus, returned to head marketing operations for General Mining. He handed over to Don Mackay-Coghill, who had joined Intergold as a managerial assistant in 1971 at the age of twenty-nine.

Mackay-Coghill had joined the Chamber originally because of its civilized approach to time-off for representative sport, including cricket. He was unlucky not to obtain international status as a Springbok fast bowler before Intergold called him from the cricket field. He now turned all his attention to grasp the opportunity given to him to develop an international marketing operation. He received vital guidance and support from Plumbridge, who was to be President of the Chamber in the years 1973–1974 and 1976–1977, and was later to become Chairman of Gold Fields. Plumbridge, a Rhodes scholar and first-class cricketer and rugby player, had been appointed to the GPC in 1969 at the age of thirty-four and took over the important new gold portfolio in 1972. As such he had special responsibility for Intergold, and guided the organization through its formative years, presiding at the first conference in Geneva which set the initial marketing guidelines. His colleagues on the GPC knew him as conservative and sound, as well as a brilliant financial analyst. When Plumbridge gave a considered nod to Intergold's plans, his older colleagues offered only token resistance to soaring budgets.

Initially, Intergold concentrated on the promotion of gold jewellery and watches, following the principle of close co-operation with the trade, and this would remain its prime function and a major area of achievement. However, in 1973, with its establishment phase behind it, Intergold would be assigned responsibility for marketing South Africa's gold Krugerrand which was to play a star role in the burgeoning coin market.

When the members of the GPC went to lunch 'under the oaks' at the Country Club in the fifties and arrived in the cool and spacious bar, it became the custom for them each to put 18s in the kitty and to toss out 'odds-and-evens'. The winner took the pool which was usually enough to pay for the drinks and the lunch. When Busschau joined the Committee, he was astonished to see his colleagues tossing *silver* coins, florins and half-crowns. He procured for them six United States double eagles, worth at issue prior to 1934, the coin's face value of US$20. The next time the drinks were called around the bar, seven ounces of gold went spinning, scintillating, in the air.[2] It was a moment of fun before more serious business, but gold coins were to become serious business, too, for the Committee and the Chamber. They would be talked about endlessly in all their guises, until all the thinking was to coalesce as the Krugerrand. Gold as money, so long removed from common view, was on the way back to the man-in-the-street.

In the early sixties thinking in the Chamber moved strongly in the direction of minting a one-ounce legal tender coin with the object of placing gold in as many hands as possible and creating an ever-widening vested interest in a higher gold price. The opportunity to turn this thinking into action came with the decision to introduce a new standard coinage as part of the decimalization process begun in 1961 which made the rand the South African unit of account.

Existing legislation had long provided for gold coins similar to the British sovereign and half-sovereign, and amendments authorized the minting of R1 and R2 gold coins of equivalent weight and gold content. These were marketed through a consortium of Swiss banks, in modest numbers to meet a modest demand. In early 1964 the President of the Chamber was Dr A A 'Attie' von Maltitz, a notable advocate of gold who was to play a significant role in events to come. Accompanied by Colin Anderson and Collie, he called on the Minister of Finance, Dr T E Dönges, and among the items discussed was the

435

inclusion of a new gold coin in the coinage of South Africa.

Von Maltitz was enthusiastic about such a coin's circulating in South Africa, pointing out that the world's major gold-producing country ought to set a good example. Dönges was not enthusiastic about this. He was afraid that, in times of financial crisis, the gold coins might be smuggled abroad on a scale that would constitute a serious outflow of gold. However, he showed interest in a one-ounce coin that would earn foreign exchange, saying that he had been told that there might be demand overseas for a coin heavier than the R2, such as the French louis-d'or of nearly one ounce. In the course of the discussion, Anderson took out and passed around the one-ounce double eagle that Busschau had obtained for him and other GPC members a decade before. Dönges responded by inviting the Chamber to give evidence on the point to the Parliamentary Select Committee set up to review the proposed new standard coinage.[3]

The Chamber's Special Sub-Committee on the Disposal of Gold met in the Chamber on 23 March 1964, under the chairmanship of Anderson, and considered a draft memo of evidence to the Select Committee, prepared by Collie and H Devonport, the Committee Secretary, which proposed inclusion in the official coinage of a one-ounce gold coin with a face value of R25, or around the value of an ounce of gold at the time. Those present were Dr J E Holloway, former Secretary of Finance, who was an economic adviser to Union Corporation, M W Richards (Union Corporation), F J L Wells (JCI), A N Wilson (Anglo American), Collie and Devonport. The meeting after a wide-ranging discussion added to the memo before them the all-important touch. Together, they altered the draft memo of evidence to delete the suggested R25 face value and proposed instead 'a gold coin containing one troy ounce of gold, but with no face value'.[4] The Sub-Committee had realized that a face value in rands would suffer the historic fate of such coins of being rendered anachronistic by an increase in the price of gold. And it saw that a coin without a face value would be a prestigious innovation in world coinage. Out of this decision was to flow the package that was to make the Krugerrand pre-eminent in the fast-burgeoning bullion coin markets of the world – the mass marketing of a legal tender coin containing one ounce of gold, the value of which in terms of all currencies, could easily be checked by reference to the price fixing, commonly published in major newspapers across the world, and with a face value on the coin itself, and defined in legislation, of the weight of the intrinsic gold content, instead of in the unit of account, the rand.

Careful study of Chamber records, and consultation with those involved, makes it clear that the Krugerrand was not a one-man invention, but a corporate achievement, born of the to-and-fro of debate. All those concerned share the credit in greater or lesser degree for what the *Financial Mail*, Johannesburg, described in April 1980 as a 'concept quite brilliant in its simplicity'.[5] But no single individual had a prior, clear vision of the total concept, which was developed across a span of years. It is certain, too, that none of the participants foresaw the happy combination of the stars which would ordain, some years after the coin was first envisaged, that the Krugerrand would be delivered to the gold markets of the world in large quantities at exactly the most favourable moment in economic time.

The Chamber's proposals were in due course included in the South African Mint and Coinage Act of 1964, which authorized issue of a legal tender coin of one ounce troy, entitled the 'Trojan'. But the Government green light was withheld. The Minister was doubtful if a coin without a face value in rands would be accepted as legal tender coinage; a view held by some in the mining houses. And for a while Swiss banking authorities shared their doubts. They warned that a coin without a face value might be classified as a medallion and be subject to customs duties and other taxes from which official gold coins were exempt. The Chamber sent them a copy of the Coinage Act. After studying it, the Swiss bankers changed their minds and agreed with the Chamber that the coin, being an official coin in South Africa and legal tender for the payment of any amount of money, could be imported into European countries without taxes or duties being levied. It took still more time to convince the Minister, and there were technical difficulties in the South African Mint. Dönges was not happy about the name Trojan, and invited suggestions from the public. The Chamber proposed the Biblical Talent, but many Afrikaners proposed names linked to President Kruger, who had issued gold coins. Dönges eventually decided on the name Krugerrand. However, its introduction did not look a project of importance or urgency, and it tended to sink to the bottom of Treasury in-baskets. However, in due and measured time, there passed through Parliament and became law in October 1966 the South African Mint and Coinage Further Amendment Act. The Act established the name 'Krugerrand', revised the detailed specifications of the new coin, and, incidentally, made provision for the abolition of coins of the denomination of two-and-a-half cents.

In debate on the new measure, Members of Parliament were inclined to give more attention to the latter proposition, the final quietus given to the old threepenny bit, colloquially and affectionately known as the 'tickey', but a maverick vestige of pre-decimalization days gone by. Opposition spokesmen said that the legislation should rather be known as the 'Death of the Tickey' Bill. They wept a tear at its passing and asked 'Who killed Cock Robin?' So far as the Krugerrand was concerned MPs presumed it would chiefly be a prestige coin sold to collectors around the world. They gave the bill a cool blessing.[6]

Dönges was soon succeeded as Minister of Finance by Dr Nico Diederichs, who approved the design of the new coin – the bust of President Kruger on the obverse, with the springbok designed by Coert Steynberg and the words 'Krugerrand Fyngoud 1 oz Fine Gold' on the reverse. In due course, the Minister struck the first coin on a press dating from the days of the old South African Republic and from a die used to strike the Kruger half-crown. The historic date was 1 July 1967. It was a quiet affair with only Government representatives in attendance. There does not seem to have been any prescience that a decade later a larger party would attend the striking of the twenty-millionth coin, or that in the seventies annual sales would go as high as six million, or that the Krugerrand's contribution to the country's exports in a year would account for as much as ten per cent of the value total.

Initial sales were as unobtrusive as the launching. The Chamber entered into negotiations with a consortium formed by the three principal Swiss banks, the Swiss Bank Corporation, the Swiss Credit Bank and the Union Bank of Switzerland, and initially accepted their advice that to launch the Krugerrand in competition with well-known coins, it should be minted in limited quantities and in high-quality proof-like condition. The consortium made a modest start with the Krugerrand, selling 70 000 between October 1967, and October 1969.

However, in 1969 the Chamber set in motion the mass marketing of the coin, on the initiative of Von Maltitz, then Chairman of the Gold Study Committee. Von Maltitz insisted that it was essential to move the Krugerrand into the hands of the man-in-the-street in large numbers. Having got the nod from the Chamber, Von Maltitz, accompanied by Collie, called on the Swiss bankers. The bankers at first tried to dissuade Von Maltitz from departing from the slow build-up of the coin as an item of interest to collectors and sophisticated hoarders. The Swiss were not alone in holding this view. Coins like the sovereign, the old United States eagle and the French napoleon seemed to hold undisputed sway. There was no way that anyone could discern that the demand for gold coins was about to outstrip the availability of historic gold coins, and of modern re-strikes of them.

The Swiss argued cogently the merits of building the collector's market for high-quality coin. Von Maltitz, quiet-spoken but tough and determined, was equally adamant that the Chamber was going to market the Krugerrand as a bullion coin (as opposed to a proof coin for collectors), and in large numbers. It was moreover going to widen the distribution channels to include others than the Swiss banks. The Swiss bankers, disappointed but as ever with a shrewd eye for gold business, said 'We'll take 100 000 of the new Krugerrands. When can we expect delivery?' They were soon to take millions more.

The Chamber accordingly decided at the end of 1969 that initially 500 000 Krugerrands should be minted in so-called 'uncirculated condition', without the final cosmetic polishing to a mirror finish of the proof coin. It inquired from the Government whether the South African Mint would be able to undertake the production of the coins. The Mint could not. It was stretched to full capacity in meeting the growing demand for nickel and bronze coins. It was then that the Chamber resolved the pending impasse by producing another piece of the jigsaw.

In 1965, the Chamber had undertaken the modernization and expansion of the Rand Refinery to match the mounting flood of gold produced by the mines, and to incorporate the works of a sister company, By-Products Limited, on the Refinery site. By 1970 the new Rand Refinery, the largest in the world, was complete, and a unique industry showplace, opened, for security reasons, only to select and distinguished visitors. As a result, the

Chamber was able to offer to add an additional phase to the gold refining process – the stamping out of twenty-two carat gold blanks of one-ounce fine, ready for minting into Krugerrands at the South African Mint. The Government accepted, and the Chamber rapidly installed the required machines and technical processes.

During the 1939-1945 War the South African Reserve Bank had been given the legal function of marketing South Africa's gold, and post-war it had retained it. It still today likes to play the country's gold cards close to its chest. The law provides that all gold produced must be offered for sale to the Reserve Bank which immediately credits the mines with current value less a small handling charge. However, in 1970 the Government agreed to exclude gold allocated to meet orders for uncirculated Krugerrands, while formally retaining control on the proportion allotted to the purpose.

Thus, the mass marketing of the Krugerrand in uncirculated condition was launched in 1970 with many advantages. A lively market for gold coins was already in being, largely as a result of the activities of the Swiss banks and their specialist knowledge of investment psychology. Largely by chance, the Krugerrand reached the market as supplies of traditional coins dried up. Moreover, it sold in its newly-minted form as a bullion coin at a very low premium, and possessed a decisive image of singularity.

The coin was first launched in West Germany. Fritz Plass, then heading the Gold Branch of the Deutsche Bank AG, has recalled that he received a telephone call from his Chairman, who said: 'I have a Mr Angus Collie here from South Africa with some coins to sell. Help him.' Plass was a young man who had the acumen to see a new opportunity that many in German banks would decry. He saw that Krugerrands as legal tender would escape the twelve per cent VAT then imposed on all goods entering West Germany (including gold bars or medallions). The coin would provide Germans with the cheapest form of gold on offer and the bank with the prospects of developing a wider market for the metal.

He decided to back a hunch that the coin would 'go', and took a personal decision to order 50 000 coins. He admits to sleepless nights in the weeks before sales began. Branches were not all enthusiastic, and some sent the coins back to head office. He offered other banks a share of the coins and they turned it down. A major bank commented: 'For such a coin, there will never be any market whatsoever.'

Launch day was 13 November 1970. Plass recalls: 'A Friday and a day of ill-omen in Germany.' In the event the coins were quickly sold out. He ordered more, and 105 000 were sold in two weeks. Then the problem was to meet the demand.[7]

Plass can regard with justifiable pride the trophy in his office, presented to him by Intergold to mark the bank's purchase of the five-millionth coin in 1978. By 1980, the value of the coin in Germany would have increased tenfold, and, with the spread of marketing into other Continental countries, the number of Europeans owning one Krugerrand or more was estimated at 15 million.

Germany would remain the major market, matched only by the United States which, after a hesitant start, would prove an equally important outlet for the coins. Gold ownership in the United States was legalized only in January 1975. At that time ordinary Americans knew gold only from their history books. They remembered vaguely that the United States had gone on the gold standard in 1900, and that for more than thirty years it had been possible to trade a ten dollar bill for a gold eagle. But in 1933 Roosevelt had taken the United States off the gold standard. The minting of gold coins came to an end and private ownership of gold bullion was declared illegal. Only specialized buyers, like jewellery manufacturers, dentists or numismatists, could legally buy, sell or collect gold. Millions of Americans dutifully exchanged their gold coins for paper dollars at the fixed price of $35 an ounce. By 1975 only about nine per cent of the population were old enough to remember that once one could exchange paper dollars for gold coin. A leading American economist and Nobel Prizewinner, Paul Samuelson, had declared, only a few years previously, that gold was no more than a sideshow, of interest only to French hoarders, Arab oil sheiks and underworld gangsters. It was Intergold's achievement, in company with powerful trading partners, to make the sideshow into America's star attraction.

In the later seventies the gold price rose so far and so fast that the Krugerrand became too expensive for many of the men and women it was intended to reach. The Chamber therefore obtained the agreement of the South African authorities to the striking, in addition to the one-ounce coin, of a half-, quarter- and one-tenth-ounce Krugerrand, each containing one-half, one-quarter and one-tenth of an ounce of gold respectively. The new coins were launched by Intergold internationally on 23 September 1980, and other coin-producing countries were soon to follow suit in producing fractional coins. In 1985, sales in the four sizes minted reached the cumulative total of 50 million coins.

In that year, sales in the United States had plunged as a result of the Reagan Administration's decision to ban imports of Krugerrands as part of the international programme of sanctions and economic pressure to bring about political reform in South Africa. The Krugerrand continued to enjoy wide acceptance as an investment medium. And while it was a matter of pride to Intergold to keep its coin sales high, it mattered relatively little to South African gold producers whether or not gold buyers bought Krugerrands as long as they continued to invest in gold, either in the coins of other countries, in gold bars, small or large, or in the complexity of gold investment instruments that evolved in the seventies. The Chamber, through Intergold and its trading partners, had done much more than to perceive and exploit a favourable marketing opportunity for its product: it had succeeded in so enlarging mankind's perception of the metal as an investment, that the inhibitions harboured against it had been progressively broken down. The price of

440

gold will continue to wax and wane with the vagaries of supply and demand, but the position won for it in the seventies as a personal asset of enduring value looks to be, for the foreseeable future, unassailable.

[1] 'Leadership in the Market Place', *Intergold*, p 1. (Booklet published by the International Gold Corporation in 1981).

[2] Interview with C B Anderson, at Sandton, Transvaal, on 12 January 1983.

[3] Chamber of Mines Archives: File 'Dec. Coinage – Gen. – 1', 1964: Transvaal and Orange Free State Chamber of Mines, Gold Producers' Committee: Extract from Report on Interview with the Minister of Finance, Dr the Hon T E Dönges, in Cape Town, on 20 February 1964.

[4] Chamber of Mines Archives: File 'Dec. Coinage – Gen. – 1', 1964: Transvaal and Orange Free State Chamber of Mines: Gold Producers' Sub-Committee: Minutes of the Meeting of the Special Sub-Committee on the Disposal of Gold held in Johannesburg on 23 March 1964, p 3.

[5] 'Krugerrands', Special Report: Supplement to the *Financial Mail*, 25 April 1980, p 1.

[6] Republic of South Africa: Debates of the House of Assembly: First Session – Third Parliament: 29 July to 19 October 1966, Volumes 17 and 18, Columns 3074–3084.

[7] Interview with Fritz Plass, September/October 1981, in Frankfurt, West Germany.

CHAPTER THIRTY-SIX

All Aboard the Roller Coaster!

The seventies were years of rapid change in South Africa, and in the world, bringing for the mining industry exceptional opportunities and great risks. Harry Oppenheimer, speaking at the Annual General Meeting of the Chamber on 20 June 1972, remarked that leadership of the industry called for more than the usual courage and imagination. 'It is written, and I have always liked the saying, that wisdom lies in masterful administration of the unforeseen and ... that certainly applies to the running of this industry in these times.'[1]

In the previous December, central banks had concluded in the United States the so-called Smithsonian Agreement in a vain bid to cool currency dealings, even conceding a mini-devaluation of the mighty dollar. The official price of gold was raised to $38 an ounce, or around $6 less than the prevailing free market price. In April 1972, Chamber officials had discussions with international monetary authorities in London, Paris, Brussels, Frankfurt and Zurich, and sought their opinion on the likely trend of the free market gold price.[2] By then the price had edged up to $49.[3] Hardly any of these authorities saw the price staying up there, and nobody at all saw the take-off that lay just around the corner. The Chamber officials came home and reported that the consensus of expert opinion, almost without exception, was that the price would soon start to fall, and that, as it fell, it would find nothing to hook on in its downward slide.

What actually happened was that the price at once started to rise, reaching $70 in August. At the year-end, it looked fairly steady at $65, and there were gold market experts who believed that the price would stay at that level; there were others who still believed it would drop. They were wrong again. Speculative fever was such that the exchange markets were closed for two weeks at the beginning of March 1973, and re-opened to a new world of floating exchange rates, and a price of $80 to $90. The price passed $100 an ounce for the first time on 14 May. In June the price stood at $127. In that month, the Chamber's President, R C J ('Jeff') Goode (Union Corporation) could declare that the rapid rise had given the industry its greatest stimulus in years. The industry had been enabled to reduce steadily the grade of ore mined and to extend the life of the mines. However he warned:

Unhappily the bright prospects are shadowed by what could prove to be the highest inflation rate of the past 50 years, a rate which stems from the economic ills of the world but is being accelerated by the special circumstances of our society. ... the immediate outlook is uncertain.[4]

The long era of fixed gold prices was at an end, and the industry had entered a period in which the gold price would be highly volatile. Mine managements were confronted with a radical departure in the business of gold mining as prices reached new peaks by leaps, from which they sometimes tumbled helter-skelter. Though from now on $100 an ounce looked like a reliable floor price, the industry had to adapt to an erratic price structure, at a time of unprecedented cost inflation on a global scale.

In the last quarter of 1973 the world's economic ills were compounded by the fuel crisis that followed the Arab-Israeli War in October, sparking a chain of events that would lead to a quadrupling of oil prices. A general strategic re-orientation followed that focused fresh attention on South Africa as a supplier of a wide range of minerals, and in particular of uranium and coal, the energy minerals that offered a source of power alternative to oil marketed at escalating prices by the newly-formed oil cartel, the Organization of Petroleum Exporting Countries (OPEC).

The energy revolution found the South African uranium producers well-poised to compete for business. By 1959, some twenty-six South African mines had been supplying nearly 6 000 tons of uranium oxide yearly to the West for the stockpiling of atomic weaponry. Then output fell away in step with the decline in demand for warlike purposes.[5] By 1965 production was down to 2 500 tons and the number of producers to eight. Foreseeing the need to bid for a share of the needs of the infant nuclear power industry, the mining industry in 1967 formed the Nuclear Fuels Corporation of South Africa (Nufcor) as an associate company of the Chamber, with a Board of representatives of mining houses with uranium interests. Its function was to market uranium throughout the world, to take over and run the former Calcined Products central processing plant, and to co-ordinate the uranium industry's joint research and development programme.[6]

In 1970, as the result of retirement and resignation, Nufcor was seeking a new general manager. The Chamber advertised the post and received ninety-three applications, but did not feel able to offer the post to any of those applying. John Shilling, who was Chairman of Nufcor at the time, then turned to Reginald E Worroll, the Chamber's Legal Adviser, to fill the post. Across the coming decade, Reg Worroll would become a familiar personality among the select international group involved in the buying and selling of nuclear fuels.[7] Worroll handed over the office of Legal Adviser to Peter H Bosman, who was destined to move across to management in 1978 and to succeed David Stuart as the Chamber's fifth General Manager in 1982. David G John took over from Bosman as Legal Adviser to continue one of the key functions of the Chamber, the unremitting watch on law and taxes.

In 1971, uranium was hard to sell. A prominent member of the French uranium industry commented at the time that the uranium business was like a camel crossing a wide and waterless desert, its principal concern being somehow to complete the journey before dying of thirst. In 1972, President Brand mine completed a uranium plant at a cost of tens of millions of rand, but the prospects of business were so poor that the plant was placed immediately in mothballs against better days.

Not surprisingly, consumers exploited the position of over-supply.[8] Not surprisingly, either, suppliers responded by taking steps to avoid being taken to the cleaners by the consumers. The world's principal suppliers, excluding those in the United States which operated primarily in a closed market, met to exchange information on supply and demand.[9] Their talks led them to form privily the so-called Uranium Club. Its existence soon became known, partly through the theft of confidential papers at the Mary Kathleen mine in Australia. There followed claims in the United States that the Club was a cartel in terms of the anti-trust laws, and lengthy litigation ensued in the United States Courts. As the litigation proceeded to eventual settlement, the market recovered, the necessity for the Club disappeared and it dissolved. The need remained however for an exchange of information and a common forum. In June 1975 Nufcor and other world producers set up the prestigious Uranium Institute as a non-profit making limited company under British law, on the pattern of similar organizations serving other metal industries. Membership was soon broadened to include consumers as well as producers, and its procedures were drawn up to conform with the requirements of the United States anti-trust laws and of the EEC competition law.[10]

Nufcor used the hard times to send its salesmen world-wide to thrust amiable feet into the doorways of potential buyers. When the recovery came suddenly, in the wake of the fuel crisis, Nufcor was able to win for South Africa a full share of available business.[11] The volume of orders would fluctuate with the usual ups-and-downs of demand, and with public attitudes towards nuclear installations, but overall the picture brightened. By the early 1980s there were some 255 nuclear power stations in commercial operation around the globe, providing a vital share of the electricity consumed by ten major industrial nations. To meet actual and projected increases in demand the South African producers had already put in train a major restructuring of the industry.

The supply of uranium for the generation of electricity is a long-term business. It may take ten years to open a mine and come on stream. A contract may cover the supply of nuclear fuel for a power station across its life-time: may even provide for a loan from the buyer to finance the building of the plant. To service the business that promised, total treatment capacity in South Africa was increased nearly three-fold between 1975 and 1982. While much of the uranium oxide treated was a by-product of gold mining, there were important contributions from companies working the tailings long discarded as the waste product of gold mines, and from a new primary producer, the Beisa mine, in the Free State, which was operated by St Helena gold mine.

Nufcor was able to conclude some highly lucrative long-term contracts, and the multi-million cash flow through its Johannesburg office reached impressive levels. To producers in other countries it seemed incredible that individual South African producers were prepared, in a highly competitive business, to entrust their marketing to a co-operative. But South African producers saw this as a normal spin-off from co-operation in the Chamber, which gave a service both impartial and low in cost. In 1976, for example, Nufcor negotiated sales for immediate and future delivery worth, at money values then pertaining, in excess of $1 250 million on a budget of around $1 million, including the cost of running Nufcor's processing plant. It also negotiated loan funds to help finance the step-up in production facilities. From then output steadily expanded, and the peak reached in 1959 in the supply of uranium for strategic weaponry was surpassed in 1980 when uranium produced for nuclear power generation exceeded 7 000 tons. In an age increasingly dependent on nuclear power, South Africa's huge resources of uranium assured her a place high among the top supplier countries of the world.

Minerals generally flourished in the seventies, but the bright new star of the decade was, unquestionably, the coal industry. Production expanded rapidly to meet the escalating demand from Escom power stations, and was boosted by the crisis that followed the formation of OPEC. In the late sixties, the coal produced in South Africa was generally of a quality that was not readily saleable abroad, and there was relatively little export business. There followed advances in the preparation of coal for export which enabled collieries to tender for the supply of coal to the giant steel mills of Japan. After complex negotiations, in which South Africa benefited from Japanese reluctance to place over-reliance on the single, convenient source offered by Australian collieries, a contract was won for South Africa by the Transvaal Coal Owners Association (TCOA) to provide a consortium of steel mills with 2,5 million tons of soft coking coal a year for thirteen years.[12]

However, fulfilment of the contract involved massive investment in infrastructure, for South Africa lacked a deep-water port to accommodate the bulk ore-carriers on which the mineral export trade depended. Fortunately, the South African Railways and Harbours (SAR&H) – now South African Transport Services (SATS) – saw that it had a key role to play at the centre of the country's mineral expansion. There followed the State's decision to go ahead with the building by 1976 of a new harbour at Richards Bay, formerly a remote and sleepy lagoon on the north coast of Natal, a development which enabled South Africa to steal a march on the coal producers of the world. The coal industry took a major part in the financing of what was to be the world's most advanced coal loading terminal, and of the 525-kilometre rail line which would bring the seemingly endless coal trains from the mines of the eastern Transvaal. And TCOA took a majority share in the Richards Bay Coal Terminal Company which operated the coal terminal at the new super-port on lease from the SAR&H.

445

As the building of the railway and harbour got under way, the oil crisis erupted. Major industrial countries began a process of reversion, wherever feasible, to coal as an energy fuel. South Africa responded to the new demand and progressed rapidly to the position of a major exporter of steam coal to the West. Richards Bay coal terminal was expanded. South African collieries would not actually take coals to Newcastle, but they would sell them to the Ruhr and the United States, and vie with Poland for the role of principal supplier to the European Economic Community. Completion of the phase three expansion at Richards Bay in 1985/1986 was expected to lift South Africa into the position of the world's top exporter.[13]

In South Africa, more than half the output of collieries is consumed by Escom, and often collieries are contracted, or wholly tied, to a particular power station. Much of the remaining balance of production is marketed and distributed by the TCOA. In the past, a major *raison d'être* for the long-established TCOA had been the tight state control on the price of coal which for decades shadowed the fortunes of the industry. As the State switched to more realistic pricing policies in the seventies, TCOA could concentrate on finding the best market for each coal type, and in helping to monitor quality. In 1974 TCOA took over management of Natal Associated Collieries, which marketed steam coal for Natal collieries. Often those sitting on the Board of TCOA would doff one hat, and don another to walk over to the Chamber and sit on the Collieries Committee which dealt with all coal policy matters other than marketing. Natal interests are represented on the Collieries Committee as well, for the Chamber and the Natal Coal Owners' Society merged their interests in 1975.[14]

The coal industry now geared up for a future that was to call both for sophisticated marketing and for the expenditure of huge sums on new large collieries, on extensions to old collieries, and on high-technology mechanization. Capital exceeding R1 500 million was spent on expanding production capacity, involving the establishment of giant new mines, some of which would set both South African and world records for size, production and sophistication.[15] At the opening of new extensions and modern facilities at one old-established colliery, the remark was made that the launch party was costing more than the mine's original capitalization in coal's Cinderella days.

World events in the sixties and seventies, the rapid industrialization of South Africa and the advance of coal mining technology would transform that Cinderella image, born of the long-drawn struggle to survive on minimal profit margins. In 1961, South Africa exported 0,75 million tons. By 1981 this figure would be 30 million tons. Over the same period, the coal used for the generation of power rose from 17,84 million tons to nearly 59 million tons. Consumption by secondary industry increased considerably, and coal also provided the feedstock for conversion to synthetic liquid fuels in which South Africa leads the world through the Sasol plant established by the Government in the northern Free State after 1948, in the face of public doubt and criticism. During the seventies the State developed two new oil-from-coal plants, known as Sasol II and III, at Secunda in the eastern Transvaal, at a cost of more than R6 000 million; they were fuelled by the Bosjesspruit colliery, easily the world's largest coal mine, and one of the most technologically advanced.[16]

However, the continuing expansion of the coal industry in the eighties was accompanied by a weakening of the international market and falling prices. Colin J Fenton (Gold Fields), Chamber President for 1983–1984, noted that the strong and growing domestic market was enabling the coal industry to weather the export downturn, and to prepare for the resurgence of demand which was certain, given the inevitability of global energy shortages in the future.[17]

Overall, from 1961 onwards, the value of coal production grew fifty-seven-fold to total R3 426 million in 1984. By then coal overshadowed every mineral, other than gold, as a revenue producer and earner of foreign exchange. Thus, the coal industry registered an exceptional advance at a time when spectacular progress was the norm in the South African minerals industry. Over the same period the value of asbestos production grew five-fold; of diamonds, fourteen-fold; of chrome ore, nineteen-fold; of manganese fifteen-fold; and of copper eighteen-fold. And, as a result of the construction of a new 860 kilometre railway line from the mining area of Sishen in the north-west Cape to a new ore export harbour at Saldanha Bay, the value of iron ore produced rose a remarkable thirty-nine-fold to R372 million.[18]

The creation of Saldanha Bay Harbour on the west coast in the same year as the harbour at Richards Bay on the east coast focused attention anew on South Africa's capacity as a supplier of strategic minerals, located midway between East and West. So did the erection of more than two hundred extractive processing plants for the beneficiation of raw minerals, notable examples being Anglo's Highveld Steel and Vanadium Corporation outside Witbank which produces most of the world's vanadium steel, and Union Corporation's establishment at Springs of the Impala Platinum Refinery, the world's largest.

It was already clear to the world that the West was vitally dependent on South Africa for a wide range of minerals, not just because of the country's unique endowment of ore deposits, but because of their accessibility to the Free World. Just how vital was highlighted in an academic study published in 1977, in which the authors calculated that if the Soviet Union gained control of South Africa's mineral resources, it would then possess ninety-nine per cent of the world's platinum, ninety-seven per cent of vanadium, ninety-three per cent of manganese, the hardening, strengthening 'yeast' vital to steel making, eighty-four per cent of chrome, sixty-eight per cent of gold, fifty per cent of fluorspar, forty-six per cent of iron ore, thirty-five per cent of asbestos and thirty per cent of uranium. South Africa's shares of world production and exports of key minerals, and of unmined reserves of them, have continued to grow, while American dependency on external sources has steadily increased. By the mid-eighties, the combined South African and Soviet holdings of metals critical to the production of modern weaponry could justifiably be described as frightening from the point of view of the West.[19]

The new minerals explosion was accompanied by a general advance of South African secondary industry, and of the economy generally, which laid bare the total inadequacy of the pool of skilled and scientific personnel and of those with managerial skills. And year by year, the cost of competing for those available became increasingly preposterous. It was writ large that South Africa could not much longer continue to draw trained manpower principally from the white group. The Chamber, in common with other business associations, warned repeatedly of the need for South Africa to measure up to the challenge of educating, training and employing all its citizens to the full extent of their capacity.

For example, Dr von Maltitz in his Presidential Address on 22 June 1971, declared:

> ... South Africa dare not, through failure properly to educate, train and employ its human resources, let slip the global opportunities that the mineral explosion has placed within her grasp.[20]

Jeff Goode on 26 June 1973, said:

> ... it is no use creating opportunities for Bantu without providing the educational and training facilities that will qualify them for advancement. Similarly there is already a lack of trained people for managerial and middle-management posts, and of engineers and technicians.
>
> There is no task of greater importance today than education in all its aspects ....[21]

Robin Plumbridge on 25 June 1974:

> One of the fundamental causes of low productivity is the lack of basic education of the vast majority of the industry's workers. A much higher level of expenditure by the State on general training and educational facilities is imperative ....
>
> There is a clear need for the formulation of a new overall manpower policy for South Africa.[22]

R S 'Bill' Lawrence (Rand Mines) on 29 June 1976:

> All races should increasingly share in the rewards and opportunities that economic growth of the region will bring, and the highest priority must be accorded to ensuring that the flow of qualified men and women from high schools matches the opportunities that will be opened to them. Thus, the key to the future is an imaginative programme of education and training ....[23]

Pending a more realistic state response to the country's need of educated men

Harold Macmillan, British Prime Minister, about to go underground at West Driefontein in January 1960. In the picture (left to right, foreground, in mining kit) are Bill Busschau, President of the Chamber of Mines; Sir John Maud, British High Commissioner; Supermac; Stan Gibbs, Manager, the author, and Adriaan Louw, Underground Manager (later Chairman, Gold Fields of South Africa).

West Driefontein flood October 1968. The first written record – note sent to the surface reporting that water had broken into a stope west of No 4 shaft and had reached a depth of six inches.

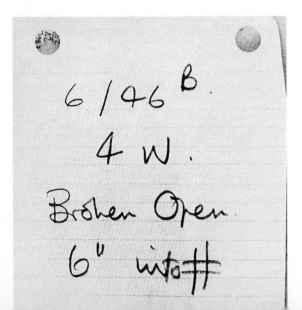

Floodwater pouring through the pipes in the main plug at West Driefontein at a rate of 85 million gallons a day.

Robin Plumbridge, the Rhodes scholar who became Chairman of Gold Fields in 1980 at the age of 45, against the background of a portrait of Cecil Rhodes who founded the company in 1887. In the early seventies, Plumbridge guided Intergold, the Chamber's marketing arm, through its formative years.

A gold rush, mirrored in these headlines, began when Britain devalued in November 1967.

Americans dutifully turned in gold for $20 an ounce when the United States left the gold standard in 1933. The price soon rose to $35 where it remained until the early seventies.

Why do people who don't believe in capital still believe in gold?

Rubles, like all other national currencies — even the "hardest" ones — are just pieces of paper. They have value only if people accept them.

Fortunately for the Soviets, the USSR is a major producer of gold. This is the foundation of their international trade. They are keenly aware of gold's inherent value. They mine it. They stock it. They sell it. Prudently. And only when they need to pay international bills.

The Soviets recognize gold as a reserve asset. Their overriding objective is to keep their gold reserves as high as possible.

If you want to be in such a strong position, you have to build up your own personal gold reserve. Gold is a hedge against the future. Valuable in good times. And bad.

Why gold?

Gold is a metal, a precious metal. It depends on no nation. On no government. As long as people prize gold — and when has it not been the most

sought after of treasures — its value will never go to zero.

Losing much — and sometimes all — of their value has been the fate of currencies, stocks, bonds and other less tangible assets throughout history. There is ample reason to believe the future will mirror the past.

The world today is balancing on the brink of a financial crisis. International indebtedness in terms of bank loans has climbed from $110 billion in 1972 to over $1,000 billion during 1982. Not just companies, but even countries face bankruptcy. "Debt rescheduling" has become the watchword of our age.

Such a situation can only favour the historical role of gold as the only truly safe asset.

Today's gold price is still relatively low and the historical trend has always been up. Now is a good time to secure a substantial portion of your assets through regular purchases of gold — your personal protection against the uncertainties of the immediate

and not-so-distant future.

The most convenient form of gold investment is Krugerrand gold bullion coins. Each Krugerrand coin contains exactly 1 troy ounce, 1/2 oz, 1/4 oz, or 1/10 oz of pure gold.

There are more than 38,000,000 standardized Krugerrands in circulation. They are the most widely traded gold bullion coins in the world. Krugerrands sell at the daily gold price plus a very small premium. You will be glad to know that Krugerrands can easily be resold to banks virtually anywhere in the world.

To make Krugerrands an even more enduring investment, each coin contains one ounce of pure gold... plus just a touch of alloy. That's why Krugerrands are harder, more durable than unalloyed gold coins.

How do you invest in Krugerrands? Nothing could be easier. You may buy a single coin or any quantity — with complete discretion — through most banks, stock brokers and bullion coin specialists.

For additional information, please write to:
International Gold Corporation,
1. rue de la Rôtisserie, 1204 Geneva, Switzerland.

KRUGERRAND
Buy gold to hold.

Pan-European Krugerrand ad poses pertinent question, urges investors 'Buy gold to hold'.

Charismatic Life-President Hastings Banda of Malawi visits Western Deep Levels in August 1971.

Representatives of Mitsui and the Transvaal Coal Owners Association signing a contract for the export of South African metallurgical coal to Japan from 1976 to 1986. The signatories are (left to right) Alan Tew (TCOA), George Clark (Gencor), and Y Iimura of the Nippon Steel Corporation.

High tech in action as a giant dragline shifts overburden to expose the coal.

A heavily-laden coal carrier leaves the east coast port of Richards Bay.

In the seventies coal mining shed its Cinderella image. These workers at Arnot Colliery, looking like space explorers, carry out mechanized stone dusting.

The mines have been producing outstanding sportsmen for many years. Peter Ngobeni, of West Driefontein, was regarded as one of the world's best sprinters after equalling Paul Nash's South African record for the 100-metre sprint in 1984.

Daniel Mapanya of Western Holdings mine won the middleweight title of South Africa in February 1978.

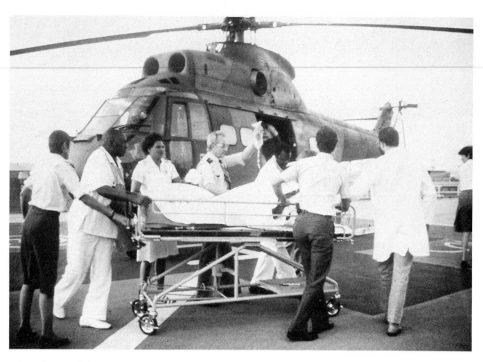

Injured miner is brought by helicopter to the Rand Mutual Hospital, Johannesburg.

GPC members and Chamber officials at a tape-cutting ceremony in Tokyo at the opening of the 1985 Japan Gold Jewellery Show. From left to right: George Nisbet (JCI), T I 'Naas' Steenkamp (Gencor), Don Mackay-Coghill (Chief Executive, Intergold), Junichiro Tanaka, President of Tanaka Kikinzoku Kogyo, Peter Bosman (General Manager, Chamber of Mines).

and women, the industry turned to husbanding the human resources available to it. Priority was given to the training of unskilled and semi-skilled workers to enable them to progress to higher-level jobs, an investment in productivity that would cost an annual R48 million by 1981.[24]

Training of skilled miners had long been carried out at the branches of the Government Miners' Training College. In 1980 the name was changed to Chamber of Mines Training College, reflecting the reduced Government share of costs. Artisans received training at fifteen Group and industry training centres specializing in the engineering trades. The Colliery Training College, founded by the Chamber in 1961, was geared up to meet the increasing skills required by the coal mines.

The industry also committed itself to a new emphasis on research and development. In July 1974 the Chamber announced a crash programme of research and development, at a rate of R15 million a year for ten years. In the event, by 1984, its research programme would be costing more than double the initial target rate.

The aims of the programme were: better use of available labour; safer and more comfortable working conditions; greater opportunities for employees; lower working costs; longer lives for gold mines and bigger profits. The Chamber's President, Dolf W S Schumann (General Mining), in announcing the scheme, summed up its purpose: 'We intend that the man with the shovel will give way to the man with the machine.'[25]

At that stage the Research Adviser was Dr Miklos D G Salamon, who had taken over from Dr W S Rapson as head of the Research Organization at the start of the year. The Organization had at its disposal the knowledge garnered from a generation of dedicated research into rockbursts and rock falls, which were the chief cause of injury underground.[26]

As a result, South African mining scientists tended to be ahead of the rest of the world in the science of rock mechanics which had developed since the 1939-1945 War. Salamon himself was a recognized world authority on deep-level mining technology, and in particular on rock mechanics and the rockburst phenomenon. Awards conferred on him included the South African Institute of Mining and Metallurgy Gold Medal in 1964 and its Certificate of Merit the following year; in 1971 he was joint recipient of the Associated Scientific and Technical Societies' National Award with Gold Medal, which is the premier scientific award of South Africa. In 1983 he was presented with America's top award for advances in the application of rock mechanics to mining, receiving the AIME (American Institute of Mining, Metallurgical and Petroleum Engineers) Rock Mechanics Award at a ceremony in Los Angeles.

Rockbursts (also called pressure bursts) have been defined as the uncontrollable disruption of rock associated with a violent release of energy. The bursts arise from the cracking or fracturing of the earth's crust under stress caused by natural weakness or man-made excavations. Study of the science of rock mechanics by the industry's engineers and scientists made it possible to predict the likelihood of rockbursts in various mining situations. By converting this knowledge into computer models, mining engineers were guided in formulating the safest possible layout. Scientific planning of this kind did not eliminate rockbursts, but it reduced their frequency. To protect men from rock falls that could not be prevented, the Organization by 1970 was already developing the rapid-yielding hydraulic prop. Its characteristic was the ability to yield rapidly to the irresistible force exerted by rockbursts while continuing to provide its original support to the overhanging rock.[27] More than 300 000 would be bought by mines by 1985 at a cost in excess of R70 million. Their installation represented the first breakthrough of modern technology in deep stopes.[28]

Salamon restructured the Research Organization to provide a separate concentration on research into rock mechanics, stoping technology, coal mining, engineering in all its aspects, into the distribution and valuation of grade in ore, and into human resources.[29] A search was launched for engineers and scientists in a wide range of disciplines and the research staff built up to more than six hundred people.

Mines have long used refrigeration to cool the air pumped to working places in deep mines through the ventilation systems. Among early achievements of the expanded Research Organization was the discovery that chilling the service water pumped underground for routine mining purposes would help appreciably to cool the working environment. The work of Dr A Whillier, Director of the Environmental Engineering Laboratory, in developing the system was recognized in 1977 by the award of the Gold Medal of the Associated Scientific and Technical Societies. By 1984, the system would have been installed in twenty-four large gold mines. As a natural follow-up, there followed experiments with the use of ice pumped underground on a large scale to cool working places further.

In 1978, the Premier Award in the Engineering Products Category of the Shell Design Awards was granted to the Chamber's researchers for the development of a two-way radio receiver able to provide communication through solid rock. Manufacture of the transceiver in collaboration with an electronics company provided valuable aids in fighting underground fires and in solving other communication problems.[30] The Organization also conceived and designed a portable gold analyser for the detection and assay of gold in unmined rock, which was 'developed, miniaturised and ruggedised' by an American company at Oak Ridge, Tennessee.[31]

The Organization has been geared, on a scale impressive by international standards, to develop in association with mining equipment manufacturers, new systems of mining, and of engineering. Above all, the Chamber set its sights on the development of non-explosive methods of mining. Mining with explosives is basically inefficient, wasteful and costly. An alternative method would make possible continuous mining, improved labour productivity and mining at greater depths because of improved strata and environmental control. Through the seventies a major concentration of effort was directed towards evolving a drag-bit rockcutter; later the emphasis shifted to an integrated system incorporating a hydraulically operated impact hammer moving along a guiderail linked to a conveyor for handling broken rock.

But finding a new method, practical and economical, to mine the narrow reefs following their unpredictable paths through the hard rock of gold mines has proved a tough nut to crack. The problem was unique in its complexity, and no assistance could be found, as in coal mining, from borrowing and adapting machines used in other mining countries. The pattern has been that of a steady contribution to the advance of mining technology and to the improvement and safety of the underground environment, which has justified increasing expenditure on research, and added to the bank of scientific expertise. Part of this process has been the advance made in harnessing the hydraulic pressure generated by the hydrostatic head of water used for cooling a mine, and in the development of hydraulic rockdrilling, employing a water-based fluid in place of compressed air.[32] Researchers are actively engaged in a pursuit which holds out the promise of a new source of power underground that will permit the design of smaller, quieter, more efficient machines.

The Research Organization has also provided the industry with a new communications channel between mining companies and workers. The Human Resources Laboratory was assigned the role of obtaining factual information on the attitudes of migrant workers and other employees to the rapid social, technological and economic changes taking place. Its scientists have helped to create effective methods of evaluating the aptitudes of workers and placing them in suitable occupations. They have helped novices to adapt to underground conditions, and to become aware of the hazards of the mining situation. Its teams of interviewers produce regular opinion surveys, offering guidelines for action by mine managements.[33]

When the distinguished State Mining Engineer, Sir Robert Kotzé, directed attention to the high level of deaths from accidents on gold mines in 1907, the rate stood at 4,7 per thousand employees per annum. On the formation of the Chamber's Prevention of Accidents Committee (PAC) in 1913 the rate stood at 3,81. Thereafter, it fell steadily, year by year, reaching a low of 1,20 by 1968. The progress made in accident prevention was the sum of state regulation and of safer mining practice, backed by the campaigning of the PAC. The reduction in fatalities reflected, too, the steady advance of the medical services of the industry, and the rapidity with which injured men were accorded sophisticated medical care. A notable role was played by first-aid in which all white workers underground are required to be proficient. First-aid training was made available, too, on a voluntary basis to black workers. Huge numbers volunteered and returned to their home territories with a valuable proficiency in the saving of life. In June 1960 certificate number one million was presented to David Motyaleni, a team leader, at Durban Roodepoort Deep, by Dr A J Orenstein, the pioneer of the industry's medical services, on behalf of the Red Cross. In May 1972, shortly before his death, he presented the two-millionth certificate to Snowdeni Dearsoni, a loco driver from

Malawi.[34] The three-millionth first aid certificate was awarded in October 1982 to Johnson Bukhosi, a team leader from the Transkei.

Despite the advances made in safety, and in the saving of lives, it was evident by the early seventies that the industry was close to the limit of progress by existing methods. The law of diminishing returns was operating. Moreover, mines were getting deeper, and in periods of expansion and drive, or when large numbers of novice labourers were employed under inexperienced supervisors, accident rates tended to drift upward. Then, in 1976, the industry became aware of the development, principally in the United States, of the techniques of loss control management which imply the control not only of accidents causing personal injury but also of all incidents that cause damage to material and equipment, and cause other losses, for the reason that they all originate from similar causes.

Early in 1978 Frank E Bird, Executive Director of the International Loss Control Institute in Atlanta, Georgia, together with South African mining officials, spent many weeks developing what is now known as the International Safety Rating Programme. There was some reluctance to participate at first, but soon large numbers of managers and senior officials of mines and head offices were attending the series of five-day courses for which Bird was brought to South Africa annually. A Diploma in Loss Control Management, introduced in 1979, had been awarded to 1 784 candidates by the end of 1984.

Mines are evaluated annually by auditors from the Mine Safety Division which the Chamber created from its PAC Secretariat in 1981. The Division's auditors also provide assistance to mines in developing loss control programmes. The audit covers the twenty-two separate elements of mine management involved in loss control. Arising from these audits, mines can be awarded from one to five stars. For a five-star award, it must achieve at least ninety per cent compliance in all twenty-two elements and have a frequency rate for fatalities and reportable injuries of approximately twenty-five per cent below the average for that class of mine.[35] The record shows that the reportable injury rate declined dramatically after 1978. The fatality rate was slow to follow, reflecting the inability wholly to engineer out the hazard of rockbursts, but in 1984 the rate at last fell below the record low of 1968. The figure for collieries in that year was also the best yet. In 1985, mines improved again. The fatality rate on gold mines fell to 1,03 per thousand at work per year, and that on collieries to 0,42. The rate for all mines fell below 1,00 for the first time to 0,89. In the same year, a total of twenty-nine gold, platinum, coal, and base metal mines qualified for five-star ratings under the International Mine Safety Rating Scheme at the advanced level. A further twenty-two received four-star ratings. In addition a record number of twenty gold mines and seven collieries won the Chamber's 'millionaire shield' by recording more than one million fatality-free shifts. Despite the successes, the need for substantial further progress was admitted, and there was top-level pressure for a continued safety drive. George Y Nisbet (JCI), President for 1984-1985, commented:

452

In an industry as vast and complex as the South African mining industry it would be naive to imagine that accidents can be completely eliminated. Research has done much to alleviate the major problems associated with the great depth of the gold mines, namely increased pressure and heat, and the Chamber's Research Organization is a world leader in this field. But no amount of technical innovation can make a mine accident-proof. Here it is a question of management control, motivation and training of every individual mine worker.

The South African mining industry is meeting this challenge by spending millions of rands annually on major educational and training programmes, including literacy and numeracy courses ....[36]

It was clear that the human factor remained dominant in accident causation. Major future advances in safety, as in so much else in mining, would depend critically on bridging the education gap to enhance the skills and status level of the workforce; and on increasing the numbers of long-service black mineworkers settled on or near the mines employing them.

[1] Eighty-Second Annual Report of the Chamber of Mines of South Africa, 1971, p 16.

[2] Eighty-Third Annual Report of the Chamber of Mines of South Africa, 1972, p 39.

[3] *The Krugerrand Directory 1981*, p 56. (International Gold Corporation.)

[4] Annual Report of the Chamber of Mines of South Africa, 1972, p 7.

[5] 'The Pattern of Uranium Production in South Africa', *Mining Survey*, No 81, No 2 of 1976, p 17.
Uranium: South Africa's Mineral Wealth, p 1. (Chamber of Mines of South Africa and the Atomic Energy Board of South Africa.)

[6] *Uranium: South Africa's Mineral Wealth*, p 8.

[7] 'Reg Worroll: Walking tall in the Uranium World', *Mining Survey*, No 1/2, 1983, p 29.

[8] Eighty-First Annual Report of the Chamber of Mines of South Africa, 1970, pp 9-10.

[9] Annual Report of the Chamber of Mines of South Africa, 1971, p 7.

[10] 'What the Uranium Institute is about', Chamber of Mines Report: November 1979, p 3.

[11] 'Reg Worroll', *Mining Survey*, No 1/2, 1983, pp 30-31.

[12] 'The Changing Face of the South African Mining Industry', Chamber of Mines' Newsletter: March/May 1982: Mining Congress Issue and 1981 Review, p 3.

[13] 'Coal Exports bring Heaps of Prosperity', *Mining Survey*, No 1/2, 1981, p 7.

[14] Eighty-Fifth Annual Report of the Chamber of Mines of South Africa, 1974, pp 7-8.

[15] 'Expansion – South Africa's Coal Industry is geared to produce more and more Coal', *Mining Survey*, No 1/2, 1981, p 13.

[16] *Ibid*, pp 15, 17.

[17] Ninety-Fourth Annual Report of the Chamber of Mines of South Africa, 1983, pp 7-8.

[18] 'The Changing Face of the South African Mining Industry', Chamber of Mines Newsletter, March/May 1982, p 4.
Memorandum dated 5 March 1986, from Information Services: Statistics, Chamber of Mines, to the author.

[19] W C J van Rensburg and D A Pretorius, (H Glen, ed), *South Africa's Strategic Minerals: Pieces on a Continental Chessboard*, pp 132–134.

'Strategic Importance of SA Minerals', Chamber of Mines Newsletter: March 1984, pp 7–8.

[20] Annual Report of the Chamber of Mines of South Africa, 1970, p 16.

[21] Annual Report of the Chamber of Mines of South Africa, 1972, p 14.

[22] Eighty-Fourth Annual Report of the Chamber of Mines of South Africa, 1973, p 13.

[23] Eighty-Sixth Annual Report of the Chamber of Mines of South Africa, 1975, p 13.

[24] W S Oosthuizen, 'Abstract: The Training of Unskilled and Semi-skilled Workers in the Mining Industry', ed H W Glen, *Proceedings, Twelfth Congress of the Council of Mining and Metallurgical Institutions, Johannesburg, 3-7 May 1982*, Volume 2, p 1022.

[25] 'Gold Mining Sows a R100 million Seed', *Mining Survey*, No 75, October 1974, pp 16, 21.

[26] 'Providing the Incentive to eliminate Mine Accidents', *The Chamber of Mines of South Africa: Ninety Years of Achievement*, p 67.

[27] 'Rockburst', Chamber of Mines: April 1978 Report, pp 3-7.

[28] 'Research', Chamber of Mines of South Africa: 1984–1985 Review.

[29] *Idem.*

[30] 'Chamber Research: Engineering: A Quiet Revolution in Mining', *The Chamber of Mines of South Africa: Ninety Years of Achievement*, p 21.

[31] Advertisement, *The Chamber of Mines of South Africa: Ninety Years of Achievement*, p 18.

[32] Ninety-Fifth Annual Report of the Chamber of Mines of South Africa, 1984, pp 17-18.

[33] 'Human Resources – providing the Data for Valid Decision Making', *The Chamber of Mines of South Africa: Ninety Years of Achievement*, pp 25, 27.

'Scientific Study of Viewpoint of Black Mineworker', *Mining Survey*, No 83 - No 4 of 1976, p 21.

[34] '1 000 000 First-Aid Certificates Issued', 'Mining's Part in the Growth of Union', *Mining Survey*, No 71 - Vol 11, No 2, 1960, p 27.

Mining Survey, No 71, October 1972, inside front cover.

[35] 'Mines get Star Ratings: Seventy Years of Safety and Loss Control Endeavour in the Mining Industry', *Mining Survey*, No 3/4, 1983, p 8.

[36] Annual Report of the Chamber of Mines of South Africa, 1984, p 20. (From the Presidential Address of G Y Nisbet, President, 1984-1985.)

See also p 35 of this report for a speech made by G W H Relly.

CHAPTER THIRTY-SEVEN

Ringing out the Old

In August 1971 Dr Hastings Banda, Life President of the Republic of Malawi, made a state visit to South Africa. The visit reflected Prime Minister Vorster's more outward-looking policy in Africa, and was a watershed event. Banda, a doctor of medicine, had returned to Malawi in 1964 after forty-three years abroad, to lead his lovely 'Land of the Lake' out of the colonial past, and into an uncertain future. Under his sole leadership, supported by a one-party legislature which favoured private enterprise, Malawi progressed economically. The annual income per capita was low, amounting to US$88 in 1971.[1] However, it was rising quite quickly, and Malawian citizens would be thought rather better off than those in neighbouring countries.[2]

Banda came to the mining industry on 18 August, making what was for him a sentimental journey. As a teenager in the twenties, he had walked 1 500 kilometres to the Rand to earn money for his education. He was chased off a mine property on the East Rand, but found work on another at a lowly wage. Later he worked underground because the pay was a little better. Prior to his return in 1971, he expressed the wish to visit these old mines, and it was arranged for him to see something of modern mining as well. The most elaborate preparations were made by the South African Government, and the most meticulous precautions put in hand for the safety of the visitor. These required the Police to close, and to render secure, the road the presidential cavalcade would travel from Jan Smuts Airport to the old mine site at Brakpan which was the first stopping point on the itinerary.

The Chamber official present will for ever recall with joy the look on the face of the Police brigadier in charge when the cavalcade was halted 400 metres from the airport, and a message was passed back to inform him that Banda did not wish to go to Brakpan first, but wanted instead to be taken in quite a different direction to another mine site, also of nostalgic memory. With commendable dispatch the Cadillacs were re-routed along an unplanned and unsecured route.

Later, Banda and his official suite visited the Rand Refinery. After luncheon there with the President, John Shilling, and members of the Executive Committee of the Chamber, Banda and his entourage were flown to Western Deep Levels in a flight of army helicopters. The ladies at the mine had prepared an elegant and scrumptious tea on tables by the sports field selected as the landing pad. Unhappily, a chopper flew too close, and the blast of its rotors swept the spread of teacups, cakes and sandwiches spiralling from the boards. Without tea, Banda, accompanied by the Minister of Mines, Dr C de Wet, drove to the mine dance arena, where he addressed 5 000 wildly enthusiastic Malawian mineworkers assembled from mines in the Transvaal and Orange Free State.

It was not only his fellow-Malawians whom Banda impressed. The charismatic Life President, with the fly whisk and the happy smile, made a remarkable impact on the white public as well, and his successful tour of the country served to promote the acceptability, as well as the importance, of closer social and diplomatic ties with the emergent states of Africa. The visit also seemed to augur well for the continued employment on a large scale of Malawian citizens on the mines. Fate would decide otherwise.

On 4 April 1974 a Skymaster aircraft, belonging to the Wenela Air Services and carrying time-expired repatriates from the Wenela air terminal in Francistown in Botswana to Blantyre in Malawi, crashed shortly after take-off. The captain, two members of crew and the seventy-four Malawians on board were killed. The tragic accident was the first resulting in loss of life in the twenty-two years in which Wenela Air Services had operated. The services were however at once suspended by the Chamber pending an inquiry into the disaster, and repatriates were sent home by Air Malawi.[3] The inquiry cleared Wenela Air Services of culpability. The cause of the accident was found to be the contamination of the fuel supplied to the aircraft by the oil company concerned.[4]

Banda, however, had suspended the engagement of Malawians for the mines immediately after the disaster, and despite the exoneration of the air service he continued the ban. Dissatisfaction with the treatment of Malawi citizens on the mines has been suggested as the reason.[5] However, more plausibly, the underlying motivation was the industry's too avid absorption of Malawians willing to sign on for wages which were not only high by local standards but rising rapidly; and the disruptive effect of the long absences of 129 000 young men out of a population of 5 000 000. Recruitment was resumed in 1977 on a more sensible basis and the numbers employed thereafter totalled about 16 000.

The cessation of recruiting in Malawi starkly exposed the over-dependence of the gold mines on foreign labour; and the need to restore the balance was to be underscored by events in Moçambique. The Portuguese Administration there had been embattled with guerillas out of Tanzania and Zambia for a decade. In 1974, as the guerilla forces pressed southwards, the Portuguese Government in Lisbon was overthrown by a coup, and its successor brought hostilities in Africa to an end. The liberation movement, Frelimo, took over in Moçambique in 1975 and, under the leadership of President Samora Machel, established a Marxist state firmly linked to the Soviet bloc. In the upheaval that accompanied independence, many Moçambicans sought the security of mine life and the numbers employed on the gold mines rose to a

456

record of 115 000. Thereafter, a working relationship was established between the industry and the new Government, but the departure of the Portuguese left administrative gaps, and a slow-down in the issue of travel documents dammed the flow of men to the mines. In 1976 the number employed fell to 32 800. Moçambicans had gone mining in South Africa for more than a hundred years, and developed an aptitude for the work. The disruption in recruiting involved a loss not only in numbers of men but in key workers whom the mines found hard to replace.

By then the Chamber had already launched a drive for South Africans to replace foreigners as they reached the end of their contracts. In November 1974 James Gemmill retired and Tony C Fleischer, a former General Manager of South African Associated Newspapers, took over as head of WNLA and NRC, to orchestrate a new broadly-based recruitment campaign. He was joined by Errol A M Holmes, from the diplomatic corps, who would succeed to the post in 1984. In 1977, the two mine labour organizations would be amalgamated to form The Employment Bureau of Africa (TEBA), but for millions in tropical areas to the north and in Moçambique TEBA remains familiarly 'Wenela'.

Prior to the Malawian cut-off the South African component of the labour force had fallen as low as twenty-two per cent. By the end of 1975 the proportion had increased to forty-three per cent; and at the Annual General Meeting on 29 June 1976, Bill Lawrence could set a target of fifty per cent. A year later his successor, Robin Plumbridge, could announce that the target had been exceeded as 'a result of the more competitive wages paid and the improved conditions on mines, the general economic situation in the country and the enhanced recruiting effort'.[6] An attempt to attract men from Soweto and the Rand townships was the only signal failure of the recruiting drive. Early in 1978, as a severe recession gripped the whole country, a flood of black workers sought employment. In the years ahead, full labour complements would become the norm, and sixty per cent of the men on gold mines, and seventy-five per cent on collieries would be engaged in South Africa and national states formed from it. The remainder would be drawn mainly from Lesotho and Moçambique, with lesser numbers from Botswana, Swaziland, Malawi, and, for a time, from Rhodesia (Zimbabwe).

A rapid increase in the wages paid to blacks had been under way since 1972. On 24 June 1975 Harry Oppenheimer at the Chamber's Annual General Meeting noted that the major factor in rising costs was wages, particularly black wages, where the minimum and average wages had been multiplied four times over the previous two years.

Now, that is something which is satisfactory. It is also a bitter comment on the extremely low level of wages which was forced on this industry by the fact that our product was fixed at a price of $35 for more than a generation, and we have got to remember that, even after multiplying these wages four times, the wages we pay are still not equal to those paid by employers in other sectors, to black workers for comparable work. There is still room to grow.

The time has clearly gone by, never to return, when we sought to control the level of costs in the industry by keeping wages down. We have got to control costs in future, not by low wages, but by high productivity ....[7]

At that time the gold price had fallen steeply from the peak of $200 an ounce reached in December 1974, and would not recover that position for three-and-a-half years, the price averaging $160 in 1975, $124 in 1976, and $147 in 1977. The decade after 1968 was a momentous one for gold in the international monetary system with the metal travelling a full circle from official recognition to demonetization back to effective remonetization. The United States has pursued the demonetization of gold, believing that this would remove its mystique and reduce it to the category of a simple commodity. But the seventies showed that the mystique of gold could not be removed by the edict of a handful of learned economists. The more the wise men argued that gold was too vulnerable to market manipulation to be appropriate as the basis of the monetary system, the more people around the world continued to vote with their savings for gold as the unbeatable store of value in a troubled world. And the demand for it sent its free market price soaring away from US$42,22 which was the official price observed by central banks for the valuation of the gold holdings in their national reserves. Moreover, the employment of these holdings was shackled by agreements reached at the IMF. In due course, central banks came to oppose the American view, and to press for the un-freezing of their gold holdings. The nations which the banks represented argued, in effect, that their gold reserves should be remobilized and usefully employed, and their view was to prevail.

The Second Amendment to the IMF Articles of Agreement ratified in April 1978 abolished the official price of gold and gave final clearance to central banks to value and use their gold reserves as they saw fit. The central banks, including the South African Reserve Bank, proceeded to revalue their gold reserves at market-related prices and to use them freely in international transactions. The South African gold mines benefited at once from an improved cash flow. Prior to the agreement they had received only the official price of $42,22 on the sale of their gold to the Reserve Bank; and had had to wait until the month-end for the premium on gold sold on their behalf in private markets. There was no premium paid to them on the gold the Bank elected to retain in its reserves or to use for monetary transactions. From now on mines received the market price, set initially at $163,27, immediately on the sale of their gold to the Bank. Mines benefited in another way because under the long-standing Moçambique Convention with Portugal, the Bank was obliged to transfer in gold at the official price the balances which became due to Moçambique in consequence of deferred earnings paid by WNLA, on behalf of the mines, to mineworkers on their return to that territory. The mines were now absolved from the need to provide the South African Reserve Bank with gold for this purpose at other than the market price. Additionally, the Chamber tried hard to obtain for the mines a slice of the bonanza that accrued to the Bank and the Treasury through the revaluing at $163 and upwards of gold bought from the mines at no more than $42,22, but in vain.

Parallel with these monetary developments, trading in gold for industrial and investment purposes world-wide had adjusted well to a moving gold price, and continued to do so despite large official sales onto the open market from the gold reserves of the United States Treasury and the IMF. In 1978 the price averaged $193, and in 1979 it jumped to $305, the platform for a take-off that would see small quantities of gold change hands at $850 in January 1980, the crest of the faltering wave of speculation. The price then collapsed $250 to complete the greatest rise and fall in the history of the precious metal markets. Thereafter, following further displays of volatility, it would settle for a time close to $500 before testing the depths around $300.

However, the price obtained was buoyant enough to encourage the further expansion of the industry, despite tax rates that on some mines exceeded seventy per cent of profits. Mines continued to raise wages in real terms, and to advance significantly in narrowing the wage gap between skilled and un-skilled workers. Migrants were enabled to save impressive sums of money, and the flow of cash back to home territories escalated. By the mid-eighties some black workers were saving as much as R4 000 in a single tour, the duration being on average about fourteen months and ranging up to two years. In an instance recorded early in 1984 a mineworker, ranking as one of the second lowest paid on the mines, collected a cheque for R10 000, his savings over four years. Capital spending on amenities increased rapidly as well so that mineworkers benefited from the upgrading of the board and lodging, medical and recreational facilities, traditionally provided at no cost to the worker.

A happy augury for the future dismantling of discrimination in labour laws was the passage of the Workmen's Compensation Act of 1977 which elimin-ated the racial differentiation in the structure of workmen's compensation benefits. Compensation of men injured at work in the mining industry had long been administered in terms of the law by the Rand Mutual Assurance Company, the Chamber affiliate founded in 1894, which paid benefits addi-tional to the statutory. The Rand Mutual could now conduct this insurance of workers on a common basis for all races. In 1981, it would add an insurance scheme for black miners providing, at a cost on average of a little over R1 a month, a benefit equivalent to two years' earnings, payable on death from any cause.

The Rand Mutual also administers two hospitals in Johannesburg, the Chamber of Mines Hospital at Cottesloe and the Rand Mutual Hospital near Booysens station which replaced the old WNLA Hospital, regarded in its day as the finest hospital for blacks in the country. By the early seventies the hospital was growing old. It was falling behind accepted standards, and was at times dreadfully overcrowded. The decision was taken to build and equip an entirely new hospital, both economically and to the highest standards, at a cost of R13 million. The new hospital of 500 beds serves as a central specialist hospital to which the fifty-one mine hospitals send cases requiring sophisticated specialist treatment they cannot themselves provide. In an article on the hospital published in 1983, Raymond Louw, formerly Editor of the *Rand Daily Mail*, wrote:

> The Rand Mutual Hospital, opened in 1979, is now firmly established as a specialist hospital with exceptional standards of excellence; a fitting monument to the priorities of a hard yet socially concerned industry.[8]

In March 1986 it was announced that the hospital would be expanded by a further 200 beds.

Unfortunately for shareholders, the drive to lift black wages from the low base of the sixties did not bring with it the hoped-for increase in the productivity of the workforce. The result was that mine costs increased much faster than the country's high inflation rate. Moreover, in the early seventies it was not yet politically feasible to talk of scrapping the colour bar. The Chamber did what it could to maintain pressure on the Government and the white unions for relaxations in the restrictions on the employment of blacks. The Government, unable longer to deny the need for higher productivity, consented to the 'adjustments of labour practices within the framework of its overall policy'.[9] However, the Government stopped short of putting pressure on unions to fall in line. It preferred to leave such changes to the Chamber and unions to negotiate, observing progress – or non-progress – from its position of advantage on the political fence.

In manufacturing industry the climb of black workers up the skills ladder was relatively fast, partly because of the creation of new avenues of employment not barred to them by law or custom. But any break in the strict caste lines of mine labour was looked at with the greatest suspicion by mining unions. However, some advances were registered, and there were changes in the pattern of labour representation.

In January 1973 the industry's winding engineers, the key men who drive the mine hoists, lowering and lifting men and materials, decided by referendum to accept an offer from the Chamber of conversion from the status of union men to that of officials. They were joined by reduction plant workers in a new officials' association, the South African Technical Officials' Association (SATOA). As a result 2 400 union men became officials.[10] However, their chosen representatives did not at once doff the militancy of their trade union past.

Without the hoist drivers and reduction workers there remained on the gold mines a union labour force of 16 435, the main categories being 7 738 miners holding blasting certificates who belonged to the MWU, and 6 492 artisans, members of craft unions which co-operated under the umbrella of the Federation of Mining Unions (FMU).[11] Later in 1973 the Chamber was able to negotiate a deal with the MWU by which, in return for higher pay and fringe benefits, the Union agreed to delegate certain limited duties to black team leaders on gold mines and collieries, under the supervision of union members. The Chamber also negotiated a deal with the FMU which, in return for similar agreements on pay and benefits, agreed to the introduction of black artisan aides. These aides were not appointed to jobs previously held by whites, but were permitted to perform only certain fractions of the artisan's work, again under his direction. There was a further agreement with the South African Engine Drivers', Firemen's and Operators' Association widening the circumstances in which blacks were permitted to drive locomotives underground.[12]

The new arrangements involved training courses of up to eight weeks for thousands of men in a specified portion of the work of either electricians, journeymen, boilermakers or miners, and called for an industry-wide effort. The change brought higher pay for the men selected and, though the advance was no more than modest, it confirmed the capacity of black workers quickly to absorb new skills and their eagerness to do so. The change seemed to hold the nucleus of more meaningful advances in the future. At this time, too, mining companies ceased to enforce legally the contracts migrant workers were required to sign, and this was confirmed by the withdrawal of penal provisions by amendment to the Masters and Servants Act in 1974. Workers could and did break contract and return home. The pattern now was for mining companies to offer incentives for men to complete the contract period, and to return to their jobs after a holiday at home, thus encouraging increasing numbers to take up mining as a long–term career. A ladder of grades was introduced, with progressive increases in pay.

Through most of the seventies the Chamber negotiated with trade unions in a search for a productivity formula that would permit the introduction of a five-day week without major reduction in output. Back in the sixties, Hermie Koch, at a lunch given by the Chamber for the Mining Unions Joint Committee, had reminded the trade union leaders of the Biblical injunction, 'For six days shalt thou labour'. It raised a laugh, but proved prophetic. After seemingly endless talk, culminating in ministerial intervention and a commission of inquiry, management and labour were obliged to settle for an eleven-shift fortnight. Its advent increased the opportunities for week-end leave, especially for migrant workers fortunate enough to work within easy reach of their homes, such as the Basotho on the Free State gold-field.

Ironically, but perhaps not surprisingly, a period of hopeful progress in pay and promotion was punctuated by sporadic outbreaks of unrest on the mines. More than fifty riots in the years 1972-1975, resulting in 132 dead and more than 500 injured, were subsequently examined by an inter-departmental committee of inquiry. Its report was not made public, but copies surfaced at an ILO conference in Geneva and a summary of its contents appeared in the Press. The report found that seven riots arose from perceived anomalies in wages paid on various mines or to different classes of worker. None of the remaining riots was motivated by grievances with management, and there was little dissatisfaction with the accommodation and other facilities provided. Inter-tribal clashes accounted for thirty-three riots; a further seven arose from resentment over the imposition of compulsory deferred pay by the Lesotho Government; and four from anxiety on the part of Malawians to return home after the cut-off in recruiting.[13]

The violence of the outbreaks was attributed to a complexity of factors, but especially the strains implicit in the migratory system and the inter-tribal friction that arose among the thousands of single men living in mine hostels. At a time when unrest was endemic in the country and beyond its borders, inter-tribal jealousies fed readily on reports or rumours of preferential treatment. Another factor was a growth of awareness of rights and prospects on the part of blacks. The commission noted, too, a high consumption of liquor in the new mine bars, induced by the frustrations of hostel life, and facilitated by the increasing means with which to buy it.[14] The rioting, and the lack of early warning of mounting tension, led to a new concentration on communications within the industry, including the setting up of liaison committees representative of workers and management. Part of this process of improved two-way communication was the launching by the Chamber of a fortnightly newspaper for black mineworkers, *Mining Sun*, and enhanced monitoring by the Research Organization.

Unrest on the mines had subsided by 1976, but the year, one of economic downturn, was marked by riot and protest elsewhere across the country. Political tension mounted throughout Southern Africa, weakening investor confidence in the region and contributing to a fall in the inflow of foreign capital. The disturbances did not spread to the mines which continued to operate normally.

However, the nature of the black workforce on the mines, and its accommodation on mine property, which tended to isolate it from township opinion, posed increasing problems of its own. Migrancy is common worldwide,[15] and it occurs wherever there is unequal economic development. In Southern Africa mineral deposits have been the most powerful agency of economic advancement, but unfortunately they have almost invariably been discovered far from concentrations of population and usually where there is a minimum of infrastructure. In consequence, the story of the Rand has been characterized by massive development in the provision of services and associated industries, and by the attraction of migrant workers from far afield in ever-increasing numbers. The migratory system was entrenched in the early days and persists. It has been, and will continue to be, the subject of intense controversy, and understandably so.

Some revisionist, neo-Marxist historians have seen the fact that the mining industry managed to thrive despite its dependence on migratory labour as proof that the system has really been in the interests of capital. Kantor and Kenney have pointed out that it means nothing of the sort. They see this neo-

Marxist thesis as a classic example of generalization on the basis of a single instance, and argue that the neo-Marxists, had they looked northward, could have found instances in which migrant labour was promoted for wholly non-capitalist reasons, as well as highly successful examples of capitalist development in which migrancy was deliberately rejected.[16]

> Perhaps it may even be that migrant labour is detrimental to capitalism. Perhaps it can fairly be concluded that South African capitalists are doing as well as they can in the face of severe constraints on profit maximization imposed by a compulsory pattern of migrant labour.[17]

Beyond question, the migrant system that took root on the Rand has involved positive disadvantages for the workers, and for the families and communities from which they are separated for long periods. It has also involved positive disadvantages for the mines in high labour turn-overs, the constant need to retrain, and low productivity. Clearly migration has brought to the societies that supply labour positive economic advantages in the form of vital cash flows, as well as disadvantages. Clearly, too, there was a time when migrancy met well enough the needs of the mines for large numbers of unskilled workers at low rates of pay. But as the needs of the mines for more skilful workers increased, the benefits of migrancy declined and its costs in terms of lost economic opportunity increased. Nevertheless, whatever the sum of disadvantage to all concerned, migrancy is an established system that cannot be wished away. The need to provide work for the growing millions of the sub-continent, as well as the need to man the mines, is likely to remain fundamental.

However, the mine-owners have pressed increasingly for the stabilization of a larger proportion of the black labour force, including in particular those in key supervisory positions. As has been related earlier, Anglo American in the early post-war years endeavoured to develop its Free State gold mines on the basis that ten per cent of the workforce should be housed, with their families, in villages, on mine property, but was thwarted by the insistence of Dr Verwoerd that those permanently housed should not exceed three per cent. In the post-Verwoerd era the Chamber pushed for an increase to ten per cent for all mines, and it urged on the Inter-Departmental Committee of Inquiry into Riots on Mines the importance of a large, stable family element in permanent residence on or near mines. A succession of government ministers listened to the Chamber's advocacy of increased stabilization and seemed sympathetic. Unfortunately, the state bureaucracy concerned with apartheid or 'separate development' showed a great propensity for in-depth resistance to sensible change, and little progress was made on gold mines. Collieries with high technology and small workforces were more fortunate.

In the eighties, as the reform of apartheid laws got under way, the prospects for a larger permanent labour force, housed on or near mine property with their families, brightened. At the same time, it looked likely that migrants would continue to predominate for some time to come. The provision of family housing calls for capital investment that some mines could not afford. Housing apart, urban settlement involves expenditure on a large scale for education, health and recreation. Settlement on any major scale is unlikely to be encouraged on mines with a short life expectancy, or on those which constitute the only form of economic activity in remote areas. Moreover, a large proportion of migrants come from independent countries which are dependent on the cash flow from their citizens on the mines, and whose governments would not be likely to agree to their settlement in South Africa. Again, large numbers of migrants wish to retain their stake in their tribal land and would not want to settle in mining areas. The modern mining industry and the territories from which men travel to the mines have indeed inherited a cruel dilemma, for the change to a more skilled, stable workforce could result in the shrinkage of jobs in a sub-continent short of work for its exploding population. In the early eighties huge numbers of applicants for unskilled work were turned away from TEBA recruiting offices. Fortunately, there is a potential for mining and industrial expansion that could in time change this picture.

In the shorter term the emphasis will remain on the progressive settlement of key workers on or near the mines, and on the continuing improvement of the working, living and leave conditions of those who continue to be migrant. Mining houses have begun to press the Government to make freehold land available to those skilled mine workers who want to settle with their families near their place of work; and to call for the abolition of regulations inhibiting their right to choose.[18] The move to further stabilization is likely to be accelerated by the removal of discrimination because there is a contemporary as well as an historical link between the colour bar and the perpetuation of migrancy. Long absences from the job, high turnovers and constant, costly retraining, may be acceptable for lowly-paid, illiterate labourers, but are hardly sustainable for educated, skilled men in a high technology environment.

464

[1] 'Malawi', in *The New Encyclopaedia Britannica, Macropaedia,* Volume 11, *Knowledge in Depth,* 15th edition, pp 360, 363, 364.

[2] *TEBA 1983,* p 22. (Published by TEBA Limited.)

[3] Annual Report of the Chamber of Mines of South Africa, 1973, p 10.

[4] Annual Report of the Chamber of Mines of South Africa, 1974, p 31.

[5] 'The Secret Mine Report', *Financial Mail,* 7 July 1978, p 31.

[6] Annual Report of the Chamber of Mines of South Africa, 1975, p 10.
Eighty-Seventh Annual Report of the Chamber of Mines of South Africa, 1976, p 12.

[7] Annual Report of the Chamber of Mines of South Africa, 1974, p 19.

[8] 'Heliport aids Mine Hospital Patients', *Mining Survey,* No 3/4, 1983, p 13.

[9] Annual Report of the Chamber of Mines of South Africa, 1971, p 11.

[10] Annual Report of the Chamber of Mines of South Africa, 1972, p 10.

[11] *The Complete Wiehahn Report: Parts 1-6, and the White Paper on each Part, with Notes by Professor N E Wiehahn,* p 694. (Table II (a))

[12] Annual Report of the Chamber of Mines of South Africa, 1973, p 28.

[13] 'The Secret Mine Report', *Financial Mail,* 7 July 1978, pp 30-31.
Lipton, 'Men of Two Worlds: Migrant Labour in South Africa', p 110.

[14] *Idem.*

Idem.

[15] Lipton, 'Men of Two Worlds: Migrant Labour in South Africa', p 91.

[16] B S Kantor and H F Kenney, 'The Poverty of Neo-Marxism: The Case of South Africa', *Journal of Southern African Studies,* Volume 3, No 1, October 1976, pp 27-29.

[17] *Ibid,* p 29.

[18] See, for example, Annual Review for 1985 by the Chairmen of the Transvaal Gold Mining Companies of Anglo American Corporation, E P Gush and T L Pretorius.

CHAPTER THIRTY-EIGHT

Ringing in the New

Mining is the ultimate South African experience. The way of life of all South Africans is wedded to it, for better for worse, for richer for poorer; and this is so, whether or not they are directly engaged in mining or wholly unaware of their involvement in its fortunes. Universities, industries, business, cultural pursuits, charities and the arts, as well as the fiscus, are nourished by it. And to the outside world South Africa's mineral wealth is the measure of her strategic worth in the community of nations.

The Chamber of Mines for a hundred years has been an advocate of the mining interest and, as such, has played a key role in watershed events in the country's history. This role has been and is misunderstood, even by many who should be knowledgeable about it. The Chamber has not dominated governments; nor political parties; it has not exercised unfair influence on the Press or in public affairs. And it does not, of course, run mines or make profits, but continues as a private enterprise co-operative to carry out the functions assigned to it.

These functions, it will have been seen, are essentially three-fold. It provides services to the mines and the public that are the envy of the mining world in range and quality;[1] it formulates policy for the industry as a whole on the matters of general concern assigned to it; and it serves as the advocate of that policy to the general public, and at the interface with Government and with organized labour. In the pursuance of these roles the Chamber employs a staff of some fourteen hundred, and its affiliated companies employ another five thousand three hundred in Southern Africa and around the globe, in the recruiting of unskilled workers; the training of skilled men; in the refining of gold and silver; in insuring workers and providing hospitals for them; and in the marketing of gold and uranium. The cost of the Chamber to the industry in 1985 was estimated to be nearly R70 million, and of the associated companies about R359 million.

The Chamber has endured because it is a flexible organization which can expand services or reduce them as required. It does not generate work for itself, but responds to the needs of the mines expressed through mining house nominees on policy committees. The Chamber's steady and, more latterly, rapid expansion suggests that the regular mining house in–depth assessment

466

of its role serves generally to confirm its cost–effectiveness.

As the spokesman for the total mining industry, the Chamber has striven to create conditions in which mining can flourish, with varying success. Advocacy for mining, confronted by a voracious Fiscus and intransigent politicians, has its full share of frustrations, and has never been the sinecure that some onlookers and theorists suggest. For in advocacy of a special interest the rule applies: some you win and some you lose. Some have been won to the immeasurable benefit of the mines and the country. Some have been lost, and minerals that might have been mined remained in the ground. Capitalists have not enjoyed the say in government in South Africa or elsewhere in the world that the Marxists claim.

> There is a thread that runs consistently through the whole Marxist (and neo-Marxist) analysis. Politics is a derivative of economics. Politicians jump to the attention of the capitalists and do as they are told. In real life, of course, things are less simple. Political goals and economic goals may clash and there is nothing in the nature of things which says that economic factors are necessarily decisive.[2]

In a deeply researched study, *Capitalism and Apartheid: South Africa, 1910-84,* published at the end of 1985, Merle Lipton entered the debate on the interaction of economic interests and racial policies. Although critical of mining's historical role as an employer of migrant labour, she concluded, *inter alia*:

> SA development since Union does not support the thesis that the state was the instrument of capital. The interests of the economically dominant mining and urban capitalists were often overridden when they were in conflict with those of white labour or the bureaucracy or of economically weaker agricultural capital.[3]

The mining record shows clearly that in clashes between economics and politics in South Africa economics has often been the loser. There is of course a special relationship between the State and the mining industry, because of mining's central economic importance, and always will be, whoever governs. But this relationship is quite different in kind to the more intimate relationship between the State and, for example, agriculture, which is of central political as well as economic importance. In resolving conflicts of interest in the past, successive governments have attended assiduously to their power bases, and have consistently yielded to the political pressure groups thought to be most essential in terms of votes cast at the ballot box; and governments will no doubt continue to do so. In consequence, capitalists in South Africa, and especially in the mining industry, were destined to suffer long the constraints of the colour bar.

However, the breakthrough came at last as a result of a switch in Government policy. By 1977 the economic pressure arising from the need to make full use of the country's manpower potential brought all major political groupings to concede that job reservation based on race was no longer defensible or practical. In July 1977 the Government appointed a multiracial commission of inquiry under Professor N E Wiehahn to examine thirteen major statutes governing industrial relations practice, and to recommend a fresh foundation for labour relations. Dr P J Riekert, Economic Adviser to the Prime Minister, was subsequently appointed as a one-man commission to investigate all legislation affecting the utilization of manpower not covered by the Wiehahn Commission.

Without awaiting the reports of the Commissions, the Government set the tone by the declaration that all persons had an equal right to be trained and to qualify for any position. The Chamber welcomed the inquiries, and in its submissions called for the scrapping of statutory and customary restrictions on employment. And it called on the Government to give legislative expression to the change in policy as soon as possible.[4] The Chamber's submission to the Wiehahn Commission also called for the extension of trade union rights to all black workers, other than foreign migrants, and included a minority recommendation, on behalf of two mining houses, calling for the inclusion of foreign migrants as well. The submission of a minority recommendation was an unusual departure for the Chamber which strives for unanimity, giving each mining house, large or small, equal weight in deliberation. However, the words *after discussion*, the Committee agreed' in the minutes of a meeting can cover a deal of verbal in-fighting. The almost invariable achievement of consensus sometimes conceals a divergence of opinion, not perhaps surprising in one of the world's large industries constructed of major components each with its own philosophy of change, in an age of change.

Both the Wiehahn and Riekert Commissions speedily reported, recommending fundamental changes in Government policy and a movement away from constraints towards a dismantling of racial discrimination in the workplace, the freer and fuller utilization of labour and the fuller participation of all employees in the free enterprise system.[5] The Wiehahn Commission, with the greatest ground to cover, produced its findings in a series of six reports. It recommended the unionization of all blacks, including foreign migrants, and, after some hesitation, the Government agreed. The Commission left the thorniest problem, that of the colour bar on the mines, to the sixth and final report, completed in November 1980. In its historical review in that report of the structuring of the industry into skilled whites and unskilled or semi-skilled blacks, the Commission commented:

While it is clear that there was a strong economic and market rationale in the formation of this original profile of labour in the mining industry, it was subsequent practices and political intervention that hardened the profile into something economically irrational, ethically unjustifiable and injurious to the industrial relations in the industry. The instruments of this hardening, in simplest form, were the white trade unions and the intervention of successive Governments in defence of the white worker.[6]

The Wiehahn Commission had already had evidence of the continuing opposition of the MWU to allowing blacks access to skilled work, for on 7 March 1979, three weeks after publication of the Commission's first report, the Union began a wildcat strike, withdrawing its labour without warning from the gold mines. There was at the time no dispute on the gold mines between the Union and the Chamber. It subsequently transpired that the strike was to demonstrate support for members of the Union who had begun a legal strike at O'Okiep Copper Mining Company in the north-western Cape, on the grounds that the Company had taken on four Coloured artisans on work which had previously been undertaken by white artisans. The Chamber stood firm. It had a strong case, and speaking out loud and clear, as well as quickly, it at once won public opinion to its side. And it told the Union that its members, by participating in an illegal strike, had automatically broken their signed employee agreements, and if re-engaged would forfeit certain benefits for prior service. The MWU then contended that the strike now revolved around reinstatement of the benefits to be forfeit, but for once the Government did not intervene, and the strike collapsed on 14 March.

P A von Wielligh (JCI) in his Presidential Address the following June commented:

> ... it has been suggested that much of the support for the strike arose from fears of the impending changes which could result from Government implementation of the Wiehahn and Riekert Commission reports.
>
> No employer, least of all the mining industry, can accept the use of the strike weapon as a means of influencing Government labour policy or of generating support for political attitudes. The strike was in fact totally unnecessary in terms of its alleged objective, for White workers in the mining industry need have no fear about the security of their jobs.
>
> Clearly, convincing them of this is going to be one of the most important tasks for employers in the months and years that lie ahead.[7]

With a new era opening up in labour relations, the Chamber had reorganized to meet it. For many years conditions of employment and negotiations with employees' representatives had fallen under the Technical Department, headed latterly by Alec B Daneel as Chief Technical and Labour Adviser, and Gordon Grange as Technical Adviser. Serving a rapidly expanding industry, they together handled an astonishing workload, or overload, with equanimity and good humour. In 1977 the labour function was transferred to the newly-formed Industrial Relations Department headed by Johann Liebenberg as Industrial Relations Adviser. Daneel retired the following year and Grange took over as head of the Technical Department. Liebenberg, the son of a man who was president of a number of trade unions, grew up in a trade union atmosphere. He started working life as a career diplomat, then switched to the motor industry where he began to specialize in labour relations as Secretary of its Industrial Council. He joined the Chamber in 1975, his brief being to familiarize himself with labour practices in the mining industry, and to create the new department.[8] He did so, just in time to meet the challenge of rapid change on the labour front. The Department was to play a crucial role and grew rapidly in numbers and sophistication.

The end of the decade saw the advent of a long-awaited revival in the South African economy, somewhat assisted by hopes aroused by P W Botha who, since becoming Prime Minister in 1978, had propagated a new philosophy of reform in race relations. The economic revival was destined to subside in 1982, before the combined onslaught of drought, inflation, falling foreign exchange reserves and global recession. But it endured long enough to expose the paradox of rapidly increasing unemployment for the unskilled, accompanied by a crippling shortage of people qualified to fill vacancies in the skilled, professional and managerial fields. Dennis Etheredge (Anglo American), President of the Chamber for 1979-1980, revealed that in the first quarter of 1980 the shortfall of skilled personnel on the gold mines was nearly equivalent to the entire complement of skilled men to man two medium-sized gold mines. The manpower problems of the industry, Etheredge observed, 'cannot be over-stated'. In that same year, as the Government faced up to an inescapable switch to multiracial employment, the Chamber and the mining houses wrote to all white employees promising proper consideration of their position and credible safeguards wherever necessary. Over the nine months to March 1981 the number of vacancies in skilled jobs on the gold mines increased further by more than forty per cent.[9]

In the following month P W Botha was returned to power and affirmed that he would pursue a policy of progressive reform. In November 1983, in a national referendum, he obtained substantial white electoral support for a new tri-cameral parliament, providing representation for Coloureds and Indians. He subsequently was elected State President with the executive powers provided by the new constitution.

Government acceptance of many of the recommendations of the Wiehahn Commission had earlier cleared the way for young men of all races to become apprenticed on the mines. At the end of 1981 agreement was reached between the Chamber and the Federation of Mining Unions, and a start was at once made with the indenturing of apprentices of all races in the whole range of artisan crafts. On 29 June 1982 Lynne W P van den Bosch (Gencor), in his Presidential Address, declared that the industry had spent more than R145 million on training the previous year:

> ... five major engineering trades training centres to serve the mines have recently been completed or are in the construction or planning stages. The cost of these centres – three of them training apprentices of all races in shared facilities at the outset – will total almost R30 million.[10]

By May 1986 101 black, Asiatic and Coloured artisans were in service and another 357 were under training on the gold mines and in the Chamber's Colliery Training College. In accordance with the mining industry's non-discriminatory pay policy, all races received the same pay under training and after qualification.[11]

In June 1983, the Minister of Manpower withdrew Job Reservation Number 27 which had reserved for whites, on the insistence of the MWU, the jobs performed by officials in the sampling, surveying and ventilation departments of mines. It was the last to go of twenty-nine such determinations made in South Africa since 1956. Its scrapping followed an agreement between the Chamber and the Underground Officials' Association (UOA), endorsing the principle of equal pay for equal work, and providing guarantees to quell white fears of loss of employment. The Association, formerly exclusively white, opened its membership to underground officials of all races.[12] By August 1984, 295 blacks, Coloureds and Asians were engaged as learners or assistants in these jobs, formerly barred to them, along with 350 whites. In the same month a further 545 black, Coloured and Asian employees were employed in jobs recognized as being covered by the UOA or the Mine Surface Officials' Association (MSOA).[13] The MSOA opened membership to all races as well, and the South African Technical Officials Association (SATOA) was opened to Coloureds, though it remained closed to Asiatics and blacks. However, the Mine Officials' Pension Fund was opened to officials of all races, and negotiations, likely to be prolonged, were begun to open the Mine Employees Pension Fund, to which white union men belonged, to all union men.[14]

With the scrapping of job reservation there still remained on the statute book the provisions in the Mines and Works Act, and regulations made under it, which limited the acquisition of certain certificates of competency to 'scheduled persons'. These certificates included the blasting certificate, which effectively denied blacks jobs ranging from miners and developers to mine managers. The Government in 1981 committed itself to replacing the 'scheduled person' definition with a non-racial definition of a 'competent person', but, and it was a big but, on the old, familiar terms that agreement must first be reached on security of employment with the white unions.[15] The proviso confirmed that the MWU continued in lively defence of the blasting certificate as a white preserve, and was still regarded warily by the Government. Predictably, the negotiations between the Chamber and the MWU were long-drawn-out. However, in May 1985 the Minister of Mineral and Energy Affairs, D W Steyn, said in Parliament that whether or not agreement was reached by the end of the year, the Government would enact legislation in the 1986 session to effect the necessary change. On 8 December 1985 Clive Knobbs (Rand Mines), President for 1985-1986, was quoted by *The Star* as saying that the Chamber was following through on its third initiative in these negotiations. 'The important point is that we are still talking.'[16] Agreement however remained elusive, and the Minister entered the negotiations, seeking to draft legislation acceptable to the Chamber and the unions. Mine managements waited hopefully for the final act which would ring down the curtain on the colour bar and enable them, at long last, to fill all jobs on the mines on the basis of competency instead of race.

Parallel with advances in job opportunities on the mines went the beginnings of trade unions for blacks, Coloureds and Asians. The Chamber in evidence to the Wiehahn Commission had urged that white unions should open their ranks to all races in appropriate work categories. Six did, but three others, the MWU, the South African Engine Drivers', Firemen's and Operators' Association and the Amalgamated Engineering Union, remained closed to other races. The Chamber had told the Wiehahn Commission that if this happened they would support blacks becoming members of new unions.[17] Subsequent Government action paved the way for the extension to all workers of freedom of association in trade unions. An early arrival on the mining scene was the Federated Mining Union which satisfied the statutory requirements for registration. The Union initially concentrated on signing up Coloureds working as vehicle drivers, handymen and painters, and achieved a sufficient number of members to win recognition by the Chamber on two mines in September 1982. In December of that year the Chamber relaxed its initially stringent criteria for the recognition of unions so that the main consideration became not whether the union had been formally registered by the State, but whether or not it was sufficiently representative of workers. A recognition agreement followed on 9 June 1983, with the National Union of Mineworkers (NUM), the union which had made the most progress in signing up black workers. W W Malan (Anglo Vaal), President for 1982-1983, commented:

> The recognition of these two unions enabled the leaders of unions representing blacks and coloureds to negotiate with the Chamber wage increases for approximately 6 000 of their members employed on nine of the forty-one gold mines – a milestone in the history of the gold mining industry.

> During the negotiations, the Chamber conveyed ... its commitment to the elimination of discrimination based on race, sex or religion in work practices and measures, and agreed to continue discussions on other conditions of employment ....[18]

The membership of the NUM increased rapidly thereafter and by mid-1985 79 000 were paying union subscriptions by deduction from pay; and the NUM, ably led and administered by General Secretary Cyril Ramaphosa, was claiming a membership of 100 000. In May 1986 the paid-up membership was 135 000, and the NUM had become the largest union in South Africa. It was clear that a new and potent union force had entered the classic struggle between employee and employer.

The Chamber's decision to withdraw its longstanding objection to trade unions for unskilled black workers had been a daring one, not reached without

472

some trepidation. There were those to whom it seemed the industry was opening Pandora's Box of troubles, and that it would not be able to control events. Nobody knew where the decision would lead, and even the most optimistic had few illusions. They could be sure that they were in for a hard and bumpy ride; but the consensus was that an open, enlightened approach would pay off in enhanced communications and sound industrial relations in an industry which in the twenty-first century, or even before then, would be increasingly in the hands of black people.

In January 1985 the Chamber, in a joint declaration with Die Afrikaanse Handelsinstituut, the Association of Chambers of Commerce, the South African Federated Chamber of Industries, the National African Federation of Chambers of Commerce, and the Steel and Engineering Industries Federation, strongly opposed sanctions and other forms of economic intervention from abroad which they said would undermine the economic momentum vital to reform. The employer groups, providing eighty per cent of jobs in South Africa, reiterated their commitment to an on-going process of economic and political reform, and they declared that this should include, in addition to a free and independent trade union movement, the grant of universal citizenship, full participation in the economy, and meaningful political rights for blacks.

A year later these objectives had been incorporated in a new reform initiative by the Government. In April 1986, there followed the abandonment of the hated pass laws, and the promise of a policy of orderly urbanization in the place of influx control. Unhappily, as the Rand prepared to celebrate the centenary of the proclamation of the gold-fields, there was no slackening of external pressure on South Africa, nor any appreciable diminution in the unrest and violence in black and Coloured townships which had resulted in the loss of hundreds of lives through 1985. The country continued, too, in the trough of depression, and unemployment was widespread. Almost the only lightening of the general gloom came from the strength of the minerals industry.

The gold market, buffeted by storms through the seventies, had emerged substantially stronger, so that by the mid-eighties the retrospective impression was of the robustness of demand for the metal in an uncertain world. Aided by the weakening rand exchange rate, gold mining members of the Chamber earned R14 billion in 1985, and paid an estimated R3,4 billion to the State in tax and share of profits.[19] Mining houses felt confident enough of the future to earmark around R12 billion for capital expenditure on gold and uranium mines in 1985-1990, creating the potential of 50 000 new jobs.[20] The mining of other minerals, and the markets for them, had expanded rapidly as well, so that at a time when business was generally at the lowest ebb, the total industry employed 700 000 people and earned some R26 billion.

In good times or bad, mining is well equipped to absorb the shocks of radical change, and to impart a lively resilience to the country as a whole. Through the fateful days ahead of transition from the old South Africa to the new, mining will sustain the country economically, and offer the leaders of her diverse peoples the incentive of the extraordinary opportunities that lie beyond the settlement of their differences.

Johannesburg, 20 June 1986.

[1] Annual Report of the Transvaal and Orange Free State Chamber of Mines, 1964, p 18. (Speech by Dr D H McLaughlin, Chairman, Homestake Mining Company, USA, at the Annual General Meeting held on 28 June 1965).

[2] Kantor and Kenney, p 31.

[3] M Lipton, *Capitalism and Apartheid: South Africa 1910-84*, p 370.

[4] Eighty-Eighth Annual Report of the Chamber of Mines of South Africa, 1977, p 11.

[5] Eighty-Ninth Annual Report of the Chamber of Mines of South Africa, 1978, p 12.

[6] The Wiehahn Report, pp 677-678.

[7] Annual Report of the Chamber of Mines of South Africa, 1978, p 12.

[8] 'Profile of Johann Liebenberg', *Gold Pannings*, 31 March 1985, p 3. (Intergold Quarterly Newsletter.)

[9] Ninetieth and Ninety-First Annual Reports of the Chamber of Mines of South Africa, 1979 and 1980, pp 11 and 12, respectively. Annual Report of the Chamber of Mines of South Africa, 1984, pp 35-36.

[10] Ninety-Second Annual Report of the Chamber of Mines of South Africa, 1981, p 14.

[11] J Liebenberg, *'Arbeidsbetrekkinge in die Mynbedryf'*, p 10. Speech made at the Congress of the Afrikaanse Handelsinstituut at Johannesburg, 20 May 1986.

[12] Ninety-Third Annual Report of the Chamber of Mines of South Africa, 1982, p 17.

[13] 'South African Gold Mining: A Review of the Labour Situation – Part 2', *Gold Pannings*, 30 June 1985, p 2.

[14] Annual Report of the Chamber of Mines of South Africa, 1983, pp 21, 22-23, 43.

[15] Annual Report of the Chamber of Mines of South Africa, 1984, pp 35-36.

[16] 'Doing well, but costs will become "horrific"', *The Sunday Star*, 8 December 1985.

[17] 'Industrial Relations', *Mining. A Survey*: Supplement to the *Financial Mail*, 23 September 1983, pp 38, 40. 'South African Gold Mining: A Review of the Labour Situation – Part 1', *Gold Pannings*, 31 March 1985, p 3.

[18] Annual Report of the Chamber of Mines of South Africa, 1982, p 16.

[19] Chamber of Mines: Analysis of Working Results: October-December 1985, pp 4, 5.

[20] Chamber of Mines Newsletter: March/May 1985, pp 1-2.

Sources

ARCHIVAL SOURCES

TRANSVAAL ARCHIVES DEPOT, PRETORIA
Argief van Staatsekretaris (SS).

MINING HOUSE ARCHIVES
Gencor Limited, Johannesburg: Union Corporation Archives.

CHAMBER OF MINES ARCHIVES
Letterbooks
Letterbook of the Old Chamber, 1888.
Letterbooks of the Witwatersrand Chamber of Mines:
    1888–1890
    1890–1893
    1891–1892.

Minute Books
Executive Committee:
    6 November 1902 – 25 February 1904
    1907–1912
    May 1912 – September 1916
    1916–1920
    1920–1953.
Gold Producers' Committee:
    1922–1925
    1926–1940.
Association of Mines of the South African Republic:
    Annual General Report, 1896.

Files
137 Ch 16: *Chinese Labour No 1.*
M4 1908, CVI4: *Mining Industry Commission.*
    Bravery of Mine Employees: 1915–1920.
F4(b): *Finance: 1916-1920 inclusive.*
40 1917 (G8): *Government Commission re Van Dyk Deep Strike.*

6 1919 *Colour Bar*.

61 1919 *White Labour - Miscellaneous*.

23 1919 *Gemmill, W (Private)*.

33(1) 1920: *International Labour Conference, Washington, USA*.

75 1920: *Status Quo*.

Position of the Industry - General, 1921.

43 1923: *Mining Regulations - Crown Mines Case*.

28a 1925: *Conciliation Board - SA Mine Workers' Union and Mineworkers (Minimum Rates of Pay) Bill (de Villiers Award)*.

89 1925: *Mineworkers (Minimum Rates of Pay) Bill*.

19 1926: *Economic and Wage Commission*.

88 1927: *Mining Industry Arbitration Board: Arbitrator's Report*.

33a 1930: *ILO Silicosis Conference: Minutes and Reports*.

49 1939: *Internal*.

107 1939: *Obituary*.

128 1939: *SAMWU - Internal Dispute*.

64b 1946: *Meetings of the Chamber and Reports (2): Special Meeting 25 10 46*.

106c 1946: *Native Labour - Miscellaneous (3)*.

108 1946: *Native Labour - Native Trade Unions*.

109a 1946: *Native Labour - Native Trade Unions - Strike (1)*.

109b 1946: *Native Labour - Native Trade Unions - Strike (2)*.

109c 1946: *Native Labour - Native Trade Unions - Strike (3)*.

109d 1946: *Native Labour - Native Trade Unions - Strike (4) (Press)*.

125 1949: *MUJC - Commission - 40*.

126 1949: *MUJC - Commission - 41*.

Coalbrook Disaster - General, 1960.

Dec Coinage - Gen. - 1, 1964.

Chamber of Mines Annual Reports

Witwatersrand Chamber of Mines – First to Eighth Annual Reports for the years 1889 to 1896 inclusive.

Chamber of Mines of the South African Republic – Ninth to Eleventh Annual Reports for the years 1897 to 1899 inclusive.

Transvaal Chamber of Mines – Twelfth to Sixty-Third Annual Reports for the years 1900–1901 to 1952 inclusive.

Transvaal and Orange Free State Chamber of Mines – Sixty-Fourth to Seventy-Seventh Annual Reports for the years 1953 to 1966 inclusive.

Chamber of Mines of South Africa – Seventy-Eighth to Ninety-Fifth Annual Reports for the years 1967 to 1984 inclusive.

Chamber of Mines Analysis of Working Results, Newsletters, Monthly Reports, and Annual Reviews

Chamber of Mines: Analysis of Working Results:

October – December 1985.

Chamber of Mines Newsletters:
  March/May 1982: Mining Congress Issue and 1981 Review
  March 1984
  March/May 1985.

Chamber of Mines Monthly Reports
  April 1978
  November 1979
  Chamber of Mines of South Africa: 1984-1985 Review.

Chamber of Mines Publications
Evidence and Reports to Commissions of Inquiry, Books, Booklets and Pamphlets.
  The Mining Industry. Evidence and Report of the Industrial Commission of Inquiry. (Compiled and published by the Witwatersrand Chamber of Mines, Johannesburg, 1897.)
  Gold Producers' Committee of the Transvaal Chamber of Mines: Pamphlet entitled *Party Programmes and the Mines: A Business Statement*, Johannesburg, 2 June 1924.
  Mining Men: 1910-1960, Johannesburg, 1961.
(Transvaal and Orange Free State Chamber of Mines.)
  Rand Refinery. (The Chamber of Mines of South Africa: Public Relations Department Series No 255, Johannesburg, 1980.)
  Intergold. (Booklet published by the International Gold Corporation in 1981.)
  The Krugerrand Directory 1981, London, April 1981.
(Published by the International Gold Corporation.)
  Uranium: South Africa's Mineral Wealth.
(Chamber of Mines of South Africa and the Atomic Energy Board of South Africa: Chamber of Mines Public Relations Department Series No 262 – May 1982.)
  TEBA 1983. (Published by TEBA Limited.)

Periodicals
  Gold Pannings (Intergold Quarterly Newsletter) – issues of 31 March and 30 June 1985.
  Mining Survey – from 1960 to 1983.
  The Reef
  Volume L, No 595, March 1965 (for article entitled Harry Haynes – The Crusading Philosopher).
  Volume L, No 598, June 1965 (for articles entitled *The Progress of The Reef: 1915-1965* and *The Early Years of The Reef*).
  February 1967 (for article entitled *Prevention of Accidents Committee Personality* [J A Gemmill]).
  November 1981 (for article entitled *Die Helena van St Helena*).
  January 1983 (for article entitled *Harry Oppenheimer: A Profile*).

OFFICIAL PUBLICATIONS

Debates of the House of Assembly (Hansard)
Union of South Africa:
  Fourth Session, First Parliament,
30 January - 7 July 1914.
  Second Session, Fifth Parliament,
13 February - 25 July 1925: Volumes 3 to 5.
  Fourth Session, Sixth Parliament,
18 November 1931 - 27 May 1932: Volumes 18 and 19.
  Third Session, Twelfth Parliament,
15 January - 20 May 1960: Volumes 103 to 105.

Republic of South Africa:
  First Session, Third Parliament,
29 July - 19 October 1966: Volumes 17 and 18.

Books
Union of South Africa: Bureau of Census and Statistics, Pretoria, *Union Statistics for Fifty Years: 1910-1960: Jubilee Issue.*

Reports
Report of the Transvaal Concessions Commission dated 4 April 1901: 1 Dynamite Concession.

Union of South Africa: Report of the Witwatersrand Disturbances Commission, September 1913 (UG No 55 - 1913).

Union of South Africa: Judicial Commission of Inquiry into Witwatersrand Disturbances: June - July 1913: Minutes of Evidence (UG No 56 - 1913).

Union of South Africa: Report of the Native Grievances Inquiry, 1913-1914 (UG No 37 - 1914).

Union of South Africa: Report of the Economic Commission: January 1914 (UG No 12 - 1914).

Union of South Africa: Report of the Select Committee on Gold Mining Industry, 1918 (SC No 3 - 1918).

Union of South Africa: Report of the Influenza Epidemic Commission, 1919 (UG No 15 - 1919).

Union of South Africa: Interim Report of the Low Grade Mines Commission, 1919 (UG No 45 - 1919).

Union of South Africa: Report of the Low Grade Mines Commission, 1920 (UG No 34 - 1920).

Union of South Africa: Report of the Mining Industry Board, 1922 (UG No 39 - 1922).

Union of South Africa: Report of the Martial Law Inquiry Judicial Commission, 1922 (UG No 35 - 1922).

Union of South Africa: Report of the Economic and Wage Commission (1925) (UG No 14 - 1926).

Union of South Africa: Report of the Low Grade Ore Commission, 1930

478

(UG No 16 - 1932).

Union of South Africa: Department of Labour: Findings and Recommendations of the Mine Workers' Union Commission (1941).

Union of South Africa: Report of the Mine Workers' Union Commission of Inquiry, 1946 (UG No 36 - 1946).

Union of South Africa: Report of the Mine Workers' Union Commission of Inquiry, 1951 (UG No 52 - 1951).

Transvaal Ordinances

The Transvaal Labour Importation Ordinance, 1904 (Government Printing and Stationery Office, Pretoria).

NEWSPAPERS AND JOURNALS

The Diggers' News, Johannesburg - issues of 1889 and 1896.

The Eastern Star, Johannesburg - issues from October 1887 to April 1889.

Financial Mail

7 July, 1978. (Article entitled *The Secret Mine Report.*)

Krugerrands: Special Report: Supplement to the *Financial Mail,* 25 April 1980.

Mining. A Survey: Supplement to the *Financial Mail,* 23 September 1983.

Rand Daily Mail, Johannesburg - issues from 1903 to 1946.

The South African Mining Journal - issues from 1891 to 1897.

The South African Mining and Engineering Journal - issues from 1921 to 1949.

The Chamber of Mines of South Africa: Ninety Years of Achievement: Supplement to *The South African Mining and Engineering Journal,* July 1979.

The Star, Johannesburg - issues from May 1889 to October 1961.

The Sunday Star, Johannesburg - 1985.

The Transvaal Leader, Johannesburg - 1907.

Appelgryn, M S, *Die Ontdekking van Goud aan die Witwatersrand*, Kleio, II, 2 October 1970.

Appelgryn, M S, *Die Ontstaan van die Eerste Gesondheidskomitee van Johannesburg*, Kleio, III, 2 October 1971.

Appelgryn, M S, *The Naming of Johannesburg - A Radical Theory*, Kleio, VII, 1 May 1975.

Blainey, G, *Lost Causes of the Jameson Raid*, Economic History Review, 1965, Volume 18.

Collender, K G F, and John, K G, *Engineering versus Tuberculosis*, The Transactions of the South African Institute of Electrical Engineers, Volume XXXII, 1941.

Denoon, D J N, *Capital and Capitalists in the Transvaal in the 1890s and 1900s,* The Historical Journal, 23, I (1980).

Fenske, G A, and Main, T R N, *Labour and the Gold Mines.* (Review Note: Wilson, F., Labour in the South African Gold Mines, 1911-1969), The South African Journal of Economics, Volume 41, No 3, September 1973.

Fouché, L, *Johannesburg in South African History*, South African Journal of Science, XXXIII, March 1937.

Franzsen, D G, *Monetary Policy in South Africa: 1932-1982*, The South African Journal of Economics, Volume 51, No 1, March 1983.

Frost, A, McIntyre, R C, Papenfus, E B, and Weiss, O, *The Discovery and Prospecting of a Potential Gold Field near Odendaalsrus in the Orange Free State, Union of South Africa*, Transactions of The Geological Society of South Africa, Volume XLIX, 1946.

Gemmill, W, *The Growing Reservoir of Native Labour for the Mines*, Optima, June 1952, Volume II, No 2.

Gemmill, W, *The International Labour Conference, 1919*, The South African Quarterly, Volume II, No 3, June 1920.

Grundlingh, A M, *Black Men in a White Man's War: The Impact of the First World War on South African Blacks*, War and Society, Volume III, No 1, May 1985.

Hagart, R B, *National Aspects of the Uranium Industry*, Journal of the South African Institute of Mining and Metallurgy, Volume 57, No 9, April 1957.

Jeeves, A, *Aftermath of Rebellion - The Randlords and Kruger's Republic after the Jameson Raid*, South African Historical Journal, No 10, November 1978.

Jeeves, A, *The Control of Migratory Labour on the South African Gold Mines in the Era of Kruger and Milner*, Journal of Southern African Studies, Volume 2, No 1, October 1975.

Kantor, B S, and Kenney, H F, *The Poverty of Neo-Marxism: The Case of South Africa*, Journal of Southern African Studies, Volume 3, No 1, October 1976.

Kenney, H, Review Note: *The Emergence of Modern South Africa: State, Capital, and the Incorporation of Organized Labour on the South African Gold Fields, 1902-1939*, by David Yudelman, The South African Journal of Economics, Volume 52, No 4, December 1984.

Kubicek, R V, *The Randlords in 1895: The Reassessment*, Journal of British Studies, XI, 1972.

Lipton, M, *Men of Two Worlds: Migrant Labour in South Africa*, Optima, Volume 29, Number Two/Three, 28 November 1980.

Mawby, A A, *Capital, Government and Politics in the Transvaal, 1900-1907: A Revision and a Reversion*, The Historical Journal, XVII, 2 (1974).

McLean, C S, *The Uranium Industry of South Africa*, Journal of the Chemical, Metallurgical and Mining Society of South Africa, Volume 54, No 10, April 1954.

Mendelsohn, R, *Blainey and the Jameson Raid: The Debate Renewed*, Journal of Southern African Studies, Volume 6, 2 April 1980.

Oppenheimer, H F, *Sir Ernest Oppenheimer*, Optima, Volume 17, September 1967.

Oppenheimer, H F, *The Orange Free State Gold Fields*, The South African Journal of Economics, Volume 18, No 2, June 1950.

Palmer, G F D, *South Africa's continuing 'boom' demands revised labour policies*,

Optima, December 1963, Volume 13, No 4.

Stokes, E, *III Milnerism,* The Historical Journal, V, I (1962).

Stuart, D N, *The Supply of the Raw Material Requirements of the Uranium Programme,* Journal of the South African Institute of Mining and Metallurgy, Volume 57, No 6, January 1957.

Van-Helten, J J, *Empire and High Finance: South Africa and the International Gold Standard: 1890-1914,* Journal of African History, 23 (1982).

BOOKS, ARTICLES, THESES, DISSERTATIONS, PAPERS, SPEECHES, AND OTHER SOURCES

Arndt, E H D, *Banking and Currency Development in South Africa (1652-1927),* Cape Town, etc, 1928.

Balfour, I, *Famous Diamonds.* (Published by De Beers Consolidated Mines Limited.) No date.

Bawcombe, P, and Scannel, T, *Philip Bawcombe's Johannesburg,* Johannesburg, 1973.

Bonham Carter, V, *Winston Churchill as I knew him,* London, 1965.

Bonner, P L, *8. The 1920 Black Mineworkers' Strike: A Preliminary Account,* Bozzoli, B, ed, *Labour, Townships and Protest Studies in the Social History of the Witwatersrand.* Johannesburg 1979.

Boydell, T, *My Luck was in: With Spotlights on General Smuts,* Cape Town, no date.

Breitenbach, J J, ed, *South Africa in the Modern World (1910-1970): A Contemporary History*, Durban, 1974.

Cameron, T, and Spies, S B, eds, *An Illustrated History of South Africa,* Johannesburg, 1986.

Cartwright, A P, *The Corner House: The Early History of Johannesburg,* Johannesburg, 1965.

Cartwright, A P, *Doctors on the Mines: A History of the Mine Medical Officers' Association of South Africa: 1921-1971,* Cape Town, etc, 1971.

Cartwright, A P, *Golden Age: The Story of the Industrialization of South Africa and the part played in it by the Corner House Group of Companies: 1910-1967,* Cape Town, etc, 1968.

Cartwright, A P, *The Gold Miners,* Cape Town, etc, 1962.

Cartwright, A P, *Gold Paved the Way: The Story of the Gold Fields Group of Companies,* London, 1967.

Cartwright, A P, *West Driefontein - Ordeal by Water,* Gold Fields of South Africa Limited, no date.

Chilvers, H A, *The Story of De Beers,* London, etc, 1939.

Churchill, W S, *Ian Hamilton's March*, 2nd edition, New York, etc, 1900.

Cope, R K, *Comrade Bill: The Life and Times of W H Andrews, Workers' Leader,* Cape Town, no date.

Creswell, F H P, Pamphlet: *The Chinese Labour Question from Within: Facts, Criticisms, and Suggestions: Impeachment of a Disastrous Policy,* London, 1905.

481

Current Biography 1973, New York.

Davenport, T R H, *South Africa: A Modern History,* second edition, Johannesburg, 1981.

De Jongh, T W, *The Marketing of South Africa's Gold.* (Address delivered on 15 November 1974, on the occasion of the Annual Dinner of the Pretoria Branch of the Economic Society of South Africa.)

De Kiewiet, C W, *A History of South Africa Social and Economic,* London, 1978.

Denny, G A, *The Deep-Level Mines of the Rand,* London, 1902.

Denoon, D N A, *A Grand Illusion: The Failure of Imperial Policy in the Transvaal Colony during the period of Reconstruction: 1900-1905,* London, 1973.

De Villiers, R M ed, *Better than they knew,* Cape Town, etc, 1972.

Dictionary of South African Biography
Volume I, Cape Town, 1976.
Volume II, Cape Town, 1983.
Volume III, Cape Town, 1977.
Volume IV, Durban, 1981.

Doxey, G V, *The Industrial Colour Bar in South Africa,* Cape Town, etc, 1961.

Duminy, A H and Guest, W R, eds, *FitzPatrick: South African Politician: Selected Papers, 1888-1906,* Johannesburg, etc, 1976.

Duminy, A H, *The Political Career of Sir Percy FitzPatrick, 1895-1906,* unpublished Ph D thesis, University of Natal, Durban, 1973.

Emden, P H, *Randlords,* London, 1935.

Etheredge, D A, *The Early History of the Chamber of Mines: Johannesburg: 1887-1897,* unpublished M A dissertation, University of the Witwatersrand, Johannesburg, 1949.

Farman, C, *The General Strike: May 1926,* London, 1972.

Fisher, N, *Harold Macmillan,* London, 1982.

FitzPatrick, J Percy, *The Transvaal from Within: A Private Record of Public Affairs,* London, 1900.

Forsyth, J (Morgan Grenfell & Co Ltd), *A Diversified Reserve Situation - The Role of Gold.* (Speech made at a Conference on World Gold in the 1980s, held in Montreux, Switzerland, on 12 and 13 June 1979.)

Frankel, S H, *Investment and the Return to Equity Capital in the South African Gold Mining Industry: 1887-1965: An International Comparison,* Oxford, 1967.

Frankel, S H, *The Railway Policy of South Africa: An Analysis of the Effects of Railway Rates, Finance and Management on the Economic Development of the Union,* Johannesburg, 1928.

Fraser, M, and Jeeves, A, *All that Glittered: Selected Correspondence of Lionel Phillips: 1890-1924,* Cape Town, 1977.

Fredrickson, G M, *White Supremacy: A Comparative Study in American and South African History,* Oxford, etc, 1982.

Glen, H W, ed, *Proceedings, Twelfth Congress of the Council of Mining and Metallurgical Institutions, Johannesburg, 3 - 7 May, 1982,* Volumes 1 and 2.

(Published by The South African Institute of Mining and Metallurgy, and the Geological Society of South Africa, 1982.)

Gordon, C T, *The Growth of Boer Opposition to Kruger (1890-1895)*, Cape Town, etc, 1970.

Gray, J, *Payable Gold: An Intimate Record of the History of the Discovery of the Payable Witwatersrand Goldfields and of Johannesburg in 1886 and 1887*, Johannesburg, 1937.

Green, T, *The New World of Gold*, New York, 1981.

Gregory, T, *Ernest Oppenheimer and the Economic Development of Southern Africa*, London, etc, 1962.

Grey, P C, *The Development of the Gold Mining Industry of the Witwatersrand: 1902-1910*, unpublished D Litt et Phil thesis, University of South Africa, 1969.

Grundlingh, A M, *Die Suid-Afrikaanse Gekleurdes en die Eerste Wêreldoorlog*, unpublished D Litt et Phil thesis, University of South Africa, 1981.

Gutsche, T, *No Ordinary Woman: The Life and Times of Florence Phillips*, Cape Town, 1966.

Hammond, J Hays, *The Autobiography of John Hays Hammond;* Volumes I and II, New York, 1935.

Hancock, W K, *Smuts: 1 The Sanguine Years: 1870-1919*, Cambridge, 1962.

Hancock, W K, *Smuts: 2 The Fields of Force: 1919-1950*, Cambridge, 1968.

Hancock, W K and Van der Poel, J, eds, *Selections from the Smuts Papers: June 1902 - May 1910*, Volume II, Cambridge, 1966.

Headlam, C, ed. *The Milner Papers: South Africa: 1899-1905*, II, London, etc, 1933.

Henry, J S (Siepman, H A ed), *The First Hundred Years of the Standard Bank*, London, etc, 1963.

Hessian, B, *An Investigation into the Causes of the Labour Agitation on the Witwatersrand, January to March 1922*, unpublished M A dissertation, University of the Witwatersrand, Johannesburg, 1957.

Hirschon, N, *The Naming of Johannesburg as an Historical Commentary*, Johannesburg, 1974.

Hobson, J A, *Imperialism: A Study*, second edition, London, 1938.

Houghton, D H, *The South African Economy*, fourth edition, Cape Town, 1980.

Hyam, R, *Elgin and Churchill at the Colonial Office: 1905-1908: The Watershed of the Empire-Commonwealth*, London, 1968.

International Labour Office, *International Silicosis Conference, Johannesburg, 13-27 August 1930: Reports*, Geneva, 1930.

Jenkins, A, *The Rich Rich: The Story of the Big Spenders*, London, 1977.

Jeppe, C, *The Kaleidoscopic Transvaal*, Johannesburg, etc, 1906.

Johannesburg Stock Exchange, *The Story of the Johannesburg Stock Exchange: 1887-1947*, Johannesburg, 1948.

Johnstone, F A, *Class, Race and Gold: A Study of Class Relations and Racial Discrimination in South Africa*, London, etc, 1976.

Katz, E, *A Trade Union Aristocracy: A History of White Workers in the Transvaal and the General Strike of 1913*, African Studies Institute, University of the Witwatersrand, Johannesburg, 1976.

Kennedy, B, *A Tale of Two Mining Cities: Johannesburg and Broken Hill: 1885-1925*, Johannesburg, etc, 1984.

Kenney, H, *Architect of Apartheid: H F Verwoerd - An Appraisal*, Johannesburg, 1980.

Keppel-Jones, A, *South Africa: A Short History*, fifth edition, London, 1975.

Krüger, D W, *The Making of a Nation*, Johannesburg, etc, 1961.

Kubicek, R V, *Economic Imperialism in Theory and Practice: The Case of South African Gold Mining Finance: 1886-1914*, Durham, N C, USA, 1979.

Lamar, H, and Thompson, L, eds, *The Frontier in History: North America and Southern Africa Compared*, New Haven, etc, 1981.

Le May, G H L, *British Supremacy in South Africa: 1899-1907*, Oxford, 1965.

Lewsen, P, *John X Merriman: Paradoxical South African Statesman*, Johannesburg, etc, 1982.

Lewsen, P, ed, *Selections from the Correspondence of J X Merriman: 1870-1890*, Cape Town, 1960.

Leyds, G A, *A History of Johannesburg: The Early Years*, Cape Town, 1964.

Liebenberg, J, *Arbeidsbetrekkinge in die Mynbedryf.* (Speech made at the Congress of the Afrikaanse Handelsinstituut at Johannesburg on 20 May 1986.)

Lipton, M, *Capitalism and Apartheid: South Africa, 1910-1984*, Aldershot, England, 1985.

Long, B K, *Drummond Chaplin: His Life and Times in Africa*, London, 1941.

Longford, E, *Jameson's Raid: The Prelude to the Boer War*, Johannesburg, 1982.

Marais, J S, *The Fall of Kruger's Republic*, Oxford, 1961.

Marks, S, and Trapido, S, *Lord Milner and the South African State*, Bonner, P, Working Papers in Southern African Studies, Volume 2, Johannesburg, 1981.

Marshall, J R, *From Heidelberg to Rachan*, Edinburgh.

Mason, R J, *Prehistoric Man at Melville Koppies, Johannesburg*, Johannesburg Council for Natural History: Occasional Paper 6, March 1971.

Mawby, A A, *The Political Behaviour of the British Population of the Transvaal, 1902 to 1907*, unpublished Ph D thesis, University of the Witwatersrand, Johannesburg, 1969.

Men of the Times: Pioneers of the Transvaal and Glimpses of South Africa, Johannesburg, 1905.

Muller, C F J, ed, *Five Hundred Years: A History of South Africa*, third edition, Pretoria, 1981.

Muller, C F J, Van Jaarsveld, F A, Van Wijk, T, and Boucher, M, eds, *South African History and Historians: A Bibliography*, Pretoria, 1979.

Murray, B K, *Wits: The Early Years: A History of the University of the Witwatersrand, Johannesburg and its Precursors: 1896-1939*, Johannesburg, 1982.

Murray, R W (Snr), *South African Reminiscences,* Cape Town, 1894.

Naudé, L, *Dr A Hertzog: Die Nasionale Party en die Mynwerker,* Pretoria, 1969.

Neame, L E, *Today's News Today: The Story of the Argus Company,* Johannesburg, 1956. (This is a condensation of a fully detailed history of the Argus Company, compiled for record purposes by Rosenthal, E.)

Oberholster, A G, *Die Mynwerkerstaking: Witwatersrand, 1922,* Pretoria, 1982.

O'Meara, D, *The 1946 African Mine-Workers' Strike in the Political Economy of South Africa,* Bonner, P L, ed, Working Papers in Southern African Studies: Papers presented at the ASI. Studies Seminar, African Studies Institute, University of the Witwatersrand, Johannesburg, 1977.

Orenstein, A J, ed, South African Council for Scientific and Industrial Research, *Proceedings of the Pneumoconiosis Conference held at the University of the Witwatersrand, Johannesburg: 9 - 24 February 1959,* London, 1960.

Pakenham, T, *The Boer War,* Johannesburg, etc, 1979.

Phillips, L, *Some Reminiscences,* London, 1924.

Pirow, O, *James Barry Munnik Hertzog,* Cape Town, no date.

Praagh, L V, ed, *The Transvaal and its Mines,* London, etc, 1906.

Reeves, J A, *Chinese Labour in South Africa: 1901-1910,* unpublished M A dissertation, University of the Witwatersrand, Johannesburg, 1954.

Rhoodie, D, *Conspirators in Conflict: A Study of the Johannesburg Reform Committee and its Role in the Conspiracy against the South African Republic,* Cape Town, 1967.

Richardson, P, *Chinese Mine Labour in the Transvaal,* London, etc, 1982.

Rose Innes, J (Tindall, B A, ed), *James Rose Innes: Chief Justice of South Africa, 1914-1927: Autobiography,* Cape Town, etc, 1949.

Rosenthal, E, *Southern African Dictionary of National Biography,* London, 1966.

Rosenthal, E, *You have been listening...: The Early History of Radio in South Africa,* Cape Town, etc, 1974.

Sauer, H, *Ex Africa,* London, 1937.

Shapiro, H A, ed, *Pneumoconiosis: Proceedings of the International Conference: Johannesburg: 1969,* Cape Town, etc, 1970.

Shilling, J W, *Historical Review of Certain Aspects of the Taxation of Gold Mines in the Transvaal and Orange Free State,* unpublished research report for the Higher Diploma in Tax Law, University of the Witwatersrand, Johannesburg, 1982.

Shorten, J R, *The Johannesburg Saga,* Johannesburg, 1970.

Spies, S B, *Methods of Barbarism? Roberts and Kitchener and Civilians in the Boer Republics: January 1900 - May 1902,* Cape Town, etc, 1977.

Strakosch, H, *The South African Currency and Exchange Problem,* Johannesburg, 1920.

Taylor, J B, *A Pioneer Looks Back,* London, 1939.

Taylor, J B, *Recollections of the Discovery of Gold on the Witwatersrand and the*

Early Development of the Gold Mines. (Written at Lancelevy, St James, Cape, October 1936, at the request of the Director of the Africana Museum.)

Trollope, A, *South Africa,* London, 1878. (Two volumes.)

Van der Horst, S T, *Native Labour in South Africa,* London, 1971.

Van der Poel, J, *The Jameson Raid,* Cape Town, etc, 1951.

Van der Poel, J, *Railway and Customs Policies in South Africa: 1885-1910,* London, etc, 1933.

Van Onselen, C, *Studies in the Social and Economic History of the Witwatersrand: 1886-1914: 1 New Babylon,* Johannesburg, 1982.

Van Rensburg, W C J, and Pretorius, D A (Glen, H W, ed), *South Africa's Strategic Minerals: Pieces on a Continental Chessboard,* Johannesburg, 1977.

Walker, E A, ed, *The Cambridge History of the British Empire, VIII, South Africa, Rhodesia and the High Commission Territories,* Cambridge, 1963.

Walker, E A, *A History of Southern Africa,* third edition, London, etc, 1957.

Walker, I L, and Weinbren, B, *2000 Casualties: A History of the Trade Unions and the Labour Movement in the Union of South Africa,* Johannesburg, 1961.

Warwick, P, and Spies, S B, eds, *The South African War: The Anglo-Boer War: 1899-1902,* Harlow, Essex, England, 1980.

Watson, L, *Lightning Bird: The Story of One Man's Journey into Africa's Past,* London, etc, 1982.

Webber, H O'Kelly, *The Grip of Gold: A Life Story of a Dominion,* London, 1936.

The Complete Wiehahn Report: Parts 1-6, and the White Paper on each Part: With Notes by Professor N E Wiehahn, Johannesburg, etc, 1982.

Wilson, F, *Labour in the South African Gold Mines, 1911-1969,* Cambridge, 1972.

Wilson, M, and Thompson, L, eds, *A History of South Africa to 1870,* Cape Town, etc, 1982.

Wilson, M and Thompson, L, eds, *The Oxford History of South Africa, II: South Africa: 1870-1966,* Oxford, 1971.

Yudelman, D, *The Emergence of Modern South Africa: State, Capital and the Incorporation of Organized Labour on the South African Gold Fields, 1902-1939,* Westport, Connecticut, USA, etc, 1983.

Selected Index

487

Associated Scientific and Technical Societies of South Africa: 271, 295; National Award with Gold Medal, 449; Award of Gold Medal, 450

Association of Chambers of Commerce, 412, 473

Association of Mines of the South African Republic, 98, 104, 105, dissolution of, 111

Association of Mine Managers, 80, 341

Association of Scientific and Technical Societies of South Africa (*see* Associated Scientific and Technical Societies of South Africa)

Atomic Energy Board, *see* South African Atomic Energy Board

Augmented Executive, 292, 301, 303, 304, 305, 307

Aurora mine, 41

Australia, 19, 145, 184, 191, 209, 210, 226, 261, 266, 330, 341, 356

Bagot, Major the Hon W L, 158

Bailey, Sir Abe, 11, 95, 97, 181, 201, 361, 390

Baillie, A C, 30, 41

Bain, Dr G W, 371, 372

Bain, James, 214, 217, 218, 221, 226

Bain, S T, 41

Baker, Sir Herbert, 236

Balfour, A J, 152, 167, 169

Balfour Declaration, 1926, 334

Ballinger, Mrs Margaret, 382

Ballot, J, 86

Balmoral mine, 41

Banda, Dr Hastings, 455, 456

Banks:

 Bank of Africa, 35

 Bank of England, 77, 240, 241, 259, 261, 428, 431

 Banque Française de L'Afrique du Sud, 77

 Cape of Good Hope Bank, 35

 Deutsche Bank A G, 75, 77, 439

 Natal Bank, 35, 105

 National Bank, 50, 93, 124, 218

 Reichsbank, 240

 South African Reserve Bank, 262, 428

 Standard Bank, 21, 35

 Swiss Bank Corporation, 438

 Swiss Credit Bank, 438

 Union Bank of Switzerland, 438

Bantjes, Jan, 19, 23

Barberton, 11, 12, 17

Barberton Mining and Commercial Chamber, 32, 69

Barbour, Sir David, 137

Barkly, Sir Henry, 11

Barlow Rand, 415

Barlow, Thomas, 415

Barnato, Barney, 9, 38, 75, 85, 97, 101

Barnato Brothers, 9, 178, 181

Barnato's Buildings, 50

Barnato, Harry, 9

Barotseland, 397, 398

Barry, George, 365

Barsdorf, A and Company, 152

Basal Reef, 361, 388

Basutoland, (Lesotho), 167, 195, 233, 379

Beattie, Sir John Carruthers, 312

Beatty, G H, President of the Chamber 1936-1937, 1939-1940, 360, 364, 365, 366, 368, 370

Bechuanaland, (Botswana), 55, 79, 91, 92, 397

Bechuanaland Rail Strip, 94

Beckett, T W, 21

Beit, Alfred, 8, 19, 30, 62, 64, 92, 102, 114, 137, 164, 165, 194, 247

Beisa Mine, 444

Benoni, 215, 216, 217, Market Square 217, 218, 219, 245, 306, 380

Bennett, J M, 245

Bernstein, B L, President of the Chamber, 1955-1956, 398

Bethlehem, 12

Bettelheim's Buildings, 50

Bettington, Colonel R, 151

Berlin Handelgesellschaft, 75

Beyers, General C F, 124, 226, 231

Beyers, F W, 327, 329, 334

'Big Ten' finance houses, 9

Birchenough, Henry, 155

Bird, Frank E, 452

Birkenruth, E S, 114

Bissett, W, 23

'Black Manifesto', 336

Black mineworkers, grievances: inquiry by H O Buckle, 1913, 235, 236, 262

Blainey, Professor Geoffrey, 100, 101, 321.

Blantyre, 456

Blasting certificate as a white preserve, 471

Bleloch, W, 136

Blinkpoort Gold Syndicate, Ltd, 388

Bloemfontein Conference, 1899, 114

Bloemfontein Convention, 1854, 6

Bloemfontein Customs Conference, 1903, 142, 149, 150, 151

Bloiff, Jas, 46

Blyvooruitzicht, 354, 392, 400

Boers, 4, 6, 17, 35, 55, 56, 87, 91, 95, 96, 112, 124, 150, 156, 168, 173, 175, 180, 229, 265

Boer Rebellion, 308

494

McArthur-Forrest Cyanide Process, 63, patentees, 64, court case, 65

McCallùm, W, 136

McCann, C J, 302

McCormack, Major Michael, OBE, MC, 287

McDermid, A, 278, 302, 307

McLean, Calvin Stowe, President of the Chamber 1945-1946, 1948-1949, 1952-1953, 295, 296, 352, 369, 371, 372, 374, 375, 378, 385, 393, 394, 395

Mears, G, 380

Melbourne, 330

Melville, 17

Melville Koppies, 1, 2, iron smelters, 3, 84

Mendelsohn, Richard, 101

Mendelssohn, Emmanuel, 26

Menell, S G, 354, 376

Mercantile Association, The, 95, 96

Merriman, John X, 8, 9, 39, 48, 56, 95, 97, 174, 176, 200, 211, 213

Merriespruit, 419

Messina, 2

Meyer, Johannes Petrus, 20, 36, 44, 69

Meyer and Charlton mine, 125, 270

Meyer's Camp, see Natal Camp

Mfecane, 4 see also Difaqane

Middelburg – Belfast area, 138, 248

Migratory labour, 77-80, 126-127, 139-140, 194-197, 233, 234, 462-464. (See also Employment Bureau of Africa, The; Labour, black; Wages: black mineworkers; Witwatersrand Native Labour Association; Native Recruiting Corporation.)

Mills, Stephen, C M G, 330, 331

Milne, A Tracey, 369, 394, 395, 426

Milne, Arnold Statham, 395

Milner Administration, 135, 167, 176, 179

Milner 'Kindergarten', 135

Milner, Lord, 101, 112, 113, 114, 115, 122, 125, 128, 132, 133, 134, 135, 136, 137, 138, 140, 141, 142, 145, 147, 149, 151, 152, 156, 163, 164, 165, 167, 168, 169, 170, 175, 177, 207, 243, 248, 318

Milton, W H, 150

Mine Accidents, prevention of: Role of Mines and Works Act, 207-208; formation of Prevention of Accidents Committee, 225; 451-453

Mine Employees Pension Fund, 379, 471

Mine Guard, 125, 129

Mine Officials' Pension Fund, 378, 379, 471

Minerals industry, importance of: 425, 445; earnings 1961-1984, and West's dependence on South Africa, 447

Mine Workers' Union, see South African Mine Workers' Union

Miners' Medical Bureau, 341, 342

Miners' phthisis, 224, 225, 340, 341

Miners' Phthisis Board, 274

'Miner's Victoria Cross' see Bronze Medal

Mine Safety Division, 452

Mines and Works Act, 207, 208, 209, 210, 254, 333, 471
  See also Colour Bar

Mines and Works Regulations, 334, 471

Mines Benefit Society, 358

Mines, Department of, 32, 36, 61, 222, 281, 333

Mines Engineering Brigade of the South African Engineering Corps, 368, 369

Mines Fund, 126

Mines Police Force, 122, 123, 124, 129

Mines' Rescue Brigade, 407

Mines Stores Department, 369, 393

Mines Stores Sub-Committee, 367, 369, 395

Mine Surface Officials' Association, 252, 471

Mine Workers' Union (MWU) – see South African Mine Workers' Union

Mine Workers' Union, Commission of Inquiry, 1946, 377

Mines, Works and Machinery Regulations Ordinance, 163

Mines, Works, Machinery and Certificates Bill, 191, 192

Mining Commissioner, 23, 36

Mining houses: formation and function, 74-77

Mining Industry Arbitration Board, 328

Mining Industry Board, 308, 311

Mining Industry Commission, 190, 191

Mining industry and the State, relationship, 188-189; with Milner, 132 et seq; 321, 322; migratory labour factor, 462, 463, 467

Mining Leases Board, 198

Mining News, 421

Mining Regulations Commission, 187, 190, 191

Mining Sun, The, 462

Mining technology, 167, 244, 341, 354, 389, 399, 400, 466. See also Chamber of Mines Research Organization.

Mining Unions Joint Committee, 357, 358, 369, 376, 377, 396, 461

Minnaar, Stephanus Johannes, 19

Mint, The Royal, 261

Mint, The South African, 412, 437, 438, 439

Moatize Colliery, Moçambique, 407

Moçambique, 2, 54, 56, 57, 81, 82, 145, 146,

499

27, 77, 138, 139

Witwatersrand Co-operative Smelting Works Ltd, 261

Witwatersrand Council of Education, 164

Witwatersrand Geological System, 12, 17-19, 77, 138, 423

Witwatersrand Gold Mine Employees Provident Fund, 357, 378, 379

Witwatersrand mine, 42

Witwatersrand Native Labour Association, 126, 145, 146, 147, 149, 153, 154, 158, 162, 177, 192, 194, 195, 196, 234, 243, 325, 342, 365, 379, 397, 398, 457, 458

Witwatersrand Native Labour Association Hospital, 459

Witwatersrand Technikon, 164

Witwatersrand Trades and Labour Council, 179, 211

Witwatersrand, University of the, 165, 248, 282

WNLA, *see* Witwatersrand Native Labour Association

Wolhuter mine, 191

Wolmarans, J M A, 72

Wonderfontein Valley, 353

Woodbush, 80

Wordingham, J, 278, 302, 307

Workers' Charter, 223

Worker, The, 218, 223

Workmen's Compensation Act, British, 1897, 51

Workmen's Compensation Act, 51, 197, 223, 359, 459

Worroll, Reginald E, 443

Wright, H, 30, 32, 33, 35

W T & L C, *see* Witwatersrand Trades and Labour Council

Wybergh, W J, 114, 136, 154, 155

Xhosa, 1

Yeoville, 201

Yudelman David, 188, 189, 269, 270, 271, 321, 322, 356

Zambesi River, 55, 132, 397, 398

Zambia, 456

ZARPS, The Transvaal Republican Police, 113, 122

Zimbabwe, 5, discovery of ruins, 6

Zulu Kingdom, 3

Zululand, 55, 146

Zurich Gold Market, 431